Sorensen's
Guide to Powerboats

Sorensen's
Guide to Powerboats

How to Evaluate Design, Construction, and Performance

Eric W. Sorensen

International Marine / McGraw-Hill

Camden, Maine • New York • Chicago • San Francisco
Lisbon • London • Madrid • Mexico City • Milan • New Delhi
San Juan • Seoul • Singapore • Sydney • Toronto

International Marine

*A Division of The **McGraw·Hill** Companies*

10 9 8 7 6 5 4 3

Library of Congress Cataloging-in-Publication Data
Sorensen, Eric.
    Sorensen's guide to powerboats : how to evaluate design, construction, and performance.
        p.   cm.
    Includes index.
    ISBN 0-07-137955-X
        1. Motorboats—Evaluations. 2. Boats and boating. I. Title.

VM341 .S646 2002
623.8′231′0297—dc21   2001007969

Questions regarding the content of this book should be addressed to
International Marine
P.O. Box 220
Camden, ME 04843
www.internationalmarine.com

Questions regarding the ordering of this book should be addressed to
The McGraw-Hill Companies
Customer Service Department
P.O. Box 547
Blacklick, OH 43004
Retail customers: 1-800-262-4729
Bookstores: 1-800-722-4726
The author can be reached at EricS1@attbi.com

This book is printed on 60 lb. Computer Book by R.R. Donnelley & Sons,
    Crawfordsville, IN
Design by Carol Gillette, Communications Graphics
Production by Eugenie S. Delaney and Dan Kirchoff
Photographs courtesy of Eric W. Sorensen unless credited otherwise
Line art by Bruce Alderson unless credited otherwise
Edited by Alex Barnett, Jonathan Eaton, Bill Brogdon, John Snyder,
    and Constance G. Burt

Contents

Preface

This book is meant to help fellow boating enthusiasts understand more fully how small craft are built, why they perform the way they do, and which types of hulls and layouts are best suited to various needs. Much of what a curious owner might want to know about boats, from the significance of which resins are used in the hull, to helm station ergonomics, the elements of seaworthiness, ride quality, and handling, is discussed and explained in detail.

The boating industry is market-driven, so boaters get what they ask for, ultimately, through that final arbiter, consumer demand. The key, of course, is for intelligent, informed boat buyers to *know* what exactly to ask of their next boat, and that no, the 18-inch bow railings, poor helm station visibility, kidney-jarring hull design, and 5-foot, 10-inch berth really aren't worth buying. There are many fine boats available today, from bass boats to megayachts. But there are also many that are lacking in safety, ergonomics, construction quality, hull design, systems accessibility, and seaworthiness. A close reading of this book will help the buyer become more discerning when evaluating a boat's design, construction, and performance.

The buyer must also be aware that although some improvements are essentially free (they don't cost the builder any more to produce), like wider side decks or a better hull design, others, such as higher-quality resins, more responsive steering systems, and added fire and flooding resistance, will cost the builder, and the consumer, money. If heightened awareness on the consumer's part results in closer attention being paid to these and other areas by boatbuilders, and ultimately leads to a better product, so much the better. In the final analysis, that's my intent.

Enjoy the book!

Acknowledgments

First of all, like other authors of nonfiction, I am indebted to the many experts who took the time to review sections of the book. Naval architect Eric Sponberg provided many helpful insights and offered corrections for the chapters on seaworthiness, fiberglass construction, and hull design, as did Alan Gilbert, Lou Codega, and Jeff Leishman. Core manufacturer engineers Rob Mazza, Keith Walton, and Marco Zvanik also reviewed the fiberglass construction chapter, zeroing in on scintillating topics like shear modulus and ultimate elongation until I actually knew what they were talking about, and offered spirited commentary regarding the relative merits of their products.

Don Blount, a leading authority on planing hull design and propulsion systems, has been generous with his advice and insights over the years, and I have learned from him and through reading his professional papers. The planing hull chapter especially benefits from Don's expertise. Don's fellow planing hull pioneer, Dan Savitsky, whose equations are used by naval architects worldwide, did me the courtesy of reading through the chapter on that subject.

John Kiley talked freely about his long experience designing catamarans. Walter Hahn, Lee Dana, Phil Kimball, Dave Martin, Chuck Husick, Bruce Hays, David Wilson, Steve Settles, and Dave Gerr were all helpful and encouraging. Yacht designers Michael Kasten, Steven Pollard, Bruce Roberts, and Broward Marine's Richard Arnold were kind enough to review the chapter on steel and aluminum construction. *Principles of Yacht Design*, by Lars Larsson and Rolf E. Eliasson, and *Seaworthiness: The Forgotten Factor*, by Czeslaw A. Marchaj, are superb resources and contributed substantially to the chapters on seaworthiness and hull design. Hamilton Jet, Bennett Trim Tabs, Grady-White, ATC Chemical, Eric Greene, Tiara, Viking, and Nordhavn were among those who provided detailed illustrations. Finally, my son, David, has taught me you're never too old to learn from youth.

Part 1 How Boats Work

CHAPTER 1

Introduction

Wear the old coat and buy the new book.
—Austin Phelps

Welcome to the wonderful world of boating! You may be getting ready to buy your first boat, or maybe you've owned a series of yachts over the last forty years. But whether you're new to the game, or an experienced boater, the more you understand about powerboats and yachts, the better. That's what this book is all about—helping you to better understand powerboat design, construction, and performance; in short, what *really* makes a boat tick. You'll learn more about the boat you own now—maybe why it porpoises at high speed, whether your hull is likely to blister, or why the bow rises excessively on plane. Or why a semidisplacement hull is really what you've been looking for all along, or the effect of bulwarks on dynamic stability. And of course my hope is that the reader will be a little more discriminating, and have higher expectations, next time around.

Choosing your next powerboat or -yacht can be a perplexing process. There are hundreds of models to choose from, and most of the magazine ads say pretty much the same thing; that Brand X is the best, a revolutionary advance over the competition. Talk is cheap, however, and results speak volumes. Two boats, one well-designed and engineered and the other anything but, might look very similar during a quick tour at a boat show. But taking a closer look in the right places, asking the right questions, and insisting on a prepurchase sea trial will reveal the great gulf that may lie between the two boats'

quality, performance, reliability, and longevity.

Even the smallest, simplest boats interact with wind and waves in complex ways. And even if it's basically a hull, an outboard, and a 6-gallon gas tank, you'll want your boat to perform well and to last a long time with minimal maintenance. The bigger the boat, the more complicated it gets with all the extra systems that make life afloat more enjoyable.

Whichever boat you end up buying, the more you know about the hull design's capabilities and limitations, the methods and materials used to build it, the propulsion system that makes it go, and the systems that provide fuel, ventilation, electricity, and fresh and salt water, the better off you'll feel about the experience. And feeling good is what owning a boat is all about.

Philosophy

The first half of the book, chapters 1 through 14, discusses the theory and engineering underlying good powerboat design, with plenty of illustrations to flesh them out. Here we explore questions such as what makes a boat seaworthy, whether a displacement or planing hull is best for you, what propulsion system is most appropriate, what to look for in topside safety, engine compartment access, helm station design, accommodations, and so on.

In places this book is opinionated. It reflects, among other things, the philosophy about boats

I've developed and refined over recent years evaluating boats for consumers, magazines, and boatbuilders. And, perhaps more fundamentally, it reflects the twenty years I spent in the coast guard and navy, where safety was always the driving concern in our operations. Chapters 2 and 12 are dedicated to seaworthiness and safety afloat.

Not that I confuse a destroyer with a walkaround very often, but there are elements of design that are common to both, and there is much that the builders of pleasure craft can learn from military and commercial vessels. So the book is informed, among other things, by navy and coast guard design practices and assumptions, and ventures to say where they reasonably apply to your boat. Likewise, I will bring in standards applied to commercial vessels issued by regulatory bodies such as the American Bureau of Shipping (ABS) and the Maritime and Coast Guard Agency of Great Britain (MCA).

In a few places I may sound annoyed with boats that are, to put it charitably, unwisely designed—for instance with 18-inch-high bow railings that are placed just right to catch your ankle; with foredecks that slope like ski jumps; with an absence of flotation foam or compartmentation to limit flooding; or with helm stations designed by stylists rather than ergonomics experts. It *is* frustrating to see how close some models come to being really superb boats—if just a little more thought and care had gone into their design. It generally doesn't cost any more to build a boat that's practical and safe as well as good looking. On the other hand, it's the rare boat that doesn't have at least a few positive traits going for it, and most have a lot going for them. Even with a problematic boat, it could be that the judicious investment of a relatively small amount of money could bring it up to snuff.

Perception and perspective are what I hope you will gain from a close study of this book. You can skim through the chapters in any order you like, of course. But, if you read it in order, from the Seaworthiness and Other Mysteries chapter through the Finding Your Next Boat chapter, you'll find that each chapter, to some degree, builds on the last. For instance, it helps to understand the difference between static and dynamic stability (in chapter 2) before brushing up on weight distribution, propeller pocket design, and dynamic instabilities (in chapter 4).

Picking the right *type* of boat is also key to getting the most enjoyment out of it. Center consoles are great fishing boats, but you wouldn't want to spend a weekend on one. A deep-V is often the way to go offshore, but forget about cruising the Erie Canal in one. An express cruiser eliminates the ladder to the bridge, but you give up a climate-controlled saloon, and so on. As we'll see, it's important to first clearly define your expectations and needs, and then find a boat whose layout, features, and hull form best meet them.

Just like the foundation of a house, the hull of a boat, including its shape, is the entering argument as to its suitability for your purposes. A boat might have the perfect cabin layout, great helm visibility, and a family-safe topsides, but you'd better check out the hull design before making a decision. That 35-footer with the extra cedar-lined locker and bigger berth in the forward stateroom probably gained the extra cabin volume by widening the hull forward, and the result will be a really roomy boat with a rough ride. As you'll see in the planing hull chapter, you can't have the biggest 40-footer in the marina *and* get a smooth ride. So the choice depends on your requirements and having realistic expectations; do you want to keep up with that Blackfin 33 and run comfortably at 25 knots in a three-foot chop, or do you want the biggest cabin in your boat's class?

Boat speed depends on many things, but, along with available *horsepower*, *weight*, and *hull form* are at the top of the list. With few exceptions, a lighter boat goes faster than a heavier one of the same shape. To make a boat light is easy and cheap—you just use less fiberglass and smaller structural members. But to make it both light *and* strong takes time and costs money, as we learn in the chapters on construction. Weight aside, a boat with a flatter bottom goes faster than a deep-V, as we see in chapter 4. But while the 30-foot deep-V will slice through a stiff chop at 25 knots without spilling your coffee, the 50-foot flat-bottom boat will have to slow down to trolling speed to prevent serious injury, let alone discomfort, to its occupants. We'll also look at the relationship between *beam* and *ride quality*: given similar hull forms and propulsion packages, a longer, narrower boat will be consistently faster, smoother riding, and more fuel-efficient than one that has the same interior volume but is shorter and wider. Whether at displacement or planing speeds (assuming both have planing hulls), the longer, narrower boat is simply easier to push. The laws of physics and economy tell us that, in spite of those glossy brochures, you can't get something for nothing.

Reality

The second half of the book is a market survey in the form of boat reviews, where we take all the theory we have learned and apply it to actual boats. We will look at all the major powerboat types—from center consoles to pilothouse motor yachts—to see what each type does well (and not so well) and what to look for in each. There are far too many models on the market to cover all of them in a meaningful way. Instead, you will find in-depth evaluations of representative boats, both new and old, to use as a starting point to assess design, construction, performance, comfort, and safety. All reflect my own independent analysis, judgment, and opinions. Some include performance data, and one may just be of the boat you're looking for. The inclusion of a boat among these reviews means that I have a generally favorable impression of it, even though I am sometimes pretty critical—you should see the reviews we left out! Supplementing these full-length evaluations, you will find briefer "snapshot" reviews that cover related models.

A great many boatbuilders, kindly and without reservation, provided photos for use in this section of the book.

So what's the difference, really, between a name-brand and a no-name? It depends. The fact is, between large, premium-brand builders and their small, relatively unknown counterparts, modern manufacturing techniques and materials have tended to level the playing field to a large degree. Using advances like vinylester resins, core bonding putties, simplified vacuum-bagging techniques, and computer-aided design, the little guys can, and often do, turn out excellent products. (Construction techniques are discussed in chapters 6 and 7.) Some little-known boats—especially small boats powered by outboards and stern drives—are better than some of the pricier marquee names. So while that premium-brand cruiser may give an owner bragging rights with their dockmates, the shopper who takes the time to peer through the hype and haze can maybe buy a better boat for less money or a bigger boat for the same expenditure.

There is often a direct correlation between price and quality. Some well-known builders produce wonderful, long-lasting boats, and their prices reflect it. But their sticker prices also reflect the ego appeal and prestige of the *brand*, as well as the boat. A name-brand boat will tend to hold its value better over time, which is an important factor. Top-end boatbuilders may also have higher standards for their dealers than others and keep close tabs on buyers' selling and service experience through customer satisfaction surveys.

You should also factor the dealership into the equation. I'd rather have a decent boat backed by a good dealer than a better boat sold by one who's incompetent or indifferent. You'll feel the same when your starboard cooling pump breaks on a Friday morning just as all your relatives are arriving in town for a long weekend.

I'd even be prepared to pay more for a boat if it's sold by a good, reputable dealer. Dealers need to make a profit, without which they wouldn't be able to afford the people and facilities needed to get your boat back up and running by Friday afternoon. The same goes for working with a broker—find one with a good reputation, and he or she will stay with you and watch out for your interests as you trade up, or down, over the years. We cover boat shopping in chapter 14.

Finally, boatbuilders aren't just competing against each other for your discretionary income—they're also up against golf and ski resorts, travel agents, campgrounds, and motor home manufacturers. And whoever delivers the most satisfaction for harried, hurried, hard-working families gets the nod. The recreational boating industry is in the business of luring people to the boating world, so it's not surprising that marketing and styling sometimes take on an inflated importance.

In the best boats, however, form and function blend seamlessly to make them safe, reliable, durable, attractive, and ergonomically engineered for the user's pleasure. Building safe and user-friendly pleasure boats isn't rocket science. It's a matter of applying common sense and care in their design and construction.

There are many terrific boats out there. Let's find out what makes them tick.

CHAPTER 2

Seaworthiness and Other Mysteries

First rule of sailing:
Keep the ocean out of the boat.
                                    —*Anonymous*

A lot has been written about the subject of what makes a vessel "seaworthy," or literally "worthy of the sea." One legal definition says that a vessel is *seaworthy* if she can carry out the mission for which she was intended. Usually, the operative phrase is "fit for her intended purpose." Therefore, a coastal cruiser can be very seaworthy for coastal cruising, but not necessarily offshore voyaging. Yet she is still considered seaworthy for the use for which she is intended; it all depends on which "sea" we're talking about.

For our purposes, though, we apply a more stringent definition. The bottom line? Seaworthiness refers to a vessel's *survivability*, including its ability to resist capsize, and to its behavior, including its controllability and predictability, in rough water. When any vessel puts to sea, it must be able to provide its occupants a high degree of safety and security en route to its destination, and be able to take severe conditions of wind and sea in stride. The farther offshore a vessel travels, and to some extent the slower its speed, the higher the expectations for its seaworthiness, since safe haven may well be unreachable in time to avoid heavy seas and high winds. An adjunct to seaworthiness is the matter of *seakindliness*, as we discuss below, which acknowledges the importance of crew comfort to maintaining a vessel in a seaworthy condition.

Every vessel is the end result of a series of competing interests that must be compromised to

The Palmer Johnson 151-foot yacht *Turmoil* is the essence of seaworthiness. A high bow with substantial reserve buoyancy, generous freeboard, and a relatively small superstructure, located aft, are all great features in a blow. The open foredeck sheds green water overboard rather than letting it crash against the forward deckhouse. The same concept at 50 feet would work equally well, for the same reasons. PALMER JOHNSON

achieve the desired mix of qualities. To create enough interior volume to make a yacht attractive to some buyers, a designer may opt for a large deckhouse and full, blunt bow sections, both of which tend to make a vessel less seaworthy. In this and many other cases, a design objective may pull against the interests of seaworthiness. You can't have everything in a boat, no matter what the advertisers say.

Few vessels are designed with just one or two priorities, such as high speed or shallow draft. Most boats can accomplish several missions quite well but are utterly unsuited to some other purposes. By analogy, consider a sports car. A Ferrari can go 180 mph, but it would not be your choice to carry a load of plywood home from the lumberyard. Its utility is limited—and it costs a lot. You buy a Ferrari for speed, not for its climate-control system.

The SUV, on the other hand, represents a host of compromises and is much more useful. It can carry a load of passengers, it goes about half the speed of the Ferrari, it costs far less to buy and maintain, and it even pulls a trailer. But, it also guzzles gas and is far more susceptible to rollover than the Ferrari. Most pleasure vessels are more like the versatile SUV, representing a chain of compromises that produce the desired effect.

Ultimately, it is important that you understand and fully appreciate a boat's capabilities and limitations, and where compromises have been made that affect seaworthiness. In this chapter we look at the essential elements of seaworthiness and the effect on seaworthiness of the many competing design interests. We also point out a few important details to look for when choosing your next boat.

When heading offshore, and especially when your intended track takes you more than a few hours from the nearest safe refuge, safety considerations ought to be at the top of the priority list. For our purposes, *offshore capability* doesn't necessarily imply transoceanic range, simply the capability to operate with a high degree of security in the open ocean, many hours from shelter. For the run from Ft. Lauderdale to the Bahamas, for example, I for one would want offshore capability.

Keep in mind that range alone doesn't convey seaworthiness. There are plenty of boats out there that carry fuel enough to cruise many hundreds of miles, but in which I personally wouldn't want to cruise more than a few hours' distance from shore. When you're shopping for seaworthiness, range is an important part of the equation, but only one part.

Now let's consider how stability, roll damping, flooding resistance, steering, and speed, among other things, affect a vessel's seaworthiness. You'll see that naval architects have a language all their own, but the concepts are clear enough, so hang in there as we discuss a few of them.

Stability

For a vessel to be seaworthy, it must first of all resist capsizing under the most severe conditions that it can reasonably be expected to encounter. The term *stability* refers to the tendency of a hull to return to an even keel, or equilibrium, after an upsetting force is applied; stability is the result of the opposing forces of buoyancy and gravity working together. A boat *lists* when one side is more heavily loaded (by gear, equipment, fuel, or even green water on deck) than the other, and it *heels* when a dynamic movement, like a sharp turn or a wave, is introduced.

Seaworthy vessels have both *initial stability*, determined largely by the shape of the hull, and *ultimate stability*, governed more by weight distribution vertically within the boat. A boat derives stability from the *righting arm* (RA) created by the opposing forces of buoyancy and gravity. The longer the righting arm, and the greater the vessel's displacement, the more stable it will be.

If this is as clear as mud, don't worry: we'll return to it in a moment. First, however, let's have a look at a few key terms you'll need to understand to know what's going on when your boat rolls and pitches, and keeps coming back to an even keel.

Center of Gravity

Whether you're talking about a boat, an airplane, or a standard poodle, each has a *center of gravity*, called simply the CG (naval architects love acronyms). This is the exact point at which all the weights can be considered to be concentrated, or focused. A boat suspended from its CG would hang sedately in equilibrium, neither listing nor out of trim. So the CG is an absolute point within three dimensions—length, height, and breadth—and its position has three respective components: *vertical*

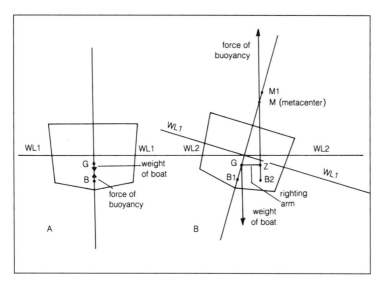

force of
buoyancy

M1
M (metacenter)

WL1

WL1   WL1   WL2   WL2

G   weight   G   Z
B   of boat   B1   B2   WL1

force of   righting
buoyancy   arm
                                               weight
                                               of boat

A   B

This diagram shows a boat on an even keel and at an angle of starboard heel. The center of gravity (G) does not move as the boat heels to 10 degrees, but the center of buoyancy (B) shifts to starboard (B2). If we were to draw a vertical line straight up from B2, it would intersect another line drawn up from the hull's centerline (like a mast) at a point called the metacenter (M). The amount of force available to return the boat to an even keel (the righting moment) is determined by the boat's weight and by the distance from G to Z, which is a point above B2 and level with G. Through the first few degrees of heel, M (an indicator of initial stability) falls in about the same place as B moves outboard. But as the boat heels beyond about 10 degrees, M ceases to be an indicator of stability since it no longer focuses about a single point above centerline. In other words, M1 migrates substantially from its consistent low-heel-angle position (M).

ADAPTED FROM ARMSTRONG, *GETTING STARTED IN POWERBOATING*

(VCG is usually measured from the keel or design *baseline*), *longitudinal* (LCG can be measured from either the transom or the bow at the waterline), and *transverse* (TCG is measured from a vessel's fore-and-aft centerline).

To get us thinking spatially, a typical express sportfisherman's LCG might be located 40 percent of the waterline length forward from the stern, the VCG will be near the top of the engines, and the TCG should be exactly on the centerline. In a planing powerboat, the VCG will be well above the waterline. On a deep-draft sailboat with a ballasted keel, the VCG will often be below the waterline. On a typical displacement hull, the CG will be farther forward and deeper than in the sportfisherman.

Designers list all the weights in a boat, including the hull, superstructure, engines, fuel, water, cabinetry, appliances, and so on, and record their centers of mass to determine precisely (from a sum of vectors) where the CG should be. Since the height of the VCG is so critical to stability, a builder can conduct an *inclining experiment* to confirm it; more on that in a moment. But to be considered seaworthy, a vessel's VCG has to be low enough to ensure adequate stability.

Buoyancy

Archimedes had it figured out in 250 B.C. The force of buoyancy acting on an immersed object equals the weight of the water displaced. So, just as gravity pushes down, buoyancy pushes up. In fact, a vessel floats because the pressure or buoyancy acting on the hull equals the weight of the boat. It doesn't matter whether the hull is made of wood, fiberglass, or steel; the buoyancy is determined by the *volume* of water the hull skin displaces. When a boat is at rest, gravity and buoyancy are in equilibrium. Add more weight, and the hull sinks lower until the added buoyancy, and upward pressure, reaches a new equilibrium.

Just as a boat has a center of gravity, it also has a *center of buoyancy*. If you were able to freeze the water your boat is floating in, and then magically lift the boat out with a crane, the hole your boat left in the ice would have a certain shape and volume. If you were to fill the hole in the ice with Perrier and let *it* freeze, it would equal the weight of the boat. Now lift the frozen block of Perrier out of the ice, and you will find that it, too, has a center of gravity, in three dimensions, just as the boat does. And that point corresponds to the center of buoyancy (CB), the exact point at which all buoyant forces acting on the hull are concentrated. The three dimensions of that point correspond to the hull's *longitudinal center of buoyancy* (LCB), *vertical center of buoyancy* (VCB), and *transverse center of buoyancy* (TCB), respectively.

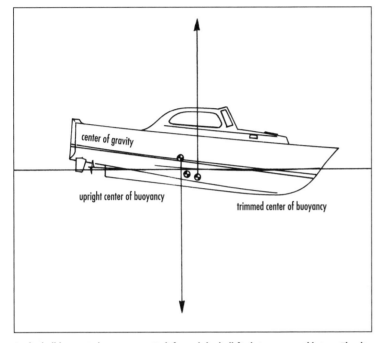

As the hull buries its bow or stern, B shifts and the hull finds its new equilibrium. The distance from G to ever-changing B determines the righting arm (GZ) that works to return the hull to equilibrium. Concentrating weight amidships also results in a boat that buries its bow and stern less in rough water. Less pitching (and rolling) make a boat not only faster, but more comfortable (seakindly) in a seaway.

ADAPTED FROM LARSSON AND ELIASSON, *PRINCIPLES OF YACHT DESIGN*

Trim

Trim refers simply to the boat's fore-and-aft attitude, viewed from the side, with respect to the water surface. A boat is said to be at zero trim when it is floating on its design waterline. Trim can vary due to weight being added or removed in the bow or stern. It can also be affected by the dynamic lift of water flow along the bottom of a moving hull. A boat with a lot of extra weight aft is said to be trimmed down by the stern. A planing boat at cruising speed invariably runs with the bow raised

in relation to the stern—say at a 4-degree trim angle (with the bow angled 4 degrees upward)—since the *center of dynamic lift* (CDL; see page 28) is (or should be) forward of LCG.

LCG always corresponds with LCB, which means the total force of gravity is balanced with the total force of buoyancy, and the boat rests at a corresponding depth and trim angle in the water. As weight is shifted forward and aft or side to side inside the boat, the center of buoyancy shifts to match the new CG. If you haul a 900-pound tuna through the transom door, the boat's LCG shifts aft, and so does the hull's LCB as the volume of water displaced aft increases to compensate for the added weight. When a new equilibrium is reached, you'll be trimmed down by the stern a degree or two.

Longitudinal Center of Flotation

A couple more buoyancy terms, and we're ready to move on. The *longitudinal center of flotation* (LCF) is the center of the vessel's waterplane area, or "footprint" at the waterline. It's the point in the vessel longitudinally at which weight can be added without changing the fore-and-aft trim, and the point about which the hull rotates longitudinally when weight is added or removed fore or aft. LCF acts like the pivot point in the middle of a seesaw.

We already know that the LCB is the same as the center of gravity of the water displaced by the hull, or our block of frozen Perrier, and the LCF is the center of the hull's waterplane. But unless we're talking about a floating shoe box, the LCB and the LCF won't line up at the same spot, since hull shape changes from the waterplane on down to the keel.

How much the hull immerses and trims (rotates) longitudinally with weight changes is also of interest to naval architects, so they've come up with a couple more catchy names for us to remember.

Adjusting Trim

Trim behavior may be intuitively obvious: add weight forward of the LCF and the bow trims down; add weight aft, and the stern settles. If the added weight is far enough forward, the stern will also come up, and vice versa. The effort, or moment (force times distance), that it takes to change the trim a total of an inch (adding up the changes forward and aft) is called the *moment to trim* an inch, or MT1. If the bow immerses 1 inch, and the stern emerges 1 inch, the trim has changed 2 inches. If a moment equal to MT1 is applied, the total change in trim is 1 inch, for instance when the bow goes up ½ inch the stern goes down ½ inch. The math is simple; moving 400 pounds 2 feet aft anywhere in the boat creates an 800-foot-pound moment. Knowing MT1 can help if you decide to relocate a heavy object in your boat, like a generator or water tank. When estimating MT1, a coefficient based on the hull form under consideration can also be used. For a rough approximation, you can multiply 0.38 by the waterplane squared divided by the waterline beam. Let's see how this works out for the 44-foot planing boat in the accompanying text. The waterplane area is an estimated 336 square feet. Square 336, divide by the 12-foot waterline beam, and multiply by 0.38, and you find that the MT1 is 3,575 foot-pounds. So, for example, adding a 500-pound weight 7 feet forward of the LCF will change the trim 1 inch. Since the LCF is roughly 36 to 40 percent forward of a planing hull's stern, weight added at the stern of a planing hull will raise the comparatively narrow bow more than it will sink the wide stern. In our example, the bow might rise 0.6 inch while the stern sinks 0.4 inch.

A figure called *pounds per inch immersion* (PPII) tells us how much weight has to be added at the LCF to make the boat settle an inch deeper in the water. Accurate PPII and MT1 figures should be available from the designer of your boat. It is a good idea to consult a naval architect before shifting or adding a significant amount of weight on the boat. To estimate PPII for a planing boat, you first need to estimate waterplane area. Multiply length times maximum beam (at the waterline) and multiply that product by 70 percent. So, a 44-foot boat with a 40-foot waterline length and a 12-foot waterline beam would have a waterplane of about 336 square feet (70 percent of a 40- by 12-foot rectangle). A cubic foot of seawater weighs 64 pounds, and a 1-inch-thick slice of that cubic foot weighs 5.33 pounds. Multiply 336 by 5.33 and we get 1,791 pounds-per-inch immersion for our 40-footer. For a displacement vessel, the figure to multiply the L × B rectangle by might be closer to 65 percent, yielding a waterplane of 312 square feet and a PPII of 1,163. The PPII usually goes up as a hull sinks into the water, as the hull tends to get wider above the design waterline.

Initial and Ultimate Stability

Now that we know some terminology, let's take a look at how stability works. The water supports the boat, at rest in calm water, with a buoyant force equal to the weight, or displacement, of the vessel. In the accompanying figure, as the hull rolls to one side, the center of buoyancy (CB) shifts outboard to CB^1, immersing the down side of the hull and raising the opposite side. Because the center of buoyancy shifts while the center of gravity does not, a righting arm (RA) is created that works to return the boat to an even keel. The righting arm is determined by the distance from the center of gravity to a point Z, which falls above the new center of buoyancy. For this reason, the righting arm is referred to on the stability diagram graphically as GZ (but mathematically it's the RA). Gravity pushes down and buoyancy pushes up, with both forces working to return the boat to an even keel. As the roll increases initially, so does the magnitude of the righting force represented by GZ.

Any seaworthy boat is stable to some degree. But it's important to understand the relationship among buoyancy, gravity, and the boat's VCG, and the two different but connected ways we speak about stability. It turns out that hull shape has the most to do with influencing stability as it starts to tip to one side; this early phase of the roll we call *initial stability*. But once the list reaches around 10 degrees or so, VCG starts to matter *more* (though hull *shape* still matters) since its height begins to have an increasing influence on stability; so *ultimate stability* refers to a vessel's tendency to right itself from more extreme angles of heel. A planing boat can *feel* deceptively stable when compared with a round-bilge displacement cruiser of the same size, but the latter will invariably be able to survive a far greater roll than the former.

The boat itself knows nothing at all about these arbitrary terms, and there is no magic point at which different laws of physics apply. It's just that with a dramatic shift sideways in CB, hull shape has the most effect on the hull's initial tendency to return to equilibrium with the water's surface. That's why a convertible sportfisherman *feels* so stable—it has a relatively flat, wide, and shallow bottom—in spite of its fairly high VCG. But as RA increases with greater angles of list, it's easy to see that the CG's height above the keel, or VCG, has a greater bearing on stability. That convertible will capsize when the displacement hull is still picking up righting moment.

So, naval architects refer to initial stability as the tendency of a vessel to right itself from small angles of heel due to the shape of the hull bottom. Initial stability is also referred to as *form* stability, because the length of the righting arm developed depends on the shape, or form, of the hull. It's called *initial* stability because hull form predominates in the stability equation only through the first ten or twelve degrees of list. After that, weight distribution (VCG) starts to have relatively more to say about stability. Initial stability is usually calculated for a hull at rest or at slow speeds in calm water. It remains predictable at speed, but only as long as the wave train (the varying waterline created by the hull-generated waves along the hull) is known and does not substantially alter the buoyant forces.

The shape of the hull determines the height of its *metacenter*, commonly and cleverly called M for short, and M is the first thing to establish when determining initial stability. M is the point where lines drawn vertically from the upright center of buoyancy (CB) and the centers at various small angles of heel intersect. These lines tend to converge about the same point until the hull reaches 10 or 12 degrees of heel, and then they start to scatter and become useless as a stability indicator. M can be determined mathematically using the hull lines drawings, since the hull shape, or area exposed to the water at various angles of heel, can be calculated. The distance GM is called the *metacentric height*. The greater it is, the higher the initial stability.

Again, the horizontal distance from CG to a line drawn vertically from CB (a point called Z) represents the righting arm (RA) working to right the vessel. The magnitude of the righting arm, labeled GZ in the drawing, varies with the angle of heel.

Engineers conduct an inclining experiment to find, or verify, the height of VCG, just in case they miscalculated when adding up all the vessel's component weights prior to or during construction. In an inclining experiment, weights are placed off-center to make the vessel list to one side, usually up to three or four degrees. Knowing precisely how much the vessel displaces (weighs), how much the inclining weights themselves weigh, and how far off-center they're placed, the designer can calculate the effort the hull is making to resist listing. This effort is reflected in the hull's righting arm multiplied by the vessel's displacement, which equals the *righting moment*.

At this point the designer knows the magnitude of the righting arm and thus the length of GZ and can pinpoint the heeled center of buoyancy from hull shape. From this information the vertical center of gravity can be located so as to calculate the righting arm magnitude, GZ. Now the designer can calculate GM, which is the distance from M down to VCG, and once the height of VCG is

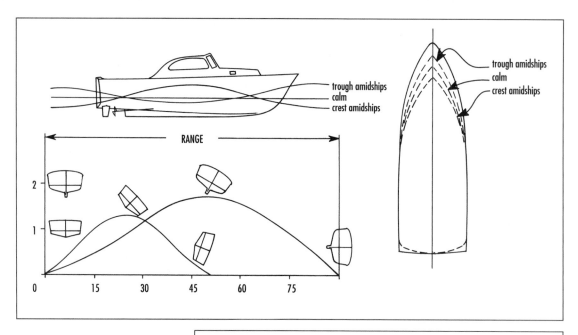

Above: A typical righting arm curve for a displacement hull that peaks at about 46 degrees and reaches its point of zero stability at some 85 degrees. If this vessel is heeled, say, to 60 degrees, the area to the right inside the curve represents the energy remaining to keep the vessel from capsizing. The planing hull's righting arm falls to zero at 50 degrees of heel or even less. **Right:** Shows the great difference between static stability calculations and actual dynamic stability, particularly when running downsea, in waves the same length as the hull (which will move at nearly the vessel's displacement hull speed, incidentally). Few owners, and, for that matter, not all boat designers, factor in the loss of (dynamic) stability that occurs when running in a seaway, straddling the crest of a wave.

TOP: ADAPTED FROM LARSSON AND ELIASSON, *PRINCIPLES OF YACHT DESIGN*
RIGHT: ADAPTED FROM MARCHAJ, *SEAWORTHINESS*

known with certainty, *ultimate stability* can be accurately calculated and displayed on a chart called the *curves of stability.*

Remember that GM is only useful in evaluating the vessel's *initial* stability. That's because M, the

spot where B intersects initially, starts to scatter at higher inclination angles.

Ultimate stability is also referred to as *weight stability* because vertical center of gravity (VCG), rather than hull shape, is most important at more extreme heeling angles. Beyond 10 degrees or so of heel, depending on hull shape in cross section, the metacenter starts to move. At this point, the naval architect uses VCG and the transverse center of buoyancy (TCB) to establish the righting arm (or RA, shown as GZ on the diagram on page 9). Then, RA is multiplied by the vessel's displacement to determine the righting moment (RM) at successive angles of heel. The stability curve is the product of those calculations, showing in graphic form the vessel's righting moment plotted successively through the stability range. Stability curves for ships and large yachts are usually drawn for light-, half-, and full-load displacements.

As the accompanying diagrams indicate, a vessel's stability curve is typically somewhat bell shaped, with the maximum righting arm developing about halfway to capsize. Some vessels' stability curves are irregular, reflecting the equally irregular shape of the hull and superstructure as they pick up buoyancy while listing. A vessel's ultimate stability, then, is the angle at which the righting arm retreats to zero. This point of no return, or point of vanishing stability, is the angle of heel at which neutral equilibrium is reached, and at which capsize is likely to occur; this point is represented by the right-hand side of the curve where the righting arm intersects the zero-righting arm line.

RM (righting moment) represents the energy available to return a hull to an even keel. Hence the importance of knowing a vessel's exact displacement when calculating its stability curves. And displacement is crucial to seaworthiness: all else being equal, a heavier vessel is more seaworthy than a lighter one of similar size and shape, since RM is a function of vessel weight. As mentioned, metacentric height is no longer a consideration when we're working with angles of heel past 10 degrees.

For some cruising sailboats and displacement trawlers, the range of positive stability can reach 130 or more degrees of heel. Some rescue craft and sailboats are stable at all angles of heel, even fully inverted, with a low center of gravity and a high, watertight and buoyant superstructure allowing them to roll 180 degrees and quickly return to an even keel. For navy destroyers, and many other ships, the figure is closer to 60 to 70 degrees. These displacement hulls have a low CG and moderate GM (metacentric height). Planing powerboats might have a range of stability as low as 45 degrees or even less.

Moderate GM

Depending on the hull, there is always an acceptable range of GM; it can be too low or too high. In fact, the most seaworthy vessel is one with moderate GM and low CG; too much GM is not a good thing for ultimate stability. Excessive GM indicates a hull that relies on great beam, rather than a low CG, for its stability. For that reason, ultimate stability in high-GM vessels drops off more quickly compared with those of moderate GM.

High GM makes a vessel follow wave slopes more closely, which means it will heel over farther as it rides up a wave crest, and then be more susceptible to capsize when hit broadside by the water jet produced by a breaking wave. High GM also makes for a stiff, uncomfortable motion with high roll and pitch accelerations. The snap roll created by these high accelerations can be dangerous as well as uncomfortable. Moderate GM, on the other hand, makes for a very long, deep roll period and low accelerations. The significant form stability of a high-GM hull is a double-edged sword, then, acting to make the hull conform more readily to wave action, and less resistant to capsizing in heavy seas.

As a general rule, seaworthy displacement hulls vessels have moderate GM, a relatively narrow beam, deep draft, and heavy displacement, which results in a longer roll period, a greater range of stability, and the ability to resist capsize much better than other vessels.

Planing versus Displacement Hulls

Planing boats have relatively wide, flat, shallow bottoms with hard chines (the corners formed by the intersection of the hull sides and bottom) that create great initial stability, but their ultimate stability, the point at which the forces working to right the boat reach zero, generally occurs below 50 degrees. The ultimate stability of most planing vessels is limited by their relatively high VCG and shallow hulls. By contrast, as discussed, a well-designed displacement hull might have a range of positive stability of 130 degrees or more.

As a typical planing hull heels to one side, the

hull's buoyancy outboard increases rapidly (more rapidly than a round-bilge hull) as the chine submerges. That's why a flat-bottom *planing* hull has a shorter, stiffer, less comfortable roll period than a displacement hull, and a deep-V will roll more than a modified-V. The flatter the bottom, and the beamier the boat (and the correspondingly greater the GM value), the stiffer the roll and the greater the initial stability.

Displacement hulls rock and roll more easily, because the shape of the bottom doesn't resist rolling nearly as effectively. Unlike a planing hull, there are no hard chines to create lots of buoyant force or lift outboard, just slack bilges (with a large, gentle radius at the bottom–hull side intersection) that are designed to minimize resistance to forward motion. In other words, because the hull is rounded in cross section, the volume of water displaced at the boat's extreme beam changes very little as the hull starts to incline to one side. Since the center of buoyancy doesn't shift outboard as dramatically in a roll, there's less righting moment created at small angles of heel to return the vessel to an even keel. But even though deep, narrow, round-bottom displacement hulls roll easily initially, they can, and usually do, have tremendous *ultimate* stability because of their lower centers of gravity.

Since a planing hull is relatively shallow, the VCG can only get so low in relation to total hull volume. A deeper-draft trawler-style displacement hull can use fuel, liquid ballast, machinery, and even fixed interior or keel-mounted ballast to make VCG very low. This creates a strong righting moment that, working with the hull's shifting center of buoyancy, results in tremendous ultimate and reserve stability. (When looking at a stability curve, the area to the right of the present angle of heel is *reserve stability*; this represents the energy, in the form of righting moment, that remains to prevent capsize.) Although a sportfisherman or express cruiser's stiff roll period makes it feel more stable, most displacement hulls keep gaining righting arm long after a planing hull's stability starts to drop off. Once again, the center of gravity—not the hull shape—is the fi-

nal arbiter of ultimate stability at angles of heel past 10 degrees. That's why it's important to keep heavy weight low in the boat and to minimize weight additions above the center of gravity.

Surviving a Roll

Rollover capability is touted by some displacement trawler builders, and the ability to survive a roll of 360 degrees certainly adds substantially to a vessel's seaworthiness. But this claim needs a reality check. Any vessel with a 360-degree range of positive stability must have a low center of gravity as well as significant buoyancy high in the hull and superstructure. To maintain this buoyancy as the vessel rolls to 180 degrees, windows, doors, and hatches must be watertight. They must remain watertight, too, and be able to withstand the significant forces caused by the static pressure and tremendous dynamic impact of seawater.

Most yachts have large windows in the saloon and pilothouse, and these are the most vulnerable during a rollover. And of course the larger the window, the more susceptible it is to breaking. Either the glass must be very thick, or they must be covered (before the rollover, obviously) with storm covers or shutters of fiberglass, metal, or acrylic. A better solution, from a seaworthiness perspective, is to keep the windows small and the glass thick, but unfortunately portholes in a dimly lit saloon don't sell boats. Nevertheless, smaller, thicker windows would eliminate the need for window covers, which would not likely be installed in time in the normal course of events, anyway.

Machinery must keep running after a rollover, and the amount of water shipped into the engine room must be limited by the aggregate volume of gooseneck combustion air intakes. Obviously, furniture and all other large objects must be secured to the deck, or storage space inside lockers must be provided in such a vessel, and seat belts should be provided for all passengers. Spare handheld radios and GPS receivers will also be a good idea, since their antennas are likely to be lost in a rollover.

It's important to remember that initial and ul-

The larger the window, the thicker the glass should be to resist breaking by wave impact. This Nordhavn's saloon windows are a full ½ inch thick. NORDHAVN

timate stability figures are applicable only to vessels in an *intact* condition, meaning they have suffered no structural damage that leads to hull flooding, like a hole in the bottom, that would affect stability. When a hull floods, even partially, significant stability and reserve buoyancy are lost. And, of course, initial and ultimate stability figures are only accurate for a vessel in the static condition—that is, when the vessel is not being tossed by seas and buffeted by wind.

Dynamic Stability

Static stability calculations are only the starting point when determining seaworthiness. *Dynamic stability* is an entirely different kettle of fish. The position of a hull on a wave, whether astride the peak (which diminishes stability) or in the trough (which increases stability); the area and shape of the hull exposed to tremendous breaking-wave energy; the synchronicity between a hull's roll period and the relative wave period; and the variation in trim as a hull pitches—all these are elements that affect a vessel's actual stability. They're also very difficult to predict accurately, which accounts, in part, for their relative obscurity. However, relying solely on static stability calculations to determine a vessel's seaworthiness can have disastrous results.

Storm windows made of impact-resistant Lexan are a great thing when the weather deteriorates at sea. These sheets bolt on from the outside, so it's important to get them mounted well before the strong winds hit. NORDHAVN

Dynamic stability can be defined as the tendency of a vessel, by virtue of its displacement, mass distribution, and shape, to return to equilibrium after being upset by the forces of wind and sea. It is possible for a vessel that has impressive static stability to be dangerously unstable dynamically. The stability curves produced by inclining experiments and hydrostatic calculations are a good start for determining a vessel's stability and seaworthiness, but they are useful mainly for comparing similar vessels to one another. They are not meant to be predictive of real-life vessel behavior. Broaching, rolling, and capsizing are *dynamic* events that have no sympathy for carefully calculated stability curves. When your boat is at sea in high seas and strong winds, that calculated 70-degree (or whatever it is) angle of vanishing (zero) righting arm in no way ensures that it will actually survive a dynamic roll to that angle without capsizing.

A hull with a very large, lightweight superstructure may be stable when inclined at the dock, but take it offshore and put it beam-to a 50-knot wind, and watch that windage go to work! In an 80-knot beam wind, a navy frigate will reach some 30 degrees of semipermanent heel, using up half its stability range even before wave action is taken into account. So while a vessel with a large superstructure may have as large a static righting arm as the low-profile trawler in the next slip, it'll be the first to capsize in extreme offshore conditions. Likewise, a wave is a moving force, and imparts its *inertia* (resistance to changing velocity or direction) to any hull it comes into contact with. Both wind and wave forces will diminish stability, making the stability curves, predicated on static conditions, unreliable in a seaway.

Another way of looking at it is that dynamic forces reduce reserve stability. Your yacht's stability curve may indicate that positive RA is present up to a 70-degree list. However, the inertia from a relatively small wave impacting the hull at the wrong time—say, when the hull is rolling away from the breaking wave at a 50-degree angle of heel at the time of impact—can easily capsize the vessel. If that same vessel was rolling *toward* that breaking wave when they met at 50 degrees of heel, its chances of surviving are greatly improved. Once again, the inertia created by the vessel's lateral movement opposes the inertia of the wave in this case, adding to its effective dynamic stability. Likewise, changing course induces a heeling moment as the rudder is put over, and the results are predictable in calm water. But when a boat turns to head upwind while running down the face of a wave in a quartering sea, the results can be anything but predictable or controllable. The same thing goes for a strong gust of beam wind at just the wrong moment.

It's important to distinguish between the two kinds of inertia at work in any vessel. *Mass inertia* is the energy stored as a result of the vessel's weight and weight distribution. *Waterplane inertia* results from the area, or the size and shape, of the hull at the waterline. Both influence vessel motion and seaworthiness.

Pitch, Roll, Yaw, Heave, Surge, and Sway

A boat is capable of a combination of six motions in a seaway. The first three are rotations about an axis: the bow (and stern) *pitches* up and down (about a transverse axis), the boat *rolls* from side to side (about a longitudinal axis), and the boat *yaws* about a vertical axis (the boat changes direction, or course, about a pivot point). The remaining three are linear, or nonrotational. *Heave* is a vertical movement, such as when a vessel is rising bodily on a wave. *Surge* is a fore-and-aft movement, and *sway* is a transverse or side-to-side movement. Combinations of these movements are felt at sea: riding up and over a wave would produce both heave and pitch; being hit by a wave amidships would create both roll and sway movements, for instance. A particularly exciting combination would be a roll and a yaw, which, when running down a wave, may result in a *broach*, with the stern being thrown ahead by a following sea while the bow digs in and stays put (relatively speaking).

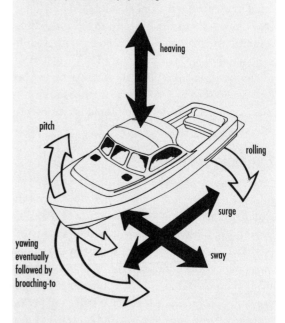

The vessel's motions in all these directions determines its seakindliness and controllability in a seaway.

ADAPTED FROM MARCHAJ, *SEAWORTHINESS*

A vessel's displacement has a great deal to do with its seaworthiness, for reasons of static stability as well as resistance to movement. As discussed, whereas a light, shallow boat will quickly conform to a wave gradient, and will be easily overwhelmed by a breaking wave, a heavy, deep vessel puts up a lot of resistance, through sheer mass and inertia, to being buffeted about. It conforms much less readily to a wave face. Grab hold of a 25-foot outboard and push it away from the dock, then do the same thing to a 60-footer. It takes a lot more effort to get the bigger boat moving, water and air resistance notwithstanding.

Another factor that plays a role in calculating capsize probability is the vessel's *roll moment of inertia* (RMI): its resistance to being rolled by outside, dynamic forces such as waves. The vessel's mass, and especially its mass distribution, is the main factor. In this regard, the boat behaves much like a flywheel. A larger-diameter flywheel resists changes in speed more than a smaller one of the same weight, and therefore is able to store more inertia in the form of rotational energy.

If significant weights are located well away from the center of gravity and the boat's roll axis, RMI increases. For instance, a tuna tower, though relatively light, extends a long way from the center of gravity, so it tends to add significantly to the roll moment of inertia, and can therefore work to resist a boat's initial roll movement caused by wave action. A hull with a larger RMI better resists roll *accelerations*, just as the larger flywheel does—it takes more effort to *start* it rolling.

A good analogy is the figure skater; when they pull their arms in, reducing the mass moment of inertia, the spin increases in speed. The 1979 Fastnet disaster, in which an offshore sailboat race was caught by a powerful storm, provides an illustration of the effect of *roll inertia* on dynamic stability. Severe weather caused many dismastings and—counterintuitively—it was discovered that dismasted yachts had a *greater* tendency to roll over than yachts with intact masts. Tank tests later confirmed this observation.

Roll Damping

All vessels have a certain amount of *damping* ability, which is the resistance to roll and pitch created by their mass and moment of inertia and by the drag of surrounding water. The more a hull is able to attenuate the energy from wave and wind action, the less it will roll, and the more stable it will be. Full keels, fixed bilge keels, fin stabilizers, paravanes, rudders, running gear, and, to a great extent, hard chines all dissipate roll. This is because of their mass and moment of inertia about the center of gravity, as discussed above, and because of their frictional drag underwater. A hull carries along with it a *boundary layer* of entrained water, known when headway is on as *frictional wake current*. This layer of water creates an additional damping effect caused by the fric-

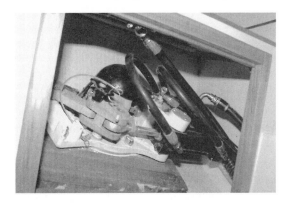

The brains and muscle behind an active fin stabilizer, viewed from inside the hull.

tional drag, or resistance, to the hull's movement. A hull with a larger underwater surface area carries more entrained water along with it, and this added drag makes the vessel less susceptible to wave action, and diminishes accelerations in all directions.

Planing hulls are susceptible to dynamic forces all their own, and the way in which a particular boat handles these forces has a direct bearing on its seaworthiness. The hull essentially flies on the surface of the water, with more of the vessel's weight supported by hydrodynamic pressure than buoyancy. Planing hull dynamics, stabilities, and instabilities are covered in more detail in chapter 4.

Complicating this matter of dynamic stability further, if the frequency which with waves impact a hull is in *resonance* with the vessel's natural roll period, a relatively low sea state can end up capsizing an otherwise seaworthy boat. If conditions produce a relatively modest sea on the beam every four seconds, and the vessel happens to have a four-second roll period, this synchronous timing will roll the boat a little farther with each cycle. The same accentuated oscillations can occur in pitching as well as rolling. Fortunately, nature seldom delivers waves hullside with such regularity. The easiest way to avoid this condition is to aggressively alter course or speed to change the frequency with which waves are met. As mentioned, vessels can also either passively or actively reduce, or *dampen*, roll period and amplitude with their keels, fixed bilge keels, paravane "flopper stoppers," or active fin stabilizers.

Stability Works Both Ways

In a sense, stability can be your friend or your foe; it all depends. Within the range of positive RA, buoyancy and gravity are our friends; outside this range, past the angle of maximum righting arm, they work to cause capsize. The same forces that keep a hull on an even keel in calm water act to roll it when inclined on the surface of a wave. A hull beam-to a large wave will try to keep itself on an even keel in relation to the wave surface; a boat floating perpendicular to a 10-degree wave gradient is at equilibrium when heeling at 10 degrees. That's why the most seaworthy hulls have narrow to moderate length-to-beam ratios; they won't seek equilibrium with steep-faced waves as readily as wide-beamed hulls, resulting in a more moderate roll amplitude and, ultimately, a more stable vessel.

Seakindliness

I grew up fishing on semidisplacement boats, operated both planing and semidisplacement rescue boats as a coast guard coxswain and surfman, then spent the better part of fifteen years aboard displacement ships of 4,100 to 10,000 tons. I then started evaluating boats for a living—mostly high-

speed, hard-chined, planing boats. Then one day I found myself back on a semidisplacement Down East–style lobster yacht—a Dyer 40—in a stiff Narragansett Bay chop. The fact is, I'd forgotten how comfortable these semidisplacement boats can be. The Dyer rolled easily in the 2- to 3-foot seas, not too deeply, and certainly not stiffly like the average hard-chine planing hull with its pumped-up GM. The Dyer can't do some things as well as a modern planing hull, such as going fast with high efficiency, but it sure is a comfortable boat to go to sea in.

A seakindly yacht like our redoubtable Dyer 40 is, well, kind to her crew. A physicist, or naval architect, would say that *accelerations* in every direction are within a comfortable range. Such a boat does not pound or snap roll, and in general has an easy motion. Neither does it roll too deeply or pitch too heavily as a boat with a lot of weight up high or in the ends might do. The amount of weight spread out on her waterplane (footprint at the waterline), called *bottom loading*, is within a certain range of moderation; a boat that is too light for its waterplane will bob and heave rapidly and dramatically, while one that is too heavy will lurch and surge about heavily and will require a prodigious power plant to plane. Heavier boats have an easier motion because of their added inertia, or resistance to movement, and diminished accelerations in all directions. Note that you don't see many lobstermen working all day from hard-chine, light hulls. Their round-bilge, moderate-beam (and moderate GM) boats have an easy motion that's lacking in their hard-chine, beamier cousins. Lacking accelerometers, seakindliness is difficult to quantify, but like a good performance of a Brahms piano concerto, you know one when you experience it.

As a rule of thumb, the wider, flatter, and lighter a boat is—or the more extreme in any one of those elements—the less comfortable it will be, at speed or at rest. If you want comfort and seaworthiness, there's just no substitute for a narrow, deep, and heavy vessel. Deeper hulls simply dissipate pitch and heave energy more effectively than shallow hulls. Heavy hulls, as we've seen, are more stable because *ultimate stability* comes from the righting moment, a function of GZ times displacement, so it takes more energy to bring such a vessel to capsize. In terms of comfort, a heavier hull's greater mass is also less susceptible to the accelerations and inertia of wave action.

We talk about moderate length-to-beam ratios in the next two chapters, but keep in mind that a 40- by 12-foot boat, while having no more interior volume than a 32- by 14-footer, will deliver a much more comfortable ride, be a better sea boat, and run more efficiently.

A fine example of a seaworthy pleasure boat, made so by a sharp entry, ample deadrise throughout, and a moderate beam-to-length ratio (44 feet, 6 inches by 11 feet, 4 inches), this Dave Gerr–designed Westbourne 44 express yacht will keep steaming in a stiff chop when other boats head for the barn. She's also faster and more easily driven—much more so—than a shorter, wider boat of the same size (volume). The steering station is comfortably far aft, where vertical motions are less pronounced.   DAVE GERR

The Nordhavn displacement trawler yacht has great reserve (weight) stability, but little form (hull shape) stability. The hull form of this long-range cruiser necessitates an easy turn of the bilge to reduce wavemaking resistance at its cruising speed of about 8 knots. When these outriggers are lowered, and flopper-stopper paravanes deployed, the roll amplitude is greatly reduced by the tension on the outrigger cables.   NORDHAVN

Enhancing Stability

Now we know why hulls roll, but it's also nice to know something can be done about it, at least on displacement vessels. All roll-reducing devices work by introducing a *heeling* moment opposite to that created by sea conditions. The two most common are *paravanes*—mini wings suspended over the side from outriggers and towed through the water—and fixed or active *bilge stabilizers*. Nothing's free in life, though: any appendage added to the bottom of a boat or hauled through the water suspended from

outriggers will add drag, slowing the vessel and diminishing propulsion efficiency. They are also subject to impact damage from grounding or striking submerged objects.

Paravanes

Commonly seen on shrimpers and trawler yachts, paravanes, or flopper-stoppers, passively reduce motion by creating a resistance to a vessel's natural tendency to roll. Suspended from long outriggers to create a significant lever arm, a pair of small paravanes can work wonders. They even dampen roll

A paravane roll dampener taking a break.　　　NORDHAVN

stabilizers to work effectively, the vessel must have headway on, and the more the better. Fin stabilizers jut out from the bottom of the hull, so they're susceptible to damage by grounding or striking an underwater object, and, like paravanes, they add some drag. They also are susceptible to mechanical failure. But both paravane and active bilge stabilizer systems help address the antiroll needs of a vessel with limited initial stability, which describes the typical full-displacement hull. Depending on the size of the vessel, a fin stabilizer might be 18 inches wide and 36 inches deep. Vosper, Naiad, Wesmar, and Seabrace are a few prominent fin stabilizer manufacturers.

Bilge Keels

Fixed bilge keels or fins project at right angles from the hull at the turn of the bilge. They extend between one- and two-thirds the length of the hull and might be a foot or more deep on larger yachts. They aren't as effective as active stabilizers but, like paravanes, they reduce roll passively and with minimal drag if they are designed right, which they by no means always are. Bilge keels are generally considered more effective in large ships (about 10 percent dampening, according to some sources) than in small boats (closer to 3 to 5 percent dampening). The lever arm, or amount of useful work they do, is a function of the distance from the center of the bilge keels to the roll axis. Their effectiveness results from the hydrodynamic resistance they create while effectively being pushed sideways through the water as the hull rotates about its roll axis. Bilge keels can be hollow, allowing them to serve as auxiliary fuel tanks, or permitting the addition of lead ballast at their ends, which further reduces rolling through damping, thanks to the addition of mass well away from the roll axis and center of gravity.

Other roll-inhibiting methods include oversized transom-mounted trim tabs that flap up and down independently to minimize roll, and antiroll tanks that rapidly move mass (seawater ballast) from side to side out of phase with the vessel's natural rolling motion (see photo page 65). (Active

with no way on—say, at anchor—but they steadily become more effective as speed is increased. The great advantage of paravanes is that there is no machinery or hydraulics involved, so they're more reliable than active stabilizers. Disadvantages include that you have to go on deck to deploy them, potentially a problem in rough water. They also slow the boat down, perhaps a half knot or so, which can be significant on a six- or seven-knot vessel over a few thousand miles at sea. In rough conditions, they will also walk in toward the boat on the high side of the roll, and can actually make contact with the hull and get stuck against it by hydrodynamic pressure. In extreme conditions, especially if set too shallow, they can pull free of the water and go flying toward the boat.

Active Stabilizers

Mechanical bilge stabilizers act like adjustable wings to generate roll-reducing lift at the turn of the bilge. They're mounted at the turn of the bilge and linked to gyros that sense the vessel's motion and continuously adjust the *active* stabilizer fins to counteract roll. When the vessel rolls to port, for instance, the port fin changes its angle of attack to generate upward lift, and the starboard fin angles down to create a downward force. For active fin

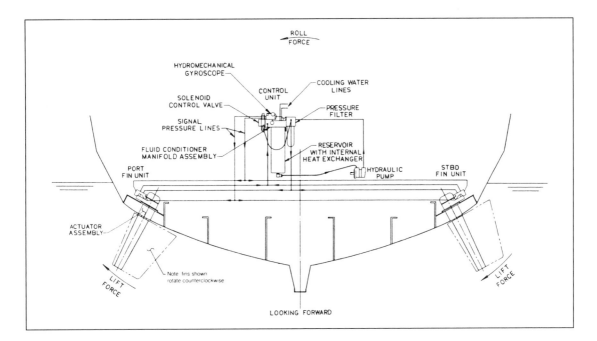

Example of an active stabilizing system. Working similarly to the ailerons on a plane, the fins can actually make a boat roll to either side, much as an airplane banks. A gyroscope senses true vertical and directs the fins to produce a counterroll opposing the natural roll induced by the hull's reaction to wave motion. The result is near-level cruising. NAIAD STABILIZERS

tanks use pumps and passive tanks use sluice valves.) Icebreakers have tanks on either side of the ship that are rapidly filled and emptied sequentially to create a rolling action to help break up ice.

Whichever type of roll stabilization is selected, a boat with more initial stability will always roll more as it tries to remain square to the slope of the waves. A deep, heavy, long, and narrow displacement hull will have the more comfortable motion, since it is less reactive to wave slope influences. It is also possible to add too much weight, or ballast, down low in a hull, resulting in a stiff, jerky motion and too-short roll period. Adding weight above VCG increases the roll period, whereas adding weight below has the opposite effect.

The Effect of Trim on Stability

Static stability calculations also assume that a vessel will not change its fore-and-aft trim as it rolls, but will rotate evenly around a longitudinal axis, like a roast on a spit. This isn't a valid assumption; unless the hull is perfectly balanced in displacement and cross section, trim will vary as a vessel heels. The imbalance is most significant when, for instance, a hull has a narrow bow and full, wide stern. This hull will initially trim by the bow when heeling because of the greater buoyancy in the stern as one side of the hull immerses and the other emerges. This tendency will significantly diminish ultimate stability.

This trimming effect is accentuated in boats that are overly beamy for their waterline length and asymmetrical forward and aft. Trimming moments, in fact, tend to *reduce* actual stability below the figures established using conventional static stability calculations. So, the most seaworthy hulls, while certainly not symmetrical, have well-balanced fore and aft sections, so that trim isn't dramatically altered as they heel over. In practice, the fore-and-aft asymmetry common to any hull form results in changing trim as a vessel heels, and this is usually taken into account in the righting arm curve.

The Effect of Freeboard on Stability

The lower the hull sides, the sooner they will be submerged on the low side of a roll. Higher freeboard continues to pick up buoyancy as the hull rolls; low freeboard would result in buoyancy-derived stability dropping off as soon as the gunwale submerges (assuming the absence of a full-beam, watertight superstructure). There is also a dynamic consideration when a steep wave rolls a boat and then starts to break against the hull side. Higher freeboard on the *low* side may allow the hull to slide sideways rather than tripping. The tripping effect of a submerged gunwale will make any vessel more susceptible to capsize, even if plenty of static stability remains (theoretically) in the righting arm curve. But this, too, is a double-edged sword: the higher freeboard that encourages the low side to

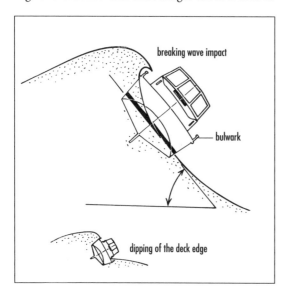

breaking wave impact

bulwark

dipping of the deck edge

There are many dynamic influences acting on a vessel's stability that aren't accounted for in a stability curve. A high-velocity, high-pressure wave jet from a breaker taken broadside can have calamitous consequences. The higher the freeboard, the more surface area on the up-wave side of the boat will be subject to the enormous force of a breaking wave. High freeboard on the down-wave side is a good thing, since the hull will better resist dipping its deck edge and be less prone to "tripping," which would hasten capsize. Should high bulwarks submerge, they may scoop up tons of seawater high on deck. ADAPTED FROM MARCHAJ, *SEAWORTHINESS*

slide down the wave rather than trip over it also exposes a larger surface with which to suffer the energy of the breaking wave on the high side.

Bulwarks can be a mixed blessing, too. They do a good job of keeping water off the deck when running into a sea, and add buoyancy initially in a roll. But if the top of the bulkhead is immersed in a roll, tons of water can be trapped temporarily before the scuppers have a chance to drain it overboard, dramatically, if temporarily, causing CG to rise. If a breaking wave jet upwind catches the hull when the lee bulwark is immersed, the tripping force, and lever arm, are intensified, increasing the chances of a capsize.

The same goes for the superstructure; the added buoyancy on the lee side is offset by the added surface area exposed to the breaking wave jet on the windward side. For the one to offset the other, the deckhouse has to be not only watertight, but built stoutly enough (including the doors and windows) to resist impact with solid water. The worst combination, from a dynamic stability perspective, is a combination of a wide beam (and high GM) and low freeboard, since the wider boat will more readily conform to the wave slope gradient, and therefore immerse its lee (low freeboard) gunwale sooner than a narrower hull of moderate GM.

Staying Afloat

The captain of one of the navy cruisers I served on liked to say that the ocean belonged on the outside of the ship, and it was our job to keep it there. I can appreciate his point! The fact is, unless certain precautions are taken during its design phase, a boat can sink very easily. When a hull is ruptured, usually through collision with an underwater object, the ocean will flow in until the water level inside and out is equalized, or the vessel sinks. Whether the hull stays afloat, although deeper in the water than usual, or sinks, depends on its built-in flooding resistance. If the hole, or crack, is of any significant size, don't count on the bilge pumps doing much more than slowly recirculating water from the bilge back into the ocean. So for any boat to have a chance of staying afloat despite a large hull penetration, it must be designed with adequate reserve buoyancy and stability. So, you ask, just how do designers build in flooding resistance to resist sinking in a damaged condition?

When floating normally, on its design waterline, the hull displaces an amount of water equal to its own weight, and so stays afloat. If water floods the hull, something inside the boat must create enough buoyancy to keep the boat from sinking, even with the added weight caused by flooding. So, positive flotation is built in by one or more clever methods.

A happy-looking crew—nothing quite calms the nerves when the waves get higher than the half-tower so much as knowing your boat's unsinkable. Boston Whaler delivers in this area with all its boats, including its bulletproof Defiance 34 flagship.

BOSTON WHALER

Many small boats have low-density foam flotation pumped into the voids between the hull and deck liner during construction, so even with a hole in the bottom, the boat will only settle so far before finding equilibrium. The foam fills up the space, or at least enough of it, that flooding would otherwise fill. In fact, boats under 20 feet in length must have sufficient buoyancy, usually provided by foam, to keep the boat not only afloat, but floating *level* after being holed. All that foam, even though of low density, contributes to the hull's *impact resistance* as well, and may prevent an underwater collision from penetrating the hull in the first place. Foam replaces belowdecks storage capacity, for sure, but maybe

you only need to balance your family's security and your peace of mind with the ability to stow more junk onboard.

Compartmentation

Pumping a 50-footer full of foam is a different story, though. All that foam is heavy, for one thing (believe it or not), and a bilge space full of foam represents more lost storage space than most owners are willing to give up. Foam also prevents inspection of the hull's structural members and components, and hides any mischief (like wood rot) that may have been caused by moisture. These are reasons why well-designed larger boats depend on *compartmentation*, the division of a vessel into separate watertight compartments using structural bulkheads. Of course this represents another compromise, since the more watertight compartments there are, the harder it is to get around below decks.

From a survivability perspective, the more compartments the merrier, since a single hole in the bottom, whether caused by a rock or a missing rudder, will flood a correspondingly small percentage of the hull's volume. That leaves more reserve buoyancy, and stability, to keep you afloat. At one extreme, navy ships longer than 300 feet are "three-compartment ships," which means that any three adjacent compartments can flood completely and the ship will stay upright and afloat in moderate sea conditions. This might require ten watertight bulkheads, dividing the ship into eleven compartments.

Navy ships in the 200-foot range are usually two-compartment ships, since there's a practical limit, based on habitability considerations, to how small watertight compartments can be. Large oceangoing yachts settle for fewer watertight subdivision bulkheads to make getting around more practical, and those designed to meet shipbuilding standards organizations' requirements for commercial vessels will typically stay afloat with any one compartment completely flooded. Unfortunately, many oceangoing yachts do not meet a one-compartment standard, though they should.

Any boat over 30 feet or so should have, at a

minimum, a collision bulkhead forward, watertight bulkheads forward and aft of the engine room, a watertight lazarette bulkhead, and, in a perfect world, watertight, dogged hatches in the cabin sole, with this deck serving as a double bottom to contain flooding. This modified compartmentation arrangement will make a boat more apt to survive an underwater collision or other hull breach. In the case of the engine room, the most likely location of failed through-hull fittings and hoses, watertight bulkheads will contain the flooding.

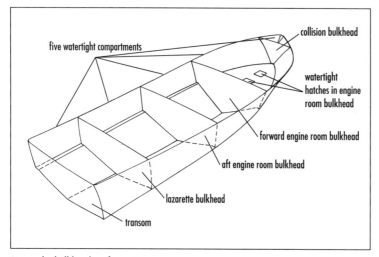

Seaworthy bulkhead configuration.

You can ask your boatbuilder if buoyancy and stability calculations, or real-world testing, have been done to determine if the boat would stay afloat with any one compartment completely flooded. I wouldn't head too far offshore without a definitive, positive answer, either in writing from the builder, through a design analysis, or by a commonsense inspection of the boat's bulkhead arrangements. Otherwise, proceed with the understanding that any hull breach will likely result in your boat sinking either slowly or quickly, depending on the flooding rate.

The number of compartments, and how far apart the watertight bulkheads are separated, are reflected in a figure called *floodable length*, which is the length of the hull that can be breached and still

maintain adequate reserve stability and buoyancy to remain afloat in moderate sea conditions.

The worst situation is to find yourself on a damaged boat that has no compartmentation, with little or no foam flotation built in. If the hole is larger than the bilge pumps can keep up with (and it doesn't take much of a hole to overwhelm a couple of 5,000 gph bilge pumps), then the boat will sink. I've heard boat salesmen boast about being able to pour a cup of coffee in the bilge under the forward berth and have it drain quickly aft to the lazarette, where it gets pumped overboard. This is not a boat you want to head offshore in, for obvious reasons. Ironically, many boats come very close to achieving subdivision, but, incredibly, builders often cut holes for shafts, wires, or plumbing in the otherwise basically watertight bulkheads. If the public demanded boats that were built with a higher level of survivability, and people were willing to pay for these improvements (which in some cases would require very little modification), all of this would change for the better.

Some will say that these are yachts we're talking about, after all—not coast guard or commercial ships—so what's all this fuss about compartmentation? The fact is, the recreational marine industry could learn much from the commercial and military sectors. When a boat is taking on water or has caught fire, the same principles of sound design would have obvious benefits.

Probably the biggest reason for Boston Whaler's early and continued popularity is their boats' quality of "unsinkability." Whalers have much to commend them, but they're certainly no better built than some other similar brands. Whaler sells itself, and distinguishes itself from its competition, by its generous use of structural foam that provides worst-case positive buoyancy. Look at the recent ad for their 34-foot Defiance, settled in the water with seacocks fully opened up and a crowd of people onboard smiling nonchalantly at the camera. In this industry, that's a big boat to be unsinkable. It's a good feeling to know that, no matter what you run into, or what runs into you, and whatever the other merits of the boat, your boat is going to stay afloat. And good feelings are what recreational boating is all about.

Many trawler yachts marketed as "oceangoing" have engine rooms that stretch a third or more of the hull's length, making it difficult or impossible for them to stay afloat with adequate buoyancy and stability margins in the event of major engine room flooding. Adding an athwartships watertight bulkhead somewhere in the middle of the engine room (machinery layout permitting) to such a vessel would make it much more able to survive flooding in this area. It would also make routine maintenance less convenient, but you'll sleep better. Deck hatches below the waterline must also be watertight to restrict flooding to the bilge area.

On a boat with a large engine room, installing a bulkhead fitted with a watertight door would be a next-best solution, making it easier to get around, but make sure to keep the door dogged shut when it's not in use. The compromise is, then, one of habitability against seaworthiness. But few would disagree that the degree of subdivision, and its ramifications, ought to be a matter of intelligent consideration by a forewarned owner.

So what's reasonable for the average boat owner to expect? Boats smaller than 20 feet are required by the coast guard to have positive buoyancy, usually derived from low-density flotation foam between the hull and deck liner, when swamped with a predetermined load onboard. A boat between 20 and 35 feet, based on a reasonable and prudent standard, should have a combination of foam and compartmentation to keep it afloat. And larger boats can also be made unsinkable (at least from a single hull penetration) with a combination of compartmentation, foam, and watertight hatches and doors.

Dewatering

Substantial pumping or dewatering capacity is highly desirable. Propulsion engine cooling pumps can have bilge suction pickups installed for dewatering. These two-way valves should be designed to prevent backflooding of the bilge by closing off the through-hull when the bilge suction is open (for more on this see chapter 10). Larger electric bilge pumps can have Y-valves for secondary use as backup fire pumps. Main drainage systems can remotely pump out watertight compartments using a common pump and remote-operated valves. In any event, most regulatory and advisory standards for dewatering capacity are grossly underprescribed, if they're mentioned at all, and do not at all take into account the real-world flooding rates of even small holes just below the waterline.

The fact is, four out of five boats that sink do so at the dock, for the excellent reason that that's where they spend most of their time, and there's no one onboard to stop the leak. Not surprisingly, failed stuffing boxes and shaft logs, stern-drive seals, through-hull fittings (I'd avoid plastic through-hull fittings), hoses and clamps, and self-bailing cockpits with scuppers plugged and the boat sunk by rain or snow are among the leading causes of sinking dockside. Any through-hull on a powerboat that would be immersed when the boat heels 7 degrees or more should have a seacock. A single intake sea chest, which is essentially a distribution reservoir in the bilge of the boat with a through-hull supplying water to it, is a great way to go, since through-hull fittings are minimized. Engines, genset, air-conditioning, saltwater washdown, and other users can all tap into it.

Learn how to tie your boat up, since being caught under a dock on a rising tide is a surefire way to sink a boat. Make sure the freshwater system hooked up to a dockside connection is sound, or your boat could fill up with nice, clean, potable water and sink right to the bottom. You can install a bilge pump counter to find out how many times the bilge pump cycles on in a given period; excessive pump operation tells you to look for a persistent leak, and all it takes is for the float switch to stick on or the battery to drain to sink the boat. A manual bilge pump operated from the cockpit is a smart feature, since you can contribute to the dewatering effort even if a bilge is flooded and inaccessible. Well-designed larger yachts have a main drainage system, which consists of a pipe running through the watertight compartments with remotely operated valves that allow, say, the engine-driven seawater pump to dewater the bilge under the forward accommodations.

Many small boats that sink at sea do so because of low freeboard, particularly in the case of outboards, when their transoms are so low that waves are essentially invited onboard, or their motor well drain holes are too small to quickly shed water. Worst case, of course, is a transom-mounted outboard without a motorwell. Talk about feeling pooped! That's why I like bracket-mounted outboards and solid, full-height transoms. If the cockpit deck is too low, so is reserve buoyancy, so the boat will have little chance of surviving a multiton wave over the stern. Raw-water cooling system failure is another culprit, as is the old bugaboo of trailered boats, the missing drain plug.

If you think a 2,000 gph (gallons per hour) bilge pump is ample security against minor flooding, then consider that with typical static head pressure and hose restriction losses, you actually have a 1,000 gph bilge pump, which translates to a piddling 16 gpm (gallons per minute). All it will really do is keep ahead of incidental leaks and accumulations, and many small cruisers have pumps of less than half that capacity. Note that bilge pumps are marketed and rated in gph rather than gpm because the higher figure sounds a whole lot better. Commercial dewatering and firefighting pumps are rated in gpm, because it's a more useful figure. For a reality check, the accompanying chart gives approximate flooding rates in gpm versus hole size and depth below the waterline.

If you were to consider a hole as small as 2 inches in diameter, the size of most fathometer transducers, 2 feet below the waterline, the flow rate

Approximate Flooding Rates in Gallons per Minute

Hole Size	Depth below Waterline			
	6"	12"	24"	36"
1/2"	4	5	7	18
3/4"	8	12	16	20
1"	14	20	28	35
2"	55	80	110	140
4"	220	320	450	550
6"	500	700	1,000	1,250

into the boat would be about 110 gallons per minute, or 6,600 gallons per hour! A boat equipped with *three* 2,000 gph bilge pumps in the flooded compartment (allowing for their *actual* pumping rate) would only pump water over the side at half that rate. Now if this vessel is equipped with a bilge alarm, it would at least be able to warn those on board (or ashore) of a problem and give them precious time to find and plug a hole that may have otherwise gone unnoticed until too late.

From the builder's perspective, once again, the consumer has to demand that this equipment be installed and be willing to pay for it. If owners continue to put more emphasis on accommodations, furnishings, and speed than they do on seaworthi-

A manual backup bilge pump can be a valuable commodity in the event of a power loss far offshore. NORDHAVN

ness, the status quo will continue unabated. Boatbuilders are in business to sell boats, after all, not to be missionaries to an uninformed public with misplaced priorities. So don't condemn a boat that lacks this equipment or these design features—just pay to have them fitted on your next boat, preferably during construction, to the degree possible.

Other Seaworthiness Factors

Now that we've got concepts like stability, seakindliness, and flooding control down pat, we'll take a look at some of the other elements of seaworthiness. What follows applies to *any* boat, whether a full-displacement or a high-speed planing hull. Note the interactive relationship among such elements as freeboard, scupper or freeing port size and placement, bulwarks, free-surface effect, reserve buoyancy, and VCG, all of which contribute to a vessel's seaworthiness.

Reserve Buoyancy

Adequate *reserve buoyancy* is determined by compartmentation and the height of the watertight weather deck above the waterline. If you take green water on board, you can't have too much reserve

The Grady-White 223 dual console is a superb little offshore boat—the author once owned one—with a great ride delivered by its C. Raymond Hunt Associates–designed hull. Note the generous freeboard that adds seaworthiness while at the same time providing a high cockpit coaming *and* a self-bailing cockpit well above the waterline.   GRADY-WHITE

buoyancy, since that's what keeps your boat floating while scuppers free this unwelcome ballast overboard. And a low VCG combined with a moderate GM will help keep you from rolling over while all that liquid weight on deck drains overboard. The higher the freeboard and watertight deck, and the greater the volume between the hull and deck liner, the more watertight volume or reserve buoyancy your vessel has built in. Competing interests are at work in a sportfisherman's cockpit, for instance, which must be low enough for a crew to comfortably handle gamefish close aboard, yet high enough to afford adequate reserve buoyancy aft in the event significant water is shipped over the transom.

This Trophy's motor well is integrated into the hull, extending its running surface for improved ride quality, seakeeping, and efficiency. What is effectively a full-height transom forward of the motor well adds seaworthiness.

Free-Surface Effect

When a hull floods, all that water sloshing around has momentum, or inertia, that causes the vessel to lose stability as well as reserve buoyancy. As soon as the boat rolls slightly, all that liquid rushes to the down side, exaggerating the roll. This liquid movement is what naval architects call *free-surface effect*, and it wreaks havoc on a boat's ability to resist capsizing. The higher the liquid is in the vessel (and seawater on deck is a worst-case scenario, making bigger *scuppers* or freeing ports is better), the more stability is impacted. The stability-robbing inertia of free-surface effect is a function of the square of the beam, another seaworthiness argument for narrower vessels. If you've ever been in a dinghy or canoe half full of water, you've experienced free-surface effect firsthand.

Even worse is when the hole is off-center and water is free to flow in and out of the vessel as it rolls and pitches. Called *free communication*, this makes the stability situation even worse. Even if a yacht has enough reserve buoyancy to stay afloat with one compartment flooded, the lack of stability caused by free-surface effect can sink it if the ocean's too rough. Stability-wise, a vessel is better off with a tank, or compartment, completely full of liquid rather than half full, since the free-surface effect will disappear when a tank is full. Incidentally, it's never a good idea to put a watertight bulkhead down the centerline of a boat, since uneven flooding would result, and the chances of capsize would increase. The free-surface effect is also why fuel and large water tanks are baffled with inner, perforated walls to limit liquid movement; tons of fuel or potable water moving around unchecked would also diminish stability.

Freeboard

A high *freeboard* (height of the hull sides and transom) combined with higher, watertight decks adds reserve buoyancy, helps keep solid water from reaching the deck, and can make for a drier ride. High freeboard can also help reduce tripping when beam-to a breaker; tripping is the effect caused by a gunwale submerging on the low side of a roll while a breaker impacts the opposite side. In modern convertible sportfishermen, the low cockpits needed for convenient handling of fish alongside reduce seaworthiness. At extreme angles of heel, low hull sides aft will allow water to ship into the cockpit, greatly reducing stability until the water drains back overboard, and buoyancy aft is lost due to the cockpit's low deck. On the other hand, CG moves higher as freeboard increases, and there are the detrimental effects of added hull and superstructure exposure to wind and breaking waves to be considered.

Longitudinal Center of Gravity

A properly located *longitudinal center of gravity* (LCG) allows a vessel to float in trim on its design waterline. Weight must be distributed precisely from bow to stern so the boat floats neither bow- nor stern-high. This includes cargo, gear, stores, and liquid loads, including fuel and water. A bow-down trim angle, for example, can cause course-keeping instabilities.

Center of Dynamic Lift

For a planing hull, a well-balanced *center of dynamic lift* (CDL), or *center of pressure*, is crucial. A planing hull is supported by buoyancy when at rest or at slow speeds. But when a planing hull transitions "over the hump" to planing speed, vessel weight is supported predominantly by the dynamic lift generated by the bottom of the hull. The center of this area of lift must be precisely located just forward of LCG so that the vessel runs at the proper trim, or bow-high attitude, for best efficiency (two to five degrees of trim) or ride quality (zero to two degrees of trim). The shape of a planing hull and proper weight distribution are essential to achieving dynamic stability at all speeds and in all sea conditions. We discuss planing hull dynamics in chapter 4.

Sail Area

Low *sail area*, or top hamper, in relation to the hull's underbody cross section, will help keep a boat from being too susceptible to the effects of wind. An above-water-to-underwater profile ratio of 2.5:1 or less is to be preferred for offshore vessels, and less is better. A boat with an excessively large, high superstructure and hull freeboard and shallow draft will be difficult to control, especially at slow speeds. Such a vessel has too little underwater lateral plane to offset the sail area exposed to the wind. A strong beam wind can cause such a ship or boat to heel dramatically, or even capsize, in severe conditions. On the other hand, a small-displacement vessel with a staysail rigged aft will be easier to steer into the wind and, as on a sailboat, will dampen the rolling effect of wind and wave.

Redundancy

A high degree of machinery and systems integrity, reliability, and redundancy is desirable. If it's man-made, it will eventually break, but some components are simply built better than others and will last longer before failure. To maximize reliability and longevity, machinery should be accessible so it's easy to work on properly. Mechanical systems should be well engineered with the best quality water valves, pumps, hoses and pipes, compression-type fuel fittings and lines, heavy, well-supported and protected underwater gear, and so on. Bronze or stainless-steel through-hull and plumbing fittings and components can generally be expected to hold up better than synthetics. Although less economical to buy and operate, two engines and two shafts are, all else being equal, more reliable than one. In single-screw vessels, a backup means of propulsion is highly desirable, such as a generator that can be tapped electrically or mechanically to turn the shaft. It's very important that the auxiliary propulsion is powerful enough to make good headway in a strong wind. It is also a good idea to have an engine-driven generator or high-capacity alternator to back up the generator set—if not two gensets. Putting propulsion engines and backup auxiliary generators or engines in different watertight compartments increases reliability.

Adequate Scupper Size and Placement

The bigger the scuppers, the faster the deck drains. They should also be located where water is likely to collect, at the deck's low point. Larger scuppers are also less susceptible to clogging with debris. MCA regulations call for scuppers, or freeing ports, to be a certain size in relation to the length and height of the bulwark. Same goes for the drain lines in deck hatch gutters (which are, unfortunately, increasingly relied on for deck drainage); drain lines of under 1-inch inside diameter are far more likely to clog with debris ranging from striped bass scales to pine needles.

Directional Stability

Good *directional stability*, or *course-keeping ability*, refers to a boat's inclination to maintain its heading, in any orientation to the seas, with minimal helm input. A boat's ability to track well, or tendency to run in a straight line, is largely a function of hull form. A deep-V hull, with a large angle of deadrise at the transom, tracks better than a flat-bottomed, keel-less boat downsea. (We discuss deep-Vs in detail in chapter 4.) If a boat has a too-high VCG, it will yaw excessively. And if weight is concentrated too far forward, it will also cause excessive yaw or bow steer.

Most boats run straight enough in a head sea, but the true test is in a quartering sea. As discussed previously, a vessel with a fine bow and wide, buoyant stern will trim by the bow when rolling, especially with a hull that's wide for its beam. This works against directional stability, since the boat will tend to change its heading as it rolls. A moderate length-to-beam ratio also works to improve directional stability.

The Blackfin 29 flybridge has a deep-V, fine-entry hull form that delivers an exceptionally comfortable ride, the open-ocean speed potential for wave-avoidance in nasty weather, and a low-profile flybridge to enhance stability. BLACKFIN

A boat that is too directionally stable, though, will be hard to maneuver, with a very large keel providing great resistance to the rudder's turning effort. A balance must be found between directional stability and helm responsiveness.

In a following or quartering sea, wave speed relative to hull speed also has an impact on steering and on directional stability. As wave speed approaches or exceeds boat speed, the effectiveness of the rudder(s) and the inherent directional stability of the hull are greatly reduced, because the relative speed of the water moving across the rudder(s) drops, reducing the lift the rudder(s) can generate. A full keel can actually cause the boat to be thrown off course in these circumstances. And a hard-left rudder with a wave impacting it from astern can actually cause the boat's head to fall off to starboard. The only way to avoid these vulnerabilities is to be in a boat that can travel faster than the waves coming from astern, which is not always possible in a displacement hull.

A deep-V is a better-running boat downsea than a flat-bottom boat because of its larger area of *lateral plane*, or the underwater area in profile (viewed from the side). When the center of this area of lateral plane corresponds with the boat's LCG, it will tend to track better. That's because the inertia of the vessel, centered on its LCG, as it tries to naturally resist being thrown off course by a passing wave, is balanced by the center of lateral plane directly below, and any yawing tendency is reduced.

Seaworthiness can have a direct correlation to speed capability. The Bertram 60 convertible, for example, is a well-regarded, time-tested modified-V planing hull with generous deadrise and a sharp entry that allows it to maintain relatively high speeds in rough water. This provides a measure of storm-system and local wave avoidance lacking in less capable hulls. BERTRAM YACHTS

Speed and Maneuvering

Adequate speed and acceleration allow a vessel to better avoid approaching storm systems when offshore, as well as immediate hazards such as breaking waves. When trying to avoid bad weather or a sudden squall, there's no substitute for speed, and this speed capability must be usable in less-than-ideal conditions. It does little good to own a boat that will run fast in calm water, but, due to a poor hull design, must slow down to bare steerageway speeds in moderate to rough conditions.

Steering responsiveness should be proportional to the vessel's speed capability. The faster the boat, the more responsive (fewer turns lock-to-lock) the steering should be so that evasive maneuvers to avoid damage or personal injury can be carried out effectively. Steering should also take minimal effort, so that the boat can be operated for many hours without undue fatigue. Rudders should travel an arc of 70 degrees from full port to full starboard to provide an optimum turning rate, and rudder size

Trochoidal Wave Speed

Speed, knots	Length, feet	Speed, knots	Length, feet
6	20	12	80
7	27	14	109
8	35	16	142
9	45	20	222
10	55	25	347
11	67	30	500

This table illustrates the speed-to-length relationship of a wave in deep water. Note that the hull speed of a displacement vessel is identical to that of a wave of the same length. This explains why displacement hulls are limited in speed, since they start to create a bow wave that's longer than the hull and, by adding power, futilely try to climb up the back of it. PHILLIPS-BIRT, *NAVAL ARCHITECTURE*

Imagine coming alongside a canoe being paddled through the water. Give the bow a shove, and it veers off course. Same with the stern. But give it a shove amidships, and it merely slides sideways a few inches while pretty much staying on course.

should be proportional to the hull's dimensions, displacement, and speed. For more on steering systems, see chapter 9.

Deicing

For cold climes, *deicing capability* is important. This usually concerns only true passagemakers operating many hours or even days from safe harbor. When spray makes its way onboard, and the seawater and air temperature are freezing, expect ice to start forming. CG will slowly start to rise as ice accumulates on deck, on the superstructure, and (especially dangerous) in the rigging, and the vessel will eventually capsize if stability is diminished sufficiently. If there is no exterior heating system installed, the only solution is to remove the ice manually with chipping tools, and minimize the amount of spray coming aboard by reducing speed or heading downwind. According to IMO recommendations, in extreme conditions, such as in the Bering Sea, adequate stability must be provided to compensate for ice accumulation of about 1.3 inches on deck and 0.33 inch on the superstructure and hull sides.

Scantlings

Structural members supporting well-built, high-strength hulls, decks, and superstructures have large enough *scantlings* to prevent heavy seas from causing structural damage (*scantling* refers to the *size* of the structural member). It's no good having the best design in the world if the vessel can't stand up to the stresses imposed by the worst conditions of wind and sea. Large scantlings ought to extend to any windshields, windows, and portholes (using thicker, high-strength glass, and intermediate window supports) and to any storm covers that might be subject to wave impact in severe sea conditions.

Fire Resistance

Fire protection or resistance is both passive and active in nature. Passive or structural resistance to fire results primarily from the construction materials used to build the vessel. A steel vessel is the most capable of surviving a fire, since it won't burn and won't melt until it reaches about 2,800°F. Aluminum, which melts at 1,220°F, is the next most heat-resistant material, followed by fiberglass composite and wood, which, with combustion temperatures in the neighborhood of 500°F, are the least able to resist burning.

Compartmentation is also vital to a vessel's ability to survive a fire, regardless of its construction material. Any steel vessel that lacks watertight bulkheads also usually lacks fire boundaries and is susceptible to fire spreading throughout the vessel's length. Even if it doesn't sink, the result is a floating, burned-out steel hulk.

Active fire protection can be provided by several means. In its simplest form, fire extinguishing is provided by water hoses with which to cool and smother class A fires (wood, mattresses, or anything that leaves an ash residue). Class A materials should be broken up and resoaked to extinguish any embers remaining. A low-velocity water fog, when skillfully applied, can also be used in a pinch to put out class B fires (liquid fueled, usually fuel or lube oil). Water and foam should not be used on class C (electrical) fires due to the electrical shock potential.

Carbon dioxide (CO_2) fire extinguishers are effective on small class B fires, but best used on electrical fires, since they don't transmit electrical shock as water and foam will. CO_2 also won't permanently damage electrical equipment. Compared with water or foam, however, CO_2 is less effective at putting out class A fires since it dissipates quickly and has little residual cooling effect.

Dry chemical fire extinguishers are also commonly found aboard small boats, and they work well enough on class A and B fires. They leave a corrosive residue, though, so they're a last resort for electrical fires.

Active fire suppression is also created by fixed foam or water sprinklers; both act to cool hot surfaces and thereby prevent a fire reflash. Foam is especially effective at smothering class B fires, leaving an oxygen-depriving blanket over the fuel in the bilge or whatever the source of the fire may have been.

Halon (or substitute) gas systems that flood or saturate the air in a compartment, preventing combustion, are the most commonly used firefighting systems on recreational craft. Both portable and fixed Halon extinguishers are in use. Unlike water and foam, Halon has little or no cooling effect of its own, so it must remain in high enough concentrations during the postfire cooldown period to prevent reflash. For this reason, Halon is much better at putting out class B (liquid) and C (electrical) fires than class A fires; glowing embers retain heat. Halon works by interrupting the free radicals in a fire triangle (heat, fuel, and oxygen), or inhibiting the chemical reaction of fuel and oxygen.

These systems ought to be carefully sized to provide concentration levels that will extinguish a fire and then prevent reflash for a long enough period of time for the space to cool down. The most effective Halon systems in machinery compartments include audible and visual alarms to warn of impending discharge and automatic solenoids that shut down operating machinery and close air intakes in the affected space. These systems have time delays that shut down machinery and close ventilation sources and then automatically discharge the Halon. Both flame and high-temperature sensors can be used to activate Halon and foam or water bilge sprinkler systems.

As mentioned, it's important to keep in mind that even if the initial Halon discharge is sufficient to put the fire out, sufficient concentration must remain for the fire to stay out in spite of hot metal surfaces that could otherwise reflash the fuel or whatever caused the fire initially. To this end, the space should not be entered for at least 15 to 30 minutes (according to some standards) after the fire has been extinguished; opening a door admits fresh oxygen and allows the Halon to dissipate, creating a reflash potential. For the same reason, machinery—especially propulsion diesels that consume enormous amounts of air—must not be restarted too soon or left running, since to do so would quickly dissipate the remaining Halon.

A Halon-type gas system has the advantage of being breathable, at least insofar as you won't lose consciousness after a couple of deep breaths, as would be the case with a fixed CO_2 flooding system. Higher Halon concentrations are toxic, perhaps even carcinogenic, but that is probably an acceptable risk in return for surviving a fire. CO_2 is effective, but anyone caught in a CO_2-flooded space is liable to suffocate before they can escape.

It's important to know where all your vessel's fire extinguishers are located, to have frequent fire drills with varying fire type and location scenarios, and to make sure they're properly maintained. The same goes for fixed fire suppression systems—know how they work, what takes place before discharge (engine and ventilation shutdown, usually), and how the system is locally, remotely, and manually activated or overridden. Make sure your vessel is equipped with remote fuel shutoff valves so this potential fire source can be contained. When you eventually reenter a space after a fixed system has extinguished a fire, make sure you have a portable fire extinguisher with you in case of reflash. The longer you wait to reenter, the less the chance of a reflash.

Habitability

Habitability is the ability of the vessel to provide a safe and comfortable environment fit for human habitation. People require bunks that are actually long enough to stretch out on, heaters in cold climates, provisions for food storage and preparation, convenient and safe access to the boat's various compartments, a seakindly hull that produces low accelerations (comfortable motion) in a seaway, and so on. The *human factor* recognizes that the most seaworthy yachts in the world are ultimately only as good as their crews. An inexperienced, unfocused, inattentive, or just plain tired helmsman, in conjunction with adverse sea conditions, can capsize a boat in weather that it might well have ridden out comfortably otherwise. On the other hand, the most experienced, judicious, and attentive crew in the world can't make a manifestly unseaworthy vessel safe to put to sea.

CHAPTER 3

Displacement and Semidisplacement Hulls

Difficult do you call it, sir?
I wish it were impossible.

—Samuel Johnson

Choosing the right hull type for a boat is like building a house on a good foundation. Both are fundamental elements which help determine the success of the end product. No matter how pleasing the accommodations or how perfect the joinery, if your boat has a poorly designed hull or one that is not well suited to your purposes, you'll never be happy with it.

In this chapter we take a look at the capabilities and limitations of displacement and semidisplacement hulls. The next chapter, which covers planing hulls, builds on this discussion, so it's a good idea to read this one first.

There are three basic hull classifications: *displacement, semidisplacement,* and *planing.* Our focus here will be on monohulls, or single-hull vessels, mostly because of their popularity and dominance in the pleasure craft industry. We have a look at catamarans in chapter 5 and see why they are enjoying burgeoning popularity in pleasure, military, and commercial applications. These craft all have their advantages and disadvantages.

Displacement Hulls

Slow, heavy, and seaworthy, with deep draft and moderate beam—these are the qualities that typify a well-found displacement hull. A displacement vessel travels through the water rather than on top of it, displacing or pushing water to the side as it moves along—hence the name. With their slack, or rounded, bilges and gently upswept buttock lines aft, displacement hulls create little disturbance in the water at their low cruising speeds (see the accompanying figure). Displacement hulls, including trawler yachts, tugboats, and large ships,

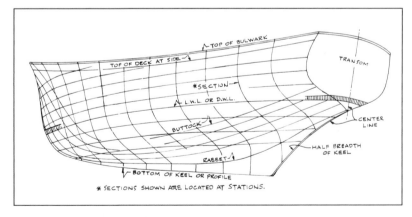

A typical deep-draft displacement hull, with round bilges and upswept buttock lines aft. The transom is mostly above the waterline, which minimizes drag at displacement speeds. Note the *stations, waterlines,* and *buttocks* used to define a hull's shape in three different planes.

STEWARD, *BOATBUILDING MANUAL*

are valued for their comfortable rides, easy motion, and, if well designed, their high ultimate stability and seaworthiness.

Displacement hulls excel at moving cargo, since added weight has relatively little impact on their resistance and efficiency. It takes only modest power to move a displacement hull at its design speed, so the propulsion plant can be quite small and inexpensive relative to the size of the boat. The downside (there's always a downside) is that a displacement hull's speed is limited by its waterline length, and although there are design tricks to squeeze a bit more speed out of a monohull of a given length—mostly involving a narrower hull with finer sections—there's no getting around this limitation.

Displacement Hull Power Requirements

Displ.	Length	bhp for 10 knots	Speed for 200 bhp
20	40	185	10.3 knots
20	45	140	11.0 knots
20	50	120	11.3 knots
27	50	185	10.3 knots

The advantage of length in a displacement hull. Listed are power requirements for 40-, 45- and 50-foot, 20-ton hulls, and a 50-foot, 27-ton vessel to make the same speed, or achieve max speed with 200 hp. The longer the 20-ton hull, the less power it takes to drive it at 10 knots. And both the 20-ton 40-footer and the 27-ton 50-footer need 185 hp to make 10 knots. The same principle applies to planing hulls: longer-narrower is generally faster for a given power, as well as being more seakindly, than a shorter-wider boat of the same size and displacement.

ADAPTED FROM PHILLIPS-BIRT, *NAVAL ARCHITECTURE*

Wave Speed and Length

All waves, including the wake from a vessel, travel at a speed proportional to the wave length, which is the perpendicular distance from one wave crest to the next. An open-ocean wave travels at 1.34 times the square root of its length; thus, a wave that is 300 feet long will travel at 23.2 knots, and a 100-foot wave will travel at 13.4 knots. A vessel's wake, specifically the bow and stern waves gener-

ated by a hull traveling through the water, propagates according to the same formula. Once any vessel (and its bow wave) is going fast enough for the length of the bow wave to equal the length of the hull, the boat cannot go any faster without *climbing up over* its bow wave, which is indeed what a semidisplacement or planing hull must do as it speeds up. That's why waterline length is the ultimate determining factor when it comes to a displacement hull's top speed. The longer the hull, the faster it can go before the bow wave reaches the length of the hull, but a displacement hull can't climb its bow wave. A displacement hull can travel at a speed-to-length (S/L) ratio of about 1.34, equivalent to the speed of a wave of the same length, and this is the point at which the bow is starting to rise and the stern to sink significantly. At S/L of 1.34, the hull will have one wave crest at the bow and a second at the stern, with the length of the wave the same as the underwater hull.

So hull speed-to-length ratios are based on the square root of waterline length; a 36-footer at six knots is running at a speed-to-length ratio of 1, at 12 knots the S/L ratio is 2, and so on. A displacement hull has a theoretical top hull speed of 1.34 S/L (1.34 times the square root of the hull's waterline length in feet), due to the hull's wavemaking characteristics (more to follow on this below). So a displacement hull with a waterline length of 36 feet can be driven up to about eight knots (6 × 1.34 = 8.04). A vessel 64 feet long at the waterline could make 10.7 knots, and if you need to make 13.4 knots, set your sights on a hull that's 100 feet at the waterline. So, length is (nearly) everything when it comes to a displacement hull's speed potential.

You can look at it this way. A bow wave is pushed up and out as water is displaced by the hull. As the bow wave leaves the high-pressure area forward, gravity takes over and it starts to fall back into the surrounding water. In a short hull, the stern catches up to where the bow just was in short order, so the speed at which the hull tries to climb its bow wave is low. A longer hull can get away with producing a higher bow wave (generated by its higher speeds), since the wave has to travel farther to reach the stern. So the longer hull can be pushed faster before the bow-climbing tendency is manifested.

Driving a displacement hull faster than displacement speed is an exercise in futility, requiring exponentially more horsepower and reducing propulsion efficiency. Reaching somewhat higher speed-to-length ratios is possible with displacement monohulls that are designed to go fast, but you'll pay a penalty in load-carrying ability and form stability.

Resistance

At slow speeds, well below hull speed, the friction created by water flow along the hull creates most of the propulsion resistance. A layer of water called the *frictional wake current*, or boundary layer, is dragged along with the hull, increasing in thickness aft and down along the hull. A clean bottom and faired underwater fittings and running gear appendages help reduce frictional drag.

Beam influences drag, since the wider the hull, the more surface area underwater and thus the greater the frictional resistance. A wider hull also increases the amount of water displaced, and therefore the amount of work the propulsion plant has to do to push the vessel. A short, wide hull requires more power to move through the water than a long, narrow hull of the same interior volume (or displacement).

In short, the less disturbance a hull makes as it runs through the water, including the water it drags along with it and the waves it generates, the less resistance it offers to forward motion. The smoother the hull, and the smaller the wake, the less the resistance.

Displacement Hull Characteristics

Let's see what characterizes an easily driven displacement hull. The accompanying figure shows a moderately deep-draft displacement hull drawn by Robert Beebe. There are three *views* in the *lines plan*, each one telling us something more about the design. In the *half-breadth view* (top), the curved lines above the fore-and-aft centerline are *waterlines*, representing horizontal slices through the hull. Counting outward from the centerline, the third waterline is the *design waterline*, on which the boat is intended to float; the other waterlines represent parallel slices through the hull above or below that one. In the *sectional view* (middle), the curved lines are transverse *sections*, or slices through the hull at regular intervals from bow to stern—like slices in a loaf of bread. In the *profile view* (bot-

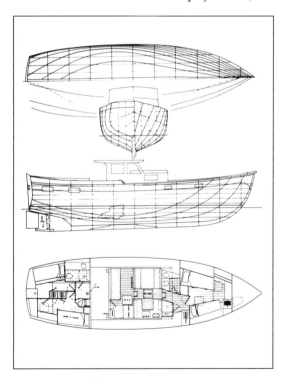

Robert Beebe's *Passagemaker*, an offshore boat with a deep, full-bodied, displacement hull. BEEBE, *VOYAGING UNDER POWER*

tom), the curved lines are *buttocks*, representing lengthwise vertical slices through the hull. These appear as straight lines in the sectional and half-breadth views; by the same token, the waterlines are straight in the sectional and profile views, and the sections are straight in the half-breadth and profile views. The round bilges seen in the sections deliver a comfortable, gentle motion in a seaway, and the easy waterlines and buttocks hint at how easily driven this hull would be at its sedate cruising speed. (At the same time, all three features testify to the futility of trying to move this hull above displacement speeds.) The hull's midsection is deep and full, and this mass low in the water is one of the qualities that make this type of vessel so seaworthy. The entry at the bow is fine, but not so sharp that a hollow waterline is created. By this we mean that, when looking down at the hull's *waterplane*, or footprint at the waterline, the bow should have slight convexity from the stem to the midships area of maximum beam. Otherwise, a secondary bow wave will be developed where a concave section creates a high-pressure region between the stem and the point of maximum waterline beam. For this reason, a hard-chine displacement hull's chines should, in the interests of reducing wavemaking drag, be entirely above or entirely below the waterline for the length of the hull. The deckhouse on this vessel is also low in profile, decreasing topside weight and improving stability, while minimizing windage for added seaworthiness.

Displacement hulls should have a certain amount of balance or geometric symmetry end to end, with buoyancy spread fairly equally as you work your way forward or aft from the midships area. This requires a gentle curvature to the buttock lines forward; hard curves there would indicate a blunt bow, which would cause excessive pressure (and a high bow wave), increasing resistance. The advantages of a balanced hull are also discussed in chapter 2. Aft, the buttock lines sweep up gradually to reduce drag and turbulence at the transom, which should be above the waterline. A submerged transom increases resistance as the smooth water-

flow is interrupted at the stern, creating drag-inducing turbulence. It follows that a displacement hull that leaves less commotion behind is going to

Speed/Length Ratio	Prismatic Coefficient
1.0 and below	0.525
1.1	0.54
1.2	0.58
1.3	0.62
1.4	0.64
1.5	0.66
1.6	0.68
1.7	0.69
1.8 and above	0.70

Optimal prismatic coefficient (Cp) as a function of hull speed.

BREWER, *UNDERSTANDING BOAT DESIGN*

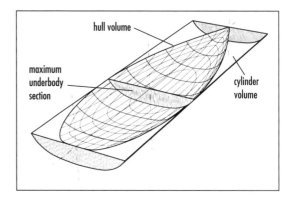

The prismatic coefficient is the ratio of the volume of a hull below the waterline to the volume of a "trough" having the same length as the hull and a uniform cross section matching the hull's fullest station. This coefficient is used to measure the fullness of a vessel at its ends. The fuller the ends, the larger the Cp. The most appropriate value depends on the desired speed of the vessel.

LARSSON AND ELIASSON, *PRINCIPLES OF YACHT DESIGN*

be easier to push through the water. A waterline length-to-beam (L/B) ratio of four or higher is favored for propulsion efficiency and enhanced seakindliness.

These easy lines reflect a displacement hull's *prismatic coefficient*, which is the ratio of the actual below-the-waterline volume of the hull to the product of the hull's largest cross-sectional area below the waterline multiplied by its waterline length. A boat with fine ends and a correspondingly low prismatic coefficient (around 0.53) is best suited to slow hull speeds below a S/L ratio of 1.0. A semidisplacement hull will have fuller ends, and therefore a higher prismatic coefficient—generally in the 0.55

to 0.68 range. A planing hull with its deep, wide after sections will be in the 0.70 or higher region. The hull form, and therefore its prismatic coefficient, is usually chosen to produce maximum propulsion efficiency at the design cruising speed.

The longitudinal distribution of weight in a boat has to be watched carefully as well. In an effort to open up more room amidships for accommodations, some builders shift heavy weights such as engines and fuel and water tanks into the ends of the hull. Although the overall weight distribution is the same, its effect at sea is a different matter. Too much weight forward results in excessive pitching and a tendency to bury the nose in a following sea. Too much weight in the stern, especially with fine lines aft, increases the risk of pooping. In general, boats that have their heavy weights concentrated more nearly amidships pitch less, handle better at sea, and have a more comfortable motion.

Tricks of the naval architect's trade include bulbous bows that decrease resistance and increase effective waterline length, adding speed potential (see sidebar next page). An overhanging counter stern, which allows the buttock lines to continue farther aft than they would in a squared-off transom stern, also adds waterline length, increases buoyancy aft in a following sea, and avoids the drag-inducing turbulence of an immersed transom.

So clearly, propulsion resistance isn't the only factor a naval architect must consider when designing a displacement hull. Load-carrying ability, initial stability criteria, volume for accommodations, and draft constraints are just a few elements that must also be considered.

In particular, a hull with fine lines forward may deliver an exceptional ride in a head sea. But with little buoyancy in the bow to balance a wide, buoyant stern, it may be squirrelly in a quartering or following sea. That fine entry with deep forefoot can turn into a fixed bow rudder (which is a lot more powerful than the rudders back aft) with a mind of its own when it digs into the back of a following sea, and it will lack the necessary buoyancy to lift the bow with the waves abaft the beam, making a

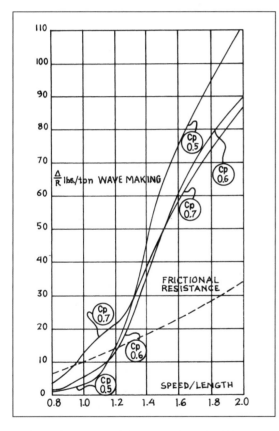

The higher the vessel speed, the greater the Cp should be to minimize wavemaking resistance.

PHILLIPS-BIRT, *NAVAL ARCHITECTURE*

Bulbous Bows

Bulbous bows are definitely in with the big (over 70-foot, generally) displacement trawler crowd, and if nothing else, they impart a big-ship allure to a small boat. Bulbous bows add to the effective overall waterline length, even though they're below the waterline, increasing speed potential. If properly designed, they can reduce the height of the bow wave and move it forward off the stem. These appendages have been extensively tank-tested to come up the shape that offers the least resistance to forward motion. But few full-size boats spend much time in the calm waters of a test tank, preferring instead the open ocean, where drag is often a secondary concern after course-keeping ability and predictability in a heavy seaway. Since they are buoyant and have mass, bulbous bows can also reduce pitching in a head sea. However, they can create downsea handling problems if the bow effectively turns into a fixed rudder, working against the efforts of the movable rudder in the stern. Yawing can become more pronounced, and a broach more likely.

broach (slewing broadside to the waves), or even a *pitchpole* (somersault) in extreme conditions more likely. At the other extreme, a owner may insist on a roomy stateroom forward, but this will compromise ride quality when running into the seas at speed, since fuller sections forward are needed to provide a wider waterline beam. On the other hand, a full bow will tend to behave well downsea thanks to its greater buoyancy, which prevents deep immersion and loss of steering control.

The Result

A displacement hull's slack bilges and relatively narrow beam at the waterline make it quite comfortable in a seaway, with a longer roll period and deeper rolls. Accelerations in general are reduced (and comfort levels increased), thanks to its diminished form, or hull, stability, to the hull's finer ends, and to the vessel's greater weight for its waterplane area. A wider, lighter boat with hard chines or harder (more tightly radiused) bilges will be more uncomfortable because the motion will be quicker and snappier, the roll of a shorter period, and the range of stability less. The displacement hull's greater roll amplitude belies its greater range of stability. And since it moves through rather than over the water, a displacement hull is not nearly as affected by added weight as a planing vessel.

These full-displacement Nordhavn trawlers have very deep forefoots and round bilges for enhanced seakeeping and a smooth ride offshore. Very little dynamic lift is developed forward (or aft) due to the shape of the hull. The high bows add significant reserve buoyancy, helping to make these hulls very seaworthy.   NORDHAVN

Displacement powerboats have a few advantages over sailboats, which are also usually displacement vessels. A powerboat doesn't need a large keel to resist lateral movement due to wind pressure on the sails, or from which to suspend external ballast. So a powerboat's keel can be smaller, reducing frictional drag, which is the dominant power absorber below a S/L ratio of 0.90 or so. Nor do powerboats have to be as wide as sailboats, which must have sufficient initial stability to counter sail pressures, so the powerboat's narrower, more efficiently driven waterlines are an advantage.

The accompanying table shows the performance curves for the Krogen 39, a full-displacement trawler yacht; the relevant figures here are speed and nautical miles per gallon. This boat has a waterline length of 36 feet, 8 inches, or 36.66 feet, giving it a theoretical hull speed of 8.1 knots. A single,

115 hp diesel pushes this boat to a half knot higher than that, or 8.6 knots, at 1.4 nmpg. The Krogen takes less than half as much horsepower (look at the fuel flow to estimate horsepower output; a diesel develops roughly 20 hp for every gallon burned each hour) to make 7.7 knots, so above 8 knots the hull is starting to dig a hole in the water as it tries to climb its bow wave, with little success. You can see that it only takes about 36 hp (1.79 gph × 20) to drive the hull at 7 knots, a

Krogen 39 Trawler Performance Results

RPM	Speed, knots	Fuel Usage, gph	Nautical mpg	Range, nm
1,000	5.3	0.85	6.2	3,928
1,200	5.6	1.08	5.2	3,267
1,400	6.3	1.34	4.7	2,962
1,600	7	1.79	3.9	2,464
1,800	7.3	2.33	3.1	1,974
2,000	7.7	2.94	2.6	1,650
2,200	7.9	3.88	2.0	1,283
2,400	8.3	4.83	1.7	1,083
2,600	8.6	6.3	1.4	860

Tests are with a single, 115 hp John Deere diesel engine.

S/L ratio in this case of about 0.86. Drop down to 6 knots, and only 1.2 gph, or 24 hp, is required, and range goes up correspondingly.

Although the Krogen 39 conforms to the hull-speed rule, other displacement vessels can achieve speeds in excess of S/L 1.34. The Krogen has a hefty molded beam of 14 feet, 3 inches for increased accommodations and carrying capacity, and its L/B ratio of 2.7 holds it back in terms of speed. Trim the beam down to 10 feet or so and give the hull a lower

prismatic coefficient with finer ends, and speed may well pick up by a couple of knots. Semidisplacement and planing hulls, as we shall see, require higher prismatic coefficients with fuller ends to achieve their higher speeds, but in a displacement hull—which lacks flatter buttock lines aft, an immersed transom, and a bottom shape that provides dynamic lift—finer ends reduce wavemaking resistance and help speed. The Krogen represents a design compromise: a marketable boat with the interior room and range people want and a top speed they can live with.

Semidisplacement Hulls

As the name suggests, a semidisplacement hull is capable of traveling in excess of hull speed by developing some hydrodynamic lift—enough to be partially supported by waterflow-induced pressure under the hull. It occupies a transition zone between displacement hulls, which even at top speeds are supported mainly by buoyancy, and true planing hulls, which, as we shall see in chapter 4, are largely supported by hydrodynamic lift at planing speeds. The semidisplacement (or *semiplaning*, if you prefer) vessel makes an excellent cruising yacht. It enjoys much of the full displacement hull's efficiencies at low speeds while offering reserves of higher speed to put more destinations within reach and to avoid bad weather.

A typical full-displacement hull form, like this Krogen 39's, easily makes hull speed—in this case, about 8 knots, but going any faster takes an exponential increase in power. All the power in the world couldn't get this boat to plane, with its emerged transom and highly swept buttock lines aft. But at displacement speeds, the same hull form characteristics make this yacht easily driven, with low wavemaking characteristics.   KROGEN

Even a brick will plane with enough power, but the choice of hull form on a yacht ought to be appropriate to the owner's speed requirements. Here's what is nominally an 18-knot, semi-displacement, round-bilge, full-keel Maine-style hull being driven to just under 30 with twice the power it really ought to have under the deck.   JONATHAN KLOPMAN

Another view of this Carroll Lowell–designed semidisplacement lobster yacht. The deep, fine entry prevents pounding, and the round bilges aft provide an easy motion. Oversized power plants are wasted, though; the planing surface aft is half of what it would be on a hard-chine planing hull, and the round bilges prevent efficient waterflow separation at speed.

The Maine-style lobster yacht, with its full keel and round bilges, is probably the best-known type of semidisplacement hull today. Semidisplacement hulls can often attain speed-to-length ratios of 2.5 or greater, so a semidisplacement hull with a 40-foot waterline length could reasonably be expected to achieve a speed of up to about 16 knots with moderate horsepower. Of course, larger engines can make it go faster still, but at the price of increased fuel consumption compared with a hard-chine planing hull. If you want to go fast—say, 25 knots—efficiently, you want a keel-less, hard-chine hull. A semidisplacement has fuller bottom sections than a planing hull and a shallower, flatter bottom than a displacement hull. A well-designed semidisplacement hull is seaworthy and has a more comfortable motion than a planing hull (if somewhat less so than a displacement hull).

A semidisplacement hull needs a larger waterplane than a displacement hull, in order to develop the necessary hydrodynamic lift to rise up on the surface of the water. This calls for a wider beam at the waterline, especially aft, and a fuller, flatter bow with chines that emerge from the water forward to increase dynamic lift. These hulls either have hard chines, or they have "hard" bilges with a smaller ra-

dius of turn from bottom to side than one sees in a displacement hull. This widens the bottom's effective lifting surface and, in the case of the hard chine, contributes to waterflow separation, reducing drag at higher speeds. Hard chines or small-radius bilges also increase buoyancy outboard in the hull, increasing metacentric height (GM) and shortening the roll period. Back aft, the buttock lines are flatter than in a displacement hull, generally just 2 to 4 degrees from horizontal, and they terminate at a

A shoal-draft Roberts trawler with a hull designed to operate well into the semidisplacement speed range. The hard chines and buttocks are nearly parallel with the waterline, allowing the boat to leave a clean wake astern at cruising speed. Note the twin skegs protecting the running gear.   BRUCE ROBERTS

lift-generating submerged transom that prevents excessive squatting at speed.

The semidisplacement hull's prismatic coefficient is higher than that of a displacement hull, with more buoyancy (and dynamic lift at speed) in the hull's ends. Nothing's free in life, so the trade-off is a loss of efficiency at displacement speeds thanks to increased wetted surface and a higher wave-generating underwater shape.

Note that we said that semidisplacement hulls are speed limited. The fact is, if you put enough power in them, they'll go faster, all right. But to make a heavy 42-foot Maine-style hull move along at the same speed as a 42-foot planing hull is a questionable endeavor. It takes an inordinate amount of power to push the hull at planing hull speeds (above S/L 2.5), and dynamic instabilities can be a problem. Some of the working lobster boats entered in races along the Maine coast each summer achieve speeds well above 40 knots, but they do so by stripping all excess weight, adjusting trim, substituting souped-up power plants for their workaday engines, experimenting with exotic fuel mixes, and in general pushing the envelope any way it can be pushed. In the summer of 2001 one of these full-keeled boats flipped spectacularly during competition in a moderate chop—a graphic example of dynamic instability. (Fortunately, no one was seriously injured.)

Not long ago I had an opportunity to observe these limitations close up when I was asked to eval-

The Krogen 49

The semidisplacement Krogen 49 measures 48 feet on the waterline, so its hull speed is about 9.3 knots. At 9 knots, she's using 5.1 gallons per hour of fuel, which translates into about 100 hp worth of propulsive power and an efficiency of 1.8 nmpg. Back off a knot and a half or so to 7.6 knots, and fuel consumption is cut in half to 2.5 gph, or a 50 hp output with 60 percent better mileage. On the other hand, if you want to take advantage of this Krogen's semidisplacement speed potential, crank it up to a fast cruise speed of 16.6 knots, at which point the hull is "semiplaning" at a S/L ratio of 1.8, and the 300 hp Cats are delivering about 550 hp between them while propulsion efficiency drops to 0.65 nautical mpg. This speed capability, in fact, is the biggest advantage of any semidisplacement hull.

A semidisplacement hull running essentially at planing speed. This Krogen 53 express cruiser leaves a clean waterflow down her side, a low wake astern, and runs at a moderate 3 to 4 degrees of bow rise, indicating an efficiently driven hull form. KROGEN

Krogen 49 Performance Results

RPM	Speed, knots	Fuel Usage, gph	Nautical mpg	Range, nm
800	5.7	1.6	3.6	1,924
1,000	7.6	2.5	3.0	1,642
1,400	9.0	5.1	1.8	953
1,600	9.8	8.0	1.2	661
1,800	10.3	11.9	0.86	467
2,000	12.4	15.7	0.79	426
2,200	14.2	19.9	0.71	385
2,400	16.6	25.5	0.65	351
2,600	18.4	30.3	0.61	328
2,780	19.7	35.5	0.55	300

Tested with twin 350 hp Caterpillar 3116 engines.

uate a high-end, nearly completed, 42-foot lobster yacht that was not performing up to expectations (see photo top right, opposite). The semicustom boat's builder started with a sound, well-known, Maine-style hull with a large, 15-foot beam, a gently radiused round bilge, a full hollow keel curving gently into the hull bottom, moderately fine entry, and flat sections aft. This boat would run well with a single 600 hp diesel at the speeds for which it was intended, in the S/L region of 2.5 to 3. But as we and the owner discovered, trying to make a semidisplacement hull perform like a planing hull with double that much power is a costly undertaking.

This semidisplacement hull was unsuited to meeting its advertised performance potential from the start; you can't just keep adding power to get satisfactory planing-hull performance. First, a radiused bilge combined with a hollow keel reduces the effective lifting surface (the flat area remaining between the radius of the keel and that of the bilge) to about half of what it would be on a true, hard-chine planing hull. This boat also had a full keel that was trimmed off back aft to reduce frictional drag and improve its turning characteristics. The problem is, since this hull is flat-bottomed aft, it needs a keel for directional stability, so it handled unpredictably in a quartering sea. Steering took a full 6.7 turns (3–4 turns is called for in a boat of this speed capability) lock-to-lock, which compounded the handling problem downsea.

Instead of the low, flat wake normally seen leaving the transom of a Maine-style hull, our boat's wake was much higher, due to an excessive running angle of 7 degrees and to the boat's heavy displacement. The high trim at speed was likely due to the LCG being too far aft, and to the minimal dynamic lift aft produced by the hull's relatively small planing surface. Filling the fuel tanks resulted in increased bow-down static trim, so as fuel is consumed, the bow will steadily rise in relation to the stern at speed. Ideally, the fuel is positioned over the *longitudinal center of flotation* (LCF) so trim remains constant regardless of fuel state. With the large trim angle, a 6-foot, 3-inch operator standing at the lower helm station couldn't see clearly over the bow at cruising speed. Plus, the boat pounded more in a head sea, since slamming loads increase as trim angle goes up.

Powered by twin 635 hp Cummins QSM11 diesels, this 38,500-pound lobster yacht had a top speed of 25.3 knots, at least 4 to 5 knots slower than all that horsepower led us to expect. It might be instructive to compare this semidisplacement boat to a similar-size planing hull like the ones we discuss in chapter 4. A Viking 43 convertible, with its bona fide hard-chine planing hull, makes for an interesting comparison. The Viking 43 is close to our lobster yacht in length and beam, and it's no lightweight, weighing in at a hefty 42,000 pounds, nearly two tons more than our lobster yacht. Nevertheless, with a pair of 625 hp Detroit Diesels, the Viking 43 reaches 33.6 knots at full throttle. Viking's modified-V hull design, with 15 degrees of deadrise (see chapter 4) at the transom, develops significant dynamic pressure at high speed, lifting the hull vertically a foot or more out of the water and reducing the wetted surface and frictional drag. The hard chines improve flow separation, further reducing drag at planing speed. The Viking also has a more efficient drivetrain and a flatter trim angle at speed.

The lesson learned here is that the boat should have been more moderately powered to achieve a below-20-knot cruising speed. A cruise speed of 18 knots at full load, possibly achievable with just one of those Cummins, would likely have produced a fine cruising yacht that would take full advantage of its hull shape's excellent rough-water ride and handling qualities. Push a semidisplacement hull shaped like this one too fast, a S/L of 4 in this case, and not only will fuel consumption be off the charts, but dynamic instabilities may well result. We cover planing hull design in depth in the next chapter.

CHAPTER 4

Planing Hulls

In this country it's a good thing to kill an admiral now and then to encourage the others.

—Voltaire

You'll probably get more from this chapter if you read chapters 2 and 3 first. Many of the concepts discussed here are explained in those earlier chapters, and reading them will help you gain a more complete understanding of what makes a planing hull work.

Good planing hulls are amazing creations. They have to run reasonably well and handle predictably at displacement speeds *and* be capable of climbing up on plane and skimming along the water's surface. Besides the *static* pressure of buoyancy acting on any partially submerged body, planing hulls are subject to the *dynamic* forces of rapidly moving water. The ski boat, convertible sportfisherman, express yacht, and outboard-powered center console are all examples of planing boats.

Whereas displacement hulls can move huge amounts of cargo slowly while using very little fuel per ton of cargo, *planing* hulls can move small cargo loads, including people, very fast and very inefficiently, using a lot of fuel in the process. Though *semidisplacement* hulls can rise partially on plane, a planing hull can essentially fly on the surface of the water and reach tremendous speeds. We'll see why in this chapter.

Planing hull dynamics can be remarkably complex, and the study of these forces keeps some of our best naval architects busy. Why the complexity? For one thing, unlike a displacement hull, a hull's behavior on plane is nonlinear and therefore

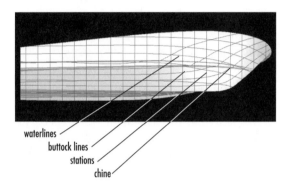

waterlines
buttock lines
stations
chine

A computer–generated perspective rendering of the bottom of a Proteus Engineering–designed sportfisherman showing waterlines, buttock lines, stations, and chines.   PROTEUS ENGINEERING

hard to predict. This means that steady changes in dynamic influences, like *trim*, have an inconsistent influence on the boat's behavior. Increasing trim by two degrees instead of one does not necessarily mean that lift is doubled, nor does dropping the bow a degree have the opposite effect of raising it a degree. A one-degree increase in trim may suddenly cause a dynamic instability like *porpoising*, while a three-knot increase in speed, say from 25 to 28 knots, may suddenly result in *chine walking*. So while the static buoyant forces acting on a displacement hull can be accurately predicted, *why* a planing hull acts the way it does under all conditions at high speed is another issue. We'll take a closer look at porpoising and chine walking on pages 70–71.

It would seem obvious, then, that designing a planing hull is a job for an expert with a thorough understanding of hydrostatics and hydrodynamics. But in fact many boats are designed by people who apparently rely on their boating experience and their intuition rather than on a comprehensive study of the principles of planing hull dynamics. The problem with this approach is that the behavior of planing hulls can be counterintuitive or evade intuitive powers altogether. So, while many planing boats are marvels of engineering, more than a few are inappropriately designed for their intended purpose. Others are designed to satisfy market demand for the roomiest possible boats for a given length, with wide, relatively flat bottoms and full, blunt entries. These floating condos should never venture outside calm, sheltered waters.

Planing Speed

In chapter 3 we saw that a vessel is considered to be in the semidisplacement mode at speed-to-length (S/L) ratios between 1.34 and 2.5 (8.5 to 15.8 knots for a boat with a 40-foot waterline length, for instance). A boat is generally considered to be fully planing when traveling at speeds in excess of S/L 2.5 to 3 (for a boat 40 feet long at the waterline, that means over 15.8 to 19 knots). Concrete evidence of a boat on plane, though, is a noticeable rising of the hull relative to the water—that is, the boat has "emerged" from its hole in the water. A hull planes because it has a suitable shape and sufficient power; when going fast enough, it's supported primarily by dynamic rather than buoyant pressures. Dynamic lift (see below) tends to dominate the force of buoyancy at speeds over 25 knots in larger planing hulls.

Speed-to-length ratios notwithstanding, a heavily loaded boat may still be in semidisplacement mode at S/L 2.5, while the same hull lightly loaded may be on plane at a S/L ratio of 2.3. The speed at which a hull actually rises bodily out of the water depends to a large degree on its bottom loading.

If, upon achieving a certain speed, a 42-foot, 20,000-pound lobster boat rises vertically at the stern as well as the bow and leaves a clean wake

This fast-moving Mako 21 center console shows a rise in CG and a significant reduction in wetted surface, both of which define a hull on plane.

astern, is it on plane? The answer is yes, since there has been a rise in CG, and a clean wake indicates that significant dynamic pressures (lift) are being developed. But what about the same hull, now 18,000 pounds heavier with a load of fish on board and running at the same speed? Probably not, since the same dynamic forces acting on the bottom of the hull aren't likely to be sufficient to lift the hull vertically and make it plane. The only way to add dynamic lift is to add speed, and that requires more power. If it's available, the boat will plane.

So, although S/L ratios are useful for calculating wavemaking resistance, they aren't the whole story when it comes to predicting planing speeds; this is where the *volume Froude number* comes in. Naval architects use the volume Froude number, rather than the S/L ratio, or another Froude number based on length or beam, when evaluating planing craft. That's because the ability to plane is partly a function of the vessel's displacement, especially in the transition stages from semiplaning to planing.

Planing Hull Overview and Terminology

Let's consider first in broad-brush strokes how a planing hull works, and then we'll go into more detail with clear definitions of the terms used. Since boats have mass (weight), they have to be sup-

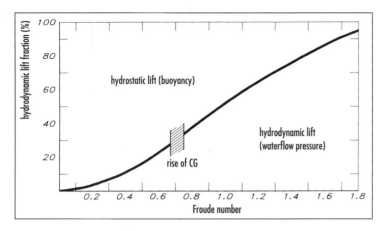

The faster a planing hull goes, the more it's supported by dynamic forces, and the less by buoyancy. This chart shows the relationship between speed (divide the Froude number by 0.298 to get S/L), the rise in CG (center of gravity), and the ratio of buoyancy-to-dynamic lift at various speeds. LARSSON AND ELIASSON, *PRINCIPLES OF YACHT DESIGN*

ported by something. An object that floats, including a planing hull, is supported by buoyancy when at rest, or at low speeds. When a planing (or semi-displacement) hull is moving above displacement speed, dynamic lift created by the pressure of moving water along the hull supports an increasing portion of the vessel's weight. Once a hull is moving fast enough, and this speed depends mostly on the hull's length and weight, dynamic water pressure predominates over buoyancy, doing most of the work of supporting the vessel. At this point we say a boat is "on plane."

We'll also see that a planing hull's overall dimensions mean little when it comes to its performance; what really matters is the *wetted* hull length and chine beam. And this wetted area, the part of the hull that's in regular contact with the water, is surprisingly small in relation to the boat's overall size.

Let's now define a few concepts that are critical to understanding how planing hulls work, and why some hulls perform much better than others.

Deadrise

Deadrise is the angle of the hull bottom (keel to chine) upward from the horizontal in station or cross-sectional view. The first place to look is the transom; a flat-bottom boat has no deadrise (0-degree deadrise) while a deep-V racing boat typically has 24 degrees of deadrise at the transom. The more deadrise, the smoother the ride. It's simple physics, based on the distribution of energy over time when a hull impacts a wave. When landing on a wave, a deep-V absorbs the energy incrementally, and decelerates slightly slowly than a flatter bottom, reducing the *vertical accelerations* felt by the boat and its human occupants. Larger angles of deadrise result in a smoother ride, allowing a hull to slice through the waves. However, as we shall see, this improvement in ride quality (see page 60 for ride quality explanation) comes at the expense of dynamic lift, propulsion efficiency, and form stability. The flatter the bottom, the more easily a boat is pushed along the surface of the water. But calm-water speed is gained at the expense of rough-water

The angle of deadrise on a 65-foot Viking Sport Cruiser at station 4, or about 40 percent of the way aft of the bow. The convex sections above the waterline increase interior volume. BERNARD OLESINSKI

speed, because the low-deadrise boat will have to slow down sooner as the waves build to avoid pounding.

Transom deadrise, while an important at-a-glance indicator of how a boat will ride at speed, is by no means the whole enchilada. In fact, it's possible for a boat with 16 degrees of transom deadrise to ride better than the boat in the next slip with 22 degrees of transom deadrise, if the deadrise farther forward is greater. Deadrise in the bow and midship sections is important to ride quality because this is where the hull first meets the waves (except in ultra-high-performance racing boats, which can often become airborne and land stern-first). Planing hulls can have *constant-deadrise* or *warped-V* hulls, as we'll see.

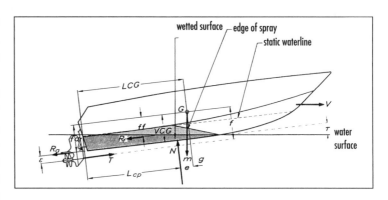

A side view of a planing hull at work, marked to show the major forces to be considered by the yacht designer. G is the center of gravity. The center of pressure caused by dynamic lift and buoyancy is N, and engine thrust is T. Resistance due to hull frictional drag is R_f; lower unit appendage drag is R_a. N, R_f, and R_a tend to trim the boat by the bow (bow down). The propeller thrust tends to trim the boat by the stern (bow up). The boat trims at an angle where all these forces cancel out. Compared to optimal trim (usually 2 to 5 degrees, depending on hull form), a lower trim angle reduces bottom pressure (spreads it out more evenly) but also increases wetted surface and frictional drag, and buoyancy will take more of the load. More bow rise reduces the wetted surface, but increases form drag, slowing the boat.

LARSSON AND ELIASSON, *PRINCIPLES OF YACHT DESIGN*

Longitudinal Center of Gravity

If one element is crucial to planing hull performance, it is *longitudinal center of gravity*. As we saw in chapter 2, LCG is defined as the precise location between bow and stern from which a boat would balance if suspended in the air. When a boat is designed, the weight of the hull, superstructure, decks, machinery, auxiliary equipment, fuel, water, furnishings, appliances, and everything else that will be placed in the finished boat must be precisely accounted for to ensure a well-balanced LCG. That's because the location of LCG is key to a planing hull's performance.

Longitudinal Center of Buoyancy (LCB) and Longitudinal Center of Flotation (LCF)

The *longitudinal center of buoyancy* (LCB) is the center of the buoyant forces acting on the hull; or to put it another way, it's the LCG of the water dis-

placed by the hull. An immersed body is buoyed up by a force equal to the weight of the displaced fluid, and the fore-and-aft center of buoyant force (LCB), determined by the underwater shape of the hull, lines up precisely with the fore-and-aft center of the boat's weight (LCG). If you add 500 pounds of weight aft, the LCG will move aft and so will the LCB, and the boat will trim down by the stern accordingly. The *actual* LCG must be located directly at the hull's design LCB, or center of the hull's submerged volume, for the boat to float properly at its design waterline.

The *longitudinal center of flotation* (LCF) is the longitudinal center of the hull's waterplane area (or *footprint* on the water's surface) about which the hull trims. Weight added *at* LCF will cause the hull to settle without any change in trim.

Center of Dynamic Lift

So a planing hull not only floats—it flies on the surface of the water. The pressure created by high-velocity water flow has a longitudinal center of ef-

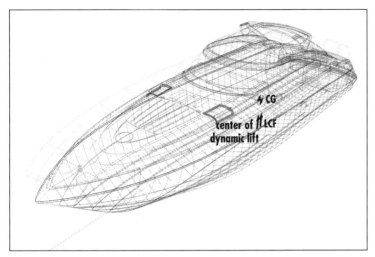

A port-bow computer rendition of a 65-foot Viking Sport Cruiser express yacht, designed by Bernard Olesinski. The center of gravity (CG), center of dynamic lift (CDL), and longitudinal center of flotation (LCF) are shown. These drawings can be fed to a computer-controlled 5-axis milling machine and turned into a flawless mold.   BERNARD OLESINSKI

shifted toward the stern. And if the boat is riding bow-down, low pressures (below the pressure of buoyancy) can develop forward in the hull, causing dynamic instabilities. If bow-high, for example, porpoising can result. So the interplay between CDL and LCG is all important; the hull has to have the right shape and trim angle for proper lift, LCG influences trim, trim affects CDL, overall displacement affects wetted surface and lift, and around and around we go. And the faster the boat, the farther aft LCG should be to maintain control and prevent instabilities at high speed. That's why some repower jobs get into trouble; high-horsepower diesels are installed, LCG doesn't shift aft, and the boat becomes a performance and handling nightmare.

fort that's called the *center of dynamic lift* (CDL). It's called *dynamic* lift simply because it depends on the constant motion of water flow to be present. The dynamic pressure acting on the planing hull varies from point to point along the bottom; it's high forward where the bottom first makes contact with the water, while back aft, near the propellers, it's quite a bit lower, in terms of pressure-per-square-foot of hull surface. CDL is determined by the shape of the bottom and the vessel's trim. Trim, in turn, is determined by CDL and LCG, so all these elements are interdependent.

If LCG is too far forward or aft in relation to CDL, the boat will run off trim, handling poorly and running inefficiently. CDL also changes with trim; it moves forward when weight is added at the bow, and aft when weight is

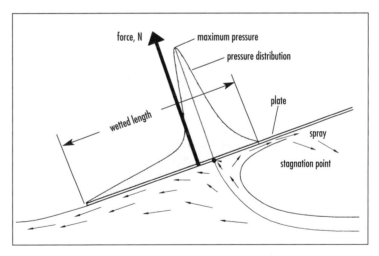

Bottom pressure concentration versus waterflow angle of incidence on a flat plate. N represents the center of pressure acting on the hull. From the hull's forward-most wetted surface to the transom, the peak pressure occurs just aft of the stagnation line. The sum of these pressures determines CDL. CDL (the focus of pressure) in relation to LCG (the focus of weight) helps determine running trim, with the weight of the hull balancing on the center of dynamic lift.

LARSSON AND ELIASSON, *PRINCIPLES OF YACHT DESIGN*

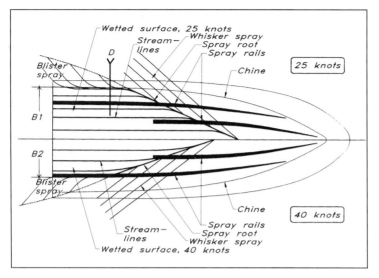

The bottom of a planing boat, showing the interaction between the hull and the water surface at 25 and 40 knots. Note how less of the hull is in contact with the water, but the pressures increase on the smaller area to support the weight of the boat. Forward is the spray developed by the hull's motion, and the immersed V-section shows the area of the hull in contact with solid water. Because of the "hump" in the bottom pressure curve, seen in the bottom illustration on page 47, the center of lift (CDL) is forward of the *center* of the waterplane area shown here.   LARSSON AND ELIASSON, *PRINCIPLES OF YACHT DESIGN*

Trim

Trim is the fore-and-aft inclination of the vessel, measured in degrees, and is often referred to as *bow rise* when on plane. A planing boat has a static trim (at the dock) and a dynamic trim (when on plane). When a boat runs with its bow raised 3 degrees higher than when floating (on its design waterline) at the dock, it is said to be running at 3 degrees of trim. For a given hull shape, static trim is determined by LCG. Dynamic trim is determined predominately by LCG, and also by CDL, with the latter in turn influenced by the direction and location of propeller thrust, and the shape of the hull, in particular its buttock lines. LCG is a moving target, since it changes as fuel is consumed (on most boats) and as people and gear move around.

Trim directly affects ride quality and propulsion efficiency. Planing hulls tend to run best in a trim range of 2 to 5 degrees (on warped-V and constant-deadrise hulls respectively), depending on

bottom type. The most efficient trim angle is, up to a point, the one that minimizes wetted surface, and therefore frictional drag.

But most efficient doesn't mean most comfortable; a bow-up attitude is more efficient than bow-down, but the latter delivers a smoother ride. The trick is to find the sweet spot, which will depend on how rough it is, what direction you're running in relation to the seas, and how fast you're going, that delivers a reasonable combination of efficiency and ride quality without causing instabilities and poor handling.

Excessive bow-high trim increases slamming loads (vertical accelerations), increases the tendency to porpoise, increases fuel consumption, and interferes with visibility from the lower helm station. Bow-down trim increases wetted surface and frictional drag, slowing the boat, although it produces a smoother ride in a chop. Bow-down trim also creates a tendency to bow-steer (a deeply immersed bow reduces the rudder's ability to control heading), so things can get out of control quickly in a following sea, and you'll be in for a wetter ride with spray developing farther forward. Running with a slightly bow-high attitude reduces drag by reducing wetted surface. Running with a degree or two less trim slows the boat a whisker, but reduces vertical accelerations in a chop. The longer a hull, and to an extent the greater the length-to-beam ratio, the flatter it tends to run. This make it easier to see over the bow of some 60-foot express cruisers than some 35-footers.

Buttocks

The shape of the buttock lines in profile can create or prevent dynamic instability, and in fact is the primary design factor distinguishing displacement,

Running with close to zero trim angle at high speed minimizes slamming loads, but it also increases wetted surface forward, slowing the boat and making for a wetter ride. This high-end 11-meter Aprea Mare runs at higher trim ordinarily, but caught a wave just as this picture was snapped.   APREA MARE

The first Don Blount–designed Albemarle 41 getting ready for launch. A deep forefoot, ample deadrise midships, and moderate waterline beam produce a smooth ride in sloppy weather, much like Blount's missile boats and megayachts.

A smooth, dry, and stable ride is the hallmark of any C. Raymond Hunt Associates hull, including this Chris Craft 26. A quick look at the sharp entry on this boat tells us why. Note also the modestly proportioned strakes and chines that deflect spray without making the boat pound.

A Bernard Olesinski–designed Viking Sport Cruiser's excellent ride is due to its refined forefoot, deep and fine, with high chines forward and radiused strakes and chines.

semidisplacement, and planing hulls. Waterflow at high speed very nearly follows the buttock lines, so their shape has a great deal to say about how a hull will perform. As we saw in chapter 3, a displacement hull's buttock lines sweep up aft to reduce the hull's wavemaking at slow speeds. The planing hull's buttock lines, on the other hand, must run parallel, or nearly so, to the waterline, in order to detach waterflow from the hull aft, to develop dynamic lift without an undesirable degree of bow-up trim, and to prevent the stern from squatting at speed.

Chines

The chine is the corner formed by the intersection of the hull's bottom and its sides. Planing hulls typically have "hard" chines, with true corners, although there are also round-bilge planing hulls. The gentle radius seen on displacement hulls and sailing boats is properly referred to as a *round bilge*, not a soft chine.

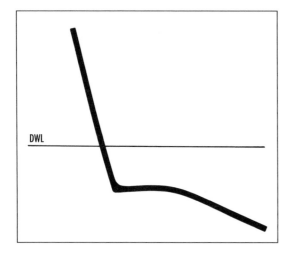

A gently radiused chine flat on a Viking Sport Cruiser deflects spray effectively and adds buoyancy high-up and outboard for added form stability.   BERNARD OLESINSKI

The hydrodynamic purpose of the chine is to provide waterflow separation from the bottom of the hull, which reduces frictional drag. And, since the chine forward projects farther outboard than the corresponding section of a round-bilge hull, the hard chine flattens the buttock lines forward, which helps prevent dynamic instabilities (see below). In a round-bilge hull, the intersection of hull side and bottom, seen in section, is a radiused curve. With no chine to separate the waterflow, when the round-bilge hull is running at high speed, water tends to flow outward around the turn of the bilge and up onto the hull sides, and negative pressures can result. If the hull is light enough and properly trimmed, this problem can be overcome and the hull will run perfectly well. Spray rails can be added forward to reduce spray and improve waterflow separation along the hull sides. For more information, see Round-Bilge Planing Hulls on page 62.

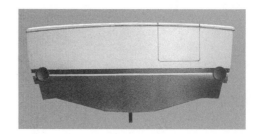

Viking Yacht's signature convertible transom, with reverse lower chines, or chine flats, for added dynamic lift and spray deflection, double chines to reduce wetted surface at high speed and add stability at rest, and a nearly flat "fairbody" section on centerline.

STEPHEN DAVIS DRAWING, COURTESY VIKING YACHTS

Some boats have double chines, which are intended to increase wetted beam at rest (with the upper chine submerged) and, once up on plane, reduce wetted surface and drag (with the upper chine clear of the water). Chine flats, in which the deadrise flattens out or even reverses downward a few degrees, like a flap, are *de rigueur* in modern planing hulls. These surfaces are usually four to eighteen inches wide at the stern, depending on the size of the boat, and narrow toward the bow. They add buoyancy outboard, which increases form stability, and they deflect water and spray at planing speeds, increasing dynamic lift and contributing to a drier ride. The original deep-Vs, like the Bertram 31, which did not have chine flats, could run like the wind when slicing through a choppy sea, but were notoriously tender at rest since the chines were clear of the water at rest.

Forefoot

A hull's entry, or forefoot, plays a crucial role in determining both ride quality and course-keeping ability, which is the vessel's natural tendency to stay on course at all speeds and in all directions to the sea. Regulator, Buddy Davis, and Blackfin sportfishing boats have deep, fairly fine entries that essentially eliminate pounding in a head sea. It is possible for a forefoot to be *too* deep and fine, resulting in a boat that bow-steers in a following sea. A destroyer-like (long and narrow) bow with low displacement forward may develop too little buoyancy initially when immersed below its static waterline, such as when the stern is raised by a quartering sea. Especially when the stern is wide and fairly flat, this imbalance results in a boat that is difficult to keep on course when running downsea; the bow digs in, and the broad, buoyant stern gets thrown around.

A broad and shallow bow entry will often result in a faster, more easily driven hull, and one that handles well running downsea (since there's so little bow to dig in and trip the stern), but will also be far more susceptible to pounding in a head sea. A balanced hull has a moderately fine and deep entry to deliver a smoother ride in a head sea, but one that's not so deep and sharp that it scares the daylights out of you running downsea, or so full and blunt that it pounds your kidneys out upsea.

Boats powered by waterjets require special care in the shape of the entry: with no underwater gear aft to keep them going in a straight line, these hulls are inherently susceptible to fickle tracking downsea. A waterjet-propelled hull must have fairly shallow sections forward, with the hull radiused at the keel to help keep the bow from digging in downsea.

In addition to forefoot geometry, the overall

This midcabin express cruiser has a fuller, flatter entry than the Chris Craft 26, so ride quality will suffer, but the hull will also be easily propelled compared with a deep-V.

A waterjet-powered Little Harbor bottom. The forefoot is fairly shallow to help prevent bow steering downsea. Note Ted Hood's scalloped "quiet chines," designed to minimize wave-slapping noises dockside.

hull shape, LCG, and rudder design are all factors in good course-keeping. Moderation is the key here: a boat that resists any course changes will be difficult to steer, and one that changes course too easily will require constant rudder corrections.

Flare

Flare is the concave curvature in a hull in section view: a hull with flare curves inward between the chine and sheer. Flare makes a boat look better, of

This New Jersey–built sportfisherman, the Jersey 40, is fast for its power, making 30 knots with just a pair of 300 hp GM 671s. But the speed comes at the expense of a smooth ride—note the shallow, full and flat entry that increases pounding.

This Davis 45 has a superb, Don Blount–designed running surface with considerable flare, North Carolina style.

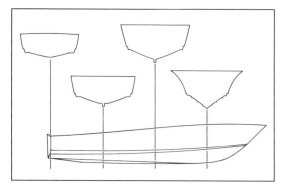

A Viking 52 profile with selected stations showing the change in shape from bow to stern. Viking uses double chines, which, when on plane at high speeds, reduce wetted surface by effectively narrowing the beam. The lower chines angle down a few degrees for added lift, and their buoyancy outboard improves form stability at rest. Note also Viking's flat "fairbody" sections along the keel aft, which add lift at speed, and also raise the hull's center of buoyancy slightly for added stability. The Viking 52, capable of speeds approaching 40 knots, has considerably more deadrise forward than its 1980s predecessors to accommodate the extra speed.

VIKING YACHTS

course, but more importantly it adds buoyancy as the bow submerges; no amount of flare, though, can make seaworthy a hull that is too fine forward at the waterline to start with, or that has its LCG too far forward. And relying on flare alone to provide a dry ride is also an exercise in futility; the geometry of the bottom and the placement and shape of the bottom strakes and chines have a greater influence on whether a hull will deliver a wet or dry ride. Exaggerated flare sometimes hints at a boat's heritage, such as that of a North Carolina–built sportfisherman. Too much flare, though, and you only have to look at a few of the custom sportfishermen to find examples, just makes the boat look a little silly, though; a lot like a car with a huge tail fin. And pity the crew of such a boat that stuffs its inordinately wide foredeck in a following sea!

Section Shape

The shape of the hull bottom in cross section is also important to ride quality and dryness. Underwater hull sections can be *convex* in cross section, making for a ride that is smooth yet wet. *Concave* hull sections produce a dry ride but are hard-riding in a seaway, since water gets trapped in the hollow sections, especially when the hull is heeled over. *Straight* sections are often a good compromise, offering

a reasonable combination of smoothness and dryness. Some sophisticated hulls are bell shaped in cross section, with convex curvature near the keel (to soften wave impact) and concavity near the chines (to deflect spray), mixing the best of both worlds for a smooth and dry ride.

Hook and Rocker

Hook and *rocker* describe the curvature, in profile (viewed from abeam), in the aft 10 to 25 percent or so of the boat's buttock lines. Hook is a concave curvature; rocker is convex. Adding hook or rocker

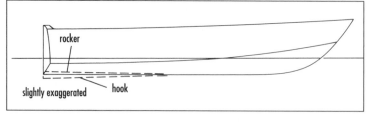

Hook and rocker (exaggerated).

is a good way to control trim. Hook makes a boat run flatter by shifting the center of dynamic lift (CDL) aft, thus raising the stern slightly. Rocker makes the hull run lower at the stern, trimming up the bow and shifting the CDL forward. A designer might add a little hook to compensate for a large amount of weight in the stern. Both hook and rocker can help correct dynamic instabilities, but some designers avoid rocker because it increases stern drag at lower speeds and its effects at higher speeds are not always readily predicted.

Length-to-Beam Ratio

This is the relationship between the boat's length and beam, usually at the waterline. Along with deadrise, displacement, and longitudinal center of gravity (LCG), the L/B ratio has a profound effect on ride quality in a seaway. A longer, narrower boat will have more comfortable motions and lower accelerations in rough water, and be more efficiently propelled, than a shorter, wider boat of the same size and displacement. The long and narrow vessel may not have a lot of room for its length, but it has ample room for its *displacement.* A short, wide hull may have more room for the LOA, but it will burn more fuel than its longer, narrower cousin and will have to slow down more and sooner when the going gets rough. The long-and-narrow advantage applies both to planing hulls and to displacement hulls. Unfortunately, market forces have driven the demand for shorter-wider boats, which is too bad since most people have no earthly idea how smoothly and efficiently a same-size, but longer-narrower, boat can run.

Speed-to-Length Ratio

The S/L ratio is the ratio of a hull's speed in knots to the square root of its waterline length. A boat that is 49 feet at the waterline makes 7 knots at a S/L of 1, or 21 knots at S/L 3. Maximum S/L is often used to define which category a hull belongs to; in general terms, with sufficient power, a displacement hull can reach S/L 1.34 and a semidisplacement hull S/L 2.5, while a planing hull theoretically has unlimited speed potential.

Resistance

The drag caused by a hull's interaction with the water is called *resistance,* which we break down into three types, just to make it interesting. *Frictional resistance* results in a boundary layer of water that the hull drags along with it due to the friction of the hull's surface disturbing water molecules in the immediate vicinity. This boundary layer gets thicker as a hull gets longer and deeper in the water, and may reach 4 to 6 inches on a sportfisherman and 18 inches on a navy destroyer. Where it contacts the hull, the boundary layer moves along as fast as the boat, but it slows gradually until at its outer edge the surrounding water remains undisturbed. Frictional resistance is largely a function of the immersed hull's surface area and roughness along with the size and shape of its appendages. *Wavemaking resistance* is caused by the hull's displacement of water as it moves along. Hull shape and trim have the biggest influences on wavemaking resistance. *Appendage drag* is the resistance caused by struts, shafts, rudders, and propellers sticking out into the waterflow. Then there's aerodynamic drag, caused by the above-water hull and superstructure moving through the air; a modestly proportioned displacement hull will hardly notice a stiff head wind, but a broad-beamed convertible with a flybridge brow and tuna tower might easily be slowed 4 or 5 knots by air drag when running upwind.

Hard-Chine Planing Hull Types

Planing hulls come in a variety of shapes that make each one well suited to a particular set of tasks and ill suited to others. Now that we've defined some terms, let's look at the boats. In this section we look at the various hard-chine planing hulls; in the next we compare these with the round-bilge planing hulls.

Flat-Bottom Hulls

Flat-bottom planing hulls are generally found on skiffs and other small craft that ply calm bays and lakes. Able to carry a lot of weight, the easiest to push through the water, and the most stable at small angles of heel, flat-bottom boats also produce a kidney-jarring ride in a chop.

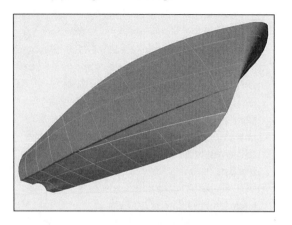

The hull lines of the Ward Setzer–designed Lyman Morse 74. The planing hull's 4:1 length-to-beam ratio, fine forefoot and modified-V aft sections deliver excellent ride quality in rough water. Radiused, moderately proportioned prop pockets, also seen in the rendering, reduce draft and shaft angles without detracting noticeably from buoyancy, or dynamic lift at speed.   WARD SETZER

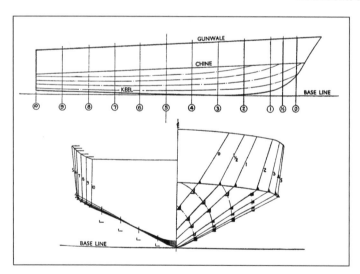

An early Ray Hunt–designed deep-V, the smoothest-riding planing boat around in its day. Modern refinements missing here include chine flats and a padded keel, which would add form stability and planing efficiency. This hull became an early Bertram and is the paradigm for all modern planing hulls.

BREWER, *UNDERSTANDING BOAT DESIGN*

Deep-V Hulls

The *deep-V* hull is the most common planing hull out there today. It is seen in its most basic form in the Bertram 31, the Ray Hunt hull that started it all. A deep-V typically has 20 degrees or more of deadrise at the transom, with 24 degrees a common standard on very high speed hulls. The deadrise angle on a deep-V is constant from the stern forward for over half of the boat's length, and then starts increasing from slightly forward of amidships, rising to the stem, where the chines start to rise out of the water and narrow up.

The great advantage of the deep-V is the smoothness of the ride in a rough chop at speed. A deep-V can keep on charging when a more flat-bottom boat has a slow to a crawl. That's because the *time* (in milliseconds) over which a hull impacts a wave is spread out over a longer period of time. A deep-V hull meets a wave incrementally—first the keel, then the garboard, then the midsection, and finally the chines. A flat-bottom hull, on the other hand, meets the same wave all at once—wham! Both boats follow the surface of the waves, but the deep-V adjusts to the contour of the water's surface with a lot more ease and finesse; the difference in terms of comfort between the physical effect of a deceleration that's spread out over a few milliseconds, and one that's virtually instantaneous, is significant.

The deep-V's high angle of deadrise, carried all the way back to the transom, allows a boat to slice smoothly through the waves. A deep-V can maintain speed without pounding in sea conditions that force boats with less deadrise to back off. On the flip side, all that deadrise tends to rob speed, because with more deadrise, less lift is developed. The best way to get some of that speed back is to reduce weight, and some builders have done a great job of doing so, without sacrificing strength, through the use of composite sandwich construction (see chapter 6). Deep-Vs can also gain speed through refinements that add lift, like reverse chines and padded keels (see below). But for two otherwise identical boats, the one with less deadrise will go faster in calm water since a flatter bottom is the more efficient lifting surface.

For high-performance craft that cruise fast

This deep-V hull is similar to the early Bertrams, with its chines emerged above the waterline at rest. Without the immersed reverse chines, or chine flats, seen on most modern V-bottom hulls, this boat will lack form stability and be on the tippy side at rest.

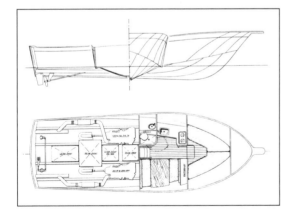

The Gerr 34's lines. That she's a smooth ride in rough water is apparent at a glance. A pair of 300 hp Cats pushes this 12-foot-beam, 19,000-pound sportfisherman to 32 knots and delivers a 28-knot cruise. The keel flat and radiused chines widen toward the transom, adding lift and stability.

GERR, *THE NATURE OF BOATS*

enough to emerge most of the length of their bottoms on a regular basis, a deep-V bottom is the way to go. These very fast (50-knots-plus) hulls often become airborne in rough water, and when they land on the aft 30 to 40 percent of their bottoms, they need every bit of that 24-degree deadrise back there to smooth out the landings. The extra deadrise aft also helps a deep-V to track better downsea, since the hull shape tends to grab hold of those waves more tenaciously, creating its own railroad track as it goes. Well-known, superior deep-V hull designs include the original Bertrams, the Regulator- and Contender-type center consoles, and Formula's cruising and race boats.

Modified-V Hulls

Modified-V planing hulls typically have between 12 and 18 degrees of deadrise at the transom and 20 to 25 degrees amidships. This design works well with larger, heavier planing hulls that need all the dynamic lift they can get back aft and rarely come more than half their length out of the water at high speed. The flatter sections usually extend farther forward, as well, than in a deep-V hull. Deadrise is constant in the aft half of the hull, with the keel and chines running essentially parallel to the waterline. Buoyancy is centered higher in the hull, so the modified-V hull has greater initial stability than a deep-V, which helps on boats carrying a lot of weight topside. Unless a boat rides with half its length out of the water at cruising speeds, a modified-V is often a good choice for a designer.

Warped-V Hulls

The *warped-V* is so named because deadrise changes along the length of the vessel, lessening all the way to the transom. While the keel remains very nearly parallel to the waterline, the chine continues to run downhill as it approaches the stern, resulting in a *warp*, or twist, to the bottom. A planing hull with a warped-V bottom will run at a flatter trim than a constant-deadrise deep-V, since the CDL is farther aft, with more lift developed by the stern's flatter sections, thanks to the bottom's

The C. Raymond Hunt–designed Chris Craft 26's fine entry twists, or warps, out to moderate deadrise aft. The chine continues to run downhill slightly most of the way to the stern, as it does on Hunt's Grady-Whites and other designs. This produces, without tabs, a modest trim angle for improved efficiency, and a good view ahead from the helm, thanks to plenty of buoyancy and dynamic lift aft to support the stern drive.

slightly twisting sections. And because the warped-V hull's chines are deeper in the water at the transom, LCB shifts aft as well, making this hull form an excellent candidate for an aft engine room with V drives. The warped bottom also produces an excellent lower-unit-powered boat, since the added buoyancy in the stern can easily accommodate the weight of a stern drive or a pair of big engines cantilevered off the stern on a transom bracket.

Warped-V hulls have gotten a bad rap because excessive warp, such as in some of the WWII PT boat designs, produces a lousy hull design with low dynamic pressures aft in the hull on plane. Designers have since learned how to get it right. C. Raymond Hunt Associates of Boston, Massachusetts, in particular, has designed some of the finest warped-V planing hulls in the world. These designs are improvements on the original 1960s-era constant-deadrise deep-V hulls designed by Ray Hunt, since they combine the soft forward entry of a deep-V with the added buoyancy and lift aft of a moderate-deadrise hull. With their superb ride quality and excellent propulsion efficiency, Eastbay, Alden, Palmer Johnson, Grady-White, and some of the latest Chris Craft retro-yachts are examples

Running at about 24 knots, a S/L of 5, this Albemarle 26 deep-V express sportfisherman is well up on plane with CG considerably higher than its static position. On a 25- to 30-knot-cruise hull like this one, which infrequently becomes airborne, it's the deadrise in the forward half of the hull and the waterline length-to-beam ratio that matter most when determining ride quality, not so much transom deadrise. ALBEMARLE

The Hunt-designed Dettling 51 has a high-tech-construction, moderate-weight hull that rises well up on plane. The slight warp in the bottom produces a low trim on plane, improving ride quality, helm visibility, and running efficiency.

The Donzi 39's steps are designed to present three small, wide, low-drag surfaces to the water at high speed rather than one big one.

of the C. R. Hunt warped-V hull form done right. Trim tabs, incidentally, are to some degree superfluous with these hulls, since they climb on plane and run at a low trim naturally.

Stepped Hulls

Short, wide (high-aspect) surfaces are more efficient than long, narrow (low-aspect) ones in terms of frictional drag on water. Lift generation is just far more efficient with a large beam-to-length ratio surface. So, the idea behind a stepped bottom is to reduce wetted surface by allowing the hull to plane on two or three high-aspect planing surfaces rather than one large, low-aspect surface. And the popular notion that any added speed from a stepped bottom is due to a layer of bubbles blanketing the hull bottom is true to a degree but generally exaggerated. Entrained air bubbles undoubtedly reduce frictional drag to some extent, but the real saving is in minimizing the hull area in contact with the water, specifically by presenting two or three wide and short surfaces to the water instead of one long, narrow one.

Like any true design advance, though, the technology can be misapplied. While stepped bottoms work admirably on high-performance boats, they do little or nothing to improve performance on slower boats. In general, data indicate that if a boat can't cruise easily at close to 30 knots or more, it can't go fast enough to ride up on hull steps, so steps would only add drag. More specifically, this means that a gas-powered family cruiser with steps should be able to cruise fully loaded at 30 knots, not just reach this speed at full throttle. Otherwise, the extra cost of tooling and the added time and cost spent laying up a stepped hull is wasted, and the stepped bottom is just a marketing gimmick. Some runabout builders even carve out a little scoop

A view looking aft of the Regal stepped bottom. Note the large air intake area at the chines, intended to keep the air flowing on the inboard side of a sharp turn.

at the chine amidships, which I suppose is meant to suggest that the bottom is stepped, when in fact the bottom is as straight as an arrow.

Assuming that it has enough power to cruise in the 30-knot range, what's the downside to a stepped hull? Well, since stepped bottoms create localized areas of high pressure (dynamic lift) at the steps and

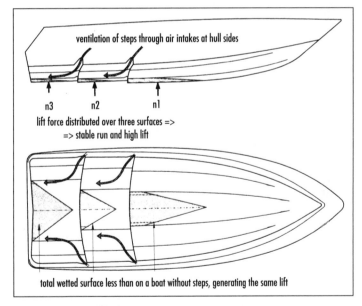

Bottom steps reduce wetted surface and drag, and pressure is distributed over three small, wide surfaces. Trim locks in at high speed, so trim tabs, lower unit angle, and changes in LCG have less effect than on a conventional hull. The stepped bottom tends to follow the water's surface (up and down waves) with great tenacity.

LARSSON AND ELIASSON, *PRINCIPLES OF YACHT DESIGN*

at the transom, these boats tend to make up their own minds about trim angles. Fore-and-aft stability is significantly increased compared to a nonstepped hull, and stepped bottoms tend to follow wave contours more closely. Even in an outboard- or stern-drive-powered stepped-hull boat, at least at higher speeds, you can forget about raising the bow by trimming the lower units up in a following sea.

The area behind each step has to be adequately ventilated, and the airflow must not be cut off by waves, turns, or rolling. If airflow is lost, resistance is immediately created that can sharply reduce speed or, if airflow is cut off to one side of the hull only, the vessel may turn suddenly and unexpectedly. Builders often provide large inlets to the areas behind the steps, and a few even provide air paths through ducts that lead to the trailing vertical edge of the steps.

Planing Hull Dynamics

As we've discovered, a planing hull not only floats, but when traveling fast enough, it also skims along the surface of the water. When on plane, the bottom of a hull acts, to a limited degree, like an airplane wing. Water moving at high speed impinges on the hull, and since for every action there is an equal and opposite reaction, *dynamic lift* is created. A planing hull is unlike an airplane wing in that the latter mostly generates lift by creating a low pressure area along the top of the wing. This low pressure, and consequent pull upward, is due to the curvature, in cross section, of the top of the wing. This curvature causes the airflow to accelerate (and create lift from the resulting low pressure) along the top of the wing, since it has to travel a greater distance than the air on the bottom of the wing before it reaches the wing's trailing edge. See more below under Dynamic Instability.

Dynamic Lifting Surface

The *dynamic lifting surface* is the wetted surface of the hull that supports the vessel when on plane. It is bounded by an area termed the *stagnation zone* for-

ward, by the spray rail or chines to the sides, and by the transom aft. On high-speed planing hulls, this surface is roughly triangular in shape and may be only 20 to 30 percent of the boat's length. The dynamic pressure on this small area equals the displacement of the boat. And ultrafast surface drive–powered boats may also be supported partially by the surface-piercing propeller's considerable vertical lift.

The stagnation zone is where the high-speed waterflow is tangent to the hull surface, with waterflow breaking off both ahead and astern. Since the waterflow impinges at a right angle to the hull, dynamic pressure is greatest here. This is called the *stagnation zone*, or *line*, since the water hitting the hull along this line, for the briefest moment, is not moving in relation to the hull. Dynamic pressure on the hull drops off both forward and aft of this region—rapidly forward, as water is deflected and turns to spray, and more gradually aft.

A Balanced Planing Hull

A planing hull's longitudinal center of buoyancy (LCB) is generally about 35 to 40 percent of the way forward of the transom at the waterline—farther aft than on a typical displacement hull. Why the difference? The planing hull's buttock lines aft must be nearly horizontal, or parallel to the waterline, so the hull can plane efficiently. On a displacement hull, the buttock lines normally sweep up aft to reduce drag and equalize fore-and-aft buoyancy at displacement speeds. Such a hull will lack the dynamic lift necessary to plane. The hull at the waterline must also be wide enough back aft to develop sufficient dynamic lift so the vessel can get up on plane. The planing hull also has its *longitudinal center of flotation* (LCF) farther aft, which reduces the impact of fuel level on trim when the fuel tanks are near the stern. The fullness of the planing hull's waterplane is reflected in its *prismatic coefficient* (see pages 36–37). Compared to its displacement and semidisplacement cousins, with their finer ends, the typical planing hull has a large Cp of about 0.70 or greater, which it needs to achieve dynamic lift.

The bow sections of planing hull must be full and buoyant enough so that when the stern is lifted by a following sea, the bow is not excessively immersed. If the bow roots, or digs too far into a following sea, yawing (or in extreme conditions, broaching) is introduced, with the bow turning into what is effectively a fixed rudder forward. The stern can't be so wide and buoyant that the bow tends to stuff when running downsea, and the bow shouldn't be so full (wide at the waterline forward) that it makes the boat pound upsea in a stiff chop.

Speed versus Deadrise

As increasingly powerful lightweight diesels boost a boat's speed capability, it's essential that the deadrise in modern designs increase proportionately to keep slamming loads down. A sharp entry for the first 20 percent of the waterline length isn't enough; the increased deadrise must continue aft to the hull's midbody, because that's where most of the wave impact is taking place at higher speeds. For most hulls, there must be at least 15 degrees of deadrise at the transom, and 25 to 35 degrees in the hull's midsection. There's no way around the need for deadrise here.

Over the years, many production boatbuilders like Tiara, Grady-White, and Viking have steadily increased deadrise forward as their boats have evolved from cruising at 16 to 20 knots in the 1970s to 32 knots (or faster) today. But these boats and yachts aren't lightweights, so there's a limit to how much deadrise is practical with a 30-knot cruising speed in demand. Bertram and Viking both opt for transom deadrise in the 15- to 18-degree range, delivering good lift at speed, but with enough deadrise for a smooth ride and improved course-keeping. The Bertram 46 (a stretched 43), as much as any other convertible of its size, is a smooth-as-silk marvel at speed in a chop.

Speed versus Weight

Since adding weight and deadrise reduces speed, all else being equal, a boat's speed can be increased by keeping the weight down. But two boats of similar size can vary in weight for a variety of reasons; the heavier boat isn't necessarily stronger or better built, but it may be. If Brand A's 36- by 12-foot express cruiser weighs significantly more than Brand B's, ask the builder to spell out specifically why that is. Is it because Brand A is heavily built with fiberglass-encapsulated plywood stringers and bulkheads, a solid glass hull, and plywood-cored decks, whereas Brand B benefits from advanced composite engineering with foam-cored stringers and bulkheads and a resin-infused, postcured, cored epoxy hull and deck laminate? Or are the two boats built pretty much the same, except for the thinner laminates and smaller scantlings in the hull grid system of the lighter one? Find out!

If two boats of similar dimensions weigh about the same and have similar drivetrains, and one is

Update Those Old Hull Designs!

The problem with some boats on the market today is that their hull designs originated thirty or more years ago. In the late 1960s, a 42-foot, low-deadrise sportfisherman might be fitted with a pair of 300 hp, 2,800-pound GM 671 diesels and would run along nicely at 16 to 20 knots. Nowadays you can fit 610 hp MAN diesels in about the same space as the old 671s, and suddenly a decent 16- to 20-knot fishing boat is transformed into a hard-riding, flat-bottom 32-knot race boat.

Some of the venerable New Jersey–built sportfishermen, like the Post 42—a well-engineered and beautifully finished boat otherwise—and the Jersey 40, are prime examples. They're fast for their size and power precisely because of their relatively flat bottoms. But with their low-deadrise bottom sections forward, they pound noticeably in a stiff chop; there's no way to get around the laws of physics! With low or no deadrise aft, boats with similar hull shapes also tend to wander about their course with seas abaft the beam unless trimmed bow-up (which is possible only with plenty of fuel in the undercockpit fuel tank and trim tabs raised). If you value speed in calm water above all else, these boats may be right for you. But don't expect to comfortably keep up with the rest of the fleet when the wind picks up.

still significantly faster than the other, the reason is likely to be found in the deadrise. I'll take the deeper-deadrise, slower boat over the flatter, faster boat, since the first will deliver solid all-weather comfort and performance while the second will be a miserable ride in a chop.

The bottom line is that if a manufacturer claims that their boat is the fastest around with a given power plant, you should pull the string and find out why. If the boat isn't a whole lot lighter, it's probably because it has a flatter bottom than everyone else. You should care deeply about this if you plan on heading out past the jetties when the wind's blowing. Adding horsepower to an older hull, as we'll see, can also introduce dynamic instabilities if LCG isn't carefully managed during the repower.

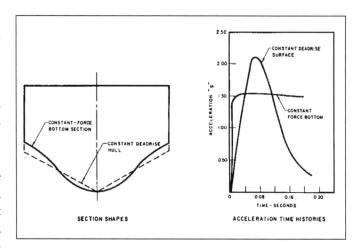

SECTION SHAPES

ACCELERATION TIME HISTORIES

Deadrise isn't everything, as this diagram by planing hull authority Dan Savitsky shows. The shape of the hull, in section view, has a significant impact (so to speak) on slamming, or pounding, which is measured as vertical accelerations. A bell-shaped hull section significantly reduces G-forces upon wave impact, when compared with a straight section. The downside is that more spray is generated. DAN SAVITSKY

Ride Quality

As mentioned earlier, *ride quality* refers to the comfort of a boat's ride measured in vertical accelerations, or *slamming loads*. As a hull encounters waves at high speed, impacts of varying degrees occur repeatedly. These impacts are measured as accelerations using the force of gravity as a standard. A boat

This typical express cruiser is fully up on plane, but it's a harder-riding boat in a chop than, say, an Albemarle 26 or Formula 27, due to its also flatter, fuller forefoot. That makes a boat like this well suited to inshore waters, but not to running at speed in rougher water offshore.

high and dry in a parking lot subjects its cradle (and its occupants) to a G-force of one. But if the same boat is slamming into a wave with sufficient impact to produce a G-force of 1.5, a 200-pound person standing in the bow of the boat will momentarily feel as if he weighs 300 pounds. Standing near the stern of the same boat, since the boat effectively moves vertically about a fulcrum just aft of amidships when pounding through small waves, the same man would experience less G-force and consider the ride more comfortable. Thus, where you happen to be standing in a high-speed boat is important to your morale. Remember if you are sitting farther aft than your passengers that they are being subjected to higher accelerations than you are, especially in a bowrider.

Course–Keeping and Handling

Course-keeping and boat handling have to do with the ability to control a boat at both high and low speeds. High-speed course-keeping is largely a function of hull form, which determines whether or not a boat will naturally tend to track in a straight line with minimal helm input. Here again, the deep-V has a distinct advantage over a boat with flatter sections aft, since a flat bottom tends to wander more about the desired heading, especially with seas abaft the beam. A full keel on a flat-bottom boat helps, but the added wetted surface increases drag and slows you down, and dynamic instability can occur at high cruising speeds. That's why a deep-V is so much better suited to waterjet propulsion (which has less directional stability than other drives) than a flat-bottom boat.

The LCG must not be too far forward, nor the VCG too high, to permit good seakeeping. In fact, if there is one other element in hull design that is most crucial to good performance, and this includes handling at speed and course-keeping, it's proper placement of the LCG. Put it too far forward and the boat rides bow down, making it directionally unstable and wet to boot. Too far aft, and the boat takes excessive power to propel through the water, decreasing range and wasting fuel, to say nothing of the bad effect on visibility from the lower helm station. A VCG that is too high will make the boat wallow and yaw excessively in a following sea, too.

The best test for course-keeping is a quartering sea some 20 to 40 degrees off the stern. If a boat tracks well in such a sea, then hats off to the designer and builder for getting weight distribution right. Most boats handle better running at a greater trim angle (bow up) in a following or quartering sea, while lowering the bow by depressing trim tabs makes for a smoother if wetter ride in a head sea.

Good *handling* characteristics presume rapid response to throttle and helm inputs and a hull that is not so directionally stable that it's hard to turn. For throttles to respond well, horsepower alone is only the beginning. Just as important, or more so, is how the power is delivered to the water. Larger reduction ratios with larger, slower turning propellers almost always respond better to low-speed clutch and throttle commands than smaller gear ratios with smaller, faster turning props. The volume *and* velocity of water being moved by the propeller is the key to responsiveness. Just try docking a typical 40-foot express cruiser with its shallow (1.64:1) gear ratio and too-small (22-inch) props; the boat hardly moves when you put an engine in gear at idle. While docking such a boat in Florida a few years ago, I backed the starboard engine only to have the bow fall off to port until I applied a strong burst of power. The same boat and engines with deeper gears and larger props would undoubtedly handle much more responsively and would likely reach the same cruising speed, though top speed (a mostly irrelevant and academic figure) might fall off slightly.

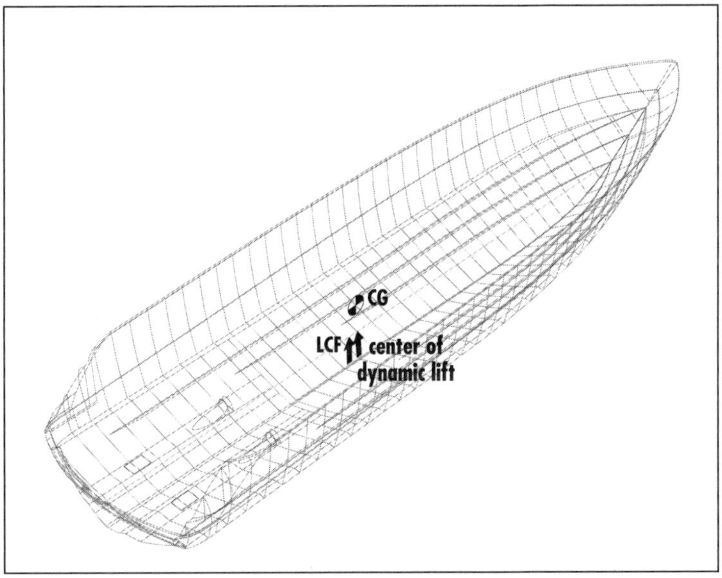

Another computer-generated 3-D wire drawing of the 65-foot Viking Sport Cruisers motor yacht shown in the figure on page 47. This is one of the best-running hull designs in the industry. Note the positions of CDL, CG, and LCF, the point about which the hull trims statically.

BERNARD OLESINSKI

Round-Bilge Planing Hulls

Though they are the most efficient at high speeds, not all planing hulls have hard chines. Some have round bilges (radiused chines), which have their own advantages, such as producing an easier, more comfortable motion in a seaway, and reducing resistance at slower speeds. Or a hull may have hard chines aft (to increase lift) and round bilges forward (to improve ride quality). A hard-chine planing hull creates more wavemaking resistance at displacement speeds and requires more power for a given displacement speed than a round-bilge craft. The round-bilge hull will tend to require less power to achieve a given speed up to S/L 2, whereas a hard-chine vessel will require less horsepower, and be more stable dynamically, above S/L 2.5. If the priority is low-speed efficiency and range, the round-bilge hull is the best choice. The larger waves created at slow speeds make the hard-chine planing hull a poor choice for operating extensively in no-wake zones such as canals and other protected waters. This is especially true of deep-V hulls, which leave a large wake and plane at higher speeds than flat-bottom boats.

There's no significant difference between round-bilge and hard-chine hulls of similar dimensions and displacement in pitch and heave at semi-displacement speeds. However, round-bilge vessels do have more comfortable motions at displacement speeds, and hard-chine planing hulls have superior ride quality at planing speeds. The hard-chine vessel rises significantly out of the water due to dynamic pressures, increasing the hull's effective freeboard, improving visibility from the helm station, and helping to keep spray and solid water off the deck. (As we've seen, length-to-beam ratio has a significant effect on crew comfort in a head sea, since vertical accelerations are greatly diminished in longer, narrower hulls of all persuasions.)

Compared to the round-bilge hull, the hard-chine vessel at planing speed will have better directional stability or course-keeping, especially with seas abaft the beam, and will be less prone to broach when operating near wave speed. The hard-chine

craft will also have a stiffer, shallower roll and will tend to ship less water on deck in rough water. A hard-chine vessel running downsea at displacement speed will yaw more than a displacement hull, due to its flat buttock lines aft, wide transom, and buoyant stern. It will also squat less when coming up on plane, and once planing. And because of its superior course-keeping, a hard-chine, deep-V hull is generally better suited to waterjet propulsion than a round-bilge hull.

A round-bilge hull would need a full keel for acceptable directional stability, and possibly bilge keels or active stabilizers to reduce roll, all of which add drag to the hull. Naturally, there's a relation among course-keeping, yaw, and roll, since a single degree of yaw in a round-bilge hull can develop up to five degrees of roll. In fact, reducing roll angle in any vessel does wonders to improve course-keeping. And with a round-bilge hull's greater buttock lines curvature forward, as we'll see in the Dynamic Instability section below, bow diving becomes more likely.

The hard-chined Little Harbor Whisperjet 44 is waterjet-propelled.
BILLY BLACK, COURTESY LITTLE HARBOR

Hybrid Hulls

One type of hybrid hull starts with a round bilge forward, the radius of which decreases gradually until a hard chine appears near the stern. The hard chine adds buoyancy and dynamic lift aft and reduces squatting at low planing speeds, helping to turn a semidisplacement hull into a planing hull. The hard chine aft also contributes to directional

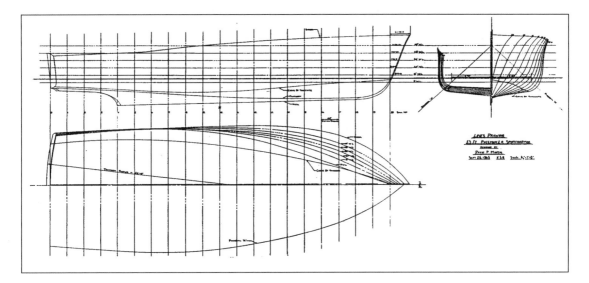

A 1960s-vintage Pacemaker designed by Dave Martin, who also has the Ocean Yachts line to his credit. This low-deadrise, round-bilge hull was well-suited to its day, when 16- to 18-knot speeds were made for a fast boat. The entry is reasonably sharp forward where most wave impact takes place on a moderate-speed hull like this.

DAVE MARTIN

stability, improving course-keeping at higher speeds. Another hybrid design puts it the other way around, with the round bilge aft and the hard chine forward, a combination thought to improve course-keeping as well as transverse dynamic stability at semidisplacement speeds.

Other hard-chine design advantages include greater internal volume than a round-bilge craft of the same dimensions, improving load-carrying capacity and habitability. And since the hard-chine hull has greater form stability, it can carry more weight up high with greater impunity.

Large Planing Hulls

Large planing hulls, over about 75 feet, tend to run too flat in trim at high speeds, increasing frictional resistance and diminishing the vessel's handling. An easy way for the designer to drop the stern (and raise the bow relative to it) and improve matters is to put a little rocker in the buttocks aft. On many hulls, trim can be varied within a range of some five degrees in this manner. Savvy designers can also lock in optimum trim by shifting the LCG a bit farther aft than usual (remember that too-far-forward

LCG is curtains for a planing hull) and then adding a little hook (concavity in the buttock lines) aft to raise the stern a whisker. In fact, hook in the buttocks aft acts like a big set of trim tabs by shifting the CDL aft. Hooked buttocks minimize drag at low speed (and are generally to be avoided on high-speed planing hulls), straight buttocks minimize it at intermediate speeds, and slightly convex buttocks (a little rocker) produce the least drag at high speeds.

A Refined Bottom

Besides waterline L/B ratio, the secret to efficiency and ride quality lies in refinements to the hull shape, including deadrise distribution from bow to stern; hull shape in station view (whether concave, straight, convex, or bell-shaped); the precise shape and size of the chine flats; the shape, size, and location of bottom strakes or spray rails; and the hull trim resulting from LCG and bottom hook or rocker. A padded keel, also known as a ski or delta pad, is a flattened keel section that adds lift, reduces tripping in a high-speed turn, and shifts buoyancy from the keel area to the chines, increasing stability. Chine flats (which improve form stability and add dynamic lift) can also improve a planing hull design. Expect most modern planing hulls, whether modified-Vs, warped-Vs, or deep-Vs, to sport a combination of these refinements.

Hull shape and refinements influence ride quality, handling characteristics, and optimum speed, and so do underwater appendages such as shafts, struts, strikes, fins, keels, and rudders. These appendages should be faired to minimize drag and to provide a smooth flow of water to the propellers and rudders.

Bottom Strakes and Spray Rails

Bottom or *running strakes* add dynamic lift and deflect spray, but their real purpose is to define the boundary of the hull's wetted surface when running on plane. The lift generated by bottom strakes can be significant forward, where water and spray direction is at an outward angle from the hull's centerline. Farther aft, waterflow lines up with the hulls' keel, or centerline, so dynamic lift from strakes is minimal or nonexistent, though they may still contribute to a small degree to tracking and roll attenuation.

Bottom strakes, like those we typically see on

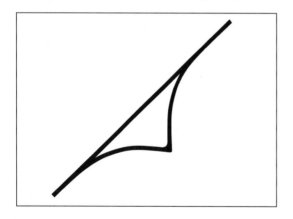

Spray rail detail from the 65 Viking Sport Cruisers. The soft inside corners have lots of advantages, including easier fabrication, greater strength, less frictional drag, focused spray deflection, and decreased slamming in a seaway at speed. The hard outside corner produces clean waterflow spearation   BERNARD OLESINSKI

a deep-V hull, look great and, if properly designed, can improve performance. It seems intuitively obvious that a soft radius in the inner corner of a bottom strake deflects spray most efficiently and effectively. Water tends to "crunch" up against strakes with hard inside corners, increasing slamming loads. It's also important that the edge away from the keel comes to a sharp point so waterflow breaks cleanly away, minimizing drag. Bottom strakes have to be carefully positioned, or they can create channels for air to flow to the propellers, struts, rudders, through-hull connections, waterjet inlets, and transducers farther aft, as we'll see in the Dynamic Instability section following.

Some boats—especially round-bilge, semidisplacement hulls—incorporate *spray rails* that deflect spray and add lift forward. These spray rails are something like oversized bottom strakes, and a single pair is usually fitted starting well above the waterline at the stem and gradually sloping down as you move aft. They may terminate just forward of amidships or continue to the transom. Overly large spray rails may increase slamming loads, and when improperly shaped and located on the hull may generate spray as well as deflect it. But all in all, they're indispensable when it comes to controlling spray forward, they generate lift forward, and they can encourage waterflow separation at the bilge aft.

Trim Tabs

Trim tabs are small flaps, usually made of thin stainless-steel plate, mounted to port and starboard on the transom just above the bottom of the boat. They're controlled from the helm station via a hydraulic piston that projects through the bottom of the boat or from the transom. In the Up position, they are on the same plane and at the same level as the hull bottom. When lowered, they generate lift by increasing their angle of attack. The effect of this lift, then, is to raise the stern and lower the bow.

Planing hulls can use trim tabs to advantage in order to run at optimum trim through any likely combination of speed, loading, and sea state. Trim

A trim tab slightly depressed. Well offset from centerline, trim tabs, or flaps, acting in consort, can lower the bow by raising the stern, or individually correct for a small amount of heel. Adequate tab surface area is necessary to produce lift efficiently, and tab-angle indicators, which take the guesswork out of tab positioning, are great to have.   BENNETT

tabs can be used to correct for heel (caused by wind) or list (caused by uneven weight distribution), to decrease time to plane, to help stay on plane at lower speeds, or to depress the bow in a head sea to reduce slamming loads. Trim tabs will also increase a boat's speed range at low planing speeds.

Depressing the tabs might allow a planing vessel to slow down a couple more knots without falling off plane, a useful attribute in rough water since a hull on top (planing) at 13 knots is much more efficient than one that's fallen off plane. Tabs, then, can be used to "finesse" a boat's trim, meaning the skipper can tweak the angle of the hull so it operates at its most fuel-efficient, best-handling, smoothest-riding attitude.

Some boats need a lot of tab not only to get on plane in a reasonable time, but to correct for inappropriate LCG (too stern-heavy) once *on* plane. With these boats, trim tabs are used to help compensate for poor design. Though there are exceptions, if a boat needs tabs just to run well when normally loaded in calm water, or to get on plane without aiming for the clouds, something was amiss in the design phase.

Tabs can be lowered and raised together or in-

dependently. When both are lowered, the stern comes up and the bow drops, shifting the CDL aft. Lowering the bow smoothes the ride in a head sea by immersing the sharper bow sections and shifting wave impact forward. Wetted surface and drag are also increased when depressing the bow, slowing the boat and increasing the amount of spray generated forward. In a following sea, a depressed bow will often lead to bow steering and degraded directional control.

When only one tab is lowered, that side of the stern is raised and the opposite bow is depressed. Using a single tab is a good way to correct for a small list caused by uneven weight distribution (say, with a 1,000-pound tuna to port), single-engine propeller torque, or a strong beam wind. Interestingly, a boat running on plane often tends to heel into the wind rather than away from it. That's because a small amount of rudder is needed to counteract the wind and keep the boat going in a straight line, and this *steering effort* induces a lever-arm that tends to heel the boat. So, depressing the starboard trim tab in a strong starboard beam wind will often return the boat to an even keel, using one trim tab to counteract that right-rudder lever arm.

Some larger boats are designed so the fuel tanks are centered over the LCF, which means that trim won't change noticeably as fuel is consumed. Such a boat needs trim tabs, then, only to adjust trim to suit the sea state and wind conditions. It's rare to see a sportfishing convertible with its fuel tanks over the LCF, though, since that's where the oversized diesels reside. A convertible's main fuel tank is usually under the cockpit, well aft of the LCF, so that as fuel is consumed the stern comes up significantly. Many convertibles, at least those over 50 feet, have a smaller fuel tank forward that they burn off first so they don't get into a bow-down attitude offshore. Trim tabs can help compensate for a stern-heavy loading, but nothing can help when a boat is running bow-heavy other than a weight shift aft. The problem, then, is that trim tabs won't raise the bow if the LCG is too far forward to begin with; all they can do is raise the stern and depress the bow.

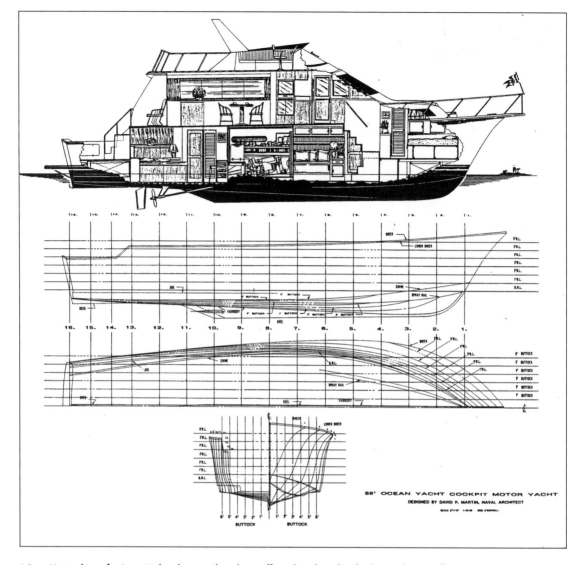

A Dave Martin design for Ocean Yachts planes easily and runs efficiently with modest deadrise and narrow, flat stern sections. DAVE MARTIN

As discussed elsewhere, getting the LCG right during the design of a boat is crucial to proper performance and handling. If a boat runs excessively bow-high during all conditions of loading, the LCG is simply too far aft. Such a boat needs trim tabs at all times to achieve its best running trim, and having to rely on trim tabs can be a Band-Aid approach for ill-conceived boats. On the other hand, a few, usually well-designed planing boats (like the Hunt designs mentioned) don't even come with trim tabs, running naturally at their 2- to 5-degree trim angle, but you give up the ability to offset list or depress the bow in a stiff chop. Length usually helps to minimize bow rise when accelerating up on plane, so a 70-footer will aim for the sky less than the 30-footer, all else being equal.

And tabs can help a boat get up on plane in less time while burning less fuel and with better visibility from a lower helm station, thanks to less bow rise. Certain dynamic instabilities can sometimes

This mid-1990s 34-foot Egg Harbor convertible has lots of room and comfortable amenities on the inside, but its beamy hull and low deadrise produce a fairly bumpy ride in a chop. The ride quality, or smoothness of ride, is further diminished by the vessel's bow-high running trim, due to the linear relationship between trim and slamming loads. The laws of physics are intransigent; you just can't have both generous interior volume *and* superior ride quality.

be corrected with trim tabs. For instance, porpoising can usually be controlled by dropping the tabs a bit, shifting the CDL aft.

It can be aggravating to run a boat that needs trim tabs to operate acceptably, only to find that the tabs are too small or that there are no trim tab angle indicators. The tabs must be large enough to actually lift the stern at cruising speed. I tested a Chris Craft 300 (a nice-running and handling boat otherwise) fitted with tabs that managed only to slowly turn the boat when depressed individually. There was no noticeable difference in trim when depressing both tabs until the engines were running over 3,500 rpm, which is above their cruise rpm. So, if you don't see three to five degrees of change in trim from full-up to full-down tabs when running at a comfortable cruise rpm, they're probably too small for the weight and length of the boat.

Bennett Marine, the largest trim tab manufacturer in the world, recommends an inch of tab width per side for each foot of boat length, but also takes boat weight and speed into account. So there would be 30 inches (called *span*) of trim tab width per side for a typical 30-footer. Their tabs are usually 9 inches long (fore-and-aft length referred to

as *chord*) but are available up to 12 inches long for heavier, slower boats, or if space for mounting the tabs on the transom is limited. Speed is an important issue when sizing tabs, since those that would be large enough to work well at slower speeds could cause the boat to get out of control at, say, 50 knots.

Trim tab angle indicators are usually not included by the builder, but I wouldn't want to leave home without them. That's because it can be pretty tormenting fooling around with the tab rocker switches at the helm without having a clue as to their actual angle. These handy little tab angle indicators uses a series of LED lights to show the angle of each tab, which depress 20 degrees when fully lowered.

Trim Control with Outboards and Stern Drives

Outboard and stern-drive power offer a natural advantage with regard to trim: the ability to control the direction of propeller thrust vertically as well as horizontally. It's the ability to trim the lower unit up (raising the bow) that separates a stern drive or outboard from an inboard-, surface-drive-, or waterjet-powered boat. Raising the lower unit allows an operator to find the hull's sweet spot, where wetted hull area and drag are minimized but the boat is still not porpoising, or to select a bow-up attitude for better following-sea control. Even though you can trim the lower unit down to raise the stern, trim tabs get the job done more efficiently, allowing the propeller to run level and just push the boat.

Of course, trimming a drive down will depress the bow as trim tabs do. The inefficiencies of a stern drive or outboard's smaller propeller and complex, energy-robbing bull-gear arrangement are offset by this ability to adjust propeller thrust to a more horizontal inclination, and by the lessened drag of the lower unit in comparison with an inboard's fixed gear (shafts, struts, and rudders). It's also worth noting that in a small boat, three or four people moving from stern to bow or filling a fish box and livewell will alter trim significantly, and a lower unit's ability to compensate for a bow-heavy condition due to these variable loads is a welcome feature.

Though its ability to "dial in" optimum trim gives a lower-unit-powered boat with poor weight distribution a speed advantage, an inboard with optimum LCG can perform nearly on a par with the stern drive or outboard, giving up at most 10 percent speed. The result is a boat that will run at its sweet spot all day long without trim tabs, with the tabs still available to depress the bow in a chop, raise the stern when the fish box or livewell are filled, or correct for heel or list. Provided you don't need an outboard's light weight and you get the weight distribution right, the cheaper, more corrosion-resistant inboard just might be the ticket to your boating Nirvana.

Dynamic Instability

Predictability is greatly favored by astronauts and boaters alike. No one appreciates the unexpected happening when traveling along at cruising speed. When things get out of control, it's invariably because of outside forces acting in an unanticipated way.

As we mentioned earlier, a planing bottom can develop low-pressure areas that destabilize handling and controllability. To understand how underwater hull shape produces positive and negative pressures, we return to our airfoil analogy. Note that the buttock lines on a planing hull describe a similar curve forward (seen in profile) to the top of an airplane wing (seen in section). The wing, which is more highly curved at the top than the bottom, develops lift not so much because of the high pressure on the bottom of the wing, but from the low pressure on the top. Low pressure develops on the wing's top surface because the air has to travel farther and therefore faster along its curved upper surface, creating a low-pressure region of aerodynamic lift.

Now here's where the bottom of a planing hull acts like the top of an airplane wing. Normally just the aft half of a planing vessel is in contact with the water, with the bow high and dry on plane in calm

Fuel Tanks

While we're on the subject of LCG and trim, let's see where fuel tanks fit in—literally. From a performance perspective, the optimum location for tanks is about 5 percent of the waterline length ahead of the full-load LCG. Bow-up trim tends to increase as fuel is burned off and the LCG shifts aft, and tends to decrease as speed picks up with the loss of weight. The result of these opposing forces is a net trim change of zero. The problem is, it's just about impossible to get this balance just right on a marketable boat, since fuel tank location isn't as high on the average owner's priority list as, say, closet size and squeezing in that stackable washer-dryer unit.

Saddle tanks installed outboard of the engines is one way to get the tanks close to the LCG, but this also cramps the engine room and reduces maintenance accessibility. Saddle tanks usually force the engines closer to the hull centerline, and this of course reduces the boat's maneuverability at low speed, with the propellers and rudders being closer together. This tank location also places the tanks higher in the boat, raising the CG and decreasing ultimate stability.

The convertible's largest fuel tank must usually be placed under the cockpit, which is well aft of the LCB. As a result, most convertibles will change trim markedly as fuel is consumed, and fuel has to be pumped between forward and after tanks to compensate. In nonsportfishing layouts, V-drive configurations with the engines mounted well aft have a lot to commend them. This allows the large fixed weights (the engines) to be in the stern and moves the variable weight of fuel forward, nearer the LCG. But an aft engine room arrangement, which also isolates machinery noises and vibrations more effectively from living spaces, is not practical if the design calls for a cockpit or aft cabin.

water. But when the forward hull bottom is immersed—when the stern is lifted by a following sea, or the hull is heavily loaded, or trim is too low, or the boat is slowing down—low hydrodynamic pressures are created forward even if this area of the hull is at a positive angle of attack relative to the surrounding waterflow. Under these circumstances, the forward bottom sections may actually develop pressures that are less than atmospheric, pulling the bow down.

These negative, less-than-atmospheric pressures may be exacerbated when bow-down in a roll, since the roll presents the most negative pressure-inducing hull profile to the water. As a result of the loss of lift forward, the CDL shifts aft, the bow dives farther, and the boat becomes dynamically unstable. High pressures also develop at the bow, but the net change is a bow-down trim. You'll see the same effect if you dangle a spoon under a running faucet; it takes some effort to separate the spoon from the waterflow, even when the spoon surface seems to be at a positive angle of attack.

Dynamic instability—called *bow diving* (the bow pitches down deeply into the water in the absence of a clear cause, such as waves acting on the hull)—is compounded in a heavily loaded hull because the forward sections are already more deeply immersed at speed. The more highly curved the buttock lines forward are, the less lift is developed, so the bow of a poorly designed and overloaded planing hull can be literally drawn down into the water by low pressure that's insufficient to support the hull's weight. In fact, one of the reasons a hard-chine hull makes a better planing boat than a round-bilge hull is that there's less curvature in the buttock lines forward, because the hard chines provide a natural place for the buttock lines to terminate. Low pressure can also develop locally due to depressions in a metal hull's plating or a fiberglass hull's imperfect tooling. The result can be chine walking, bow steering, and bow diving, which we discuss below.

In simple terms, a dynamically unstable vessel is one that, when up on plane and supported by the pressure of fast-moving waterflow, does not run like it's supposed to. This usually means the boat porpoises, chine-walks, runs bow-down, heels over to one side, yaws unpredictably, or is subject to some combination of these motions. The reason it runs at the wrong attitude (in trim, yaw, and heel) probably has to do mostly with hull shape and weight distribution and the resulting distribution of dynamic pressures (or lack of pressures) acting on the hull, hence the term *dynamic* instabilities. (There may be other reasons, too, such as appendage problems, loose steering, and improper handling.)

As we've seen, the area of the hull bottom where the water pressure is greatest is called the *stagnation zone.* This is the forward area of the hull at the on-plane waterline where waterflow impacts with and is perpendicular to the hull bottom. Dynamic pressure drops off quickly aft of this point, but there should be some degree of positive pressure all the way aft to the transom. Certain underwater areas of the hull are under normal pressure while others, due to inappropriate hull curvature or hull-skin irregularities, can actually be under less-than-atmospheric pressure (slight vacuum). When

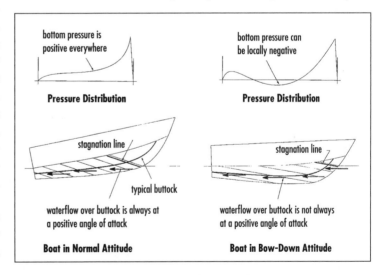

Naval architect Lou Codega, who designed such well-regarded boats as the Regulator and Carolina Classic, has long studied planing hull dynamic instabilities. These drawings show the relationship between hull trim, buttock lines, and dynamic lift. Excessive buttock curvature in the bow acts a little like a spoon held under a faucet, actually developing negative pressures forward that produce bow steering and other planing instabilities.   LOU CODEGA

you sum these pressures, their distribution and intensity don't combine to support the hull in its proper attitude. A normal, dynamically stable vessel, on the other hand, is suitably supported by the sum of hull pressures and will return to a state of equilibrium (usually an even keel) by restoring pressure or forces after being subjected to wave action. In displacement and semidisplacement craft, dynamic pressures rarely build to the point of causing instabilities, unless you count dynamic events like broaching, which is one reason designing a fine planing hull is such a complicated business.

So what factors are believed to cause a boat to be unstable dynamically? Speed is at the top of the list—the faster a boat can go, the more apt it is to become unstable. That's one reason why driving a semidisplacement hull to planing speeds can be a bad idea. Depending on hull length, dynamic lift generally starts to predominate over the static lift of buoyancy at about 25 knots. Instabilities resulting from dynamic forces alone are relatively uncommon below this speed. *Hull loading*, or the psi (static and dynamic) acting on the bottom of the hull, is another factor; the heavier the loading, the greater the chances of an instability developing. LCG is also critical: putting it too far forward will invariably result in a dynamic instability. It's worth noting that adding a cockpit extension effectively shifts LCG forward (as a percentage of waterline length), which can easily be a recipe for introducing dynamic instabilities, so this common hull-form alteration must be carefully engineered.

Too much buttock line curvature forward, excessive hook or rocker aft, and underwater hull appendages can also contribute to dynamic instabilities, as we'll see, and rudder and trim tab movement can upset the stability apple cart. Dynamic instabilities may also result when VCG, LCG, or displacement are wrong for the hull's shape and dimensions. So, a high-powered, heavy boat with a forward LCG, highly curved buttock lines forward, and ventilated appendages is likely to disappoint in terms of stability on plane. Sometimes the solution is simply to slow down a couple of knots.

Some dynamic instabilities result from putting too much power in an older design. Production builders are taking older hull designs, which behaved well with moderately sized engines and repowering with 75 to 100 percent more horsepower. Adding power usually necessitates shifting LCG aft (usually by moving the engines aft), but this requirement is all too often ignored. Now these boats are really operating in an altogether different performance regime, and their builders and owners seem to wonder why they're no longer well-behaved at speed.

Oscillating Instabilities

Instabilities can be either oscillatory (varying, moving back and forth) or constant. Oscillatory instabilities include *chine walking*: this is a roll oscillation in which the boat heels over on its chine, rights itself to an even keel, and then repeats the cycle. The cure for chine walking in outboard-powered boats may be as simple as tightening up the steering or shifting the LCF aft. Repowering with larger engines without moving the LCG aft can also result in chine walking.

Porpoising is an oscillation in pitch and heave, with the bow alternately rising and falling. The center of dynamic lift (CDL) changes as speed increases and trim and the area of the immersed hull change; porpoising results when the CDL constantly shifts forward and aft relative to a stationary LCG. Both chine walking and porpoising are associated with hard-chine hulls (chine walking is also sometimes found in certain boats with long length-to-beam ratios), and the intensity of these oscillations is often a function of hull speed. They can occur in calm or choppy water without any helm or throttle input from the operator, and they are often predictable.

Porpoising, in fact, like other oscillatory instabilities, can be anticipated by the operator once it's happened the first time, since it's based on a known combination of speed, trim (and trim-tab or drive position), and weight distribution. The operator may learn that her boat will never porpoise below

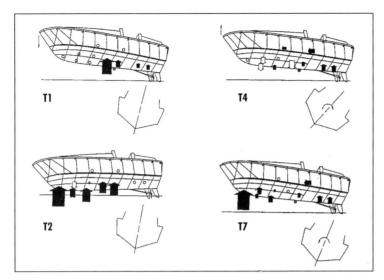

The relative pressures acting on a problematic planing hull's bottom set up dynamic instabilities at speed. At **T1** the boat is running normally, with positive pressure (black arrows) providing lift; at **T2** it slams downward, plowing into a wave; at **T4** it rolls, as negative pressure (white arrows) takes control of the hull; and at **T7**, it returns to normal operating trim. The "dots" depict atmospheric pressure, while the midsection views show rotation.

LOU CODEGA

ated entirely by internal influences such as a vessel's weight, weight distribution, and shape, or they can be triggered by external forces like wave action. A broach while traveling down the face of a wave is a dynamic instability in yaw and roll, for example. A broach can be initiated by a static instability if a hull is moving at the same speed as the wave supporting it, but the hull's inertia makes things worse. Sometimes, a one-in-a-thousand combination of wave impact, rudder angle, trim-tab setting, and LCG will cause a dynamic instability in an otherwise satisfactory boat.

While this discussion may give the impression that naval architects have a good handle on dynamic instabilities, this is not always the case. The interface between wave and hull, and the other elements that influence boat behavior in a seaway at speed, are complex. It may be easy to recognize a dynamic instability when it happens, but most of these phenomena are poorly understood even by those who make a living studying them.

a certain speed or engine trim setting. An owner may relocate her outboard from the transom to an aft bracket; this weight shift would tend to increase the chances of the boat porpoising. Porpoising can be stable at a constant speed and trim, or it can be unstable, increasing while these conditions remain constant. A naval architect's ability to accurately predict the conditions in which a new boat design will porpoise, before it ever hits the water, is limited, but it's also one of the best understood planing instability phenomena.

Constant Instabilities

Constant dynamic instabilities usually occur on large, relatively fast-moving, heavily loaded craft with LCGs that are too far forward. These instabilities are potentially the worst kind, since they can occur rapidly and unexpectedly under pushing-the-envelope conditions of weight and speed, and the results, including broaching and erratic helm response, can be dangerous. Instabilities can be cre-

Low Speed Instabilities

Instabilities at semiplaning (semidisplacement) speeds are often caused by static as well as dynamic pressures, and can diminish both directional and transverse stability. Loss of transverse stability, for example, can result when gravity, acting on the bow wave, creates a deep trough alongside the midbody of the hull, diminishing form stability by exposing the turn of the bilge to the sea breeze (and low atmospheric pressure). In fact, positive and negative pressures distributed along the underwater portion of the hull affect planing and semidisplacement, and round-bilge and hard-chine hulls.

When round-bilge hulls are pushed to semidis-

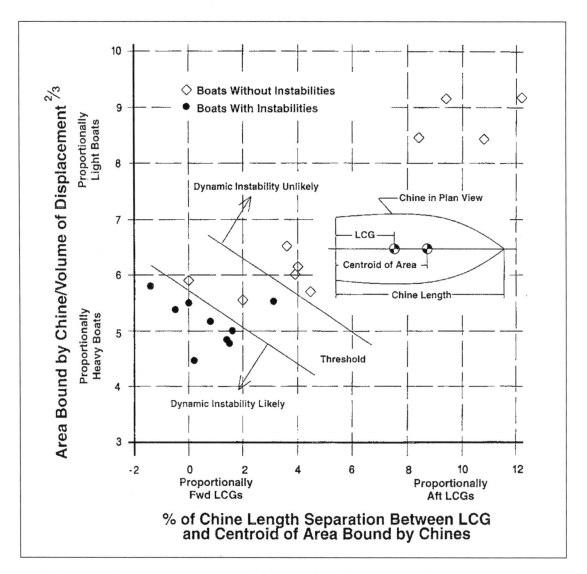

Naval architect Lou Codega's investigations into planing hull instabilities have resulted in this diagram showing the relationship between hull displacement and chine length relative to LCG placement, and the propensity for a hull to be dynamically unstable.

Hulls with lighter bottom loadings and proportionately aft LCGs in relation to the wetted chines are less likely to be dynamically unstable.

LOU CODEGA

placement or planing speeds, the boat's GM (its metacentric height, the measure of initial stability derived primarily from hull shape), is decreased because of the positive and negative pressures and changing waterlines that develop. In fact, some dynamic inclining experiments show a 20 to nearly 40 percent loss of GM at a speed-to-length (S/L) ratio

of 1.7 and 3, respectively, resulting in a high degree of roll sensitivity. A reserve of static stability must be designed in to compensate. Round-bilge boats that roll excessively at speed usually benefit from increasing bow-up trim, either by shifting the LCG aft, reshaping the hull by adding rocker aft, or adding wedges forward, just aft of the stagnation zone. Much as lowered trim tabs create lift at the transom, wedges forward provide lift at the bow, especially on the side more deeply immersed by heel and roll, thus countering excessive roll.

Ventilated Appendages

Hull spray strakes, which can as easily channel air as water, must be carefully positioned so they don't direct air to propellers, rudders, and underwater appendages. This may be counterintuitive, but if struts and rudders ventilate, they can cause dynamic instabilities, including roll moments and bow-down trim angles, by generating lift at the stern. An off-center ventilated strut or rudder will also cause the vessel to roll, potentially initiating a yaw or broach. The designer also has to make sure that cooling-water inlet through-hulls, depth sounder transducers, and waterjet inlets get a clean supply of solid water. Ventilation problems are best addressed by closing off air paths and reducing local disturbances with improved appendage fairing (streamlining).

Rudders can ventilate (and cause the stern to lift) when they're located too close to the transom. The low pressures created by the rudders can suck air in and cause the rudders to stall as well as generate lift. The best fixes are to move the rudders farther forward away from this ready air supply, to install horizontal cavitation plates above the rudders that project aft of the transom, or to notch out the rudders' upper trailing edges. Speaking of rudders, adding larger rudders or skegs to solve course-keeping problems will probably prove ineffective if the root cause is low-pressure regions forward in the hull.

A Viking 47 stays somewhat in the middle of the channel in the serpentine Bass River despite having the author at the wheel. There's no question about this boat being on plane. VIKING YACHTS

Solutions

Dynamic instability fixes that may work include shifting weight aft, building rocker into the hull to depress the stern, widening the chines or adding running strakes forward, fairing hull appendages, and adding wedges at the bow to introduce air to ventilate the wetted surface, eliminating the low pressure areas. Naval architects can conduct tests to determine the causes of dynamic instabilities, including a trim-speed test to look for low dynamic pressures forward that produce bow-down trim at speed, and dynamic inclining experiments to measure changes in transverse stability from dead in the water to full-speed. Older, overpowered hull forms need to be replaced with newer designs that can accommodate today's powerful diesels. The simplest fix, though, may be just to throttle back and enjoy the scenery.

CHAPTER 5

The Power Catamaran

God is a comedian playing to an audience too afraid to laugh.

—Voltaire

P ower cats have taken off in a big way over the last ten years in the United States, and with good reason. A proper cat offers an excellent ride, with a well-designed 25-footer purring along as smoothly in a 2- to 3-foot chop as a deep-V 5 to 10 feet longer. For many years, cats have been especially popular in countries—including Australia, New Zealand, and Norway—where fishing grounds can be a long way from safe harbor and where avoiding rough-water transits is not an option.

In the United States, small 20- to 30-foot outboard-powered cats are niche boats to a certain extent, often intended for the hard-charging offshore fisherman who requires a trailerable package. Many of these hardcore anglers would never consider going back to a monohull once they've lived with a cat for a while in rough water. Larger performance cats in the 30- to 40-foot range are also being produced for the offshore fishing crowd. Some cruising families, including former sailors, are even buying trawler cats for the extended voyages to which these craft may be well suited.

A cat's smooth ride is due to simple physics. Two narrow hulls are presented to a wave instead of one wide one, so vertical accelerations are minimized—as long as it's not so rough that the tunnel "roof" bottoms out. Cats have great form (initial) stability and, with their often-generous beam, offer a lot of open deck space for a given length.

Although cats are wonderful boats, they can't

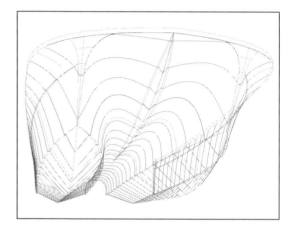

The lines to a John Kiley 40-foot cat show the hull shape nicely.

JOHN KILEY

do everything—include look good, according to a few pundits. Some cats are seriously homely, to be sure, but others, like the 36-foot Benchmark and 38-foot Hydratech, are as good looking (to these eyes) as they are smooth riding. As with any boat, there's no substitute for length when it comes to creating beautiful lines. The stylists are making improvements in the 22- to 30-foot outboard cats as well, and you sometimes hardly notice that these *are* cats at a casual glance.

Cats also have their quirks and limitations. Some of them have a tendency to "sneeze" when air compresses in the forward part of the tunnel and blows spray out over the bow. Though cats do indeed run very well in a light to moderate chop, they can't run at 30 knots in 15-foot seas like some builders would have you believe. They have to slow down when seas get short and steep enough, just like any other boat, though usually not as early.

Partly because they have a relatively high center of gravity, cats tend to lean *away* from a turn at speed, which can be disconcerting to the uninitiated and makes hanging on more imperative. The cat's two narrow hulls present more resistance to *lateral movement*, or sliding, in a turn than a monohull, which further works against any tendency to bank into a turn. Some cats manage to stay on an even keel in a turn, or even lean into the turn ever so slightly, but they are the exceptions.

The Achilles' heel of any cat is its tendency for the tunnel to bottom out in certain conditions, usually involving overloading and rough conditions. The whole boat, in fact, is designed around the tunnel's height requirements, though this is not as much of a problem with some asymmetrical cathull designs that have small tunnels to start with. Let's look at some of the challenges a cat designer faces.

Design Considerations

While the main deck above the cat's tunnel is impressively roomy, it can't be any lower than the top of the tunnel. This means the hull freeboard has to be high enough to provide adequate cockpit freeboard, which further raises CG. The result, at least in a small cat (under 35 or 40 feet) with standing cabin headroom, is a boat that's aesthetically challenged (with its high freeboard) from the outset.

Most cats have a smaller waterplane area than monohulls of the same length, which means they'll settle deeper in the water with a weight addition. With their lower pounds-per-inch-immersion figure, the tunnel will settle closer to the waterline with just a moderate amount of weight, which can quickly add up in the form of fuel, passengers, and gear. With the tunnel closer to the waterline, and closer to the tops of the passing waves, ride quality

diminishes rapidly, and the added wetted hull surface slows the boat down. A monohull, on the other hand, just slows down and can actually ride more smoothly with added weight onboard.

The Sea Sport 32's hull form is clearly seen in this bow-on view.
JOHN KILEY

A power cat is inherently heavier than a monohull of similar length, since its hull has much more surface area, and the tunnel especially has to be strongly built to absorb not only wave-slamming loads, but the wracking of the two hulls, which try hard to head off in different directions. A Glacier Bay 26, for instance, has seven structural bulkheads in the tunnel area to resist stresses and add stiffness. These bulkheads, which should cross over the tunnel "roof" from hull to hull for optimum strength, have to be securely tabbed in place to resist the significant stresses encountered in a seaway at speed. The challenge is to build a cat strong enough to resist these added stresses while keeping the boat light enough to perform properly. Some builders keep the weight down by using advanced composites and vacuum bagging or, better yet, resin infusion systems (see chapter 6).

So the trade-offs are starker with a cat. Add weight, and the tunnel bottoms out, increasing frictional drag and slamming loads. Make the tunnel higher, and the deck above it is raised just as much. Raise the deck, and the hull sides also have to be higher if interior (cockpit) freeboard is valued. The more things you raise, the higher the CG gets, the less stable the boat becomes (dynamic stability is especially affected), and the more awkward and homely it looks. An outboard-powered cat, especially, has a high center of gravity, and weight additions in the form of passengers, fish, and gear raise VCG higher still, since they will usually be concentrated on or above the main deck, which is already quite high atop the tunnel. Some owners may have a false sense of security about their boat's stability. Remember the difference between initial (form-derived) stability and ultimate stability. With its high CG, an outboard-powered cat may well capsize at a lower angle of heel than a conventional monohull.

Once you get up above 35 feet or so, the design

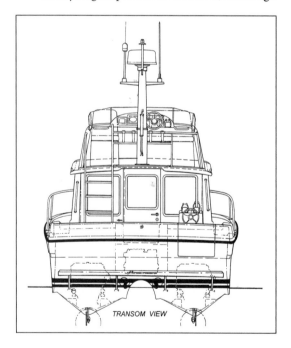

The John Kiley–designed Sea Sport 32 as seen from astern in this drawing. Engines are low in the twin hulls, the cockpit deck is as low as possible over the tunnel top, and the slight asymmetry is noticeable aft. JOHN KILEY

possibilities start to open up. A longer cat doesn't have to look disproportionately high, since the length-to-freeboard ratio becomes more pleasing. This is also the point at which inboards become the clear power of choice, and the hulls can each accommodate a small stateroom forward and individual engine rooms aft.

A small cat's cabin is often one of its weaknesses; there's precious little room to do anything with the tunnel running down the centerline. What you would expect to end up with on a boat like this is a very large berth forward over the tunnel, and on either side inside the twin hulls will be standing headroom areas, with the head to one side and the galley on the other. All in all, cat builders have gotten good at making the most of the breed's shape and putting the available room to good use. The boat's seakeeping and seakindliness more than make up for cabin design limitations for most owners.

Planing and Semidisplacement Cat Hulls

Recreational power catamarans come in both planing and semidisplacement versions. Some of these "displacement cats" are not so easy to categorize, though they tend to have round-bilge sections and very little flat lifting area on their bottoms. When the hulls narrow to a L/B ratio of 10:1 or more, as they do on many cats, all bets are off when it comes to traditional displacement speed limitations. Quite a few power cats with radiused hulls (in cross section) develop practically zero dynamic lift. That makes them displacement hulls by definition. But, thanks to their low wavemaking resistance, these narrow cats actually run at planing speeds.

At 25 knots, a cat with a 25-foot waterline length is running at a speed-to-length (S/L) ratio of 5, rather than the S/L ratio of 1.34 that displacement hulls are usually limited to. That's why a "slenderness" ratio is a valid component when discussing hull form and speed potential. The displacement cat becomes a semidisplacement cat,

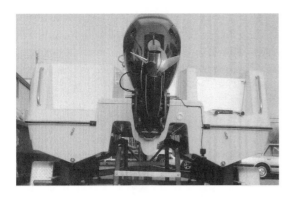

This Sea Gull outboard cat has modified-V full-planing sponsons and a transom pod for mounting the single engine.   SEA GULL

technically, if there is significant vertical rise at speed.

The planing cat often has hard chines and moderate deadrise amidships and aft where the dynamic lift is produced. At least theoretically, the planing cat has to be built (to heavier scantlings) to withstand the higher G-forces that result from higher slamming loads at speed. The planing cat rises vertically at speed like any other planing hull, and this adds welcome clearance between the bottom of the tunnel and the water surface.

Some builders of high-performance cats use asymmetric hull sections, which provide both planing surface and the interior room needed for inboard diesel power. The wider, flatter inboard hull sections allow machinery to be easily mounted over the primary planing surface—essentially like a deep-V installation—while also making running gear installation more monohull-like and providing more planing surface. On the outboard sides of the hulls, which are more exposed to wave action (and this is the asymmetry), the deadrise is sharper. Some asymmetric designs actually bank slightly into a turn, a significant advantage from a human engineering perspective. This feature is due to the lift generated by the outboard hull's shape and the lesser lateral resistance produced by the inboard hull.

High-performance racing cats often have split-V hulls, which look a lot like a deep-V monohull

A Glacier Bay cat's twin sponsons deliver a soft ride with their radiused bottom sections, but pick up lift at speed with their inboard chine flats. Getting tunnel height right is an art form, since a tunnel that bottoms out regularly produces a poor ride. When the hull climbs up on plane, the tunnel's added elevation provides extra clearance for waves to pass under.

sliced down the middle and separated by the tunnel. This design, while not as efficiently propelled as the asymmetric design, produces the smoothest possible ride at speeds that can exceed 100 mph.

The width of the tunnel varies markedly from cat to cat, and so does their sensitivity to added weight. Given the narrow tunnel and extra beam of some asymmetric designs, their pounds-per-inch immersion values may actually be very similar to a mono of the same length, making them well suited to commercial applications requiring moderate load-carrying ability.

Many cats have a small, V-shaped nacelle, or pod (like a mini deep-V hull), located at the forward end of the tunnel, which helps prevent slamming below planing speeds while remaining well clear of the water at speed. The trailing edge of this pod may have an air channel built in to provide airflow in the tunnel even when the bow of the boat is immersed. World Cat, for one, gets around the sneezing problem by also raising the tunnel (and hull freeboard) forward.

Though most cats are trim-sensitive to weight

changes, some planing cats with wide hulls forward actually have *more* waterplane area forward than a monohull, increasing resistance to trim changes. In a quartering sea, cats with narrow hulls are more susceptible to broaching since the lee hull, with its minimal buoyancy forward, will bury its nose deeply and tend to trip the boat in extreme conditions.

Cat Performance

Twin outboards are a natural power plant for a small cat, with each motor mounted on a hull, and a fuel tank for each motor inside its hull. The same goes for inboard power in larger cats; each hull is designed to be just the right size to hold a lightweight diesel engine. (In fact the width of a hull must be designed around this consideration.) A cat with outboard power will have a higher center of gravity than one that's inboard powered, all else being equal, since the engines sit higher on the boat.

Cats provide a great ride running into a stiff chop, but they also can do well running downsea, especially if LCG is far enough aft for the hull shape, and often don't slow down as much as a monohull when climbing the back of a wave. Many displacement cats also run well at 10 to 20 knots, speeds at which a monohull deep-V runs and handles sluggishly. This quality gives the operator more latitude in adjusting speed to match sea state. The better displacement cats, in fact, hardly notice the transition to plane, meaning you can operate easily at virtually any midrange speed. Some planing cats, depending on the make, also offer a degree of midrange versatility.

Cats are known for being efficiently driven, but this is not always true. Grady-White, for instance, made both monohull and (for a short time) cat 26-footers, and the mono was more efficiently driven in calm water. That's not surprising when you consider that the power cat has more windage (sail area) and more wetted surface than the monohull.

The 26-foot Glacier Bay is typical of the outboard-powered recreational cat; in a 1-foot chop, it slices through the waves like butter at any speed.

With the waves running higher, say at 2 to 3 feet, 25 knots or so of speed definitely helps improve ride quality, since the boat rises vertically, creating more clearance for the waves passing through the tunnel.

Seaworthiness

A catamaran's twin hulls can add passive protection against sinking if the hulls are separated from one another by a watertight longitudinal bulkhead on centerline. The chances of maintaining adequate reserve buoyancy, and staying afloat, increase if each hull further is subdivided with watertight transverse bulkheads, the more the better. If each hull has significant compartmentation or generous flotation foam built in, the damaged angle of heel will be minimized and the boat's ability to survive

A view you don't see too often—a cat hanging from its lifting eyes. The hull shape of this Sea Gull is clearly visible, as is the outboard deflector pod intended to provide clean waterflow to the single engine. SEA GULL

single-compartment flooding greatly improved. Ask the builder if tests have been conducted to prove a boat's ability to stay afloat with one hull ruptured.

Since the small to midsize cat must be built high off the water, windage is higher than on most monohulls of the same length and absorbs a higher percentage of propulsion power as speed increases. On the other hand, the two narrow hulls create more resistance to lateral (sideways) movement through the water, so the cat may or may not be as susceptible to a crosswind.

Though variation in beam is more pronounced in sailing catamarans, a wide power cat (with the hulls set far apart) will have more deck space for its length, greater initial (form) stability, and less rolling. It will also be harder to turn, and finding a slip can be a problem.

Lessons Learned from Sailing Cats

The widest sailing cats are nearly as wide as they are long and are just as liable to pitchpole as to capsize in a strong wind. They must have their decks, or underwings, suspended higher off the water, since the hulls span a greater distance, making it easier for waves to build up between them. Narrower cats are much easier to maneuver and moor. The fastest sailing cats have narrow hulls (to minimize resistance) set far apart (to maximize form stability). A power cat isn't so concerned about the form stability as its sail-powered cousin, since there's no sail to support in a strong wind. But since cats don't have the *ultimate stability* of a full-displacement monohull, they arguably don't belong in extreme offshore conditions of strong winds and high seas, offshore racing trends notwithstanding. Once a sailing cat heels far enough to raise one hull out of the water, it can pass through the angle of maximum righting moment in an instant, and the crew must react quickly to prevent capsize from a sudden gust of wind or rogue wave. The most seaworthy

displacement and semidisplacement monohulls, on the other hand, can develop positive righting arm at over 120 degrees of heel, and in some cases even when fully inverted.

Nevertheless, the fastest sailboats used in round-the-world races are 100-foot-plus cats and trimarans. A cat or trimaran will beat a monohull every time, *if* it survives capsize, broaching, pitchpoling, and structural failure. To do so, these offshore cats rely on highly skilled crews, sound structural engineering, high-tech construction, and a good bit of luck—the latter augmented with escape hatches in the bottoms of the hulls and inverted living arrangements for use while awaiting rescue. Some of these high-performance, high-tech, lightdisplacement sailing cats are giving the breed a bad name, but only because they are pushing the speed envelope in extreme offshore conditions.

The *most seaworthy* (though not the *fastest*) cats have adequate tunnel clearance, moderate freeboard, and moderate beam. In chapter 2 we saw that any vessel (including a cat) with too much form stability is both uncomfortable and unsafe, since it is too eager to conform to the water surface (wave and swell) gradient, and it will also tend to have less ultimate stability.

Should You Own a Cat?

Cats are winners in many areas, and have developed a following accordingly. Part of the key to the cat's success in the U.S. market, certainly, is familiarity, or conditioning, on the part of the public. Builders of trailerable, outboard-powered cats are doing a lot to improve the cat's popularity. And who hasn't admired the incredibly smooth ride and thrilling speed of a 50-knot passenger ferry? If the cat's layout limitations, looks, and occasional handling quirks are of little concern, and ride quality is everything, a cat may be just the ticket for you. Whichever cat strikes your fancy, be careful about keeping extra gear, passengers, and fuel to a minimum, and add weight judiciously.

CHAPTER 6

Construction with Fiberglass and Cold-Molded Wood

I choose a block of marble and chop off whatever I don't need.

—Rodin

F iberglass is the clear choice of material for most production boatbuilders, and it has been since the 1960s. It's strong, impact resistant, relatively immune to deterioration, easily shaped, easy to repair and maintain, and fairly inexpensive. Fiberglass production boats take their shape from female molds, which allow fast, high-volume output and ensure uniformity from one boat to the next.

This chapter explains the basics of production and custom fiberglass boatbuilding so that you're better equipped to ask the right questions and look in the right places when shopping for your next boat.

If you have the means to pay, and the time to wait for a custom boat, the world's your oyster. Custom builders can use "one-off" construction methods to build one-of-a-kind or semicustom yachts out of fiberglass or cold-molded wood-epoxy. Most of these methods involve building a throwaway framework, or male mold, which gives the boat the desired shape and size, removing the hull from the form, and finishing it off. All these methods can produce excellent craft, and each has its distinct advantages.

One-off means that only one boat is built from a temporary mold, while *semicustom* (or *semiproduction*) refers to a product that is produced in smaller quantities and retains some potential for customization. For instance, a semicustom builder might use a single hull but completely customize

This modern Ocean 70 convertible can climb several feet vertically when on plane and make close to 40 knots, in large part because of the builder's wide-ranging use of weight-saving composite and flat hull sections aft.

the interior arrangement and deck plan. It is also possible to produce hulls of different lengths from a stock mold: the hull mold is dammed off aft with a transom mold that can be positioned farther forward or aft according to the desired vessel length.

Whether building a production or one-off custom fiberglass vessel, though, certain fundamentals apply to ensure a well-found, long-lasting boat. A wide range of resins, fiberglass reinforcements, core materials, bottom-support structures, and manufacturing processes can be used. So, it's important when evaluating a boat to know how these elements interact to affect quality, strength, seaworthiness, and longevity.

The Basics of Fiberglass Construction

A fiberglass hull consists of a matrix of fiberglass reinforcements (see below), hardened resin, and, often, a core material. The fiberglass provides the strength and impact resistance; the resin keeps the fiberglass locked in the matrix and transmits loads within and between the layers of fiberglass. Without the hardened resin, the fiberglass would just flop around, lacking strength and rigidity in any direction but direct tension. Core materials, such as end-grain balsa wood and foam, are often added to increase the strength and stiffness of a fiberglass panel with minimal weight gain. A solid fiberglass panel, with no core material, is technically a composite—a combination of resin and fiberglass reinforcement—so we will use the term *sandwich* to mean a combination of fiberglass skins surrounding a structural, lightweight core. The term *fiberglass* can refer to the dry woven or knitted material still on the roll, or the finished lamination of the fiberglass reinforcement in a matrix of catalyzed resin. The more accurate term for the latter is GRP, or *glass-reinforced plastic*, also known as *fiberglass-reinforced plastic*, or FRP.

In any fiberglass panel, or laminate, the physical properties of the fiberglass reinforcement—including its ability to stretch, which is referred to as *elongation*—may differ greatly from the resin that binds it. If the resin can't elongate as much as the reinforcement before yielding, the resin will fail first when under high stress. If less expensive, and more brittle, polyester resins are used to build a boat—and these are the most commonly used—the designer has to add enough fiberglass reinforcement so that the overall laminate stress is kept within acceptable limits.

The adhesion between layers, or *plies*, of fiberglass reinforcement, called *interlaminar bonds*, must be very strong. As we'll see, the overall strength and integrity of the laminate, including the interlaminar bonds, varies widely depending on the materials and methods used in their construction.

Why use a core material? A single sheet of fiberglass is tough and resilient, but it's not especially stiff. But when two relatively thin skins of fiberglass are bonded to both sides of a thick, lightweight core material, the result is a sandwich panel that is far stiffer and stronger than the two skins alone would be, and one that's much lighter than a solid lamination of fiberglass achieving the same overall thickness. Sandwiches have wonderful advantages, but they have to be built carefully and with the right materials, as we shall see.

Fiberglass Reinforcements

Fiberglass is sold in a variety of weights and fiber orientations. Fiberglass gets its name because it's composed of molten glass extruded, or drawn, into filaments of 5 to 25 microns in thickness. These filaments are coated with a sizing that protects against abrasion and helps to bond the fibers together when they're wet out with resin. Then the filaments are combined to form strands, which become the basis of the many different types of fiberglass reinforcements. When a roll of fiberglass is made, strands can run with the roll in the *warp* direction, and across the roll in the *weft* direction. They can also run diagonally at a 45-degree angle.

Fiberglass comes in different grades. E-glass is relatively inexpensive and fairly strong, so it is most commonly used. S-glass, which costs a lot more, is more fatigue resistant and some 30 percent stronger. S-glass is sometimes used in high-tech applications when high strength is required, as are more exotic nonfiberglass reinforcements such as carbon fiber.

Chop and Mat

Chop and mat fiberglass are similar types of low-strength reinforcement consisting of short strands of fiberglass (1 or 2 inches long) oriented at random. Mat comes in rolls, with the strands of fiberglass held together by a soluble binder that dissolves when it comes into contact with the styrene in polyester and vinylester resins. (Stitched mat must be used with epoxy resin, which has no styrene to dissolve the binder.) Chop is applied by a device called a *chopper gun* that chops up fiberglass strands, mixes them with catalyzed resin, and shoots them out under pressure. When the mixture hits the mold, it does so in a random pattern.

The end result is pretty much the same, though chop, lacking any binders to interfere with thorough saturation, can arguably be more thoroughly wet out, reducing the chances of osmosis (see sidebar, page 100) when used as a skin coat. On the other hand, if the chopper gun doesn't thoroughly mix the catalyst with the resin, and an incomplete cure results, blisters can occur. Mat typically results in a layup of more uniform thickness. Although chopper guns have gotten a bad reputation, there's nothing wrong with a boat laid up in part by a chopper gun controlled by a skilled operator, as long as it's not substituting for stronger fiberglass reinforcements. Though relatively weak in their own right, chop and mat are good for filling the valleys between layers of heavier fabrics, building thickness quickly and cheaply—while adding significant weight. Many boatbuilders also apply a layer of mat or chop immediately underneath the

gelcoat as a skin coat to prevent "print-through" of woven fiberglass reinforcement. Boatbuilding resins shrink, both during the cure and afterward, allowing the underlying woven roving or other reinforcement to telegraph its impression to the gelcoat (this is called *print-through*). This is most noticeable when dark gelcoats are used. It also occurs more often when the resin is added under high pressure, as with the various vacuum techniques discussed below.

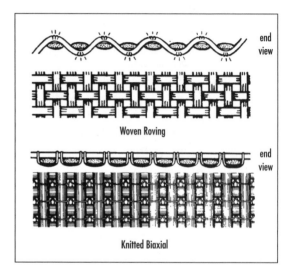

Woven Roving

Knitted Biaxial

In a woven roving the fibers are loaded out of plane, making the reinforcement less efficient, structurally, than a nonwoven, or knitted pattern. This type of weave pattern is weaker for much the same reason that a knot is weaker than the rope with which it is tied. A nonwoven reinforcement is therefore better able to absorb loads parallel to the fibers. ERIC GREENE

Woven Roving

Woven roving, the most commonly used reinforcement, is made of flattened bundles of strands woven together in a coarse pattern, with slightly more fiberglass running in the warp than in the weft direction. The weave pattern makes woven roving thicker (of higher profile) and stiffer than unwoven reinforcements of the same weight. Woven roving generally affords good impact resistance, precisely because the fibers are woven together: under impact, individual fiber bundles have to be broken for an object to penetrate a woven laminate, while knitted reinforcement (see below) tends to split apart more readily. The woven reinforcement's higher profile means more resin must be used to fill the voids between layers of reinforcement, making for a more resin-rich and therefore brittle laminate. Resin is a lot cheaper than fiberglass, so it costs less to get a stiff panel with lots of resin than it does with more tightly compacted knitted reinforcements.

Because woven roving is made of interwoven fibers, which continuously change direction as they snake around crossing fiber bundles, its strength in the direction of the fibers is reduced compared with knitted reinforcements, which lie flat. High strain in tension (imagine pulling on a rope) will tend to straighten the fibers out, and high strain in compression (the 4-by-4s holding up your deck at home are under compression) will tend to make the fibers crimp further. In the real world, however, the polyester resins used by most builders will give out long before these fiberglass fibers are fully stressed.

Knitted Reinforcements

Boatbuilders couldn't take full advantage of the potential of fiberglass until knitted reinforcements—also called stitched or unidirectional—were developed in the mid-1970s. Knitted reinforcements employ strands of the same thickness as woven roving but, instead of being woven together, the strands lie flat and run in a single orientation; a light stitching holds them in place. Knitted reinforcements allow the fiberglass strands to be fully loaded in tension; they are not crimped like the interlocking fibers of woven roving. For a given laminate thickness, knitted fabric is stronger than woven roving because the reinforcement fibers are already straightened out and the fiberglass is denser. And, since the voids between the layers of material are smaller, less resin is needed to wet out

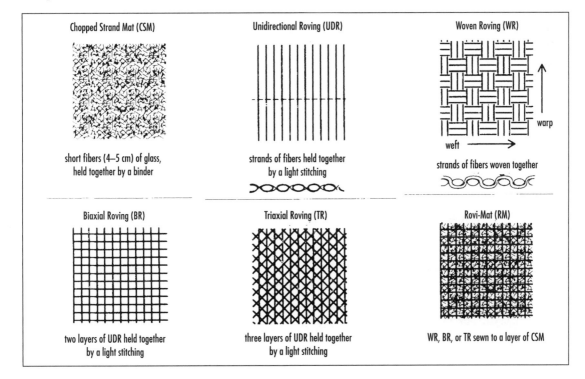

Chopped Strand Mat (CSM)

short fibers (4–5 cm) of glass, held together by a binder

Unidirectional Roving (UDR)

strands of fibers held together by a light stitching

Woven Roving (WR)

warp

weft

strands of fibers woven together

Biaxial Roving (BR)

two layers of UDR held together by a light stitching

Triaxial Roving (TR)

three layers of UDR held together by a light stitching

Rovi-Mat (RM)

WR, BR, or TR sewn to a layer of CSM

Various reinforcement weave patterns, including woven and non-woven, or stitched, materials. The closer the fibers align with the stresses in a structure, the more efficiently it can do its job.

LARSSON AND ELIASSON, *PRINCIPLES OF YACHT DESIGN*

A Tiara hull takes shape in Holland, Michigan. The hull mold tilts from side to side, which makes it easier for the laminators to get to their work, and helps prevent resin from puddling. TIARA YACHTS

A cross section of a Viking convertible's keel. A solid filler and heavy fiberglass laminate provides the necessary grounding-load impact resistance. VIKING YACHTS

the reinforcement, improving the final glass-to-resin ratio.

Reinforcing fabrics are the structural backbone of a fiberglass boat, and they work by absorbing loads within the matrix. For this reason, the direction of the fiberglass strand orientation is very important. Reinforcements are selected based on the stresses anticipated in different areas of the boat. The simplest kind of knitted reinforcements is unidirectional, with the strand bundles running in a single direction. Unidirectional (0-degree) fiberglass has little strength in the weft direction, but is very strong in the warp direction. Unidirectional reinforcement is used where loads in a single orientation are expected, such as on the tops of hull stringers where tension and compression loads are absorbed, and for keel and stem strengthening.

When one layer of unidirectional reinforcement is stitched to another running in a different direction, a biaxial reinforcement is created. This allows a single roll of reinforcement to absorb stress in two directions simultaneously. Biaxial, triaxial, and even quadaxial knitted reinforcements, consisting of two, three, or four layers of strand bundles stitched together in 0-, 90-, or 45-degree directions, are commonly available to reduce production time

and to provide strength in the appropriate orientations. A 0/90 orientation means that a layer of fiberglass runs in both the warp and weft directions, while 45/45 indicates two fiberglass layers oriented with a 45-degree offset from the direction of the roll and at right angles to each other. A 45/45 reinforcement might be used in the sides of a long, narrow, low-profile offshore racing boat to better absorb the global loads present when running in a seaway at high speed. Fabrics defined as 45/45 also tend to conform to sharp corners, making them well suited for tabbing purposes (such as tabbing a bulkhead to a hull side). Knitted reinforcements are also available with fiberglass mat prebonded on one side to speed up production.

Cloth

Fiberglass cloth resembles a very fine woven roving. Because of its low profile, or smooth surface, cloth is usually used for finishing surfaces. Though very strong for its weight, it's not often used as a structural material because it can take as many as 50 layers to build up 1 inch of thickness. Cold-molded boats, which are built of wood bonded with epoxy resin, are often finished with layers of fiberglass cloth wet out with epoxy resin.

Bulking Materials

There's no substitute for thickness when it comes to making a panel of a given material stiff, so some boatbuilders try to save weight and money by using bulking materials. Bulkers are thinner than proper sandwich cores (which we discuss below) but the objectives are the same: to increase thickness and stiffness while adding little weight. Bulker mats are made from polyester or other synthetic fibers, and are sometimes combined with plastic microspheres to thicken the resin. Since the fibers are less dense than fiberglass, and microspheres weigh less than resin, bulker mats weigh less. Since they are weaker than fiberglass, bulker mats are always used as the core in a fiberglass sandwich, where they do the least amount of structural work (like the web of an I-beam), primarily absorbing shear loads. Used properly, bulker mats improve a hull's resistance to impact, fatigue, and blistering. Bulkers added to otherwise thin laminates, such as hull sides and center consoles on small boats, help prevent flexure or oil canning, reducing gelcoat cracking and crazing. Many builders also use bulking materials, along with a skin coat of mat or chop, to prevent gelcoat print-through. Coremat, BaltekMat, Spherecore, and Matline are all examples. They cost more per pound than fiberglass, but labor and resin savings offset the added expense. A syntactic foam called SprayCore, which contains resins and hollow glass microspheres, can be sprayed on and will block print-through like a bulking fabric, according to Omega Chemical, the manufacturer.

Exotic Reinforcements

Boatbuilders also have at their disposal expensive, high-strength reinforcements for special applications, such as aramid and carbon and graphite fiber. Generally such materials are used when great strength is required with minimal weight gain. The most often used aramid fiber is DuPont's Kevlar, which is lightweight and boasts significant resistance to fatigue and impact. It is not as strong in compression as fiberglass, though, and if left untreated, it will absorb water more readily than fiberglass. Aramid fibers can be wet out using either vinylester or epoxy resin, and since they deform significantly before ultimate failure, they can resist damage well.

Carbon fibers and graphite fibers are very stiff, strong, and temperature-resistant. Because of their stiffness, when these materials fail, they do so decisively. These fibers are expensive and must be wet out with epoxy or epoxy-based vinylester resins (which we discuss below), though carbon fiber may be wet out with vinylester resin if it's treated with the proper sizing. Their cost usually limits their use to high-stress areas and to parts where a combination of very high strength and low weight is needed. Both carbon and aramid fibers are stronger in tension than E-glass and S-glass, and carbon is nearly as strong in compression as tension, which gives it a significant advantage over Kevlar.

Fiber	Density lb/in^3	Tensile Strength psi x 10^3	Tensile Modulus psi x 10^6	Ultimate Elongation	Cost $/lb
E-Glass	.094	500	10.5	4.8%	.80-1.20
S-Glass	.090	665	12.6	5.7%	4
Aramid-Kevlar 49	.052	525	18.0	2.9%	16
Spectra 900	.035	375	17.0	3.5%	22
Polyester-COMPET	.049	150	1.4	22.0%	1.75
Carbon-PAN	.062-.065	350-700	33-57	0.38-2.0%	17-450

The relative physical properties of various reinforcements. Note the ultimate elongation of E-glass fiberglass, used most commonly in boats, compared to the resins in the chart on page 87. Vinylester and epoxy resins produce a far stronger matrix since they "stretch," or elongate, roughly the same as fiberglass.

ERIC GREENE

Another option for designers is Spectra, a high-density polyethylene reinforcement made by Allied Chemical. Its resistance to abrasion and its physical properties at room temperature are superior to Kevlar; in fact, it has the highest strength-to-weight ratio of any fiber. Resin adhesion is not good, however, so it's used mostly in sails, but seldom in boatbuilding.

The Laminate

The laminate "schedule" can combine these reinforcements with resin (as well as core materials) in a variety of ways. Some builders prefer woven roving since its higher profile, or more pronounced weave, builds up thickness and stiffness quickly. Woven roving also has excellent damage tolerance and impact resistance. Fiberglass boats were originally built with alternating layers of woven roving and mat or chop. The roving provides the strength and toughness, while the mat fills in the valleys in the roving's coarse weave patterns, improving the interlaminar (between the layers) bond between layers of roving. Without the mat, only the high spots of the layers of roving would come into contact, producing a weaker interlaminar bond. When building a boat, it is important to squeeze out excess resin in order to bring the layers of reinforcement in close contact; this is reflected in the *glass-to-resin ratio*. Mat or chop can generally be dispensed with if a laminate consisting only of woven roving is cured under pressure (with the use of a vacuum bag), compressing the layers of roving and ensuring good interlaminar bonds.

Other builders prefer knitted fiberglass for its lower profile and good interlaminar bond properties and for its higher glass-to-resin ratio. To save production time, combination reinforcements have also been developed that consist of a layer of mat bonded to the woven roving, allowing both to be applied and wet out at the same time. With four or more layers of woven fiberglass prebonded together, these "combination goods" can be applied quickly with relatively unskilled labor, and they cost less than knitted reinforcements. These fabrics are a

good choice for building a solid fiberglass (non-sandwich) hull.

Resins

Resins are the glue that holds the laminate together; they bond the reinforcements together, fill the voids between the reinforcement strands and fibers, and create a solid composite matrix that allows the reinforcement fibers to absorb and distribute loads efficiently. Resins come in a variety of chemical compositions, including, in ascending order of overall quality and price, orthophthalic (general purpose) polyester, isophthalic polyester, vinylester, and epoxy. Since resins are intended to lock the fiberglass in a matrix, those that most closely match the physical properties of the fiberglass (in particular its tendency to stretch) and adhere best to other, cured fiberglass components result in the best product.

Polyesters

Orthophthalic polyester resins are the most widely used by boatbuilders, followed by isophthalic resins. These resins are cured—transformed from a liquid to a solid—by adding an accelerator and a catalyst. Cure times can be regulated by carefully controlling the amount of these additives used, and ambient temperature, humidity, and the thickness of the laminate are all factors affecting cure time.

Orthophthalic resins, which have been around longer, are relatively cheap and easy to use. They have the lowest tensile strength of the common boatbuilding resins: they break more easily when pulled under strain. They are also relatively brittle, so they won't stretch (elongate) very far before failing. A volatile chemical in the resin called *styrene* is released to the atmosphere during the building process, both through evaporation if the resin is sprayed and from the high heat generated during cure. When the styrene flashes off, microscopic voids are left in the resin. As a result, laminates made of orthophthalic resin are the least solid and the least resistant to *osmosis* of the boatbuilding

Resin	Tensile Strength psi x 10^3	Tensile Modulus psi x 10^5	Ultimate Elongation	1990 Bulk Cost $/lb
Orthophthalic Atlas P 2020	7.0	5.9	.91%	.66
Dicyclopentadiene (DCPD) Atlas 80-6044	11.2	9.1	.86%	.67
Isophthalic CoRezyn 9595	10.3	5.65	2.0%	.85
Vinyl Ester Derakane 411-45	11-12	4.9	5-6%	1.44
Epoxy Gougeon Pro Set 125/226	7.96	5.3	7.7%	4.39
*Hardness values for epoxies are traditionally given on the "Shore D" scale				+

This chart shows why the kind of resin used plays a crucial role in determining laminate strength and impact resistance. Vinylester comes the closest to matching the elongation of fiberglass rein-forcement, making it a much better choice, from a physical prop-erties perspective, than ortho, iso, or DCPD resins. ERIC GREENE

resins. Most production boats are built primarily or entirely with orthophthalic resin. This microscopic permeability can be addressed with proper quality control during the building process.

Compared with orthophthalic resins, iso-phthalic polyester resins generally have higher me-chanical properties, which means they have greater tensile strength, over twice the elongation, and ad-here better to previously cured fiberglass, resulting in superior secondary bonds. Isophthalic resins have better chemical resistance and, because they are more resistant to osmosis than orthophthalic resins, are sometimes used as a barrier coat under the gelcoat to help prevent osmotic blistering.

DCPD

A DCPD, or *poly dicyclopentadiene*, resin blend is sometimes used by boatbuilders because of its lower styrene levels. Too brittle in its pure form for boatbuilding use, DCPD is blended with or-thophthalic (and sometimes isophthalic and vinylester) resin to allow builders to meet increas-ingly tough Environmental Protection Agency (EPA) styrene emission levels. Because there's less styrene (33 to 38 percent in a DCPD blend versus orthophthalic's 42 to 46 percent), there's also less shrinkage during cure. So, DCPD is often used in the first layer of fiberglass to minimize print-through of the underlying fiberglass reinforcement to the gelcoat. DCPD blends offer somewhat bet-ter osmotic blistering protection than pure or-thophthalic resin, and cure faster, so a part doesn't have to stay in the mold as long.

Some builders use DCPD resin for the whole laminate since the time the part has to stay in the mold is reduced. The downside is that DCPD resins are the most brittle of all when cured, even more so than orthophthalic resin. DCPD-based lami-nates can also be hard to repair; chemical linkage in a secondary bond is impeded since the resin cross-links so completely and so quickly. The win-dow for creating secondary bonds can be as little as 24 hours, and less if exposed to sunlight. (As a re-sult, early DCPD laminates experienced problems with bulkhead and liner installations failing to ad-here to the cured hull.)

This contrasts with orthophthalic and isoph-thalic resins, which, though the great majority of the cure occurs within a few hours, can take months to harden completely. Repairs to DCPD resin lami-

Secondary Bonding

You get a secondary bond when you add a fresh layer of fiberglass to a previously cured fiberglass surface and rely on the adhesion of the resulting mechanical bond to glue the parts together. This wet-on-dry process is a weak link in fiberglass construction. In a perfect world, the whole hull laminate would be laid up and impregnated with resin at the same time, cross-linking the entire laminate with a primary, chemical bond at the molecular level. (This is, in fact, what SCRIMP and other resin-infusion processes do: all the resin is drawn through by vacuum in a single step, eliminating secondary bonds in the hull and, in some cases, in the supporting bulkhead landings and stringers as well. See pages 100–102.)

In conventional fiberglass construction, boatbuilders typically lay up one or two layers of fiberglass at a time, let it cure, sand it, and then apply another layer. Or peel ply, a layer of plastic that leaves a textured, bondable surface when removed, can be applied to the wet-out fiberglass. When the part cures, the peel ply is removed, the area lightly sanded, and follow-on laminates applied. To ensure that these secondary bonds are solid and secure, mechanically preparing the surface with sanding, grinding, or chemical preparation is essential. Some builders will apply a layer of mat to areas that are to be ground after curing in preparation for a secondary bond; this extra step protects the underlying layers of reinforcement, such as woven roving, from damage by heavy grinding. In reality, polyester resins take longer to harden completely, so a secondary bond applied 72 hours after the resin has cured to the touch may still establish some chemical as well as mechanical bonding.

Secondary Bond Joints

A secondary bond should include a tapered, or beveled, edge to maximize the bonding area, and provide an even transition for stresses being transferred from one part to the other.

ERIC GREENE

nates thus call for large scarfs, or tapers, and correspondingly larger bonding surfaces when a damaged section is being prepared for a patch job. Using DCPD resin in the repair job is also thought by some to be a good idea since the patch's flex and expansion characteristics will then match that of the original DCPD part.

Vinylester

Vinylester resin, though applied in much the same way as polyester resin, is a far superior material with excellent fatigue and impact resistance. It will elongate 5 to 12 percent before failing, allowing the fiberglass reinforcement to absorb maximum loading, increasing its impact resistance and ultimate strength. Vinylester resins adhere very well to cured fiberglass, making them a good choice for many secondary bonds.

Most excess styrene in vinylester resin crosslinks with itself during cure, rather than flashing off and leaving microscopic holes as in orthophthalic resin. So vinylester is more solid and has superior resistance to osmosis, which results in excellent, proven protection against osmotic blistering. For this reason, some builders use a skin coat of three ounces of chop or mat applied over the gelcoat in the mold (i.e., just under the gelcoat in the finished hull) and wet out with vinylester resin to prevent blistering. Many well-built, high-end boats are constructed using vinylester resin throughout the laminate, resulting in the best laminate you can get short of using epoxy.

Polyester and vinylester resins are usually air-inhibited, which means they won't cure when exposed to air. The resin remains chemically receptive for 12 hours to a week, allowing a small degree of primary bond cross-linking during this time.

Air-cured resin has paraffin wax mixed in, which rises to the surface during curing to form an air barrier, allowing the resin to cure completely. This paraffin film presents a secondary bonding (see below) problem when subsequent layers of fiberglass are applied to the cured laminate. The fiberglass must be sanded and washed with a solvent to remove the paraffin film so that freshly applied fiberglass will adhere to it. Polyester resins bought at the local hardware store or marina are usually air-cured and therefore air-inhibited.

A Viking Yachts convertible hull being lifted from the mold with stringers and bulkheads already installed so the hull will keep its shape.　　　　　　　　　　　　　　VIKING YACHTS

The ultimate elongation of E-glass—the amount it will stretch before failure—is about 4.8 percent, which is less than the ultimate elongation of vinylester and epoxy resins. That's a good thing, since the fiberglass is allowed to come under full strain without the weaker resin failing first, which is what would happen with far more brittle polyester resin. This is one of the reasons why a laminate of vinylester or epoxy resin and E-glass works so well structurally; the physical properties of the resins more nearly match that of the reinforcements.

Epoxy

Epoxies are the best resins used in the boatbuilding industry and, as you might expect, they're by far the most expensive. Although the various epoxies differ in their physical properties, as do the members of all resin families, they are all tough and strong, and elongate before failure more than other resins, resulting in the toughest, most impact-resistant and resilient fiberglass matrix. Epoxy is also the best possible glue, adhering tenaciously to a properly prepared, previously cured fiberglass surface. It is often advisable to use epoxy to make re-

pairs to damaged polyester or vinylester fiberglass components. Epoxy resin has no styrene, making it the most solid and blister-proof of all resins. Extremely resistant to osmosis, an epoxy hull can be expected to live a very long life blister-free. Epoxy resin is usually hand-applied with rollers or brushes, unlike polyesters and vinylesters, which can easily be sprayed.

Core Materials

People often equate stiffness with strength, but the two are not the same. A panel may have plenty of strength but inadequate stiffness. Walk on a limber deck and you think it's weak, when in fact it could easily hold your car. On a boat, however, it is very important that panels be designed to provide adequate stiffness. A panel may be strong enough to resist impacts with waves and underwater objects but, if it flexes excessively, fatigue will eventually set in, weakening the laminate over time. In addition, flex-

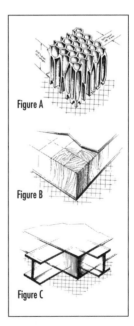

A close-up view of several sandwich panels, showing the relationship between the I-beam and the components (skins and structural core) of a composite sandwich. The integrity of the bond between the fiberglass skins and the core material is crucial. BALTEK CORP.

relative stiffness	100	700	3,700
relative strength	100	350	925
relative weight	100	103	106

The relationship between thickness, strength, and stiffness in three different panels.

LARSSON AND ELIASSON, *PRINCIPLES OF YACHT DESIGN*

ing in the skin of the hull will present an unfair surface to the passing water, adding drag and possibly creating dynamic instabilities.

Before composite sandwiches became commonplace, a boatbuilder just added more layers of fiberglass to get the necessary thickness for a strong and stiff structure. However, beam theory tells us that two relatively thin skins held fixed in relation to each other a small distance apart is a much more efficient use of materials. So boatbuilders began to use two relatively thin layers of fiberglass sandwiching a lightweight core material to create the same effect—strength and stiffness with light weight. The two thin skins of fiberglass, like the flanges of the I-beam, are separated by a core material, which acts like the web of the I-beam and holds the skins in place. In addition to reducing weight, cores add thermal and acoustic insulation, reducing condensation and noise levels, and help to attenuate vibrations. A cored hull also needs fewer support members, so more room is available for interior accommodations.

The I-Beam Effect

Let's look quickly at how beam theory works in this case. When a force pushes against an I-beam, the flanges (fiberglass skins) of the beam absorb tension and compression loads, and the web (the core material) keeps the flanges from separating in *shear* (one piece of paper sliding over another is move-

ment in shear). If the two I-beam flanges were able to move, or slide, in relation to each other, the I-beam would lose its strength and stiffness.

A core is used to form a "sandwich" consisting of two fiberglass skins bonded to a lightweight core, usually made of balsa, foam, or honeycomb. A sandwich of two ¼-inch layers of fiberglass separated by a 1-inch-thick core is far stiffer than a single layer of ½-inch-thick fiberglass. In a solid laminate, stiffness increases with the cube of the thickness; in a composite sandwich, the stiffness increase is somewhat less, but still significant, and depends on the core material used. Just as the web of an I-beam prevents its flanges from moving in relation to each other, the core material absorbs *shear stresses* between the two layers of fiberglass. Thickness also contributes to panel strength. Strength in a solid laminate is a function of thickness squared; strength in a sandwich is, again, somewhat less than that, depending on the core type.

Although we select core materials because of their light weight, the density of the core is also important. Strength and stiffness in a sandwich laminate are both directly proportional to the density of the core material, whether it's foam or balsa. A denser core is also more resistant to compression. So a dense, strong, and stiff core material can be thinner than one that's less so and still get the same job done. Put another way, a less-dense core must be thicker to achieve the same load-carrying capacity as a denser core. However, a thinner, denser core material will not deliver the dramatic gains in stiffness that a thicker sandwich will. So it's generally more practical to increase the panel's thickness, using a lightweight core, than to find a core material of high density. Dense cores are often used selectively in highly loaded areas, such as hull bottoms, where shear loads are higher.

Building a Sandwich Laminate

A stiff panel experiences high tension and compression stresses in its fiberglass skins, so selecting the right materials and resin is critical.

Knitted reinforcements are often preferred to roving woven because they permit lighter, thinner skins without sacrificing strength. As for the laminating resin, a vinylester or epoxy resin—with its greater ductility, elongation, and adhesion—will produce a better composite sandwich than is possible with orthophthalic polyester resin. If the resin that bonds the skin to the core is brittle, then the whole sandwich structure is brittle itself. Some isophthalic polyester resins have good elongation, and a hybrid orthovinylester resin can also produce an acceptably rugged, resilient sandwich at a lower cost than vinylester alone.

Although the fiberglass skins around a core could be thin and still absorb the loads generated by slamming into waves, the outer skin has other responsibilities, including resistance to collision impacts, so it must be made thicker. In fact, a sandwich bottom with two ¼-inch fiberglass skins will have significantly higher impact resistance than a solid ½-inch laminate, especially if the core is one of the more plastic and ductile foams (see below). That's because the sandwich panel can absorb energy from the collision and bounce back, whereas the solid glass laminate is more brittle and more likely to shatter.

The bond between the skins and the core (the "skin-to-core" bond) has to be sound, and things get complicated because dissimilar materials with different physical properties are being joined together. When a sandwich hull or deck is built, the gelcoat is typically sprayed into the female mold first, followed by a skin coat and then the outer skin laminate. Then the core material is bedded to the outer laminate, either in a bed of resin-rich fiberglass or with a specially formulated core-bonding adhesive supplied by the core manufacturer.

If the core is to be bedded in fiberglass, the cured fiberglass outer-skin surface is ground smooth to minimize hills and valleys. Then, wet mat or chop is applied to the sanded fiberglass to fill in the remaining valleys. The core is primed with partially catalyzed resin and applied to the wet fiberglass. This priming resin seeps into the open pores of the foam or balsa core better than core bond adhesive can, providing a far better mechanical bond when it cures. If a core-bonding putty is used, the putty is troweled onto the partially or completely cured outer skin of fiberglass. The core is then squished into the adhesive and hand rolled to remove air bubbles or, preferably, vacuum bagged to ensure a sound bond. In general, the best results are often achieved with a combination of resin and bonding putty.

Tiara hulls fresh out of the mold, getting ready to receive mechanical, electrical, and other major-component installation. Bulkheads and stringers are installed before removal from the mold so the hull keeps its shape. TIARA YACHTS

Any gaps in the core material itself or between sections of core must be filled to maintain structural integrity. In particular, the builder must be certain that there are no gaps or air voids in the hidden joint between the outer fiberglass skin and the core material. The best way to produce a solid skin-to-core bond is to use precoated core, a core-bonding adhesive, and a vacuum bag to apply great pressure evenly to the core while the bonding material is setting up. (Vacuum bagging is discussed on page 99.) Once the outer bond line has cured, the inner layer of fiberglass can be applied to the inside of the core, wet-on-dry. Vacuum bagging is not required here, as the builders can see what they're doing.

The problems of skin-to-core bonds have dis-

Core Material Evaluation Comparison Table

	Balsawood	Honeycomb Plastic	Linear PVC (Airex R63.80)	Cross-Linked PVC	SAN (Core-Cell)
Closed Cell Structure	3	1	10	10	10
Resistance to fresh/salt water	3	6	10	10	10
Resistance to Water Vapor Transm.	2	-	9	9	8
Resistance to Rot/Deterioration	2	9	9	9	9
Resistance to Gasoline/Diesel Oil	7	6	9	9	10
Resistance to Styrene	10	6	4	8	7
Outgassing Tendency	8	-	10	1	10
Compression Strength	10	3	2	4	3
Flexural Modulus	6	4	4	6	8
Shear Strength	10	3	7	8	7
Impact Strength*	5	5	10	3	9
Fatigue Strength*	3	-	3	7	10
Resistance to Crack Propagation	8	5	10	2	9
Heat Distortion Temperature	10	4	3	6	5
Thermal Insulation	5	4	7	8	7
Damping Characteristics	4	3	8	4	7
Burning Characteristics	8	2	5	5	4
Smoke/Toxic Emission	8	6	3	3	4
Versatility in Boatbuilding	5	2	3	5	10
Weight (at common useage)	5	6	8	7	8
Economic Criteria/Price	9	10	5	7	6
Totals	134	85	139	127	161

Core materials are rated on a scale from 1 - 10, 10 being the most desirable, or best property. The ratings are our estimates, and are based on our general experience as well as data sheet values.

ATC's estimation of the relative merits of different core materials (ATC is the manufacturer of Core-Cell). Although other manufacturers would undoubtedly assign higher values to their own products, this chart is an excellent starting point for any discussion of core material suitability. ATC CHEMICAL

couraged many production manufacturers from building boats with cored bottoms, since a failed bond line here means a failed hull. That's too bad, because coring a bottom is a great way to keep weight down, increase bottom panel thickness, reduce framing requirements, and add insulation against water noise and condensation. And it's not that hard to do right using vacuum bagging and special skin-to-core bond adhesives. The problem is that some builders have insufficient quality controls in place to ensure a high-quality bond line during construction.

Although coring the bottom is a challenge, most builders do use coring on the hull sides, deck, and superstructure. It's a simple matter of saving weight and gaining stiffness at the same time, and a skin-to-core bond line failure likely won't have catastrophic consequences in these locations.

Balsa Cores

End-grain balsa is the most commonly used core material, offering excellent physical properties and low cost. The wood is cut from the tree like slices of bread from a loaf, so that the grain runs from fiberglass skin to skin. Balsa is resistant to compression along the direction of the grain, and it is excellent at absorbing the shear stress to which cores are subject. Balsa is available in a variety of densities from 4.5 to 15.5 pounds per cubic foot, from suppliers including DIAB and Baltek. It comes in rigid sheet form or in shapeable panels that are sliced into small squares and held together with a fiberglass mesh on one side, so that they can conform to curved surfaces. It's important that the gaps between the squares be filled with resin or bedding compound to maintain the structural integrity of the finished sandwich. This applies to both balsa and foam cores. Balsa should also be hot-coated, or coated with resin that is allowed to catalyze, before being fiberglassed in place. This prevents the lamination resin from being wicked out of the reinforcement and weakening the skin-to-core bond.

With the outer fiberglass skin and end-grain balsa core laminated in place, the next step is applying the inner skin, which is in progress on this Great American Concepts project. BALTEK CORP.

Because it's commonly used in higher densities than foam, balsa typically has greater shear strength. (High-density foam is actually stronger than low-density balsa, but most balsa comes in a density of 10 to 12 pounds per cubic foot, versus 4 to 5 pounds for most structural foams.) The strength and stiffness of balsa make it a good candidate for decks and other rigid surfaces.

Due to its compressive strength and stiffness, however, balsa is not as good at absorbing impact energy as the more ductile foams. Under impact,

say with an underwater piling, balsa will transfer the load directly to the inner fiberglass skin. This is why a resin that can stretch, like vinylester, will do a better job of holding the sandwich together at the skin-to-core bond than a more brittle polyester resin. Wave impact load attenuation with a balsa core is quite good, though, since the material's compressive properties transfer energy efficiently from one fiberglass skin to the other.

Like most organic materials, balsa is susceptible to rot in the presence of moisture, oxygen, and rot-causing spores. If the balsa core stays dry, it won't rot. If it becomes wet, it will rot and eventually delaminate from the fiberglass skins as the water migrates along the skin-to-core bond line. The cross-grain structure of the balsa coring slows down the permeation process, as do the resin- or putty-filled voids between the balsa scrims. Needless to say, the importance of keeping the balsa core dry is hard to overrate. That means you don't drill holes through deck, superstructure, or hull components cored with balsa without taking elaborate precautions.

Foam Cores

Structural foams are often used as core materials and are available in a wide range of densities to suit different applications. Compared with balsa, foam cores are generally lighter and more resistant to rot—or even rot-proof, depending on whom you believe. They are also more expensive.

The degree of molecular cross-linking (or interlocking of molecules) is a major factor in the behavior of foams and their desirability in different applications. Most structural foam cores are cross-linked to some extent. Foams with the most cross-linking, such as polyvinyl chloride (PVC) cross-linked foams, offer the greatest shear strength and stiffness, but they are also relatively brittle. Examples are Divinycell and Klegecell. As with balsa, the stiffness of PVC foams makes them a good choice for decks and rigid surfaces.

Foams with the least cross-linking are commonly referred to as *linear*. Airex, for example, has the least cross-linking of the major boatbuilding

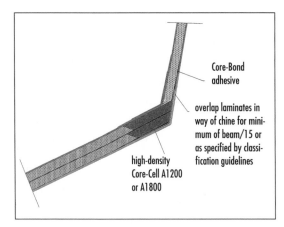

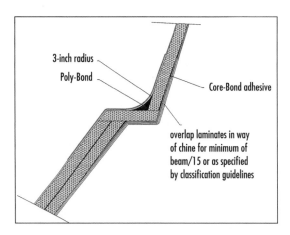

The double-core in this hull bottom allows the desired total core thickness to be achieved, even in the absence of a suitably thick material. Note the use of higher density foam at the chines, which, like the keel, will be subject to high localized loads from lifting straps.   ATC CHEMICAL

Detail of a stepped chine showing how core materials can be used to negotiate complex shapes. The inside corner of the upper chine is radiused (in this case with a fillet of Poly-Bond) to spread out loads and to make sure the fiberglass reinforcement lays down smoothly and void free.   ATC CHEMICAL

foams. It has the least shear strength, but it is the most ductile. So although an Airex core gives less strength and stiffness to the panel than balsa or cross-linked PVC foam, it can yield and distort further—and absorb much more energy—before failing entirely. In a collision, a ductile core will absorb more energy than a brittle core, limiting damage to the fiberglass skins, the core itself, and the skin-core bond. And as long as the inner skin remains intact, the boat will not take on water. Airex is sold in 3.8- to 8.7-pound densities.

Blurring these categories is a linear foam called Core-Cell. Core-Cell has stiffness close to that of PVC cross-linked foam, but its ductility is close to that of Airex, giving Core-Cell some of the best qualities of each. Its physical properties make it suitable to use throughout a boat, from hull bottom to superstructure and decks. Core-Cell tends to stretch as it fails, helping to keep the hull intact after impact. In addition, its heat tolerance makes it well suited for use in sunlit decks. Core-Cell is made by ATC Chemical and sold in densities from 3 to 12 pounds.

In general, the denser the foam, the higher the stiffness and weight, since there is more, or tighter,

cross-linking with more core material and less air per unit volume, and the greater the cost. A very dense foam might be used in the transom of an outboard or stern-drive boat, where high compression loads are expected, while lighter foams could be used in the hull sides.

Not surprisingly, some boatbuilders use a combination of different core materials for different applications in the same boat. Out on the water you can find boats with solid fiberglass bottoms and balsa-cored topsides, boats with Airex-cored bottoms with Divinycell topsides, and boats made entirely with balsa, Core-Cell, and Divinycell sandwich panels.

Foams also respond differently to heat. The heat distortion temperature (HDT) of a foam—or any core material—is the temperature at which the core will lose its strength and shape and begin to deform. Balsa and cross-linked PVC have higher HDTs than linear foam, so they're a good choice for surfaces subject to heating from the sun, such as decks and the topsides of dark hulls. Linear foams such as Airex should be avoided in these surfaces, since the sandwich will more readily lose its stiffness when heated.

Foam cores are available in solid sheets and as flexible sheets of little blocks. Solid sheets are preferable, since there are no cuts to the core, but they can only be used on flat or very gently curved surfaces. With solid sheets, builders have to take great care that there are no gaps in the bond between the foam core and the fiberglass skin. Some solid-sheet foams can be thermoformed, or heated, to conform to a curved surface. The alternative is to use sheets of foam sliced or cut into little blocks and held together with a scrim on one side. The contour-cored core is used around curved areas, since the slits between the blocks will open up to allow the core to follow the shape of the mold. Again, these slits and voids have to be filled with resin or putty during construction to maintain the structural integrity of the core and prevent any water that gets into the core from migrating through the hull.

Honeycomb Cores

Honeycomb cores are extremely light, high-end materials derived from the aerospace industry. Marine applications have to be engineered carefully because of the potential for water absorption and because of the difficulties of bonding the surface of the honeycomb to the fiberglass skins. High-end boats, like some of the America's Cup contenders, use honeycomb cores because they deliver the lightest possible composite. At the top end is Nomex, a very expensive honeycomb made of aramid fibers, widely used in the aircraft industry. Sandwiches using paper or plastic honeycomb core are more affordable. Plastic honeycomb like Nida-Core has been used in decks, bulkheads, and even hulls. Tricel, a paper honeycomb, produces interior furniture, joinery, and nonstructural components at a fraction of the weight of solid plywood. Sandwiches with plastic or paper honeycombs have very good sound-dampening qualities, so they work well as saloon decks above engine rooms.

The Challenges of Cores

Sandwich composite laminates are marvelous creations when they are properly engineered and constructed. However, poor design or construction can have disastrous results. While it's relatively hard to screw up a laminate of solid fiberglass, which can be made stronger and stiffer just by adding more layers of reinforcement, sandwiches are complex and unforgiving. Premature failure will result if incompatible materials are used or if proper procedures are neglected during construction. As we have seen, the various core materials have different properties, so they must be carefully matched to the application.

Core materials, particularly those made of foam, are comparatively weak in compression, and the core must at all costs remain dry. High-density foam cores can be used in areas where compression loads are anticipated, but any areas that will be drilled for through-hull fittings should be solid fiberglass. Otherwise, the through-hull's bolts will compress the core and may crush the fiberglass, and the holes will become susceptible to water leaking into the core with disastrous results.

If a sandwich hull or deck section must be drilled through, the core must be removed in the immediate vicinity of the hole and the resultant void filled with a fiberglass filler, preferably using epoxy resin, which has superior bonding properties. Alternatively, the inner skin and the core can be cut back and a scarf created from the inside of the hull by grinding down the surrounding area to a

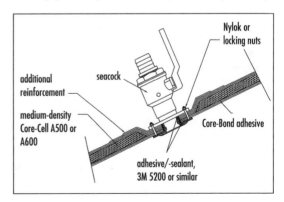

Section at a through-hull fitting, which should always be surrounded by solid fiberglass to resist compression when the mounting bolts are tightened and prevent water from leaking into the core. ATC CHEMICAL

gradual taper to the inside surface of the outer skin. This scalloped-out area is then laid up with solid fiberglass and the hole is drilled through the new fiberglass.

Going to all this trouble and proper planning should guarantee that water never gets into the core, an eventuality that would likely result in core delamination and water absorption over time.

The bigger the boat, the harder it is to keep the weight down. The balsa core in the bottom of this Viking convertible is being bonded to the outer fiberglass skin. Note that the hull is solid fiberglass wherever a through-hull fitting or penetration is to be located, such as cooling water seacocks and shaft strut pads.   VIKING YACHTS

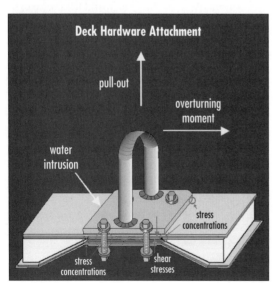

Proper deck hardware installation, with some of the stresses that are to be expected indicated.   ERIC GREENE

The deck and superstructure of a balsa-cored boat is actually more likely to become water-soaked than a balsa-cored hull, if for no other reason than an owner is more likely to drill holes topside than elsewhere. Also, water can enter the core through both the inner *and* outer skins. All those little side-curtain fasteners, for instance, are a prime source of water intrusion, as are any other holes drilled into the skin. For this reason, most builders use marine plywood instead of balsa or foam as a core material around railings, cleats, and other areas of the deck where fixtures are likely, reasoning that the plywood will absorb the bolts' compression loads better and is more resistant to water penetration. While plywood is certainly more resistant to compression, the problem is that marine plywood will *also* delaminate and rot if it gets wet. And if a hole is drilled through a cored deck or hull section, it's almost guaranteed to leak during the boat's lifetime. Pressure-treated plywood is a better choice for this reason, though some experts report problems bonding permanently to pressure-treated plywood with polyester resins.

One alternative to plywood in this application may be a material called Xtreme Composites, made by Penske Plastics, which was originally developed for use in luggage frames and shipping containers. It's made of continuous-strand, nonwoven fiberglass in a matrix of foamed polyurethane resin. Fiberglass will stick to it, preventing water migration to the surrounding core material, and it's very compression resistant. As you might guess, it's more expensive than plywood. Whatever material is used to substitute around penetrations, a mistake sometimes made by builders is failing to carry the high-density core material and extra reinforcements far enough beyond the fitting to adequately spread out the loads to the surrounding hull or deck structure.

The challenge of weight reduction is not limited to hull structure. Interiors account for 25 to 30 percent of the average luxury yacht's gross weight, and can reach even higher percentages in very large yachts. A range of cored panels with excellent stiffness-to-weight ratios and good acoustic properties allows an architect and builder to achieve significant weight reductions. The use of these lightweight panels requires new techniques and a reevaluation of traditional carpentry skills.

Cores in Conclusion

Cores allow builders to produce lighter, stronger boats that go farther and faster on less fuel. As you dig into the engineering arcana of fiberglass sandwich construction, you quickly discover that there are differing opinions—firmly held and well-substantiated—among engineers about which core materials are best for a given application. There are a lot of different ways to build a good boat with core materials. However, none of these experts would disagree that, whichever materials are chosen, they must be properly matched and carefully constructed to be successful.

Building a Production Boat

Female molds are used to build all of the major components of a production fiberglass boat, including the hull, deck, superstructure, and countless hatches, doors, and other small components. Once the builder has created this mold (or *tooling*, as molds are called in the industry), it can be used repeatedly to build the pieces of the boat. That is what makes this method of boatbuilding fast and relatively cheap. The fewer parts that make up a completed boat, the better, too. For instance, many builders make their deck-superstructure-cockpit liners out of a single fiberglass part, eliminating a few leak- and squeak-prone joints and speeding up assembly time in the process.

Making the Mold

Fiberglass tooling is usually made by first building a male "plug" of the same shape and size as the desired component. Plugs can be built by hand, using wood or steel frames and usually wood or plywood planking. The wood surface is faired, and fiberglass cloth may be applied and the surface faired again.

Plugs can also be built using computer-aided design and computer-aided manufacturing (CAD-CAM). A special computer data file created from the naval architect's drawings is used to control a five-axis milling machine that carves the hull or other component shape out of a large block of foam. The foam plug is then coated with a thick layer of denser filler and milled again to very close tolerances, within thousandths of an inch.

Some builders use a combination of CAD-CAM and conventional methods, for example using CAM to cut out the hull plug's frames to within very close tolerances and then planking over the framework and fairing the plug manually.

Once the plug is finished to a mirror-smooth finish, it's time to build the female mold. The plug is waxed several times and a mold release agent may be applied, which creates a nonstick film on the finished surface. Next, layers of gelcoat specially formulated for mold building are applied to a combined 30- to 40-mil thickness (1 mil = 0.001 inch). Next follows a thick laminate of fiberglass chop or mat (which, being omnidirectional in reinforcement orientation, won't distort the mold surface) followed by layers of reinforcing fiberglass fabric. Molds are sometimes cored to add stiffness and strength, just like in the boat itself. A stiff supporting framework is then added to the outside of the mold to keep it from deforming, or changing shape, once it's lifted clear of the plug. Large hull molds often have "rocker" foundations that allow them to be rolled from one side to the other as alternating sides of the hull are laid up.

The completed mold is then lifted free from the plug and made ready to produce a fiberglass part, whether it's a hull, deck, or flybridge. The mold is waxed and, depending on the builder, coated with a special mold-release coating to help keep the part's outer layer, the gelcoat, from adhering to it. Some builders rely solely on the wax to assure the part lifts off easily, finding that the mold release agent leaves a visible pattern in the gelcoat surface.

The plug for a Sea Sport 32 catamaran mold starts to take shape. These rough plywood stations define the shape of the hull. They are then covered with sprayed-on foam, which is milled to shape using a computer-controlled five-axis router. The final result is a smooth plug, ready to produce a mold.

Laminating the Hull

Once the mold is prepared, a pigmented gelcoat is sprayed on to a thickness of 20 to 30 mils and allowed to gel and partially harden. The gelcoat is what you see on the finished, unpainted product, since the hull is laminated from the outside in. The gelcoat gives the hull its smooth, gleaming appearance and color and helps protect the underlying substrate of fiberglass.

Next comes a "skin" coat, usually made up of a couple of layers of chop (sprayed from a chopper gun) or hand-laid mat that forms a resin-rich barrier layer over the gelcoat. Chop or mat is used here because either cures uniformly, being random in fiber orientation. The resulting cure won't shrink the gelcoat, causing print-through once the hull is separated from the mold, as a heavy-weave roving might do. Low-profile DCPD resin is often used in the skin coat in topside areas. The mat layer and the following plies of reinforcements are wet out either with a spray gun or by using rollers and brushes with buckets of resin.

With either method, the resin must be carefully catalyzed so that adequate working time is provided and so the resin doesn't "kick" too quickly; the proper amount to use is largely a function of ambient air temperature. Using too much catalyst, or an overly thick laminate, will produce an excessive exothermic reaction, meaning that too much heat is given off by the chemical reaction of the curing process. The result may be reduced osmotic blistering resistance and distortion and print-through of the fiberglass reinforcement.

The layup process is straightforward. A fresh, thin layer of resin is applied to the mold or to the previous layer of cured reinforcement. The reinforcement is laid out dry over this wet coat of resin, positioned in place, and then wet out with spray- or roller-applied resin. Grooved metal rollers and squeegees are used to remove excess resin and air bubbles from the laminate. This process also ensures that the reinforcement is completely wet out.

Depending on the builder, and on which part is being laminated, the reinforcement material can be precut on a table in a cutting room, rolled back up, and delivered to the molding room. Then, when it's rolled out on the hull in the proper location, it'll fit perfectly as it's being wet out. Some fiberglass vendors even deliver the material precut in kits to reduce production time on the lamination floor.

Vacuum Bagging

Vacuum bagging is often used to hold core materials firmly in place when bonding a core to a cured fiberglass skin. The goal is to produce a consistent, high-quality secondary bond. The area to be bonded is covered with a plastic bag, the edges are sealed, and a strong vacuum is applied until the part sets up. Since the outer side of the core in contact with the vacuum bag is not wet out, this process is called *dry bagging*. A perfect vacuum of up to 14.7 psi would result in over 2,100 pounds per square foot of pressure applied uniformly to the entire surface being laminated, far more than can be applied using weights. In the real world, a vacuum of around 10 to 12 psi is more realistic in large molds.

Wet bagging applies the same procedure to wet laminates. However, in this case it is necessary to draw off excess resin before it gets to the pump that produces the vacuum, so a bleeder material that allows excess resin to drain off and a film that keeps the plumbing from sticking to the cured fiberglass are needed. Wet bagging results in a higher glass-to-resin ratio by removing excess resin, removes entrained air in the laminate, and eliminates interlaminar voids by compressing the layers of fiberglass against each other firmly, greatly improving the quality of the final product. Some builders lay up large parts like hulls and decks manually, but use vacuum bagging on cored saloon decks and bridge hardtops because they are easier to handle.

Impregnators and Prepregs

Keeping the glass-to-resin ratio consistent is a concern for boatbuilders, as is the speed with which large amounts of thick, multilayer fiberglass reinforcements can be wet out. Machines called "impregnators" address both of these points and are used by builders of very large fiberglass craft. An impregnator passes the dry fiberglass reinforcement, which comes in rolls up to 60 inches wide, through a pool of catalyzed resin and then through a pair of rollers that squeezes out the excess, precisely controlling the amount of resin saturating the material. Another pair of rollers controls the speed at which the fabric passes through. Glass content of 55 percent (relative to resin) can be attained using an impregnator. The impregnator is usually mounted on an overhead crane or gantry, which can be positioned directly over the part being laminated, accelerating production time significantly. Smaller, portable impregnators can also be used.

Preimpregnated reinforcements, or prepregs, are delivered to the boatbuilder wet out in partially cured, tacky epoxy resin, ready to be laid up in the mold. Prepregs, which are much more expensive than traditional reinforcement materials, require special handling; they must be stored in a freezer until they're used and then they must be postcured (allowed to harden) by putting the vessel, or part, in an oven set between 140° and 350°F, depending on the prepreg. Only a few custom boatbuilders use this method, but the advantages include a consistent glass-to-resin ratio, the ability to bond effectively to honeycomb cores, and a strong, lightweight structure. High-end boatbuilders like this method because of the material's easy handling, low styrene emissions (even when styrene-free epoxy isn't used), longer working times, and better quality and consistency. Many America's Cup sailboats, around-the-world race boats, high-end power- and sailboats, and high-performance hydroplanes are built using prepregs.

Resin Infusion and Other Specialized Techniques

If you're considering a boat that's built using one of the available resin-infusion processes, you'd be buying bragging rights to one of the best-built boats around.

Bottom blistering has been a recurring problem with fiberglass boats since the 1970s, supposedly when resin manufacturers changed their formulations with unfortunate results. Technically, osmosis is the migration under pressure of a solvent—in our case water—through a film, or barrier, that separates areas of varying salinity concentration. Blistering starts when moisture passes through the gelcoat and into the fiberglass substrate beneath by osmosis. Water finds its way into tiny air- or styrene-filled voids in the fiberglass, interacts with soluble chemicals left over from uncured resin and other vagaries of the construction process, and then expands under pressure, peeling off little—or not so little—bits of hull bottom.

It turns out that fiberglass hulls are surprisingly porous, especially when built using general-purpose orthophthalic resins. Water can migrate into the fiberglass hull structure at the microscopic level, or it can find resin-starved fiberglass strands and wick its way into the substrate. Water can also penetrate into the fiberglass from the inside, from the bilge. (Boats with water-soaked flotation foam have been known to develop osmotic blistering from the inside of the hull.) At the same time, a fiberglass hull can absorb moisture and *not* blister, provided there are no voids and no soluble chemicals for the water to react with.

There are a number of causes of osmotic blistering. An incompletely wet-out fiberglass skin coat will leave voids and dry glass fibers, which will carry water into the laminate by capillary action. The skin coat should be composed of mat or chop, thoroughly wet out to produce a resin-rich barrier against moisture. (The first few ounces of laminate is often called a *barrier* coat for this reason.) A low-quality gelcoat, or a gelcoat that is damaged or poorly applied, will not resist moisture penetration well. A poor bond between the gelcoat and the fiberglass beneath will allow water to pass through to the laminate more readily and cause the gelcoat to delaminate.

In the case of polyester resins, if too much catalyst is used in the resin, or the resin is not thoroughly mixed, unreacted chemicals may be left over in the laminate that will react with water. If the resin cures too quickly, microscopic (or larger) pathways can be left in the laminate that water will quickly find. Other causes include impurities or solvents in the fiberglass or the resin and damp, cold conditions during hull lamination. Left untreated, blistering can be counted on to worsen, with tiny blisters growing larger and larger and water wicking farther into the laminate until a resin-rich barrier is reached. In rare cases blistering can destroy the bottom of a boat structurally, or at least make it a very expensive proposition to repair.

Blistering can be prevented by using high-quality resins and careful quality control; in particular, builders must ensure complete saturation of the fiberglass and proper curing of the resin. Boats built of conventional, general-purpose orthophthalic resin are the most susceptible to blistering because this type of resin is less cross-linked at the molecular level, although with good quality control a hull built of orthophthalic resin can certainly be blister free. Some builders use isophthalic resin or vinylester resin in the barrier or skin coat because these resins are chemically more cross-linked at the molecular level and are significantly less porous. A vinylester skin coat is to be preferred over an isophthalic skin coat. Orthophthalic, general-purpose polyester resin is often used for the remainder of the laminate since it's cheaper. In terms of blister resistance, the ideal laminate would be all-epoxy, followed by all-vinylester.

Some dealers will tell you that their boats have a vinylester barrier coat, but that may just mean that a couple of coats of vinylester resin were sprayed over the gelcoat when the boat was laminated in the female mold. Unfortunately, such a thin layer can easily be ground off if bottom paint preparations are done carelessly. Or a builder may point to their premium gelcoat

Rather than adding hand-laid layers of fiberglass reinforcement to previously cured layers, resin infusion processes usually involve laying up all the reinforcement (except the skin coat) in one stack, including stringers and bulkhead landings, and infusing resin under vacuum pressure in one shot, eliminating the weaker secondary bonds.

SCRIMP

SCRIMP stands for Seemann Composites Resin Infusion Molding Process. SCRIMP uses either epoxy or vinylester resins to infuse the fiberglass hull, stringers, and bulkhead landings under very high vacuum all in one step, eliminating secondary bonds and carefully controlling the glass-to-resin

as their answer to blistering protection, but that 20- to 30-mil layer of gelcoat is susceptible to cracking, either from impact or from being applied incorrectly, or to being ground through during bottom paint preparation. Once the relatively brittle gelcoat is penetrated, the underlying fiberglass barrier coat better be built right, or watch out. A much better barrier coat consists of 3 ounces of mat or chop wet out with vinylester resin and applied over the gelcoat (i.e., "over" the gelcoat in the mold, and immediately under the gelcoat in the finished boat). Be sure to ask about blistering coverage in the warranty.

Osmotic blistering is mostly a problem with vessels that are kept in the water year-round, but some boats develop blisters after being left in the water for just a couple of months. The warmer the water, the greater the tendency to blister. Even after a boat has been hauled out of the water for months, water may still be present in voids and blisters and continue to permeate the hull laminate's glass fibers. If you discover blisters on the bottom of your boat, and try to fix things by just sanding it and applying a couple of coats of epoxy and bottom paint, you can actually make things worse by sealing the water *in*. The gelcoat and underlying fiberglass laminate have to be completely dried out before repairs are attempted, and this might take the application of hot air for a prolonged period.

Fixing a badly blistered bottom properly is a difficult undertaking. Doing the job right is an extensive, time-consuming process, usually involving the removal of the gelcoat and part of the fiberglass mat or chop substrate using a machine-mounted "peeler," or electric planer. Then the hull is thoroughly dried and several layers of specially formulated epoxy are applied (although some tests show that vinylester works even better over bare fiberglass). In no event should a hull be sandblasted, since this will leave the bottom more pocked than ever—and more susceptible to blisters later on.

The True North 38 deck and superstructure being built using the SCRIMP resin infusion process. The reinforcements and sandwich core materials are stacked dry and covered with a plastic film bag. A vacuum is applied and catalyzed resin is drawn from the buckets in the foreground until the resin has completely saturated the fiberglass reinforcements. The bag is removed when the resin has cured, revealing the completed part.

ratio. It's an excellent way to build a boat, but it's expensive, licensed to users by patent-holder TPI, and limited to high-end builders, at least for now.

Here's how it works. The mold is prepared, coated with gelcoat, and a skin coat of mat or chop is applied and allowed to cure. Next, the dry reinforcements, core materials, stringers, and bulkhead landings are all carefully positioned in place. A plastic bag is placed over the whole affair, carefully sealed around the edges, and the stacked reinforcements can be leisurely checked for proper positioning before the resin starts to flow. Then, a precisely measured amount of catalyzed resin is drawn by vacuum through the laminate until it's completely wet out.

The vacuum, which is significantly higher than that used for standard vacuum bagging, assures as-good-as-it-gets interlaminar bonds (between the layers of reinforcement) and skin-to-core bonds (between the fiberglass skins and the core material). The pressure also compacts the laminate, removing excess resin while achieving glass-to-resin ratios of 70:30 with woven roving and as high as 75:25 with unidirectional knitted reinforcements. Air is completely removed from the laminate, eliminating the tiny voids that otherwise reduce flexural strength by up to 10 percent. In a crucial step to ensure a thoroughly wet-out and air-free laminate, core materials are perforated to allow resin to flow to, and air to bleed off from, the outer skin.

The excellent interlaminar and skin-to-core bonds result in a stronger, lighter, and more durable laminate compared with conventional hand layup or even vacuum-bagged prepregs. A boat built using SCRIMP has twice the flexural (the ability to withstand flexing without structural failure), compressive, and tensile strength of hand-laid laminates. In addition the tensile strength and elongation properties of an epoxy-based laminate can be nearly doubled after the laminate has cured by heating in an oven at 140 to 250°F for three or more hours.

The J/125 high-performance sailboat built by TPI Composites, owner of the SCRIMP process, is an excellent example of a SCRIMP-built boat. Kevlar and fiberglass are used on the outer hull skin and two layers of carbon fiber are used on the inner skin; these materials provide lighter, thinner skins than would be possible using fiberglass alone. The hull is cored with thermoformed (heat shaped) Core-Cell, which is perforated to allow air pockets to bleed off from under the core and to provide a path for resin to flow from inner to outer skins. TPI turns out J/125 hulls that can vary less than 1 percent in weight, thanks to the control of resin use.

Another resin infusion process, now being used to build some of the larger composite sandwich vessels, is DRIP, or DIAB Resin Infusion Process. The foam core used in this process is scored only along the surface, and these grooves allow the resin to flow evenly through the entire part's inner and outer skins. DIAB offers this process free of charge to builders, making their money by selling the foam.

UIP

Another excellent resin-infusion process is VIP, for Vacuum Infusion Process, developed by Intermarine. This process was, quite generously, published by Intermarine, which means that it can't be patented and is therefore available to any builder to use without a license fee. The process involves scoring ⅛-by-⅛-inch grooves in both sides of the core material on 1-inch centers, and these grooves act as channels for the resin to flow through, completely wetting out the laminate. The core, then, acts as the resin transfer medium.

This process eliminates the need to perforate the core to wet out the inner skin, as is the case with SCRIMP. Vinylester is the resin of choice, since its chemistry can be adjusted to control the cure rate carefully, ensuring complete laminate wet-out. Intermarine has successfully resin-infused three 123-foot yachts with 2-inch coring using the VIP process, along with many smaller projects.

Intermarine's VIP (vacuum infusion process) system sucks resin under high vacuum through a dry stack of fiberglass, using scored core material as the primary resin channel. The company generously "disclosed" the process so it couldn't be patented, making it available for all to use without a license fee.   INTERMARINE

Resin Transfer Molding

Some high-quality boatbuilders use a process called Resin Transfer Molding (RTM) to build small components like deck hatches and topside cabinet doors. The reinforcement and core are stacked dry inside a two-sided mold to which gelcoat may have been applied, which is closed and sealed tight with a pair of gaskets around the perimeter. A pump draws a carefully measured amount of resin (which may be tinted) into the closed mold, which completely

Glass-to-Resin Ratio

Glass-to-resin ratio, or *fiber-to-resin* if you prefer, refers to the ratio, by weight, of a cured fiberglass part's fiberglass reinforcement to its resin. The ratio common in conventional hand-layup construction is about 35 to 40 percent fiberglass to 65 to 60 percent resin—not very impressive when you see what's possible with SCRIMP and vacuum bagging. Measuring the same ratio of glass-to-resin by volume is a different kettle of fish—a 50:50 glass-to-resin ratio by weight amounts to a 34:66 ratio by volume.

By using knitted rather than woven reinforcements, and by vacuum bagging the laminate before it cures, this ratio can be improved markedly in favor of the glass. A greater glass-to-resin ratio makes for a more efficiently laid-up hull, less wasted resin, and a lighter boat for the same strength. With high-tech vacuum resin infusion methods like SCRIMP, the ratio can be reversed to as much as 80:20, but be careful! At extremely high ratios, there won't be enough resin to saturate the voids and bind the fibers together in the matrix. Since too little resin can be a bad thing, preventing the fiberglass from being completely wet out and adhering to the surrounding matrix, vacuum during construction has to be carefully controlled. Glass-to-resin ratio can be measured by a burn test, which involves taking a cured fiberglass sample, weighing it, burning away the flammable resin, and weighing the (inflammable) reinforcement that remains.

---

wets out the reinforcements and bonds them to the core. When the part has cured, the mold is opened, much like a waffle iron, the part removed, and the edges trimmed and polished smooth. The result is a high-quality, lightweight part that's tooled on both sides and around the edges, with the core completely sealed by the surrounding fiberglass.

VEC

Genmar Holdings, currently the world's largest boatbuilder, opened a new plant in 2000 that uses a patented closed molding process called VEC, which stands for Virtual Engineered Composites. VEC is an advance over the RTM process with a very high degree of automation. Dry fiberglass reinforcements

and core material are laid up in a two-piece mold that is closed and sealed before being placed in a vat of water. Both the pressure and temperature of the water can be controlled. Then resin is injected into the closed mold. Instead of a vacuum, water provides the pressure (some 50 psi) and the water temperature controls the rate of exotherm (resin curing). The process is managed by computers that monitor hundreds of variables such as resin temperature, viscosity, and flow rate. The molds themselves are fairly light; they get their structural rigidity from the surrounding water, just as an aluminum soda can is stiff while pressurized by carbonated water.

VEC produces high-quality components with excellent consistency and strength at less weight while using less labor. That's in part because, as with SCRIMP and RTM, the amount of resin is tightly controlled, resulting in a relatively low glass-to-resin ratio, and the interlaminar and skin-to-core bonds are tight and sound. VEC parts achieve 98 percent cure within 24 hours, much faster than with open-molded fiberglass components. The VEC plant runs around the clock to produce hulls four times faster than open molding could—it takes a little more than an hour to build a VEC hull. VEC also reduces volatile organic compounds (VOCs) by some 75 percent, and this figure may improve as the process is refined.

Genmar's up-front investment in the technology was considerable, but these may well prove to be the best-built boats (Glastrons and Larsons for starters) of their kind anywhere, since hulls and decks are molded in a single process, eliminating secondary bonds in a sealed hull-and-deck structure. All visible surfaces are tooled fiberglass thanks to the two-part molds, for a better looking, easily maintained boat.

Though not yet used in the pleasure boat industry, Picken's Plastics of Jefferson, Ohio, has developed a proprietary Closed Cavity Bag Molding (CCBM) process. A standard mold is used to lay up the fiberglass reinforcement, and a second, more flexible hard-body fiberglass mold, rather than a plastic film, is used to cover the reinforcement from

lon, and polypropylene. Very rugged and forgiving of impact, these boats have a definite place in the recreational marine marketplace. The molds are expensive to produce initially, but thermoplastic boats can be produced much more quickly and with less labor than those made of fiberglass.

ABS (acrylonitrile butadiene-styrene) plastic is a promising material for the small-boat industry. It can be thermoformed, shaped with a heat gun, glued, drilled, machined, welded, and bent. It's durable, impact resistant, abrasion resistant, light, and can be ordered with the color impregnated throughout the thickness of the material. Leisure Life Ltd., of Grand Rapids, Michigan, builds an electric-powered pontoon boat of Centrex/ABS plastic, for instance, while AB Inflatable builds a line of lightweight RIBs (rigid inflatable boats) using ABS plastic.

Genmar's Triumph boat line builds polyethylene plastic boats using a proprietary closed rotational-mold technology called Roplene. Triumph boats are durable and seamless, built much like a plastic gas tank and with the same compelling advantages of structural integrity, toughness, simplicity, and indefinite life. A polyethylene powder is poured into a high-temperature mold, which is rotated on two axes, horizontally and vertically, in a computer-controlled process. The powder melts, evenly covering the inner mold surfaces, and is soon

the inside. Resin is drawn through ports into the laminate and out through vents in the mold. This process results in a very smooth finish on both sides of the part, and it's probably the closest thing to the VEC process. Picken's has successfully laminated one-piece, 30-foot bus sides with this process. VEC and CCBM eliminate the need for bleeder materials and vacuum bags, which makes for less garbage to be disposed of after the lamination process is complete.

Thermoplastics

Small boats can be built of heat-formed plastics, or thermoplastics, most commonly polyethylene, ny-

A Triumph boat under construction—you just can't see it yet. Polyethylene powder fills the cavity in the steel hull mold, heat is applied, and a one-piece, continuous hull-and-deck is Roto-molded into existence. Impact resistance, durability, and strength are high, and maintenance is as low as you want it to be.

transformed into a one-piece boat—with the release of little or no VOCs. The hull color is molded into the plastic, so there's no gelcoat to crack or chip, and the material is impervious to osmosis.

Triumph claims that their boats have five times the impact resistance of fiberglass (although that statement would have to define both materials to be very meaningful). In any event, the company says you can hit one of their boats with a sledgehammer and use a propane torch or other heat source to remove the dent. Triumph sounds like the perfect boat for the lousy boat handler. The company points out that although their boats aren't the only ones that can be sawn into parts and still float, they're the only ones that can be readily welded back together again. Triumph puts its money where its mouth is, too, backing their boats up with a structural hull and stringer warranty that's good for as long as the original purchaser owns the boat. We'd like to see other boatbuilders go as far out on the same limb.

Hull and Deck Support: Bulkheads, Frames, and Stringers

Even with core materials, every fiberglass hull still needs additional support, usually in the form of an interlocking network of bulkheads, frames, and stringers. Bulkheads are essentially solid walls that run transversely (from side to side) in a hull. They are usually made of plywood, which is tabbed to the hull on both sides and the bottom (see below). Bulkheads can also be made of cored fiberglass. Bulkheads are designated as watertight if they are solid and prevent water from flowing from one section of the hull to the next. "Intermediate" bulkheads give structural support to the hull but are not watertight, as they are not as high as the deck above. (Viking Yachts, for instance, uses intermediate bulkheads to support its engine beds.) Nonstructural bulkheads, which are not fiberglassed to the hull and therefore contribute little if any strength to it, are used to support furniture and other subassemblies.

Stringers are support members running fore and aft in the bottom of the hull. They can be made up of foam, wood, or plywood beams encapsulated in fiberglass, or they may be molded as a single grid work, or *grillage*, which includes landing spots for bulkhead and transverse frames, and then lowered into the hull and fiberglassed or bonded in place while the hull is still in the mold.

Transverse frames would be called *ribs* in a wooden boat. They stiffen the hull skin and, with the stringers, define the size of the bottom panels. While the bottom is essentially a continuous layer of fiberglass, in an engineer's mind it is also divided into panels defined by the spans between the interlocking network of bulkheads, frames, and stringers. The thickness of the bottom laminate and the sizes of these panels are engineered according to the anticipated weight and speed of the boat. For a given laminate thickness, a faster, heavier boat requires smaller panels (i.e., more support). On the other hand, the use of a core material permits larger panels to be used. The strength of the individual support members must also be carefully calculated to match the anticipated loads on the hull. And the support members must be securely and permanently bonded to the hull skin.

Bulkheads and stringers should be fiberglassed in place while the hull is still in the mold. Otherwise, the hull may deform and lose its shape before its structural supports are installed. The secondary bond between stringers and bulkheads and the hull skin is a weak link in the hull structure, and it's important that these members be ruggedly attached and that the inside corners where they meet are radiused to reduce high stress concentrations.

Engine beds are usually integral to the stringers. Twin-engine boats, for example, usually have four stringers that also serve as engine beds. Stringers should have either a wood or a dense foam as a core. A denser wood or foam core helps to absorb and dissipate engine vibrations and resists the compression loads of engine mounting bolts better than a less-dense foam core. If the engine beds are tall, they

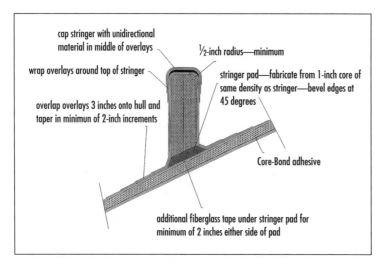

cap stringer with unidirectional material in middle of overlays

wrap overlays around top of stringer

overlap overlays 3 inches onto hull and taper in minimun of 2-inch increments

½-inch radius—minimum

stringer pad—fabricate from 1-inch core of same density as stringer—bevel edges at 45 degrees

Core-Bond adhesive

additional fiberglass tape under stringer pad for minimum of 2 inches either side of pad

A typical stringer done well, with mitered inside corners that distribute the stresses over a greater area. The unidirectional fiberglass used on top of the stringer runs in the direction of the stringer, and efficiently absorbs tension and compression loads caused by the hull hogging and sagging or just resisting local loading from wave impact in a seaway. This foam-cored stringer is strong, stiff, lightweight, and rot resistant. The foam pad between it and the hull skin (essential with a wood-cored stringer) spreads out wave impact loads.

ATC CHEMICAL

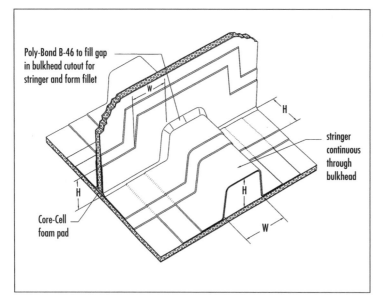

Poly-Bond B-46 to fill gap in bulkhead cutout for stringer and form fillet

W

H

stringer continuous through bulkhead

H

H

Core-Cell foam pad

W

The way a hull should look with the continuous stringer passing through a slotted bulkhead. Note the foam pad landing between the bulkhead and the hull skin, the overlapping tabbing securing the bulkhead, and the radiused inside and outside corners.

ATC CHEMICAL

should be supported by gussets or knees to prevent racking. The engine beds must be strong enough to support the engines' weight and thrust and also rigid enough to prevent shaft movement, which could damage the drivetrain.

Bottom structural members, such as stringers, should be continuous in order to take advantage of their beam effect. If short stringer sections are butted against bulkheads rather than running continuously from bow to stern, the hull skin could be subject to greater flexing at the bulkheads, eventually leading to skin failure due to fatigue. Failing continuous runs, effective connections at the ends of short stringer sections and additional transverse frames can mitigate the hull-skin flexing problem. The worst case is an egg-crate plywood network of fiberglass-encapsulated stringers and frames without continuity in either direction.

Securing Bulkheads and Stringers

Since a hull skin is relatively thin and subject to severe wave impact loads at high speed, it's important to avoid hard spots where bulkheads and stringers support the hull bottom. Plywood bulkheads should never actually come into contact with the skin; rather, the bulkhead is held a small standoff distance away from the hull skin and tabbed in place with fiberglass. Many good builders install a "landing strip" of foam or endgrain balsa along the hull around the bulkhead's perimeter, and ra-

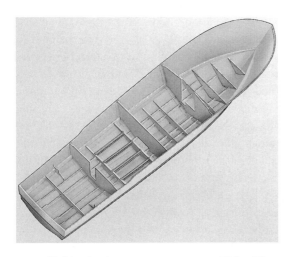

A typical bulkhead and stringer arrangement on a 72-foot Viking convertible. The steel engine beds are supported by low, intermediate bulkheads inside the engine room's main structural bulkheads.   VIKING YACHTS

A Tiara 50 express hull with stringers installed *(top)*. This is one of the most advanced production hulls being built in the United States, with an all-epoxy laminate postcured in an oven. This results in a very strong, but lightweight yacht that's ruggedly bonded together and impervious to osmosis. Bulkheads are then positioned *(bottom)*. The metal fixture provides very accurate placement, and the bulkheads are tabbed in place to the hull.   TIARA

dius all inside corners. The bulkhead tabbing (see below) then covers the landing strip where it makes the turn from bulkhead to hull skin. This distributes the bulkhead-induced stresses much more evenly along the hull skin.

Wherever a bulkhead meets the fiberglass hull, a sharp corner is created. To secure the bulkhead, multiple layers of fiberglass reinforcement called *tabbing* are wet out and bonded both to the bulkhead and to the hull surface, over the seam. (The same technique can be used for stringers or anywhere else members need to be securely bonded at similar angles.) The corners should be radiused to spread out loads and to ensure that the fiberglass reinforcement can lay down without voids. Some builders use angled cant strips of wood ripped at a 45-degree angle, sandwiched in fiberglass and pushed into the inside corners, ensuring a more gradual transition from the bulkhead to the hull. Others use a putty to create a radius (called a *fillet*) at inside corners. When applied at the right radius, tests show that this results in a stronger joint than the cant strips. A foam or balsa landing strip accomplishes the same end while relieving the hard spot under the bulkhead edge.

Tabbing is typically cut from a roll of biaxial fiberglass in strips 4 to 8 inches wide. Opinions differ as to which orientation is best in the fiberglass. Although some prefer 0:90, 45:45 knits will more easily conform to small radii, and both plies contribute strength to the tabbing. In any event, either reinforcement orientation works well enough if secondary bonding preparations to the cured fiberglass surfaces are done properly so good adhesion is assured.

If a plywood bulkhead is to be tabbed to a fiberglass hull, the plywood should be coated with resin, which is then allowed to cure, at least partially, before the tabbing is applied. This ensures that the plywood doesn't wick the resin out of the tabbing as it cures. It is also important that the edges of the successive layers of tabbing don't terminate along the same edge, or a hard spot susceptible to delamination will result. The edges of the successive layers of tabbing should be staggered by one of a variety of methods to produce a tapered edge. In fact, *peel* is the most ready failure mode in a fiberglass laminate, and it's best prevented by eliminating reinforcement-edge hard spots, using higher-elongation resins (like vinylester), and by proper surface preparation, including liberal grinding of the surface to be bonded to.

Taking the time to do it right prevents the hull skin from being fatigued over millions of impact cycles by spreading impact loads more evenly and gradually over a wider area. This can be easily checked during a boat inspection with a little time crawling around in the bilges. Most importantly, if you find tabbing that, due to the absence of cant strips or fillets, actually buckles, or tucks, under the gap between the bulkhead and the hull, expect it to fail sooner rather than later. Find another boat.

Molded Bottom Grids

Some builders mold one-piece, bow-to-stern bottom-support grids that include the stringers, transverse frames, and bulkhead landings. The grid is then placed into the hull and bonded in place with adhesive or fiberglass tabbing. A bottom grid, or grillage, is usually the most complex and difficult-to-build part found in a boat, so it's expensive to produce. You don't necessarily save weight, and the builder probably doesn't save money, but what you gain, besides a very strong bottom, is a uniform and consistent foundation on which to support the engines and accommodations. And builders love consistency, since it speeds up production.

These grids are usually bonded by applying an adhesive to the bottom flanges of the structure

Edgewater Powerboats' high-strength hull grid system includes a one-piece Permagrid part bonded to the hull and deck liner. It is bonded to the hull while it is still in the mold. In the bottom photo, the Permagrid has been bonded to the hull and is having foam injected in any remaining voids. The deck liner will then be bonded directly to the top of the Permagrid without relying on the low-density foam structurally.   EDGEWATER

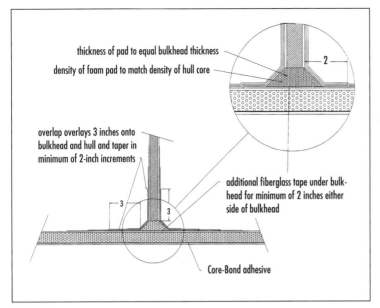

thickness of pad to equal bulkhead thickness

density of foam pad to match density of hull core

2

overlap overlays 3 inches onto bulkhead and hull and taper in minimum of 2-inch increments

3

3

additional fiberglass tape under bulkhead for minimum of 2 inches either side of bulkhead

Core-Bond adhesive

One good way to bond a bulkhead to a hull. The beveled landing strip or pad of foam serves as a hull-skin cushion. Note how the fiberglass tabbing edges are staggered to prevent stress concentration and weak spots. ATC CHEMICAL

and then pressing the whole assembly against the hull interior. Weight, or pressure, is applied until the adhesive cures. The potential downside is that, with some grids, the interior flanges can't be seen, so the builder is relying on a consistent fit between grid and hull to ensure a solid bond. Depending on their design, other grids are suspended an inch or so above the hull in a jig and tabbed in place with fiberglass rather than relying on an adhesive.

A preformed structural shape called Prisma is produced by Compsys, Inc., to be used as stock for prefabricated stringer and bulkhead landing systems of various shapes and sizes. They come ready to install with dry reinforcement material attached to the urethane foam-cored stringer. There's enough reinforcement extending beyond the stringer for tabbing them to the hull. The manufacturer claims time is saved in installation and that parts are more consistent and stronger, which is certainly plausible. Some boatbuilders using SCRIMP use these stringers and bulkhead landings,

eliminating secondary bonds in these crucial structural components. With their foam cores, these stringer and bulkhead landing systems are efficient from an engineering perspective, unlike a lot of plywood-cored structures, since the foam serves mostly as a form and a sandwich core, and the fiberglass is allowed to do the structural work.

Stick–Built Supports

Another way to support a fiberglass boat's bottom is by "stick building" foam or wood stringer and transverse frame cores, bonding them in position, and then encapsulating them in fiberglass. Foam-cored stringers and other support members are lighter than wood, and it's mostly the fiberglass that does the structural work anyway, so this makes good engineering sense for many applications.

A foam-cored, high-hat stringer (a tall stringer with a trapezoidal cross section) might have a thick

This large Grady-White gets lightweight Prisma stringers, which are preformed with a foam core and dry fiberglass reinforcement casing, including tabbing, ready to be wet out. Prisma components are also commonly used in SCRIMP and other resin infusion methods, since they lend themselves to being wet out in one shot along with the hull's primary laminate. GRADY-WHITE

Construction with Fiberglass and Cold-Molded Wood

layer of unidirectional fiberglass along the top to absorb tension and compression loads. This box-beam structure works like an I-beam, with the top of the high-hat and the bottom of the boat serving as the I-beam's flanges and doing the brunt of the structural work. Since the foam core is essentially a male mold on which to lay up the load-bearing fiberglass, eliminating wood is a great way to gain strength and stiffness at moderate weight.

Even though foam-cored stringers save weight, using a wood core where the stringers do double-duty as engine beds is often a good idea and a common practice among boatbuilders. The added mass of the wood absorbs and attenuates engine vibrations before they reach the rest of the boat. Wood also resists the compression loads of engine mounting bolts better than medium-density foam could, though high-density foam could also be used here.

As mentioned, stringers (most boats have four) should be continuous from bow to stern, with slots cut out of the bulkheads to receive them. This continuous-stringer method provides maximum load distribution and helps prevent hull skin flexure where stringers meet bulkheads. Noncontinuous stringers are much weaker in way of their bulkhead joints than continuous stringers, and the bottom skin is consequently subject to greater stress and fatigue.

Limber Holes

Limber holes in stringers allow water to drain to the lowest part of the bilge where it's pumped overboard. How the limber holes are installed is important not only to ensure complete drainage but to ensure that water is unable to penetrate into the stringer core, whether it's wood or structural foam. In fact, the special bugaboo of wood-cored stringers, bulkheads, and transoms is the ingress of water and consequent rot.

If the tabbing joining the wood to the hull skin is continuous, and limber holes are thoroughly sealed against moisture penetration, then properly installed wood cores will last indefinitely. But that's a big "if," since water is tenacious when it comes to finding a way through cracks, screw and bolt holes, and other unnoticed openings. Pressure-treated plywood is becoming more widely used for this reason, as the wood itself is rot resistant. Even if the wood doesn't rot, though, water migrating into the fiberglass-wood interface can eventually delaminate the bond between the two.

Completely encapsulated foam-cored stringers, bulkheads, and high-density-foam-cored transoms are catching on for marketing as well as engineering reasons. But foam cores also have to be waterproofed, since water can soak into exposed, lower-density closed-cell foam given enough time.

Wood's bad rap is almost wholly due to shoddy quality control during construction or to inept attempts to seal water out. Some builders will drill a hole through a stringer and just paint the raw exposed wood with gelcoat or resin. This is a completely ineffective way to get the job done, since wood contracts and expands depending on ambient moisture content, even if it's completely encapsulated in fiberglass. Remember that fiberglass is porous at the molecular level. Once the wood changes dimension, even slightly, the less flexible gelcoat or resin cracks and allows water to enter. PVC pipes or half-rounds can be used to line limber holes. Polyurethane adhesives like 3M's 5200 adhere very well to PVC, but fiberglass doesn't, so glassing them in isn't the best solution.

A *good* way to get the job done is by cutting out the limber holes before the wood or foam part is installed in the boat, replacing the excised material with fiberglass, then fiberglass tabbing the stringer into position in the hull. This way, when the limber holes are cut, they're cut through solid fiberglass. Fiberglass tubes can also be used to line limber holes and then be sealed with the fiberglass tabbing.

Plywood

Plywood has been used as structural material in fiberglass boats for a long time. To form the core of stringers and egg-crate bottom support networks, plywood can be assembled and suspended from a jig while it is tabbed in place. The jig is removed after the tabbing cures, and the plywood is then completely encapsulated in fiberglass. In this case, the plywood is the primary structural material, with the fiberglass reinforcement serving primarily to bond the plywood to the hull and to seal the wood against moisture and rot. The inside corners where the plywood meets the hull, and outside corners along the tops of the stringers, must be radiused so the reinforcements can drape tight against the wood without air voids forming during the curing process.

Some boatbuilders use foam to core hull stringers except around the engines, where the added mass of plywood (or high-density foam) does a better job of absorbing engine vibrations and engine mounting bolt compression and shear loads. Even when fully encapsulated in fiberglass, the moisture content of the wood will change depending on the boat's environment, whether it's in the water or in dry storage on land. Though dimensionally stable, especially when compared with conventional timber, plywood will change thickness as its moisture content varies, making the fiberglass susceptible to cracking and moisture penetration. And plywood isn't the easiest surface to get polyester resin to stick to in the first place.

Plywood-cored transoms have been known to last decades when properly installed. They're probably better known for failing, though, sooner rather than later, due to water getting in through stern-drive and bolt openings. A cottage industry has grown around the need for new transoms in otherwise sound boats. This helps explain the increasing dominance of high-density foam core and other synthetic transoms.

Plywood is also commonly used to replace foam and end-grain balsa cores in way of bolt penetrations in decks, since the plywood is much more dense and therefore resistant to bolt compression loads. As discussed, since marine plywood will rot when exposed to moisture, penetrations must be completely sealed against leaking.

Component Installation

Once a hull structure is complete, the builder installs the propulsion and steering systems, generators, mechanical systems, fuel tanks, rough wiring and plumbing, cabin and furniture subassemblies, appliances and other large components, and the deck over the engine room. Better builders tab the subassemblies—such as enclosed heads, dinettes, and staterooms—to the hull and cabin sole; this fixes these large components securely, and can even add a bit of strength to the hull. Next comes the deck and superstructure, usually in one piece, molded just in time for installation as soon as the hull is ready.

Hull-to-Deck Joint

One critical area to ask about when shopping for a boat is how the hull-to-deck joint is fastened together. When a boat runs through a rough sea, the hull and deck are constantly doing their best to part company. They work hard at it. Viewed from a macro level, the boat's uppermost deck and hull bottom act as flanges of an I-beam, and the hull-to-deck joint has to be able to absorb significant shear stresses in a seaway as a result. So it's important that the hull and deck are firmly held together, and that the joint doesn't ever develop leaks.

The most common hull-to-deck joint is the shoebox type, which, you guessed it, looks like a lid covering a shoebox. Builders typically use a bonding putty or run a thick bead of death-grip adhesive—such as 3M's polyurethane 5200, methacrylate (Plexus), or epoxy—along the top edge of the hull (the gunwale) and also along the inside of the deck lip. It's important that the adhesive be applied liberally, since the mating surfaces might well have irregularities, so that the flanges actually make continuous contact evenly. The adhesive also acts as a sealant to keep the inside of the boat dry. A flanged joint, consisting of two flat surfaces, improves the chances of the adhesives making complete contact through the length of the joint.

Once the adhesive is applied, the deck is low-

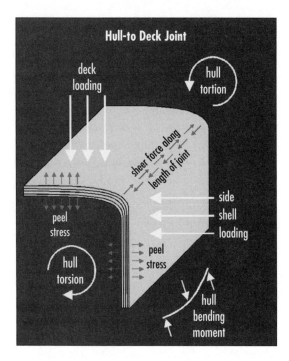

Hull-to Deck Joint

deck loading

hull tortion

sheer force along length of joint

side shell loading

peel stress

peel stress

hull torsion

hull bending moment

The significant stresses to which a hull-to-deck joint are subject.

ERIC GREENE

ered to mate with the hull. The next step, commonly, is to fasten self-tapping screws every 6 to 8 inches all around the boat. At this point the screws are clamping the adhesive between the two fiberglass parts to ensure it sets up with a good bond. Once the adhesive sets up, the screws become largely superfluous. That's because the structural adhesives should adhere so well that the fiberglass itself may well shred into little pieces before the adhesive lets go. In the absence of a significant backing pad for the screws to tap into, self-tapping screws in fiberglass can't be counted on to hold their grip for very long, so using such tenacious adhesives is a good thing.

For long-term security, many good builders also fiberglass the hull-to-deck joint from the inside, which further strengthens this critical area. Some builders add a row of closely spaced bolts, which, unlike self-tapping screws, should stay locked in position for the life of the boat. The next step is to fasten the rubrail in place, and this in-

volves yet another row of screws, or better yet, through-bolts. With the rubrail sealed with a silicone or similar sealant, the job is done. Perhaps the most practical rubrails are made of heavy PVC, which is strong and resilient and doesn't require maintenance. Stainless rounded stock, often used over wood rubrails, looks great, but it's hard to straighten out after an impact. Figure that a ding means replacement may be called for.

Flotation Foam

Urethane and polyurethane foams are commonly used in nonstructural small craft applications for positive flotation, either poured or blown in place or as blocks. Boats under 20 feet long are required by the coast guard to float level when swamped, although there is no analogous criterion for remaining afloat after a hull rupture. These foams have low strength and are not generally considered structural materials, although Boston Whaler, for one, relies on relatively low-density urethane foam to bond its hulls and deck liners together. Whaler also adds solid fiberglass shear-stress-absorbing supports between hull and liner to back up the foam. Whether a hull will stay afloat when ruptured depends on the weight of the boat and the buoyancy provided by the foam and any intact compartments.

Besides contributing positive flotation to a hull and a sense of security to its owner, poured or blown-in foam greatly reduces wave-slapping noises

Here's one of those great Boston Whaler marketing shots—a boat that's cut in two but keeps on truckin'. The two skins (hull, and deck liner) are laid up in steel molds, clamped together, and foam is injected under pressure. What you give up in storage space you gain in peace of mind in your unsinkable Whaler. BOSTON WHALER

against the hull and adds weight, which—to a point—tends to improve ride quality in a chop. When foam expands inside closed cavities, like those created by the hull and deck of a boat, significant pressure is applied as the foam begins to cure. This pressure also makes the deck feel stiffer underfoot and adds to the hull's impact resistance. In general, a boat should be designed without the stiffening effect of foam calculated in. Panels should be stiff and strong enough without the foam. (The exception is Boston Whaler, which has been using low-density foam for structural purposes for decades.)

If urethane foam is used, it must be kept dry. Urethane foam is referred to as *closed-cell*, but that doesn't mean that the foam won't absorb water. If foam is exposed to water for an extended period, it will become waterlogged—water will permeate right through all those little closed cells. The results of waterlogged foam can range from lost buoyancy and a gain of thousands of pounds in water weight, to a loss of structural integrity. Water-soaked foam can also cause osmotic blistering in the hull and the liner, from the inside, and well above the waterline. Leaking fuel tanks bedded in foam can also saturate the surrounding foam with gasoline, turning it into a thick, sticky paste that's a huge production to remove (see below). Unfortunately, the only fully effective cure for waterlogged foam is to remove it, reapply fresh foam, and seal up the original leaks.

As with soaked end-grain balsa core, the cause of waterlogged foam is usually holes drilled in the boat after delivery to its owner. In my experience, for instance, Boston Whaler dealers screw down a battery tray to the cockpit deck aft on their smaller, open-deck models, and if the screws aren't well bedded, the foam core in this area can gradually get soaked with water. Improperly bedded holes drilled in the decks and coamings for canvas side curtain snaps are a common water source affecting even the best boats. In addition to sealing off water entry points above, the builder should provide plenty of drainage below. Remember that limber holes used to drain foam-filled compartments can work both ways, and a high bilge water level backflooding through limber holes into a foam-filled compartment over a period of time can cause saturation. If the edge of the poured foam is trimmed before the compartment is sealed, a face of open cells results, making the foam act like a sponge. Sealing the foam edges with thickened epoxy (polyester and vinylester resins will eat the foam) is one method of reducing water penetration. Some builders have tried coating exposed foam with latex house paint that serves to seal the foam surface while adding a measure of fire resistance (urethane foam is highly flammable and releases toxic gases when burning). C-Hawk, a North Carolina builder of rugged little fishing boats, has a novel solution: using planks of foam that, if water is poured on them, shed it readily into the bilge.

Fuel Tanks

Most tanks are made of aluminum, fiberglass, or plastic, with aluminum most prevalent. For reasons that will become clear, my preference is for plastic fuel tanks when the desired capacity is under about 100 gallons per tank. Water and holding tank materials and installation are less critical from a safety perspective. (Clean-tasting water is obviously important to the boatowner, as is keeping sewage contained in its proper place until discharge. Fiberglass and plastic tanks are well suited to these purposes.)

Aluminum fuel tanks dominate in the boatbuilding industry because they're relatively inexpensive, boatbuilders are familiar with them, and they're easy to buy in a wide range of shapes and sizes. But aluminum tanks are also susceptible to corrosion resulting from improper installation, with moisture getting trapped inside or outside the walls of the tank.

Aluminum tanks are better off left unpainted, since the metal naturally forms a protective oxide coating when it's left exposed to the air. This coating is not allowed to form when the tank is painted. Aluminum fuel tanks are usually built of 5052-grade plate in either 0.09- or 0.125-inch thickness; the coast guard holds that tanks made from mater-

Fire Resistance

We considered the relative fire resistances of steel, aluminum, and fiberglass in chapter 2, but let's take a look at what happens when fiberglass boats, with their varying construction methods and materials, burn.

Yachts over 500 net tons or 50 meters that carry more than twelve passengers and are built to the standards of the American Bureau of Shipping (ABS), the Maritime and Coast Guard Agency of Great Britain (MCA), and comparable regulatory bodies are required to meet *structural* fire protection standards. Structural standards ensure that the choice of building materials and the vessel's design are taken into consideration when deciding how resistant to fire a vessel must be for its intended service. A cruise ship that accommodates five hundred overnight passengers on offshore passages logically warrants a higher standard than an inshore, unoccupied barge, for instance. While yachts carrying fewer than twelve passengers, for instance, don't have to meet these regulations, those that do may be able to command a higher resale value, depending on the market. And the owner has the added peace of mind.

An MCA-classified yacht under 164 feet (50 m) would have gas-tight engine rooms designed to contain fire and smoke during a 60-minute burn test. (To pass a burn test, the structure must remain intact after being subject to high temperature for an hour.) Engine room ventilation and fuel supply lines must have remote shutdown capability. Accommodations spaces must have two means of escape. Fire detection and alarm systems are required in the machinery and galley spaces. U.S. Coast Guard Subchapter T regulations require the use of fire-retardant resins in certain passenger-carrying vessels.

The vast majority of recreational craft are not subject to any of these regulations, however; they only have to meet minimal coast guard standards and American Boat and Yacht Council (ABYC) recommendations regarding fire extinguishers, flammable gas tank shutoff valves, cooking stove design, smoke stacks, and so on. That's apparently because most unregulated pleasure boats are small, so fires are easier to detect and escape. Meeting the higher standards of rules-built vessels would also add to the builders' cost to manufacture boats. Few builders of fiberglass pleasure boats choose construction materials with fire resistance in mind. Unlike commercial vessels with their trained crews, most recreational craft are operated by people who have no knowledge or experience of firefighting. This fact should argue for a higher structural fire-resistant standard, and for better firefighting equipment standards, than are currently applied. This is especially true on fiberglass boats powered by gasoline. (Diesel fuel, of course, is inherently safer than gasoline, which gives off highly explosive vapors.)

The most fire-prone areas on a vessel are the machinery compartment (engine room) and galley area. The key points are: to have automatic fire suppression systems that work as intended; and to keep the fire contained. Even if a fire is contained, if it is not put out in short order, temperatures can quickly reach the point at which surrounding decks and bulkheads will collapse.

Since it's the resin that burns in a fiberglass composite, not the fiberglass reinforcement itself, the choice of laminating resin has more bearing on a fiberglass structure's ability to withstand the intense heat of a fire. The fiberglass reinforcement actually

ial of these thicknesses will last an average of 6.5 and 17.4 years, respectively, but these numbers vary widely in the real world. To put the issue into perspective, the coast guard requires inspected passenger-carrying vessels built under Subchapter T regulations to have their tanks built of at least 0.25-inch aluminum, which is twice the thickness used in most pleasure boats today.

Whatever the actual figure for a given boat, the point to keep in mind is that few aluminum tanks can be expected to last the life of the boat. A means for their removal must be provided, or the owner will be in for a costly fuel tank replacement process. Some builders of small craft provide a removal hatch directly above the fuel tank, and they don't foam the tanks in place. These hatches are bolted around their perimeter and caulked with a nonadhesive sealant. A less expensive approach is to mark a cutout perimeter with a nonskid-free two-inch-wide swath around the tank. This makes it easier to cut out the right section of deck, replace the tank, and glass the deck back in place with a neat cosmetic finish.

Aluminum tanks weigh about a third as much

acts as a thermal insulator during a fire, unless we're dealing with thermoplastics, which can actually accelerate a fire's spread. Polyester resin is more flammable than vinylester or epoxy, but in the presence of an external fuel source such as gasoline or even diesel fuel in the bilge, the difference becomes academic. Very few builders use flame-retardant additives in their resins. Such additives add cost and can also degrade the strength and bonding properties of the resin, and can actually increase smoke production during a blaze. Core materials will generally impede the spread of fire, if only because they act as insulation to delay the time at which the far-side sandwich skin also heats up, softens, and fails structurally. Foam softens before balsa burns, but neither will burn until the fiberglass skin is burned through.

The best thermal protection comes in the form of insulation batts, including mineral wool and refractory materials, which are mechanically fastened to surrounding bulkheads and decks. These, in conjunction with special thermal-insulating treatments, can be designed to achieve a 60-minute fire rating in a fiberglass vessel. Other precautions against fire that will make any pleasure boat safer include: carrying plenty of working fire extinguishers; installing a fixed fire suppression system that shuts off ventilation and shuts down machinery before discharging; using high-pressure fuel lines instead of rubber hoses with hose clamps; holding regular fire drills; making sure engine room bulkheads are watertight so that smoke cannot spread and fire will spread to adjacent compartments less readily; and using the bilge blower every time before starting a gasoline engine.

as those of steel, are 20 to 30 percent lighter than fiberglass, and are reasonably priced. When properly installed, they will last many years. However, many aluminum tanks are installed in a way that guarantees they'll corrode through in just a few years. When water is allowed to stand against the aluminum, it deoxygenates and corrosion inexorably sets in. The tank must be able to breathe, with ample air circulation provided, and dry off if wetted. Tanks usually corrode from the outside, although it is possible for a tank to corrode from within (see below).

According to the coast guard and the ABYC, any material that comes into contact with an aluminum tank must be nonabsorbing. Neoprene strips, which won't collect moisture and which also provide chafing resistance, are commonly used in lieu of carpet or wood strips under aluminum tanks both to cushion them and to admit air between the tank and the underlying structure. Tanks should be mounted so they don't flex as a boat moves through rough water. Mounting tabs or brackets can be welded to the tank, preventing water from collecting along the tank bottom and preventing chafing.

The life of an aluminum tank is often directly proportional to its thickness, so the thicker the better. High-quality aluminum fuel tanks start at 0.125-inch thickness, but many used in small boats are only 0.09 inch thick, since the thinner plate is cheaper for the builder. One high-quality aluminum boatbuilder, which builds aluminum components, including fuel tanks, as a sideline, is Winninghoff Boats of Rowley, Massachusetts. This company starts with 0.125-inch-thick stock on smaller tanks of up to 50 gallons, and increases to 0.16-inch plate for tanks in the 75- to 125-gallon range and 0.19 inch for larger tanks. (As mentioned, passenger-carrying vessels built to the USCG's Subchapter T regulations have tanks that are at least 0.25 inch thick.) Tanks should also be baffled at least every 30 inches.

When a new tank is installed in an older boat, and the capacity is changed, make sure you know what the effect on LCG and the static trim angle will be before proceeding. It could be that the tank will have to be relocated to avoid interfering with proper static and dynamic trim angles. On the other hand, if the original tank was improperly located, you may have a chance to fix the problem.

Aluminum tanks that are foamed in place have a couple of strikes against them from the outset. The coast guard requires that the bond between the foam and the tank be stronger than the foam itself. This is difficult to achieve in practice, and the result is that moisture can easily get trapped between the foam and the tank. The water is unable to drain off when the foam completely fills the fuel tank space, preventing the tank from drying. That's when corrosion starts, from the outside, and it's only a matter of time before the tank corrodes through and starts to leak.

Fuel tanks that are supported, as well as surrounded, by foam are especially vulnerable. The foam used to bed tanks can also compress and wear away over time, exposing the bare tank bottom to a hard fiberglass foundation that will probably eventually rub a hole in the tank. Foamed-in fuel tanks are also impossible to inspect, so you don't know what shape the tank is in short of removing it—and removing a foamed-in tank is a bear. If tanks are foamed in, the top of the tank should be higher than the surrounding foam so water is able to drain off the tank and, hopefully, into the bilge. Although welds are an aluminum fuel tanks' weak spots structurally, they rarely fail and cause leaks.

Some manufacturers mount the fuel tank on a flat shelf or platform, and water collects on the platform. Without proper drainage, the water stands against the bottom of the tank and you can bet corrosion will kick in.

Although corrosion from the outside is more common, if gasoline is allowed to stand for a long time while the boat is in storage, and water in the fuel settles to the bottom of the tank, then the tank can corrode from the inside, a problem that alcohol additives in the fuel can make worse. The newer reformulated oxygenated gasolines, especially those modified with ethanol, also increase the rate of corrosion in aluminum fuel tanks, because water precipitates out and settles to the bottom more readily.

Plastic fuel tanks, on the other hand, will never corrode, and if properly installed will last the life of the boat. Most plastic tanks are made of polyurethane or polyethylene in a seamless rotary molding process. The plastic actually absorbs minute amounts of the fuel, and the coast guard requires that the tank space be ventilated if the permeation rate is above a certain level. Plastic fuel tanks expand slightly when they are first filled with

A fiberglass fuel tank being installed in a Viking convertible. The rot- and rustproof tank, which conforms to the hull's shape, is bedded in bonding putty in the bilge and fiberglassed directly to the hull stringers. It's no lightweight, but it will last forever.

fuel, so the tank's installation must allow for this. These tanks must also be protected from chafing, but this is easily accomplished with a little forethought.

All fuel tanks have to pass the same 2½-minute fire test for permanently installed tanks without leaking, and plastic tanks do just as well as aluminum tanks. Plastic tanks in the 25- to 55-gallon range weigh about the same as their aluminum counterparts, and many shapes and sizes are available up to about 100 gallons. Larger plastic tanks can be ordered on a custom basis from companies like Kracor, Inc., of Milwaukee, Wisconsin.

Fiberglass tanks are often used in high-end yachts, and they have the advantages of being corrosion proof and, if properly built, very rugged. A fiberglass fuel tank, then, should never need to be replaced. Well-built fiberglass tanks are usually fiberglassed to the hull stringers and may sit in a bed of fiberglass putty, adding impact resistance locally to the hull bottom. Chances are that a fiberglass tank will be heavier than one made of aluminum, so the boat's speed may be slightly reduced, but the trade-off is a worthwhile one.

Wrapping Things Up

Once the hull and superstructure are permanently mated together, the rest of the components, sys-

An increasing number of builders are using frameless windows, and that's good for several reasons. Window frames are typically made of aluminum, which is a perennial source of corrosion, so eliminating them will save you a lot of aggravation. Window frames also tend to leak, so leaks become a thing of the past. Frameless windows are installed in rabbeted window openings after a strong adhesive has been applied (the rabbet is a groove cut along the window frame opening that allows the glass to sit flush with the outer fiberglass surface). Pressure is applied until the adhesive has cured. This is all very well, of course, until it comes time to replace a broken frameless window, which takes a lot of patience and time to remove. But with chemically strengthened laminated glass, a frameless window will probably never break, nor will it leak or corrode.

tems, and finishing touches are completed, including cabin liners, electrical fixtures, joinery, carpeting and exterior railings, hatches, windows, steering and engine controls, and davits. The bottom is painted, the name is painted on the transom, and the completed boat is rolled out of the final assembly building ready for its first dip into the water.

Once all the systems are checked out, the boat is launched, sea trials are conducted, and a detailed "punch" list of deficiencies needing correction before delivery is written up. The more trouble-free a boat is upon delivery, the lower the builder's warranty claims, the less the dealer has to do to fix the builder's oversights, and the happier the customer. When the process works, another boat is ready to provide many hours of enjoyment to a proud new owner.

By now you should be well on your way to being able to ask all the right questions and look in the right places to evaluate the quality of a fiberglass boat's construction. As we've seen, the methods, materials, and the level of quality control used to build your boat make all the difference in the world.

One-Off Custom Boats

Custom fiberglass boats, called *one-off* because they're one-of-a-kind, can be built by a variety of methods. Most of these involve building a temporary, upside-down male framework that defines the shape of the hull, fastening planks made of fiberglass or core materials to the frames, and laminating layers of reinforcement over the structure. The hull is then removed from the framework, turned right side up, and fiberglassed on the inside. Support structure is added to the hull, the interior finished, and machinery and other components installed. The downside of these one-off methods is the extra work that goes into building a boat from scratch. The hull has to be faired and painted, which takes many hours of painstaking and unpleasant labor. The decks, superstructure, and furniture all take longer to build and install since they are either stick-built on the spot, or molds have to be custom made for one-time use. The upside is that owners can have the exact boat they've always wanted, the boat of their dreams.

Seemann Fiberglass makes a fiberglass plank called C-Flex, consisting of fiberglass rods and fiberglass reinforcement. The rods allow the planks to assume a fair curve as they're attached to the mold framework, and the reinforcement forms the foundation of the fiberglass laminate that follows. These rods also have good rigidity and may require fewer mold frames and longitudinal supports.

Likewise, Baltek makes DuraKore planking material for one-off construction. It's composed of two layers of $\frac{1}{16}$-inch hardwood veneer glued to an end-grain balsa core that's sealed with resin to minimize resin absorption from the reinforcements. The planks are 8 feet long by 12 inches wide and are finger-jointed at their ends to make it easier to join one plank to the next. These planks can be used in one-off construction using male molds as a framework, with epoxy gap-filling adhesive used to bond the edges of the planks together. Once planking is complete, fiberglass reinforcements are added to the outside, and then the inside of the hull is fiberglassed and faired to the desired finish. DuraKore can also be used as hull stringer cores. ATC Chemical's bead-and-cove planking is also available for relatively easy one-off construction.

ATC Chemical's high-density foam-core planking system, called bead-and-cove. It's a tongue-and-groove plank arrangement in which plank edges fit together securely, making it easier to smooth the hull before fiberglassing inside and out.   ATC CHEMICAL

Cold-Molded Construction

Many high-end custom sportfishermen and other pleasure boats are made of wood encapsulated in epoxy. The wood delivers the strength, and the epoxy bonds all the wood pieces together, effectively forming a sealed, one-piece or *monocoque* hull. The process is often referred to as *cold-molded* since it's done without using heat or steam to bend the wood into shape. There are many variations on the cold-molded theme, but the usual procedure is to build a male mold consisting of station molds or frames (which define the hull's cross-sectional shapes), over which ribbands, or temporary wood straps, run fore and aft. The hull is built upside down, with the first layer of planking laid up over the ribbands or in some cases directly on the mold frames. Layers of overlapping plywood (whose width depends on the hull curvature) or wood strip

planks are bonded together with epoxy resin and then sheathed on the outside with fiberglass or other reinforcing cloth. The hull is then lifted off the mold, turned right side up, and finished off.

Wood-epoxy composite boatbuilding is a tried-and-true method of one-off custom construction. It produces a very strong, long-lasting hull of light to moderate weight that requires little maintenance. Wood has one of the highest ratios of stiffness and tensile strength to weight of any material, and the one problem that has always plagued wooden boats—rot—has been solved by epoxy resin saturation. Neither the spores that cause rot nor the water and air needed for the rot to spread can penetrate epoxy. Another problem with wooden hulls—poor abrasion resistance—is addressed by the epoxy sheathing on the outside of the hull. With a wood core, these boats are insulated naturally and don't sweat like a solid fiberglass hull. Wood boats are also quiet, with the wood acting as an acoustic insulator. The wood core (strip planks on laminated frames) also makes for high impact resistance when compared with some conventional sandwich layups.

Compared with a traditionally built wooden boat, the cold-molded process is superior for its durability, strength, low maintenance, and resistance to rot. A traditional wooden boat's planks are not bonded to each other (other than by their caulking), only to their frames. The planks, then, are on their own, structurally, in the event of impact. If the hull hits a log, the one plank impacted either has the strength to resist the impact or it doesn't; there's little load sharing with surrounding structure. The cold-molded hull is far stronger and also better able to handle the longitudinal stresses imposed by heavy seas and uneven weight distribution. This means that the wood-epoxy hull can be built lighter than a traditional wood boat for the same impact resistance and overall strength. Built to the same scantlings, or wood component size, the boat will be far stronger. Further, a traditional wooden hull is only as good as its fastenings, which can corrode, work loose, and fail over time. In a wood-epoxy hull, on the other hand, the fasten-

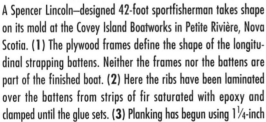

A Spencer Lincoln–designed 42-foot sportfisherman takes shape on its mold at the Covey Island Boatworks in Petite Rivière, Nova Scotia. **(1)** The plywood frames define the shape of the longitudinal strapping battens. Neither the frames nor the battens are part of the finished boat. **(2)** Here the ribs have been laminated over the battens from strips of fir saturated with epoxy and clamped until the glue sets. **(3)** Planking has begun using 1¼-inch strips ripped from clear fir 2-by-12s. **(4)** Here the planked hull has been sanded smooth and is getting its first coat of epoxy resin before the heavy, epoxy-saturated fiberglass cloth sheathing goes on. **(5)** Sheathing is complete and the frames and battens have been removed, but the hull is still upside down on the strongback. **(6)** The wood-epoxy Covey Island 42 sportfisherman is well on its way to completion.

ings are often superfluous once the epoxy has set up.

After a conventionally built wooden boat is launched, the planking below the waterline soaks up water and swells, which tightens up the seams, reducing or stopping leaking. The problem here is that the wood planking gets heavier and weaker as it absorbs water. The constant stresses and strains imposed on the hull at sea eventually loosen its fasteners, which have to do their job while holding to this weaker wood. Over time, the boat's planking starts to loosen up and the hull strength diminishes as it loses rigidity. In a wood-epoxy boat, on the other hand, the 8 to 12 percent moisture content present in the wood during construction is largely maintained by epoxy encapsulation, allowing the wood to retain its original weight and strength.

CHAPTER 7

Aluminum and Steel Construction

Everyone complains of his memory, none of his judgment.

—La Rochefoucauld

S ome of the finest yachts in the world are built of metal. Aluminum is the prime metal for yachts and small boats and has some distinct advantages over fiberglass. Steel is the only choice for large ships and many heavy-duty commercial vessels like fishing boats, tugs, and barges. But, steel also has its merits as a hull material for yachts and small craft.

A rendering of the Bruce Roberts–designed metal 16-meter (52-foot) Euro cruiser. STEVE DAVIS DRAWING, COURTESY BRUCE ROBERTS

Metal Basics

Steel weighs 490 pounds per cubic foot, costs about 35¢ a pound, and melts at 2,796°F. It has a yield strength (the force at which it starts to permanently deform or stretch) of 36,000 psi and an ultimate strength (the force required to make it separate or fracture) of 60,000 psi, so it has a relatively large "plastic" region of 24,000 psi, or 40 percent. In other words, steel is quite ductile. Its large "plastic" range means that it dents easily in relation to its ultimate strength, but this ability to stretch also allows it to absorb more impact energy before rupturing. Steel is relatively immune to fatigue resulting from the millions of stress cycles a vessel is exposed to over time. Steel welds are almost as strong as the members they join together, eliminating weak links in a steel vessel's construction. It's no secret that steel rusts when left unpainted; in fact, steel ships are built with thicker plating than a new ship actually needs, allowing for corrosion-related

strength loss over the life of the hull. Steel is very hard and therefore highly resistant to abrasion. This is an important attribute, especially for a commercial vessel that's subject to lots of abuse. Steel's hardness and abrasion resistance also make it harder to cut during the construction process.

Steel is the material of choice for the largest yachts—say, over 300 feet—and for commercial ships and small craft that are apt to take a beating. Steel has its limitations for small craft construction, however. A 35-footer is probably as small as you'll want to go with steel, but the thin steel plating (10 gauge, which is just over ⅛ inch) needed to allow such a small boat to actually float is difficult to weld without significant distortion. Thin plating also has little margin for corrosion built in, so it would have to be absolutely rustfree to last. A 45-footer, on the other hand, has enough displacement to allow heavier, and more easily welded, ³⁄₁₆-inch plate to be used. Smaller vessels have been built of steel, but they have to be squat, beamy little ducklings to float all that weight.

Depending on vessel design steel can be a great choice, especially for amateurs. It is the cheapest of all boatbuilding materials and is relatively easy to weld. For those new to welding, most high school adult education programs offer courses. Using a kit to build a steel boat is by far the best plan of attack; most useful is a kit that comes with all the pieces clearly labeled and computer cut so that all the parts fit together with precision. Steel construction is dirty work, but I haven't met many people who'd say that grinding fiberglass is a lot more fun. A steel hull is bulletproof once the boat is finally floating, and for some, that security alone justifies the effort. A steel hull is likely to win arguments with ice, logheads, or floating debris that a fiberglass hull might lose, and it will probably survive running aground on rock or coral quite nicely. This is especially true at the displacement speeds to which most steel hulls are limited. Guarding against rust through proper surface preparation, especially on the inside of the hull, is a tedious but essential step during the construction process. Many books are available to take the amateur through the building process and guide them through electrical work, joinery, insulation, mechanical installations, and other details. Steel and aluminum are sold by the pound, so estimating the cost of materials is relatively straightforward.

Derived from bauxite, aluminum is a silvery-white, ductile metal with excellent corrosion resistance. It is conductive and has thermal properties that make it a good choice for casting and welding. Aluminum has a melting point of 1,220°F. It weighs 170 pounds per cubic foot, just over a third as much as steel, and costs $1.90 per pound. Although aluminum's strength varies depending on the alloy selected, commonly used marine-grade 5083 H-32 aluminum plate has a yield strength of 34,000 psi and an ultimate strength of 45,000 psi, with a plastic region of 11,000 psi, or 25 percent. Since it is more brittle than steel, aluminum will start to yield at about the same loading as steel, but it fails before denting as deeply as steel and is more susceptible to fatigue. Aluminum welds are about 60 percent as strong as the members they join. Since aluminum welds are weak links, backing plates and longitudinal stiffeners to distribute loads beyond the welds are added to compensate. Aluminum hull plates are also butted in between, rather than at, the frames to minimize stress at these structural hard spots. Since aluminum is more susceptible to fatigue than steel, special care must be taken to increase scantlings (the dimensions of hull plating and support structures) in areas subject to high loading and vibration, such as around machinery beds.

Aluminum vessels do not need to be painted above the waterline—since a corrosion-resistant

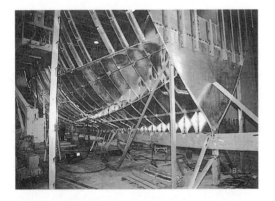

A Palmer Johnson 151 takes shape with her aluminum frames and bulkheads being put in place. PALMER JOHNSON

The framing for a Palmer Johnson 151-foot expedition yacht lends form to the hull in the early stages of construction. PALMER JOHNSON

A Palmer Johnson 151-foot aluminum expedition yacht being plated. PALMER JOHNSON

Aluminum versus Steel

An aluminum vessel's scantlings need to be about 50 percent beefier to achieve the ultimate strength of a similar vessel built of steel, but the aluminum vessel will still be about 30 percent lighter. Consequently, aluminum, which pound for pound is stronger than steel, will provide a vessel with greater cargo and fuel capacity. The aluminum vessel will require less power to go the same speed as the steel craft, consuming less fuel in the process and increasing the vessel's range.

A 151-foot Palmer Johnson aluminum yacht's lower deck, showing the hull and main deck framing. PALMER JOHNSON

layer, or film, of aluminum oxide forms naturally on the untreated surface. Although unpainted aluminum vessels are relatively low-maintenance, many owners prime and paint the gray aluminum, considering it well worth the added cost to pay for a glossy, hard-as-nails finish that looks good for years. Aluminum is also subject to crevice corrosion, so it must be painted anywhere moisture would naturally collect and stand.

Aluminum is not as abrasion resistant as steel, but lighter and tougher than fiberglass or wood. It is relatively easy to cut, even with ordinary hand tools and the right blades. Its light weight and builder-friendly qualities make this versatile metal the choice for thousands of bass boats, canoes, and other small craft every year.

Compared with an all-steel vessel, a steel-hulled yacht with an aluminum superstructure will be more stable due to its lower center of gravity, a result of less topside weight. A product called *tri-clad*, a strip of aluminum pressure-bonded to steel, is used to join the steel hull and the aluminum superstructure together.

An aluminum vessel may weigh considerably less than steel, but aluminum costs about twice as much. There are, however, trade-offs: carbide tools can be used for cutting, and welding goes quicker so labor costs will likely be less. When the added cost of a steel yacht's heavier propulsion machinery, ground tackle, bow thruster, and other equipment is considered, the scale starts to balance.

Over the years, an aluminum yacht will cost less to maintain and operate, and its resale will be higher. This is especially true if the hull is left un-

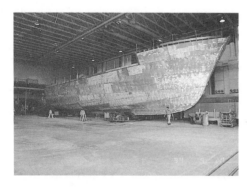

Designed to cross oceans, this 151-foot Palmer Johnson was doing just that a year or so after this photo was taken of the fully plated hull. PALMER JOHNSON

painted. The inside of an aluminum boat can be left unpainted, like the outside, so the initial cost of preparing and painting can be avoided altogether, while a steel boat has to be sandblasted, primed, and painted inside and out.

Some builders say that once you add it all up a painted aluminum boat costs slightly more to build than steel whereas an unpainted aluminum vessel may actually cost less.

As we've seen in chapter 2, many factors contribute to a vessel's seaworthiness. The most seaworthy displacement hulls are heavy, of moderate beam, and deep; steel is a great material for building such a boat. A beamy boat with lots of form stability will benefit from a heavier steel hull to dampen the roll period. Also, the heavier a boat is for a given waterplane area, the gentler the vertical accelerations and the more comfortable the motion, at least to a point.

Metal versus Fiberglass

How does metal compare with fiberglass as a boatbuilding material? Since you can't lay up metal boats in a mold as you can with fiberglass, the hull and deck will take more time and often more money to build. But the cost of a yacht's hull, decks, and superstructure are only a fraction of the total price, so the difference in the drive-away price may be less than you think. This makes metal an excellent choice for custom, one-off boats, since the cost of a highly finished female mold is prohibitive for a single fiberglass boat, whereas a one-off fiberglass boat built over a male mold requires hundreds of hours of fairing before it's ready to paint. Properly welded and framed, an aluminum or steel boat requires minimal fairing or none at all, depending on the finish quality expected.

When it comes to fire resistance, steel, which as we've noted melts at 2,800°F, is superior. Aluminum is next at 1,220°F, while fiberglass burns at only 500°F. With their higher melting temperatures, aluminum and steel vessels easily meet IMO fire containment standards, unlike fiberglass composites. And what's more conducive to peace of mind hun-

Two Megayachts

Since the same design issues apply to all yachts regardless of size, let's consider a study done by naval architect Dick Boon, who has designed Palmer Johnson megayachts, among other multimillion-dollar pleasure ships. Boon compared a 164-foot, all-aluminum displacement yacht with a vessel of the same size having a steel hull and an aluminum superstructure (for more on yachts that mix metal with other materials, see below). Built to Lloyds rules, the aluminum hull weighs 86.8 tons compared with 206 tons for steel/aluminum. The steel hull's extra weight includes the larger engines, 2,665 hp versus 2,055 hp, needed to achieve the same speed. The steel bottom plating is 8.2 mm thick versus the aluminum at 10.4 mm, and the hull sides are 6.7 mm and 8.4 mm, respectively. When all is said and done, the strongly built aluminum version weighs 450 tons versus 584 tons for its steel-aluminum counterpart, a 23 percent weight savings, and draws 6 inches less water.

At hull speed (16.35 knots for both), the all-aluminum version has a range of 3,773 nautical miles compared with the heavier steel-aluminum yacht's 2,973 miles, due to the latter's greater displacement, increased wetted surface and frictional resistance, and larger power plant. At 12.2 knots, the aluminum yacht will use just 500 hp and achieve a range of 8,750 miles, whereas the steel-aluminum yacht would use 585 hp and have a range of 7,700 miles; these numbers reflect the heavier vessel's 29 percent higher propulsion resistance. In reality, such a light load at these speeds would damage the engines over time unless two smaller engines per shaft and controllable pitch propellers are fitted, but these illustrations make for a fascinating comparison nonetheless.

One of Boon's 151-foot Palmer-Johnson designs uses thicker aluminum plating still, and he notes that an underwater collision that would puncture 10 mm steel would just dent the 12.7 to 15.8 mm aluminum used in the bottom of this 151-footer. A 151-foot Palmer Johnson is shown on the back cover of this book.

dreds of miles at sea than built-in, passive fire and flooding protection?

Metal boats have other advantages. You can weld a cleat, towing eye, or chock directly to the

A bulbous bow in the making on a Bruce Roberts trawler.

deck, hull, or bulwark. Hull-to-deck joints are welded together, a structural improvement over the screwed-and-bonded joints normally seen on fiberglass boats. Welded decks don't leak, and there's no hull or deck core to rot and delaminate after becoming saturated with water. Also, metal boats don't get bottom blisters. A surveyor can inspect weld integrity using ultrasound and X-rays and determine plate thickness using an audio gauge. There's little guesswork involved in determining the structural integrity of a metal yacht; what you see is what you get, unlike fiberglass composites.

Modifying metal yachts is also simple—just weld on the new part (and any necessary supports), whether it's a davit or a cockpit extension. Whereas a secondary bond on a fiberglass structure will never be as strong as the original wet-on-wet laminate, a weld is there to stay.

Aluminum yachts are also more amenable to aft–engine room designs than those made of steel—and this layout offers distinct advantages. Because an aluminum hull weighs less, the aft sections can be made a little deeper and fuller, producing enough buoyancy in the stern to support the weight of propulsion machinery. An aft engine room isolates machinery noise in the stern and frees up the midships spaces for comfortable accommodations at sea, away from the propellers, where noise and vibration are minimized and the yacht's motion in a seaway is most comfortable. Propeller shafts and exhaust pipes can be shorter, lighter, and thus less expensive. An alternate means of engine room access (and emergency egress) may

be provided through the lazarette or transom. This arrangement also allows the fuel tanks, which represent the vessel's largest variable load, to be carried over the hull's longitudinal centers of buoyancy and flotation, so that little if any trim adjustment is needed as fuel is consumed. The midships area is also the deepest portion of the hull so any fuel tankage located there contributes more stability.

To summarize, both steel and aluminum offer excellent impact resistance. They are easily repaired as compared with boats built of fiberglass or cold-molded wood. Aluminum boats can essentially last forever if properly cared for, and they don't take a lot of work to keep in good condition. Metal boats face special threats from corrosion and electrolysis (corrosion specifically caused by the interaction of dissimilar metals), but with proper maintenance these are not insurmountable problems. Regardless of the material selected, construction costs rise more or less with the cube of a vessel's displacement, while the relative costs of hull, machinery, equipment, and furnishings vary depending on the quality of the components and the level of finish selected.

Framing Methods

Metal vessels are built in a variety of ways, but they generally fit into one of three categories. Vessels built with only transverse (side to side) framing are fairly common in Europe. In this approach, only the transverse frames, or ribs, support the plating, and no longitudinal (fore and aft) frames are used. As a side note, old wooden ships and boats are transversely framed, with the planking constituting the longitudinal support.

Transverse framing in combination with longitudinal stringers is the most common modern metal construction method. Usually, the longitudinals will be half the depth of the frames but have the same thickness. In fact, the American Bureau of Shipping (ABS) requires that transverse frames be twice the depth of the cutouts that allow the longitudinals to pass through uninterrupted. Longitudinal frames effectively absorb and distribute the great tension and compression stresses to which a hull is subjected in a seaway, and they also reduce the loads on the plating welds of an aluminum boat. They may permit the use of thinner plating, thus reducing weight overall.

Hull and deck frames of an aluminum Bruce Roberts—designed yacht.   BRUCE ROBERTS

The third approach incorporates web framing with longitudinal stringers. This is a system of webs (deep transverse frames, or semibulkheads) supporting fairly beefy longitudinal stringers. In some cases the large webs alternate with smaller intermediate frames that support the longitudinal stringers. Web framing is often used on lightweight vessels, including racing sailboats.

So-called frameless boats take their shape from the plating during construction and derive much of their strength from it when the vessel is completed. But *frameless* turns out to be a relative term; there are invariably frames, but there are fewer of them. This method can work without frames if the plating is thick enough, but only at a huge weight penalty, with the added skin thickness weighing more than the framing it replaces. There are certainly legitimate ways to reduce framing, including the use of bulkheads and carefully engineered internal furnishings that become structural members. A fair hull can be welded over a temporary jig, or framework, with framing inserted after the jig is removed. This method prevents prefixed, slightly misaligned frames from distorting the fair curve of the plating, but the result is still not a frameless boat.

Whatever method of framing is used, the design usually specifies a plating thickness based on the vessel's size and intended use, and that thickness in turn guides the frame spacing. Longitudinals, if used, are sized according to the size of the vessel, their spacing, and the distance they span between frames. Then frame size is determined by vessel size, frame spacing, their spans, and their need to be at least twice the height of the stringer cutouts. When longitudinals, or stringers, are used, the transverse frames support the longitudinals, which in turn support the hull plating. In the absence of longitudinals, the framing must be spaced more closely in order to adequately support the plating. When a longitudinal is large enough to become the dominant strength member locally, such as an engine bed support, it is called a *girder*.

Unlike fiberglass boats, metal boats have a real keel for a backbone, imparting longitudinal strength and impact resistance and providing a foundation for ballast in heavy displacement yachts and a landing for frames and hull plating. The keel can also help form integral fuel, potable (drinking) water, and ballast water tanks. Bilge keels can be easily attached to metal hulls, and ballast can be added to the keel and bilge keels, further increasing the vessel's roll moment of inertia, or inertial resistant to dynamic rolling influences.

When fuel and water tanks are built in as part of the hull structure, they can create a double bottom that strengthens the hull longitudinally and locally, adds significant watertight integrity in case of a holing, makes excellent use of internal space, and lowers the center of gravity with all that liquid as low in the hull as possible. On larger yachts, manhole covers in the top of each tank section allow complete access for hull inspection, maintenance, and tank cleaning.

Hull Plating and Design

Both aluminum and steel come in flat plates, which can be bent or twisted into simple or *developable* curves (around a single axis) with relative ease. Try to bend a plate into a *compound curve* (around two axes), however, and you will find the going much harder. Grab a sheet of plywood with someone else holding the other end, and you will find that you can twist the sheet or bend it in one direction, but you can't do both. Metal boat builders are subject to these same limitations unless they employ hydraulic presses and rollers. Because of the challenges and costs of bending plates into compound curves, the hulls of most commercial vessels, and many yachts, contain only developable curves.

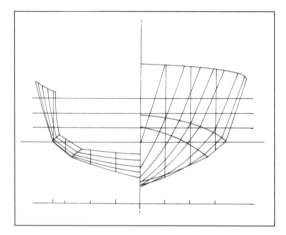

The developable curves on this multichine hull approximate a compound-curve hull while eliminating the need for heavy plate-forming presses. STEWARD, *BOATBUILDING MANUAL*

Metal hulls come in several basic designs, including single-chine, multichine, radius-chine, and round-bilge. (Remember that a vessel's chine is the angle formed by the intersection of the topside and bottom hull plates.) Single-chine hulls are the simplest and cheapest to build since they essentially involve joining cut plates to each other along the chine while bending the plating to the framing. Because of its simplicity, single-chine construction is most often chosen for lightweight aluminum plan-

ing hulls, but it also imposes the most limitations on hull form. Some appreciate the simplicity of the single-chine form, while others feel the absence of compound curves extracts too great an aesthetic price to be worth making. So what are the options?

Double-chine hulls, also drawn to plans incorporating developable curves, are one step up in complexity and expense. They involve an additional plate intersection to cut and weld on either side of the hull, providing the semblance of a round bilge. Add yet another angled strake (metal plank) at the turn of the bilge, and you've got a multichine hull. These are even more time-consuming and expensive to build, and may require a lot of fairing to achieve visually appealing curves. Some feel that multiple chines merely emphasize that a vessel is built from flat sheets of metal, but the hull shape is hydrodynamically improved.

Radius-chine hulls have rounded bilges surrounded by and joined to flat plates bent into developable curves on the hull's topsides and bottom. Imagine running a two- or three-foot-diameter pipe from stem to transom along the chine and welding the hull plating to its outside surface and you've got the idea. This combines something of the round-bilge boat's pleasing appearance with the hard-chine hull's ease and simplicity of construction. While this is not a true rounded hull, it is visually appealing and more closely resembles the real thing. Some designers even claim greater strength, lighter weight, and higher resale value. Since only the chine is rounded, or radiused, computer-aided design is needed to produce the right shapes to make all the pieces fit together while producing a fair surface. This is especially important forward, where the angle between the hull bottom and topsides gradually becomes less acute, a highly visible area where appearance is important.

Using the right equipment, designers and builders aren't limited to developable curves. Plates can be formed into compound curves by the application of pressure. Plates are often rolled or deformed into convex or concave shapes that actually stretch the metal. In this way, the hull can take on

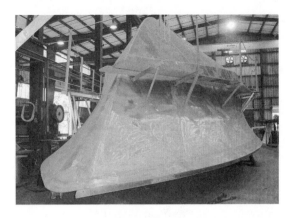

A Broward motor yacht hull, having been framed and plated upside down, is ready to be rolled upright for finishing. BROWARD MARINE

curvature that creates less hydrodynamic resistance below the waterline and is more aesthetic above. When faired, the rounded hull looks like it might have come out of a fiberglass mold. It takes a lot of pressure to distort heavy steel or aluminum plates, and it takes a lot of skill to get it just right, but fortunately for the builder, even a rounded metal hull is mostly made up of developable areas.

Rounded metal hulls are more costly, but for many, the possibilities of real bow flare, tumblehome, and canoe and fantail sterns are well worth it. In addition to the obvious aesthetic advantages, this ability to shape the metal offers a seaworthiness payoff as well, creating a well-balanced, double-ended displacement hull with minimal drag aft and good following-sea characteristics.

In the absence of rollers and presses, a curved steel or aluminum hull can be built by running narrow metal plates, perhaps one to two feet in width (depending on hull size), along the length of the hull. The plating can also run diagonally to more readily adapt to a hull's three-dimensional curvature. Additionally, a builder might press and offset one edge of a sheet inward and lap the next plate over it much like a lapstrake wooden boat. This also adds stiffness and strength longitudinally, since the plate is twice as thick at the overlap.

Just as with fiberglass boatbuilding, there are plenty of strongly held opinions out there about these different metal boat designs and construction methods. Some designers favor a single chine and put the savings into a longer, roomier, more easily driven hull. A longer single-chine hull will have higher hull and cruising speeds and achieve the same speed with less power than a shorter rounded hull. Any measurable loss of propulsion efficiency caused by the hard chine's slightly greater drag will be more than made up for by simply building it longer.

While aluminum boats used to be limited, in practice, to single- or multiple-chine designs, CAD-CAM has made round-bilge aluminum hulls more feasible. With a computer figuring out the best plate shapes, life gets a lot easier for the builder. In general, CAD-CAM has greatly increased the speed and accuracy of cutting all the parts needed to build a boat. Cutting metal parts with computer-controlled equipment can now shave the hours needed to complete a hull in half. The cutting goes faster, the more precisely cut parts go together quicker, and the resultant plating surfaces are smoother and require less fairing. And once the computer files are saved in the computer, the same boat, or, say, a stretched version of it, can be built over and over with the same program.

The Challenges of Metal Boats

Coating Systems

Epoxy paint systems are preferred to prevent corrosion in metal boats, with six or more coats of primer and topcoats applied to build up a durable finish. The final coats are often a tough polyurethane paint that holds its luster for years. The metal is first cleaned with a solvent to remove oil and other contaminants from the surface. Steel vessels should be sandblasted to provide good adhesion for the first coat of primer, which is typically applied shortly after blasting. Plates are often ordered preprimed from the supplier to minimize surface preparation. Aluminum calls for gentler sandblasting in preparation for the primer coat, since the metal is much softer than steel. As mentioned, aluminum surfaces don't need to be coated for other than aesthetic reasons, notable exceptions including below-the-waterline surfaces of boats left in the water. Crevices should be filled in or faired where attachments have been welded on to prevent standing water from leading to crevice corrosion.

For ultimate protection against corrosion, steel hulls can be flame sprayed with molten aluminum or zinc as long as the surface is not subsequently abraded through to the steel. After a thorough "white metal" sandblasting, molten aluminum-zinc or aluminum is sprayed on the steel surfaces. This process seals the steel against moisture and oxygen penetration and is followed by an elaborate epoxy paint process. Regardless of the finish, it is essential that the integrity of the paint system be maintained.

Rust inside a steel hull is more of a concern than rust on the outside surfaces. There are so many hidden nooks and crannies where water can collect and accelerate corrosion. It's very important that the bilges be accessible for routine maintenance over the years. And of course, when steel starts to rust, it's obvious. Wood and fiberglass boats might look great, but have real rot or delamination problems lurking below the surface.

After primer coats are applied, two-part fillers are used to fill in the valleys to create a mirror-smooth finish above the waterline. The fairer the plates are to start with, the less filler (and extra weight) is needed to produce a smooth surface. That's where CAD-CAM technology can help, along with highly trained welders who know how to minimize plate distortion. A final coat of epoxy primer goes over the filler, followed by several polyurethane topcoats. Below the waterline, the builder is more concerned with sealing the metal against seawater than achieving an absolutely fair surface. Several barrier coats are applied, followed by primer coats and then topcoats of antifouling paint. Most builders stay away from copper-based antifouling paints, while some don't hesitate to use it on the premise that the barrier coat remains intact.

Corrosion

Corrosion, of course, is the archenemy of metal. Introduce a metal surface to an *electrolyte* through which ions can flow, and some degree of corrosion will result. (Corrosion is often confused with electrolysis, but to be strictly accurate the latter is what happens to the electrolyte, not to the metals involved.) Atmospheric moisture is itself an electrolyte, as any child who has lost a bicycle to rust can understand, but seawater is a far more powerful one, awash with loose ions to carry electrical currents. Expose a single pure or alloyed metal to an electrolyte and you get *electrochemical corrosion*, which proceeds extremely slowly. But the flow of electrons, or electrical current, that occurs when two dissimilar metals that are connected metallically—either by direct contact or by a conductor—are immersed in the same electrolyte is more problematic. Once this interaction is established, one of the metals—acting as the *anode*—will lose ions and corrode at an accelerated rate, while the other metal (the more "noble" in the galvanic series) will be unharmed. *Galvanic corrosion*, as it is known, can be combated effectively by the use of *sacrificial anodes*, which are usually made of zinc. Zinc falls at the very bottom of the galvanic series, so when a zinc anode, known simply as a *zinc*, is connected to another metal part, the zinc will always be the primary target for galvanic corrosion, leaving the other metal unharmed until the zinc is consumed.

If you introduce a stray electrical current or two from other sources into the electrolyte—say from an improperly grounded appliance on a boat, or abraded wiring insulation in bilge water, or a busy marina—you have the potential for *stray-current* or *electrolytic corrosion*, which can proceed hundreds of times as fast as galvanic corrosion.

Electrolysis is always a concern on boats, but it is an especially acute problem on metal boats. Builders strive to isolate every dissimilar metal fitting using plastic bushings and pads, thus preventing metal-to-metal contact. On a metal hull, sacrificial zincs should be placed at intervals from bow to stern to protect the bottom and running gear, and must be inspected regularly. Galvanic activity picks up significantly if bare metal is exposed to the water, so it's important to keep the bottom paint and underlying primer in sound condition. Aluminum is at the bottom of the galvanic-action food chain (only zinc and magnesium are lower), so it must be rigorously protected against galvanic corrosion.

Metal boat builders and owners have to be fanatical in preventing ground pathways for stray electrical current. Shore power should pass through an isolation transformer, and floating ground systems are recommended so that negative DC wires are not directly or indirectly (attached to the engine or through-hull, for instance) in contact with the hull.

Intriguing Hybrids

Hybrid steel boats with fiberglass or aluminum decks and superstructures make good use of both materials. They offer some excellent advantages, marrying a rugged hull with strong, lightweight, and low-maintenance topside structures.

A company called Safe Boats takes a novel approach to boatbuilding with their RIB-like aluminum hulls supported by tough, chemical- and water-resistant polyethylene foam collars. The aluminum hull makes the boats tough and durable, and the deflation-proof foam collars provide tremendous positive buoyancy and act as a built-in fendering system. The system is used by the U.S. Coast Guard and other law enforcement agencies on their vessels, a testimony to their beefy construction and ability to take abuse.

Another company, Hy-Lite, builds composite aluminum boats with a sandwich of two-inch foam bonded to inner and outer sheets of aluminum skin. The foam acts as the flange of an I-beam, stiffening the hull, decks, and superstructure and adding acoustic and thermal insulation. The company claims that repairs are easily made in the event of damage. The boats are washed in a series of acid baths, primed with three coats of epoxy, and finished with three coats of polyurethane paint.

Home–Built on a Budget

Steel and aluminum hulls lend themselves well to home construction for the family on a budget, especially kit boats. Kits come with all the pieces precut and ready for assembly. Even when contracting with a professional boatbuilder, the welds do not have to be ground smooth, and you can skip fairing the hull and deck surfaces, saving a bundle. The result is a rugged, functional pleasure boat; it's just not a seamless yacht.

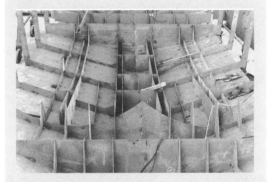

All the pieces of this Roberts hull kit, which are precut by CAD, fit together practically perfectly. BRUCE ROBERTS

Thanks to CAD-CAM technology, some companies are offering kit boats that can be built in either aluminum or steel; again the pieces are precut, marked, and ready for assembly. The computer-controlled cutters are so precise that the pieces fit together perfectly (within several thousandths of an inch), further reducing construction time and effort. Most of these kits involve setting up a framework to give the hull its shape during construction, but some take their shape from the plating itself.

Insulation

Any metal vessel must be insulated, both to eliminate condensation inside the hull and to provide thermal insulation against heat and cold. Blown-in polyurethane foam insulation works well as a thermal insulator and provides good acoustic insulation, but it's important that it adhere well to the primed metal, sealing it off completely. If applied to a properly prepared and primed surface, the foam can prevent corrosion; if not, it will just hide any corrosion that gained a foothold through faulty surface preparation.

Blown-in urethane foam is susceptible to absorbing water, so it must be kept dry. It also absorbs odors. Urethane foam is flammable, and when burning emits toxic vapors. A fire-retardant paint will help matters here. Closed-cell urethane is also available in panels and can be easily cut to fit. Urethane foam can be bought in a fire-retardant, non-toxic chemical formulation. It should be applied in a thickness of 1 to 2 inches, and coated with a surface skin that repels water.

Metal Boat References

A good resource for more detailed information on metal boatbuilding is yacht designer Michael Kasten's Web site www.kastenmarine.com.

Thomas E. Colvin, *Steel Boatbuilding: From Plans to Bare Hull,* 2 vols. (Camden, Maine: International Marine, 1985, 1986).

Glen-L Marine Designs, 9152 Rosecrans Ave., P.O. Box 1804WA, Bellflower, California 90706, 562-630-6258, info@glen-l.com, www.glen-l.com/.

Gilbert C. Klingel, *Boatbuilding with Steel,* including *Boatbuilding with Aluminum* by Thomas Colvin, 2nd ed. (Camden, Maine: International Marine, 1991).

Stephen F. Pollard, *Boatbuilding with Aluminum* (Camden, Maine: International Marine, 1993).

Bruce Roberts-Goodson, *The Complete Guide to Metal Boats: Building, Maintenance, and Repair.* (Camden, Maine: International Marine, 2001).

Robert M. Steward, *Boatbuilding Manual.* 4th ed. (Camden, Maine: International Marine, 1994).

CHAPTER 8

Propulsion Systems

The universe is full of magical things,
patiently waiting for our wits to grow sharper.
—Eden Phillpotts

nyone researching their next boat purchase may face a bewildering choice of power plants: inboards with conventional submerged propellers, stern drives, outboards, surface-piercing propellers, and waterjets. In this chapter, we examine the particular strengths and weaknesses of each propulsion package.

In the United States more boats under 21 feet are sold annually than all others combined, so it is no surprise that outboard-powered craft lead in number of units sold. The propulsion system best suited to *your* boat, however, depends on its hull design, size, and intended use. As with any choice, there are almost always trade-offs involved. For instance, an outboard on a center-console sportfisherman might be a good choice for its light weight, ease of trailering, and speed, but having the motor sticking out 4 or 5 feet past the transom is sure an impediment to fishing.

For larger vessels, above 30 feet or so, conventional inboards with submerged propellers are the usual choice. The drivetrain (propeller, propeller shaft, shaft log, seal, struts, and rudder) is relatively inexpensive, reliable, and efficient within its operating range, but all that underwater gear adds drag at higher speeds. The angle of thrust (shaft angle plus hull trim) also results in a loss of efficiency. Compared with waterjets and surface drives, conventional submerged props are located well below the waterline, and consequently can be counted on to maintain thrust in all but the most severe conditions.

Waterjets, whose popularity was once driven by consumer whim, are now gaining acceptance based on actual merit. They function by drawing in water through an inlet grate on the hull bottom, accelerating it through an impeller, and shooting it out the stern through a steerable nozzle. Waterjets make sense on very small craft, such as Jetskis, and on larger inboard-powered vessels where speed, maneuverability, and shallow draft are primary concerns.

A surface-piercing propeller is as the name suggests only partially submerged. Excellent efficiency and performance at high speed are gained by eliminating much of the drag caused by underwater running gear.

Waterjets and surface-piercing propellers are significantly more expensive than conventional propulsion packages. In terms of efficiency, conventional propellers are generally best for operating speeds below 25 knots, waterjets from 25 to 40 knots, and surface-piercing propellers for sustained cruising speeds above 40 knots. Complexity, maneuverability, and other issues also enter into the equation.

Real-World Speed

Speed sells, and consequently boatbuilders place a great emphasis on it in their marketing. To be properly informed, you need to understand the conditions under which advertised speed predictions were calculated. For example, was the calculation based on flat-out speed in ideal conditions or was it cruising speed into a headwind while fully loaded with fuel, gear, and passengers?

The speed you see bandied about depends a lot on the builder and on the class of boat being sold. A center console or runabout builder is likely going to talk about flat-out speed in miles per hour as opposed to knots, since speed in miles per hour is a more impressive-sounding figure. (Based on the nautical mile—the equator divided by 24,000, or 6,076 feet—1 knot equals 1.15 mph. Or multiply mph by 0.869 to get speed in knots.) On the other hand, a builder of luxury convertibles is likely to advertise fully loaded speeds in knots and usually knocks off a knot or two from their measurements to avoid disappointing the customer. A new owner who is told to expect 30 knots at 2,000 rpm is going to be pleasantly surprised when the boat consistently makes 31 or 32 knots. (By the way, the legitimate argument for advertising speeds in miles per hour is that freshwater boats are traditionally rated this way, but any boatowner who operates in a marine environment ought to be thinking in knots.)

Many factors can influence speed. Just painting the shiny gelcoated bottom of a big convertible can drop its speed by two knots due to the added frictional drag from a rougher surface finish. Imagine what happens when slime and barnacles build up over the season, not to mention the accumulation of provisions and extra gear. Even adding a tower on a big boat or a bimini with full enclosure on a smaller one can slow a boat by 2 to 3 knots. Builders usually plan ahead by installing props that are slightly undersized originally so that additional weight and bottom fouling won't prevent the engines from achieving their full rated rpm.

So when you hear "it'll run 55 mph" at your local boat dealership, do some mental math. What this usually means is that, when normally loaded with fuel, provisions, crew, and gear, the "55-mph boat" will actually cruise at 23 to 26 knots. That's with a gas inboard turning 3,000 rpm or an outboard operat-

ing at a comfortable 3,500 rpm. Maybe the boat can make 38 to 40 knots wide open. If the dealer questions your math, you could always make his estimate of cruising speed a condition of the sale to be proven during sea trials. Question advertised speeds.

So with gasoline-powered engines, whether outboard or inboard, a boat's speed at wide-open throttle (WOT) is a pretty meaningless figure. Pushing the engine at full throttle, or "wide open," will burn it out in short order. When boat salespeople talk about "wide-open" speed, what they're often talking about is a boat's speed with a quarter tank of fuel, a waxed, unpainted bottom, and a 90-pound twelve-year-old driving in a three-inch chop. In my experience, small powerboats very rarely go as fast in normal operating conditions as advertised.

What really matters with speed is how fast a boat will go normally loaded and with bottom paint at its cruising rpm. Newer, more powerful engines—including compact, lightweight diesels—have made it possible for cruising and sportfishing yachts to cruise at well in excess of 30 knots fully loaded. In fact, boatbuilders design new models around the available power as the market continues to demand more speed. Hull forms have been refined accordingly to include finer entries, greater deadrise, and more rugged construction in an effort to accommodate the higher horsepower available. But make sure that the power plant complements the hull. Unfortunately, some builders continue to construct flat-bottom hulls better suited to the 20-knot speeds of a decade ago than the 35 to 40 knots that these new powerhouses are capable of delivering.

As we saw in chapter 4, there's no substitute for deadrise to deliver a good ride. If you buy an older boat with the intention of repowering it, it's important that the hull shape and structure can support the extra speed, and that CG be shifted farther aft the faster the boat is capable of going.

With any planing hull, it's essential that the boat run easily on a plane, fully loaded and with the engine(s) turning no faster than their continuous cruise rpm rating. Otherwise, the engines will be pushed too hard, burn excessive fuel, and die prematurely. Some boats with inadequate power fall short of getting up on a plane at cruising rpm. In many cases, another 10 percent horsepower increment would make them good performers, but a sea trial is not the time to be figuring that out. Beware of the price-point 35-foot cruiser sold with big-block V-8 gas engines; these boats are priced to get you on the water, but most are just too heavy for gas engines and will only lead to a disappointing ownership experience. Pay the extra money for the diesels, buy used, or get a smaller boat.

Outboard Engines

The most popular small boat engine is the outboard. It is light, fast, and easy to maintain and replace. Compared with inboards of like horsepower, outboards are typically louder (though four-stroke engines are quieter than the ubiquitous two-strokes), more expensive, and shorter-lived, with 800 to 1,200 operating hours being about average. To put engine hours in perspective, the average boater puts well under 150 hours on their engine each season. Diehard fishermen and cruisers might log several hundred hours, but they're the exception.

The design of an outboard's lower unit is more streamlined than an inboard's running gear (shafts, struts, and rudders), creating less drag at high speeds. The engine's thrust is closer to horizontal than an inboard's, resulting in additional propulsion efficiency. On the downside, the outboard's smaller propeller with its oversized hub is inherently less efficient than an inboard's, especially when pushing heavier boats, and there is a 4 to 5 percent loss of engine power in the 90-degree turn from driveshaft to prop in the lower unit. But the engine's trimmability (ability to raise the bow) and its ability to operate continually at a higher percentage of its full power usually give it a speed advantage over same-horsepower inboard engines. With few exceptions, outboards run on gasoline, not diesel fuel.

An advantage of outboards is that it is easy to adjust hull trim, or running angle, by pivoting the motor up or down. Raising the motor will change the thrust angle downward, depressing the stern and lifting the bow; lowering it will accomplish the opposite. This control over trim angle is a wonderful thing since you can minimize the hull's wetted surface, thereby reducing frictional drag and achieving optimum speeds. Stern drives offer similar benefits, but with an inboard engine, you can't raise the bow, though you can lower it by depressing the trim tabs. Outboards also offer excellent maneuverability because the propeller thrust is used to steer the boat as well as propel it. This makes an outboard more responsive to the helm at low speeds, especially in reverse.

Outboards come in different shaft lengths to accommodate varying transom heights, allowing the lower unit to be submerged enough to give the

This quiet-running four-stroke Yamaha slides up and down on its Flats Jack. A jack plate like this is a great way to adjust lower unit immersion (and overall draft) without having to tilt the drive up.

prop a good bite on solid water, preventing cavitation and ventilation, but not so much as to induce excessive drag. For high-performance and shallow-water fishing boats, optional power mounts called jack plates allow a motor to be raised and lowered vertically to adjust prop depth. Unlike pivoting the motor up or down with its trim-tilt motor, raising or lowering it with jack plates does not alter the thrust angle.

Outboards are mounted either directly on the boat's transom or on a bracket extending several feet aft. Transom-mounted outboards have less effect on static trim (since their weight is farther forward) and are less of an obstacle when fishing; they are also easier to reach for routine maintenance. Bracket-mounted outboards, on the other hand, can be faster, since they often balance the V-bottom hull's weight distribution more favorably, and they operate in a slightly cleaner waterflow. Because they are mounted farther aft, they are quieter and tend to minimize exhaust fumes in the cockpit. Since the motor is cantilevered farther aft of the hull's center of dynamic lift when planing, the boat

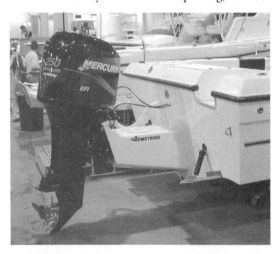

An aluminum Armstrong bracket supports this 250 hp Mercury. The transom must be very strong to take the cantilevered weight, as well as the thrust, of the outboard. The cockpit will be a bit more smoke-free, the noise levels will be lower, and the bow will trim higher as a result of this arrangement, compared to transom-mounted power.

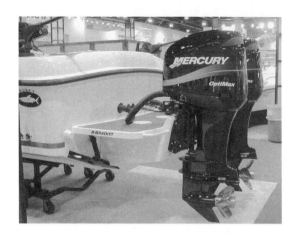

This Dusky twin outboard is equipped with a B-Bracket motor mount, which adds buoyancy, but no dynamic lift at speed; the bottom of the bracket is above the hull's running surface. A ruggedly built transom is needed to hold nearly 1,000 pounds of engine and several hundred horsepower-worth of thrust.

can be trimmed higher by the bow, which can reduce wetted surface and increase speed. A bracket-mounted outboard eliminates the transom cutout, which makes for a stronger transom that is also less prone to swamping (pooping, actually) in a following sea.

An outboard on a bracket moves a boat's center of gravity farther aft and therefore increases the speed needed for a hull to get up plane, thus reducing midrange performance. Bracket-mounted outboards also submerge more readily, since a wave coming from astern will immerse the engine before lifting the boat. In contrast, an inboard will tend to stay on plane and operate more efficiently in the 12- to 18-knot range.

Outboards have simple internal cooling systems that pump water through an intake grid in the lower unit, through the engine, and out the propeller hub. A small "telltale" stream of water is visible from the side of the lower unit to indicate that water is flowing freely through the engine and that the cooling system is working properly. All outboards are raw-water-cooled, which means that they use the water the boat is floating in—as opposed to a closed, recirculating freshwater supply—

to cool the engine directly. Unless you're operating on a lake or river, it's important to flush your engine with freshwater after each use since salt water is so corrosive.

Two-Stroke

The majority of outboards are two-stroke (intake and compression on one stroke, power and exhaust on the other). These are light, relatively inexpensive engines in which the lubricating oil is mixed with the gas. Oil is either poured into the fuel tank on each filling in a ratio recommended by the manufacturer, or injected into the fuel from a reservoir via a variable ratio oil (VRO) pump mounted on the motor. These pumps supply oil at the rate the engine actually needs, depending on engine speed and demand, so they run cleaner than engines using premixed fuel.

Older outboards are usually carbureted, the fuel being crudely mixed with combustion air and mechanically injected into the cylinder for ignition by the spark plug. These engines are cheaper to buy but more expensive to operate, since they burn more fuel. The oil is mixed with the gas, so some of the oil ends up unburned in the exhaust, making them real polluters by comparison with four-strokes.

Outboards with electronic fuel injection (EFI) accurately meter fuel to the cylinders; compared to a carbureted engine, this increases efficiency and makes for easier starting, smoother running, and less smoke resulting from incomplete combustion.

Direct injection is the latest and greatest technology to hit the two-stroke outboard market, and the most fuel-efficient, clean-running two-stroke. Fuel is introduced as a fine mist at the top of each cylinder, preventing unburned fuel from escaping.

Four-Stroke

Four-stroke outboards are increasingly popular. Like car and inboard boat engines, four-stroke outboards have a four-step cycle: (1) intake, (2) compression, (3) expansion, and (4) exhaust, or, to put it a little more memorably, suck, squeeze, bang, and

Talk about redundancy and power combination options. This Trophy walkaround sportfisherman can steer easily on its pusher outboards, or on one or two of the mains.   TROPHY

blow. (As mentioned, two-strokes combine steps 1–2 and 3–4.) They are more expensive and heavier than two-strokes and don't deliver the same snappy acceleration, but they are significantly quieter.

By most accounts, four-stroke engines are more reliable and durable, as reflected in the longer warranties many manufacturers offer. They are also usually more fuel-efficient (although direct-injected two-strokes are very competitive) and gentler on the environment, since there is no oil discharge and little or no smoke to pollute the air. Environmental considerations make the four-stroke the clear choice for many boaters today, especially for boats operating on inland waters, rivers, and lakes. New EPA regulations effective in 2006 have all the outboard manufacturers rushing to produce cleaner-burning, nonpolluting engines.

Outboards are great for smaller boats because

A study in excess: Surely there's a better way to make a boat go fast.

they typically weigh 300 to 500 pounds less than inboards of similar horsepower, which among other things makes trailering significantly easier. But even outboard engine weights can vary considerably by horsepower. A 115 hp Honda four-stroke tips the scales at a hefty 496 pounds, while the 115 hp Johnson two-stroke is a bantam 319 pounds. Two 225 hp two-strokes push the scales at around 1,000 pounds.

Diesel outboards are also available, and they're typically used in commercial applications where many hundreds of hours are put on an engine each year. Yachts and commercial ships sometimes carry tenders fitted with diesel outboards to avoid the necessity of having to carry gasoline onboard. They're very durable, and heavier; Yanmar's 27 and 36 hp models, for instance, weigh 207 and 256 pounds, respectively.

Stern Drives

Stern drives are essentially outboard lower units connected through the transom to inboard gas or diesel engines. MerCruiser and Volvo (in that order) are the two leading stern-drive manufacturers. Although significantly heavier than outboards, stern drives offer similar speed and trim advantages. And these advantages are maintained despite their smaller props' inherent inefficiencies, and an 8 to 10 percent loss of power to friction in the two 90-degree gears located at the top and bottom of the lower unit. Particularly when mated to diesel inboards, stern drives enjoy superior fuel economy.

Stern drives are especially popular in freshwater, where the inability to raise the lower unit out of the water when not in use, as you can with an outboard, is much less consequential with regard to corrosion. A stern drive allows an operator to enjoy the maneuverability of an outboard combined with the quiet, efficient, out-of-sight operation of an inboard. The engine can be shut off and the lower unit can be raised higher than the bottom of the hull, making it possible to bring a boat into shallower water using a kicker or human power.

Stern-drive engines, like outboards, are usu-

ally cooled by taking water in through a grill in the lower unit and circulating it through chambers in the engine block, as with other raw-water-cooled engines. A freshwater-cooled stern-drive or inboard engine, on the other hand, pumps raw sea or lake water through a heat exchanger (mounted on top of the engine), which cools a closed-loop supply of freshwater mixed with antifreeze, much like a car engine. The freshwater is then circulated through the engine block, minimizing corrosion and prolonging engine life.

A Volvo KAD44P EDC diesel bolted to a Volvo DP (duo-prop) stern drive, a combination meant to deliver exceptional efficiency, speed, and maneuverability.

Manufacturers including Volvo Penta and MerCruiser make lower units of varying propeller size and reduction gear ratio to suit the application, and most stern drives have a single propeller, which is the cheapest, simplest design. Counterrotating propeller-drive systems have two props mounted one in front of the other that turn in opposite directions, thus canceling the side forces and eliminating the spiraling helix (which represents wasted energy) from the propeller wash. MerCruiser's Bravo 3 and Volvo's DuoProp are examples. The result is improved propulsion efficiency, greater speed and acceleration at a given rpm, and better handling. A counterrotating drive will also eliminate the tendency of a single-engine boat to heel at speed and to pull the steering wheel to one side. Finally, boats with counterrotating propellers turn and back exceptionally well. A few outboards are also available with counterrotating props.

Volvo has recently come out with a synthetic composite stern drive lower unit that eliminates any worries about corrosion. As of this writing, it's available for 160, 205, and 250 hp gas engines. Volvo says the drive is about 40 pounds, or 20 percent, lighter than the aluminum lower unit it replaces, and that its streamlined profile reduces drag by some 20 percent. It is available with both stainless and composite DuoProps. Sounds promising.

5.7GXi with SX
Aquamatic drive

A 5.7-liter, 315 hp gasoline engine built by GM, marinized by Volvo, and mated to a Volvo SX stern drive.   VOLVO

A stern-drive engine is usually installed in the stern, with its transmission just forward of the transom. It is possible, and sometimes desirable, however, to fit an intermediate jackshaft between the transmission and the lower unit using universal or CV joints, thus moving the engine farther forward to improve weight distribution, open up the cockpit for anglers, and in some cases eliminate the engine box.

Larger cruising and racing boats often use twin stern drives when a single engine can't deliver sufficient power. However, twin engines—be they stern drives, outboards, or inboards—add cost, complexity, weight, and drag, and twin stern drives and inboards crowd the engine room and impede access. For instance, a single 300 hp engine would be significantly faster, cheaper to buy and operate,

and more efficient than a pair of 150 hp engines. For these reasons, when a single engine can deliver sufficient power, it is often the better option.

On the other hand, twin engines offer redundancy as well as significant maneuvering advantages. On a boat with twin engines sufficiently offset from the centerline, one engine can be put in forward and the other in reverse, turning the boat in its own length. The trick when maneuvering dockside with twin stern drives or outboards is to leave the rudder (helm) amidships and let the engines do the turning to best effect.

Twin engines with completely separate fuel systems, including tanks and filter-separators, provide maximum redundancy. But even so, a bad load of fuel can contaminate both tanks during a single fill-up. Alternatively, small single-engine boats can benefit from the installation of a "get-home" kicker, a small outboard mounted to one side of the main engine that will get you home at displacement speed if the main engine dies. Don't make this engine too small, since a surprising amount of thrust may be needed just to point the bow into the wind, let alone buck a headwind and opposing current. The kicker can be mechanically connected to the main engine—whether inboard, outboard, or stern drive—enabling you to drive from the steering wheel. It can also be used for everyday trolling or other standard slow-speed operations thus reducing fuel consumption and wear and tear on the main engine. Since it draws less water than a larger outboard or stern drive, it will let you into shallower water with relative impunity.

Some boats are equipped with dedicated "kickers" called *wing engines* for routine slow-speed operations. These may be outboard or inboard, and twin wing engines may also be fitted. An inboard wing engine can either turn its own fixed or feathering propeller or turn the main prop shaft via belts, gears, or hydraulic hoses.

One interesting variation on the stern-drive theme is Dorado's single-engine, twin-stern-drive arrangement. A single Volvo engine drives a dual-output transmission connected via carbon fiber

This wing engine provides enough power to push a boat along at 4 or 5 knots, or to help keep it headed more or less into the wind in a stiff breeze. An engine-mounted hydraulic motor provides the motive force.   NORDHAVN

jackshafts to a pair of Volvo stern drives. In the standard configuration both drives shift in unison; though independent shifting is available, the maneuvering benefits of this setup are limited since the drives are quite close together, so much of the twin-screw's twisting effect is lost. But, the manufacturer claims excellent performance with this system, combining a single diesel's efficiency with trimmable stern drives for optimum performance.

Outboards and stern drives are rarely found on boats over 35 feet, other than on light, high-speed racing boats. Their smaller props just can't develop enough thrust to get heavier boats on plane efficiently. Inboards, on the other hand, can be very effective on boats as small as 20 feet. Consider the ski boat, which is almost always inboard powered (with its forward weight distribution producing a flatter wake) and usually in the 20-foot range.

Inboard Engines

Inboard engines, whether driving conventional submerged props, surface-piercing propellers, or waterjets, are the overwhelming choice for larger boats. Compared with outboards, they're available in higher power ratings and produce more power at the shaft for each gallon of fuel consumed. Their weight is centered deeper in the hull, lowering the vessel's center of gravity and improving stability. They also tend to last longer, a critical factor for larger boats that spend more time underway each season.

When well-designed inboard boats are running with optimum trim, efficiency, and drag, they can match the speed of same-horsepower stern-drive- and outboard-powered boats. But, since trim can change significantly with weight movement fore and aft, especially on smaller boats, the ability of outboards and stern drives to control trim usually gives them a speed advantage in the real world.

Gasoline Inboards

Gas inboards are usually more efficient, quieter, cheaper, and longer lasting than two-cycle outboards. Largely because of their added weight, farther-forward center of gravity, inability to trim the bow up, added drag, and shaft angle inefficiencies, the inboard is usually not as fast at cruise speed as an outboard of the same rated horsepower.

Gas inboards are marinized versions of automotive engines and are made mostly by GM and Ford. They differ from their car-bound brethren in that they're raw-water-cooled (either directly, or indirectly through a heat exchanger) and have non-sparking electrical systems. They come in three basic configurations: carbureted, fuel-injected, and multiport fuel-injected. Carbureted engines are cheaper to buy and simpler to maintain, but their mechanical fuel delivery system is less precise and therefore less efficient than injection.

In an engine with electronic fuel injection (EFI), an electronically metered charge of fuel is sprayed under pressure into the cylinder or the intake manifold, increasing the percentage of fuel that is actually burnt (versus being discharged in the exhaust). EFI systems lack points, rotor, cap, and condenser, and therefore require less maintenance. They are generally easier to start when cold, run smoother, and offer lower fuel consumption for a given power output. Spark advance is adjusted automatically to meet changes in air temperature and barometric pressure. Multiport fuel injection, which includes a separate fuel injector for each cylinder, helps meter fuel even more precisely for maximum horsepower output and cleaner emissions.

On any of these gas engines, water pumps are preferably gear driven by the engine, not by a belt, eliminating another weak link in the system.

This 8.1-liter HO MPI (multiport injection), which puts out 425 hp and over 500 foot-pounds of torque at full throttle, is the GM 7.4-liter 454 CID big-block engine's replacement. CRUSADER

Gas engines are inherently more dangerous than diesels, since gasoline fumes are far more explosive. The most dangerous gas engines are inboards and stern drives mounted in enclosed compartments, since gasoline fumes are heavier than air and will collect in the bilge. Outboards with portable gas tanks mounted on deck are much safer for this reason. Whenever a gas tank or gas engine is installed in an enclosed compartment, the potential exists for a hose or fitting to come loose, allowing gas or gas fumes to flow into the bilge.

Any boat with belowdeck gas tanks should have a mechanical bilge blower installed with the suction hose reaching to the lowest point in the bilge. The blower should be allowed to run for several minutes before starting the engine and after refueling to exhaust the fumes and introduce fresh air. This points to the need for a well-engineered and properly installed fuel system that meets USCG standards for hose and fittings and for proper grounding,

I almost always favor diesels over gas engines simply because of their greater inherent safety. It's not that gasoline installations can't be made safe (and they're usually quite reliable), since thousands of these boats have been running around for years without incident. But why add an additional hazard to boating if you don't have to?

Gas engines require clean fuel (although they tolerate contaminants better than diesels), so there should be a fuel filter–water separator between the tank and the engine. Water can condense in the tank (especially a partially empty one) or may be introduced during fueling. Sediment, a real risk from "dirty fuel," can find its way from the tank and clog fuel lines. The clear bowl on the bottom of a good filter-separator allows you to detect any water or sediment. These contaminants can then be drained off into a container for proper disposal ashore.

As discussed, inboard gas engines are generally considered impractical on boats larger than 35 feet, since even big-block V-8's strain mightily to get such heavy boats up on plane. In spite of the temptation

A Racor gas filter–water separator with sediment bowl. Don't leave home without it. RACOR

of a lower base price, if you get yourself a 35-foot-plus boat, or one that weighs over about 16,000 pounds, you'll be a lot happier with the diesel.

Electronic fuel injection and ignitions systems are improving both inboard and outboard gasoline engine efficiencies. Gas engines run cleaner and emit fewer pollutants than they used to. One well-known gas inboard brand, Crusader, is available carbureted or in two EFI configurations: TBI (throttle body injection), which has two fuel injectors and burns about 15 percent less fuel at cruise than the carbureted model, and MPI (multiport injection), which has eight injectors and is 17 to 18 percent more efficient at cruise. Both EFI models burn 40 percent less gas at trolling speeds. According to the manufacturer, there is little difference in engine life among these models. Since GM no longer manufactures its 7.4-liter, 454 CID block, the 8.1-liter engine used in Suburbans and GM pickups is now the big block engine of choice.

Note that the reduction ratios available for these gas engines run from 1.25:1 to 2.8:1 (for more on reduction ratios, see below). Depending on the boat, the steeper gear ratio will almost always produce better midrange performance, since it will drive a larger-diameter, slower-turning propeller—provided you can get one. The larger propeller, shaft, struts, and other components will cost the builder more, so they're rarely standard equipment and may not even be available as an option. A smaller, faster propeller generally gives less responsive overall performance and less speed at cruise, especially when a boat is fully loaded, so if you're repowering, the added cost of changing to a deeper-ratio gear may be well worthwhile.

Diesel Inboards

Diesels are invariably the best choice for boats over 35 feet and 16,000 pounds, as well as for boats that run more than 200 to 300 hours annually. Gas engines, lacking the midrange torque of a diesel of similar power, just aren't suited to pushing larger boats. The potential life of a diesel is much longer than that of a similar-sized gas engine, too, so

diesels start to pay for themselves after several hundred hours of running time annually.

Diesel engines are becoming more popular in small pleasure craft because of their shrinking size, superior fuel economy, and above all their greater inherent safety. A diesel-powered boat is significantly more expensive to buy, but it will retain more value and may well be easier to sell on the used market. It's also a lot more expensive to rebuild come overhaul time—up to three times that of a same-horsepower gas engine.

Compared with gas engines, diesels are louder, since they rely on compression rather than spark to ignite the fuel, thus they require more extensive sound-deadening systems. Their exhaust odor is more objectionable than gas, though underwater exhaust systems do a good job of burying the fumes. Diesels are the hands-down choice for displacement vessels, including heavier diesels, since weight isn't a critical factor. Diesel engines are durable, increasingly quiet, and becoming so light that they can produce more usable, continuous power than a gas engine of the same weight, making them well suited even to small, fast planing hulls. Some diesels from MAN, Isotta Fraschini, and Yanmar reach a pounds-per-horsepower ratio

Detroit Diesel is now selling this 70-series electronically controlled marinized truck engine to the marine industry. Any engine that can run over a million miles in an 80,000-pound truck ought to last a while in a boat. DETROIT DIESEL

of 3:1 or less, an accomplishment unheard of just a few years ago.

A diesel engine can last anywhere from 800 to 20,000 hours or more between major overhauls. The exact figure depends on how well the engine was built and much horsepower is squeezed out of it each cubic inch of displacement. Fastidious maintenance and consistent running (the less downtime, the better) also add hours. Some 1,200 to 3,000 hours may be a more realistic average life span for diesels that are run hard continuously at close to their rated power.

Diesels may have a well-deserved reputation for lasting tens of thousands of hours in certain commercial applications, but on yachts and other pleasure craft they are often used infrequently. In yacht applications they may also be run at slow speeds under minimal loading for many hours, then run hard before being shut down for days on end. This sort of operation shortens the engine's life to an amazing degree (often under 1,000 hours on poorly maintained, infrequently or lightly used diesels) since diesels like to be run moderately hard and often.

Diesels are inherently more reliable than gas engines in part because they don't have electrical ignition systems, relying on compression rather than spark plugs to initiate combustion. But diesels are especially susceptible to being shut down by dirty fuel, largely because the clearances in their injectors are so small. Also, they can't tolerate water in the fuel as well as gas engines. So, high-quality, high-capacity fuel filter-separators are essential. A dual filter, with two units lined up in parallel, allows the engine to keep running while filters are shifted "on the fly."

A modern, high-speed, turbocharged, intercooled diesel can operate at as much as 90 percent or more of its rated rpm all day long, while a gas engine may wear out prematurely and burn lots of fuel in the process if run above 65 to 70 percent of its rated speed. A turbocharger uses the engines exhaust gases to drive a blower, or fan, that increases the amount of air forced into the cylinders. A su-

How Slow Can It Go?

Whichever power plant is selected for a cruising boat, it's important that continuous engine loading and long-range cruise speed are considered. If a semidisplacement trawler capable of a 14-knot cruise is throttled back to produce an ocean-crossing, 6-knot cruise speed, it may be operating at 20 to 25 percent of its capacity, which will eventually result in damage to the engine. A better arrangement is to have smaller twin engines driving controllable pitch propellers, or perhaps two engines driving a single shaft with a controllable pitch propeller, so that the engine in use can be sufficiently loaded. For large yachts, an electric propulsion system offers several advantages: between two and four diesel generators can be used to drive two electric propulsion motors while at the same time providing the ship's electrical power. More generators can be fired up, depending on the ship's speed and the electrical demand for house services. An electrical power management system is necessary to provide overall monitoring and control.

The compact Cat 3126, available in ratings up to 440 hp, is widely seen in 30- to 40-foot pleasure and commercial boats.
CATERPILLAR

percharger does the same thing, but since it's mechanically driven by the engine, there's less lag time before you get a boost when the throttle is advanced. An intercooler uses the engine cooling water to also cool the air being injected into the cylinders, and since cooler air is denser, the engine can develop more power.

When you put it all together, a 200 hp diesel

This dual Racor diesel fuel filter-separator has shift-on-the-fly capability, so an engine never has to be shut down to clean a filter.

RACOR

MAN is well known for producing diesel engines that are small and light for their power. The D2842LE404 is rated at 1,300 hp and weighs 3,905 pounds. MAN

will likely cruise your boat as fast as a 300 hp gas engine could (since their continuous power ratings are similar), last a lot longer, and burn around 40 percent less fuel in the process. In any event, what's most important in any discussion of engine power is continuous horsepower output at the propeller.

Cooling system maintenance is crucial to any engine, especially diesels that are turbocharged, aftercooled, or intercooled. In fact, cooling problems are directly responsible for many a premature en-

gine overhaul. The complex wet cooling systems for these modern diesels have to be kept working efficiently for efficient heat transfer, or you can kiss long engine life good-bye. Installing a temperature sensor with an alarm in the rubber exhaust line between the engine and the muffler is a good idea. That's because running the engine dry due to loss of coolant can quickly soften and melt the exhaust hose, and an exhaust fire and bilge flooding (if the exhaust outlet is partially below the waterline) could result.

An increasing number of diesel manufacturers offer electronically controlled (EC) and monitored engines. These engines are advertised as having a number of advantages. An EC diesel is designed to burn fuel more efficiently, run smoother, produce more power, and smoke less on cold startup and during normal operation. In fact, horsepower output can be controlled by tweaking the electronics, allowing diesel manufacturers to increase power output on newer engine models a little at a time once an engine has proven its durability at lower settings.

The operating parameters of many EC diesels are recorded so the manufacturer can more readily troubleshoot, even via a computer modem. They can also tell if the operator has been running the engines at too high a power setting for too long, which

This 500 hp marine diesel, like the rest of the Yanmar lineup, is a leader in power-to-weight ratio and compactness. YANMAR

PERFORMANCE CURVES

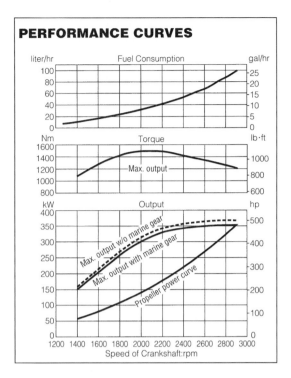

The 500 hp Yanmar's performance curves. Yanmar recommends running their engines at just 200 rpm off the top, maximizing available continuous power, in this case about 400 hp at 2,700 rpm. Note the fairly consistent 20 hp per gph fuel ratio in this curve. A 600 hp diesel typically burns about 31 gph wide open. Note that the marine gear (reduction gear) absorbs about 3 percent of the engine's power.   YANMAR

Caterpillar's 3412E has grown to 1,400 hp, thanks to engine-state-sensitive electronic monitoring and controls.   CATERPILLAR

A joint venture between DDC (Detroit Diesel) and Germany's MTU has produced several families of engines, including the V-8, V-12, and V-16 2000-series. The top-of-the-line 16V2000, pictured here, is rated at 2,000 hp with electronic monitoring and controls.

DETROIT DIESEL

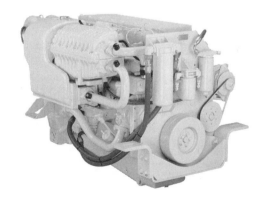

At 635 hp, the electronically controlled Cummins QSM11 diesel is the manufacturer's power-to-weight champ and first lightweight engine in this horsepower range.   CUMMINS

has the ancillary effect of keeping owners from abusing their engines and voiding the warranty. Some electronically controlled diesels accelerate less quickly than their mechanically controlled stablemates, because their electronics are designed to limit smoke by regulating acceleration. EC diesels also depend on these sophisticated electronics to start and operate, adding yet another component with a potential for failure. Notwithstanding such drawbacks, however, EC diesels have many advantages and are clearly the wave of the future.

Many diesel (and gas) engines in recreational boats corrode internally before they wear out. This is especially true in the absence of freshwater cooling. A ten-year-old oceangoing boat's gas en-

The venerable GM 671 (6 cylinders, 71 cubic inches per cylinder) two-stroke diesel was originally developed by Gray Marine for one-way trips to the beach in WWII landing craft. The engines proved so durable, some of the originals are still in operation 55 years later. Output ranges from the original's 165 hp, naturally aspirated with a two-valve head, to a jacked-up 485 hp with turbocharger and aftercooler. Guess which version lasts longer?

gine with 400 hours of running time may be near the end of its service life, whereas a gas engine that's used every day in commercial or charter service might easily run 1,200 hours or more.

Gas versus Diesel

Since diesels are preferred on most boats over 35 feet, the real sales contest is for boats in the 28- to 34-foot range. Both gas and diesel engines will get the job done, but each has specific advantages over the other.

When you consider that many people operate their boats between 50 and 150 hours each season, gas engines often make sense due to their lower initial cost. They won't last as long and they're less efficient, but you may be able to buy two or three gas engines in succession for the price of a single diesel. Gas engines also tend to fare better when standing unused for long periods of time. While diesels are more reliable, electronic fuel injection in gas engines has closed that gap. And some owners still prefer carbureted gas engines because they're cheaper and simpler to work on.

A gasoline inboard can't match a diesel for continuous cruise speeds. An inboard gas cruiser that

makes 37 knots wide open (4,400 to 4,800 rpm) would likely cruise at around 24 knots at 3,000 to 3,200 rpm, while a 37-knot diesel-powered boat could likely cruise at 30 to 32 knots. The diesel can cruise at a higher percentage of its maximum rpm and deliver a lot more torque while doing so.

Gas engines are a good choice for boats that are used under 200 hours annually or that usually make short trips of an hour or less. Diesels win out when maximum range is needed, since they burn at least 40 percent less fuel for a given power output. Engines that develop high torque at lower rpm (diesels) are better suited to heavier displacement and planing hulls, since they can develop enough power at intermediate speed settings to deliver good midrange performance. But, as mentioned, diesels not only cost more to buy, they cost much more to service, especially if an overhaul is needed.

Bear in mind that the greater the horsepower rating from a given engine block, the less time it will run between overhauls, and this goes for diesel as well as gas engines. The old, naturally aspirated

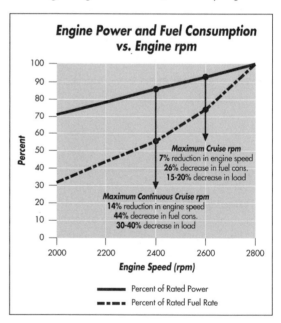

Cat has developed this little chart showing the reduction in fuel consumption when backing a few hundred rpm off from full throttle.

CATERPILLAR

(nonturbocharged) GM 871 diesel rated at 325 hp would easily run over 10,000 hours in a commercial fishing application, but when the same engine is pumped up to over 500 hp, it may well need to be rebuilt before reaching 2,000 hours.

Cooling Inboards

Inboard engines have either wet or dry exhausts and are almost always water- rather than air-cooled. A wet exhaust system discharges a mixture of cooling water and exhaust gases through a common muffler and horizontal hose that exits at or near the transom or though the bottom in case of an underwater exhaust. A dry exhaust system pumps the water over the side and discharges the hot exhaust gases through a muffler and out a vertical metal pipe high in the rigging.

A raw-water cooling system pipes water from outside the hull, usually through an internal filter, then the water pump, the engine block cooling passages, and back overboard. For a boat operating on the ocean, this means that the engine itself is constantly in contact with corrosive salt water. Any engine operating in salt water will last a lot longer if it's freshwater cooled. In a freshwater-cooled inboard engine, the cooling water treated with antifreeze circulates through the engine block from an engine-mounted expansion tank and heat exchanger in a closed loop. This freshwater is in turn cooled by seawater pumped through the heat exchanger via a through-hull fitting and a strainer, then discharged overboard through the exhaust system. Because the seawater never comes in contact with the engine itself, a freshwater-cooled engine lasts longer. If you operate in salt water, don't be stingy when it comes to selecting freshwater cooling as an option.

Gas engines built by Crusader (a well-thought-of marine conversion) come with 170-degree thermostats when freshwater cooled and 143-degree thermostats if raw-water cooled. The lower setting minimizes scaling for boats used in salt water. Crusader recommends that owners using their boats exclusively in freshwater choose the 170-degree unit

Rotary Engines

Rotary Power International and Rotary Power Marine manufacture rotary engines for marine use. Rotary engines eliminate many of a conventional engine's moving parts, including pistons and camshafts. RPI is gearing up to produce diesel-fueled engines of up to 3,000 hp, and RPM is selling Mazda-based marinized gasoline engines for small craft. The big advantages of a rotary engine are its power-to-weight ratio and its smooth, low-vibration operation. A 1,000 hp rotary engine, for instance, weighs just 2,200 pounds, largely because there are no pistons and cylinders to add to its weight.

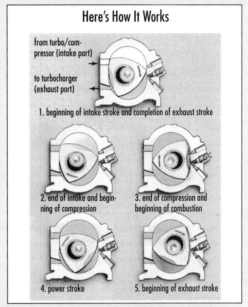

Here's How It Works

from turbo/compressor (intake part)

to turbocharger (exhaust port)

1. beginning of intake stroke and completion of exhaust stroke

2. end of intake and beginning of compression

3. end of compression and beginning of combustion

4. power stroke

5. beginning of exhaust stroke

Rotary Power International is gearing up to produce large diesel-fueled rotary engines for marine and industrial use. Short of a gas turbine, this may be the ultimate engine in terms of power density and engine weight per hp. This is an RPI chart showing the rotary engine cycle—sans pistons and cylinders.

ROTARY POWER INTERNATIONAL

even for a raw-water-cooled engine, since their gas engines run more efficiently at the higher temperature. Crusader also recommends running their engines at 75 percent of maximum rpm, so an engine that turns up 4,400 rpm wide open can be cruised as high as 3,300 rpm continuously. A raw-water-cooled Crusader gas engine is said by the manufacturer to last an average of 1,000 to 1,200 hours, whereas its freshwater-cooled counterpart has a typical life span of 1,500 hours.

Seawater used to cool the engine combines with the engine exhaust at the exhaust riser before the hot gases reach the muffler and rubber exhaust hose. Without the seawater, the exhaust gases would quickly melt the rubber hose, so it's important to ensure a continuous stream of water all the way through the system. If cooling waterflow is lost, you can usually tell right away by the sound of the exhaust, which changes pitch and becomes throaty as it exits the transom.

A wet exhaust usually exits the hull aft and above the waterline, but underwater exhausts are not uncommon. These usually include a relief valve to vent the exhaust to the atmosphere should excessive backpressure threaten to harm the engine. When the boat is moving at speed, a venturi plate just forward of the exhaust outlet reduces the pressure at the outlet to below atmospheric pressure, helping to draw the exhaust out and greatly reducing engine backpressure. Underwater exhausts can be very quiet and generally do a good job of burying fumes below the surface long enough for the boat to pass them by. But the hot gases can damage a fiberglass hull under extreme conditions, and the exhausts must be located in such a way that they don't aerate and ventilate the props and rudders.

Although the cooling systems described above are inside the hull, slow vessels commonly employ an externally mounted heat exchanger—the so-called keel-cooler. This is nothing more than a series of pipes mounted on the outside of the hull, through which the engine's fresh cooling water circulates. Seawater passes around the pipes, cooling the water inside. Naturally, the system works better (with the improved heat transfer) when the boat is moving, and the tubes must be kept clean inside and out for efficient cooling. Keel cooling adds drag, but it's negligible at displacement speeds. The system is simpler, since only one circulating pump—the one for the freshwater—is needed. Keel cooling systems are paired with dry exhaust systems, since there's no seawater to pipe through a wet exhaust hose.

Dry exhaust systems are popular with commercial vessels and some trawler yachts. Some commercial builders consider them to be safer than wet exhausts, since the exhaust gases only come into contact with metal pipes, not rubber hoses. Exhaust fumes are piped out a metal pipe (sometimes incorporated inside or attached to the mast) and into the atmosphere high above deck, while the cooling water is piped directly overboard. This minimizes or eliminates exhaust fumes and engine noise in the cockpit. Nothing's perfect, though; dry exhaust system piping also gets very hot, takes up interior space, and can interfere with accommodations above the engine room. These systems must be carefully designed, shielded from combustibles, and made of durable materials to prevent fire.

As with freshwater cooling, this is not a place to cut costs. When an exhaust manifold and risers fail due to corrosion, water can get into the cylinders, ruining an engine. If you end up with one of the manifolds leaking after a few years of use, replace them both, since the other won't be far behind.

Inboard Drivetrains

A conventional inboard drivetrain consists of an engine under the deck or engine box, a reduction or reversing gear to slow the prop down and allow it to operate in reverse, a propeller shaft and struts to support it, the propeller, and a rudder. The engine is fastened to mounts, which are usually soft or flexible to absorb vibration and are in turn bolted to rigid engine beds. This combination of soft mounts and rigid engine beds (themselves usually part of the hull's stringer system) works well to attenuate vibrations.

Whatever the power source, the propeller shaft angle should be no more than 12 degrees from horizontal, and less is better. The higher the angle of thrust, the less efficient the propeller becomes, especially as boat speed increases. A shaft angle of 13

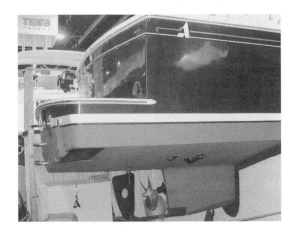

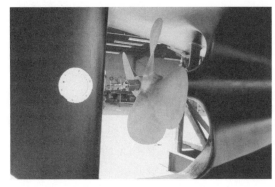

This trawler prop will have nice clean waterflow, thanks to the careful fairing in the aft end of the full keel. No chance this prop would be harmed in a grounding.   NORDHAVN

This Albin 32 had its running surface extended by two feet to add buoyancy and dynamic lift aft, necessitated by the weight of a V-drive diesel mounted in the stern under the cockpit. The built-in swim platform was a bonus. Note the full keel protecting the single-screw running gear.

to 14 degrees is not much concern to a boat that cruises below about 18 knots, but any boat capable of cruising above 30 knots wants a shaft angle below 12 degrees, and 8 to 10 degrees is needed for a 40-knot vessel. High shaft angles can result in excessive bow-up trim, which increases drag and creates a higher, power-absorbing wake.

Finally, consider that a 14-degree shaft angle, when combined with a hull trim angle of 8 degrees, will result in a propeller spinning through the water offset from the horizontal by 22 degrees! The result will be an inefficient drivetrain, to say the least, and excessive propeller vibration.

Drivetrains come in two main varieties: in-line drives and V-drives, with the former being the more common. In an in-line drivetrain the engine, reduction gear, and propeller shaft are laid out in a straight line often spanning half the boat length. A V-

drive greatly reduces this length requirement by turning the engine 180 degrees and putting the reduction gear at its forward end. The propeller shaft then runs back under the engine and out through the shaft seal. For hulls with sufficient buoyancy in the stern to support the weight of the engine, the V-drive is an excellent way to make room for larger accommodations amidships, while still maintaining an acceptable prop shaft angle.

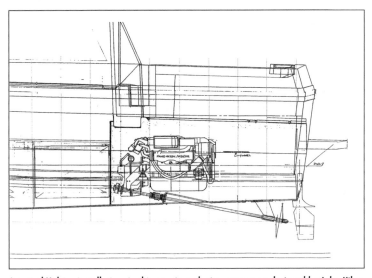

A typical V-drive installation, in this case in a planing catamaran designed by John Kiley. With the shaft exiting the aft end of the engine, as in an in-line configuration, the engine would have to be moved forward an engine length. Of course, that's the whole idea behind the V-drive, which opens up room forward for accommodations or fuel.   JOHN KILEY

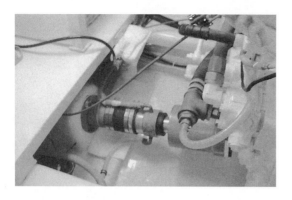

The dripless shaft seal on this Davis 58 keeps the salt content in the engine room to a minimum. Most modern yachts come with these dripless shaft seals, which lubricate the through-hull bearing supporting the shaft where it exits the hull.

A valid argument against V-drives used to be that they were less efficient at transmitting engine power to the propeller shaft. However, modern designs have eliminated this difference. Both transmissions operate at 97 percent efficiency, which is largely a function of the number of pinions in the reduction gear.

Since the propeller shaft is usually at an angle of eight or more degrees, a *down-angle reduction gear* can be used used in an in-line drivetrain to allow the engine to be mounted level, or close to it. The input shaft from the engine to the gear is hori-

zontal—on a plane with the engine—while the output shaft, which bolts to the propeller shaft, angles down from 7 to as much as 10 degrees on larger engines. A horizontal engine has a lower profile and allows the deck above to be mounted lower. Gears with vertical and horizontal offsets are also available for special applications such as catamarans and quadruple-engine power plants.

Most modern powerboats employ reduction gears to reduce the rpm of the propeller below the rpm of the engine. That's because a prop that turns as fast as the engine would have to be so small that it

The cutaway keel and streamlined strut of Shamrock's KeelDrive provide clean waterflow to the prop and minimal drag. The flat plate atop the rudder prevents ventilation and actually increases the lifting efficiency (steering force) of the rudder. SHAMROCK

The Tiara 50 Express's V-drive propulsion and dripless shaft seal are evident in this close-up. With the right hull form, the engines can be situated well aft in a boat, freeing up space for larger accommodations forward.

Shamrock's PocketDrive, which dispenses with the keel in favor of a recessed prop pocket for reduced draft. Shamrock is one of the very few inboard boat manufacturers in the 21- to 29-foot range. SHAMROCK

would be inefficient and produce very little thrust. A gear ratio of 1.5:1, in which 1,500 rpm from the engine delivers 1,000 rpm to the prop shaft, is considered "shallow." A ratio of 3:1, in which 1,500 rpm from the engine delivers 500 rpm to the shaft, is considered "deep," at least by small pleasure craft standards. In most cases, deeper reduction gears and larger, slower-turning propellers are preferable. Gear ratios up to 2.5:1 are commonly available with gasoline engines and smaller diesel engines, but builders usually select shallower gears, at least in part because engines with shallow reduction gears use smaller (and cheaper) props and shafts. In fact, the majority of pleasure boats on the market today would perform better with deeper gears and slower-turning propellers, especially when running fully loaded at cruising speed, and dockside engine responsiveness would be greatly improved.

Reduction gears come in three basic flavors: direct-mounted in-line, direct-mounted V-drive, and remote V-drive. Direct-mounted means the gears are bolted directly to the back of the engine. Direct-mounted in-line drives are the most common, and they take up the most room since the shaft is attached to the gear at the aft end of the engine. Direct-mounted V-drives have the gear mounted at the same point on the engine, but the engine is turned 180 degrees, placing the gear forward as described above.

The third configuration, which offers significant advantages, is the remote-mounted V-drive. The engine faces forward as in the direct-mounted V-drive, but the transmission is mounted several feet forward of the engine on its own foundation. A jackshaft connects the engine to the top of the remote gear, and the propeller shaft runs aft under the engine from the bottom of the gear. This allows the gear to absorb the propeller thrust, so the engine can be soft-mounted on its bed, reducing vibration. Placing the gear well forward also helps ensure a moderate shaft angle. Remote-mounted gears are identical internally to an engine-mounted gear, so they create the same 3 percent or so loss in propulsion efficiency. Considering their advan-

This inboard's main (aft) and intermediate shaft strut pads are *bolted onto*, rather than being *recessed into*, the hull, adding drag and turbulence forward of the propellers. Flush pads would help here.

tages, it is surprising that more yachts don't use remote-mounted V-drives, but shaft alignment issues are likely to be one explanation. Builders may also be deterred by the added complexity of installation, although modern constant-velocity and universal joints actually make shaft alignment less problematic than with direct-mounted in-line drivetrains.

The running gear of a conventional inboard-powered boat turning a submerged propeller adds significant hydrodynamic drag. In planing craft, more than 20 percent of the total hull resistance can be caused by these underwater appendages, and in vessels that cruise at over 60 knots, submerged appendage drag can be nearly as high as the drag from the entire hull. In addition, conventional underwater gear limits the size of the propeller: a clearance of 8 to 20 percent of the propeller's diameter is generally needed between the tips of the propeller blades and the bottom of the boat. However, both of these limitations—underwater drag and prop diameter—can be reduced if the propeller is partially recessed inside a pocket that closely matches its diameter. More on propeller pockets below.

Propellers

The propellers familiar to most of us operate completely submerged in the water and are driven by outboards, stern drives, and conventional inboards.

While most boats have three- or four-bladed propellers, five to seven blades are sometimes found on exotic large yachts whose owners don't mind paying extra for diminished vibration levels. While there are certainly exceptions, a three-bladed prop will often deliver a higher top-end speed than a four-blade, but the latter will run smoother, produce superior mid- and low-range performance, and often deliver a better "hole-shot," or acceleration, thanks to its greater blade surface area.

The idea behind any well-designed propulsion system is to accelerate as much water as possible while keeping the speed increase (in relation to the surrounding water), or slip, as low as practical. That's why a relatively large, slow-turning propeller is more efficient than its small, fast-spinning counterpart. The larger prop moves a greater volume of water at a lower velocity with less slip.

Prop Terms

Propellers are identified and classified by several characteristics, one of which is their rotation. Viewed from astern, a right-handed propeller turns clockwise when going forward; a left-handed prop turns counterclockwise.

Diameter is the overall dimension of the pro-peller from tip to tip. For a given vessel speed and available thrust, the bigger and slower-turning the propeller, the greater its efficiency.

Pitch, measured on the pressure face of the propeller, is the distance the propeller would travel, with no slip, through the water in a 360-degree rotation. Think of turning a wood screw a full turn; the distance it sinks into the wood is the pitch. In the real world, propellers slip from 10 to 20 percent or more due to the boat's drag and resistance.

Slip is simply the difference between the distance the boat actually advances through the water with one propeller revolution, and the propeller's actual pitch; a propeller with 30 inches of pitch that moves a boat 24 inches forward with one revolution has a 20 percent slip.

A propeller will usually be stamped with its diameter and pitch on the hub; for example, a "26 × 28" prop has a diameter of 26 inches and a pitch of 28 inches. In a *square propeller*, the diameter equals the pitch—say 30 by 30. An over-square prop has more pitch than diameter, and is usually found on high-speed boats. A tugboat or displacement trawler prop would tend to have significantly more diameter than pitch.

Inboard propellers can be either fixed or con-

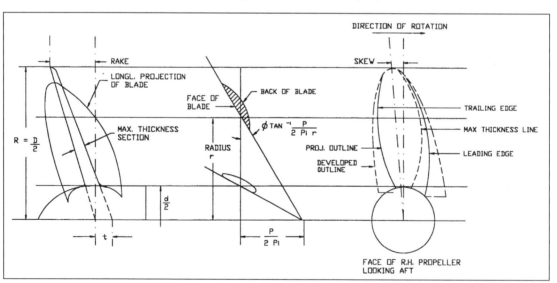

Propeller terminology.

TEIGNBRIDGE

trollable pitch. A *fixed* pitch prop is cast or machined from a single block of metal, and the blades are fixed relative to the hub and each other. A *controllable pitch* propeller (CPP) has articulated blades that are able to rotate on their hub, so pitch can be varied depending on the vessel's speed and engine load. Because CPPs have moving parts, they're more expensive, and they need larger hubs to accommodate the internal actuating gears; they are therefore less hydrodynamically efficient. The propeller shaft must also be hollow to accommodate the pitch actuating linkage between engine room and propeller. CPPs work very well on vessels that have multiple engines driving the same shaft and on vessels, such as tugs, that have widely varying loads. They allow the engines to be loaded efficiently throughout their rpm range.

A *highly loaded* prop has a great deal of pressure on each square inch of propeller blade. When a lot of power is delivered to a relatively small propeller, high *blade loading* results. Increasing the propeller size for a given horsepower lowers the blade loading and decreases cavitation, as we'll see below.

A propeller's *developed area ratio*, or DAR (also known as its *expanded area ratio*, or EAR), is the ratio between the total area of its blades when flattened out and a solid disk of the same diameter. A DAR of 0.7 means the area of the flattened blades would be 70 percent of the total disk area, as is common for a high-speed, highly loaded propeller. A tug or displacement fishing boat might have a DAR of 0.55. The higher the DAR for a given prop diameter, the less blade loading per horsepower, since there's more blade area to absorb the thrust. Thus, when propeller diameter is restricted by hull clearances, a prop with a higher DAR will deliver more horsepower before it cavitates.

Rake is the angle, measured in degrees, at which the propeller blades slant forward or aft relative to the hub when viewed from the side. Props with aft rake are often used in high-speed applications and tend to work well with ventilating propellers.

A propeller's *bore* is the diameter of the tapered hole in the middle of the hub. The hole is tapered to match the taper at the shaft end, so that more force just drives the prop on tighter. A slot in the shaft lines up with a slot in the propeller hub, and a key is inserted in the aligned slots to prevent the prop from rotating independently of the shaft. Two nuts tightened on the shaft end hold the prop in place, and a cotter key is used to fix the second nut. Propellers are available in different classes, Class 1 being more precisely made than class 4. All else being equal, a class 1 prop will run smoother and more efficiently.

Ventilation and Cavitation

These are two often-misapplied terms that are actually quite simple to explain. *Ventilation* occurs when ambient air is drawn in to the propeller, such as in a sharp turn or with an outboard that is mounted or trimmed too high. It can also happen when spray strakes direct air into the propeller. The propeller loses its bite, and engine rpm shoots up very quickly. A high-speed boat can also ventilate its prop when jumping out of the water from wave to wave, and the rudder can ventilate if mounted too close to the transom.

A propeller *cavitates* when it is highly loaded. The suction (forward) side of the propeller blade is under very low pressure and water vaporizes in this low-pressure region adjacent to the blade surface. The water is able to boil and vaporize at the relatively low temperature of the surrounding water because a liquid's boiling point decreases with atmospheric pressure. As the propeller cavitates, tiny steam bubbles are formed and then collapse upon reaching the higher-pressure region at the tips of the blades. These bubbles actually collapse in contact with the surface of the propeller, a little like a million tiny jackhammers banging away and gradually eroding the propeller. Excessive cavitation can also cause higher vibration levels and a loss of speed and efficiency. Some thrust is lost by moderate cavitation, but this is actually compensated for by the diminished power needed to turn the cavitating propeller.

Prop Materials

Most inboard propellers are made of bronze or a strong alloy such as nibral (*nickel-bronze-aluminum*) that's tough enough to hold its shape after absorbing tremendous water pressure but easy enough to manufacturer and repair to be economically feasible for the boatowner. A bronze or nibral prop falls between aluminum and stainless steel in both cost and strength. Very-high-performance propellers might be made of stainless steel, but these are expensive and more difficult to repair when damaged. Being harder, they also transmit impact energy more readily to the rest of the drivetrain, which is not a good thing.

Outboard and stern-drive propellers are commonly made of aluminum, stainless steel, or composites. Aluminum props are cheaper and lighter, and generally don't perform quite as well as stainless steel. But they also break and deform much more readily, reducing the chances of impact damage to the lower unit if you hit a rock. A stainless steel prop offers excellent performance in part because the blades can be thinner yet remain stronger and stiffer (deforming less under load) than aluminum. It is rugged and durable, but it also costs the most and is most apt to cause damage to the lower unit gears upon impact. On the other hand, a stainless prop stands up much better to abrasion from contact with sand and pebbles.

Composite propellers for outboards and stern drives are usually made of fiber-reinforced plastic (FRP) or another synthetic material. Like aluminum props, they are cheaper and more forgiving on impact than stainless props. I've tested composite propellers made by Piranha Propellers and found that they offer distinct advantages over both stainless steel and aluminum. They performed about as well as a stainless prop and better than an aluminum prop on my 22-foot Grady-White powered by a 225 hp Yamaha. Each composite blade is detachable from the aluminum hub, so if you damage one it can easily (and cheaply, at about $20 per blade) be replaced. The blades are made of a composite fiberglass-nylon material called Verton that

the manufacturer says has a tensile strength 10 to 15 percent greater than aluminum, and each blade comes from the same mold, helping to ensure that they're the exact same dimensions and shape to minimize vibration when running. I wouldn't hesitate to use one of these composite props over a metal one on a stern drive or outboard.

Side Forces

Propellers generate side force as well as thrust. That's because the blades get more bite, or meet more resistance, in the higher-pressure water at the bottom of their arc and because of the corkscrew effect caused by the angle of the blades as they rotate through the water; this refers to the tendency of the prop, free of its shaft, to follow the path of least resistance in the direction of its blade surface. A right-handed propeller going forward will want to

Piranha's synthetic propeller blades are cheap and easy to replace one by one. In the author's experience, they perform at least as well as aluminum props and about as well as stainless steel.

PIRANHA PROPELLER

pull the stern of the boat to starboard, giving the boat a slight tendency to veer to port. The same propeller will pull to port in reverse. This walking effect is why an outboard or stern drive with a single prop will turn more easily (with manual steering) one way than the other; the propeller tends to pull the lower unit to one side or the other depending on its direction of rotation. A single-screw inboard with a right-handed prop will turn sharper to port when running ahead and will also back to port more readily for the same reason.

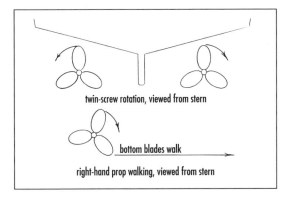

twin-screw rotation, viewed from stern

bottom blades walk

right-hand prop walking, viewed from stern

The outboard-turning props in most twin-screws twist the boat more effectively since side forces are complementary.

GERR, *PROPELLER HANDBOOK*

Side forces are canceled out in boats with twin props rotating in opposite directions and also with counterrotating props on a single shaft. On boats with two propellers, the props nearly always turn in an outboard direction, with a left-handed prop to port and a right-handed prop to starboard. The combined and complementary walking effects of the twin props, when they're running opposed with one engine ahead and the other astern, increase the turning ability of a twin-screw boat, twisting the vessel in its own length.

Since for every action there's a equal and opposite reaction, when a single-screw inboard's propeller rotates through the water, it transmits its torque to the hull, which tends to rotate in the opposite direction. That's why at high speed, some single-engine boats will heel to one side in the ab-

sence of a weight shift or wind and wave force. If the prop rotates to the right, the boat will tend to rotate (or heel) to the left, or port. This effect is more pronounced with larger propellers that develop more torque. In a twin-screw installation, the torque is canceled out.

With a counterrotating propeller, two props are mounted on a single engine, one directly behind the other, and they rotate in opposite directions to cancel out side forces. Counterrotating props also improve the efficiency of the engine by taking the twist out of its discharge race. They are used on some single-engine stern drives from MerCruiser (Bravo 3) and Volvo (DuoProp), and also on a few outboards.

Propeller Efficiency

In all but very-high-performance boats, larger, slower-turning propellers are more efficient, faster, and more responsive than small, fast-turning props. Still, many builders use smaller props and run them faster to save weight, reduce draft, or just cut costs. You'll notice a big difference in the slow-speed maneuvering responsiveness of your boat with the same engine(s) fitted with 3:1 rather than 1.5:1 ratio gears. Larger props will invariably produce less slip and a cleaner wake, since more water is being moved at a slower speed. Because of its greater blade area, a larger prop also allows the same overall power to be applied with less pressure per square inch on the blade's surface, reducing risk of blade overload and cavitation.

A safe rule of thumb is to get the largest gear ratio and biggest propeller you can fit. Blade tip speed should be kept to 150 feet per second to avoid blade tip cavitation. To find blade tip speed, multiply your propeller diameter (in inches) by pi (3.1416), divide by 12, multiply by shaft rpm at full throttle, and divide by 60.

The relationship between diameter and pitch is worth mentioning, too. In the average propeller, an inch of diameter will absorb about as much engine power and torque as two inches of pitch. For example, if your engine is under-revving at full throttle by two hundred rpm, decreasing pitch by two inches would have about the same effect as shaving off an inch of diameter. Blades can also be *cupped* at their trailing (aft) edge, which increases the engine's load and therefore the boat's speed by increasing the velocity of the waterflow off the blade tip. Adding cup to a propeller is often a good way to improve performance without changing to a larger prop, assuming the engine has enough power to turn it.

Unless deeper gear ratios are taken to extremes, don't worry about running out of pitch. The right balance between pitch, diameter, cup, DAR, and number of blades will produce the appropriate cruising speed and the responsiveness. Hatteras, for instance, uses very deep gears and six- or seven-bladed props with enormous pitch relative to diameter.

Propeller Pockets

Propeller pockets are a poorly understood and sometimes poorly designed feature of modern inboard planing boats. Proper pocket design is critical to boat performance and handling but is often overlooked or misunderstood by both builder and owner.

Prop pockets should not be confused with propeller tunnels, which are deep recesses in the hull that more or less enclose a propeller, like on the old Penn Yan tunnel drives. A prop pocket, depending on the boat, might be a quarter to a third of the propeller diameter in depth. Properly shaped and matched to the propellers, prop pockets reduce propeller shaft angles, decrease draft, and allow engine placement farther aft. They can even increase propulsive efficiency, since a pocket will accommodate a larger, more efficient propeller even while permitting a reduction in draft.

In contrast, poorly designed prop pockets will decrease propulsive efficiency, detract from handling, increase vibration and, because they reduce buoyancy and dynamic lift, cause a boat to run with an excessive bow-high attitude.

The differences between good and bad propeller pockets concern their shape, volume, and dimensions. A prop pocket has to be long enough to

The pad at the base of this Tiara's shaft strut is nicely contoured to match the propeller pocket radius, and it's flush with the hull to minimize drag and waterflow disturbance around the prop.

provide a smooth transition for water flowing into its forward end at high speed, but not so long as to compromise dynamic lift and buoyancy. The pocket's cross-sectional shape is also crucial to good performance, and should be properly radiused to conform to the arc of the blade tips. When pockets are properly shaped with the same radius as the prop, prop tip clearance requirements are reduced dramatically—in theory to zero, but in practice to just a few percent of the propeller diameter—allowing larger, more efficient propellers to be used while still decreasing overall draft.

This minimal clearance contrasts favorably with a pocketless design, which requires a 15 to 20 percent clearance between the tip of the blade at the top of its swing and the flat hull bottom above it. Without such clearance, vibration levels would be unacceptable. Put another way, propellers run smoother in a radiused pocket since the blades operate in a smoother, more even waterflow, and localized areas of high pressure (caused by flat-bottom sections above the prop) are largely eliminated. Since propeller pockets reduce shaft angles, propulsion thrust is closer to horizontal and more efficient. And with the propeller closer to the hull bottom and the shaft exiting the hull at the forward end of the pocket, both the shaft and its supporting strut(s) can be shorter, reducing appendage weight and drag.

The tight blade tip clearances of a good pocket also greatly reduce *tip loss*, which is the lost thrust of water flowing centrifugally outward rather than aft off a propeller. By focusing the discharge race aft, a pocket increases forward thrust and efficiency.

A planing hull with propeller pockets is a tricky thing to design properly. As we saw in chapter 4, planing boats have flat buttock lines aft and therefore run most efficiently at a trim angle of 2 degrees (for a warped-bottom design) to 5 degrees (for a constant-deadrise, deep-V design). The problem is that deep prop pockets detract from dynamic lift aft by forcing a large volume of water to flow up into the pocket rather than aft undisturbed along the flat buttocks. The resultant loss of dynamic lift causes the stern to squat and the bow to rise, increasing fuel consumption for a given speed or power setting.

Some boatbuilders produce prop pockets that are ill shaped for their purpose. Take a peek under the bottoms of some of these boats and you'll see propeller pockets that are excessively deep relative to the propeller diameter, with nearly vertical sides and flat tops. These deep, slab-sided cross sections can detract from performance and handling, and their shape and excessive volume decrease buoyancy at rest and dynamic lift at planing speeds.

This frequently results in a boat that will "aim for the sky" when coming up on plane, and once over the hump will ride with an excessively bow-up attitude. The operator of such a boat will lose sight of the horizon at least some of the time, and may have to stand up to see over the bow even when trim tabs are lowered. Large pockets also add significantly to wetted surface, further increasing drag. Builders can decrease trim angle by reducing the "exit region" area of the tunnel aft of the propeller, thus accelerating the discharge race and deflecting it downward, but this too can be taken to extremes and will cause a dynamic instability with excessive bow-down attitude if carried too far.

The tops of deep prop pockets come closer to the waterline, and this too can be a problem. In extreme cases, backing down will introduce air into the pocket, and the resultant ventilation can cause the propeller and rudder to lose their bite.

Some of us have been on cruisers that responded bizarrely to steering and engine commands. Just fire up one of these shiny new propeller pocket–impaired beauties and head down the middle of the basin. When you back the starboard engine at idle, the bow falls off to port. Or, idling along with both engines in gear, put the rudders over full to port and observe as nothing discernible happens. Finally, throttle up and watch the boat head for the stars as the stern stalls underfoot and it struggles up on plane. The problem isn't with the engines; it's in the way the engine power is transmitted to the water via gear ratio, propeller size, and prop pocket design.

Now try running a well-engineered boat like a Fairline 65 from the lower station, and you'll never lose sight of the horizon at any speed. When I ran sea trials on this boat for the first time a few years ago, the bow rose less than four degrees when coming up on plane even without using trim tabs. Try the same stunt with a lot of 40-footers, with or without pockets and with half as much foredeck to interfere with your sightline. You won't see the horizon in front of you for a half-dozen boat lengths as you struggle to come up on plane.

At three effortless turns lock-to-lock, the Fairline also responded crisply to the helm. Fairline has broken the code on prop pocket design (along with hull form, rudder design, weight distribution, etc.). The imported Viking Sport Cruisers built by the United Kingdom's Princess Yachts, and also designed by Fairline's naval architect, Bernard Olesinski, is another brand that offers comparable performance.

So, to sum up, when prop pockets are reasonably shallow (no more than 40 percent of the propeller diameter) and radiused in cross section, and engines are mated to steeper gear ratios and larger propellers, we consistently see improved throttle and clutch responsiveness. Additional benefits include increased propulsion efficiency, faster cruising speeds, faster time to plane, lower vibration levels, less loss of buoyancy and dynamic lift aft, and better operator visibility. Steering is also improved without the excessive directional stability imparted by slab-sided prop pockets fighting the rudder's effort to turn the boat.

Waterjets

Waterjets have taken off, literally and figuratively, like no other small-craft propulsion system. Designed to work most efficiently at speeds of about 25 to 45 knots, they're maneuverable and can operate in shallow water that would leave other boats high and dry. Dealers of waterjet-propelled boats make a point of driving over rather than around lobster pot buoys to make their point about the absence of conventional running gear. For the same reason, waterjets are far safer to swim from than conventional inboards. They also offer superior efficiency for high cruising speeds. So how do they do it?

Waterjets, which can be powered by diesel, gas turbine, or gas engines, operate by drawing water in through a grate in the bottom of the boat, pumping it at high velocity with an impeller (a type of propeller in a tunnel) in a precisely shaped tube and discharging it out the stern through a steerable nozzle. The shape of the inlet is crucial to achieving optimum performance, since peak efficiency depends on capturing as much as possible of the frictional boundary layer of water traveling along with the hull. Since the boundary layer has already been accelerated by the hull's friction, the impeller can more easily accelerate it to the required propulsion velocity.

One reason waterjets are more efficient than submerged props at high speeds is that a propeller has to work harder due to its interaction with the hull. The waterjet impeller's discharge is focused and directed exclusively aft, while the conventional propeller loses efficiency as water spills off the blade tips.

The nozzle is fitted with a bucket that drops down and deflects water forward to stop or reverse the boat. This backing capability allows a waterjet-powered boat to stop quickly, since the engine need not be slowed and shifted into reverse. Triple or quadruple waterjet applications usually eliminate the steering nozzles and reversing buckets on the inboard engines.

Because water is drawn up and into the waterjet housing, and the thrust is high relative to the vessel's center of gravity, the hull tends to run at a lower trim angle than with a conventional submerged propeller. This should be factored into the hull's design and weight distribution.

Waterjets have distinct advantages in boats capable of full-load cruising at 25-knot-plus speeds. Eliminating the conventional inboard's running gear enhances high-speed efficiency, and vibration and sound levels are a lot lower than with submerged propellers for a couple of reasons. Since the engines do not absorb the impeller thrust (the waterjet housing does), they can be soft mounted and allowed to "dance" around freely. Also, the impeller is enclosed in a housing and receives an even flow of water, unlike a submerged propeller, which is inclined at the shaft angle and subject to uneven waterflow and variable loading through its arc of rotation.

Once you get the hang of it, it's hard not to show off a little when maneuvering a twin water-

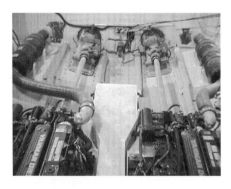

A Little Harbor Whisperjet drivetrain, with twin 420 hp Yanmars driving Hamilton waterjets through jackshafts and CV joints.

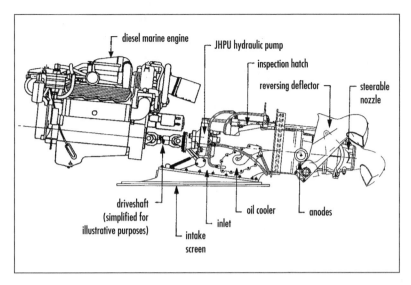

The various components of a Hamilton waterjet.   HAMILTON

jet. They're a kick to drive and, in the right hands, much more maneuverable than a twin-screw conventional inboard. In fact, you can walk many twin waterjet boats more or less sideways, assuming the waterjets are mounted far enough apart.

So why isn't every boat waterjet propelled? There are several answers, including hull form, midrange performance, and rough-water capability.

Hull Design

A waterjet-powered boat needs a hull that's specifically designed for it. This is important if it is to handle and run well, especially in a following sea. The hull must be designed to achieve adequate directional stability in the absence of underwater struts and rudders, and the formula includes buoyant (with modest deadrise and not too fine an entry) bow sections to prevent bow steering, a moderate beam-to-length ratio, and enough deadrise aft (usually at least 16 degrees) to help the boat track relatively straight with seas abaft the beam. The trade-off is that in order to prevent bow steering in a waterjet-powered hull, you'll likely have to give up the deep, fine Blackfin-like entry that would produce a great headsea ride.

Besides directional stability, another design

consideration is preventing air from getting to the impellers with resulting reduced waterflow and thrust. Waterjets require a smooth, uninterrupted flow of solid (unaerated) water through the intake grates, which are mounted flush with the hull bottom. If the bow is too blunt (or shallow, with low deadrise), the water passing back to the impeller intake may be heavily aerated, causing impeller ventilation. Adequate deadrise amidships and aft helps to direct air outboard before it reaches the waterjet inlets, and running strakes must also be positioned so that they don't direct airflow to the intakes.

The waterjet also must be deeply enough submerged (with the top of the tunnel below the waterline) to keep it primed and to ensure a good, air-free bite on solid water in a chop. The hull's buoyancy aft must suffice to accommodate the added weight of waterjets (full of water) in the stern, and in some hulls this mandates shifting the engines farther forward to maintain proper static trim. These requirements make some hulls not very well suited to waterjet propulsion, such as flat-bottom boats and most traditional Down East–style hulls.

Though waterjets clearly do not enjoy the directional stability of a conventional keel- and rudder-equipped inboard (especially in a quartering sea), there are fixes available. Builders like Hinckley install hull fins just forward of the transom to control the tendency of some waterjet-propelled boats to spin out, or to bank excessively in a hard turn. Oversized fins might trip a boat in a hard, high-speed turn, however, so they must be carefully tested. Perhaps the best but most expensive solution to squirrelly directional stability is retractable rudders, which can be lowered for more control at slower speeds and in following seas, and raised to reduce drag in more favorable running conditions.

Sea State Limitations

When a hull becomes airborne in rough water, the waterjet loses its prime and propulsive power is momentarily cut. For this reason, any boat that routinely operates offshore and in rough water at high speeds will likely be better off with submerged propellers. Another consideration is that rough water requires running at slower, semidisplacement speeds, speeds at which waterjets generally fare poorly.

Low-Speed and Midrange Performance

The amount of horsepower a waterjet impeller can absorb at intermediate engine speeds is much less than that of a propeller. That means that an engine driving a waterjet has to turn a lot more rpm to match the thrust and speed of a conventional inboard of the same power. In fact, the waterjet typically doesn't begin to develop similar thrust until it's close to full throttle. Take, for example, a 700 hp diesel running at an easy 1,850 rpm cruise; a submerged propeller will absorb 470 hp and the waterjet only 360 hp. In fact, the waterjet doesn't absorb 470 hp until the engine reaches 2,000 rpm. Its relatively small impeller just can't get as much "bite" at slower speeds, and responds sluggishly to midrange throttle adjustments. This lack of midrange thrust also increases the potential for cavitation, since there is a limit to how much the small inlet's waterflow can be accelerated in such a confined area. Thought of another way, once the hull gets on plane, the water velocity at the waterjet inlet is already high, and thus experiences a lesser acceleration through the impeller. This means less pressure reduction and therefore less cavitation on the backside of the impeller blades.

Selecting a large enough waterjet unit is important, since the cavitation produced by too small a unit (for the boat's displacement) can erode the aluminum impeller housing and the impeller itself. For this reason, waterjet manufacturers recommend against operating in the midrange any more than necessary.

So what does this mean for the boatowner? If you compare two identical hulls with the same power, one with waterjets and the other with submerged props, the latter will generally perform far better in the 8- to 22-knot (plus or minus) range. That can be a problem for waterjets if sea conditions mandate these lower planing speeds.

And since a waterjet doesn't start to operate most efficiently until it climbs above 25 knots, a boat must have enough continuous horsepower to cruise at (not just reach) these high speeds with a full load.

Waterjets only come into their own at relatively high planing speeds. They have to work hard to get up on plane, and they tend to run inefficiently below 22 to 25 knots. For high-performance planing hulls, one of the greatest difficulties is designing a waterjet-engine combination that will both get the boat up on plane and then perform well at high cruising speeds. The 25-knot figure (a generally agreed upon number in the industry) is the point at which the low drag and propulsion efficiency curves start to cross.

A hull fully on plane creates a lot less drag than one climbing onto plane. Getting past hump speed is the hardest work a propulsion engine has to do, and it's even more of a milestone for a midrange-impaired waterjet. This illustrates the advantage of a two-speed gear; a prop can be chosen for optimum high-speed performance, and the two-speed gear allows the engine to turn faster and develop sufficient power while getting up on plane.

Waterjet boats are less able than conventional prop-driven boats to carry significant weight through midrange speeds and especially onto plane. If a new waterjet boat exceeds design-displacement estimates at launch, it may not be able to plane at all. Enhancing this unfortunate prospect is the fact that larger-diameter waterjets are costly and add still more weight, so the builder's natural

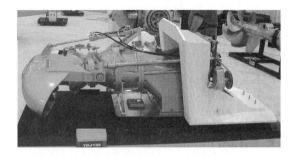

This Twin Disc waterjet is all shined up for presentation at a boat show. In clear view on top of the unit is the hydraulic cylinder used to control the backing bucket to the left.

With this Sunseeker high-performance cruiser, the surface drives are incorporated into the hull overhang in the original design, a more satisfactory solution, perhaps, than bolting on an 8-foot swim platform.

tendency is to fit the first hull of a model line with a smaller unit and hope to meet the owner's expectations for performance. Little Harbor Yachts, a leading waterjet-powered yacht builder, often installs the next bigger waterjet in the first hull of a series than the computer-generated performance prediction numbers called for, just to make sure the boat meets performance specifications.

Waterjet-powered boats tend to get blown around a lot due to their lack of running gear and keel. They take some getting used to since they can handle unpredictably and sluggishly at low speeds. Hinckley has developed a patented JetStick to ease these handling chores, and the device works well. Use of the JetStick allows you to dock and undock a boat without your hand ever leaving the single control lever.

The waterjet impeller is susceptible to fouling by floating sea grass or other debris. A fouled jet can be cleaned by reversing the impeller and blasting the debris out, or hand cleaned from an internal access port. Designers also have to accommodate the added weight of the waterjet drive system and the water entrained in the tunnel. And to top things off, waterjets cost big bucks.

If you don't plan to do a lot of rough water cruising, if you value low vibration levels and minimal draft, if you operate in waters choked with pot buoys or debris, and if you want to cruise at 25-plus knots and stop on a dime, waterjet propulsion may be just the ticket. You'll be able to "hotdog" around

the bay once you get the hang of the handling the boat, and it'll be hard not to show off a little.

Surface-Piercing Propeller Drives

For cruising speeds above 40 knots, nothing beats a surface-piercing propeller. The faster it goes, the more efficient it becomes compared with other drives, since it creates so little drag. The surface-drive (SD) concept goes back to the nineteenth century, but Howard Arneson is largely responsible for developing the idea into the best high-speed propulsion system, and one used by fast yachts and patrol boats around the world today. Surface drives are also the most expensive propulsion systems in use on recreation craft, in part because the specialized prop is so expensive.

With only half of the propeller submerged, the running gear and associated drag of a conventional inboard are eliminated. Some manufacturers and propulsion engineers claim that as much as a 50 percent reduction in drag is realized as a result. A surface-drive propeller can be much larger than a submerged propeller, since it's not buried below the hull, taking full advantage of a larger propeller's in-

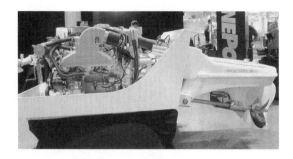

A novel setup, this PulseDrive surface-piercing unit is delivered ready to install as a unit, like a stern-drive package, with the platform above integral to the drivetrain.

Another view of an Arneson surface-piercing drive.

herent efficiency. A deeper gear ratio and a larger, more lightly loaded, slower-turning propeller is the key to SD performance.

The thrust developed by a surface-piercing drive has both horizontal and vertical components. In fact, vertical lift from the spinning surface-piercing propeller is as much as 80 percent of the forward thrust. This huge vertical lift component raises the stern and contributes to the ease with which a SD-powered boat planes, the equivalent of a shift forward of LCG. The vertical lift component is accentuated by the surface-piercing propeller's usual location 5 or 6 feet aft of the transom, creating a substantial lever arm. LCG should then be well aft, just 35 to 40 percent of waterline length forward of the transom, to help compensate for this significant dynamic lift at the propeller.

Two pistons generally support the SD shaft and propeller; one controls side-to-side movement, and the other, vertical movement. The first is what allows the boat to be steered, while the second allows the height of the propeller—that is, its immersion depth—to be regulated. The deeper the propeller is in the water, the more thrust it produces. Consequently, the surface-piercing operator is effectively able to vary the diameter of the propeller and the load on the engine.

Since the engine can produce only so much power at a given rpm setting, propeller immersion is matched to the rpm setting, much like a controllable-pitch propeller. If the boat's trim or load

changes, the propeller can be raised or lowered to compensate. When accelerating over the hump to get on plane, the propeller can be raised to decrease the load on the engine. This permits more rapid acceleration and eliminates the need for a two-speed transmission, a frequent requirement of submerged-propeller drives that are overloaded in their low to middle performance range.

Cavitation is a recurring problem in most high-speed applications with significant blade loading. If unchecked, it causes blade erosion, vibration, and loss of speed. The SD gets around this problem by using a super-ventilating propeller that introduces air bubbles into the low-pressure region on the leading (forward) edge of the blades where cavitation develops. Each time a blade slices down through the surface of the water, it takes along ventilating air bubbles with it that shroud the blade, cushioning the blade's surface and preventing the harmful effects of cavitation.

At low speeds, as with waterjets, surface-piercing drives steer less surely than conventional inboards. Backing can also be a problem, especially in some race boats that use highly raked cleaver props. A more rounded prop design takes a couple of knots off the top end, but time-to-plane, backing, and low-speed maneuverability improve.

With the propellers churning partially out of the water five feet aft of the transom, safety is a definite concern. Stern projections or swim platforms cover the drives of most SD boats, helping to protect the boat's occupants as well as the propellers themselves.

Compared with conventional propellers, surface-piercing propellers endure far greater variation in blade loading as they rotate alternately through air and water. This generates high vibrations as well as creating higher stresses on drivetrain components and must be accounted for in the system's design. These propellers have high camber (curvature) and blade angle and essentially chop their way through the water, generating a reactive thrust from the pressure on the blades' trailing surfaces. (In comparison, a jet engine produces reactive thrust with its high-velocity gas discharge.)

Submerged propellers, on the other hand, have high- and low-pressure areas on the trailing and leading surfaces of their blades, respectively, that combine to provide thrust. Submerged propellers, in other words, act by pulling as well as pushing their way through the water.

SD propellers are very expensive. They can have from four to seven blades—five or six being most common—and the more blades, the more expensive and smoother running the system will be. SD props from 15 to 30 inches in diameter are usually made of stainless steel, with larger propellers made of a bronze alloy.

LCG is important to proper surface-drive performance, and weight studies must be done to ascertain whether a vessel is suitable to be built or retrofitted with an SD system. Twin Disc Corporation, which owns the Arneson brand of surface drive, also sells waterjets. They consult with their customers about speed, cost, and safety priorities, and then advise on propulsion system choice accordingly.

If you want high performance and like the idea of surface drives, but don't want the units projecting aft of the transom, a company called Power Vent may offer a solution. This surface-drive package fits into a tunnel system in the hull bottom, which makes the system well suited for new construction but very difficult to retrofit.

Power Vent's propellers are fixed, which re-quires that the tunnel design provide the proper water height to the props. This makes it imperative to get the installation right to start with. The drive has been used in boats up to 51 feet long, and the manufacturer claims a performance similar to that of conventional surface-piercing drives. The number of moving parts—including steering and trim cylinders, U-joints, and external seals—weight, and cost are all reduced by this system. Reliability should improve, but the ability to trim the unit is lost. The ideal candidate for Power Vent would seem to be a boat that does not vary excessively in weight (and thus, immersion and trim) from full to light load. The clear transom is a big bonus for fishing boats. As with any surface-piercing drive, excellent efficiency at high speed and shoal draft are part of the package.

CHAPTER 9

Rudders and Steering Systems

Rowing harder doesn't help if the boat is headed in the wrong direction.

—Kenichi Ohmae

Once the hull form has been perfected and the most appropriate propulsion system and drivetrain selected, the next step is to make sure the steering system is up to snuff. A rudder's size and shape, maximum turning angle, and position beneath the boat, along with responsiveness to the wheel (turns lock-to-lock), are all important factors.

Rudders

To steer the boat, rudders generate lateral, or sideways lift, which creates a turning moment about the hull's pivot point. This point is usually about one-third of the waterline length aft of the bow, but depends on the fore-and-aft location of the rudders and the shape of the hull bottom. The pivot point also changes with speed, moving forward at higher speeds and aft as the boat slows and backs down. For instance, if you're backing with significant sternway and shift the engines into forward with a little power, the pivot point may momentarily be closer to the transom than the bow pulpit.

Shape

Not surprisingly, the shape of the rudder has a great deal to do with its performance. In cross section, the rudder of a low-speed boat might resemble the cross section of an airplane wing (airfoil) with a blunt leading edge trailing aft to a long, gentle taper. This is a shape that minimizes drag. However,

the thick leading edge of an airfoil creates turbulence and cavitation when turned at higher speeds, so rudders of this shape lose lift and stall at a fairly small angle. As a result, high-speed planing hulls usually have ax-head (wedge-shaped in cross section) or flat-plate rudders, which add a little drag when centered but create more lift at higher speeds and resist stalling at greater angles of attack.

Rudders must also be balanced, with the proper distribution of surface area forward and aft of the rudderpost to minimize strain on the steering gear. Generally speaking, about 16 to 17 percent

A Luhrs 40 Open's running gear. The flush shaft strut minimizes drag, and the ax-head rudder provides a stall-free, 70-degree range of motion. The cutaway aft-top corner of the rudder prevents air from being drawn in from aft of the transom and stalling the rudder. Prop tip clearance is well in excess of the 15 to 20 percent minimum standard.

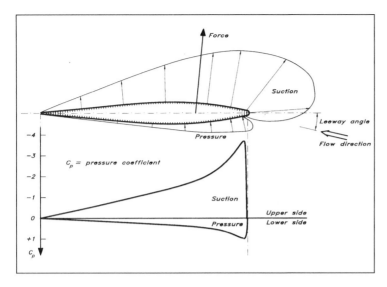

This illustration shows how lift is generated by pressure as well as suction on an airfoil-shaped rudder. The narrowing low-pressure area at the trailing (aft) edge of the rudder (when it's put over to one side) is the reason boatbuilders go to pains to prevent air from being introduced via the transom. They do this either by notching the top-aft rudder edge, by installing an anticavitation plate above the rudder, or by just locating the rudder farther forward under the hull bottom away from the transom.

LARSSON AND ELIASSON, *PRINCIPLES OF YACHT DESIGN*

of the rudder surface area should be forward of the stock. This reduces the effort required to put the rudder over at speed.

Size and Location

Rudder size is always a compromise between minimizing high-speed drag and maximizing low-speed responsiveness. If the rudders are too large, they will slow the boat at high speed. If too small (which is more often the case), helm response will be sluggish, especially at slower speeds, or outright hazardous when running at speed in a rough following sea. Generally speaking, larger rudders are more responsive, and greater rudder area confers greater low-speed maneuvering. When boats are equipped with flat-sided propeller tunnels, the rudders have to be large enough to overcome the resistance to turning created by the tunnel sides. In fact, that's another argument in favor of shallow, radiused prop pockets.

Since larger rudders add drag, slowing a boat at

high speeds, some boatbuilders tend to minimize rudder size so their performance numbers look as good as possible. You may be willing to trade off a good deal of slow-speed handling ability for a higher speed potential, but you should be aware of what you're giving up.

In an effort to keep propeller shaft angles as near horizontal as possible, builders often place a propeller as far aft as possible. This naturally forces the rudder(s) aft as well, in order to preserve its proper location aft of the propeller, where propeller wash makes it most effective. Rudders placed nearer the transom can also be a little smaller than those placed farther forward, since they do their work farther from the pivot point and thus operate at the end of a longer lever arm. But rudders should be far enough from the transom not to ventilate (draw air in by vacuum) and stall in high-speed turns, or perhaps even cause the stern to

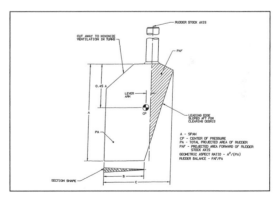

An ax-head or wedge-shaped rudder profile and cross section. CP is the center of pressure impinging on the rudders as a result of propeller discharge. The shaded area forward eases the strain on the steering gear by applying counteracting pressure *into* a turn.

DONALD L. BLOUNT ASSOCIATES

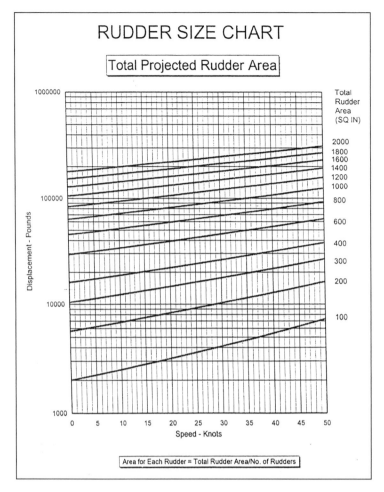

RUDDER SIZE CHART

Total Projected Rudder Area

The minimum rudder area needed for adequate steering responsiveness based on vessel speed and displacement. A bigger rudder adds drag at high speed but also adds responsiveness at slow speeds. DONALD L. BLOUNT ASSOCIATES

lift. If too close to the transom, they can be cropped at the top, trailing edge provided there is surface area to spare; alternatively, a horizontal plate can be installed on the hull bottom to extend its effective running surface aft of the transom.

Planing hulls bank into a turn in spite of the fact that the centrifugal force acting on their VCG (vertical center of gravity), which is well above the waterline, should make them bank away. This is a result of the dynamic pressures acting on the hull and the rudder(s). Thus, although a rudder of high aspect ratio (one that's deep and narrow) creates

less drag and more lift than a shorter, wider one, the rudder's turning moment also has to be considered. If the center of the rudder's side force is excessively deep, an exaggerated heeling moment can be created causing the boat to lean sharply into a turn.

A slow boat can be overtaken by a strong following sea, which might throw the rudder full left or right and swing the boat into a broach in the opposite direction. To guard against this, a displacement hull needs a deep rudder that projects downward into undisturbed water, where it will be more effective. A deeper rudder also remains more effective as the stern rises or the boat heels, ensuring better control. Slow, heavy, deep-draft displacement vessels also require larger rudders and more powerful steering gear than lighter, faster boats of the same length because their greater draft and full keels produce greater directional stability and resistance to turning.

Dynamics

The best test of a rudder's effectiveness is a boat running downsea, especially if the boat is bow-heavy and its longitudinal center of gravity is a bit too far forward. An unusually deep forefoot also complicates matters, behaving like a rudder and causing the boat to bow steer. If such a forefoot is also fine, which it usually is, the bow won't develop enough buoyancy, or dynamic lift, to prevent it from being immersed even deeper when the stern is raised by a wave, making it harder still for the rudders to keep the boat on course.

The hull itself should provide a certain amount of directional stability when it's running at speed.

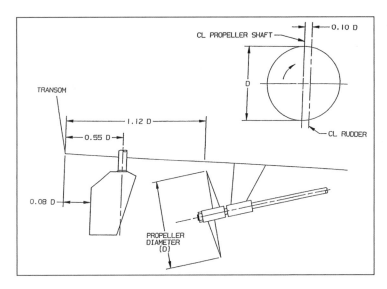

Rudder location guidelines. This rudder is placed optimally, well forward of the transom so ventilating isn't an issue, but far enough aft so that the rudders are still effective in turning the hull about its pivot point. A rudder that continues flush with the hull bottom is actually the most efficient, since waterflow or spillage off the top edge of the rudder is prevented.   DONALD L. BLOUNT ASSOCIATES

with judicious use of throttles and gears. Running offshore in a heavy following sea at semidisplacement speeds, the engine speeds can also be varied or even opposed in direction to help the boat keep on course. When I was a coast guard coxswain on a 44-foot motor surfboat, our standard procedure was to put the most seasoned boat handler on the throttles and the less experienced seaman at the wheel when towing. Steering the boat is instinctive after you've spent a couple of hours at the helm, but backing an engine to kick the stern over with headway on and without stalling is trickier, especially when the shrimper you're towing is three times your size and you're trying to keep the hawser taut.

Too little, and the boat wanders; too much and the boat will require very large rudders to overcome the hull's tracking ability. The steering system must be selected with a hull's inherent directional stability in mind.

As we saw in chapter 8, a single right-handed propeller will tend to back to port and walk to starboard when running ahead. This effect is much more pronounced when the engine is first put in gear than at faster speeds, when waterflow around the rudder increases. Dynamic pressure builds up quickly as speed increases, and any walking effect is largely masked by the hull's inherent directional stability and by the effect of the rudder. Backing a single-screw boat will invariably result in the stern walking in the direction of the propeller's side force, and it takes a big, barn-door rudder to counteract this side force until the hull gains sternway. Very few single-screw boats will back downwind, though there are exceptions.

This is one time when twin engines come in handy: they will back in any direction you want

When twin engines are installed, a boat should also be fit with twin rudders. Though rarely seen

Here's a view of transom-mounted rudders on a Blackfin 29 sportfisherman. The engines are so far aft that, in the absence of V-drive transmissions, the props have to be situated practically right under the transom. Otherwise, shaft angles would be unacceptably high. These rudders have anticavitation plates built in, and the swim platform above obviates any obstruction otherwise presented by the projecting rudders to an angler playing a fish off the stern.

these days, a twin prop/single rudder setup is problematic for responsive steering, especially in a following sea. The single rudder receives little or no high-velocity prop wash to help it create lift. Rudders need to be placed in the propellers' slip stream, or discharge race, and offset just enough to allow shaft removal.

Rudders on twin-screw boats have to be sized for special circumstances, not simply to steer a vessel with both engines running ahead. They must be capable of steering the boat with only one engine, and be able to turn the boat quickly toward the running engine up or downwind. By no means should this capability be taken for granted.

Twin rudders require special consideration when they're aligned. When a boat turns, the outboard rudder travels a greater distance. This means, for both rudders to be doing the same work, the inner rudder must be at a slightly greater angle to match the tighter circumference of its turn. This geometry requires that the rudder or tiller arms be offset so that rudder inboard to a turn will always be at a greater angle than the outboard rudder.

Rudder and Hull Protection

The bigger a rudder and the greater the hull speed, the more heavily the rudder and its foundation in the hull bottom need to be built. The rudderpost, which passes through the hull inside a bearing with a watertight seal, must of course be able to withstand normal operating stresses, but that is not enough. Bad things happen to good boats, so rudders must be designed so as not to cause the sinking of a boat that runs aground or collides with an underwater object.

Rudderposts may be machined to accept an O-ring shaft seal. This necessitates a channel perhaps ½ inch deep around the post inside the hull, which then becomes the weak link in the rudderpost. If the post fails at this point, at least the inboard segment remains to keep the rudder bearing plugged.

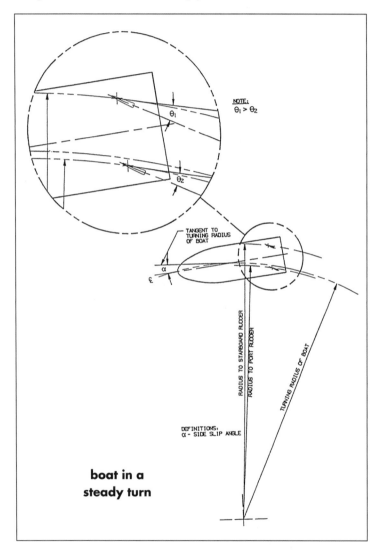

The different paths taken by twin rudders necessitate a sharper rudder angle for the inboard rudder. This angle variation is provided by the toed, or offset, tiller arm.

DONALD L. BLOUNT ASSOCIATES

The top of the rudderpost should be supported by a rudder shelf, or board, so that the entire force of a grounding or collision impact isn't absorbed by the hull alone. The effect of the rudder shelf is like holding a baseball bat at two points rather than just in the middle while someone pulls on one end. Lever arm advantage and strength are gained by supporting the rudderpost in the middle (at the hull) and at the top. This minimizes the chances of a hull rupture and flooding. See more on this subject in chapter 2.

A good way to protect a rudder in a single-engine installation is with a shoe projecting aft from the bottom of a full keel, into which the bottom of the rudderpost is secured. A full keel adds drag and slows a boat down, but the speed loss in a semidisplacement 16- to 20-knot boat is fairly insignificant. This protects the propeller is as well as the rudder, making the full keel an attractive feature for anyone who may bump bottom occasionally.

Some builders extend a rudder tube, similar to a shaft log, above the waterline inside the boat so that even if the rudder falls out the vessel won't flood. Yet another precautionary measure is to

The flat-stock rudder on this Mainship 34 Pilot is supported at both ends, while the notch cut out of the upper trailing edge prevents air from being drawn in, when on plane, from the transom by the low-pressure side of the rudder and causing it to stall. The hull of this semidisplacement boat is heavily built up around the rudderpost, which must be able to absorb heavy impact loads from accidental grounding. With the skeg projecting below the bottom of the full keel, the rudder would absorb part of any grounding loads.

mount rudder stops inside the hull that prevent the rudders from swinging too far to one side or the other. Stops can be especially important with cable steering, since a rudder can otherwise travel to a point from which cable steering can't easily pull it back.

Steering Responsiveness

The faster a vessel can travel, the more responsive its steering needs to be, because evasive maneuvers have to be carried out more quickly as speed increases. The rudder angle induced by each 360-degree turn of the wheel is key. I've seen everything from 2½ to 10 turns lock-to-lock (i.e., full starboard to full port), with the former producing four times as much rudder angle from each turn of the wheel as the latter.

In the interest of helm responsiveness, four turns of the wheel from hard-left to hard-right

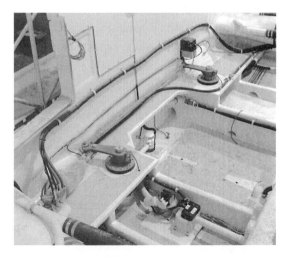

Built like the proverbial brick outhouse, this Viking convertible's fiberglass-encapsulated rudder board secures the top of the rudderposts. With the rudders held securely in two places, in the middle and on one end, the rudder should bend under impact rather than rupturing the hull and flooding the bilge compartment.

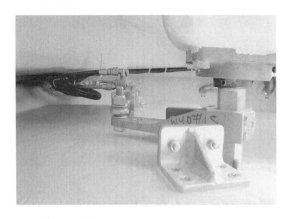

These hard rudder stops on a Nordhavn trawler prevent damage to the steering gear resulting from excessive rudder angle. (Rudders should swing through an arc of 70 degrees.) Recessed pocket above rudderpost *(top right)* provides deck access for emergency tiller. NORDHAVN

(based on a 70-degree rudder arc) is the most that should be accepted, especially on faster boats. Three or 3½ low-effort turns are even better. It simply takes too long to turn a wheel five or six turns. There's also a huge difference in driving ease when you only have to turn the wheel a quarter turn or less to make a small course correction.

There are plenty of 65-footers out there that handle much better than the average 35-foot inboard, and they do it with help from power steering. Power steering uses a small electric motor and pump, or the main engine-powered pump, to provide hydraulic pressure to turn the rudders. All the helmsman is doing at the wheel is indicating to the power steering unit and servo follow-up control valve which direction the rudder arm needs to move and how far. Typical power steering installations require just 3½ turns lock-to-lock and are truly a joy to behold.

When I take a boat on sea trials, one test includes timing a 360-degree turn to port and to starboard. (I test both directions in case the rudders turn farther in one direction than the other.) Using this method on a single-screw boat you can measure the effect of prop walk on the boat's ability to turn. For a typical inboard 45-footer, a 360-

degree turn in 25 seconds is quite good, while 50 seconds or more is sluggish. It all has to do with the steering system design and underwater hull shape.

Some boats come with rudders that only swing 25 or 30 degrees when hard over. But according to the U.S. Navy, the U.S. Coast Guard, and the American Bureau of Shipping, rudders should swing an arc of 70 degrees, or a full 35 degrees to port and to starboard. Don't be told differently. After all, the same hydrodynamic lift and stall principles apply equally to ship and small-boat rudders. Major vendors like Teleflex design their steering systems to the 35-degree standard.

The reason for the standard is simple; the farther a rudder swings (up to a little beyond 35 degrees), the more sideways lift is generated and the shorter the boat's turning radius. Anything less than a 70-degree rudder arc cannot unlock the full potential of your steering system. I've seen some poorly engineered steering systems with maximum rudder angles of as little as 22 degrees. You can easily measure your rudder arc using a protractor against the rudder arm, or by measuring the angle between the rudder stops if installed.

I've seen rudders in workboats that swing as much as 40 degrees to either side, enabling single-engine boats to turn practically in their own length. Above 35 degrees, however, the lift component of the rudder force begins to diminish while the drag from the rudder will slow or even stop the boat.

Rudders need to be balanced to minimize steering effort, but even a well-balanced rudder will take considerable effort to turn, an effort that increases with boat speed, displacement, and rudder size. A smaller rudder naturally turns more easily, which may partly account for the undersized rudders we see on many cruisers and even a few sportfishermen. Of course, maneuvering requirements are higher for sportfishermen, since they spend a lot of time with their sterns pointed at a taut line. Power steering is at least part of the answer for responsive maneuvering.

Steering Systems

The several varieties of steering systems in common usage share a common task, of course: translating steering wheel movement into rudder action. The simplest of these is a tiller, which mounts directly on the rudderpost and dispenses with the steering wheel and intermediate control linkages altogether. Probably the next most basic is cable steering, in which the turning of a steering wheel actuates the rudder(s) via a wire cable or cables. In what is known as *pull-pull* cable steering, several turning blocks, or pulleys, provide a fair lead for the two ends of the cable (one to pull to port and the other to starboard) back to the rudder, where the ends attach to the corresponding corners of a curved quadrant mounted on the rudderpost. Pull-pull cable steering is cheap, simple, and reliable as long as the cables are protected from chafing. A disadvantage of this system is that every rudder vibration along with the propeller's side force is felt at the wheel.

Outboards and stern drives often have push-pull cable steering, which utilizes a semirigid cable in a sleeve, much like engine throttle and shift cables. This single cable both pushes and pulls to turn the lower unit, or rudder, as the case may be. It's important that the cable not be bent too tightly around corners between the helm and lower unit or rudder, because friction (and steering effort) build up quickly around sharp turns. All cables wear out quickly if not properly installed.

Many boats have manual hydraulic steering, in which turning the steering wheel actuates a pump that transmits fluid (and energy) back to a hydraulic cylinder attached to the rudder arm. The direction in which the wheel is turned determines on which side of the steering piston fluid is pumped, thus pushing the rudder arm to one side or the other, and the number of turns of the wheel determines piston and rudder arm travel along with the corresponding rudder angle. Twin rudders are rigidly connected, so that the same cylinder turns both simultaneously. The hydraulic fluid is usually carried by hoses made of high-strength plastic or copper, and an integral locking valve holds the rudder's position when the wheel is not being turned.

Whatever the steering system, the work of turning the rudders is done by the person spinning the wheel unless a power steering system is installed. The helmsman is the motor and the steering head is the pump. In contrast, the steering wheel in a power system merely sends a signal to the power steering unit, which works to match the actual rudder angle with what the helmsman ordered. The effort at the helm is much less.

Tiller Arm Forward of Rudders

Tiller Arm Aft of Rudders

In order for a twin-screw rudder installation to work properly, the tiller arms are toed in so that the rudder in the inside of the turn is at a greater angle than the other. This offset accounts for the rudders' traveling through the water at different angles in a turn.

DONALD L. BLOUNT ASSOCIATES

A manual steering system is cheaper, so manufacturers can save money by installing them on boats that are really too big for them. How big is too big? That depends on a boat's displacement and speed, but 35 feet might be a good average. Since manual systems require the helmsman to serve as the hydraulic pump, extra turns are needed on bigger boats to provide the necessary mechanical advantage to keep steering effort low. Power steering, which costs more to install, not only reduces the effort but, when properly matched to the boat, is able to put the rudder over more quickly.

On smaller cable-steered boats, a no-feedback steering option incorporates a clutch in the cable steering head that prevents the torque from a propeller's side force from having its way with the wheel. The clutch acts like the no-feedback valve in a hydraulic steering system by holding the rudder in place unless the wheel is moved. It's well worth the added expense if it is only offered as an option.

For a boat with multiple steering stations, hydraulic steering is often the way to go. Unlike with a mechanical system, the amount of work done at each helm station is virtually unchanged by the number of stations fitted.

Autopilots

Many boats, even some 20-foot outboards, are fitted with autopilots that tap into the steering system. These units sense the boat's heading, usually from an electronic compass or GPS input, and steer the selected course automatically. Their sensitivity can be adjusted to match the amount of rudder angle it takes to keep the boat on course, which in turn depends on rudder size, the hull's directional stability, displacement, trim, sea state, course, etc. Obviously, the less rudder movement needed to stay on course the better, since putting the rudder over adds drag. The downside of autopilots is that they encourage a lowered vigilance, tempting the helmsman to tend to other chores or simply daydream. Horror stories of resultant accidents abound. A reliable and properly set autopilot can keep a boat on course better than a human can, especially during open-ocean transits, but there is no substitute for a pair of human eyes to avoid collision.

Emergency Steering

It doesn't happen often, but when it does, loss of steering control offshore can ruin the best of days. The ensuing panic can be reduced, or even eliminated, if you have an alternative means of steering the boat home. Small boats might have a "kicker" (small outboard) bolted to the transom that can be used to steer, after a fashion. Larger inboards with hydraulic steering do well to carry a manual tiller that will fit on top of one of the rudderposts if needed. Just make sure there's an easy means of disconnecting the hydraulic lines from the rudder arm or bypassing the lock valve so the rudder is free to travel back and forth. A six-inch-diameter access cover directly above the rudderpost permits mounting the emergency tiller while keeping the lazarette hatch closed—an important consideration when seas are running, which according to Murphy's Law will be the case when your steering fails. Also, be sure that the emergency tiller arm is long enough to give you leverage on the rudder, rather than the other way around. Finally, as long as the rudders are close to amidships (pointing straight ahead), twin engines can also be used to steer a boat home in a pinch.

Outboards and Stern-Drive Considerations

As mentioned above, no-feedback steering is especially important on outboard and stern-drive-powered boats. That's because the side force of the propeller tends to pull the lower unit to one side with significant force, and the operator ends up wrestling with the steering rather than enjoying the ride.

Inboards steer by deflecting prop wash off the rudders, whereas outboards and stern drives steer with their propeller's thrust as well as with the rudder effect of the submerged drive unit. As a result, steering response is more immediate and an outboard offers the further advantage of much better control while backing down. An outboard with a right-hand prop will still tend to back to port, like an inboard, but the stern can be jockeyed in the right direction by turning the lower unit if sternway and momentum are carefully controlled.

On the other hand, outboard and stern-drive-powered boats often heel more in a turn than inboards, especially if the propeller's center of effort is lower than the inboard's rudder. This tendency to bank sharply is especially pronounced in single-engine installations, which place the propeller lower in the water than with twin installations. The deeper propeller thrust depth adds lever arm and heeling moment.

Outboards and stern drives also tend to exhibit greater steering response because the steering force is aft of the transom, while inboard rudders are usually forward of the transom. Counterrotating dual-propeller stern drives, such as Volvo's Duo-Prop and MerCruiser's Bravo 3, have exceptional turning ability. Unlike single-propeller drives, they turn with equal facility to port and starboard, since the counterrotating props cancel out side forces.

Waterjets

Waterjet propulsion, like outboards and stern drives, offers an advantage in maneuverability over a propeller-driven inboard in that thrust is vectored from side to side through a steering nozzle. When the engine is shifted into reverse, a deflector scoop drops down over the waterjet discharge race, redirecting the flow forward. The steering effect is the opposite of what you'd expect; back down with the wheel to port and the stern pulls to starboard, and vice versa, due to the geometry of the reversing deflector. Once you get the hang of it, however, a waterjet-powered boat is more maneuverable than even an outboard. Single and twin waterjets have steerable nozzles and reversing deflectors, while triple and quadruple waterjets only include the steering and backing mechanisms on the outboard engines.

Surface Drives

Surface drives come in at least two basic flavors, steerable and fixed. Those that are free to rotate from side to side steer using propeller thrust. Fixed units have a rudder assembly mounted aft of the prop to deflect prop wash to one side or the other in the familiar fashion. Surface drives typically lack the low-speed finesse of other propulsion systems, but again, they're designed and intended to operate efficiently at very high speeds. Alas, you can't have it all.

CHAPTER 10

Engine Rooms and Onboard Systems

In theory, there is no difference between theory and practice. In practice, there is a big difference.

—Jan L. A. van de Snepscheut

W hether you're the owner of an outboard center console or a 140-foot megayacht, the systems that keep your vessel humming along are well worth your acquaintance. Murphy is alive and well, so anything man-made will eventually break. Un-

The dry exhaust system on this trawler is well insulated to keep the engine room as cool as possible. NORDHAVN

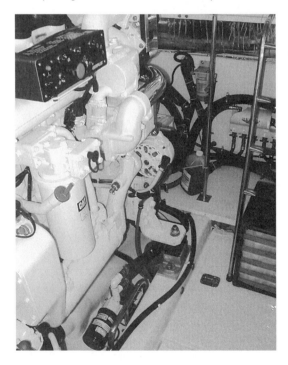

A Tiara 50 engine room showing the LOP (local operating panel) for the Cat diesel *(top left)*, centerline oil-level-check dipstick, access ladder to the bridge deck above, and the hull shaft log under the V-drive engine.

derstanding your vessel's systems, even just the basics, will put you ahead of the curve.

It's often amusing to observe new owners' reactions to their dreamboat's engine rooms. Some genuinely enjoy changing the oil, topping off the expansion tanks, and tinkering around—even cleaning the bilge. In fact, the engine room is the first place these owners want to show off to guests. Other owners couldn't care less about what goes on in the heart of the boat as long as all that mysterious machinery gets them from point A to point B. They're reluctant even to visit down there and wouldn't clean out a seawater strainer on a bet.

Modern pleasure craft, from small stern-drive-powered express cruisers to megayachts, can have surprisingly complex systems, but once you've spent a little time learning the various mechanical, electrical, and plumbing systems, things somehow don't seem quite so overwhelming.

Room to Maneuver

Builders cater to every market demand in order to sell their product, and as a result, emphasis on systems engineering varies according to the market they're trying to reach. For instance, a builder's design philosophy, even within a class of boats, makes a big difference when it comes to allocating space for the engine room. If the priority is on accommodations, the forward engine room bulkhead may be pushed aft to make room for a bigger master stateroom, another head, or a big cedar-lined closet. But if priority is placed on engine room space, then there will be plenty of room to get around, even when options such as a watermaker or extra genset are included.

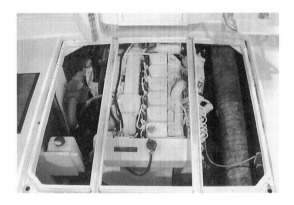

The Albin 32's V-drive diesel is accessed through a three-piece cockpit hatch, which takes two people to remove and reinstall comfortably. Hatch gutters, and the supporting aluminum channels, drain overboard. Access here is a bit tighter than on boats with larger, usually hinged, hatches.

Viking Yachts emphasizes space in their engine rooms, a fact appreciated by their engineering-savvy owners. And convertible sportfishermen owners are more likely to be involved in their yachts' mechanical system maintenance than their express or pilothouse motor yacht counterparts.

Being able to get around an engine room comfortably is important. In an emergency, you need to be able to get to the problem in a hurry. For routine maintenance, having more room means you or your mechanic is more likely to do the job right, and at manufacturer-specified intervals. Proper maintenance results in increased reliability and longevity, one area where single-engine vessels have a distinct advantage over their twin-screw counterparts.

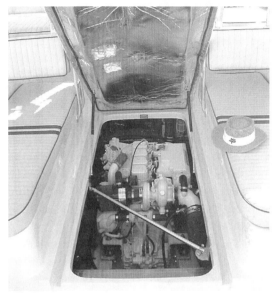

All-around access to this single engine is a little tight here, with molded bench seats restricting side access.

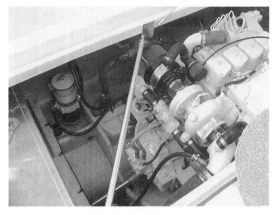

This express boat has reasonably good access to its aft-centerline maintenance points, but the fuel filter and raw-water seacock outboard to port are hard to reach.

This Krogen 39's engine room is a pleasure to work in with a single diesel amidships, a workbench with tool chest (can you believe it in a 39-footer?), and standing headroom forward under the pilothouse. KADEY-KROGEN YACHTS

The aft engine room on this Dettling 51 with its V-drive diesels is neatly laid out, with duplex fuel filters mounted to the port engine bed.

A single 600 hp diesel takes up a lot less space than a pair of 300 hp engines, leaving room to breathe for maintenance. But, many owners who are concerned about maneuverability and redundancy don't care to hear about the merits of single-screw propulsion.

Whether you have the typical convertible's roomy engine space or the more cramped variety found on many express cruisers, be sure to know where everything is and how the systems interrelate. You should also be clear about maintenance schedules and know what tools and spares will be necessary, and where they are stowed. Flat surfaces or catwalks along with sufficient overhead lighting all make for a more hospitable engine room environment. Other features bearing serious consideration are the size and location of hatches, bulkheads, and ladders.

If access hatches are exposed to the weather, be sure they're water- or at least weathertight. Any machinery or equipment mounted below the hatch perimeter will be susceptible to corrosion from leaks. Hatches and doors to machinery spaces should have gaskets to seal in as much noise as possible and to prevent rattling. Deck hatch openings should have deep gutters around their perimeters, with large (1-inch or greater) drain lines to keep things dry down below. Test for watertightness with

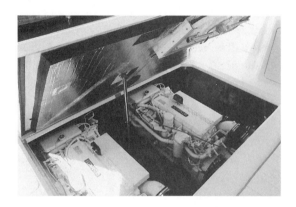

Here's an engine room hatch that opens wide—you can stand up practically anywhere below it. This Sea Ray 400 DA's V-drive diesels are mounted under the cockpit, so there will also be plenty of natural light. For quick maintenance checks, a small access hatch is built into the hinged deck.

a fully pressurized hose and a couple of buckets of water to be sure.

Engine start and stop switches and full instrumentation at the cockpit entrance for local control and monitoring are an advantage. Enclosing gensets further reduces noise levels when the main engines are shut down and electrical power is needed.

Well-planned twin-engine rooms allow you to do all routine engine maintenance, such as fluid level top-offs and filter checks, from centerline. All auxiliary equipment such as air-conditioning units,

The virtues of single-engine propulsion are seen in this marvelously accessible, cleanly laid out Maxum 27's engine room. The hatch is gasketed to minimize noise and rattle levels, and a molded gutter drains directly overboard, keeping the components below dry.

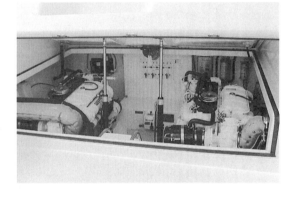

This Cabo 35 express sportfisherman's bridge deck raises about 30 inches aft, making it easy to enter the engine room. Note the gasket, which is meant to help contain engine noise and minimize rattles and squeaks.

generators, voltage isolators and transformers, inverters, batteries, watermakers, ice makers, and transfer pumps should be conveniently located. Systems and components should also be labeled to take the guesswork out of what you're looking at.

Fuel Systems

Designing an engine room, like the rest of the boat, involves a series of compromises. For instance, if the fuel tanks are placed outboard of the engines,

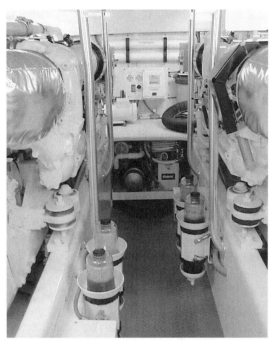

This well-lit Davis 58's engine room offers nearly standing headroom, deck support stanchions that double as handrails, a flat, comfortable deck, and accessible fuel filters.

where their effect on trim is minimized, it's often impossible to access the outboard sides of the engines. These saddle tanks are also higher up in the yacht than tanks mounted on centerline in the bilge, decreasing stability and increasing the vessel's roll amplitude.

If the main fuel tank is placed under the cockpit to make the engine room roomier, as on a convertible, trim varies significantly as fuel is consumed, impacting the boat's seakeeping ability. Builders of these yachts often rely on forward auxiliary fuel tanks and large trim tabs to help balance things out. If the battery banks are mounted in the bilge on the centerline, stability is improved but effective headroom between the engines is reduced. So, the best choice isn't always crystal clear.

Wherever the fuel tanks are located, fuel system integrity, redundancy, and reliability are all-important. Today's modern, high-speed diesels with their sophisticated electronic and mechanical control and monitoring systems are very reliable as long as clean fuel is supplied to the engines. A large fuel filter-separator should be provided for each engine and for each generator. The filter prevents contaminants from reaching the engine's injectors, which have very small openings and are easily clogged. Any water is separated from the diesel fuel and collects in a small, clear bowl at the bottom of the unit where, as the water level rises, it can be monitored visually and drained off as necessary.

Many of these units are available with alarms that let you know when they need maintenance. Some builders provide two fuel filter-separators in parallel so they can be shifted on the fly if one line becomes clogged. This allows the engine to stay running while the first filter-separator is cleaned. The filter-separators should be mounted high enough above the bilge to leave room under the clear sediment bowls for a bucket to collect the drainage. They should also be positioned so they're easy to see and access for maintenance—the closer to the engine room entrance, the better.

Look for high-pressure fuel line hoses with compression fittings connecting them to the engines, filter-separators, tanks, and fuel manifolds. Most small boats, and even some expensive yachts, have cheaper, less secure rubber hoses with clamps on their ends. These can give many years of good service, but a hose clamp is nowhere near as dependable as a compression fitting with a flare or O-ring seal. Also, the relatively soft rubber hoses are not as abrasion resistant as high-pressure hose. When hose clamps are used they should doubled up, and the nipple should be long enough that both clamps bear on it securely.

Abrasion resistance is an important consideration, especially if fuel lines are not routed out of harm's way and provided with protection from chafing. Builders sometimes use PVC pipes to route fuel lines and wiring from one part of the vessel to another. If this is done, make sure the hoses and wires are slack enough that they don't chafe against the pipe ends, which should be filed or sanded smooth to further guard against this.

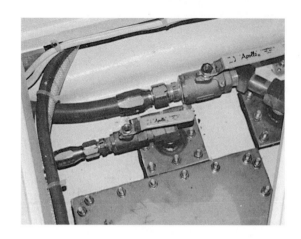

There are two basic types of fuel fittings and hoses: rubber lines held to nipples with hose clamps, and high-pressure, aircraft-type compression fittings and hoses. The latter, seen here, is much to be preferred, since compression fittings are more secure than hose clamps will ever be, and the steel-jacketed high-pressure lines are far more abrasion resistant.

Fuel supply and return lines valves ought to be remotely operated so that potential fuel sources to an engine room fire can be cut off. Remote operating gear in the cockpit (for both raw-water and fuel systems) is an excellent solution; don't leave home without it!

The fuel lines and fuel manifolds should be clearly labeled at their ends, so there's no question of where lines lead. If you have to disconnect a high-pressure fuel line from the engine, be careful not to overstress the fitting. Sometimes these are the weak links in fuel lines, so using a second wrench to relieve strain is essential. The worst combination is a rugged high-pressure line connected to ¼-inch copper tubing at the engine. A strong argument can be made for replacing any and all such copper tubing with high-pressure hoses all the way from the tanks to the engines and back. Diesel fuel supply lines are under slight vacuum since the engine-driven pump is drawing from the tank. Fuel return lines, on the other hand, are under pressure, which means a break in a return line will dump fuel to the bilge. Gas engines usually have a single fuel supply hose. Some diesels, including

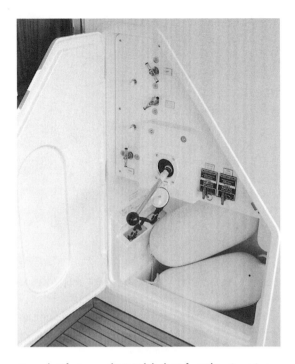

One cockpit feature on this British-built 65-foot Viking Sport Cruiser ought to be on every boat. Fuel lines supplying the engines can be remotely closed off, Halon can be dumped, and the bilge can be pumped manually. There's even room to stow a couple of fenders.

A fuel tank sight glass is the most accurate means of knowing how much fuel you have left. The one on this Nordhavn trawler is well protected from breaking by a clear plastic screen. NORDHAVN

MTU's, cool the bypass fuel at the engine and send it directly to the injectors without returning to the tank.

Electrical Systems

If you can't imagine going to sea without a CD player, microwave, or television, don't worry—there are amps aplenty, assuming your boat is properly outfitted. A simple electrical system starts with the typical outboard's battery, with or without a selector switch, to feed running lights, radio, and bilge pump. Small cruisers will usually have a 12-volt system fitted with shore power cables feeding a battery charger-inverter that also supplies power to a dual-voltage refrigerator. Larger yachts have sophisticated multivoltage AC-DC systems that provide power for everything from bunk lighting to engine starters, air-conditioning, and compressors.

Electrical systems on boats and yachts are usually divided into 12-volt DC and 120- to 240-volt AC sides, with a single electrical service panel divided into an AC and a DC side. In simple terms, an alternator on the main engine(s) charges the house and engine starting batteries. Separate battery banks are usually installed so that even if someone leaves an appliance on overnight and drains the house battery, the engine will still start using its dedicated battery. If the starting battery dies, a cross-connect or parallel switch may be provided to allow the house battery to start the engine. Many small outboards have a pair of batteries and a four-position battery switch from which you can select battery 1, battery 2, both, or off. This serves much the same purpose as more complicated systems by helping to ensure that one fully charged battery is always available to start the engine.

Unlike automotive batteries, which might use

up just a small percentage of their charge in a short surge when the car is started, deep-cycle marine batteries are built to regularly discharge a significant percentage of their stored energy before being recharged, and to withstand many cycles of such use. Liquid electrolyte and deep-cycle gel cell batteries are commonly used. Even deep-cycle batteries last longer if they aren't discharged below 50 percent of their capacity, however. Batteries are very heavy, so they should be secured to prevent movement and placed low in the hull to improve stability. They should be protected with covers that provide plenty of ventilation. Lead acid batteries under charge give off hydrogen gas that's explosive, hence the need for ventilation. Batteries will sometimes continue to work when submerged, but a spare battery high in the boat (on the bridge, for example) to power a radio for an SOS call might be worth its weight in gold one day.

Direct current (DC) 12-volt systems need both a positive and a negative (ground) side to complete the electrical circuit. DC loads usually include lighting, electronics, engine starter, refrigerator (which may run off either 12 or 120 volts), bilge pumps, engine room blower, instrumentation, and so on. Bilge pumps, float switches, and alarms should be wired on the battery side of the selector switch so that they'll still operate when the latter is shut off.

Some boats carry an inverter, usually fed by a dedicated battery bank, to convert DC to AC electrical power for operating small appliances. An inverter can only be used as long as its batteries hold a charge, but they're great for smaller boats that don't have room or weight allowance for a generator, or for big-boat owners who want to restrict generator usage to a minimum. Inverters are inefficient, requiring a lot of 12-volt DC power to make a little 120-volt AC, but they're great for handling small loads intermittently.

Dual-function battery charger-inverters are also popular, since many of the electrical components required for charging a battery and converting DC to AC are shared. Like all electrical

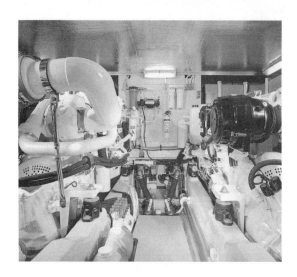

Here's Sea Ray's version of the perfect engine room, as seen on their 540 motor yacht. Plumbing and wiring are well labeled, unobtrusively routed, and protected from chafing. Maintenance points are comfortably accessed, and lighting is plentiful. A nice performance by one of the world's megabuilders.　SEA RAY

components, they should be mounted in a dry, well-ventilated area.

Many small 24- to 30-foot express cruisers and fishing boats and virtually all larger yachts have 120- to 240-volt systems fed either by shore power cables when dockside or the boat's generator when offshore. AC wiring should always be isolated from DC and differently color-coded to prevent confusion. Air-conditioning compressors, battery charger-inverters, water heaters, watermakers, ice makers, televisions, refrigerators, stoves and microwave ovens, built-in vacuum cleaner systems, and house lighting are just a few of the loads that can be served by an AC system.

Generators are the third source of AC power after inverters and shore power. A genset (generator set) consists of a prime mover, either a gas or diesel engine to conform with the vessel's main propulsion engine(s), and the generator itself. Gensets run as long as you want them to provided they're fed with fuel and air, and they're usually rated to carry a healthy percentage of the entire ship's load all at once. Modern wet exhaust systems make gensets very quiet indeed, so they're hardly noticed when running. An insulated enclosure makes them quieter still.

Overload Protection

Electrical circuits are protected against power surges by either fuses (that melt through) or circuit breakers (that trip, opening the circuit). They should be of the correct size (the same amperage rating or smaller) to match the wiring they protect (the smallest wire in the circuit) and located as near the power source as possible—the ABYC recommends within 7 inches. Without circuit protection, a fire could easily result from an overloaded or shorted circuit melting wire insulation and the copper wire itself. Electrical system failures are one of the most common causes of onboard fires. Engine starting circuits are wired separately and do not require surge protection.

Few boats have enough electrical generating capacity onboard to run everything at once, and builders are usually clear about this. Depending on their number and amperage rating, shore power cables may not provide enough power to run everything in port, either.

Marine Wiring

The heavier the electrical cables—and thus the lower the AWG number—used between power sources and their loads, the less power and voltage loss there will be. Wiring strands should be tinned to protect against corrosion, and only marine-grade wiring should be used to withstand the salt air and potentially oily environment. Unlike house wiring, marine-grade wire also provides the flexibility needed to hold up in a dynamic environment. Other precautions against corrosion, including the use of heat-shrink tubing at connections, should also be used.

Wiring terminals are often the culprits when circuit failure occurs. If incorrectly assembled, terminals can increase resistance to current flow and the demand on the power sources. Common sense dictates that wires should be kept out of the bilge

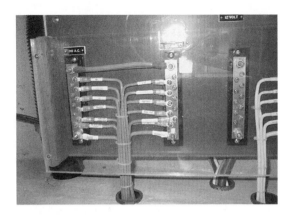

This trawler's wiring is expertly installed. The wiring bundle passes through a deck hole lined with a soft rubber grommet to prevent chafing. The ends of each wire are labeled to take the guesswork out of troubleshooting. Wire turns are neatly and consistently executed. The overall appearance is impressive. NORDHAVN

and that new loads not be spliced into existing circuits. If additional service is needed, run a new wire from the distribution panel. Each circuit should be grounded and connected to the vessel's common ground. Twisted-pair wiring, which cancels out the magnetic field created by current flow within a single wire, should be used near compasses and other magnetically sensitive devices. In general, wiring ought to be supported every 18 inches unless it runs through a conduit.

Wiring throughout the vessel should be neatly bundled and routed through protective conduits to prevent chafing. It should also be color coded and labeled on either end to facilitate troubleshooting and future modifications. Wiring should be as continuous as possible from load to power source, with breaks only at panels and switchboards as needed. Under no circumstance should wires be spliced together where they will potentially come into contact with water. Breaker panels should be sited high in the vessel and at a height above the deck that makes their use comfortable and convenient. A voltage stabilizer-transformer to provide the correct shore power voltage to sensitive ship's electrical equipment is often provided on larger yachts.

Fire Prevention and Suppression

Among catastrophes at sea, fire ranks just behind flooding in vessels lost. Safe vessel design is essential, as are intrinsically safe fuel, mechanical, and electrical systems. Once a fire does break out, the speed at which it can be extinguished and remain extinguished is crucial to a vessel's survival.

Firefighting systems come in two basic forms: fixed and portable. Portable fire extinguishers should be plentiful, of the right type for the likely classes of fire, charged, and easily accessible. There's no substitute for running periodic drills with your crew so that all hands know where the nearest appropriate fire extinguisher is and how to use it. This goes for any onboard emergency, of course, whether it's a man overboard, flooding, or fire.

Fixed fire-extinguishing systems should be installed in any space that contains machinery or fuel: the engine room, of course, but also a lazarette or similar space in which a fuel tank is installed. Fixed systems automatically detect rises in temperature or the presence of smoke and discharge an extinguishing agent.

More sophisticated and effective fixed fire-extinguishing systems shut down machinery and close off ventilation before discharging. This might incorporate a delay of anywhere from 10 to 60 seconds while ventilation is shut down and air sources isolated, but the intermediate step prevents the discharged agent from diluting before the fire is completely out or before the space has cooled sufficiently to prevent a reflash. Most systems give audible and visual alarms, which give the captain time to manually override the discharge. The system might be overridden, say, if losing propulsion power would be more hazardous than immediately extinguishing the fire.

Once an agent, such as Halon (or an equivalent gas), is discharged, the space should not be entered for a period of time. Opening an engine room door too soon might introduce fresh oxygen into the space and cause the fire to reflash. Halon and its equivalents don't cool the fire or the space as water or foam does; they just prevent combustion as long as their concentrations remain within a certain range. Waiting 30 minutes or more for the space to cool before entering is often recommended by fire-extinguishing system manufacturers and other experts.

Fixed fire-extinguishing systems should also have manual pump capabilities in case the automatic system is short-circuited. These manual controls should be located on the bridge and outside the engine room or compartment. Engine room doors should be fitted with a small inspection window so that you can tell, once the smoke has cleared, if the fire has been extinguished before opening the door.

Keeping the Water Out

The engine room is often the largest, longest space at the waterline and is vulnerable to flooding. The seacocks necessary to provide cooling water to all that machinery present a particular risk. A sea chest, which is essentially a box fixed to the interior of the hull bottom, enables you to feed multiple seawater requirements from a single large through-hull fitting. The box serves as a manifold, feeding the various sources through secondary seacocks while minimizing hull penetrations.

As mentioned elsewhere, forward and aft bulkheads should be watertight to prevent flooding into surrounding spaces. Generous bilge pump capacity should be provided, along with high bilgewater level alarms should the electric bilge pumps fall behind the flooding or fail altogether. A manual back-up bilge pump that can be operated from the deck should be installed for such contingencies.

Some builders provide Y-valves in the main engine raw-water intake line. This lets the suction be diverted from the through-hull fitting to a pick-up hose in the engine room bilge, so that the engine can serve as a pump in time of need. This Y-valve should close off one avenue as it opens the other, so that at no time does it establish a pathway from

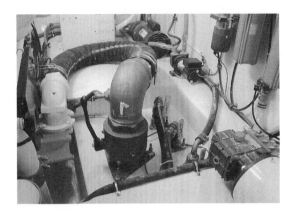

Seacocks sprouting off this Davis convertible's sea chest mean there's only *one* hole in the bottom of the boat per side versus a half dozen. That's a good thing.

This Groco through-hull fitting can take a suction on the bilge by removing the plug in its side, as long as the through-hull water path is shut off first by closing the main valve. This either-or safety feature prevents a path for water to flow from sea to bilge, potentially sinking the boat.   GROCO

the sea to the bilge. The type of Y-valve installed by many builders will open the bilge suction valve without closing the through-hull valve, which can quickly sink a boat. A main engine's pumping rate is an order of magnitude greater than an electric bilge pump's and can be measured in hundreds rather than tens of gallons per minute, provided the hoses and pipes are of adequate dimension. Bilge suction Y-valves should be located near the engine room entrance so they can be reached quickly, especially if the bilge is already flooded.

An engine power takeoff (PTO) high-capacity dewatering pump can be used to dewater a space or to provide firefighting water. A main drainage system, essentially a pipe with remotely controlled valves running fore and aft in the bilge, can also be fitted, so that another compartment, isolated from the engine room by watertight bulkheads can be pumped out remotely by opening the right valves.

Mechanical, hydraulic, or electric remote operating gear is available to allow engine room valves to be opened and closed from the main deck. The next best solution is to provide long handles that allow valves to be opened or closed from several feet above the valve. Many seacocks are mounted in out-of-the-way bilge areas, making it difficult to open or close them under the best of conditions; many are frozen. Seacock valves should be regu-

larly cycled and lubricated so they will actually work when needed. I prefer bronze over fiberglass-reinforced plastic seacocks. Bronze is stronger and more durable, and where any through-hull fitting is concerned you can't be too cautious.

My habit is always to close the engine cooling water seacocks at the end of each trip and reopen them just before starting the engines and heading out again. This practice will help to prevent a failed cooling water hose from sinking the boat and ensure that the seacocks open and close freely. The downside of this procedure is that if you forget to open the seacock before starting the engine, there is a good chance that you will burn out the seawater pump cooling impeller. Place a note or placard at the helm to remind you or your mechanic to open the valves before starting the engine.

Other Considerations
A No-Salt Diet Works Best

To minimize corrosion, keeping salt air out of the engine room is always a priority. This can be facilitated by installing demister pads in the combustion air intakes to help filter salt from the air, and by using dripless propeller shaft seals to reduce spray and bilgewater.

Machinery Overhaul and Replacement

Engines, gensets, and other major components will likely need to be replaced some day, so it pays to find out before buying a boat how involved that process may be. To facilitate removal, some builders provide patches or hatches on deck to make the process as easy as possible. Other boats will need to have holes cut in the side of the hull or in the deck above. In some hulls, even the fuel tanks might have to be removed before an engine can be replaced. If this kind of major surgery is needed, expect the job to cost more and take longer. The same accessibility issue applies to fuel tanks that are subject to corrosion or any kind of deterioration. Especially if they're made of aluminum, chances are they'll eventually need to be replaced. Fuel tanks need a way out, and a hatch directly above the tank is by far the best solution.

Fiberglass fuel tanks should last as long as the boat itself, but aluminum tanks have a limited life span: their longevity depends on the quality of the initial installation. Aluminum tanks tend to corrode from the outside where water is trapped against the tank by support members and allowed to deoxygenate. Supporting fuel tanks on neoprene strips or welded angle brackets and providing lots of breathing room for fresh air to circulate all around is a good way to prevent corrosion and increase tank life. Many experts recommend against installing aluminum fuel tanks in a bed of foam, since air cannot circulate around the sides and bottom of the tank.

Sound Reasoning

Some builders install one-piece, composite saloon decks above the engine room. This seamless process helps seal the engine space acoustically, containing most of the machinery noise. Different composite coring materials provide varying degrees of sound attenuation. Lead-and-foam foil-backed acoustic insulation helps attenuate machinery noise of different frequencies. Engine rooms with watertight bulkheads forward and aft further contain machinery noises. Since the proof of noise control effectiveness is in the pudding, take noise-level readings with a $60 RadioShack decibel meter throughout your boat at various engine speeds. Readings in the low 70 dBA range at all speeds indicate a successful noise attenuation effort on the builder's part. Continuous readings above 84 dBA at cruising speeds will necessitate the use of earplugs to prevent hearing loss from long-term exposure.

Auxiliary Equipment

Watermakers make it possible to stay at sea for extended periods. Seawater is converted to freshwater by condensing steam or by forcing seawater through microporous filters. An ability to make freshwater from seawater permits potable water tank capacity to be much smaller, increasing a vessel's speed and range.

Fin stabilizers are fitted on many round-bilge, displacement cruising vessels with minimal form stability. They're also used on a few hard-chine planing yachts whose owners want to keep rolling to an absolute minimum.

Bow thrusters are a great aid when it comes to maneuvering a yacht in tight quarters. Twin screws can walk the stern sideways while the bow thruster pushes the bow to either side on command. Essentially a propeller (or counterrotating propellers) in a fiberglass or metal tube mounted athwartships just below the waterline, a thruster is only effective when the boat is stopped or has very little way on. Some bow thrusters are powered by electric motors fed from a dedicated battery bank; others are driven by hydraulic pumps that are in turn powered by a power takeoff on one of the main engines.

Systems and Structure Accessibility

A vessel's systems and structure should be accessible throughout the length of the hull, not just in the engine room. When builders seal off portions of the bilge by putting a hatchless sole in the cabin, it's impossible to tell the condition of the wiring, plumbing, or hull structure in that area. It could be that water has gotten into that space and is rotting out structural members or causing other damage. In the event of a grounding or other impact that results in a hull puncture, it will be impossible to make temporary repairs if the bilges aren't completely accessible.

Deck hatches should allow you to see and access all of the bilge. Foam-filled compartments can trap water against wooden structural members such as bulkheads and stringers, causing the onset of rot. These concealed voids may well not have adequate ventilation or drainage, but you might not know the consequences of such poor design until you want to sell the boat and a surveyor discovers the damage. Access hatches are essential.

All machinery and equipment need adequate ventilation. AC compressors tucked under molded, nonopening bench seats, uninsulated AC ventilation ducts, cockpit washdown pumps sitting in puddles of salt water, water heater relief valves in compartments without drainage, and battery chargers-inverters mounted under leaky cockpit hatches are all examples of corrosion-related problems. Ultimately, these problems will lead to premature equipment and component failure.

CHAPTER 11

Pilothouse and Bridge Design and Ergonomics

Depend upon it, sir. When a man knows he is to be hanged in a fortnight, it concentrates his mind wonderfully.

—Samuel Johnson

If any area of a vessel can benefit from a little extra planning, it's got to be the helm station. Whether located on a flybridge, in a pilothouse, or on an express cruiser's raised bridge deck, the helm station is the heart and brain of a vessel. From here the craft is controlled and navigated, and all ships' systems monitored. The importance of visibility, comfort, and user-friendly helm console ergonomics can't be overemphasized. As we'll see, there are many practical and even legal issues to consider, and after reading this chapter you'll have a better idea of what to look for when evaluating a helm station.

Although there are many marine regulatory and advisory bodies around the world, we'll be making reference to the Maritime and Coast Guard Agency (MCA), a leading U.K. standards organization for commercial vessels and large charter yachts. MCA rules do not apply to most recreational craft built in the United States, but they spell out standards that abound with common sense and with which other agencies generally agree. Other vessel standards organizations, including some in the United States, are working closely with the MCA to develop clear, concise, sensible guidelines covering helm station visibility and other related issues.

Helm Station Ergonomics

Although some helm stations are carefully thought out, too often we find layouts that are more the province of stylists than ergonomics specialists. It's often a matter of form over function, which is too bad, since it's easy to design a helm station that works well and looks great. For instance, many builders achieve perfect symmetry of layout at the expense of practicality and utility. But if a toothbrush, vacuum cleaner, and an aircraft cockpit all are designed with ergonomics in mind, why not the helm station on a boat?

Ergonomics, by the way, is the science concerned with designing and arranging manufactured products to fit the human anatomy, and for maximum ease and efficiency of use. Physical movement, visibility, lighting, comfort, noise levels, and air quality are all ergonomic issues. Well-considered ergonomics result in greater comfort, efficiency, and safety, to say nothing of keeping your spirits up after hours at the helm.

Visibility

Many vessels are capable of great speed these days, and as a consequence the need for good visibility from the helm has never been greater. If inadequate visibility from the helm station prevents keeping a proper lookout, a requirement under rule 5 of the 1972 International Regulations for Preventing Collisions at Sea, best known as COLREGs, the odds of a collision or grounding increase, and any damage or injury could have legal consequences.

MCA rules and common sense dictate that the

Radar Arches

In addition to making a boat look snazzy, radar arches support antennas, the radar, the deck, and running lights. In fact, an arch is often the best place to put running lights for maximum visibility from other vessels. On open cruisers, radar arches also provide a handy place to attach a canvas bimini top or awning, and they offer a handhold along the side deck. All too often, these arches are large, bulky, visibility-blocking fiberglass sculptures drawn by designers who've apparently never put to sea. They take a good-sized chunk out of the horizon for the operator, hampering visibility, especially to port, from the driver's perspective. Ocean Yachts has come up with a great solution to this problem by molding their bridge arches with a glass window slot down the middle. Another solution is to build arches out of aluminum pipe, which creates only minimal sight line obstruction.

This Albin 32 has my idea of the perfect radar arch: strong, functional, and good looking, and you can even see *through* it.

conning position should provide a good all-around view of the horizon. This includes an unobstructed view of the sea surface two vessel lengths ahead and within 10 degrees of the vessel's heading. The exact length of the blind spot inside this range will depend on the operator's height of eye relative to the bow. When standing at the helm station, the operator must have a clear field of vision of at least 225 degrees, or from dead ahead to two points (22.5 degrees) abaft both beams. Visibility from a bridge

One of those sleek-looking radar arches that takes a big chunk out of the horizon. It's a little like the builder saying, "here's a 6-degree sector of the horizon you don't need to see."

wing must also extend at least 225 degrees, from 45 degrees on the opposite bow through dead astern on the same side. Blind spots created by obstructions cannot exceed 10 degrees, the clear sectors between blind sectors should be at least 5 degrees, and the total arc of blind sectors cannot exceed 20 degrees.

Window size and spacing are too often inadequately throught out by the boatbuilder, with many helm area windows too low to see through without ducking. As a practical matter, the upper window edge should accommodate an eye height of 5 feet, 11 inches (1.8 m) so that a 6-foot, 4-inch operator can see the horizon without ducking. The lower edge should be as low as possible, and in no case should it obstruct visibility ahead.

The mullions, or frames, between the windows should be kept to a minimum and should not be installed directly forward of the helm station. I see mullions as much as 6 or 7 inches wide, creating a significant blind zone for the operator. Well-engineered windshields or pilothouse windows have narrow frames, 2 to 3 inches wide, yet still provide

What a concept: a 60-foot boat with a lower station that boasts excellent all-around sight lines. This U.K.-built Viking Sport Cruiser comes up on plane with minimal bow rise, so you never lose sight of the horizon when seated at the helm. Window mullions are narrow but plenty strong. A watertight door slides open for direct weather deck access. Controls and gauges are easy to reach and intuitively located.   VIKING SPORT CRUISER

plenty of support to the surrounding structure. Don't be told by a salesperson that a 2- to 3-inch frame is inadequate to support the superstructure above—it's simply a matter of intelligent engineering. Many builders have been successfully constructing frames this way for years.

At least two of the forward-facing windows should provide a clear view in all weather conditions, a requirement that calls for windshield wipers and freshwater washers to remove glare-enhancing salt smear. It's also important that the operator's view not be blocked by the helm console, which is becoming more of a problem as consoles expand to accommodate burgeoning electronics suites. Wipers should cover the glass from at least 15 degrees left to 15 degrees right of the operator's line of sight and should sweep at a rate of two arcs per second. The blade should also be long enough to cover the majority of the glass pane from top to bottom.

The windows themselves should not be polar-

ized or tinted, as this makes it hard to identify navigational aids and running lights correctly. Area lighting around the helm station should be of low intensity, and preferably red or blue. You'll never see a white light on the bridge of a navy or coast guard ship underway at night, and for good reason: night vision is impeded during and immediately after exposure to white light. On a related note, many flat-panel LCD displays are nearly impossible to see in direct sunlight, while monochrome displays are generally easier to read in daylight than color. Also of note is the positioning of running lights. Many builders put them in the bow, on either side of the pulpit. The problem is that they are directly in the operator's line of sight, and the backscatter from these lights can also interfere with visibility. A much better solution is to mount them high above the bridge where they're out of the captain's way, and their height makes them much easier to see from, and sooner seen by, another vessel.

The operator's external view outside the vessel should be glare- and reflection-free both day and night. To minimize window reflection off the instrument panels below, MCA dictates that forward-facing windows be inclined 10 to 25 degrees from the vertical, top forward. In the real world of recreational boating, however, styling constraints often

This trawler bridge has much to commend it, but not the 7-inch-wide windshield mullions. Any place that doesn't have clear glass obstructs visibility and reduces the skipper's sight lines. These windows could easily have been made larger, and their frames smaller, while maintaining structural integrity.

The bridge of a trawler is supposed to look shiplike, and this one on a Krogen 39 comes close. A raised bench seat gives the guests a good spot from which to critique the captain's performance. A passage door leads directly to the side deck so the skipper can help the first mate with the bow line. A handrail overhead gives something to hang onto when running in the trough. The helm station itself is pretty straightforward, with a decidedly shiplike wheel, a flat-black, ergonomically angled electronics panel, and the most commonly used switches close at hand.   KADEY-KROGEN YACHTS

top, as with a sedan cruiser—is to protect occupants from wind, spray, and rain. To do its job effectively, it needs to be high enough to see through when standing up. In fact, when standing and facing forward, the operator should be able to see the horizon, not the top frame of the windshield. This means that the bottom of the upper frame should be at least 5 feet, 11 inches above deck level.

Building a windshield to this height eliminates the need for forward plastic filler curtains; these plastic windows, especially when made of standard light-gauge material, are difficult to see through and invite trouble when underway. Since windshield wipers and washers can only be used on glass, filling a large gap between a windshield and the bimini or hardtop above with a plastic filler curtain almost guarantees an awkward and hazardous piloting arrangement. Pointing again to Tiara, we can see that it is possible to build a windshield that

prevent this forward-sloping design practice. What builders can do is eliminate the gloss-white dashes that cause significant windshield glare and use a flat, darker color like tan or gray under the windshield.

Although it's a point of pride with many yacht builders to finish all pilothouse and flybridge surfaces with the brightest white gelcoat available, seamanlike pilothouses and bridges are painted a flat color throughout that prevents reflection and glare. Bright white overheads and helm consoles may look great with the boat tied up at the dock, but they impair visibility when running at night. In the sunlight, reflected glare makes running a boat with a bright white bridge impossible without sunglasses. I risk sounding strident, but bright-white surfaces around the helm area are anathema to the seasoned mariner.

Windshields are another area where form is winning over function. The function of a windshield—which can be either freestanding, as on an open express boat, or built with an integral hard-

This Trophy walkaround has room at the helm for flush-mounted electronics, and the dark console and dash area reduce reflections off the windshield above. The distances the switches, electronics, and gauges are from the operator are appropriate.

This Tiara 50's fiberglass-framed windshield is a work of art: there is plenty of glass around the helm station, the windshield frame is high enough to see under when standing up, and yet the builder has managed to keep the mullions narrow. There's plenty of room here for electronics above the engine gauges.

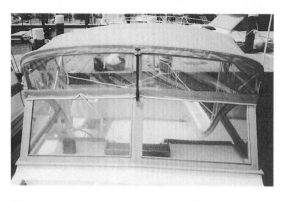

This express cruiser certainly has company with its glass windshield topped by a cheap plastic filler curtain. It's cheap because it's thin, and the thinner it is, the more distorted the view and the harder it is to actually see through. Plus, you can't use a windshield wiper on plastic curtains. Pay the extra bucks for clear, undistorted plastic. Finally, the low windshield frame will cut right through your forward sight line.

looks great and is also tall enough to keep you cozy.

Unfortunately, the side curtains offered as standard or optional equipment by most production boat manufacturers leave a lot to be desired. That's because the thin, crinkly plastic commonly used, although easy to roll up, markedly distorts vision. You'd be better off not ordering the standard-issue plastic, or deleting it from the standard equipment list for credit, and having a local canvas shop do the work for you using heavier-grade material. Examples of well-known, high-quality side curtain manufacturers are EZ2CY, Isinglas, and Strataglass. Generally speaking, the thicker the plastic, the less it will distort your vision.

Operator Position

On most small craft the operator is also the helmsman, lookout, navigator, and electronics operator. Not only must the skipper be able to see clearly outside the boat, but she must also have ready access and clear sight lines to all controls, switches, and instrumentation.

Most helm stations are designed for use by an operator who may be either standing or seated. If the helm station is to work effectively for an opera-tor in either of these positions, her height of eye should be nearly the same whether seated or standing. That's because the location of the steering wheel, propulsion controls, gauges, switches, and electronics should remain constant relative to the operator. For instance, a poorly positioned helm seat might put the operator lower and farther aft than when standing up, putting controls out of easy reach and hiding part of the electronics display behind the steering wheel.

Besides supporting you at the same height of eye as when standing, the helm seat should provide support side-to-side with contoured bolsters, especially in high-performance craft. Ideally it should adjust fore and aft and also vertically to accommodate different operators and to move back out of your way when standing up.

The helm seat foundation should be far enough aft to provide plenty of room to stand comfortably well back from the wheel. There's nothing more annoying than having your thighs jammed up against the steering wheel with your heels tight against the seat foundation. Every time the boat comes up on plane or rides over a big wave, you'll have to hang onto the wheel to keep your balance.

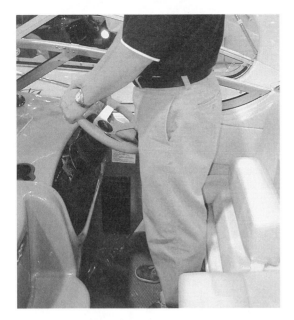

Things are a little tight at this helm. With the wheel all the way forward and the seat all the way aft, you should be able to move fore and aft a little. Otherwise, the first time you hit a wave while driving standing up, you'll be hanging onto the wheel instead of steering the boat. The seat base ought to be several inches farther aft.

The seat should be high enough to allow you to see over the bow even when coming up on plane. This is a tall order with boats that come up on plane or run at excessive trim angles. You should never lose sight of the horizon above the bow pulpit from the helm of a well-designed boat, even when coming up on plane.

Controls and Instruments

It is important for a builder to prioritize the layout of the helm, since not everything can be right at your fingertips. The most important controls are the steering wheel and the engine controls, after which gauges and electronics get a high priority. Well-designed helm consoles are tiered, with flat sections arranged according to placement priority. It's also important that the most frequently used controls and instruments not take your attention

Marinova's Jockey Seat

The Swedish company Marinova AB has produced a helm seat that allows high-speed operation in rough conditions. Resembling a saddle with a tall backrest, this unique design allows operators to support themselves partially with their feet, reducing the shock on the spine. The seat is fitted with a titanium shock-absorbing spring, further reducing G-forces, and is mounted higher than ordinary seats, improving visibility from the helm.

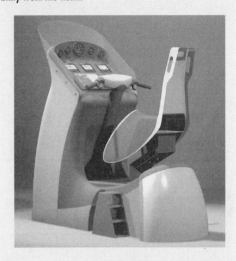

This is the Ullman seat and console, successfully used in Swedish rescue craft. A cross between riding a horse and a motorcycle, the Ullman helm station—seat has handlebars instead of a wheel, which makes a lot of sense if you need to hang on while driving in rough water. JOHAN ULLMAN

The result of this highly ergonomic design is a safe and secure operating position for the helmsman and an effective preventative for shock-related injuries. The Ullman cockpit, as it's known, also includes a motorcycle-style handlebar in place of a conventional steering wheel. This gives the operator a much better grip on the steering mechanism, which not only ensures continuous helm control but helps the operator stay put in extreme conditions. With the throttle mechanism integral to the handlebar, the operator always maintains full vessel control without having to let go. These Ullman cockpits, currently in use by the Swedish coast guard, are growing in popularity among recreational boaters in Europe.

from what's going on outside the boat, especially directly ahead. If a radar screen is mounted 3 feet to starboard, for instance, the chances of seeing a hazard directly off the bow with your peripheral vision are much less than if the display were mounted right in front of you.

The compass is often poorly placed, despite its importance. When steering manually offshore you refer to the compass constantly. For that reason it

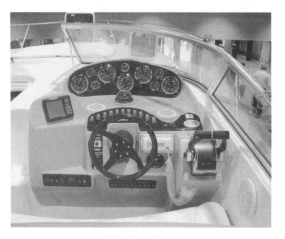

This Rinker 342 helm station has a lot for you to like. There's room for flush-mounted electronics, unusual on a midcabin express cruiser, the wheel and throttles are comfortably positioned, and the compass is right above the wheel, where you can see it either seated or standing.

should be on top of the helm console just below the horizon in relation to the operator's line of sight. The idea is to position the compass so that minimal eye movement is needed to shift between it and the horizon ahead. The height should be such that a shorter person can see it seated at the helm, and not so far away that it can't be easily read by someone with 20/20 vision. If the compass must be mounted five or six feet ahead of the operator, then it should be a more substantial model with numbers that are large enough for easy reading. The compass should be flat black so it doesn't reflect off the windshield above, and it should be lit with a red light for night use.

Since many helm stations are designed for both

seated and standing operation, the location of the controls, gauges, switches, and electronics is often a compromise. The panels should face the average operator's line of sight as squarely as possible. Otherwise, reflected glare will make the displays hard to see. If the seated and standing operator's height varies significantly, the panels should face either the middle ground or the line of sight from the more common position.

The movement of a control should be consistent with the direction of the desired response. When the throttles are moved forward, for example, the boat should move faster; when a gear shift is pulled back, the engine should shift to reverse, and so on. Knobs should turn clockwise for right turns or commands to the right, and counterclockwise for left turns or commands to the left. For switches on horizontal side consoles, forward is on, aft is off; on vertical panels, up means on and down is off.

All of the helm station's steering, engine, and maneuvering controls along with its switches and gauges should be grouped logically by purpose,

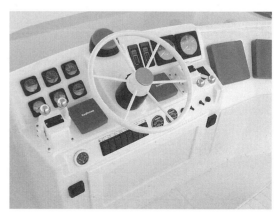

A view of the well-designed Blackfin 29 Saltshaker bridge helm station: a perfectly angled wheel and all the gauges and switches positioned in clear sight or within easy reach. The gauges are paired by function, so you can see at a glance if one engine is starting to act up. The tachs are right next to each other—rather than being separated by a superfluous synchronometer or speedometer—making it easier to match throttles. The electronics are well off to the side, the only downside of this design, depending on your preferences.

Sea Ray's answer for the person who like the sedan layout, but still wants lots of fresh air. This is a bird's-eye view of the Sea Ray 680 SS Flagship with the sunroof open. SEA RAY

significance, and frequency of use. Boat and yacht designers should also take into account temperature, vibration levels, adequate ventilation, and noise levels. Noise from machinery and other sources should not exceed 80 dBA continuously, a reasonable comfort level. Compare this with many diesel express cruisers that subject their owners to a hearing-damaging 85 dBA or greater for hours on end. When noise levels reach 85 dBA, expect a decrease in cognitive performance to follow. And wear hearing protection above 84 dBA to prevent hearing loss.

Steering Wheel

The steering wheel should be high enough to reach easily when standing, without stooping over to spin the wheel from lock-to-lock. You should also be able to reach it comfortably while seated with your back against the seat, and without leaning forward. An angle of 15 to 30 degrees from horizontal is the most comfortable and convenient, especially when shifting the rudder from stop to stop. Steering with such a horizontally inclined wheel (seated or standing) minimizes body movement and allows the shoulders, triceps, and biceps to do the brunt of the work, rather than stressing the weaker forearms and wrists.

While certainly salty looking, a vertical wheel is not a great choice; in fact, it's probably the worst ergonomic arrangement available. It's more difficult to steer with one hand, as the hand's height relative to the shoulder varies so much more than it does with a horizontally inclined wheel. The larger the diameter the more difficult this becomes, with the operator having to stoop low with each rotation. Spinning a vertical wheel through four or five (or even seven or eight) turns is not a lot of fun, and is likely to divert the helmsman's attention from the view ahead.

Tilt wheels add a great deal of flexibility for people of different heights, and you may find that different angles work better whether seated or standing. Adding a telescoping capability to the wheel makes it easy to accommodate different drivers. In the interest of ergonomics, steering wheels that tilt and telescope should be standard equipment.

Some boatbuilders inexplicably use wheels with flat, sharp-edged spokes that dig into your fingers when you're spinning them. Common sense and ergonomics dictate that spokes should be rounded to prevent this discomfort.

Steering effort should be minimal, to allow

Here's Little Harbor's idea of the ultimate helm station. I like the simple single-lever engine controls, the fairly flat wheel angle and position well aft of the console, the angled electronics flat, and the priority given to the electronics rather than the engine gauges. The windshield on this boat is huge—too big to fit in this photo. The JetStick at right controls direction of thrust of the waterjets and bow thruster. BILLY BLACK, COURTESY LITTLE HARBOR

palming of the wheel. To avoid the higher cost of power steering, however, most builders reduce steering effort by adding turns lock-to-lock or by increasing the diameter of the wheel. Both of these measures increase the mechanical advantage of the pump motor, which in the case of non-power steering is the operator. But the result, especially in a boat at high speed, is sluggish responsiveness. On smaller boats with well-balanced rudders, it's sometimes possible to find an acceptable combination of steering effort and responsiveness from manual hydraulic steering. But when you get above four turns from full left to full right rudder, your ability to respond rapidly in a collision avoidance situation is impaired. The faster the boat, the more responsive the steering should be. On any boat over 30 feet that's capable of 30 knots or more, I always recommend power steering to keep the steering both tight (around three turns lock-to-lock) and low-effort.

Engine Controls

Like steering wheels, engine controls are at the top of the priority list for helm station placement. Since most people are right-handed, the controls should be to starboard of the wheel. They should also be located within easy reach whether seated or standing, at a convenient height, and mounted 10 to 20 degrees from horizontal. Vertically mounted engine controls are uncomfortable to operate and difficult to move with any precision, since the forearm is doing most of the work; this can result in hit-or-miss boat handling in tight quarters.

I'm biased toward single-lever controls, for one simple reason: the fewer levers there are to grab hold of, the slimmer the chances of tearing up a clutch or ramming the boat in front of you. Who hasn't grabbed the shift to go from reverse to forward only to discover that you've got a firm grip on the lever with the little red knob (the throttle)? A mishap like this is especially likely when you're operating an unfamiliar boat. With mechanical or hydraulic single-lever controls, you have to put the engine in gear, or at least start to, before throttling up, so damage to the reduction gears through a high-speed shift attempt is reduced. These controls use either cables within sleeves or hydraulic lines to transmit the movement of the throttle and clutch controls to the engine itself.

Locating single-lever controls together makes the most sense, but splitting them up, with port and starboard engine controls on their respective sides of the steering wheel, is favored by some sportfishermen captains. This arrangement lets the operator turn around to face the cockpit and, with a hand on each control, precisely maneuver the boat, whether backing on a fish or backing into a slip. The downside of this arrangement is that you can't advance the throttles when heading in the other direction and steer the boat at the same time, unless you were born with three hands, or you have electronic engine controls with an automatic synchronizer. Maybe the best idea is to put single-lever controls together to starboard, on the same binnacle, but also to duplicate the port engine control to port of the wheel, thereby meeting both objectives.

Despite my bias toward single-lever controls, I must acknowledge that dual-lever controls do have a couple of advantages. They let you run the engine up to a faster idle speed, so you can maneuver a boat dockside with just the clutches and still have plenty of power at your disposal. This is especially relevant with gas and high-speed diesels with small props and shallow gear ratios that need a shot of rpm to be noticed. In the mechanical cable versions, their throttles also have more throw, or travel distance, than single-lever controls, allowing for more precise adjustment.

Since it's important for an engine to shift into gear before adding power, some electronic single-lever controls have time-delay circuitry to prevent throttle linkage movement before the engine actually shifts. Electronic controls also accommodate up to a half dozen or more control stations, and some even feature remote units with steering and bow thruster controls included that can be carried around the boat. If you want to drive from the pulpit, or (if you're psychic) from your stateroom, the world's your oyster with one of these babies.

Another consideration is mounting the engine controls so they're well away from curious or careless fingers. This sometimes means placing them outboard of the wheel, away from the companionway where people tend to stand. You also want to make sure that the engine controls aren't placed so they serve as the first thing people grab onto in a sudden turn or when hitting an unexpected bump.

Switches and Auxiliary Controls

Although most larger boats have an extensive array of switches and auxiliary controls, only a few are used frequently, and these should have front-and-center accessibility. Controls for the trim tabs, horn (painted fluorescent orange), autopilot, bow thruster, windshield wiper-washer, and searchlight switches should be at your fingertips and easy to see. The same surface that's used for the throttles can be designed to accommodate the trim tab switches, their indicator gauges, and the wiper-washer switches.

I can't figure out why so many boatbuilders provide a long row of identical shiny black rocker switches in front of the wheel, while the switches that you really need are dispersed in the background among switches for lighting, bilge blowers, stereo system, and other incidentals. Engine shutdown and Halon discharge switches should be

Here's a row of rocker switches on a nicely sculpted helm. Problem is, you can't tell the horn from the bilge blower switch at a glance. The horn, wipers, washers, and trim tabs should be separated from the rest, clearly labeled, and at the operator's fingertips.

prominently displayed and unmistakably marked. In the interest of achieving an ultraclean Palm Beach look, an unfortunate trend being followed by some convertible boatbuilders is to hide the engine shutdowns and even the engine start-stop switches out of sight under the console! This is not a great location when panic sets in and the operator forgets where these vital controls are located. So much for these come-and-go styling trends, like the foot-high Palm Beach bow rails, followed dutifully even by builders and owners who know better.

Instruments and Gauges

Engine gauges or instruments are supposed to tell you at a glance what your engines are doing. This involves a couple of important design considerations. They should be angled so they're nearly perpendicular to your line of sight, using an average of a typical person's seated and standing height of eye. The most important gauges should get the most prominent position; for example, oil pressure and water temperature gauges are more critical than ammeters and voltmeters.

Engine gauges should be large enough to read without binoculars, but not so large as to take up a disproportionate amount of space; a 2-inch-diameter gauge is just about right. If you have twin engines, the gauges should be stacked in pairs by type, with like gauges for each engine side by side so you can spot any variance—of lube oil pressure, temperature, etc.—at a glance. Corresponding annunciators (warning light or audible alarms, each of which should have a sender that's independent of the gauge) should be right next to or even inside the gauges so your eyes are drawn to the relevant spot immediately. Positioning the throttles below their corresponding gauges makes for an intuitively obvious arrangement. High-priority alarms should be within 15 degrees of the operator's line of sight so they're readily identified. Audible alarms alert the operator regardless of head or eye position; spoken alerts are best, and audible alarms should be kept to a minimum.

In any event, you're not very likely to find out

This Davis 58 convertible has a power-lift console. The idea is that you can see everything when you need to, and hide what's the equivalent of a Porsche 911 in cost away from prying eyes when you don't. (And it doubles as a high-end wind deflector!)

about an errant engine from a gauge, since mechanical casualties often happen too quickly to be spotted with the occasional glance at the instruments. That's what alarms are for, so make sure your boat has them and that they're working. Instruments should also be mounted with sealant or gaskets so they don't allow water to get behind the helm console and corrode the wiring. We've seen a lot of expensive boats with gaps under their fancy gauges that you could push a gaff through.

Large tachometers and speedometers, some of which are a whopping 3 to 4 inches in diameter, are more a function of the overactive male ego than of any practical considerations. Builders may want the potential buyer to imagine himself cruising along with those tachs and speedometers pegged to the right, but they have no real merits. One of the most counterproductive arrangements is placing a large speedometer or synchrometer between two equally oversized tachs. The intervening gauge makes it more difficult to read the tachometers. A synchrometer can be very small, placed above the tachs, and still be readable. Speedometers are for ski boats and are generally useless for the average boater. Most operators select a cruising speed based on rpm, fuel efficiency,

or sea state, and the vessel's speed through the water follows. Who thinks, "I think I'll run the boat at 28.5 mph today" and sets the throttles accordingly? It seems unlikely unless you're running a log race or have to be at a destination at a given time, and for those purposes the speedometer doesn't need to be so large or prominently located, especially on a GPS-equipped boat. Save the dash space for the electronics.

Many engine manufacturers use proprietary digital or analog (or both) instrument and control panels, and although they serve up a lot more data than you'll ever really need to know about, these may present a couple of problems. First, they serve as advertisements for their providers, so they may well be bigger than necessary and take up a lot of real estate on the console. They are also generally provided in single-engine units, so the gauges can't be paired on a twin-engine boat. The best solution we've come across is to take them apart, if possible, and rearrange the component gauges and displays in a more sensible paired layout.

Engine-related gauges and alarms should in-

This Bayliner motor yacht's bridge helm station has plenty of room for a chart plotter or radar to port, and the flat is angled nicely toward the operator. I'm not wild about the throttle mounting angle, which requires that you pull up rather than push forward, the offset compass or the bright-white finish, but this helm station's forward-swept venturi windscreen, clean lines, and simplicity are functional enough.   BAYLINER

A good spot for a running light: up high in the clear, easy to see from another vessel, and out of the operator's line of sight so nighttime visibility isn't impacted.　　　　NORDHAVN

clude cooling water temperature, lube oil pressure, lube oil temperature, voltage, exhaust temperature, and the fuel filter-separator's water-in-fuel indicator. A ship's systems monitoring and alarm panel should include alarms for fire, smoke, high bilge-water levels, carbon monoxide, and bilge pump status displayed on a schematic of the boat's layout. Other indicators, depending on the systems onboard, might include refrigerator temperature, generator status, and low fuel level.

Electronics

It's rare to find a 40-foot powerboat these days without an impressive array of electronics including a GPS and chart plotter, sonar or depth-sounder, radar, and a battery of VHF and SSB radios. Ideally, all these toys should be at arm's reach, and like the gauges, their displays should be perpendicular to your line of sight to improve readability. Many builders provide a concavely curved or angled electronics console situated at the best viewing angle. The radar and GPS chart plotter displays should be front-and-center, since they're most important to safe navigation and most frequently referred to and adjusted. Radios, depth-sounders, and other electronics should be arranged in sight and within easy reach.

CHAPTER 12

Topside
Safety

A ship in harbor is safe, but that's not what ships are built for.

—William Shedd

Small craft are called *pleasure boats* for a reason; you're supposed to be able to relax and enjoy yourself. But who can take pleasure and relax in an unsafe environment? Since boats should be as safe as they are fun, we'll look at the elements of topside safety that concern you and your family.

Marketing considerations aside, some customers have to be protected from themselves when it comes to topside design. The expanse of a shiny foredeck on a convertible may look great dockside, but it's a death trap at sea. And since boats can't choose their owners, they ought to be designed with a healthy margin of error built in for less experienced operators. Rather than catering to market demands, the best boatbuilders put safety ahead of fashion—and their astute marketing and sales departments capitalize on the results. In fact, many builders produce boats designed with safety foremost that look great at the same time.

Let's start with the basics. Recreational boats carry people of all ages, sizes, and levels of boating experience. It makes sense that safety-related features should be designed to the lowest common denominators: people with minimal strength, balance, and agility who need to get around a tossing and turning boat safely, and those lacking the experience with which to judge and anticipate naturally occurring hazards and vessel movements. Unfortunately not all boats measure up in the safety department. Instead we find slippery steps, low bow

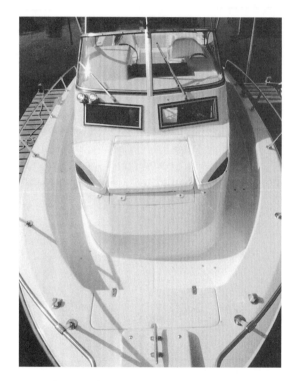

Here's why the walkaround can be such a great family boat. All the decks are recessed, flat, and safe to move around on, and the whole length is usable. You even get a cuddy cabin to get out of the weather in, or for the occasional overnighter.

railings and 18-inch-high transom doors ready to cartwheel the unwary overboard, open transoms on outboards, foredecks that drop off like ski slopes, and other safety sins abounding.

When a boat has a safety problem, it's probably due to one of the following reasons: styling has won out over function and practicality, the designer has tried to squeeze too much into a given hull length, it costs more to do it right, or no one saw the problem coming. Foot-high bow railings, for example, may look stylish, and they certainly cost less.

The goal of topside safety is actually pretty uncomplicated. For the most part it involves keeping people from falling down or, what's worse, falling overboard. Falling overboard is the leading cause of boating deaths.

Nonskid

Most production boatbuilders mold the nonskid pattern into the part (foredeck, cockpit sole, etc.) using gelcoat. This minimizes the time it takes to produce the finished deck and results in a long-lasting finish; a nonskid finish can also be painted on an existing deck. If the nonskid is aggressive, it tears up boat shoes and pants knees in short order, and it can be harder to keep clean, but it also does a good job of gripping your feet. The best aggressive nonskid is not hard to clean, though, since its patterns allow scrub brush bristles to reach down into the valleys of the tread.

A finer pattern can also grip well and be easier to scrub off. Some builders use different nonskid patterns in different areas. For instance, a convertible's cockpit might appropriately get a coarser, more aggressive treatment on account of the fish slime and scales that tend to accumulate like a fine layer of motor oil underfoot. The foredeck and flybridge deck surfaces, which are usually just susceptible to getting wet, have a finer pattern.

The American Boat and Yacht Council (ABYC) is responsible for setting standards for the design of pleasure boats, with recommendations formulated by consensus among its industry members. The ABYC stipulates that nonskid surfaces should be used in exterior walkways and companionways, shower areas, weather decks, swim platforms, ladder steps and rungs, and on walkways adjacent to

This Albin has plenty of handholds on the bridge, grabrails around the trunk cabin top, and a high (30-inch-plus) bow railing forward.

engines. The inclusion of weather decks suggests that the whole foredeck should be covered with nonskid, not just a walkway strip down either side. It's a smart recommendation, since you'll eventually walk all over the foredeck for one reason or another. Nevertheless, partly in response to market demand, some manufacturers don't incorporate any nonskid forward, valuing a glossy finish over a safe working environment.

Cockpit nonskid should extend right up to the hull or hull liner and under the toe space, since that's where your toes typically are trying to dig in when leaning overboard to gaff a fish. Cockpit

The bow of this railing-free convertible is a no-man's-land at sea. Curiously, this clean-and-uncluttered look takes precedence over safety offshore. It's too bad when a decent bow railing makes a boat uncool.

coamings, or washboards, should also have a non-skid finish. If foredeck access on an express cruiser is through an opening centerline windshield, the steps leading up from the bridge deck, the dash surface that gets walked on, and the centerline section of the foredeck, right up to and including the pulpit, should be covered with nonskid.

The term *aggressive nonskid* takes on a whole new meaning aboard coast guard ships. In the early 1970s, in the cutters I served on, we'd prime and paint the steel deck, roll out a fresh coat of paint, sprinkle on a layer of black beauty sandblasting grit, let the paint dry, sweep off the excess grit, and roll out another thin coat of paint. As a result, most of us wore out a pair of Boondocker boots every six months. In the yachting world, a two-part polyurethane paint such as Interlux's Interthane, into which a fine grit is premixed, is a better solution. It can be applied over a smooth or previously nonskid-surfaced deck.

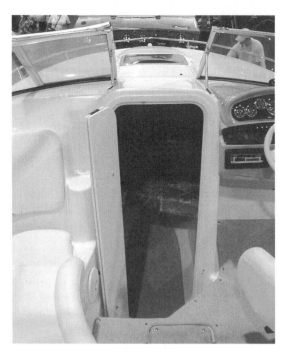

Too-small steps are provided here for safe bow access on this personal injury lawyer's dream. Try climbing back down dockside, let alone when the boat's rocking in a chop.

Railings

Bow railings, side-deck grabrails, bridge railings, and cockpit coaming heights are common topside safety concerns on many boats and yachts. On numerous midrange, cruising-style boats, if the foredecks have railings at all, they're often less than 24 inches high, making them effective tripping hazards on your way overboard! Bridges frequently have low railings overlooking the cockpit and as often as not lack railings altogether around ladder wells.

Cockpits on small outboard-powered boats typically have minimal coaming heights, no handrails of any kind, and little if anything in the way of protection aft to prevent the unwary passenger from somersaulting over the stern, even on boats capable of rapid acceleration. Transom doors on express cruisers are often as low as 18 inches, flimsily made of nonstructural plastic, and devoid of balance-enhancing toe kicks.

This Four Winns has great centerline access to the bow on these large molded steps.

There's plenty to hang onto on board this Century 32 with its full-beam hardtop, making it one of the more deck-safety-friendly center consoles. CENTURY BOATS

So, at the top of any list of deck safety requirements are rugged railings that are high enough to prevent falls overboard and strong enough to withstand the impact of someone falling hard against them. The question is, where should railings be fitted, and how high and strong should they be?

Where?

In a perfect world, railings, coamings, or bulwarks would surround all topside decks, making it tough to fall overboard anywhere on the vessel. If side decks are too narrow (as they often are) to permit extending bow railings all the way aft to the cockpit, chest-high grabrails should be provided wherever side railings aren't. Ideally, bow railings should extend from the cockpit to the pulpit. All too often there's a railless no-man's-land between the deckhouse grabrails forward and the beginning of the bow railing. I've heard salesmen explain that there is no need to go forward at sea, so why bother with bow railings that are high enough to prevent falls overboard? One can only speculate that the boats they are selling will remain at anchor or tied to the dock.

The ABYC's (minimal) recommendations call for the perimeter of weather decks normally occupied when underway to be equipped with railings, lifelines, bulwarks, coamings, grabrails, or other enclosures. That's a good start, but unfortunately the ABYC makes an exception for open boats. They also

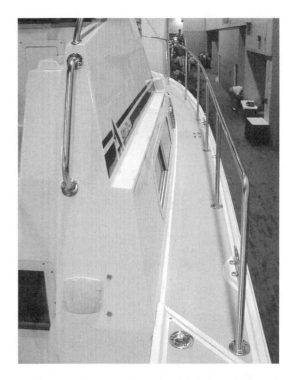

The Albin 32's side deck is easily and safely traversed. The railing is high and stiff, the deck is flat and wide, and the house sides slope inboard to give you more room.

exempt wide-open bridge ladder openings, which place the cockpit 8 feet below a single misstep away. Then there's the issue of rail height, which we'll address in a moment.

Common sense dictates that bow railings should be inboard of the rubrail at their tops as well as their bases so they aren't damaged by piling impact, an aspect of rail design that is overlooked by boatbuilders to a surprising degree. Mystifyingly, on many boats the tops of the bow railings flare several inches outboard of the rubrail. Such a design may increase the chances of a person falling overboard and further complicate the incident if the person strikes the rail while falling. The railings are also harder to reach when you're walking upright along the side decks, and they make it more difficult to stay balanced. In addition, many bow railings project well forward of the boat's stem or pulpit, further degrading their effectiveness. While

The great advantage, or one of them, of the Albin 32 + 2 is the low bridge: just four steps up from the cockpit.

poor bow rail positioning is in some cases part of the form-over-function syndrome, it seems just as likely that poor engineering is to blame.

The ABYC sensibly says that grabrails, or "handhold devices," are supposed to be provided on all weather decks intended for use underway. This includes side and foredecks, around topside seating, in companionways, and on ladders or stairways. Exceptions are made for the person at the helm, who presumably has the wheel to hold onto, and in areas already provided with railings. Grabrails should have a minimum clearance of 1¼ inches from adjacent surfaces to provide enough finger clearance.

How High?

What's a reasonable height for adequate safety in these areas? The American Bureau of Shipping (ABS) maintains a standard railing height of 39 inches (1 m) for commercial vessels, and so does Britain's Maritime and Coast Guard Agency (MCA). ABS requirements for yachts state that railing height can be as low as 30 inches, although these requirements only apply to vessels over 79 feet.

U.S. Coast Guard regulations from 46 U.S. Code subchapter T for small inspected passenger vessels under 100 gross tons are also worth paying attention to, even if they don't legally apply to small pleasure boats. Aboard ferries and excursion vessels, these regulations call for 36- to 39.5-inch-high rails, or equivalent protection, around the perimeter of all decks accessible to passengers or crew. An exception for "big-game angling" is allowed under certain circumstances, with the railing height reduced in the immediate vicinity of the angler to 30 inches. When done fishing, the higher railing requirement is back in effect. To accommodate the regulation, the removable section of railing is replaced.

The ABYC, on the other hand, requires only a 24-inch height for railings, lifelines, bulwarks, and coamings. If the railing is higher than 24 inches, an intermediate railing must be provided. In my opinion, this is an inadequate height. Flybridges are an exception, with ABYC recommending a 30-inch railing or at least a 24-inch-high perimeter seat back.

I am citing ABS and MCA standards as a point of reference—which is not to suggest that a 25-foot

With no railing aft, the sunpad on this 70 mph go-fast boat is unfit for human occupancy, unless perhaps the boat is tied to the dock.

 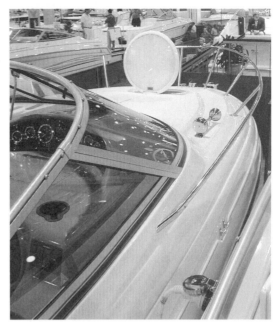

A nice, wide, but railing-less side deck on the left, and a narrow side deck with a railing that's too low (14 in.) to do any good on the right.

Here's a bow railing begging for a redesign. This one's too short, and too far outboard, to be of much use to anyone, and it actually can create a false sense of security forward.

Chris Craft must be built to the same safety standards as an 800-foot container ship. But at what point below 39 inches does a railing become too low to be effective? If you're 4 feet tall, maybe a 2-foot railing is high enough. My own practical experience indicates that a 30-inch railing is the minimum height offering a tangible sense of security, and that's still nine inches shorter than ship standards. The U.S. Coast Guard's relaxation to 30 inches for anglers seems to bear this out. Much lower than 30 inches, and the average person's center of gravity is just too high for such a low fulcrum point to be effective. If the fulcrum point, or point of contact with the leg, isn't well above the knee, a fall overboard is much more likely.

The 16- to 24-inch-high bow railings common to many small pleasure boats can actually be a greater safety hazard than none at all. A leg can easily get caught between the gunwale and the railing on one's way overboard, breaking it cleanly between the knee and foot. It's a safe bet that you'll want full use of both legs while swimming back to the boarding platform. Low railings can also lend a false sense of security.

How Strong?

The ABYC says that any pulpit, bow railing, or coaming must be able to withstand a 400-pound static load in any direction at any point. In reality, many railings could not withstand such a load, at least not without significant deformation. Railing gates have to pass the 400-pound load test and are supposed to have sailorproof latches to prevent them from opening accidentally. Railings and grabrails, usually made of aluminum or stainless steel pipe, should be between ¾- and 1½-inch outside diameter so they're easy to grip. Naturally, the larger the diameter of the railings and stanchions for a given wall thickness, the stronger and stiffer the railing.

A decent railing has to be strong, stiff, and reasonably unyielding as well as adequately high. It needs strength to resist the high-impact load of an off-balance body slamming against it. Grand Banks's Eastbay-series planing yachts are excellent examples: their 1.25-inch stainless steel bow railings supported by stanchions just 3 feet apart feel stiff and secure. Perhaps another reason for the widespread use of 24-inch railings is that larger (more expensive) pipe stock is needed to support the extra lever arm created by a higher railing.

Going Overboard in Outboards

Boats with transom-mounted outboards are also a recurring safety problem. Most outboard-powered boats are capable of strong acceleration, so an adequate railing or coaming is needed, nowhere more than across the transom. Some of these boats don't even have motor wells, just a 1-foot-high transom for the center third of the boat. This configuration offers practically no protection against falling overboard. Then there are boats with motor wells and low, nonstructural plastic gates that flip up when the outboard motor is down. These hinged gates, often less than 24 inches high, offer little security during unexpected acceleration. Any solid water making its way over the stern would easily overcome the spring-loaded retaining clips that are sometimes used to hold the gates up.

The round or rectangular plastic inspection plates in the bottom of the motor well are often made of nonstructural material and are rarely leakproof. Anything made of metal below such an inspection plate will eventually corrode. The most seaworthy outboard boat is one with a full-height transom or a permanent, full-height, molded-fiberglass motor well. Both designs offer good passenger safety and improve seaworthiness to boot.

Transom doors come in two basic varieties, one-piece and two-piece, in the latter of which the coaming and door open separately. The door section can hinge either inboard or outboard; the inboard-swinging design is unlikely to come open

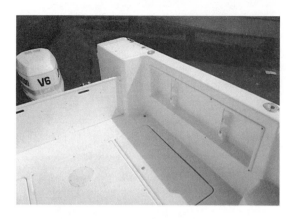

A typical budget boat from hell. There are no toe kicks along the sides, so you'll be off balance every time you lean overboard to grab a line or gaff a fish. The motor well gate is about half the height it ought to be, and there's no toe kick there, either. The scuppers are too small, with ¾-inch drain lines, so they'll drain slowly and clog readily. The stern cleats aren't recessed, so they'll attract line snags.

There is very little to keep a wave out, or you in, in this transom-free zone. No wonder it's for sale!

when running offshore, since its weight will hold it shut against its frame even if the latch works loose, and is therefore safer. An inboard-swinging transom door is also less susceptible to damage when backing into a slip, and you don't have to worry about it interfering with crossed mooring lines.

A two-piece transom door with an upward-

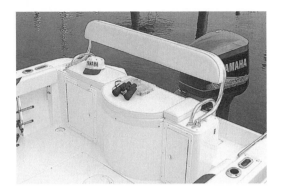

This seat back on a Cobia 250 walkaround serves double duty as a high railing to keep people from falling over the stern of the boat.

COBIA BOATS

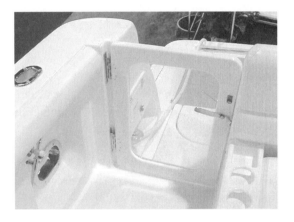

The transom door on the Tiara 50 is as high as the coaming. The stern line can be led from the cleat up to the washboard hawsehole or directly overboard through a hull-side hawsehole. Versatility is a great thing when it comes to mooring a boat. The window in the transom door gives a better view astern when backing into a slip.

swinging coaming section offers excellent security, since the coaming will provide passenger protection even if the door inadvertently comes unlatched. The strength and size of the hinges and latch should be sufficient to the task of holding the transom door securely open or closed. The transom door design ought to include a toe kick space, and the door should be as high as the surrounding cockpit coaming. It should be gasketed to admit little if any water when backing down.

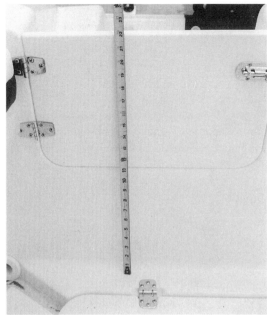

At 22 inches high, this transom door is 6 to 8 inches too low to do much good. Note the scupper at the end of the hatch drain gutter. Water will collect and turn the gutter a nice rust brown within a few weeks of delivery.

Steps and Ladders

The ABYC tells us that a change in elevation greater than 12 inches to a flybridge, companionway, or walkway necessitates a step or ladder. Twelve inches is a pretty healthy step; an 8- to 9-inch rise is preferable. The same 400-pound load tolerance mentioned for railings applies to ladders, although a permanent deformation of ¼ inch is allowable. The clearance to adjacent structures is increased to 5 inches to provide adequate toe space. Step or rung spacing should be no more than 12 inches, and handholds or grabrails are to be provided.

The wider and flatter a nonskid-treated tread is, the more comfortable and secure underfoot it will be. The most uncomfortable and least secure type is a pipe ladder, with no flat surface or nonskid at all. Fortunately, most builders who use pipe treads specify the oval-type, which has a more comfortable and secure stepping surface. Also impor-

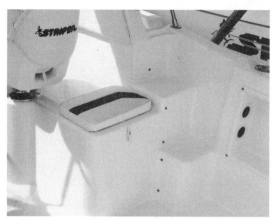

Molded steps lead up to the side decks on this small outboard. Incidentally, if all those canvas snaps around the steps are drilled into a balsa-cored laminate, expect water in the core eventually, and sooner rather than later.

A typical convertible ladder is seen on this Davis 58, with flat, level treads, a handrailing, and a slope of about 10 degrees from vertical. Its mounting design makes it easier to clean the deck below.

A close-up view of the Mainship 39 trawler's molded stairs, which make it easy and safe for kids and seniors to make it to the bridge.

tant are the rise and run, the latter being the angle at which the ladder inclines from vertical. A vertical ladder is the most difficult to climb; inclining the ladder 20 degrees or so reduces the arm strength and effort required to hold on.

Although it's a long reach from the cockpit up to the side deck, many builders neglect to provide a step, either of the molded or folding variety. A molded step can't be moved, so it'll always be there when you expect it to be. A folding step, like the ones used on the Bertram 43, will stow out of the way when not in use but deploy easily when needed.

Speaking of steps, there's often a discrepancy of an inch or more in the height of two adjacent companionway steps. Uneven steps present a tripping hazard to the unwary. Just as in a house, a boat stairway or ladder's rise and run should be consistent from top to bottom.

Boarding

The ABYC calls for a means of unassisted boarding from the water to be provided on all boats. This means that the person in the water should be able to deploy the ladder from the water and climb up it unassisted. Another obvious call is to locate

A Rinker's boarding ladder, extended. This ladder could be deployed by a swimmer, which could be an important consideration in case of a man overboard.

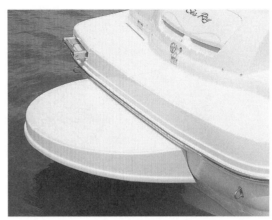

The cover over this Sea Ray's outdrive, if installed on all similar boats, would undoubtedly prevent a lot of diving and swimming accidents. SEA RAY

boarding ladders on boats with outboard or stern-drive power as far outboard as practical to minimize chances of propeller-induced injury. These boarding ladders, according to the ABYC, have to project at least 12 inches into the water, meaning only one step has to be submerged. I'd like to suggest that the standard-setters try climbing a ladder with the bottom rung just 12 inches below the surface, and nothing other than the ladder and a grab bar to hold onto!

Much less upper body strength is needed to use a ladder that projects two or more steps into the water. This is especially true when the swimmer is fully clothed and tired from swimming back to the boat. While we were waterskiing on a Cape Cod lake last summer, we spotted three teenage girls who had been blown away from shore a quarter-mile or so. They'd been hanging on to their inflatable for 45 minutes and were unable to swim back to shore. We flipped the boarding ladder down on our 17-foot lake boat and invited them aboard. Two of the three girls couldn't get up the ladder, which sticks all of 12 inches below the surface, so my accommodating, teenage weight-lifter son promptly hoisted them up, thereby achieving something of a hero's status in their eyes.

Be aware of how difficult it may be to reach up

The teak steps on this aft-cabin yacht can't be climbed without hanging onto the ladder, a decided inconvenience considering this is the yacht's main access point.

Foredecks and Side Decks

The Dettling 51 has it all together in a lot of important areas. Note the waist-high wraparound railings and the water-deployable five-step swim ladder.

In the interest of expanding interior volume, some builders have done away with side decks altogether, meaning you have to climb up on the dash and open the center windshield to get forward. These centerline-access designs can work pretty well if they include large, nonskid-covered, molded steps leading up to the dash, but a railing or handhold of some kind other than the windshield itself, which may be lightly built, is essential.

Sometimes the molded or folding steps become more of an afterthought, pushed off to one side because of the companionway opening, or there are no railings either at the windshield or along the foredeck centerline. This leads to a lurch-and-lunge routine as you try to make your way forward to the anchor in a chop—amusing to onlookers, maybe, but not to the performer. On heavily cambered foredecks, unless you are standing on the dock, it's also tough to reach the spring cleats when side decks are lacking. Not a pretty picture, but it's one that a plaintiff's lawyer would salivate over.

In the interest of expanding interior volume, especially on so-called express cruisers, functional side decks have just about been eliminated. To create more room inside, side decks are often just 3 to 5 inches wide, or are effectively reduced to the width of the railing stanchion mounts, leaving little space between the railing and the deckhouse. These boats typically have lots of pitch and camber in the foredeck to increase cabin headroom, so stepping from the cabintop down to the side deck can be hazardous.

A proper side deck is flat, covered in nonskid, and at least 10 to 12 inches wide. It should be clear of railing stanchions, antennas, and tuna-tower

and deploy the ladder from the water. Some boats have "concealed" hatches over the ladder, which would have to be flipped up out of the way to get to it.

One of the best examples of an ergonomic boarding ladder is on the Dettling 51; it merely has to be pulled from its normal stowed position leaning against the transom. This ladder projects several steps into the water, making it a relatively easy to ascend.

Express cruisers often have their stern cleats mounted externally outboard of the swim platform, thus creating a hazard to swimmers. The Eurostyled sloping transom puts the designer in a quandary as to where to mount the cleats, since there's no actual transom and the undersides of the washboards are inaccessible because of storage bins. An easy fix is to install pop-out cleats or to relocate them so they're out of the swimmers' way. Sportfishermen solve the problem with flush hawseholes leading to cleats mounted below the coaming. Either way, swimmers will be safer and anglers will appreciate the cleaner, snag-free surfaces.

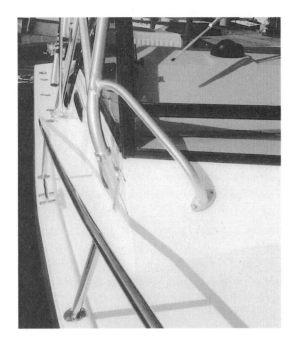

The side decks on this 27-foot express sportfish are wide enough, but obstructions like this poorly thought out half-tower leg make it hard to get by safely.

How Not to Build a Boat 101. There's only about 3 inches between this flimsy, foot-high railing and the deckhouse.

Crew Overboard

Every boat should be outfitted and its crew prepared for the likelihood of a crew overboard. A life ring, life sling, or other throwable device should be mounted both in the cockpit and on the bridge for quick use. It's a good idea to have lifesaving equipment like a MOM8 crew-overboard kit that deploys in just a few seconds. These kits include a carbon dioxide (CO_2) cartridge-inflated flotation device with 40 pounds of buoyancy, an 8-hour steady-state light, a 16-inch sea anchor, and a recovery harness. Water-activated radio transmitters and strobe lights are also available. Some of these transmitters can even be rigged to turn on an alarm and shut down the engines. Direction-finding antennas are also available to help the crew locate beacon-equipped victims.

Don't leave home without one of these close at hand.

NORDHAVN

legs. The deckhouse sides and/or bimini top should slope inboard from the side deck so people aren't caught off balance if they should lose their grip. Handrails along the deckhouse should be continuous and mounted at a height that kids and grownups alike can grip securely. If the side decks are 14 inches wide or wider, extending the bow railing aft to the cockpit is a good idea. If the boat has a trunk cabin, it should also have a handrail to supplement the bow railing.

Toe Kicks

The need for toe kick space should be obvious, but it's often overlooked. As in a kitchen, toe kick space on a boat is provided so a person can stand right up against the countertop, or cockpit coaming, without feeling off balance. Good balance on a boat is even more important than in kitchens, which are generally stationary. Toe kicks can be created by carving out a space at deck level that's 3 or 4 inches deep and high, or by fitting wide coaming washboards that project farther inboard than the interior hull sides or cockpit liner.

Toe kicks allow your thighs to make contact before the toes do. Without it, you would be off balance. The balance problem only gets worse when leaning overboard to gaff a fish or grab a dockline. As mentioned on pages 197–98, nonskid should continue right up to the liner, since your toes are usually planted at the deck edge when leaning over the side.

Boats that lack cockpit toe kicks usually do so because of the added complexity and expense of the fiberglass tooling. On production fiberglass boats, the cockpit deck and hull-side liner are almost always molded as a single fiberglass part. If the coaming washboard is also part of that same mold, a toe kick cannot be provided unless expensive breakaway tooling is used in the liner at deck level. Buyers should be aware of the trade-off here.

Better builders usually attach separately tooled washboards to the gunwale and cockpit liner. Sometimes this is a single, U-shaped fiberglass part that includes the washboard for both sides and the transom. The washboard, usually eight inches or more wide, effectively creates a toe space at deck level. This extra unit is more time-consuming and expensive for the builder to produce, but it makes for a safer boat.

Drainage

Deck drainage has perhaps more to do with a boat's seaworthiness than safety, but it can also impact passenger safety since a clean, dry deck is less slippery. In everyday use, the cockpit drainage system keeps the deck clear of standing water that results from washdowns and rainwater. In extreme conditions, green water that makes its way aboard has to be shed quickly to preserve reserve buoyancy and stability. A deck drainage system must, then, work quickly and efficiently to direct water overboard and resist clogging by debris.

For a cockpit deck to be self-draining, it must be reasonably high above the waterline; that's because most scuppers work both ways, and would just as willingly let water in as out. With a full load of fuel, passengers, and provisions and a gaggle of anglers milling around at the transom, the deck should still be well above sea level to provide reserve buoyancy and prevent backflooding. The higher the deck, the greater the reserve buoyancy and the lower the likelihood of backflooding, but a balance has to be struck in the interest of keeping the angler close enough to the water to play her fish.

The deck must have enough pitch so that water runs aft to the scuppers. To accomplish this, the forward end of the cockpit deck needs to be higher than at the transom. Deck camber, which is the slight convex athwartships curvature, or crown, helps water drain outboard as it moves aft, making for a dryer deck. Gutters are sometimes molded in at the edges of the cockpit sole to channel water aft and to the corner-mounted aft scuppers. Sometimes these gutters are too deep, however, creating real ankle twisters.

Coast guard–inspected vessels operating more than 20 miles offshore are generally required to have their cockpit decks at least 10 inches above the full-load waterline, a standard that might be relaxed only if nonreturn devices are fitted. Guidelines for scupper size are also provided.

How fast the water makes it to the scuppers is one thing, but how fast it then drains overboard is another. The speed at which it drains is a function of the number of scuppers and hatch gutter drain lines, and how big they are. The cleanest, simplest, and most reliable scupper installation consists of a pair of rectangular holes in either corner of the transom, recessed slightly below deck level to col-

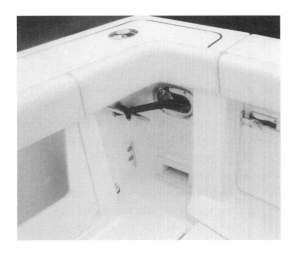

Here's a deep cockpit gutter—so deep that twisting an ankle is a distinct possibility. The rectangular scupper is not recessed below the gutter level, either, so an annoying and unsightly few ounces of standing water will remain onboard.

The hatch gutters in this cockpit drain directly to the scuppers and overboard. The stern scupper itself is not recessed below the gutter level, though, so standing water will remain. The hatch itself is flanged, and the gutter is deep, so the lazarette below should stay dry.

lect that last half a pint of water. The bigger the scuppers, the faster the deck will drain, an important consideration when operating well offshore where seas can build faster than you can get back to port.

Scuppers should extend all the way to the cockpit corners, because that's where water naturally collects. Some builders install flaps on the outboard side of the scuppers to lessen the amount of water shipped when backing down. The large-hole-in-the-transom type of scupper is the simplest and my personal favorite; it won't clog like a hose and is easy to inspect and keep clear.

Nowadays, more builders are installing flush deck drains with hoses leading belowdecks and then overboard instead of transom scuppers. The reasons given for the shift range from reducing the water shipped aboard when backing or lying-to in a trough to aesthetic concerns. This is all well and good, but be aware that drainage is not complete unless the drain plate is recessed below deck level. The slots in the drain plate (if one is installed) also reduce drainage capacity and are subject to clogging. Drain lines are also susceptible to coming loose belowdeck where you can't see them, with the

water ending up in the bilge instead of back in the ocean.

The other problem with drain lines, whether fed directly by deck drains or by hatch gutters, concerns the size of the hose used. Incredibly, some builders use hose as small is 0.5 to 0.75 inch, guaranteeing that the drain line will clog when presented with its first fistful of striper scales or pine needles. A 1.25-inch drain line, in my experience, is the absolute smallest diameter acceptable, both for its clogging resistance and for its drainage capacity. The U.S. Coast Guard seems to agree, with subchapter T regulations defining a scupper as a pipe or tube at least 30 mm (1.25 in.) in diameter leading down from a deck or sole and through the hull to drain water overboard. ABYC, on the other hand, only requires that "each scupper or freeing port shall have a cross-sectional area of at least that

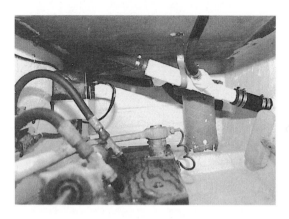

Cockpits with gutter drain systems are all the rage, but make sure the cluster of hoses belowdecks doesn't come loose. This hose exits below the waterline, which is not a good design since it adds one more way for the boat to sink.

of a 1-inch diameter circle (0.785 sq. in.). The 1.25-inch scupper has an area of 1.23 square inches, more than half again as large as the 1-inch drain.

ABYC recommendations also say that, with a cockpit full to the brim (the fixed sill height), the scuppers should be large enough so that 75 percent of the water should drain off within 90 seconds. That's by no means a very stringent requirement, as 90 seconds is a very long time to have tons of water sloshing around on deck, decreasing stability significantly with its free-surface effect. If it took half that time to drain *completely*, I'd consider that a minimal drainage capacity. You'll feel the same way if you ever have a breaker dump 6 inches of seawater in your cockpit, let alone fill it up.

When gutters are used, of course, they must be deeper at their aft ends. It sounds too obvious to mention, yet it isn't always done. I've also seen networks of six or eight deck and gutter drain lines connected to a single pair of through-hull fittings that could not possibly manage the volume of water directed to them. Also, through-hull fittings should be well above the waterline to prevent backflooding, which can be a real problem if that maze of plumbing connections in the lazarette comes loose over time. But when a deck is close to the waterline—say, within 8 inches—there's little room left

to provide sufficient slope for efficient overboard drainage.

A few convertible sportfishermen builders have taken to locating scuppers on the hull sides aft rather than the transom, reasoning that less water will be shipped when backing hard on a fish. Of course, this makes them susceptible to shipping more water when lying-to in a trough. The bottom line is that there's really no substitute for generous deck height above the waterline. I was once on a new 19-foot Boston Whaler Outrage that, with full fuel and two (big) guys onboard, floated with its cockpit deck scupper (located just aft of the console) right at the waterline. In this case, most of the reserve buoyancy (which Whaler prides itself on) comes from the watertight interior hull liner.

ABYC tells us that the minimum height of a cockpit deck, in inches, should be 0.22 times the boat's length in feet. That means our 19-foot Whaler should have a cockpit height, above the waterline, of 4.2 inches.

In summary, the elements of good cockpit drainage include adequate deck height above the waterline, a pitched and cambered deck, watertight hatches, large, clog-resistant scuppers and drain lines, and minimal belowdeck plumbing.

Coast Guard–Enforced Safety Regulations

Federal law weighs in, too, when it comes to the safety of small craft. The portion of the Code of Federal Regulation identified as 33CFR 181–183 lists federal regulations for pleasure boats; the U.S. Coast Guard administers and enforces these codes. Many aspects of life afloat are addressed, including the use of and outfitting with life preservers and other lifesaving equipment, emergency position-indicating beacons (EPIRBs), and cooking, heating, and lighting systems.

Also covered is anything that is likely to cause a fire or explosion, including gasoline fumes and electrical sparks. On boats with permanently installed inboard gas engines, this is addressed by regulations concerning natural and forced ventilation, fire extinguishers, ignition protection, backfire prevention, battery installation, wiring, grounding, and overcurrent protection. Fuel system requirements for conventional inboards and stern drives over 16 feet are meant to eliminate or minimize the chances of fuel leaks causing explosion and fire. These address fuel tanks, pumps, hoses, carburetors, fittings, connectors, and fuel tank pressure testing.

Also included in 33CFR are regulations relating to preventing swampings and sinkings of boats less than 20 feet in length that require them to float when swamped (full of water) with a full passenger load onboard. Even when these boats are swamped or capsized, they should remain floating and level to give passengers safe haven until help arrives. Note that "level flotation" doesn't even necessarily keep the gunwales above the water. The oc-

cupants have to stay seated, and the test for compliance is done in calm water. In fact, the free-surface effect (the momentum of the water in the boat sloshing around) of a boat with level flotation would have a very good chance of capsizing the boat. But level flotation does keep the boat afloat, and will also keep the boat floating higher than less stringent flotation provisions would do.

Staying with the boat is almost always the smart thing to do, since it's easier for a rescuer to spot the boat than your head or life jacket. It's also smart because people often drown trying to swim for shore. 33CFC also requires that manufacturers of most boats under 20 feet display a boat's passenger and overall weight capacities as well as maximum allowed horsepower ratings.

Information on these regulations, and on boat recalls due to safety defects, can be found online at www.uscgboating.org. This is a good Web site for any boater to become familiar with.

CHAPTER 13

Accommodations

Boating is like standing under a cold shower tearing up $20 bills.

—Anonymous

People usually think of their boat as a home away from home, at least if it's big enough to have a cabin with a galley, head, and a couple of berths. Obviously the average boat doesn't have the room of the average house, but what the builder does with the room available can make a big difference in how eager you are to get back home after a weekend afloat.

Any boat has a finite amount of interior volume, defined by the space inside the hull, decks, and superstructure. The success with which that space is apportioned depends on the artfulness of the designer. A convertible sportfisherman will have a large cockpit, since anglers need plenty of space to move around aft. Cruising yachts have smaller cockpits and engine rooms (often at the expense of machinery accessibility), and commensurately larger saloons and cabins.

Some builders have taken to installing engines with V-drives or remote-mounted gears, which allows more flexibility in engine room location (see chapter 8). The engine room and its forward bulkhead can be shifted farther aft with these drivetrains, opening up more room for accommodations forward. An aft engine room makes a lot of sense for many cruising yachts, since the machinery noise is more easily isolated from the "people compartment," making for a quieter yacht.

Obviously, the amount of space dedicated to accommodations, which we define as the interior

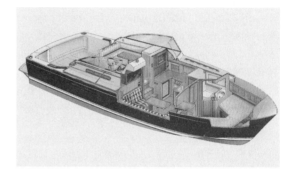

This cutaway rendering shows a Sabreline 36 layout that's pretty typical of express yachts in this size range. SABRELINE

living space of a boat, depends on the boat's intended use. A center console generally has *no* accommodations unless it's big enough to have a standup head inside the console (if you want to call that an accommodation!). A flush-deck or pilothouse motor yacht, on the other hand, has tons of interior space thanks to its large, heavy superstructure, which of course also makes it less seaworthy than a lower-profile vessel.

Just be aware of the 30- or 40-footer that's advertised as having the largest master stateroom, or saloon, or whatever in its class. That space came from somewhere, and it was likely out of the engine room. Either that, or the boat is so beamy and so full in the bow that it will be a bucking bronco terror to ride offshore.

The Ocean 40 convertible is a great example of

The Ocean 40 convertible has a unique, space-smart layout with a raised dinette forward in the saloon *(left)* creating extra headroom for the midships master stateroom below *(right)*.

OCEAN YACHTS

efficient space utilization. This boat has its master stateroom situated amidships, just forward of the engine room, instead of in the bow. This arrangement—rare or perhaps even unique in a convertible of this size—gives the owner a slightly better ride at speed in a seaway, with lower vertical accelerations. Ocean Yachts accomplished it by tucking the master stateroom partially under the saloon's raised dinette and galley countertop. The resulting layout, dominated by the centerline dinette, is a bit unconventional, but it's a trade-off that makes a lot of sense for many owners.

Companionways and Passageways

Just like at home, companionway stairs should ideally have a gentle rise and run to make descent safe and easy, and the rise, or vertical separation between the steps, should be consistent from one step to the next, which is not something you can take for granted. A variation in stair or tread height is an invitation to stumbling. A step with a rise of over 10 inches is hard to climb, and may just indicate the designer's failure to think through the problem properly. Stairs or ladders on boats should always have handrails to grab on to in a seaway.

You should be able to navigate comfortably down a companionway and through a passageway

This Albemarle 32 convertible has a comfortable saloon with galley-down, meaning it's situated a few steps down from the saloon under the deckhouse windscreen, and a step up from the forward stateroom.

ALBEMARLE YACHTS

without bumping into frames and bulkheads along the way. That calls for at least 22 inches, and preferably 24 inches, of unobstructed width. A few inches narrower may be acceptable on a smaller boat, leaving a little more room for adjacent staterooms and other compartments. Some boats have a 24-inch-wide companionway, but the sliding companionway door only opens to 19 or 20 inches, indicating a faulty design.

Saloon

The saloon, or *salon* for most of us (I happen to have an unusually highbrow editor who has appointed himself guardian of the language of the sea), is the yacht's living room. It's invariably in the middle of the boat. On a convertible, it's between the cockpit and the cabin and over the engine room. On an aft cabin motor yacht, it's between the aft cabin and the forward staterooms, and again over the engine room.

This Blackfin 29 Saltshaker is a great running boat offshore, and the accommodations are anything but austere for this class and size of boat. The cabin sleeps four comfortably on the convertible dinette and forward V-berth.

The Bertram 510's saloon has a conventional layout with settee aft and a dinette opposite the open galley forward. BERTRAM YACHTS

Saloons should have plenty of seating, generally on L- and U-shaped settees with either storage space or pull-out beds beneath. If a TV is installed, it should be viewable from the settees, or at least from one of them. On larger convertibles, the galley is often part of and on the same level as the saloon, separated at most by an island countertop. Many people like to cook with a bit of privacy, but while still remaining part of the social group, so this arrangement works well. Smaller yachts often have the galley down a few steps, under the glassed-in windshield.

Saloons usually have plenty of glass, at least on three sides, which lets in plenty of daylight while providing a good view of the great outdoors. Some trawlers and a few pilothouse motor yachts have either narrow side decks aft, outboard of the saloon, or do away with the side deck on one side altogether.

Head and Showers

Even some 26-foot walkaround models have an enclosed head these days, and that's a strong attraction for any family boat. Especially when the head doubles as a shower, with a pull-out spigot that serves as the showerhead, this makes for a great use

The asymmetrical deckhouse on this Nordhavn 57 opens up the saloon to port while providing weather deck access forward to starboard.

of interior space. On larger boats, the trend is for every stateroom to have its *own* head and shower, and builders try to meet consumer demand. But when you consider that space is at a premium on most boats, it's a questionable priority, considering how much time a head is actually occupied. Many three-bedroom homes only have one or two bathrooms, after all. While having a private head for each stateroom has its marketing appeal, and some owners insist on it, the trade-off is always less available space elsewhere. It means the staterooms, for starters, have to be smaller.

Any comfortable head needs to be at least 24 by 36 inches just to maneuver in, and a separate shower at least 24 inches square. As mentioned, many builders of smaller (26- to 40-foot) cruisers save space, making the shower part of the head by providing a bracket to hold the sink spigot so it can

do double-duty as a showerhead. With this design, make sure that the curtain provided completely encloses the person taking a shower to contain the water, and especially that it keeps water away from the head door's sill. Some of the European builders use circular shower units that are closed only when the shower is in use. These effectively contain the water and prevent the shower area from robbing head space. Inward-opening doors work better at containing shower water, since a drip flange can be fitted at the lower edge of the door, but they can be difficult to open from the outside if someone inside becomes injured or unconscious.

One variation on the head-and-shower theme that makes sense for many boats is separate toilet and shower compartments, allowing both to be used at the same time. Carver offers good examples of how to do this right, with the added nifty

Here's a typical, nicely designed head with a raised toilet platform and a separate shower with molded seat. The fewer pieces of fiberglass that make up the head-shower unit, the better, since mildew- and leak-prone joints are eliminated.

This trawler yacht's head includes a separate shower compartment with molded seat, a great feature to have when offshore.

NORDHAVN

feature of a vanity between these two compartments in many of their models. Of course, the most economical use of space is to provide two staterooms private access to the same head, opening up deck space for a larger saloon or maybe larger closets. Or, two staterooms can have their own heads while sharing a single shower in between.

Toilets range from self-contained portable toilets that are carried off the boat and dumped manually, to fancy electric vacuum-flush units with holding tanks. Some toilets are supplied with Y-valves that direct the contents either to the holding tank or directly overboard when operating offshore, but there are restrictions on these Y-valves in some areas. Holding tanks are fitted with dockside pumpout connections that allow the tank to be emptied in suitably equipped marinas.

Larger yachts do very well with a day head near the companionway door, so that anglers covered with muck don't go traipsing through the cabin en route. An exhaust fan is always a welcome feature, of course—just make sure it vents somewhere it won't come back to haunt you. AC 120-volt outlets in any potentially wet area, like the head or galley, should be GFI (ground fault interrupted) protected to help prevent electrical shock.

Berths

The builder's brochure may tell you that a boat will sleep six, but that may be a qualified statement on some boats. A lot of midcabin cruisers, for instance, have a convertible dinette that's supposed to sleep two, but the occupants had better be under 5 feet, 8 inches if they want to stretch out! Measure all the berths before buying the boat, since you don't want to be unpleasantly surprised on your first overnighter with the whole family onboard.

The minimum acceptable length for a berth is 6 feet, 4 inches, and that's really just long enough for a 6-footer to be comfortable; 6 feet, 6 inches long is better still. For a single berth, 6 feet, 6 inches long and 24 inches wide (which is 6 inches narrower than a single bed at home) is also just big

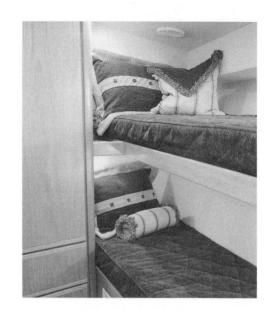

The Bertram 54's guest stateroom with stacked bunks makes good use of a small space.   BERTRAM YACHTS

enough to be comfortable. A 30-inch width is much more practical, though the foot area can be a little narrower (unless you have very large feet). Since boats are usually narrower in the bow, tapering the foot of the berth (with your head facing aft) to 16 inches or so wide can be both necessary and acceptable. For a double berth to sleep two comfortably, look for a minimum width of 46 inches (which is 2 inches narrower than the standard double bed, and 14 inches narrower than a queen). Wider is always better, all things considered.

The midships (near the fore-and-aft middle of the boat) area experiences the least amount of motion at sea, and is generally susceptible to *surge* (vertical rise and fall), but not much *pitching* action that you can feel. Rolling motions will feel more pronounced as you move outboard and up in the boat. When you put all this together, the best spot for a berth is on the centerline amidships down low in the hull.

Notwithstanding the suggestion above that a forward berth works best with the foot end forward, in all other instances a berth with the head facing forward is the best plan. If it faces aft, your

This clever, and increasingly popular berth arrangement, seen here on a Viking 55, offers a double for a couple to starboard, and a single above and to port. Which is great since it accommodates a boys' night fishing offshore, or a guest couple on a cruise. Regulator's excellent, too-short-lived 26 Express, among others, had the same sort of arrangement.   VIKING YACHTS

This Regal 2960's midcabin, tucked below the bridge deck, has seated headroom and a full-size berth.   REGAL BOATS

This Little Harbor 44's dinette converts to a double berth by lowering the table and inserting a couple of filler cushions.

BILLY BLACK, COURTESY LITTLE HARBOR YACHTS

head will be downhill when the hull is up on plane, and an athwartships (across the boat, from side to side) berth is just not as comfortable for most people offshore in a seaway. At least that's what 10 years at sea in the coast guard and navy taught me. An island berth, one that you can climb in or out from either side, is also preferable when occupied by more than one person. It's the berth arrangement of choice for bow staterooms, especially when designed for two people to sleep in, since either can get out of bed without climbing over the other.

Putting midcabin berths below the raised bridge deck on express cruisers is a great way to add sleeping capacity. Ease of entrance and exit is important, though, particularly in the event of an emergency. Having to crawl around companionway ladders, lockers, or stanchions in the dark to get up to the saloon is not a good plan. These are often the largest berths on a small cruiser, since they're essentially just filling an otherwise unoccupied void. Except for the berth being mounted athwartships, this

is the most comfortable location from a motion perspective at sea.

Look for a four-person dinette table to be at least 30 by 40 inches, since a seated person needs over 24 inches of elbowroom to be comfortable. Table dimensions are often predetermined by its other function as a drop-down berth insert, though. Just how easy the conversion from dinette to berth is should be a matter of concern; on some boats it's fast and easy, while on others you have to wrestle the foolish thing into submission.

Headroom

Headroom has an outsize psychological impact on how big a space feels, and for that reason, the more the better. For smaller cruisers of 25 to 30 feet, 6 feet, 2 inches may acceptable, but 6 feet, 4 inches should be the standard on any cruising boat. With their sloping foredecks, many midcabin cruisers have 6 feet, 6 inches or more headroom at the companionway but as little as 5 feet, 10 inches at the V-berth forward. A builder may, then, advertise, say, 6 feet, 10 inches of cabin headroom, but that will likely be only for the first couple of feet at the companionway entrance. The head, galley, and forward stateroom will likely have significantly less, depending on the design.

Seated headroom is also important, especially in the mid cabins of these cruisers. Some builders provide a table to sit at during the day, but headroom is so tight only small children could actually use it. Look for at least 38 inches of seated headroom above the seat cushion.

Hatches and Portholes

There's nothing more claustrophobic than a cabin without hatches or portholes to let in sunlight and fresh air. In the interest of meeting demand for an ultraclean look, many builders—especially of convertibles—have done away with portholes altogether. But that's unfortunate, at least in our view, since there's no substitute for being able to see the passing scenery, or at least to enjoy a little sunlight, from the galley or your berth. I can't imagine thinking, "Wow, the view is just too good through this big window. I think I'll paint half the window flat black to make it feel more like a cave."

Eliminating portholes also eliminates the possibility of leaks, which is another reason why you see so few of them, and it's also one of the reasons why convertible windshields were originally fiberglassed over. Builders then found they could put a lot of furniture, cabinets, microwaves, and large-screen TVs under where the windshield used to be,

A windshield is an indispensable feature, in this writer's humble estimation, eliminating the cavelike feel of many convertibles' saloons with their fiberglass and furniture forward. CRUISERS YACHTS

and that element soon caught on with boaters. Personally, I would take the sunlight and the view ahead over a standup refrigerator any day, but I might be the odd man out on this one.

From a safety perspective, hatches are essential as a means of emergency egress in the event of a fire or if the boat starts to sink. For that reason, having at least one 24-inch-square hatch forward in the cabin, with a ladder to climb through it with, is essential. Try climbing out a 15- or even 20-inch-square hatch, common on today's yachts, with or without a ladder, to see why we like bigger hatches. And when we speak of a hatch size, we mean the clear opening inside the frame that you actually crawl through. The average person just can't fit through these smaller hatches, and certainly doesn't have the upper body strength to pull him- or herself up without a ladder. After waking up to a saloon fire on a friend's cruiser a few years ago, the owners of a new Alden 56 we tested recently specified the installation of a 24-inch hatch and a folding ladder in their forward stateroom during the design phase. Good plan. Live and learn.

Galleys

Galleys range from being equipped with just the basics, with an icebox and a sink, to a veritable kitchen suite including stove, oven, trash compactor, dishwashers, freezer, and refrigerator. Even refrigerators on the smallest cruisers are usually dual voltage, so they can run on 12-volt DC battery power at sea and on 120-volt AC shore power when hooked up dockside.

The Carver 570's galley is open to the saloon, just the way most owners like it. Every convenience found in the average kitchen is standard on Carver's flagship. CARVER YACHTS

A common view a few years ago was that alcohol stoves were least likely to cause fires. The theory was that alcohol is nonexplosive and that an alcohol fire is easy to put out with water, but while the former is true, the latter is not necessarily so. Indeed, dousing an alcohol fire with water may serve only to "float" the fire to nearby flammable materials. Some experts, and many cruising sailors, now feel that an LPG (liquefied petroleum gas) stove is safer provided the gas bottle feeding the stove is small enough not to produce explosive fume concentrations should it leak all its contents into the bilge. This means you have to change the bottle more often, of course, but the peace of mind is probably worth the extra trouble. Another benefit of a gas stove is that it burns hotter than alcohol and thus cooks faster. Sailboats always carry the gas bottle topside in a self-contained locker that vents overboard, and this arrangement is recommended for powerboats as well.

Most larger yachts with generators have all-electric appliances, including stoves and ovens, eliminating the issue of stove fuel. Of course, this means you have to fire up the genset to cook a burger. Whatever the stove type, though, make sure

it has a solenoid switch to shut off the fuel source or the electricity when the stove lid is closed, to prevent a fire from starting.

Most boats come with a single sink, but having two, even on a smaller boat, can actually save freshwater, with one used for washing dishes and the other for food preparation. Having a covering board for one or both sinks will also increase counter space when it's needed most. A combination microwave-convection oven is a truly wonderful appliance to have onboard any small boat; if you can install a kitchen-sized, 1.5-cubic-foot microwave instead of one of those shoebox-sized units that many small-boat builders include as standard equipment, so much the better.

Fiddle rails, those slats that line the perimeter of the counter to keep everything from falling onto the deck in a seaway, take many forms. The

This Sea Ray 240 DA's cabin includes a modest galley unit with refrigerator, sink, and cooktop, a lot of soup-and-sandwich making potential for a 24-footer. SEA RAY

ones I like best fold down out of the way when in port. Drawers and cabinet doors should have push-to-open or other type of positive latches, or the drawers should be of the lift-to-open variety, so they don't come open at sea without your direct involvement.

The inside corner of a countertop is often wasted, inaccessible space, except from above. But this area is perfect for a trash container (just open the lid and sweep those potato peelings right into the can) or even an insulated icebox, which works best with a top-opening lid rather than a side-opening door anyway, since much less cold air is lost upon opening. Or you can have a lazy Susan with cabinet door access just as in some kitchens at home.

Ventilation

You can't have too much natural ventilation in a boat. Just ask anyone who has woken to the sound of a carbon monoxide detector going off, or anyone who's cruised the Caribbean in the summer. Opening doors, hatches, and windows all let in light and fresh air, but they have to be closed when the boat is underway to prevent spray from getting inside. There are hatches that hinge on both sides, giving you a choice depending on conditions. Or some boats have two hatches, one facing forward and the other aft, serving the same purpose.

Dorades are used on high-end yachts for dry ventilation, and especially on sailboats. These are essentially wind scoops that provide a path for air to enter the boat at one end of the cabin and exit it from the other. They're mounted on a baffled box that drains any water off before it has a chance to get inside the boat. Good natural ventilation will allow you to do a lot more cruising without the air conditioner turned on, saving wear and tear on the AC components and maybe allowing you to cruise without running the generator continuously.

Good natural ventilation throughout the vessel's interior is also essential for preventing mildew,

This Dettling 51 is guaranteed to have ample fresh air and daylight with all these opening deck hatches.

condensation, and rot. Bilges, lockers, closets, and voids must all be provided with a continuous supply of fresh air to prevent these evils, to say nothing of musty odors.

Storage Space

Although it may not be readily apparent at a boat show or dockside, storage space on many cruising boats is sorely lacking. If the boat is advertised as a day boat and you plan on using it as such, then all is well. But if it's supposed to accommodate the whole family for a weekend or longer, make a mental note of how much food and gear you'll be taking along and check out your next boat's available storage space to see if it's enough. You might be amazed at all the stuff a cruising family can accumulate over a couple of years.

If you see that there are a lot of inaccessible voids behind lounges, cabinets, hull liners, and under the deck, the builder isn't taking the extra time to do the job right. A separate locker for wet foul-weather gear is a great idea, space permitting, and it should be well ventilated and near the companionway to keep dripping on that nice teak and holly

Carbon Monoxide Poisoning

Besides comfort, your safety is another reason to have an effective natural ventilation system, with properly vented stoves, heaters, and engines, and plenty of carbon monoxide detectors. Carbon monoxide (CO) is the product of combustion of carbon-based fuels, such as natural gas, fuel oils, gasoline, and propane. Gas stoves and internal combustion engines on board boats are sources of this deadly tasteless, odorless, colorless gas. It weighs about the same as air, so it mixes with the air evenly in any enclosed compartment. When a person inhales CO, the lungs' oxygen-absorbing capacity is reduced, so sufficient exposure to the gas is eventually, and sometimes quickly, fatal. Depending on the CO concentrations in the air, death can come within minutes.

In a recent incident, two small boys on an anchored houseboat went for a swim, and paddled into a hull cavity where the generator exhaust was being vented. They lost consciousness and drowned, a tragic illustration of the potentially lethal effects of CO. Even if you don't have an engine or stove operating onboard, you can still be at risk for CO poisoning. For instance, CO from a boat moored alongside can have similar results if conditions are just right, and the "station-wagon effect," which is the vacuum created by a hull and large deckhouse moving along at speed, can suck CO from engine exhaust into a running boat's cockpit and interior.

Symptoms of CO poisoning, according to the ABYC pamphlet *Educational Information about Carbon Monoxide*, include the following sequence of symptoms: watery and itchy eyes, flush appearance, throbbing temples, inattentiveness, inability to think clearly, loss of physical coordination, ringing in the ears, tightness across the chest, headache, drowsiness, incoherence, slurred speech, nausea, dizziness, fatigue, vomiting, collapse, and convulsions. The solution is to make sure that your boat's ventilation, stove, heater and engine exhaust systems are properly designed and that you have plenty of CO detectors onboard, in every space capable of even temporary human occupancy.

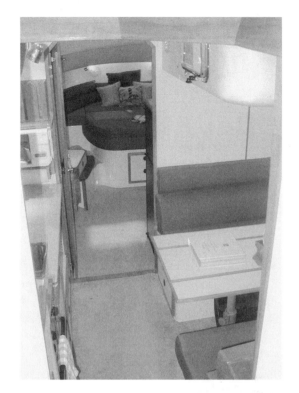

The Albin 32 + 2 has a huge cabin for a 32-footer, stretching from the anchor locker bulkhead to the cockpit. Two or three quasi staterooms are available.

sole (or carpet, as the case may be) to a minimum. Speaking of carpets, snap-in carpets on fiberglass liners are a great way to go. Unlike nailed-down carpet, which gets wet and eventually smells as bad as a barrel of pogies, they can be easily removed for cleaning and airing out, or for replacement when the time comes.

Not only is storage volume important, so is access to all that space. Many builders provide under-berth storage that makes full use of that otherwise wasted space, and a few make it easy to get to by installing hydraulic lifts that make light work of lifting the berth, mattress and all.

CHAPTER 14

Finding Your Next Boat

It is far easier to write ten passably effective Sonnets, good enough to take in the not too inquiring critic, than one effective advertisement that will take in a few thousand of the uncritical buying public.

—Aldous Huxley

Promise, large promise, is the soul of an advertisement. —Samuel Johnson

The worst and best are both inclined,
To snap like vixens at the truth.
But, O, beware the middle mind,
That purrs and never shows a tooth!

—Elinor Wylie

In this chapter, we take a look at some of the ways people try to find the boat that's right for them. We also consider the broker and surveyor's role in your decision-making process, and give you some tips on what to look for on a dockside inspection and sea trial.

Where to Look

Advertisements

Boatbuilders spend a lot of money on advertising, and for good reason, since that's one way you're likely to learn about one of their new boats on the market. Advertising is almost always part hype, so when you read that some earth-shattering, mind-boggling new technique has magically produced a boat that is faster, better riding, more luxurious, better looking, easier to maintain, and roomier than anything else in its class, reading between the lines is definitely in order.

On the other hand, you can often learn a good deal about a boat from an ad. First, its dimensions and power options might be listed so you'll know whether it will fit in your slip or squeak under a local bridge. You may find out if it's available with diesel power. Exterior and interior photography will give you an idea as to whether a closer look is warranted. An accommodations plan, or *floor plan*, will show you how the interior and deck space is divvied up and whether it matches your priorities.

From a photo, you can also learn something about bridge accessibility, helm station visibility and ergonomics, foredeck access, ease of boarding, and other design elements. You can even learn something about how a boat will ride from a photo taken from the right angle to show bottom deadrise and the fineness (or fullness) of the bow.

When you read that a boat is the fastest around for its horsepower, chances are good that it has a flatter bottom than its competitors, which will mean a harsher ride in a chop. If it's a lot lighter than its stablemates, it could be very well built of an epoxy-infused composite sandwich, or it could just be lightly made with conventional materials at low cost and with low strength margins. Another ad will say a boat is the roomiest for its length, and then go on to say it has a great ride. Unfortunately, the laws of physics tell us you can't have both. As we saw in chapters 3 and 4, more beam at the waterline equals diminished ride quality, while greater length and less beam (but the same overall volume) translates into more speed and range for the power, and much greater comfort at speed in a seaway.

Ads in newspapers, weekly advertising publications, and boating magazines are great sources of information on both new and used boats. NADA used boat pricing guides offer their view of a fair price for your next boat, and another good source for larger boats is the *Powerboat Guide*, by Ed McKnew and Mark Parker. Such guides should

drive) are likely to be in superior condition in the absence of the corrosive effects of salt water.

Negotiating is a big part of the game. Dealers can make anywhere from 10 to 15 percent (on some high-end yachts) to 40 percent (on one or two mass-produced cruisers) markup on the sale of a new boat, with 25 to 33 percent being more the norm. The dealer's *ability* to discount depends on the difference between their wholesale cost and the retail sticker price. Their *willingness* to discount depends on supply and demand for their product.

While you'll want to bargain for a fair price, all dealers need to make a profit. A profitable dealer presumably has enough money to invest in service facilities. Their ability to fix your boat's widget on a Friday afternoon before the relatives arrive for a long weekend depends on staff size and competence, parts inventory, and maintenance equipment.

CSI (consumer satisfaction index) information, rigorously tracked during and after the sale, is a big part of the follow-up for companies like Tiara, Sea Ray, Cobalt, Grady-White, and others, and has helped make them successful.

offer a good starting point for negotiations. The rubber-meets-the-road reality is that a boat is worth whatever a willing buyer will pay to a willing seller in a given geographical area. Yacht world.com and BoatTrader.com are just two of the many boat classified Web sites available. More can be found using search engines.

Remember that there can be a huge disparity in depreciation from one brand to the next. A mass-produced express boat might lose 20 to 30 percent of its original value after just one year, while a high-end sportfisherman might be worth as much after two or three years as on the day it was launched. The high-end yacht's high resale price is due to many factors, but chief among them are high-quality construction, durable engineering, and perhaps most of all, strong consumer demand and a long waiting list for a new model. Buying an older boat that has spent its life in freshwater is a fine plan; the mechanical components (e.g. the lower unit in a stern

Magazine Boat Reviews

What can you believe in a magazine boat test? Well, keep in mind that the same magazines that review boats also depend on revenue from boatbuilders' advertising, which is a built-in conflict of interest. If there's no specific criticism in a review, and the

A bargain of a boat offering a lot of bang for the buck, the Mainship 34 Pilot is a good-looking boat with a seakindly ride.

A sharp-bowed Bertram 54 slicing and dicing a light chop. BERTRAM

overall tone is glowing, then read the article as though it were an extension of the builder's marketing efforts. Some publications do make an honest effort to separate their editorial and advertising departments, though, and try to provide useful and honest assessments.

Performance graphs (such as those in *Boating*) are always useful, since they tell you something about speed, propulsion efficiency, and noise levels. Read the review carefully, though, since many such tests are conducted with the boats under lighter conditions of loading than you'll ever see as an owner. A point-counterpoint format with two or more writers participating, as pioneered in automobile consumer magazines, opens the door to healthy disagreement and is always welcome.

Most magazines feel like they have to tell a story every time they write a review, so expect 20 or 30 percent of the story to be only loosely related to the boat at hand. Do expect to hear about how the boat being tested reminds the reviewer of his granddad's 1952 Mathews, or crossing Hatteras Inlet in the same brand's product 35 years ago. These may be good sea stories, but they detract from the space available for pure test-boat-related information. In fact, it is exceedingly difficult to write a thorough and meaningful review in less than 2,000 words, especially when a third of the piece is scene-setting. But the average boat review is only 1,000 words long or less, and the trend is toward even shorter reviews, with a boat being given half a page including photos, specifications, and write-up. These "snapshots" let you know the boat exists, but don't expect any useful critical analysis.

No boat is perfect, and it ought to be evaluated in the context of its market, price, and advertised capabilities. In my own boat reviews, I'm always harder on a boat when a customer's reasonable expectations (based on the boat's size, cost, and the builder's claims) would not be met by the boat due to design, construction, or performance flaws. Some 50-foot-plus boats are wonderful in calm water, have top-drawer joinery, intelligent structural engineering, large frameless windows, and tons of room with full-beam saloons, but their flat-bottom sections also pound hard in a 1-foot chop. Such a big boat could reasonably be expected to offer acceptable performance offshore, only to disappoint when put to the test.

If you don't find any substantive criticisms in a boating magazine review—something more than the toilet paper dispenser being hard to reach or the taupe curtains clashing with the tan dinette—the magazine is probably not serious about reviewing boats. I've been on boats that had terrible visibility from the helm, or that pounded in a 1-foot chop at 20 knots, or had fuel filter-separators or seawater

Grady-White's 248 Walkaround is a great family cruising cum fishing cum water toy boat, built like a tank and running very nicely, thank you, on its C. Raymond Hunt Associates–designed bottom.

GRADY-WHITE

strainers that you could hardly see, let alone reach, or 18-inch-high transom doors and ½- inch-diameter hatch gutter drain lines. Not a word about these issues appeared in reviews of the same boats in some of the major boating magazines.

The problem is compounded by the absence of clear standards for testing boats. For instance, almost no one measures ride quality with an accelerometer, which is the only objective way of distinguishing a smooth ride from a crab smasher. Or you will read that a 35-knot sportfisherman with six-turn lock-to-lock steering handles great, which is a self-contradictory statement. My hope is that this book, and in particular the boat reviews in the second half, will be a first step toward standardizing boat reviews.

Powerboat Reports, which accepts no advertising, just loves to print horror stories! I wrote PBR's reviews for a couple of years and soon learned that I didn't have to worry about offending anyone if the criticism was justly deserved. My reviews were critical, to be sure, but I have long had a policy of sending the draft of the boat review to the manufacturer before publication for comments, corrections, or counterpoint out of fairness to them. And, like most boat reviewers, I'd rather review and report on a good boat than a poor one. In general, the major magazines won't print a review of a boat that's a real horror.

Of course, the reviewer must be competent. He or she must know what to look for, what strings to pull, what hunches to investigate, which questions to ask. Armed with that knowledge, the right equipment, and a thick skin, the reviewer is perhaps ready to write a useful review. I remember running a Bernard Olesinski–designed 65-foot Fairline for the first time in Miami five years ago; I hadn't known a boat that big could handle so responsively, track so well downsea, and ride so smoothly at 25 knots in a 4-foot head sea. I'd never been on an American-built express cruiser that handled and rode anywhere near that well. Since then, that Fairline, and other good-running boats like Eastbays, Aldens, and Viking Sport Cruisers (also British-

A Huckins 40 Sportsman will take a few old salts down memory lane with its classic lines and PT-boat heritage.   HUCKINS

built, Olesinski-designed hulls), serve as my benchmarks for evaluating other boats.

One of my favorite sources of boat reviews is *Motor Boat and Yachting*, published in the United Kingdom. The reviewers seem to know what they're talking about, and they *say what they see*. Maybe that's what the chairman of Brunswick Corporation, one of the largest U.S. boatbuilders, meant when he said that European writers are "brutal" in their reporting on boats and equipment, but that U.S. writers defer to advertisers.

Some may wonder why Brunswick, which builds over 20 percent of the boats produced in the United States, would be looking for more hard-hitting journalism. So do I. But Brunswick's Bayliner, long a whipping boy in the industry press, has made significant strides in quality, such as using vinylester resin in 3-ounce skin coat to prevent blistering. They build boats that are better in some respects than their competitors' higher-priced offerings, though they still have a ways to go in component quality.

CAD-CAM (computer-aided design and manufacturing) is a great equalizer for boatbuilders. The fact is, many midprice boats are getting better (smoother surfaces, better-fitting components), and there aren't a whole lot of ways the best boats can get much better than they already are without pricing themselves out of the market. It's analogous to the auto industry; Japanese cars are still a little more reliable than their U.S.-built counter-

Custom Yachts

If you can't find the boat you're looking for, consider having a boat built. You'll pay more for a custom boat, but perhaps not as much more as you might think. The upside is that you get exactly what you want (which isn't always a good thing in life, admittedly!), but you'll likely have to wait longer for it. The first step is to select a naval architect you are comfortable with. They will recommend yards based on what you're looking for, or even on their perception of your compatibility with the builder. Or, start with a builder you respect and feel you can work with. Figure on the designer's fee being about 5 percent of the cost of the boat itself. A good designer is worth their weight in gold; you pay now or you pay later.

parts, but not by nearly as wide a margin as they were 25 years ago. (That's when, not coincidentally, J. D. Power and Associates started reporting on quality and customer satisfaction, an activity they are extending into the marine industry as of this writing.)

Boat Shows

A boat show is a great place to investigate what's on the market and to do some quick comparisons between models. Bring along a tape measure, camera, and clipboard to take notes. Go to the end of this chapter and use the tips listed as a guideline. Then fill out the information for each boat so you'll be able to make some apples-to-apples comparisons. What boat shows are not good for is a deliberate, unhurried inspection. Salespeople are trying to move as many people through their product as possible, while culling the qualified buyers from the tire kickers.

A boat show can be a great place to get a good deal on a boat. How much you can expect to save off MSRP (manufacturer's suggested retail price) depends on supply and demand. But price isn't everything: buying a boat from a reputable dealer who takes care of their customers in the years following delivery can be worth a lot more than saving a few bucks up front.

Many boatbuilders have dealer networks with strict territories. If you're at a national show, like Miami or Fort Lauderdale, and you're in the market for a larger boat, manufacturers' representatives will almost always be present, and the boatbuilding company's owners and executives are usually available for the first few days of the show. You'll be asked where you live by the builder or one of their dealers, or where you do most of your boating, and then handed off to the dealer who covers your area. If you live in both Newport and Fort Lauderdale, both dealers for these areas may be involved in the sale of your boat and share the profits. At regional shows, such as Boston, Chicago, or New York, the builders may have reps at the show for the first day or so and after that local dealers may have things to themselves. You'll also be "qualified", or judged as to your ability to actually pay for the boat by the dealer if it's a bigger model.

The advantage of attending a show is that there are so many models to investigate, and prices may be favorable. The downside is that it can be a carnival, high-pressure atmosphere on a very busy (usually weekend) day, and you may feel like a herded Holstein at the more popular displays. Get there early or stay late, and attend on weekdays if possible and if you want to have a more leisurely look around. Collect all the information

They don't get any better than this 58-foot Merritt sportfisherman, a fabulous high-end custom boat that runs as well in rough water as it looks dockside.   MERRITT

you can, take it home and spread everything out on the kitchen table so that you can make detailed comparisons.

Brokers

You can also do well finding a used boat by working with a reputable broker. Before selecting a broker, ask around and check out their reputation for honesty and competence. Finding a broker whom you trust and can work with can be an advantage, since they should know the market, and after interviewing you, should have a clear understanding of what suits your needs and lifestyle. Internet-based brokerage services make it easy for the broker to find just the right used boat anywhere in the country.

You'll soon find out if the broker you've selected is really working for you when you see how close what you need matches up with the boats you're shown. If you need another boat in a few years, having already established a relationship with a broker will speed up the search and purchase process. Good brokers want you to be happy with your purchase, and they also want your repeat business.

Word of Mouth

Finding out what the owners in the next slip think about their boat is a good place to start if you're considering buying a vessel like theirs. Talk to everyone you know who owns a candidate boat to learn about its reliability, performance, quality, dealer and warranty service, and other issues. Both the satisfied and the disgruntled owner will have a story to tell, but especially the latter.

But even if an owner raves about their boat, that doesn't mean all is well. You sometimes have to take their praise for Brand X with a grain of salt. It is only human nature that people don't like admitting they've bought a lemon. On the practical side, the truth is many owners really don't know enough about boats in general to offer an informed opinion. They may be very happy with their boat, while the reality is that it's a terror to be aboard offshore and the bottom is blistering away underneath them. I've evaluated boats whose owners were thrilled with their craft, only to come up with laundry lists of design, engineering, and performance flaws that, properly addressed, would make their boats the fine craft they had the potential to be.

It's rare that any owner will sing the praises of their dealer if they're getting poor service, so remarks about service can more often be taken at face value. Sometimes it may be a smart idea to buy the number two boat on your list from the number one dealer in your area. Even then, there will always be those with unrealistic expectations who make petty demands of dealers, who in their turn jump through hoops to try to satisfy these perpetually disgruntled owners.

Internet

Most boatbuilders have Web sites that duplicate the copy and photos in their brochures. You'll find the range of boats, the closest dealer, and sometimes the MSRP for each model. Some Web site names are obvious, like www.bertram.com and www.bayliner.com (no space). For the rest, try "www." plus the brand name, followed by "yachts.com" or "boats.com," or use a search engine. Or, go to www.nmma.org, click on Industry Directory, and fill out the search form. Boats.com, www.motorboating.com, and yachtworld.com also have useful listing services. Be sure to check out www.jdpower.com too.

Surveyors

When the time comes to buy that new or (especially) used boat, make sure to retain a competent surveyor. You may think that a new boat doesn't need a survey, but for many new larger models, paying a few hundred dollars to find out if any systems are improperly installed or if there are other problems is money well spent. The builder usually makes up a "punch list" of discrepancies to fix before it gets shipped to the dealer, and the dealer should also go through the boat to look for what are usually quality-control problem areas. The list tends to get longer as the boat gets bigger and more complex. The surveyor may find things on your new boat that the builder either didn't catch or didn't consider to be a problem.

A used boat of any size and complexity should always be surveyed, usually after signing the purchase and sale agreement and with the actual purchase contingent on the survey findings. After all, it may be on the market precisely because of some hidden flaw.

Competence and Accreditation

I emphasize the term *competence* because not all surveyors are created equal. The competent surveyor has developed an eye for discovering problem areas that would escape the amateur's eye. He or she can often find hidden structural problems based on surface abnormalities and nondestructive inspection. This sort of understanding is generally beyond the scope of even experienced boaters. Surveyors will look at your boat with a practiced eye. They know—or *ought* to know—precisely what they're looking for, and, unlike the eager buyer, they put things into perspective dispassionately.

Choosing a surveyor belonging to an association such as NAMS (National Association of Marine Surveyors) or SAMS (Society of Accredited Marine Surveyors) is a good start. However, membership in one of these organizations alone doesn't guarantee your surveyor is the best choice, or even competent. Credentials from a professional surveyors' organization should mean that the surveyor has met at least minimum standards for technical competence. For example, NAMS members who've earned NAMS-CMS credentials must pass an extensive screening process, a day-long exam, and are held to clear ethical standards. Similarly, SAMS tests its members before awarding an AMS designation.

Naturally there's an incentive for surveyors to join an organization that conveys credibility on the part of the member, like the CMS or AMS designations following the surveyor's name. Some surveyor organizations allow the use of the term "Certified" though the surveyor may not have been screened or

The Shamrock 270, a West Coast–inspired inboard-powered sport-fish-cruiser. The enclosed pilothouse adds a month or two to the boat's practical cruising and fishing season. SHAMROCK

tested for competency. There are also associate members of NAMS and SAMS who have not met the requirements for five years of professional experience and passed a test. Keep in mind that the most competent surveyor in your area may not be a member of any of these organizations at all. Talking to boatyards, boatowners, and others involved in the industry will likely reveal a few names that come up more than once for your short list of competent surveyors.

A surveyor who does work regularly for the seller or his agents may have a conflict of interest; a surveyor (including honest, ethical surveyors), like any vendor, will tend to feel more loyalty to the repeat customer than the one-time client and it may influence their findings or the tone in which they're reported. On the other hand, the broker may be recommending someone who's a real professional. Just be wary of the broker who insists that you use one and not another.

Be sure the surveyor has experience in the type of boat you're considering; a crackerjack fiberglass boat surveyor may know little, if anything, about wooden or aluminum boats. A sailboat specialist will not be the best choice to survey a performance cruiser, and a specialist in large commercial vessels may not be who you're looking for to inspect your 30-foot walkaround. Best perhaps is the surveyor who is familiar with the builder's product line in general, and your model in particular, since design and construction problems tend to show up throughout a builder's product line. Ask the surveyor for a copy of her CV and references when you first talk to her. You'll want a list of previous clients who you can contact as references.

Once you've selected your surveyor, make sure that his rates are clearly understood up front. If you cancel without adequate warning, expect to pay him for a day's work. It is better to pay a little more for an expert surveyor than to get a bargain from an incompetent one. Surveyors' rates vary geographically and by the individual, but expect to pay a per-foot fee. This might range from $12 per foot for a 20-footer to $25 (or more) per foot for a 70-footer, plus expenses. Additional services, such as engine compression checks (often done by a mechanic, not the surveyor), boat hauling, and lube oil analysis will cost extra but are well worth doing.

There are relevant standards. The National Fire Protection Association and American Boat and Yacht Council's Standards and Recommended Practices for Small Craft should be adhered to. These minimum standards may be considered voluntary guidelines for the builder, but adherence to them is often required by underwriters. The Code of Federal Regulations applies to the inspection of commercial and passenger-carrying vessels

The Tiara 31 Open is a classic cruising boat that doubles as an open sportfisherman. This model has proven enormously popular over the years, due to its sound construction, intelligent design, good ride, and the builder's penchant for practicality.   TIARA

and not to pleasure boats, but serves as a sensible starting point for any boat. Meeting USCG requirements is also a good start but by no means ensures that your boat is either well built or seaworthy.

Types of Surveys

Surveys come in several flavors. In general, the public deals with either prepurchase surveys or underwriting inspections called Condition and Value surveys. Both the prepurchase and the C&V surveys should check for the basics like proper wiring and systems installation.

Prepurchase Survey

The prepurchase survey is the whole ball of wax, involving a full inspection of the vessel as well as test running of equipment. A prepurchase survey is conducted to assess the structural condition of the vessel as well as the proper operation and installation of its systems. It is the surveyor's responsibility to comment on condition and to put these recommendations in a logical framework based upon her client's stated interests. Make sure that all systems will be tested, that the boat is sea trialed, and that all lights, machinery, equipment, and systems (main engines, generators, windlass, battery charger, inverters, toilets, tenders, and davits) are turned on and operated.

Having a boat surveyed will give you leverage in negotiating the final price, though people can get carried away on this point. If the vessel had been represented and priced as being in "Bristol" condition, then the buyer may feel some justification in renegotiating the price based upon significant problems revealed during the survey. But it's more common that only structural repair items costing more than about $500 are renegotiated during closing. In these cases, an experienced surveyor can be a valuable consultant to help put damage repairs in perspective.

The surveyor may be asked for an opinion as to the market value of a used vessel for purposes of finance and underwriting. But the surveyor is not there to shed light on whether or not the buyer is getting a good deal. Prudent buyers do their own research and shopping around before signing a purchase and sale agreement. Nor does the surveyor verify a vessel's seaworthiness. Obviously, this would entail a far more in-depth assessment of the vessel's stability and design (well beyond the scope of a simple prepurchase survey), as well as intangibles such as the vessel's outfitting and the competence of the captain and crew.

Condition and Value (C&V)

On the other hand, the underwriting C&V inspection is generally a quickie, and it's often what sellers are referring to when they say they have a "recent survey." It will rarely answer any substantial questions for the buyer. It's common for an insurance inspection report to paint a rosier than normal picture of the vessel. Under no conditions should a prospective buyer accept a recent C&V inspection as a basis for a purchase decision.

How Long Does a Survey Take?

A thorough inspection of virtually any boat is time-consuming—for most boats it's an all-day affair. In fact, the more experienced the surveyor, the more potential trouble areas she may know to ferret out. How much time it takes to get the job done properly, of course, depends on the condition, complexity, and age of a vessel. The accessibility of bilges, voids, fuel tanks, and other out-of-the-way areas are also factors.

A well-written, comprehensive survey report will take the better part of another day to write up. The surveyor should be able to get his client a list of items that require further investigation or negotiation in short order so that he'll have something to work with during negotiations with the broker or seller. However, it is not unusual to have to wait five working days for the final written survey. So, don't expect to close on a boat the day after the survey.

The survey report should include detailed recommendations. A properly worded recommendation should (a) state the problem or condition; (b) recommend repair in detail; and (c) state the pos-

sible hazards of leaving the condition uncorrected.

Make sure any boat you're considering buying is hauled for a thorough bottom and running gear inspection. You won't know for sure what you're getting otherwise. Blistering is a big problem with some fiberglass boats, even with some boats built in the last year or so (though their builders should know better), but you won't know until too late that your boat has a blistering problem if you don't have it hauled. Stern-drive-powered boats should have their transoms thoroughly checked for water penetration and rot in the plywood core, if so equipped, as should fiberglass-encapsulated wood stringers and bulkheads. Balsa-cored hulls, decks, and superstructures should also be checked for rot and water penetration through improperly bedded bolt and screw holes. And the list goes on.

Talking and Listening

While you're at it, tell the surveyor what you plan to do with the boat: where you plan to cruise; how many people will be with you; and whether you fish, ski, or dive. Ask what she thinks about the suitability of the boat for your intended purpose. You could also ask your surveyor up front what she thinks of the model generally—its design, construction, and performance—regardless of the actual physical condition of the boat you're considering.

It's natural for a prospective owner to want the surveyor to validate her own good taste; that's where the listening part comes in, so be willing to swallow the bitter pill if it's presented to you. It may save you a world of trouble to follow their advice up front and not get involved with a boat the surveyor knows to be problematic or unsuited to your needs. Don't waste your time and money: look for another boat before you get any more emotionally involved in a lemon.

Get your money's worth and be present for the survey and sea trial. You'll learn a lot from the surveyor about boats in general, and about your boat in particular. The surveyor will appreciate it if you arrange for the two of you to be alone, without the broker or seller's agent onboard. This will allow him to speak freely without having everything he's saying refuted, and will prevent you from being distracted from what he's trying to tell you. Once you buy the boat, it's a good idea to have it surveyed periodically, maybe every two to three years. If water is getting into the balsa coring in the deck or hull, if aluminum fuel tanks are corroding, or if mechanical systems are getting ready to fail, the sooner you know about it, the better.

Surveyors can also act as owners' representatives on new boats during construction to make sure ABYC and other standards organizations' recommendations are being followed. A surveyor can be retained for acceptance inspections and sea trials and can provide litigation support and accident investigation or damage surveys on an owner's behalf.

The Dockside Inspection

Once you've narrowed your list of boat candidates, inspecting the boat is the next step. The checklists below are cross-referenced to the chapters where relevant in-depth discussions can be found.

SPECIFICATIONS *(see chapters 3, 4, 5, 6, 7)*

Type of boat (sportfisherman, express cruiser, trawler, etc.) _____

Hull design: planing __ full displacement __ semidisplacement __ catamaran __

Construction: wood __ fiberglass __ composite __ steel __ aluminum __

Dimensions: LOA ___ LOD ___ beam ___ draft___ hull displacement _____

PROPULSION *(see chapter 8)*

Number of engines: primary __ auxiliary __

Type of propulsion: inboard __ stern drive __ outboard __ surface-piercing propeller __ waterjet __

Fuel type: gas __ diesel__

Horsepower: primary _____ auxiliary_____

Fuel capacity: _____

Tank type: aluminum __ fiberglass __

Propeller size: diameter __ pitch __ blade area __

Exhaust type: wet __ dry __

RUDDERS AND STEERING SYSTEMS *(see chapter 9)*

The steering is mechanical __ hydraulic __ power __

Number of turns lock-to-lock _____

Is there an autopilot? Y/N

Number of steering stations: _____

Emergency tiller?: Y/N

ENGINE ROOM AND ONBOARD SYSTEMS *(see chapter 10)*

Is there standing and sitting headroom in the engine room? Y/N

Is there room to move around and reach components? Y/N

Are walking surfaces flat, dry, and raised above the bilge? Y/N

Is lighting adequate? Y/N

Are engine start and stop switches with full instrumentation installed at the entrance? Y/N

Can the engine(s), generator(s), compressor(s), fuel tank(s), etc., be removed without deconstruction? Y/N

Can fuel filter–water separators be switched and changed "on the fly"? Y/N

Are all hose clamps stainless steel and backed up? Y/N

Are battery banks secure, covered, installed low in the hull, and properly vented? Y/N

Is there an inverter aboard? Y/N

Is there a generator? Y/N
   gas __ diesel __
   what is its rating? __ kW

How much electrical equipment can the generator power at one time? _____

Are surge protectors installed? Y/N

Is there a shore power hookup? Y/N

Is all wiring marine grade? Y/N
   numbered at both ends? Y/N
   protected by heat-shrink tubing (connections), grommets (bulkhead passages), and chases? Y/N

Is there an automatic fire suppression system installed? Y/N

Does the automatic fire suppression system shut down the engine before engaging? Y/N

Are there watertight bulkheads forward and aft to prevent progressive flooding? Y/N

Is there a raw-water suction Y-valve installed? Y/N does it have a valve interlock to prevent flooding the bilge? Y/N

Are the raw-water strainers accessible? Y/N

Is the bilge pumping system adequate, properly plumbed, and fitted with a bilge-level alarm? Y/N

Are seacocks accessible in the event of flooding? Y/N
   can they be operated easily? Y/N

Are the fuel tanks accessible for maintenance? Y/N

Are tank fittings and hoses the recommended high-pressure aircraft type (the common alternative being rubber hoses with hose clamps)? Y/N

Is the engine room easily accessed from the saloon or cockpit? Y/N

Is there adequate soundproofing (noise level of 83 dBA or less at cruise outside)? Y/N

Can fluid levels be checked from the centerline? Y/N

Can all machinery be accessed from either side and below for routine maintenance and inspection? Y/N

Is there a "day hatch" for quick equipment checks? Y/N

Are all plumbing, electrical, fuel lines, and components properly labeled and accessible? Y/N

Is there adequate ventilation and a blower system? Y/N

Is the bilge smoothly finished for ease of cleaning? Y/N

Are the shaft, transmission, and couplings accessible? Y/N

Is the shaft fitted with dripless seals or a spray guard? Y/N

Is there a work area or bench? Y/N

Is there adequate storage for tools, lubricants, and spare parts? Y/N

HELM (see chapter 11)

Does the helm give a clear and unobstructed view of the horizon? Y/N

Do the radar arch, hardtop supports, and other structures obstruct visibility in any way? Y/N

Are the windows large enough? Y/N

Do the window mullions noticeably obstruct vision? Y/N

Are there windshield wipers? Y/N
   do they sweep most of the glass surface? Y/N
   do they have a freshwater washer installed? Y/N

Is the windshield glass strong enough and clear? Y/N

Have precautions been taken to reduce glare such as minimizing glossy white surfaces under the windshield? Y/N

Is red or blue lighting installed for night operations? Y/N

Is there adequate headroom for the operator? Y/N

Can the vessel be operated safely and comfortably whether standing or seated? Y/N

Can all gauges be viewed easily whether standing or seated? Y/N

Does the helm seat have enough support? Y/N
    is it adjustable? Y/N

Is there adequate seating for passengers/crew? Y/N

Are the steering and engine controls ergonomically positioned? Y/N

Are all switches and auxiliary controls conveniently located, easily reached, well labeled, and logically arranged? Y/N

Are the engine shutdown and fire suppression controls within reach? Y/N

Does the vessel have GPS? Y/N
    VHF? Y/N
    radar? Y/N
    depth-sounder? Y/N
    other _____

SAFETY AT SEA *(see chapter 12)*

Is the boat easy and safe to board? Y/N

Are the decks, walkways, ladder treads, stair treads, and swim platform covered with nonskid material? Y/N

Is the nonskid pattern easy to clean yet aggressive enough to grip? Y/N

If there is a swim platform, does it project past any running gear below? Y/N

Are there adequate railings? Y/N
    are they strong and high enough? Y/N

Are adequate grabrails installed? Y/N

Are the cockpit coamings high enough? Y/N

Are there sufficient mooring cleats? Y/N
    are they positioned usefully? Y/N
    are they large enough? Y/N

On outboards, is the transom cut away with a motor well? Y/N
    cut away without a motor well? Y/N
    solid (not cut away)? Y/N

If equipped with a motor well, does it drain quickly? Y/N

Are the control cables in the motor well fitted with watertight boots? Y/N

Are all inspection ports or hatches watertight? Y/N

Are transom doors gasketed? Y/N

Are the transom door and hardware strong enough? Y/N

Is there a swim ladder? Y/N
    does it extend at least two steps into the water when deployed? Y/N

Does the foredeck have excessive camber or pitch, making it difficult to walk on? Y/N

Are the side decks wide enough to walk on safely? Y/N

Are there enough PFDs and life rings? Y/N
    are they readily accessible? Y/N

Are there toe kicks provided where needed? Y/N

Is the cockpit self-draining? Y/N

Is there sufficient deck camber to facilitate good drainage? Y/N

Are there gutters in the cockpit and around all hatches? Y/N

Are the scuppers or drain lines large enough to facilitate fast draining? Y/N

Are the scuppers high enough above the waterline when the vessel is fully loaded to prevent backflooding? Y/N

Do the scuppers have backwash flaps? Y/N

ACCOMMODATIONS *(see chapter 13)*

Is there enough overall space to suit your needs? Y/N

Does the layout accommodate your needs? Y/N

What is the number of staterooms? _____

Is there enough natural light in the saloon? Y/N

Is there enough electric lighting? Y/N

Does the saloon have adequate seating? Y/N

Is there a view out the saloon windows when seated? Y/N

Is there sufficient ventilation in the saloon? Y/N

What type of ventilation is there (hatches, opening portlights, fans, etc.)? _____

If there are windows in the saloon, do they open? Y/N
are they fitted with screens? Y/N

How many berths are there? _____

Are the berths long enough (at least 6′4″)? Y/N

Are double berths accessible from either side? Y/N

Are the berth cushions thick and dense enough to sleep on? Y/N

Is there an air-conditioning system? Y/N

Is there a heating system? Y/N
what type? _____

Is the standing headroom adequate (at least 6′4″)? Y/N

Is there an overhead hatch fitted with a ladder for emergency escape? Y/N

Is the hatch large enough in diameter to accommodate passengers exiting in an emergency (22″ or greater)? Y/N

Are the doors and companionways at least 6′4″ high and 22″ wide? Y/N

Is there adequate storage? Y/N

Galley

Is the dining table large enough? Y/N

Does the dining table easily convert to a berth? Y/N

Is the standing headroom adequate (at least 6′4″)? Y/N

Is there a refrigerator or icebox? Y/N
what is the volume? _____

What appliances are installed (microwave, trash compactor, etc.)? _____

What type of stove is installed? _____

How many sinks are there? _____

Do the counters have fiddle rails? Y/N
are they open at the corners for cleaning? Y/N

Do the drawers and cupboards have secure latches? Y/N

Is there adequate ventilation? Y/N

Is a carbon monoxide detector installed? Y/N

Is there adequate and secure storage? Y/N

Is there a hot water heater? Y/N
what type? _____

What is the freshwater tank capacity? _____

Is there a watermaker installed? Y/N
GPD (gallons per day) capacity? _____

Head

Is headroom adequate (at least 6′4″)? Y/N

Does the head door have a sill to prevent flooding from the shower? Y/N

Does the head door(s) open inward? Y/N

Is the toilet manual or electric? _____

Is there a holding tank and Y-valve? Y/N

Is there mechanical ventilation? Y/N

Is there an opening portlight? Y/N

Does the head have a shower? Y/N
   can the shower area be completely enclosed? Y/N

Is the shower sump adequate to prevent flooding? Y/N

Is there adequate and secure storage? Y/N

Is access to the head adequate? Y/N

Is there a seat in the shower or over the toilet? Y/N

Is all plumbing accessible and fitted with shutoffs? Y/N

CONSTRUCTION *(see chapters 6 and 7)*

What is the composition of the skin coat (a vinylester skin coat in the first 3 ounces of mat or chop is preferred)? _____

If wood is used in the hull structure, is it marine plywood (which is susceptible to rot) or, preferably, pressure-treated, rot-resistant plywood? _____

Is the wood core susceptible to getting wet in way of limber holes or other penetrations (even if otherwise fully encapsulated)? Y/N

Are the bilges smooth, painted with gelcoat, and easy to clean? Y/N

Is the hull divided into sections by watertight bulkheads to prevent progressive flooding? Y/N

Is there plenty of ventilation around aluminum fuel tanks? Y/N
are they mounted on neoprene strips to prevent corrosion-inducing water from being trapped against the tank? Y/N

The Sea Trial

After the dockside inspection, take a sea trial. Don't forget to buy a sound-level meter at RadioShack to measure and compare noise levels in the saloon, staterooms, cockpit, and bridge. Also pack a stopwatch to time turns, and your handheld GPS so you'll know firsthand how fast your dreamboat really is at cruising rpm. Try to conduct your sea trial on a windy day in rough conditions. Otherwise, you may be disappointed in the vessel's rough-water capabilities after taking delivery. If the bottom is freshly cleaned and painted, the fuel tanks are less than full, and only a few people are onboard for the ride, make sure to deduct an appropriate amount, possibly several knots, when calculating your own cruising speed and range at a given rpm. The engines should turn their full rated speed at full load, and a little over that with the bottom clean.

HELM *(see chapter 11)*

Are instruments and controls clearly visible both standing and seated? Y/N

Do the engine shift controls operate smoothly and have positive mechanical detents so you can feel the control shift? Y/N

Do the throttles move smoothly and stay set where you leave them? Y/N

Can you drive with one hand on the wheel, leaving the other on the engine controls? Y/N

Are trim tab controls within easy reach, and do they have tab angle indicators? Y/N

Is the noise level acceptable (low 80s dBA range or less) at cruise speed? Y/N

Is the steering easy and responsive, with no more than three or four turns lock-to-lock? Y/N

Can you move around comfortably with someone seated next to you? Y/N

Does the boat need trim tabs to get on plane quickly? Y/N

Do you lose sight of the horizon getting up on plane while seated or standing? Y/N

Does a radar arch restrict visibility abaft the beam? Y/N

How close aboard can you see your wake when seated and standing at the helm? ___ yd./m

Does the boat turn as quickly in both directions (use a stopwatch to time a 720-degree turn at cruise speed in both directions)? Y/N

What is the minimum planing speed with and without trim tabs? _____ mph

If the boat is fitted with a bow thruster, is it effective in a crosswind or crosscurrent? Y/N

When averaged over reciprocal runs with and into the current, using GPS, how fast is the boat at various rpm's? _____ mph

Running into a sea (without using tabs) is the ride smooth and dry? Y/N

At what speed does the boat start to pound? _____ mph

At what speed does the motion become uncomfortable? _____ mph

If trim tabs are fitted, do they quickly produce a noticeable difference in trim and correct for list? Y/N

Does the boat track well in a following sea? Y/N

Does the boat slow down and speed up excessively in a seaway? Y/N

Is it seakindly in a trough and when the sea is broad on the bow? Y/N

Are vibrations around the cockpit or aft deck abnormally high (possibly indicating a need for prop repair or balancing before purchase)? Y/N

If a twin-engine, how fast will the boat run on one engine without overheating? _____ mph

Can you turn in the direction of the running engine? Y/N

Can you trail the inoperative shaft without damaging the gears (check with the dealer or your mechanic; if it needs to be locked up, it will increase drag)? Y/N

If a single engine, is the steering responsive enough for safe maneuvering? Y/N

Whether twin- or single-engine, can you back down with control? Y/N

Are shifting and overall engine operation smooth? Y/N

In harbor, in a single-engine boat, can you back and make sternway in the intended direction, and will the boat turn sharply in both directions? Y/N

Will the engines shift smoothly at idle and the boat not run too fast when clutched in at idle speed (trolling valves may be needed on high-powered boats)? Y/N

Backing into a slip, is visibility from the helm acceptable and can you can see and communicate with your deckhands? Y/N

Can you read all the gauges in bright daylight (arranged in pairs next to each other by function is best), reach all the controls and switches, and see and reach the electronics seated and standing? Y/N

Is the vessel's systems monitoring console clearly visible? Y/N

Can the fire suppression system be easily monitored? Y/N

At night, do the helm station electronics, gauges, and switches interfere with night vision? Y/N

Is windshield glare from sunlight or night lighting a problem (glossy white helm areas are a problem, accentuating windshield reflection)? Y/N

TOPSIDE ON DECK (see chapter 12)

Can you walk forward and feel secure with the handrails; side deck width; bow railing height, solidity, and location; and nonskid provided? Y/N

Are bow railings 30″ high, unyielding to the touch, and inboard of the rubrail? Y/N

Are there sufficient cleats (two bow, two stern, and two spring cleats minimum), and are they large enough for your standard mooring lines and a couple of storm lines? Y/N
Can they accommodate a boat moored outboard? Y/N

Do cleats or chocks have sharp edges that could chafe the mooring lines? Y/N

Is the ground tackle (anchor, anchor line/chain, and windlass) sized adequately to hold the boat securely? Y/N

If fitted with an anchor locker, does it drain completely overboard? Y/N

Is there plenty of room for the anchor rode (line) and chain, and can the anchor be secured for sea? Y/N

Can the anchor be deployed from its chute/pulpit by gravity alone, without coaxing? Y/N

Is a washdown provided for the anchor and anchor line? Y/N

If centerline access to the foredeck is provided, are the steps large enough to negotiate safely, and are there railings to hang onto as you make your way forward? Y/N

COCKPIT (see chapter 12)

Do engine exhaust fumes get sucked into the cockpit by the "station wagon" effect? Y/N

Are exhaust noise levels acceptable (high 70s to low 80s dBA range)? Y/N

Does the cockpit feel safe for human occupancy at speed (nonskid effectiveness, coaming and railing height)? Y/N

Does the transom door stay securely latched? Y/N

Is there plenty to hang onto at speed? Y/N

Does the boat have a wet ride, rendering the cockpit unusable at speed? Y/N

Is access to the bridge safe and comfortable? Y/N

Is seating provided to meet your needs? Y/N

INTERIOR (see chapter 13)

At cruise speed, are noise levels satisfactory (mid-70 dBA levels throughout interior)? Y/N

Do cabinet doors and drawers stay closed in rough water and hard turns? Y/N

Do drawer and cabinet contents stay put offshore? Y/N

Do hatches, doors, and other components rattle? Y/N

Is the stereo usable at cruising speed? Y/N

Is at least one hatch 22″ square or round, and is a ladder to climb through it provided for emergency egress from the cabin? Y/N

Are there sufficient grab bars and overhead grabrails in the saloon and cabin? Y/N

Are there unusual noises coming from the engine room or drivetrain? Y/N

Do vibrations seem excessive? Y/N

Other Considerations

WARRANTY

New-boat warranties should cover all structural defects, including osmotic blistering. The better warranties are good for 10 years or more and are transferable when the boat is sold.

Is the warranty transferable to the next owner? Y/N

What is covered by the hull-structural warranty and for how long? _____

Is osmotic blistering specifically covered and for how long? Y/N _____ yr.

When exactly does the warranty start: at purchase and sale signing, upon closing, or upon commissioning and delivery to the owner?
_____

Who warrants the vendor-supplied components like the generator, microwave, saltwater washdown pumps, and electronics? _____

Is there a dealer close by where you do most of your boating? Y/N

What is the builder's (and dealer's) local reputation for service? _____

Will the dealer or builder fix reasonable off-warranty items in a show of good faith? Y/N

Affordability and Suitability

If you have to ask, you can't afford it, right? Wrong! Make sure you ask a lot of questions about operating and maintenance expenses, especially if you are new to boating or to this class of boat. Be aware of the mileage you can expect when cruising and the price of fuel in your area. Naturally, your next boat must be *affordable* in every sense of the word, both to purchase, to operate, and to maintain (outfitting, fuel, insurance, slip fees, hauling, cleaning, storage, bottom painting, hull and exterior waxing and preservation, machinery and equipment maintenance, crew, etc). It must have the *range* to get you to your destination, and the seaworthiness and seakindliness to do so safely and comfortably. Its design must have a suitable layout to accommodate your lifestyle afloat, including sufficient sleeping accommodations and storage capacity. It must be safe for kids and seniors to move around, especially in a seaway offshore. Molded stairs to the bridge instead of a ladder might be a deal maker for you. To fish it must have a cockpit and, most likely, a flybridge and tower. If you plan to dive, a swim platform, tank storage locker, and air compressor locker will likely be needed.

Boat Buying Decision–Making Guide

A Few Questions to Ask Yourself When Considering a Boat Purchase

You will use the boat for cruising _____% fishing _____% diving/skiing/watersports _____% other _____
_____

You need accommodations for _____ people in _____ staterooms and _____ heads.

Does the boat have enough sleeping capacity, living area, and privacy for the cruising you actually do? _____

_____

How many people do you cruise or fish with?

_____

How far offshore do you routinely travel?

_____

_____

Where will the boat be used primarily, and for what purpose?_____

_____

How many days at a time at the most will you spend on the boat? _____

_____

What price do you expect to pay? $_____

to $_____

What is more important to you: a smooth-riding, efficiently driven vessel, or one with great internal volume? _____

_____

How important to you are: styling/looks _____% and function/utility _____%

Approximate boat length desired: _____ feet
Is there a size restriction due to slip dimensions, nearby bridge, etc? Y/N
draft _____ height _____ beam _____

Layout: convertible _____ pilothouse m/y _____
center console_____ walkaround _____
bass boat ___ ski ___ flush deck m/y _____
trawler _____ other _____

Propulsion: conventional inboard ___
stern drive ___ outboard ___
surface drives _____ waterjets ___

Cruising speed desired at full load: _____ knots

Range at full load: _____ nautical miles

Hull: planing _____ semidisplacement _____
full displacement _____ monohull_____
catamaran _____

If having this boat built, how long could you wait until delivery? 3 months ___ 6 months ___
12–24 months ___

Part 2 Boat Reviews

So Many Boats: A Market Survey

Whether you're a novice boater looking for your first boat or an old salt moving up, buying the boat that best suits your unique needs is equally important. If you've bought a boat before and have experience on the water, you likely have a clearer idea of what to look for—and what you don't want—than you did when you first started boating.

As we've seen, all boats are a series of design compromises, and none can do everything well. Preparing a list of priorities (see chapter 14) is a good start. Decide whether you want to use the boat mostly for fishing, cruising, diving, swimming, waterskiing, and so on. Will you be spending most of your time on the ocean or on a river or lake? Do you want to spend weekends on board or will this be strictly a day boat? If you plan to overnight, how many people will you need to accommodate? We'll look at these issues as we consider some of the more popular classes of boats on the water today.

We've included a market survey of different boat types, as well as selected full-length boat reviews I've done that have, for the most part, been published in a wide range of magazines, often in abbreviated or edited form. Some are quite critical, but I rarely list all the problems, since doing so would give the (often misleading) impression that a boat is not worth your consideration. All of the boats reviewed here are worth your consideration. Each review attempts to be balanced in terms of criticism and praise, so you have an accurate view of my overall impressions of the boat.

Some boats offer excellent accommodations but a lousy ride, scintillating speed but ear-piercing sound levels, and so on. You have to decide what's important to you, and maybe settle for a boat that has OK accommodations and a so-so ride to get the best of both worlds. I love finding boats that have very few flaws, that ride well, are built to last, have practical and safe layouts and topside arrangements, are reasonably priced, hold their value, and look great. But these boats are the exception rather than the rule, so apply what you've learned from your own experience and from reading this book so you know where to look and what questions to ask.

These reviews are not surveys; they're the result of spending a day on each boat, usually, including a dockside inspection and a sea trial. I've seen shafts come loose from transmissions, shift cables jam, steering fail, drain lines plug up, and so on, during sea trials, but there's no guarantee that a boat I give high marks to based on my inspection won't, for example, develop window leaks or gelcoat crazing over time.

Not all of the boats reviewed are still in production, since they were written over a period of several years. But they should still give you an idea of how a builder puts together current models (unless new processes and materials are being used) and of course they're applicable to the used-boat market. If prices are mentioned, make sure you check with the dealer for current figures (www.motorboating.com is a good resource for finding boatbuilder contact information).

Also worth mentioning is my own height and weight, because they color my observations. I'm a little larger than average—6 feet, 3 inches, and over 240 pounds—so my remarks regarding ergonomics, berth and seat dimensions, headroom, windshield height, and other measurements should be read in that context. That said, I'm demanding of manufacturers; a 6-foot berth is clearly unacceptable on any boat, as are gauges that can't be seen and switches that can't easily be reached. It's hard to make, say, a helm station work very well for people

that vary a foot in height and 100 pounds in weight, but I make every effort to keep my expectations realistic. If you're at the other end of the size scale, you may not be as offended by a windshield that's only 5 feet, 6 inches high, or a cabin with 5 feet, 10 inches of headroom. But keep in mind that you'll have an even harder time seeing over the bow when the boat's coming up on plane. And remember that when the time comes for you to sell that boat, you don't want to eliminate much of your potential market because the boat is poorly suited to tall people.

Finally, some of the reviews have tabular performance data, and others don't; it's mostly a function of the original venue for the review. In the tables and in text, rpm is revolutions per minute, gph is fuel flow in gallons per hour, dBA is decibels (calibrated to the human ear), nmpg is nautical miles per hour, bhp is brake horsepower, shp is shaft horsepower, and WOT is wide-open throttle.

We begin with freshwater boats, designed to run on lakes and rivers. Freshwater boats come in a wide variety of layouts, hull designs, sizes, and shapes. The features they usually share in common are utility for multiple purposes and hull designs that limit them to calm-water inshore operation. Most are either stern-drive- or outboard-powered; however, inboards are best for ski boats and waterjets power an increasing array of small craft.

Bass Boats

A very low profile, shallow draft, and huge outboard characterize the typical 18- to 22-foot, 130 to 300 hp bass boat. Bass boats are used for inland fishing, and the market segment is growing steadily. Designed for serious fishing, these craft also double as high-performance race boats capable of reaching speeds of 60 to 70 mph, considerably faster in some cases. Due to a beamy, low-deadrise hull, these boats are stable at rest; they must have clear sides all around for unobstructed fishing. Typical accessories include swivel seats, a livewell, and fish- and depth-finders. Most are built of fiberglass, though tough aluminum construction is also popular.

Boatbuilder G3 produces a line of freshwater fishing boats, including this Pro 185. The welded aluminum hull is painted white, and the package includes an electric trolling motor, depth-finder, and trailer. Decks are pressure-treated plywood. Up to 115 hp from Yamaha is available. YAMAHA

Here's a small bass boat from Javelin, the 18 Venom. JAVELIN

Here's a snazzy view of a Champion high-end bass boat. This is the builder's flagship, a 25-footer with a 250 Yamaha. Note the distinctive, chopped-off transom corners. Champion (now part of Genmar) builds shallow-water skiffs, inshore saltwater fishing boats, and fish-and-ski models. YAMAHA

The Ranger 520DVX shown here is part of the builder's Comanche series. It's a high-end, fast, graphics-intense, two-seater dual console with all the features that a serious freshwater angler could want. RANGER

The in-deck rod storage in this Lund fisherman helps keep the decks uncluttered when fishing, and a good selection of rods is available as needed. LUND

Boatbuilder Sea Ark's wide range of aluminum boats includes a 15- to 20-foot bass boat series. The ZX180 shown has a welded aluminum hull and casting decks forward and aft; the three upholstered seats athwartships are standard on this top-of-the-line model. The narrow beam improves the ride in a light chop.

SEA ARK

An offering from Tracker Marine, the Pro Craft 210 Super Pro is a side-console (dual consoles are available), low-profile sportfisherman with ample room for casting forward and aft. These cleanly configured fiberglass boats are offered as a package with a 225 hp MerCruiser, trolling motor, and trailer. Packages are popular with builders because they require less consumer decision making during the buying process, making a sale more likely. In fact, selling boats as "packages" is one reason for Bayliner's early success. Pro Crafts are available from 17 to 21 feet.

TRACKER

After Genmar bought the Stratos line from bankrupt OMC, the Stratos 19SS and 20SS models were subject to a recall to be repaired or replaced by Genmar. These high-performance boats with glitzy gelcoats look great and run fast, but they also serve as a reminder that it pays to look beneath the surface when buying any boat, regardless of manufacturer. In this case, the issue was one of dynamic instabilities at speed. STRATOS

This is how a bass boat looks when it's not racing. STRATOS

Tracker Marine makes a significant percentage of U.S. freshwater fishing and cruising boats, including its Tracker, Pro Craft, Nitro, Suntracker, Fisher, and Tahoe lines. The Tracker Pro Team 175, a welded-aluminum bass-panfish boat, is a marvel with all the comforts and amenities an angler on a budget could want. This boat comes with a 25 hp outboard, a 43-pound-thrust electric trolling motor, a fish-finder, and a matching trailer. TRACKER

Triton builds a wide range of bass, walleye, fish-and-ski, and saltwater fishing boats. The TR-20 shown here has dual consoles and forward and aft casting decks. The manufacturer's listed weight capacity of four people or 525 pounds seems minimal for a boat this size—that's just two extra-large anglers. A 225 hp motor drives this light, relatively flat-bottom boat to suborbital velocities. YAMAHA

Bowriders

A close cousin to the dual console, and basically a cuddy with an open bow instead of a small cabin, the bowrider is a popular family day boat. There are exceptions, of course, but bowriders often have carpeted hull liners or cockpits that drain to the bilge rather than overboard. As a result, the inboard freeboard is often higher than on a typical dual console. The dual console is more often a saltwater boat, meant to poke its nose offshore when the weather permits, and has a self-bailing cockpit like its cousin, the center console.

The full length of the bowrider can be used underway, and the added bow seating is welcome when the entire family tries to spread out on a relatively small boat. Plus, the bow area is a great place to sit when the boat is running along at cruise speed: the view is great, the engine noise is (or should be) practically nonexistent, and the breeze will help keep you cool. There should be railings and grab bars to hang onto because the last place you'll want to fall overboard from on a moving boat is over the bow. Larger bowriders sometimes have small head compartments under one of the side consoles, adding to the boat's popularity with families.

Sea Ray manufactures more models than any other builder, ranging from this 18-foot bowrider to a 68-foot express. This versatile stern-drive-powered sport boat is well built, plushly appointed, and smooth riding. Sea Ray offers something for everyone.

SEA RAY

A freshly styled retro runabout designed by Michael Peters Yacht Design, the new Chris Craft 25 Launch is an encouraging beginning as the builder regains its 1960s stature as an industry leader. Chris Craft builds runabout-, express-, and sedan-style boats from 20 to 40 feet, and larger models are coming.

Part of longtime boatbuilder Thunderbird Products, Formula is well known for its high-performance, high-end race boats; however, express cruisers and bowriders, like this 260, account for many of its sales. The Formula 260 is a quality product, including top-grade upholsteries and fittings and impressive fit and finish.   FORMULA

Baja produces go-fast boats, center-console fishing boats, and family bowriders from 21 to 44 feet. But Baja (not to be confused with fellow boatbuilder Baha) is best known as a race boat builder. The good-looking 252 Islander shown here is both fast and smooth-riding with its deep-V hull.   BAJA

Larson's product line includes bowriders, deck boats, and express cruisers from 18 to 33 feet. The LX190BR is built using Genmar's high-end VEC (Virtual Engineered Composites) process, which produces a very high quality boat—arguably the best in the business.   LARSON

Chaparral is a leading builder of quality express cruisers, deck boats, cuddies, and bowriders from 18 to 35 feet. The 220SSI bowrider shown here is a new model with a walkthrough transom for easier boarding.   CHAPARRAL

Rinker builds a well-established line of value-priced, open- and closed-bow runabouts, express cruisers, and deck boats from 18 (like this 180 bowrider) to 34 feet.   RINKER

Tahoe, a brand of Tracker Marine—not to be confused with Tahoe pontoon boats made by Playbuoy—produces a line of outboard- and stern-drive-powered open-bow, fish-and-ski, and deck boats from 18 to 21 feet. The Tahoe Q5L shown here is a 19-foot bowrider with MerCruiser power.   TAHOE

This is Maxum's outboard-powered 1800XR bowrider viewed from astern.   MAXUM

Maxum is positioned between Sea Ray and Bayliner in Brunswick Marine's extensive stable of boat manufacturers. These boats are reasonably well put together and priced to sell. The line includes outboard and stern-drive-powered cuddies and bowriders, including this 18SR stern drive, ranging from 18 to 23 feet.   MAXUM

Cuddies

The cuddy layout has been around for decades. The bow is covered over with a short foredeck, leaving the aft two-thirds or so of the boat open for passengers. This is the tried-and-true family cruiser layout among small boats. Forward, the foredeck creates a small (hence the name cuddy) cabin with maybe enough room to sit on the V-berth below. A full-width windshield protects the helm area and passengers forward in the cockpit. The cuddy might be just big enough for a portable toilet below the V-berth, and there will probably be room to put clothes and other sundries up forward out of the spray and wind. If you want to be able to lie down comfortably, you'll likely need a 24-foot-plus cuddy to stretch out for a nap. The cockpit may be similar to the dual console's, open and accommodating. If looks count, the cuddy's low foredeck and raked windshield give the boat undeniable aesthetic appeal. When compared to the dual or center console, though, which put the boat's entire LOA to full-time use, the cuddy admittedly wastes space that could otherwise be used for passengers. But the cuddy layout works best for some families who value a dry, private space in a small boat.

Cobalt 293

Cobalt 293 Specifications

Length overall (LOA):	28'10"
Beam:	9'6"
Draft:	19" (drive up)
Displacement:	6,950 lb. (dry)
Fuel capacity:	111 gal.
Water capacity:	31 gal.
Deadrise aft:	20 deg.

Cobalt builds some of the finest day boats being produced in the United States today. In fact, Cobalt scored highest in a 2001 J. D. Power survey of runabout owners. Beautifully finished with a high level of attention to detail, these high-end boats serve a demanding clientele. Cobalt also knows how to design a hull, and these are some of the best-running boats in their class. Perhaps there are a few minor bugs to work out, but Cobalt comes reasonably close to perfection with this day boat. For the day-boater who wants lots of room topside and can live with just the bare necessities for an occasional overnighter, Cobalt's 293 just might be what you need.

Cockpit

As you come aboard from the integral swim platform, two hatches open to expose a folding swim ladder that extends an adequate two steps into the water for comfortable boarding. I would move the ladder outboard, though, since it comes uncomfortably close to the duo-props that are less than a foot away. Inside the transom door to port (low at a 15 in. height), another door with push-to-open latches allows easy access to the shower and to an air pump for inflatable toys.

Aft is a U-shaped lounge that converts to a sunpad or extra berth by inserting a filler cushion. The upholstery is well crafted and comfortably contoured. A hatch to starboard provides access to the table legs stored inside. A cockpit hatch—which is

generally well finished but had cut-inducing rough spots below—opens for access to the 0.125-inch-thick, 111-gallon aluminum fuel tank. The tank is well secured with neoprene-lined aluminum straps. It's also installed with ample air space around the sides and bottom to prevent the development of corrosion caused by standing water. The water heater is to port on an outboard shelf, and the polypropylene waste tank is to starboard.

The bulkhead separating the engine room from the fuel tank space has several large access holes and a limber hole in the bilge; I would seal the holes and install a bilge pump in each watertight compartment to increase sinking resistance in the event of a major leak.

Forward to port is a sink and small icebox with bottle storage, a 120-volt receptacle, and a refrigerator-freezer below. The unit is nicely tooled and well organized, making efficient use of space; the color of the Lexan doors even matches the surrounding gelcoat. A grab bar surrounds the unit, giving you something to steady yourself with at sea. There's room for the cockpit table and canvas cockpit cover under the forward two-person lounge to port, the forward end of which is contoured to serve as a reclining couch for sunbathing.

Helm

The helm station is forward to starboard and is nicely finished in tooled fiberglass and faux rosewood paneling. There isn't much room for add-on electronics with the gauges spread out over the two-tiered instrument panel, but most people who buy day boats like this don't need a vast array of electronics. The speedometer and tachometer look identical at a glance, so it takes time to get used to which is which, but they're both positioned for easy visual reference. The toggle switches are lined up above the wheel; because it's used more often than the rest, I would definitely relocate the windshield wiper switch to be more ergonomically positioned, closer to the throttle.

Two moderately proportioned people can squeeze into the 32-inch-wide helm seat, but it really should be wider to accommodate two people—or just consider it a spacious seat for one. Unfortunately, it doesn't quite line up with the steering wheel, which—from the center of the seat—is offset to starboard, as is the compass mounted a full 4 feet forward on the dashboard. The helm seat also needs to be raised to provide a more comfortable seated position and better visibility when the boat is on plane. The seat bottom does fold up to serve as a bolster, but this results in the height that is needed full time. The throttle is also too high and too far aft for comfortable use when you are seated or standing; lower and farther forward would be a more natural position for both me, at 6 feet, 3 inches, and my 5-foot, 4-inch assistant.

The stainless steel–framed windshield is both attractive and solidly constructed, and the curved glass sections are free from distortion. Foredeck access is via a pair of molded steps next to the instrument panel and forward through the centerline opening window. There are no side decks due to the continuously radiused decks above the sheerline. This works well enough in calm water, but is a challenge for anyone who has to venture forward in a rough chop to drop the hook: there are no bow railings, the deck slopes down as you work your way forward and outboard, and there isn't any nonskid outboard on the cabintop. The designers would not approve, but I would extend the 2-inch-high grabrails to a full 28 inches to add an extra measure of safety forward.

Cabin

Situated in a recessed step in the bridge deck, a sliding Lexan companionway door opens 20 inches wide for entry to the cabin, which is two more steps down a stairway. During our test ride, the door slid shut because no one had dropped the retaining latch. Therefore, a latch that hooks automatically when the door is fully opened is a desirable design feature. For what is essentially an open-deck day boat, the Cobalt 293 offers a reasonable cabin layout, with 65 inches of headroom, two opening overhead hatches, and four opening side ports. The resulting effect is open and airy, especially with the light-tan motif accented by exotic-smelling and great-looking Connolly leather-covered, V-shaped dinette seats forward.

To port is a small galley with a single electric burner, sink, two drawers, a storage locker below, and cabinets with microwave oven above. Opposite is an enclosed head with an electric toilet, a sink with pull-out faucet for showering, a mirror, and a small vanity cabinet. An access plate lets you get to the underside of the instrument panel, and the wiring is neatly bundled and carefully routed inside. Just forward of the head is a small hanging locker.

A V-berth—the one with the Connolly leather —is located forward; the table is lowered on its telescoping stanchion to convert it to a double berth. The Cobalt's cabin is beautifully detailed, with more attention to detail than most boats of this genre.

Engine Room

The aft deck is elevated on a single boost lift, offering excellent access to the Cobalt's 502 MerCruiser Bravo 3 stern-drive power plant. The hatch is flanged and gutters in the surrounding deck are deep enough to keep everything dry below. Single engines in a boat this size are the way to go in my opinion, precisely because of the generous room all around that makes it easy to get to the dipstick, spark plugs, and other maintenance points. The 31-gallon water tank is to port and the two batteries (they need to have covers added), macerator pump, and trim-tilt pump are to starboard on level floors.

The bilge is finished in light gray gelcoat; a few rough edges and chop fibers should have been ground smooth at the factory. The hatch sits atop a deck section that's raised a foot higher than the cockpit, forming a natural seat for the aft lounge. Ideally, the cockpit deck would extend at the lower height all the way to the swim platform, eliminating the step up to port and the resulting 16-inch-high cockpit sides. Cobalt needs to add foot-high railings to port and aft of the lounge seat to avoid sudden acceleration-induced accidents. The transom door is only 15 inches high, so it too needs to be raised to 30 inches for sufficient safety.

Design

With a sharp entry, running strakes, reverse chines, and a healthy 20 degrees of deadrise at the transom, the Cobalt has all the ingredients for success as a performance boat. The hull bottom projects back on either side to the aft edge of the swim platform, extending the running surface for added buoyancy and dynamic lift—always a good feature in a planing hull.

Construction

Cobalt points confidently to its wood-free construction with good reason; the chances of rot—always possible in wood-framed boats built under substandard quality-control conditions—are eliminated. The trick with all-fiberglass construction is to keep the weight down, and Cobalt addresses this in part by using hollow high-hat stringers with flanges bonded to the hull with death-grip adhesive.

A good method for reducing weight is to build cored-composite hull bottoms and sides, but the cored bottom—a few of which have come apart primarily due to poor skin-to-core bonds—is a hard sell for marketing departments, with a few "bad apples" spoiling it for the rest of the industry. Compared with solid fiberglass, cored bottoms are not only lighter but also more impact resistant; however, attention to detail during construction is more critical.

A Kevlar-E-glass hybrid is used to increase impact resistance in the keel and running strakes, although impact with an underwater object could just as easily occur elsewhere in the bottom. Transoms are cored with high-density foam for high strength and compression resistance while avoiding the use of plywood. More technical still is the use of Nida-Core honeycomb coring in the decks, which has excellent mechanical properties and also does a great job of attenuating engine and wave noise. A barrier coat of premium resin helps prevent osmotic blistering, the bugaboo of some boats still being built today.

Performance Test

We had little wind for our test ride, but we sliced the occasional wake with little problem and trimmed the boat out to ride quartering wakes with positive directional stability. I highly recommend this single power plant: performance was excellent with an easy 26-knot cruise at 3,200 rpm, with four passengers and a light load of fuel and gear. We ran the engine up to 3,000 rpm, put the wheel over hard, and recorded just under 25 seconds to turn 360 degrees, which is excellent responsiveness. Steering was both tight—at fewer than three turns lock-to-lock—and very easy.

With a light load of four passengers, a quarter tank of fuel, and no empty water, our single big-block, 415 hp, 502-cubic-inch MerCruiser Magnum MPI Bravo 3 performed as given in the accompanying table.

Sitting down in the helm seat made me wish the seat were at least 4 inches higher, both for better visibility when climbing on plane and for more legroom. Folding the forward half of the seat up from that height would have made it an ideal bolster or quasi-leaning post for running at speed. I

Cobalt 293 Performance Results

RPM	Speed, knots	Fuel Use, gph	Noise Level, dBA	Trim, degrees
600	3.8	2	66	0.5
1,000	6	2.8	71	1
1,500	8.5	3.7	69	2
2,000	9.2	8.0	73	5
2,500	14.5	10.7	74	6
3,000	24.0	13.2	75	6
3,500	28.3	16.5	78	5
4,000	35.3	22.6	81	4
4,500	40.8	30.8	83	4
4,700	43.1	32.4	86	4

also would prefer more horizontal room between the wheel and the fiberglass seat box; with my heels right up against the seat when I was standing, I felt somewhat off balance.

The boat tended to trip slightly in a hard turn, possibly a consequence of the hull's V extending to a hard point at the keel. In any case, this is a handling tendency I don't often see on boats with padded keels. Overall, though, the boat handled very well, rose up on plane quickly (with little bow rise with the lower unit trimmed down initially), and rode smoothly in the light chop we encountered. One great advantage of this boat compared to many

I've tested is the absence of a radar arch, which permitted excellent all-around visibility.

The twin props on the Bravo 3 lower unit canceled out propeller side force, so the boat turned in just a little more than its own length in either direction. For the same reason, the boat also steered where I pointed it when backing down, regardless of the wind direction.

Cobalt has put together a commendable package with lots of exterior room and efficient use of available space. The warranty is better than most. Workmanship is superb, components are of high quality—such as the three-density foam used in the sculpted, wood-free seats—and the design makes excellent sense for this application. If you do a lot of overnighting, this is not the 29-footer for you; if your priorities are in day boating, give the Cobalt a close look. It's worth the money, both now and at resale time.

With the size of the power plant—the 415 hp MerCruiser Bravo 3—our test boat had ample power to please almost anyone. Options included a full bimini enclosure, mooring cover, global positioning system (GPS), rosewood dashboard, anchor windlass, holding system, electric toilet with macerator, Halon system, and trim tabs.

1998 Rinker 272 Captiva Cuddy

RINKER

Rinker 272 Captiva Specifications

LOA:	27'0"
Beam:	9'0"
Draft:	22"/36" (drive up/down)
Displacement:	5,400 lb. (dry)
Fuel capacity:	100 gal.
Water capacity:	10 gal.
Deadrise:	21 deg. (transom)
Standard power:	250 hp 5.7-liter MPI MerCruiser Bravo 3
Test-boat power:	310 hp 7.4-liter MPI MerCruiser Bravo 3

Rinker, one of the larger express-cruiser builders in the United States, understands its market well. With the 272 Captiva, the company meets the demand for larger day boats with lots of open deck area and a small cuddy cabin. The 272 neatly fits the open-air bill, with a mix of topsides and protection from the elements that will appeal to many dayboaters. You can overnight or even take a weekend cruise without feeling too deprived, but this boat shines for day use.

Cabin

We'll start the tour down below, where a 9-foot-long cabin seems like much more than just a "cuddy"—at least when length is being discussed. In the headroom department, with a maximum of 59 inches and just 54 inches a few feet forward, this is definitely a space for kids, primarily because I couldn't sit up in the 6-foot-long V-berth. The door to the enclosed head, to port of the narrow (16 in. wide) companionway, hinges on its forward side so it's easy to enter once you're already in the cabin. A portable toilet is mounted on a fiberglass liner and is held down by a light-duty, manufacturer-supplied sliding clip that I don't expect will last long with normal use. Headroom inside is limited, but you do get privacy.

Opposite to starboard is a small hanging locker that also holds the round cockpit table. Forward is the V-berth, molded in as part of the one-piece cabin liner. A good deal of storage space is lost because there are no hatches under the berth cushions. Fit and finish is quite adequate, with a smooth, padded liner overhead that is easy to keep clean. Seatback bolsters are built into the hull liner and cushions are integral to the berth and filler section. There are no overhead lights, just two adjustable reading lights outboard. Having the cabin liner means there's no carpet to mildew and mold, which is a welcome feature; it even unsnaps to air out or replace.

Cockpit

As you come on board from the swim platform, there is a recessed swim ladder, ski hitch, and shower spigot for your cruising convenience. The cockpit, or main deck, of this Rinker 272 is really what makes the boat special. First, it's very large, taking up most of the boat's usable length—about 12 feet. A large L-shaped lounge seat, part of which covers the engine, is aft and to starboard. A table mounts on a stanchion that inserts into a recessed deck fitting aft.

A 36-quart cooler fits below the seat in a recessed pocket, with a neatly tooled drain gutter leading overboard. Opposite to port are a refrigerator-freezer and a locker for a battery switch, small shore-power breaker, and 120-volt receptacles. Above is a countertop with sink and faucet, cutting board, and cup holders. Located forward is another lounge seat with storage space below and a molded plastic drain pad liner with contoured gutters to accelerate drying inside. Rounding out the long list of equipment is a cockpit trash container and a mooring-line storage compartment.

Rinker has made the boat easy to maintain with lots of removable carpet liners, such as the one covering the cockpit. If Rinker can solve the problem of water leakage into the engine room and clean up the glasswork, this will be a fine boat for its intended day use.

Engine Room

To access the power plant, you just push a button at the helm and the aft cockpit seat lifts out of the way for the single MerCruiser 7.4-liter MPI engine. Access is actually quite good; you can maneuver all around the engine for maintenance. Even working on the engine's back side is possible with open space provided by the molded, outboard-sloping transom. Excellent engine access is a feature that can't be taken for granted, especially on most twin-engine installations in this size range.

The bilges are finished in a speckled white and black gelcoat; my preference is all white to make it easier to find the dirt and grime. The polypropylene water tank is to port, next to the battery charger, and a pair of batteries is immediately to port of the engine. A plastic storage bin is to starboard, with ample room for the shore-power cable and miscellaneous necessities. Rinker should clean up some of the glasswork in the bilge, and I don't mean just the chop splinters. Whole sections of tabbing were hanging in midair near the forward bulkhead on centerline. The edge of the forward plywood bulkhead was not rounded, so the fiberglass couldn't possibly adhere to it as it should, exposing the raw plywood end grain. It made me wonder what the plywood looked like where I couldn't see it.

The tooling around the engine hatch–seat bottom is another problem. The flange around the rim is too narrow to keep the foam acoustic insulation from getting saturated with water, which was the case when I opened it. Plus, the perimeter of the vertical seat front, on which the hatch–seat bottom rests, is not flanged all the way around, making it easy—and probably unavoidable—for water to leak down into the engine room. After our sea trial, I hosed down the boat and then opened the hatch; water was dripping down, wetting everything directly below, which means the shallow flange around the rest of the hatch back aft was also only partly effective in channeling water away.

Helm

The helm is forward to starboard—no surprises there. The seat is comfortably upholstered and low to the deck. However, with trim carefully controlled by proper weight distribution and hull form, visibility is still quite good in all directions.

Our boat had fancy Faria gauges trimmed in gold; unfortunately, the large tachometer and speedometer were both fogged up by condensation. The two gauges are easily confused because they're the same size and color, and one goes up to 65 (mph) and the other to 60 (hundred rpm). You're out of luck if you want to install electronics on this boat—there's no room for anything but a radio, a stereo (which is also remotely controlled in the galley), and a small depth indicator. The rocker switches are neatly arrayed above the wheel, with the horn prominently outlined in red. The compass, mounted forward and atop the instrument panel, is partially obscured behind the nicely sculpted console—at least for anyone under 6 feet tall.

I think most people would find the small 13-inch-diameter steering wheel to be comfortably positioned, but the throttle off to the side—being high and well aft relative to the seat—is awkward to use from a sitting position. The trim-tab controls are well placed just forward of the throttle. This is certainly a fancy-looking dashboard, with gold-rimmed gauges and faux burr-elm paneling. Rinker also features a tan-colored dashboard to reduce the glare off the windshield above. The aluminum-framed windshield is made of rugged material, and its center section flips open for access to the foredeck.

Foredeck

Use due caution when moving forward on this boat. A pair of small steps is molded into the forward bulkhead next to the companionway door. Be sure the door is closed when you are ascending or descending because it gets in the way of the steps. Once forward, you'll notice there is no bow railing, just a 3-inch-high grabrail that gives you something to hang onto from the dock. The nonskid is satisfactory but, in my opinion, without a railing, this is not a safe area when you are trying to drop the hook.

The anchor locker is designed to hold the anchor, which hangs from its stocks, and the line bin is divided into two compartments by a plastic partition, which is a clever idea. When I opened the hatch on our test boat, though, I noticed that the partition was damming up a quart or so of water, keeping it from reaching the drain hole at the bottom of the locker. The 17-inch hatch to the cabin is probably just large enough to climb through for many people, but I prefer a larger opening—say, 20 to 22 inches.

Construction

The Rinker has a DCPD-blend resin skin coat over the gelcoat, followed by a solid fiberglass bottom layup of mat and woven roving (see chapter 6). The side laminate includes a layer of Coremat to reduce print-through and to build bulk and stiffness at light weight. The stringers and bulkheads are constructed of fiberglass-encapsulated plywood (pressure-treated for long life), and resin is used to seal the limber holes against water penetration. The hull-to-deck joint is fastened with stainless screws on 4-inch centers. Decks are cored with ¾-inch Klegecell foam and the bolt stanchions fasten through a plywood core that resists the bolt compression. Bolt holes are sealed with polyurethane adhesive-sealant. As mentioned previously, I noted significant quality-control problems on our test boat's hull laminate.

Performance Test

With two of us on board and half a tank of fuel, we had great conditions for a sea trial. With a fresh, 15- to 20-knot southwesterly breeze, we stayed in close to shore in calm seas, then ran out into the 1- to 2-foot chop for our seakeeping trials.

On the average of two runs at each throttle setting, our 310 hp 7.4-liter MerCruiser Bravo 3 produced the numbers listed in the accompanying table.

The boat was very responsive with Mer-Cruiser's low-effort power steering, requiring just 2.6 turns lock-to-lock. At low or high speed, the boat turned in just over its own length for a very tight turning circle. In the 1-foot chop, we had a smooth ride at 24 to 26 knots with the stern drive all the way down to lower the bow. The boat has a fine entry and enough deadrise carried aft for a smooth ride in a light chop.

Running downsea in 1- to 2-foot seas with the drive trimmed up, the Rinker ran straight with minimal helm input. The bow of the Rinker above the waterline has a lot of convexity, and this feature adds a significant amount of buoyancy and lift when the bow is buried in a following sea. We took some spray over the bow with a strong wind broad on the bow, but certainly not more than the average boat would in similar conditions.

I would get a dealer-installed windshield wiper (it's not a Rinker option), and I recommend a freshwater wash for the windshield to clear off salt smears. The windshield, at 53 inches off the deck and 13 inches high above the dashboard, offers about as much wind and spray protection as the average boat in this class; that is, not much. It is also a good idea to replace the cheap, wrinkled plastic filler curtains between the bimini and the windshield with higher-quality material. This change would provide a much better view ahead in rain or in windy, spray-filled surroundings.

Coming up on plane while sitting in the well-padded helm seat, I had an excellent view and was able to maintain plenty of blue water under my horizon by keeping the stern drive tucked in. I didn't notice much difference in trim or speed by using the trim tabs, but they satisfactorily corrected for list to one side.

The wheel was comfortable for me whether I was seated or standing; however, being fairly high

Rinker 272 Captive Cuddy Performance Results

RPM	Speed, knots	Speed, mph	Fuel Use, gph	Nautical mpg	Statute mpg	Range, nm	Range, statute miles	Noise Level, dBA	Trim, degrees
1,000	5.4	6.2	1.2	4.5	5.2	408	466	66	2
1,500	6.9	7.9	2.8	2.5	2.8	224	255	68	3
2,000	12	13.8	6.1	2.0	2.3	178	204	73	6
2,500	16.6	19.1	8.7	1.9	2.2	173	197	79	5
3,000	23.3	26.8	10.8	2.2	2.5	196	223	82	4
3,500	29.2	33.6	14.4	2.0	2.3	184	210	83	4
4,000	35.6	40.9	20.1	1.8	2.0	161	183	85	3
4,500	38.2	43.9	26.1	1.5	1.7	133	151	87	3

off the deck, the throttle was better positioned for stand-up driving. I would want to see the helm seat slide aft another 4 to 6 inches so you're not crammed between the wheel and seat bottom.

The Rinker has much to commend it for anyone looking for, first, a versatile and well-equipped day boat and, second, an overnighter. I would like to see the foredeck made safer and more accessible, better engine-hatch gutters, a wider companionway and bigger cabin hatch, and better quality control at the factory during lamination.

I like the basic family-friendly layout, the great handling, and the easy maintenance with snap-in carpets and fiberglass liners. Fuel capacity is on the light side for a boat with a big-block V-8 engine, but the 180-mile cruising range is adequate for most people in this market, and trailer weight is kept low. A generous standard-equipment list includes a nicely equipped galley, bimini top with full enclosure, power-tilt steering, VHF, depth-finder, compass, cassette radio, shore power, cockpit shower, and trim tabs.

Baja builds go-fast, high-performance boats, runabouts, center-console sportfishermen, and performance family boats like the 272 shown, ranging from 21 to 44 feet. The Baja 272 comes with bucket seats that do double duty as stand-up bolsters, fancy graphics, a small cockpit, and a big engine. BAJA

Bayliner produces runabouts nearly on par with some of the higher-priced competition. The cuddies, like the 192 Capri shown here, track well, deliver a reasonably smooth ride, have climbable three-step boarding ladders, and offer good helm-station ergonomics. They're also built to last, with pressure-treated plywood stringers; vinylester-resin bottom barrier coats to prevent osmotic blistering; one-piece, waterproof VDO gauge clusters; and corrosion-proof, high-density polyethylene (HDPE) fuel tanks. BAYLINER

As a builder of small cuddies, deck boats, bowriders, and now a 36-foot express cruiser, Cobalt has established a reputation for its high-quality, superbly detailed family cruising boats. The 263 shown is in the middle of Cobalt's 19- to 36-foot lineup and is also available in an open-bow hull model. The high-end appearance of this boat is matched by its intelligent engineering, careful construction, and fastidious attention to detail. COBALT

Formula's 280 SS, part of the builder's hybrid SS lineup, is narrower than a PC cruiser and wider than a Fastrac go-fast. A well-built, great-running family cruiser with a smooth, dry ride, the 280 has an emphasis on topside space, but the cabin is still big enough for a weekend on the water. Attention to detail is apparent. FORMULA

Maxum's 2100 SC cuddy is a versatile little cruiser for daytime boating and, in a pinch, the occasional overnighter for two friendly boaters. Skis stow away below the one-piece fiberglass cockpit deck, and fold-out sleeper seats are standard. The helm includes a nonglare finish and full instrumentation. The ride in a light chop is comfortably smooth.   MAXUM

Monterey's 218 stern-drive-powered cuddy is an appealing family day boat with a fold-out port lounge, fiberglass cockpit liner for easier maintenance, aft jump seats, and a well-designed helm station. Montereys range from 18 to 32 feet and include deck boats, cuddies, bowriders, and express cruisers.   MONTEREY

Sea Ray's 2300 Overnighter cuddy is a capable, nicely appointed family day boat with room for two to spend an occasional night onboard. A good ride with a deep-V bottom and fine entry, the Sea Ray 230 is plush on the inside and has a roomy, all-fiberglass cockpit.   SEA RAY

This photo allows you to see what a top-of-the-line wooden lap-strake cuddy looked like in the 1960s. This glass Lyman, a 25-foot reproduction, was laid up in a fiberglass mold, which was built using an original wooden boat as a plug. With a fine ride at 22 to 25 knots, the Lyman's entry cuts cleanly through a chop as long as most of the bow stays in the water. A flat bottom aft makes the hull easy to push along at these speeds; these boats also have a very comfortable motion at trolling speeds.

Pursuit's smallest model, the 2270 Kodiak, is perhaps technically a cuddy, but it's also a good all-purpose family fish-ski-cruise platform that's solidly built and ergonomically designed. The windshield is high for good wind and spray protection, the modified-V bottom delivers a smooth ride in a chop, and—like all Pursuits to 38 feet—this trend-resistant 2270 will look just as good in ten years as it does today.   PURSUIT

Regal's 2150 LSC, one of eleven models by Regal ranging from 18 to 28 feet, is a unique design with a small cabin and an unusual amount of headroom for a small cuddy. There are two available cockpit layouts, along with a gas grill and a wet bar. The deep-V hull delivers a smooth ride, and the stepped bottom reduces drag at high speeds.   REGAL

Shamrock is one of the few builders producing inboard-powered fishing boats in its size range of 21 to 29 feet. Since small inboards have so much to commend them for fishing, especially with their clear transoms (no stern drive or outboard in the way), it's a wonder there are so few of them in use. Shamrock produces some models with full keels and others with prop pockets for reduced draft; the Shamrock 220 Cuddy shown here has the former. Low-deadrise bottoms result in a somewhat bumpy ride at speed, but also produce more speed for the horsepower and increased range.

SHAMROCK

Deck Boats

Now outpacing bowrider and cuddy sales, the deck boat has a low, wide monohull supporting an equally wide deck that's open from bow to stern. The helm console is usually near amidships to starboard. Lounge seating is often provided around the perimeter of the deck, so there's room for a large gathering of family or friends. Some of these deck boats have bow and stern boarding ladders, and side gates as well as a transom door, making getting on and off the boat easier. A wide range of amenities is usually included or available as options, including a refrigerator, wet bar, head compartment with toilet and sink, rod holders, livewell, and fish box. Deck boats have planing hulls, which is what really differentiates them from pontoon boats, so they're also capable of pulling skiers or watertubes, assuming that enough power is available. If you plan to ski from any of these boats, getting the biggest motor permitted is often a good idea. Usually wide for their length to maximize deck space, and with minimal deadrise to provide a good turn of speed with a crowd on board, depending on the builder, a deck boat's hull may not deliver as smooth a ride as a similar LOA runabout.

The GS 170 shown is the smallest in Godfrey's Fundeck series, and I had experience with this boat when I lived near a lake. The ride is quite comfortable in a light chop, handling is excellent, the layout is great for a small family, and the insulated cooler niche is appealing.   GODFREY

The boatbuilder named Astro is part of Tracker Marine and makes a line of fiberglass bowriders starting at 18 feet, culminating in the 2350 deck boat shown here. A high-freeboard profile provides a safe interior, and direct access is provided from the narrow swim platform (extending it over the lower unit would be a big improvement) to the cockpit. A type of bowrider/deck-boat hybrid, the Astro 2350 has a closing center windshield section that offers good protection for passengers aft of the wraparound windshield.

ASTRO

One of the world's biggest boatbuilders, Bayliner has something for everyone—up to a 57-foot motor yacht—including a four-model line of deck boats from 21 to 26 feet. The 2659 Rendezvous shown is the largest in the class, and it has a surprisingly smooth-riding, stable, twin-sponson hull designed in-house by Bayliner. A five-year transferable warranty, a long list of standard features, a small fuel tank (57 gal.), and stern-drive propulsion (to 250 hp) are included. An options package that includes features standard on much of the higher-priced competition is a good value.   BAYLINER

Chaparral makes high-end express cruisers and runabouts up to 35 feet long, as well as a line of five deck boats from 21 to 26 feet. The exceptional 263 Sunesta shown is the queen of the fleet, with a curvy, even futuristic, design; its layout is similar to an overgrown jet-powered sport boat. The cab-forward design provides a bow seating area and a large cockpit aft of the wraparound windshield. There's not a straight line to be found topside on this boat, including the seating, which curves so people face one another. Practical features include the walkthrough transom and an extended swim platform, which provide excellent protection for swimmers diving over the stern drive. The latter feature should be imperative for any family boat builder.   CHAPARRAL

Aerospace giant Bombardier is perhaps best known in boating circles for its PWC (personal watercraft) product line and now also for its Johnson and Evinrude outboards, but it also makes a line of well-engineered sport boats from 13 to 22 feet. The Sea Doo Islandia 22 is part of Bombardier's sport-boat lineup, and its size and layout qualify it as a deck boat. The 240 hp Mercury-powered waterjet propulsion system is what separates the Islandia from the rest. Waterjet power has much to commend it: while not as fast out of the hole as a submerged propeller system, efficiencies improve at higher speeds, and there's no denying the compelling safety advantage (and minimal draft) of a propellerless propulsion system. Bombardier consistently makes a high-quality, intelligently conceived product, and the Islandia 22 is no exception.

BOMBARDIER

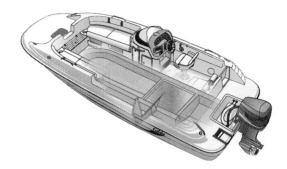

Cobia is a well-known builder of 17- to 27-foot saltwater fishing boats and a deck-boat series including 20-, 22-, and 25-footers. This well-equipped 206 shows its saltwater roots with a ruggedly built, all-fiberglass hull; generous freeboard; a one-piece, self-bailing cockpit; and dual batteries. With 11 degrees of transom deadrise, don't expect an ultra-smooth ride on most any deck boat, including this one; do expect stability and easy planing. Yamaha owns the company, which likely means that it's well run and that you'll own a Yamaha (up to 150 hp) if you buy this boat.   COBIA

This cutaway rendering shows the basics of a Cobia's construction, with fiberglass box-beam stringer systems bonded to the hull and deck, and the fuel tank nestled in a stringer cavity. Polyurethane, which is rot-proof and will last the life of the boat if properly installed, is definitely the way to go on smaller boats with fuel-tank capacities of 90 gallons or less.   COBIA

Harris Kayot has been in business for more than forty years building freshwater pontoon and deck boats. The company makes six deck-boat models, most of which (like the 228 shown here) are available with either stern-drive or outboard power. The 228 has a bowrider layout with a wraparound windshield that offers extra protection for those sitting aft. Harris Kayot maintains its reputation as a quality builder with bronze through-hulls, an all-fiberglass stringer system, sanded and gelcoated bilges, 40-ounce upholstery, and a leather-wrapped wheel. A head compartment is included for added family appeal.   HARRIS KAYOT

Fisher, also a part of Tracker Marine, builds a wide range of aluminum fishing, deck, and pontoon boats. The builder's sole deck-boat offering is this 22-footer, available with either outboard or stern-drive propulsion. The Fisher 2210 is a rugged, low-maintenance family boat with an aluminum hull (great for grounding on a pebbly beach), a pressure-treated plywood deck, and a fiberglass console. The beamy, low-deadrise bottom delivers excellent stability, a good turn of speed for the power, and—like any wide, flat-bottom deck boat—a bumpy ride in a chop. The bow is left open for anglers, and a trailer is part of the package.   FISHER

Rinker's line of affordable cruisers includes a pair of deck boats, 24 and 26 feet in length. Like many deck boats, the helm station and windshield are situated around amidships in the Rinker 24 Flotilla shown here, leaving a large bow area for passenger seating. Stern-drive power from 220 to 320 hp is available, and the boat is well equipped. Like many deck boats, which are intended for inshore use relatively close to a launching ramp, fuel capacity is quite limited at just 42 gallons. The twin-sponson hull delivers a reasonably smooth and quite stable ride in a light chop, and boarding is as easy as it gets via the open aft deck.   RINKER

Arkansas-based Sea Ark is a leading builder of aluminum vessels, from jonboats to patrol craft. Aluminum is tough and, in fact, works best for boats that are beached regularly on rocky bottoms. The 25 Sun Savana shown is a rugged, flat-bottom family boat with an outboard (up to 150 hp) mounted on a bracket for power. The railing around the raised aft seat is a safety-enhancing feature that I would like to see installed on go-fasts and similar boats with aft sunpads.   SEA ARK

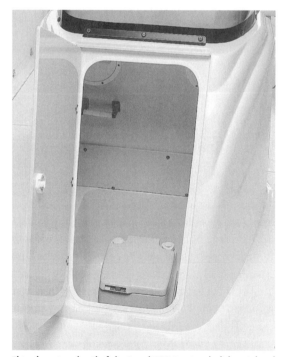

Cruiser manufacturer Regal has ventured into the deck-boat world with this single 20-foot Destiny offering. High-sided with 30 inches of interior freeboard, and built to ski and fish as well as party, the 20 Destiny offers a better-than-average ride with more deadrise and a finer entry than others of the genre. Still, there's seating for twelve, and Regal is known for producing a quality product. A head compartment is situated under the center console, which is another unique feature that makes this a fine fishing boat—most of these boats have a pair of side consoles. A bow swim ladder is handy for boarding when the boat is beached.   REGAL

This photo is a detail of the Regal 200 Destiny deck boat's head compartment with portable toilet.   REGAL

Multipurpose Boats

This is a catchall category for versatile boats that do well enough on several missions but, unlike ski or bass boats, don't excel in any single role. These boats can function as ski and fish platforms or as day cruisers in sheltered waters—sort of the SUV of the small-boat world.

Triumph (formerly Logic) is a remarkable company that builds a remarkable product. Boats from 12 to 21 feet are manufactured using roto-molded polyethylene plastic. The entire structure—hull, liner, and decks—is molded at the same time, so the boat is literally one piece, seam- and joint-free, including the integral 37-gallon fuel tank. The color impregnates the plastic, rendering gelcoat scratches a problem of the past. The process can produce boats to 21 feet, but the 186 Cool Bay shown is the most complex boat of its kind. Tough, low maintenance, and built to last indefinitely, the Triumph series is also priced to sell because labor during manufacture of each boat is minimized. Up to 150 hp is available, making the 186 Cool Bay a viable part-time ski boat.   TRIUMPH BOATS

This welded aluminum Fisher 16 Sport Avenger by Tracker is one of the builder's multipurpose, deep-V freshwater series ranging from 14 to 20 feet. The high windshield protects passengers from wind and spray; many saltwater express builders could take a cue from this little boat. Mercury outboard power from 40 to 90 hp is available, and Fisher even included reverse chines for added form stability and planing efficiency. The hull has a lifetime warranty, and a trailer is part of the package.   FISHER

Lund is a big-name, well-regarded builder of aluminum sport and fishing boats, both outboard- and stern-drive-powered, from 12 to 21 feet. The Lund 1950 Tyee shown is a multipurpose family boat with a tall, practical windshield for protection from the elements, and ample freeboard and deadrise to handle a light chop. Livewells, rod storage, fancy seats with shock absorbers, and a trolling-motor setup are included. Both outboard and stern-drive power are available.   LUND

Everyone should have his or her own private plane at the ready to fly in that spare motor.   YAMAHA

Part of the Tracker Marine boatbuilding empire, Nitro concentrates on building fiberglass bass, multipurpose, and bay boats from 17 to 22 feet, and prices them for the average family budget. The 20-foot Nitro 288 Sport shown here is a versatile little runabout, well fitted out for skiing, fishing, or just running around the lake. A 150 hp outboard is standard, and a pair of aerated livewells, a trolling motor bracket, and lockable rod storage help make this a decent fisherman.   NITRO

Smokercraft builds aluminum utility boats, jonboats, fishing boats, canoes, fiberglass runabouts, wakeboard and deck boats, and pontoon boats. The 151 Stinger shown here is an aluminum multipurpose boat with a starboard console, livewell, and seats you can swap around to different bases. The aluminum hull comes with a ten-year warranty; the pressure-treated plywood floor, which has a lifetime warranty, evidently lasts longer than the hull. Like Henry Ford's Model T, this boat is available in any color you want as long as it's black.   YAMAHA

Yarcraft builds fiberglass fishing and family boats from 16 to 19 feet. The builder's Web site emphasizes the relative weight of aluminum versus fiberglass boats, but there are many ways to build a boat from either material. Either material can produce a good-performing, low-maintenance, long-lasting boat. The 1785 Wrangler is a side-console fishing boat that's also good for the family to take a spin in around the lake. With up to 150 hp available, the boat can also pull a skier without hesitation.   YARCRAFT

For the price of a used Buick, you can have a brand-new fishing boat; namely, a Tracker Super Guide V16 complete with a livewell, a 25 hp motor, and a trailer. Despite the name's implication, *you* still have to guide the boat to catch fish. Up to 60 hp is available if you want to take the kids skiing. Set up for serious freshwater fishing, this 14- to 20-foot deep-V series consists of both fiberglass and aluminum boats.   TRACKER

Personal Watercraft and Sport Boats

PWCs, known widely by the brand name Jetski, are heaven to some and hell to others. They're fun to drive, they don't burn a lot of gas, they draw very little water, and their waterjet drives make them safe to swim around. Some are even powerful enough to pull skiers; however, a spotter is required by law to watch the skier, which can be complicated when you are simultaneously facing backward and hanging on.

PWCs have gotten a bad name for several reasons. They're loud (though the new ones, especially the four-strokes, are quieter) and they pollute (the two-cycle engine dumps a trace of fuel into the exhaust). They're also more likely to be owned and operated by novice drivers than larger boats (judging from the way some of them are operated), and when these operators are also discourteous, every-

one hears about it. Maybe all that power and pizzazz just bring out the aggression in otherwise considerate people, but they are definitely fun to buzz around in. More locales are banning PWCs, so check local regulations before you buy.

Sport boats are a little like overgrown PWCs, which is no surprise considering that many sport-boat manufacturers also build PWCs. These often have waterjets for propulsion, giving them the same safety and shallow-water advantages as their smaller cousins. Don't expect a 300 hp waterjet to pull a skier out of the water like a 300 hp inboard ski boat of the same size and weight, though. There's no substitute for a submerged propeller when it comes to low-end acceleration and pulling power.

Here's a nifty sport boat offered by the Canadian giant Bombardier, the Sea Doo Challenger 2000. Looking as if it were sculpted from a solid block of ivory, this curvaceous 20-footer is a real boat with an eight-passenger capacity, and it draws just 12 inches of water. A 200 to 240 hp with waterjet propulsion makes for a safe swimming environment. Bombardier's huge engineering and financial resources produce reliable watercraft that continue to meet market demand. The company also says it's trying to rectify the noise and pollution issues associated with these two-cycle watercraft.

BOMBARDIER

Kawasaki calls this three-seater a family watercraft, and it apparently has more than enough power (130 hp) to pull a skier with two passengers on board. That these PWCs are so performance-oriented is obvious when you consider that the engine/waterjet propulsion system is, according to the builder, capable of developing 851 pounds of thrust, which is about 160 pounds more than the bare boat weighs! That's an incredible thrust-to-weight ratio for any craft, matched only perhaps by a very few advanced jet-fighter aircraft. This is an obvious indicator (and warning) of why thorough training and good judgment are essential to safely operating one of these floating rocketships.

KAWASAKI

Here's the largest of Sea Doo's eleven-model PWC lineup, the LRV four-seater. This 13-footer (or 155-incher, in PWC-speak) has a 130 hp rotary engine driving a single waterjet. A 25-gallon gasoline tank provides a full day's worth of buzzing around the lake, and the tow eye implies that this little craft can pull a skier, at least with a light load on board. BOMBARDIER

Yamaha makes a full lineup of two- to four-person Waverunner PWCs, as well as two sport-boat models, including the 20-foot LS2000 shown here. The manufacturer, well regarded for its consistently high-quality product, claims that two skiers can be pulled together, with a pair of 135 hp gas inboards driving waterjets. Both passengers get a type of bolster to help keep them in their seat, and the forward seating is low in the hull, which—though bow railings would be a nice addition—helps from a safety perspective. Waterjets are far safer than propellers for any boat, especially one like this that will have a swarm of swimmers, and the layout makes good sense for this market. YAMAHA

Boston Whaler makes an extensive line of small craft ranging from 34 feet to this four-seater, 11-foot, 6-inch Impact model. This boat is intended for use as a yacht tender, with a small, foam-filled collar that is inflated by an internal core bladder to present a smoother appearance, attached to the gunwale. A PWC-type helm pod is built in, and Whaler says the boat, which weighs 650 pounds, has a 1,200-pound swamped capacity. Whaler's Unibond construction method, which injects foam between the hull and liner under pressure to bond the two components together, is used to build the Impact. A 25 hp outboard made by Whaler's sister company, Mercury, is—judging from one of Whaler's marketing photos—surprisingly big enough to pull a small wakeboarder with two people in the boat. BOSTON WHALER

Here's another Kawasaki three-seater offering, the 900 STX, which the builder claims is an improvement on the ride quality and handling of previous models, not to mention the new, hard-to-ignore graphics. The boat, which is 10 feet long and weighs 628 pounds dry, has room for ski or wakeboard storage, and there is an open deck area aft for changing skis. KAWASAKI

Polaris's 9-foot, 505-pound, two-passenger (370 lb. capacity) SLH is powered by a 95 hp motor that winds up to 7,200 rpm. The boat has a trim-control feature to compensate for varying longitudinal weight distribution and wave conditions.   POLARIS

Here's the four-person (or 600 lb., whichever comes first) Polaris Genesis, an 11-foot, 705-pound (dry weight) PWC with a 17-gallon fuel tank supplying a 135 hp motor. The queen of Polaris's PWC fleet, this craft sports a boarding platform aft and can pull a pair of skiers, according to the builder.   POLARIS

The 12-foot, 6-inch (the manufacturer lists the boat length in inches) SUV1200 is Yamaha's biggest PWC model, and it's powered by a 135 hp gasoline engine driving a waterjet. It can even pull a skier, according to Yamaha, but don't forget that a spotter must keep their eyes on the skier at all times.   YAMAHA

Kawasaki claims that this is the fastest PWC in production, with a 145 hp motor cranking out more than 900 pounds of thrust, which (if accurate) is an insane horsepower-to-thrust ratio for a waterjet. The fuel capacity, at just 15 gallons, is certainly on the light side, but the builder must assume you can cover a lot of ground in a short time on this little 65 or so mph two-seater craft.   KAWASAKI

Pontoon Boats

F ew vessels are more versatile than the pontoon boat. They're very stable and easily driven through the water, due to their twin (or sometimes triple) narrow aluminum hulls. A lot of clear topside space is provided, a result of the deck being attached atop the hulls. Great for partying afloat, pontoon boats are also easily beached for picnics and swimming ashore, and their aluminum pontoon hulls are very durable, which is a great feature since many are dragged up on pebble-strewn beaches hundreds of times in their lifetime.

With enough power, and especially with a third, centerline pontoon for extra buoyancy and dynamic lift, pontoon boats can also partially plane and be used to pull skiers and water toys. A wide variety of seating options may be available, and it may be surprising just how many people a pontoon boat will comfortably and safely accommodate. Either an outboard or stern-drive power option is usually available, depending on the model. Biminis or hardtops provide protection from sun and rain, head compartments may be included, and a wet bar and refrigerator may also be part of the package for long comfortable days on the water.

Bennington produces about forty different pontoon boat models, so they likely have a boat that suits you if a pontoon is what you want. Bennington's literature addresses the round versus U-shaped pontoon debate, asserting that its round pontoons are better, lighter, stronger, and more buoyant. Bennington also eschews injecting foam into the pontoons, claiming that its pontoon bulkheads provide the necessary compartmentalization without the added weight. Benningtons have 0.09-inch-thick, 23- or 25-inch-diameter pontoons with pressure-treated-plywood decks. They're backed up by a lifetime structural warranty. The LX series is Bennington's most popular and the lowest priced line, and it includes the flagship 2580 LX shown here. This big party barge can hold up to seventeen people and a 125 hp outboard.   BENNINGTON

Tracker's Fisher line of nine pontoon boats includes this 180 Fish, the smallest in the series and—like many low-frills pontoon boats—bargain-priced to make it easily affordable. This one includes a 25 hp outboard, livewell, rod holders, and a pair of swivel seats forward from which to fish.   TRACKER

Bennington's foldout head compartment makes this boat that much more attractive to the entire family.   BENNINGTON

Godfrey is one of the biggest players in the pontoon-boat market. It builds four lines and more than seventy different models of pontoon boats, with variations in layout, quality, cost, and fit and finish. The Parti Kraft Commander 220 SC shown here is rated for twelve passengers and 110 hp. Included are a convertible changing room and bow sleeper seats for the occasional overnight. The aluminum hull is guaranteed for twenty years and the pressure-treated wood deck for a lifetime.   GODFREY

Here's a Manitou pontoon boat before the deck is installed—quite simple, really, at least in concept, and probably the closest thing there is to a Winnebago on the water. Those aluminum cross members must be able to keep the two tubes lined up relative to each other, despite different weight and wave conditions on either side, while holding up the 8-foot-wide deck with a load of people and gear. The spray rails forward add dynamic lift to supplement buoyancy when the bow starts to stuff at higher speeds.   MANITOU

Crestliner builds a wide range of aluminum fishing, cruising, and multipurpose boats, as well as four lines of pontoon boats. The Crestliner CFI2285 is sleek-looking for a pontoon boat, and it's built to fish or cruise with equal facility. A temporary changing room, a pair of livewells, pedestal seats, and lockable rod storage are all included. The boat is rated for up to twelve passengers and 115 hp.

CRESTLINER

Here's a midsize pontoon boat from Harris Kayot designed for fishing. This Flote Bote 220 Fisherman comes with either 23- or 25-inch tubes and outboard power up to 120 hp, and it carries up to fourteen passengers. A long list of fishing amenities is standard or optional, and a pair of swivel chairs forward makes life quite comfortable indeed for the sedentary angler. The helm console is forward on centerline, unusual for a pontoon boat but standard for a fishing boat.

HARRIS KAYOT

Harris Kayot makes several dozen deck- and pontoon-boat models, with either outboard or stern-drive power and two or three tubes. The Harris Kayot Flote Bote Classic 24 shown here is available with a centerline pontoon and outboard or stern-drive power to 210 hp (making it a second-string ski boat), and it holds up to seventeen passengers. If you think this is big, try the 28.

HARRIS KAYOT

Sun Tracker, part of giant Tracker Marine, makes pontoon boats ranging from a basic 18-footer up to a whopping 32-foot floating camper. The midsized Party Barge 25 is designed for fishing as well as cruising with a livewell, rod holders and lockable storage, sink, gas grill, and pop-up changing room with a portable toilet. Outboards from 9.9 to 135 hp are available, and considerable buoyancy is provided by the 26-inch-diameter tubes for a fourteen-person capacity.

SUN TRACKER

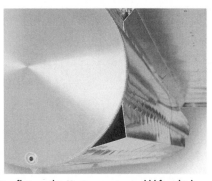

The chine flats on this Manitou pontoon add lift at higher speeds, and the keel stock at the bottom center aids in tracking. MANITOU

The Manitou Spirit 22 shown here has a conventional layout with perimeter seating and a small bow area that's kept open to minimize weight forward—as well as the chances of stuffing the pontoons in a big wave—and to provide an open diving and swimming area. The Spirit 22 has 23-inch-diameter tubes, giving the boat an eleven-passenger capacity and a 90 hp rating. Manitou makes six different lines of pontoon boats, with two or three tubes and either outboard or stern-drive power. MANITOU

Ski Boats

The ski boat is highly specialized, since the hull design, propulsion system, and layout are all geared to pulling skiers efficiently and safely. Inboard power with an in-line transmission allows the engine to be mounted farther forward in the hull, which, along with a fairly flat bottom, produces the low, flat wake favored by tournament skiers. A V-drive allows the engine to be mounted farther aft, opening up cockpit space, but LCG also shifts aft, with the natural propensity of any such hull to have a higher wake. A tow post or tower is used to pull the skier; the tower's higher position allows the skier or boarder to catch a little more air on the jumps. Whether a post or tower is used, they're positioned well forward of the transom so the boat can still steer easily with a strain on the line. The driver is supposed to keep their eyes on the road, so a rearview mirror and an aft-facing seat next to the driver are usually provided. Optimal skiing speed is 28 to 36 mph, and big power is needed to pull a pair of slalom skiers out of deep water quickly.

The Centurion Elite 22 shown is an in-line bowrider ski boat with an optional water-ballast system for use when wakeboarding. According to the builder, this boat is a compromise between a serious flat-bottom ski boat and a deep-V wakeboarder, with a little more deadrise than a regulation ski boat for a smoother rise and more beam (which takes some of that smoothness out of the ride) for a flatter wake. Engines from 270 to 340 hp are available, all-fiberglass construction promises durability, and a storage locker in the stern is included. The same basic boat is available with a V-drive designed specifically for wakeboarding. CENTURION

Although it's very difficult, if not impossible, to design a V-drive that leaves as low a wake as an in-line, many builders—including Mastercraft—are giving it a try. There's a market for layouts that dispense with the midships engine box in favor of a more open cockpit, regardless of any wake penalty. This is Mastercraft's Prostar 205V, a boat that neatly meets that market demand with seating for up to twelve. Hatches outboard of the engine compartment open to storage compartments below, and there's also a 320 hp Cadillac engine, a polyethylene fuel tank, and an air pump for inflatable water toys.

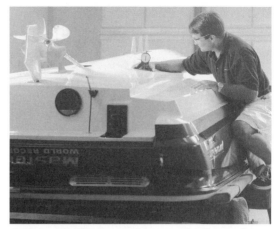

The business end of a Mastercraft is seen in this photograph. Note the low-profile prop-shaft strut and rudder that reduce appendage drag. The skegs amidships and the double-chine design help increase lateral stability. The latter feature is handy when a slalom skier is cutting the wake and trying to get ahead of the boat, helping the driver to stay on course. Note how flat the bottom is on a competition ski boat, behind which very flat wakes are highly valued since skiers tend to trip over normal-sized wakes. MASTERCRAFT

Toyota had a brief foray into the ski-boat market. Its lineup included the Epic 21—a big boat with clean styling and solid construction. This is a fairly uncommon closed-bow model—basically, you get a little storage forward instead of a bow seat—with an in-line engine drivetrain. The 300 hp Lexus automobile engine develops a lot of thrust (and relatively little noise) for an engine that weighs less than 700 pounds. All-fiberglass construction is the wave of the future—so that's how Toyota built its boats. TOYOTA

This Duvall 190 Inline Ski boat by Mastercraft is what a no-nonsense, hard-core, no-compromises tournament ski boat looks like. An in-line engine shifts LCG forward, reducing weight in the stern for a flatter wake. A flat hull aft also contributes to the ankle-high wake this boat leaves behind at high speeds. Between 330 and 425 hp is available to snap a slalom skier out of the water in a flash. Even cruise control is available as an option. Features include a digital speedometer, hinged storage compartment aft, and an in-tank fuel pump that helps keep fuel weight centered farther forward. With the Sammy Duvall upgrade package, you get a lambskin interior and fancy hull graphics, among other things. But it's the hull shape, powertrain, and weight distribution that get the job done on any ski boat. MASTERCRAFT

Here's an offering from Malibu, the Sunsetter 21 in-line, open-bow, family ski boat. The dual-console layout maximizes the boat's full beam, and aft-facing seating for the observer and transom seating for guests are provided. Flat-bottom ski boats like this one deliver a bumpy ride in a chop, so this one comes with a driver's "air lumbar support system," which is supposed to cushion the blow when you launch momentarily off some wakeboarder's wake. The all-fiberglass construction produces a durable, long-lasting product.

MALIBU

Malibu ski and wakeboarding boats are among the most popular brands. The Malibu Sunscape 23 LSV shown here has a V-drive configuration, which opens up the cockpit near the driver and shifts engine weight and noise aft. Lockable storage compartments flank the engine. This is a big ski boat at nearly 23 feet long and just over 8 feet wide, with a 55-gallon fuel tank—generous for this class of boat.

MALIBU

Wakeboarding Boats

A takeoff on the ski boat, the wakeboarding boat uses a stern-mounted V-drive engine to generate the high wake favored by wakeboard enthusiasts. Water ballast tanks add still more weight aft and help develop a higher wake. With ballast on board, the helm seat allows for standup operation so the driver can see over the bow. The desired wake is high but smooth at the rooster tail, which takes a fairly flat bottom and a heavy stern to produce. Rather than using ballast, Malibu uses adjustable foils that pull the stern down at speed and fold up out of the way when not in use. Both ski and wakeboard boats, being inboard-powered, lose the outboard or stern drive's ability to trim out efficiently at high speed, so top speed is slower with an inboard of comparable weight and power. But an inboard has stronger acceleration than a stern drive.

Centurion builds in-line and V-drive ski and wakeboard boats as a division of California-based Fineline Industries. The Eclipse V Tower (the V could designate either V-drive or V-bottom, and there is a tower) is somewhat short on seating with the engine taking up the aft third of the boat. But with its 40-gallon (about 335 lb.) ballast tank filled, it produces a respectable wake. In fact, wakeboarding boats are probably the only type that work hard to become *less* efficient, adding weight and trim to drag more water behind the boat. With the ballast tank dry and a light passenger and fuel load, this boat can also provide a reasonably low (though not competition-class) wake for a skier. All-fiberglass construction and a removable cockpit carpet liner are additional features on this well-built boat.

CENTURION

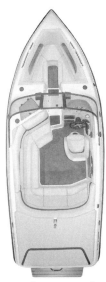

Here's a bird's-eye view of a Centurion Elite V wakeboarder. The seating is quite generous and the aft sunpad is ready to go once you drop the hook between runs. With a full load of passengers, gear, ballast, and fuel on board, it's a wonder these 20-footers can even get up on plane, let alone do so in just a few seconds.

CENTURION

Toyota, short-lived in the marine industry, produced an all-purpose runabout called the Toyota Epic 22; along with other technical features and details, it has an all-fiberglass hull-deck-liner system. The 300 hp, 628-pound Lexus engine is used in all Epic boats. A hard-core wakeboarding version of this boat is available as the Epic X22, which comes complete with a tower and 70-gallon (588 lb.) ballast tank aft. A fairly flat hull form, with 9 degrees of deadrise at the transom, delivers a flat wake at speed and—compared to a deep-V—a fairly bumpy ride in a chop.

TOYOTA

Mastercraft builds three lines of high-end wakeboard and ski boats with both in-line and V-drive propulsion configurations. The hull and deck are all-fiberglass, and voids are foam-injected for positive buoyancy and reduced wave noise. Fuel tanks are rot-proof polyethylene, and seat bases are plastic versus wood for longer life. Mastercraft's in-tank fuel pump, which pushes fuel to the engine under pressure rather than drawing it under suction from the engine, places added requirements on fuel-system integrity. The 20-foot, in-line drive X9 Wakeboarder shown here seats up to ten, according to the builder, and holds a pair of ballast tanks as needed for a big wake. Up to 425 hp and a 35-gallon fuel tank are included.

MASTERCRAFT

This 21-foot V-drive wakeboarder, the Malibu Wakesetter VLX, comes with a 60-gallon ballast tank; if more ballast is needed, the boat seats up to ten, says the builder. The tower helps the boarders get a little more air (with its higher tow power) and stows the extra boards out of the way. What if all ten passengers had their own board? An optional Corvette-based engine develops 375 hp, more than enough pizzazz to pop a heavy wakeboarder up on plane. Malibu builds a wide range of high-quality in-line and V-drive wakeboard and ski boats.

MALIBU

Walleye Boats

The walleye-boat market has seen a lot of growth as more people decide to venture farther offshore in pursuit of bigger fish. A deep-V bottom provides a good ride in the chops that these boats often encounter on large lakes, including the Great Lakes. The transom is designed to take a 9.9 to 25 hp kicker, since these boats often troll at 1.5 to 5 mph for hours on end. With more freeboard than a bass boat, the walleye boat has an added measure of seaworthiness that's welcome when you are miles from shore.

The boats are rigged for trolling aft and casting forward. Up to four aerated bait wells for different kinds of live bait, and two livewells to keep the catch fresh and healthy until weigh-in and subsequent release, may be included. Walleye boats are commonly available in lengths from 16 to 23 feet with a 50 to 225 hp outboard for power. Layouts include dual and center consoles, though some of the smaller models may have tiller steering.

Lund makes a significant percentage of the aluminum freshwater fishing boats produced in the United States each year. The 1775 Pro-V shown is its most popular walleye model, and the smallest in the builder's four-boat series. Note the generous freeboard and that the hull has more deadrise than other Lund lines to improve the ride in a chop. An SE version of this boat includes a console with windshield and an aft casting platform.   LUND

Here's the biggest boat in Lund's walleye Tournament series, the well-equipped 2025 Pro-V Magnum. This "bad boy" carries 57 gallons of gas and is rated for 225 hp, with which it ought to veritably fly. There's also a 2025 Pro-V Mr. Walleye with a tiller-steered motor (up to 125 hp); a Pro-V SE with an aft casting platform and side console; and a Pro-V IFS with a bimini and side windows, bow rails, and a walkthrough windshield. There's also a spacious rod storage locker in the 20-foot Mr. Walleye.

Lund expends a fair amount of marketing ink defending its use of rivets rather than welding its boats together. The fact is that in some applications, rivets are stronger than welds, and they join the very thin aluminum used in these small boats without distorting the material. Both bonding methods work well, when done right.

LUND

Flats Boats

The introduction of purpose-built flats boats since the late 1980s has spawned a cottage industry of specialty boatbuilders and fishing guides. Some of the best fishing is found in very shallow water, and even a modest investment in a boat can result in excellent catch rates (including some of the biggest fish around). Shallow hull draft of 7 to 14 inches and good form stability at rest are prerequisites. A few geographic areas require flat-bottom hulls with jack plates that have a very shallow draft of less than 6 inches, but this represents a minority of the market. Most flats boat owners have to run a good distance to reach their fishing grounds, so moderate deadrise is needed to deliver a smooth, comfortable ride in a chop. Too much deadrise, though, and the chines won't submerge with a normal load on board, reducing stability, so a precise balance of hull form and weight distribution is required to produce a good flats boat. Very lightweight construction also helps, and some high-end builders use a weight-saving combination of Kevlar, carbon fiber, foam cores, and vinylester resin.

A flats boat is poled from an aft raised platform in shallow water with a standard 21-foot pole, which can also be stuck in the bottom and tied to the poling platform to anchor the boat temporarily. Many fly-fishing anglers just let the boat drift rather than try to anchor it to avoid constantly changing trajectories to the fish. An electric trolling motor can be fitted on the bow, but fish won't bite—except perhaps along a shoreline—if any motor is used; hence, the versatile manual pole. The procedure is to power into the edge of shallow water and then pole in the rest of the way. The "sight" fishing that results—that is, being able to see in advance what you're going to catch—is a truly exciting sport.

Jack plates, which allow the motor to be raised and lowered vertically without tilting, can be used on flats boats. But the builder has to be very careful with the shift in LCG that results from moving an outboard that weighs up to 475 pounds half a foot or so farther aft.

Look for a flats boat to be well equipped with an insulated fish box, livewell, tackle storage locker and drawers, lockable rod stowage, depth- and fishfinders, rod holders, and a center console, depending on the model.

Action Craft makes four high-end flats boats from 16 to 20 feet, including the 1720 Bay Runner shown. The gunwales are wide to make it easy to walk forward and aft, and the minimalist console opens up a little extra deck space. A livewell, pole clips, poling platform, and a flip-down helm-seat backrest (a nice feature on long rides around the bay) are included. A premium vinylester resin is used to wet out the outer mat skin coat only, and helps protect against osmotic blistering in case your boat will be left in the water. A slight prop pocket improves shallow-water performance. ACTION CRAFT

Saltwater boatbuilder Dusky is in the flats-boat business too, with a lineup that includes a pair of 16-footers and this new, low-profile 18-footer. Sold factory-direct with a down-to-earth price and good-quality construction, the 18-footer includes a livewell; dry-storage lockers; rod racks and rod holders; a fiberglassed hull-to-deck joint; a self-bailing cockpit; and snag-resistant, pop-up cleats. The hull is no lightweight at 1,200 pounds, but you could probably buy a pair of these rugged boats for the price of a higher-end brand that weighs 600 pounds less. DUSKY MARINE

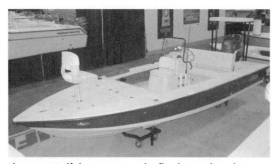

The Hewes Redfisher 18 is a popular flats boat with its clean, un-cluttered layout and sleek, low profile typical of the genre. Compared to Hewes's Bonefisher series, according to the builder, the 16-, 18-, and 21-foot "backcountry" Redfishers are designed to run farther to find fish, with added dry-storage space, livewells, and other fishing enhancements. Nevertheless, a poling platform is included above the motor. A livewell, self-bailing cockpit, rod storage, and trim tabs are included. High-density foam is used as a coring material, eliminating wood from the hull and deck structure.

Hewes's Pathfinder bay-boat and tunnel-skiff series includes this 22-footer, as well as four other models ranging from 17 to 24 feet. The 2200V includes rod racks and lockable rod storage, a self-bailing cockpit, a standup console, livewells, and dry-storage compartments. The 2200T adds a tunnel hull and jack plate for better shallow-water operation. Yamaha power up to 225 hp is available. The composite construction includes vinylester resin throughout the laminate for superior osmotic blistering protection and greater strength and impact resistance.   HEWES

Century Boats, a longtime builder of saltwater boats, offers a line of three bay boats from 19 to 22 feet. The 21-footer shown here has a low profile, a shallow deadrise (but a few degrees more than a typical flats boat for a smoother ride in a light chop), and bow and stern casting platforms. A livewell, rod racks and rod holders, a console with full-height windshield, tackle drawers, and an integral insulated cooler are standard. An all-fiberglass hull grid is injected with foam for added quiet and reserve buoyancy. Century doesn't waste time with plastic through-hulls and seacocks, which is good; bronze fittings are standard on this boat. This boat will fly with the available 225 hp Yamaha.   CENTURY

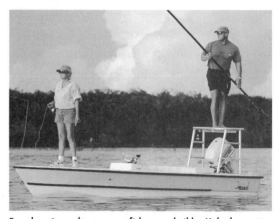

Even longtime saltwater sportfisherman-builder Mako has gotten into the lucrative flats-boat business with this pretty 15-footer, all dressed up and ready to go. A livewell, dry storage, anchor locker, and rod storage under the gunwale are included. A low-sheer, wide-open deck arrangement with forward and aft casting platforms, a poling platform, and a low, snag-resistant console are typical flats-boat features. Four models, including this 15-footer, to 21 feet are available for skinny-water fishing enthusiasts. The 12-degree transom deadrise bottom makes for a fine calm-water boat, and up to 60 hp is available.   MAKO

Hewes's high-end Maverick series from 17 to 21 feet features a high-tech, vacuum-bagged "sandwich" of structural foam, Kevlar, and carbon laminated with premium vinylester resin to produce boats that are very strong and very light for their size. Lighter weight translates into shallower draft, an appealing attribute for most flats anglers. These boats come well equipped with livewells, rod storage, trim tabs, pole holders, and tower and dry-storage lockers. Both conventional and tunnel-hull configurations (with varying fuel capacities and power ratings) are available. Note how high the motor is mounted on this tunnel boat.   YAMAHA

Pro-Line is in on the flats-boat business as well—a natural spin-off, it seems, from the builder's extensive lineup of offshore saltwater fishing boats of all descriptions. The Pro-Line 18 Flats is solidly built: it uses all-fiberglass construction, has a high-density foam-cored transom, and low-density foam is blown into hull voids for positive buoyancy. The boat has a low sheer, even by flats-boat standards, and all the features you'd expect for shallow-water fishing. Forward and aft casting platforms, rod storage, a console that is high enough to hang onto at speed, and a poling platform are included.   PRO-LINE

Catamarans

Catamarans are king for some people. It's hard to beat a well-designed cat's ride, with two narrow hulls slicing and dicing the waves with little fuss and bother. As long as the tunnel in between the hull sponsons doesn't bottom out from overloading, the cat's ride is something to write home about. It's a tough thing to make a cat look good, though some manufacturers have been doing a good job of addressing the aesthetics of a cat hull.

Cats can have displacement, semidisplacement, or full planing hulls. The shape of the bottom, the weight distribution, and the height of the tunnel, rather than the hull design, determine how well the boat works. Everything from deck boats to sportfishermen and cruising yachts have been built on cat hulls, all of which are most naturally suited to twin-engine propulsion, with an engine in or hanging from the back of each hull.

1998 Glacier Bay 2680

Among the offshore fishing crowd, power catamarans are catching on for a few very good reasons. Their small water-plane, narrow hulls push easily

through the water, climb on plane without fuss, ride smoothly in a chop, and offer terrific form stability. In the case of our Glacier Bay 2680, it was evi-

The Glacier Bay lineup is one of the most popular power-cat brands on the market. Seven twin-outboard-powered, center-console, open and hardtop cuddies, and deck-boat models built on 22- and 26-foot hulls are available. Well-built and smooth-riding at moderate (24 to 26 kt.) speeds, these boats have been well proven in off-shore service by their solid East Coast following. The 260 CC shown here has plenty of cockpit coaming height for safety, and the console holds a head compartment.

dent that the designer was also an experienced boater—one who appreciates and understands the need for deck safety, who has spent many hours fishing, and who runs well offshore when duty calls. Enough thought and expertise have gone into its conception and execution that many anglers who run long distances in sloppy weather will find much to praise. There are a few cat quirks, which I'll discuss, that make these boats too big a leap for some, but there's a lot to commend the genre—and this boat in particular.

Cockpit

Starting our tour aft, it is apparent that the Glacier Bay's cockpit gets the lion's share of the boat's square footage, and it is an intelligent layout. The padded coaming bolsters are a full 28 inches high, and the recessed liner provides an effective toe kick for excellent balance when you are leaning overboard to grab a leader. A pair of large, in-deck fish boxes (which unscrew for fuel-tank access) is guttered to drain to the sump pumps, and the hatches have gaskets to eliminate rattling at speed.

Plastic access doors aft to port and starboard

lead to the fuel filter, battery, and engine VRO (variable-ratio oil) tank kept safe and dry under the transom coaming. What makes this such a great fishing boat? Check out the sink and freshwater nozzle to port; four-drawer tackle box to starboard; rod, swab, and gaff racks under the side rails; cleats mounted vertically below flush hawseholes; and four rod holders waiting at the ready for that first strike. More attention to detail shows in the deck's side gutter, which improves drainage, although there was a tendency for water to pool forward near the helm. Cockpit courtesy lights brighten the nighttime hours, and a freshwater washdown hose coils neatly to starboard under the cockpit steps. One feature that needs to be addressed is the centerline transom opening, only 16 inches high off the cockpit deck—I would add a gate across the transom coaming.

The integral combination motor mount and swim platform is well constructed, my only reservation being the nonstructural plastic access hatches in either motor well and higher up on centerline; many builders are using these to keep water out of the bilge in rough water. Fiberglass or metal hatches are really called for when watertight integrity is at issue.

Foredeck

Foredeck access is excellent due to fixed cockpit steps leading to wide, flat, nonskid side decks. The standard stainless steel bow railing, blind-bolted for a neat look, is a full 26 inches high—higher and stiffer than on many boats 10 feet longer. The trunk cabin is a fine seat, and a molded indent accepts the cushion that snaps securely in place forward. Deck area forward is uncluttered and sizable, offering the perfect spot from which a pair of enthusiastic anglers may cast unimpeded. The terrific side decks make it a cinch to walk aft with a fish ready to gaff.

The optional windlass on our boat held the plough anchor firmly in its well-designed anchor pulpit. The only feature missing was room for a fathom or two of chain for extra holding power and chafing resistance on the bottom. Side lights are forward; I would relocate them to the hardtop, both to increase their detection range from another vessel and to remove their nighttime backscatter from the operator's line of sight.

Pilothouse and Helm

The hardtop model, enclosed on three sides by windows, affords excellent protection from the elements, making this boat well suited to extended-season fishing in the New England waters where we tested it. Under the hardtop, our test boat had a 4-foot bench seat to port with a molded-in space for an Igloo 54-quart cooler below. There's a good deal of interior space below that's difficult to reach, which could otherwise be used for dry storage. At 33 inches high, the seat affords a great view through the large windows, and a molded footrest is comfortably positioned along the lower perimeter.

Opposite to starboard, the helm was laid out sensibly with the engine gauges down low below the wheel, though I would like to see the top row angled up for easier seated viewing. The electronics are mounted nearly vertically higher up, where they are within handy reach and in the operator's line of sight. The compass sits atop the bright white dashboard (a darker, flat color would cut down on potential nighttime glare), where it is easy to see at a glance.

The tilt wheel and throttles are comfortably positioned for seated or standing operation, both set at an optimum 15 degrees from horizontal. The fixed two-piece windshield is sufficiently high and is perfectly matched by the seat's ample height for excellent visibility ahead. The side windows slide open to catch a sea breeze, and all the window mullions are narrow enough so as not to interfere unnecessarily with visibility. I found the footrest to be 4 to 6 inches too low, even with my long legs. The macerator and saltwater pump are neatly installed inside an access door to starboard of the helm seat, next to a convenient storage bin.

The helm pedestal seat sits atop a nicely tooled unit that holds a recirculating livewell with a nifty window facing aft. The top also serves as an extra seat for the mate when things slow down in the fishing grounds.

Cabin

With such an accommodatingly wide (22 in.) companionway door, it is easy to be drawn to the boat's roomy cabin. The challenge with a cat's cabin is to work around the limitations of the two narrow hulls, the problem being the limited and awkward possibilities for standing room. For a day boat, though, there's ample room to lie down and take a nap on the large 7-foot-long-by-5-foot-wide berth that takes up most of the interior. A toilet is to port, and storage bins below on centerline and to starboard take advantage of much of the interior room.

The bottom half of the cabin has a full fiberglass liner; the upper half is covered in roughly applied carpeting (the builder claims that a higher-quality carpet is currently being used), which really ought to be upgraded for a boat of otherwise fine quality. But it's still functional enough with rod racks, shelves for knickknacks, and opening hatches and side windows (which leak a few drops of standing water when you open them). A canvas covers up the interior of the helm console, a budget-minded approach to getting the job done. Wiring inside is run neatly enough, and accessibility for follow-on electronics replacement couldn't be better.

Construction

Glacier Bay starts with a premium gelcoat and vinylester skin coat to prevent osmotic blistering, followed by a solid layup (including Kevlar in the stem for added impact resistance) in the hull bottom and sides. A cat's hull is subjected to high stresses, especially in the tunnel area; seven structural bulkheads resist twisting and add stiffness. Coremat is used in the sides to prevent cosmetic print-through. The hull-to-deck joint is ruggedly fastened with bolts and polyurethane adhesive, and fiberglassed (in places) from the inside. The decks are polyvinyl chloride (PVC) foam-cored for stiffness and low weight; the transom is cored with pressure-treated plywood, which is carefully sealed against moisture penetration. If you plug the PVC-lined limber holes and other penetrations in those bulkheads, the boat will be essentially unsinkable. In fact, it already is unsinkable, according to Glacier Bay, with built-in foam flotation.

Performance Test

We had just a slight chop for our sea trial off Brant Point, Nantucket, but the ferries passing by regularly gave us a good indication of the Glacier Bay's seakeeping abilities. In what was probably a 12-inch chop, the boat rode smoothly at any speed, slicing through the waves with little fuss or motion. When the waves picked up to 18 to 24 inches, though, a clear predilection for speed became apparent. With our moderate load of four passengers and a half-load of fuel, I noticed pounding and slapping in the tunnel area in those 1- to 2-footers between 6 and 17 knots (1,500–3,000 rpm). But when we sped up to 4,000 rpm for 27 knots (and rose vertically as we simultaneously came up on plane), we entered a new world with a smooth, slap- and bump-free ride. This is not at all atypical of most other cats in this size range, so I'm not singling out Glacier Bay. Remember that the higher the tunnel, the smoother the ride; however, the boat's center of gravity also rises, decreasing stability, as does the height of the cockpit deck.

Crossing the 3- to 4-foot ferry wakes, we learned quickly that slowing down is the wrong thing to do. This boat is built for the mid- to high-20s knot range. Cats have a lower pound-per-inch immersion figure than comparable monohulls, so they're more sensitive to weight additions. That means the tunnel will come into contact with the waves more often and with greater energy when weight is added to the boat.

In a quartering sea, the boat definitely likes a bow-up attitude for good directional stability. In a head sea, 4 to 5 degrees of trim in the midrange seems to work well, both for a smoother ride and to keep "sneezing" to a minimum. Sneezing in a cat occurs when spray is caught in the forward end of the tunnel; slightly compressed air trapped inside

blows the spray forward as the boat pitches, up and over the bow.

The cat heels slightly outboard, so hang on when turning at speed—there's no equilibrium-inducing banking as with a planing monohull. Running on one engine in get-home mode, the cat ran very well indeed and much better (with less drag) than a twin-engine monohull would have run. We managed 21 knots at 4,200 rpm, a speed you wouldn't be able to maintain for long without damaging the overloaded engine. When you back off to a more reasonable 3,200 rpm, you'll manage a respectable 12 knots all the way home. Just watch for signs of overloading—getting the optional temperature gauges is a good start, since the only indication you'll have with just "idiot lights" is that you're already overheated. The gauges let you do the necessary speed-regulating in advance as the temperature starts to climb.

Backing down at 1,500 rpm into the chop, we shipped a small amount of water through the steering arm or control-cable tubes leading into the bilge. I would want to see more effective rubber boots to keep the salt water out. With four passengers and a half load of fuel, our performance test results with twin 150 hp Evinrude Ficht motors swinging four-blade stainless steel props were as listed in the accompanying table.

Speed might improve with three-blade props, but these 14½-by-17-inch four-blade props accelerate more quickly, run smoother, and back with more bite. The Evinrudes ran very quietly and smoothly.

Once you learn how to adjust balance and trim in different sea conditions, and if you run at speed, this catamaran will run smoother than most monohulls of the same displacement. On the other hand, you have to be willing to tolerate the tunnel slapping and pounding at intermediate speeds in a short chop.

Built for serious offshore anglers, the Glacier Bay offers a well-designed, solidly constructed boat with a high level of fit and finish; a sensible, safe

Glacier Bay 2680 Performance Results

RPM	Speed, knots	Speed, mph	Fuel Use, gph	Nautical mpg	Statute mpg	Range, nm	Range, statute miles	Noise Level, dBA	Trim, degrees
1,000	4.2	4.8	1.6	2.6	3.0	425	489	66	0
1,500	6.0	6.9	2.4	2.5	2.9	405	466	70	1
2,000	7.5	8.6	4.0	1.9	2.2	304	349	74	2
2,500	11.1	12.8	6.4	1.7	2.0	281	323	82	3
3,000	17.1	19.7	10.0	1.7	2.0	277	319	84	4
3,500	20.9	24.0	15.0	1.4	1.6	226	260	87	5
4,000	27.4	31.5	19.2	1.4	1.6	231	266	88	5
4,500	31.2	35.9	26.4	1.2	1.4	191	220	89	4
4,850	33.0	38.0	29.0	1.1	1.3	184	212	89	4

Test conditions: twin 150 hp Evinrude Ficht outboards, four passengers, half a tank of fuel, 25-foot-plus depth, 1-foot seas, air temperature 78 degrees, 300 pounds of gear. Test conducted on 25 June 1998 in Nantucket Sound off Nantucket Harbor, Massachusetts. Range calculated using 90 percent of the boat's 180-gallon fuel capacity. Sound levels taken at the helm.

cockpit design; adequate protection from cold and rain; and more than a few refinements compared to other models. Based on a short but instructive sea trial, I would tend to run any catamaran lighter rather than heavier, so choose your crew and cargo accordingly. Our boat was loaded up with the hardtop, windlass, cockpit bench seat, aft enclosure curtain, electric head, and freshwater system.

Mini-towers are catching on with smaller boats, especially those that have the stability to carry the extra weight topside. This Glacier Bay center console boasts a seat with a view, efficiently built into the boat's T-top. There's also lots of piping for everyone to hang onto in rough water.

Aimed squarely at the sportfishing market, the Benchmark 38 is a fine boat for anyone downgrading from a large convertible or moving up from an outboard and who wants a similar ride. A good seaboat, the Benchmark 38 also sleeps four comfortably. Power is usually twin inboard diesel, though surface drives are also available. Standard Cummins 450C diesels deliver a 33-knot top end.

BENCHMARK

A high-end power catamaran built in Toms River, New Jersey, with balsa-cored epoxy laminates, the Hydra 38 has a race boat lineage that makes it well suited to stay ahead of the competition in choppy conditions. A pair of 300 hp Yanmars with MerCruiser stern drives produces an easy 30-knot cruise, thanks to the boat's lightweight yet rugged construction. A wide range of custom layouts is available.

BILLY BLACK

World Class Catamarans builds six dual-console, center-console, deck-boat, and cuddy models on 22-, 24-, and 26-foot hulls. These boats, primarily used for (and well suited to) offshore sport-fishing, have earned a solid reputation for good performance offshore in a stiff chop. The hull form has been refined over several model generations to its present smooth-riding, crisp-handling incarnation.

GLACIER BAY

Splendor Boats, based in Silver Lake, Indiana, is owned by a bona fide industry pioneer named Doyle Heckaman. Doyle started building boats out of fiberglass in 1959, about the same time as another industry trailblazer, Leon Slikkers. After years of building tooling and components for big names like Rinker and Godfrey, Doyle started his own company building pleasure catamarans—after spending three years perfecting the design. His boats are well built, with the hull skin and stringer system all laminated within an 8-hour window, which minimizes or eliminates weak-link secondary bonds. All Splendors have positive flotation—even those above 20 feet—and they're among the smoothest-riding and most stable deck boats in their class. Many Splendor owners are older people who don't want to climb down into a boat; the deck level on this 240 (which makes 43 kt./50 mph with a 5.7-liter MerCruiser) is about even with a floating dock, making it very easy to board. The boats are sold factory-direct, and the builder will custom rig to suit.

SPLENDOR

This West Coast–inspired (and built, as it happens), John Kiley–designed Sea Sport Pacific 3200 has a unique bi-level pilothouse and a flybridge for when the sun comes out. Twin asymmetrical deep-V hulls deliver a smooth, dry ride. Power is typically twin-diesel stern drive, though V-drive inboards and waterjets are also available.

SEA SPORT

Rigid Inflatable Boats

Rigid inflatable boats (RIBs) have soared in popularity, mostly due to their seaworthiness and built-in fendering system. The air-filled (and sometimes foam-filled) collars give them positive buoyancy galore. Unless the collars are punctured in several different places, the boat will remain afloat in the worst sea conditions. This makes them especially popular for surf-rescue work.

Although most RIBs have fiberglass (the rigid part) bottoms, aluminum is also a popular choice, especially for commercial and military duty where boats tend to take a beating. RIBs with foam collars (foam with small air bladders) are puncture proof; however, they also have less buoyancy because they weigh more, and are not as popular among rescue workers for that reason.

The critical thing in any RIB is the quality of the collar and the bond holding it fast to the hull. The base cloth of polyester or nylon is impregnated with PVC, polyurethane, or Hypalon for durability and abrasion resistance. PVC is the best value, and earlier problems with longevity have been solved by the chemists. Hypalon is the longest lasting and has great abrasion resistance; its downside is its cost, and it has to be hand-glued, as opposed to PVC, which can be welded. Hypalon is used on professional boats bought by outfits like the navy and coast guard, which are more concerned with the end result than cost. More expensive than PVC or Hypalon, polyurethane coatings can be welded like PVC and may (the jury's still out) even be more durable than Hypalon.

In business for five years and affiliated with U.S.-based Brunswick Corporation, Portuguese builder Valiant makes an extensive series of pleasure, commercial, patrol, and rescue RIBs. The boat shown here is one of the portable, lightweight 250, 270, and 300 models in the Dynamic series of 8-, 9-, and 10-foot RIBs. Like most inflatables, these boats have a large carrying capacity relative to their own weight. The 8-footer Dynamic 250, for instance, weighs 66 pounds and yet can carry 880 pounds of passengers and gear.

Here's an Avon Seasport RIB displayed at a boat show. This is a Deluxe model, the builder's high-end line, which is available in 10-, 12-, and 13-foot lengths. These boats are upscale in styling and construction, and are commonly used as tenders and recreational craft. The Wales-based manufacturer, part of Zodiac, produces a wide range of civilian, commercial, and military inflatables and RIBs for the world market.

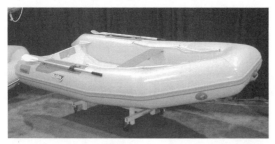

Here's a basic Achilles RIB displayed at a boat show. The company builds a wide range of inflatable boats, including tenders, dinghies, workboats, and whitewater rafters. There are three tenders like this one—9, 10, and 11 feet in length—and all are 5 feet, 4 inches wide with 17-inch inflatable tubes. They can take from 8 to 25 hp outboards and have from two to three individual air chambers for added sinking resistance.

Technically, this Triumph 1200 series tender is not a RIB, but it sure looks like one. The entire boat, including the collar, is made of a powdered, one-piece polyethylene plastic. The collar is filled with air, of course, not plastic, which adds significant reserve buoyancy. TRIUMPH

The Avon Seasport SE320 Jet is propelled to about 40 knots by an 83 hp Yamaha driving a waterjet. Waterjet propulsion in a RIB has the same advantages as in any other kind of boat: shallow draft and safety for swimmers and others in the water. The boat is well suited for use as a family runabout or tender. To ride it, you straddle the center hump and hold onto motorcycle-type handles. AVON

Zodiac makes a wide range of RIBs, including the Eclipse yacht tenders with a foam collar that's impervious to deflation and not so large that it interferes with taking passengers over the side when moored. This actually makes this particular boat more of a rigid un-inflatable boat (RUB) than a RIB, but it makes sense to list it with its close cousins. Without that big fat air-filled collar, there's also more room inside for the people who own the yachts that these boats tend. The RUB is still unsinkable (like a Boston Whaler)—though the foam-filled collar is not as buoyant as the air-filled type—impact resistant, and very high end in quality and fit and finish. ZODIAC

Apex Inflatables is another well-established manufacturer of RIBs and other inflatable boats from 8 to 18 feet. Boats range from fold-up and collapsible portables to whitewater rafts and inflatable kayaks. The A-17 shown here is quite affordable compared to some of the competition, has a deep-V hull well suited to offshore use, and it has a long cruising range of 300-plus miles with a 115 hp four-stroke outboard and a 40-gallon fuel capacity. The long range is partly due to the boat's light weight—just 800 pounds without motor. APEX

Center Consoles

The center console is by far the most popular small saltwater boat, thanks to its all-around versatility and excellent fishing layout. Catch a fish while casting forward and walk aft along either side to bring it aboard. Three or four people can easily fish from a 20-foot center console at the same time. Compared to other boats of its size, the helm station on the typical center console is situated farther aft. This means that the ride quality is much improved because vertical accelerations are less pronounced back aft. The center console likely has a flat to install flush-mounted electronics on, with plenty of storage room inside. The console is usually tall enough to offer limited wind and spray protection for one or two people, at most, as long as a tall windshield is provided.

What makes the center console so great for fishing is the clear side decks from bow to stern, which is made possible by mounting all the antennae and outriggers on the T-top above the console rather than on the gunwale.

Larger center consoles are big enough for a head and storage compartment below the helm, which makes the boat more useful when the whole family is along for the ride. The center console on many rigs, however, doesn't provide protection from the elements, particularly for guests hanging on to the leaning post or helm seat. Avoiding spray and rain can be difficult, if not impossible. With an obvious priority on clear fishing room, many center consoles have low cockpit sides. This means that your passengers will need plenty of grab bars to hold onto when operating at high speed. Installing a 30-inch tall railing back aft in front of the motor well is also a good idea—that height won't get in the way of landing a fish but will provide a railing where it's likely to be needed most, given the class's strong acceleration potential.

For children, older people, or others unused to a boat's motions, the center console may not be a great choice because of the lack of inherent cockpit safety. It's very easy to lose your balance at high speed, and just hanging on can take considerable upper-body strength and coordination. With the center console's very large market and real layout advantages, many owners wouldn't own anything but this type of boat.

Although usually outboard-powered, center consoles are also available with inboard power. This propulsion choice provides a clear, full-height transom—and the console itself serves as an engine box, making good use of deck space. Another layout pioneered—or at least popularized—by Albemarle is mounting an inboard gas or diesel engine under the console, which in turn drives the stern drive via a jackshaft. This system also provides a reasonably clear (that is, more so than the outboard, less so than the inboard) transom and the convenience of a stern drive's improved efficiency and maneuverability.

1998 Boston Whaler 26 Outrage

If you've been around boats for more than a few years, you're probably familiar with the Boston Whaler ad that shows one dismembered specimen bobbing serenely after being cut into three pieces, and another ad with the victim unceremoniously inverted, with a bulldozer perched resolutely on top of it. At the expense of ruining two perfectly good craft, a strong and memorable case was

Boston Whaler 26 Outrage Specifications

LOA:	27'10"
Beam:	8'6"
Draft:	1'3" (hull)
Transom deadrise:	20 deg.
Weight:	6,100 lb. (approximate, full fuel, water, twin 200 hp Mercury outboards)
Fuel capacity:	200 gal. (at 6.1 lb./gal.)
Water capacity:	20 gal. (optional)

made for the brand's absolute survivability. These ads are among the few that have stayed with me over the years, which certainly makes a case for their effectiveness.

Whaler is a high-end boatbuilder that has always pushed its product's safety and ruggedness, starting in the early 1960s with its stable but hard-riding twin-sponson 13- and 16-footers. Today, the same basic construction methods incorporating structural foam are used, but the hulls have evolved into smooth-riding modified-Vs. The Outrage 26 Center Console, introduced in the fall of 1997, is a case in point. With a reasonable (and trailerable) 8 foot, 6-inch beam, this Outrage promises excellent offshore capability and a real-world ability to cover serious ground in lousy weather.

With open rails and 360-degree fishing accessibility, center-console layouts are designed to appeal to hard-core anglers. As a premium manufacturer, Whaler expects you to pay relatively big bucks for its boat, and it offers high-quality tooling and meticulous attention to detail as enticements. Let's take a look at how Boston Whaler measures up.

Center Console

The helm station is probably the single most important feature for many anglers. It's easy to design a helm console so that everything fits, but it's much more difficult to make it all work ergonomically. Whaler scores well here with controls, instruments, and electronics in clear sight and close reach. This boat is designed to be driven by an operator who is

either standing up or braced against the standard leaning post, with lockable storage below the split seats, rod holders, bait-prep station, and a 96-quart insulated cooler. The inside of the leaning post under the dual seats needs more grinding, though, to eliminate the potentially painful fiberglass splinters. Dual pedestal helm seats are also available.

You can reach the tilt wheel and throttles from the seat, and the footrests are well positioned, but the fiberglass under the rubber footpads was so thin that it gave way and seemed to be on the verge of cracking under just light foot pressure. Ergonomically, the helm position works well when the operator is standing up straight, seated on the leaning post, or anywhere in between, but many deep-water enthusiasts like to take advantage of the knee's ability to double as a shock absorber when they are standing.

To start with, the Outrage's console is huge, affording sheer space needed for all the toys and gadgets. A lockable electronics box is located up high, close to eye level. Instruments are spread out low in front of the wheel, rocker switches and trim tabs are forward of the throttles, and a fixed electronics mounting panel is to starboard. Grabrails and upholders are plentiful for security and convenience, a tackle storage bin is close at hand, and the compass is directly in front of the operator about 53 inches off the deck, which is ideal positioning for most people. The console's bulk and the 67-inch-high, stainless-framed acrylic windscreen offer good protection from wind and spray.

If you want a little shade or need extra space for electronics, get the T-top with integrated outriggers like our test boat had. This framing offers even more handholds to hang onto at high speeds in sloppy conditions.

Inside the console through a door to starboard is a portable toilet; a pumpout and overboard discharge, and a full-fledged plumbed marine head with macerator, are options, as is a sink with a freshwater system. An overhead light and porthole help brighten the all-white, neatly finished interior; a countertop, drawers, and storage compartments provide a home for sundry knickknacks. However, I was surprised to see Starboard-like plastic used for a partition, cabinet door, and drawers; this is a cost-cutting measure more appropriate on price-point boats.

Cockpit

Next on the priority list is the cockpit layout, and here Whaler scores again with strong emphasis on safety and maneuverability. The coamings are a full 28 inches high, the nonskid is excellent, and toe kicks help keep passengers on balance (in my opinion, the toe-space and recessed-liner inserts ideally would extend another 4 feet forward to open up the 14-inch-wide side decks outboard of the console). Overall, there's some 6 feet of foredeck and pulpit forward and 4½ feet of the combination motor well and swim platform extending aft of the 18-foot-long main deck. This means that the usable interior of an open-transom 19- or 20-footer is combined with the hull form and ride of a 26-footer.

The cockpit is well equipped with rod racks, rod holders, courtesy lights, and two self-draining 69-by-12-by-12-inch in-deck storage and fish boxes to port and starboard. (I would like to see the pumpout drains recessed to collect the last few pints of water. Another drain leading overboard, used when the boat is at speed or on its trailer, is also positioned above the lowest point of the curved box.) Located aft is another Whaler trademark: an upholstered folding seat that quickly tucks out of the way under the transom coaming on articulated hinges. To port is a 30-gallon livewell, with

freshwater and saltwater pump and light switches just forward. The 200-gallon, 0.19-inch-thickness aluminum fuel tank is on centerline below a removable deck section with inspection plates forward and aft. These plates, made of nonstructural plastic, gave noticeably underfoot; Whaler might consider using inherently stronger fiberglass plates or specify deeper support ribbing on the underside to stiffen the plastic type.

The 28-inch-high transom door, ruggedly constructed with its own bolster, is to starboard, and it latches securely with an oversized stainless mechanism. (Many other builders cut corners here with a flimsy, too-low plastic door held shut by an easily misaligned deadbolt.) The integral combination motor well and swim platform has a handrail and hideaway stainless ladder for boarding; if you specify the freshwater system, you can rinse off with the handheld transom showerhead. Trim tabs are recessed under the transom, well out of the way of anglers and swimmers.

A fiberglass hatch aft of the transom door leads to the batteries, VRO oil tank, and a maze of wires and deck-drain plumbing that use much of the room below the swim platform; more sanding and smoothing is called for under there as well to remove fiberglass splinters. A telescoping stainless-pipe swim ladder pulls out from under a starboard side hatch and extends several steps underwater for easy boarding. A nonstructural plastic hatch inside the motor well is cause for some concern since it's relied on to maintain the hull's watertight integrity: I would specify a watertight fiberglass or aluminum hatch for an offshore vessel like this. Dual battery switches are inside a small door outboard aft of the transom door.

The forward deck area has a few pleasant surprises, starting with a boost-lifted lockable storage locker for six rods under the port seat. There's more storage under the starboard seat and below decks in a locker equipped with hatch gutters to keep the contents dry (inexcusably, there are also more fiberglass splinters). There's an optional anchor windlass to do the heavy lifting via the stainless-lined integral bow pulpit. Finally, a filler piece is available that connects the port and starboard seats to create a casting platform, or it can be raised to its full height for use as a table. If you want to do a lot of casting from the foredeck, consider raising the bow railing from its current 21 inches to a more secure 28-inch height all the way forward.

Construction

The reason Boston Whaler can claim its boats are unsinkable is the extensive use of buoyant structural foam in the construction process. The hull and the liner are laid up in separate molds; aluminum plate, phenolic board, and plywood panels are positioned to serve as backing plates for cleats and other hardware; and then the parts are clamped together while the resin is still wet. Medium-density foam injected between the two components bonds to the fiberglass. The trick is making sure the foaming process is complete with no voids.

The foam is structural because it absorbs compression loads from wave impact, the forces of buoyancy below, and people and gear moving around above. Sheer loads, which result when the hull and deck are alternately placed under tension or compression (depending on external stresses) are also absorbed by the foam. The foam keeps the liner and hull fixed relative to each other even though longitudinal stresses from hogging and sagging, for instance, try to make them move independently along the same plane. In other words, the foam acts like the web of an I-beam and the fiberglass skins act like the I-beam's flanges. The bulkheads and longitudinal stringers seen in conventional construction are eliminated.

This reliance on foam as a structural material means that the bond between the skins and the foam core is critical; if it were to fail, you would have a large mass of semirigid foam surrounded by two thin flopping skins of fiberglass. The positive by-product of this construction method is damaged-condition buoyancy in the extreme. What is lost with all that foam is storage space, and what is gained is weight along with peace of mind. This at-tribute of unsinkability is well worth the lost space and added weight, in my opinion.

Whaler's engineering department claims that this process not only results in great inherent intact buoyancy, but also adds impact resistance in case of collision with an underwater object. Furthermore, fiberglass repairs are easier with the foam acting as a natural molded surface. The company also thinks that the high heat generated during the foam-injection process, effectively an autoclave, results in an extra measure of osmotic-blistering protection. I would like to see this confidence reflected in its otherwise fine ten-year prorated warranty. Gelcoat fading, chalking, and blistering are specifically excluded because they are considered, by definition, "cosmetic and not structural and are not defective materials or workmanship." Gelcoat defects are certainly not structural in nature; however, gelcoat failure can lead to laminate-substrate failure, which would be structural. And, if gelcoat failure is not due to a defect in materials or workmanship, I'm not sure what else there is to blame. Fortunately and commendably, blistering and other defects in the fiberglass itself would be covered by the warranty, but on a prorated basis.

Design

The Outrage has a unique hull form with moderate deadrise for the aft two thirds of its bottom, transitioning or warping quickly to a sharp entry forward. Markedly convex sections (the exact opposite of concave flares) add significant buoyancy in a following sea, which should help to make these hulls much more broach-proof than otherwise. Very wide reverse chines forward also contribute buoyancy and dynamic lift, and should result in a dry ride. With 44 inches of freeboard from the washboard to the chine, this boat offers its passengers ample interior freeboard, added belowdeck volume for generous reserve buoyancy in a semi-swamped condition, and overall excellent seagoing ability for a 26-footer. Many boats of similar overall length (LOA) might have 24 inches (or more) less running surface with the underside of the motor well–swim platform clear of the water. This added waterline length, by comparison, makes the Whaler a better seaboat in less need of trim tabs and less susceptible to changes in trim with passenger, gear, and liquid load variations.

Performance Test

We had a cold, calm, and sunny day for our performance test. The new 200 hp Mercury Optimax power plants started easily, didn't smoke, and ran quietly. These are Mercury's highest-tech motors, designed for improved fuel economy and less noise and smoke.

Once we were in open water, the Outrage climbed easily on plane at 2,200 rpm and 12 knots—very impressive, due to the extended waterline aft under the motor well. The Whaler handled very well at planing speeds with excellent response to the helm at just over four turns lock-to-lock. With the helm hard over, the boat turned in a very tight circle, with no skidding and absolute directional control. The boat heeled almost perfectly for a given turning radius and speed, and the bottom design provided excellent tracking. Sea conditions were calm, so we had only our own wake to slice through, which the boat accomplished without fuss.

Visibility over the console was very good, and the location of the instruments and controls proved to be well thought out. This is a boat that actually cruises at 3,000 rpm for extended engine life and

still makes excellent time—in this case, 27 mph under our loading conditions. These engines are ideally suited to this hull, capable of high get-home speeds, as well as loafing along at more than 2 mpg at 30 mph. Load up with a boat full of passengers and gear, and you'll slow down commensurately, of course. Running on one engine with the other tilted clear of the water, the Whaler planed at 3,400 rpm for about 12 knots; however, running at this speed for any length of time is not recommended with the extra engine load. Figure on a reasonable 8- to 10-knot get-home speed.

With two passengers, a full tank of gas, and about 100 pounds of gear on board, I recorded the performance figures as shown in the accompanying table in 8 feet of calm water (range figures were calculated based on 90 percent of the boat's 200 gal. fuel capacity).

When we returned to the marina, the boat handled well backing into the slip, using just the engines with the helm amidships. The engines are positioned close together, so don't expect to do a lot of pirouetting like a twin-screw inboard—but you'll still have adequate twisting ability. The Outrage 26 has generous freeboard, so expect a crosswind to take charge quickly. However, the same freeboard allows a commendable 10-inch cockpit deck height off the water for a dry fishing platform and excellent reserve buoyancy in rough water. All told, this is an impressive fishing or cruising platform.

Boston Whaler 26 Outrage Performance Results

RPM	Speed, knots	Speed, mph	Fuel Use, gph	Nautical mpg	Statute mpg	Range, nm	Range, statute miles	Noise Level, dBA	Trim, degrees
1,000	5.9	6.8	1.8	3.28	3.77	590	679	71	0.5
1,500	7.4	8.5	4.2	1.76	2.03	317	365	74	1
2,000	9.8	11.3	7.8	1.26	1.44	226	260	81	2
2,500	18.8	21.6	9.8	1.92	2.21	345	397	83	5
3,000	23.6	27.1	12	1.97	2.26	354	407	86	4
3,500	27	31.1	15.4	1.75	2.02	316	363	86	2
4,000	30.4	35.0	18.4	1.65	1.90	297	342	87	2
4,500	33.9	39.0	21.8	1.56	1.79	280	322	88	2
5,000	37.8	43.5	31.6	1.20	1.38	215	248	89	2
5,300	40.1	46.1	41	0.98	1.12	176	202	91	2

My overall impression is of a high-quality, safe, and rugged boat that's 96 percent ready for the owner. Whaler needs to increase its quality control by sanding out the fiberglass splinters inside the hatches and doors before the boat leaves the production line and by increasing the fiberglass laminate thickness around the footrests. I would also like to see less use of plastic in the deck inspection plates, in the console drawers and partition, and especially in the motor well. To maintain its distinctive reputation, a boat in this price range should be constructed using such materials sparingly to

differentiate it from entry-level brands. This was an early-production hull, so let's hope Boston Whaler has gotten the kinks ironed out by now.

You aren't likely to find a boat that offers a greater sense of security than this big, beefy Outrage 26. Knowing that this boat will never visit Davy Jones's locker is part of the reason, and the high cockpit coamings, railings, and grab bars inspire confidence as well. Whalers are pricey to be sure, but attention to design detail and tooling is excellent, the moniker is a prestigious one, and the boats tend to hold their value well.

1998 Regulator 26 CC

Regulator 26 Center Console Specifications	
LOA:	25'10"
Beam:	8'6"
Draft:	24"/31"
Displacement:	5,000 lb. (dry without engines)
Fuel capacity:	176 gal.
Deadrise:	24 deg. (transom)

Hard-core sport anglers with the means to pay for the best need offshore transportation like everyone else; they just have a wider selection from which to choose. Regulator caters exclusively to this high-end market with a lineup of three top-notch outboards from 21 to 32 feet.

The 26-footer has been in production since 1990, and it's been the company's hottest seller for good reason. Fit and finish, design, construction methods and materials, rough-water performance, and the boat's gorgeous looks just can't be beat.

Cockpit

Would that every outboard were designed and constructed as fastidiously as the Regulator. The design is superb, with nonskid that grips fairly well yet affords easy cleanup. It's a full 6 feet, 8 inches from

the transom liner to the end of the console, so it won't be so crowded offshore when working two or three fish at once aft. Coamings are 26 inches high or better—that's on the low side for a large sport angler, but very commendable for an outboard that frequently is 2 to 4 inches lower. It's no wonder so many people fall overboard from small boats.

Toe kicks, essential to maintaining balance when leaning overboard to gaff a fish, are provided all around by the recessed liner and 9-inch-wide caprails. A shallow gutter extends across the transom liner aft, leading to recessed 5½-by-2-inch scuppers tight against the cockpit corners for quick, hassle-free hosing down. The scuppers drain down a tunnel and overboard through transom flaps, making a more convoluted path for water trying to come back on board. The cockpit deck height off the waterline also helps, providing a measure of reserve buoyancy that increases the vessel's seaworthiness.

Three separate fish boxes line the transom coaming with batteries and battery switches below. Two deck access hatches on centerline lead to the bilge aft—with flawlessly tooled fiberglass inside, incidentally—where outboard oil VRO tanks, fuel filters and flow meters, and a bilge pump are all installed with great precision. The hatch gutters seem deep enough, but just in case water spills over, a sloping Plexiglas lid protects the saltwater pumps below: more attention to detail. An in-deck bait well—with recessed drain, of course—is just forward and, in quintessential Regulator fashion, deck drains tooled into the cored deck drain aft to the gutters in the adjacent hatch and then overboard through the deck gutter. These are the details that delight this boat evaluator.

Stern cleats are recessed into the aft liner below coaming hawseholes. One of the few quality-control problems noted was a rubrail bolt projecting into the liner's path; it needs to be cut off flush with the liner.

Moving forward past the console, there's about 21 inches of clearance between the console sides and the padded coaming; walking aft with a fish on the line needn't be a balancing act. Just forward of the recessed side cleats, the deck steps up 9 inches at the forward end of the console. Port and starboard hatches open storage bins; the one to starboard holds an emergency hand bilge pump—an almost unheard of feature on any boat, even one of this class. A molded U-shaped seat arrangement—an option that's part of the deck tooling to eliminate leaks and squeaks—is forward with storage compartments below, and a huge storage area is below decks with a deep gutter to keep the eight rods and other sundries dry. With the molded seats, access to the outboard in-deck storage lockers that is provided on the flush-deck version is lost.

All the drains are recessed to get that last drop of water out as needed. There is no provision for anchoring or storing the ground tackle, although the forward bench could hold the anchor and line neatly. A hawsehole leading to the forepeak would be a welcome addition, with brackets or a pulpit to secure the anchor.

The stainless bow railing slopes up from 8 to 14 inches high, so it's only meant to be used when standing inside the boat. If you plan to be casting regularly from the foredeck, you'll want to add higher railings forward to bring the height up to 28 inches or so for adequate safety. Overall, the cockpit, including the foredeck area, is cleanly configured with excellent use of space, lots of room to maneuver, and everything is beautifully finished.

Center Console

At 37 inches wide by 76 inches long by 48 inches high, this console is large and functionally laid out. The anodized-aluminum windshield is 5 feet, 10 inches tall, providing good protection from wind and rain (I don't anticipate much spray making its way on board).

The tilt wheel controlling the Sea Star hydraulic steering is well positioned to port and set at a nominal 30-degree angle from vertical for best comfort and leverage. The twin throttles are mounted just to starboard—in fact, they're just 1½ inches away, meaning my knuckles hit the throttles at or near the neutral position while I was gripping the wheel (another inch of clearance would be just right). The compass is mounted atop the 30-by-30-inch flat top, slightly offset to starboard from the steering wheel—I would like to see it line up with the wheel and mounted slightly higher for easier viewing. That said, there's ample room for electronics inside the console electronics box, and the Plexiglas window lifts out for easy access and viewing. There's also more room on top of the console forward of the compass, so it's not necessary to order the hardtop to get enough room for everything to be mounted. The integrated engine gauges are located up high to starboard where they're easy to watch, and a row of electrical switches is at arm's length just below.

Center-Console Interior

Our test boat's head compartment inside the center console was big enough to serve its purpose. The door is narrow (for me, anyway) at just 17 inches wide; 22 inches would be great, and it's a big step—a full 24 inches—getting down into the space. This could be addressed by a folding step that would swing up, out of the way, when the occupant is seated. Like everywhere else on this boat, fit and finish is superior to just about anything else on the market. A carpet liner is neatly installed all around inside, the one-piece fiberglass floor and side liner drains to the bilge, and it all fits together with great precision.

On the aft bulkhead, a hatch flips down for access to the inside of the electronics and instrument locker. Another door just below opens forward of the operator's feet to a storage area, complete with carefully located drains. Two access plates cover the fuel tank's fuel-fill connections—there's one on each side feeding the same centerline tank so, at the gas dock, you don't have to drag the fuel hose across the boat. Wiring and engine control cables are neatly run and bundled and then routed through anti-chafe grommets below decks. It's a pleasure to see all these tooled surfaces where they are least expected; that is, in the bilges and other out-of-the-way areas. Many other supposedly high-quality builders don't even sand the fiberglass splinters out of the chop before delivering the boat to the dealer, much less provide tooled surfaces down there.

Design

The Regulator 26 has no pretensions about being the lightest boat available. What it does have is a sharp, true, deep-V Lou Codega–designed bottom along with the mass of a conventionally constructed fiberglass hull, the combination of which will slice through seas as few other boats on the market can. The reverse chines are narrow, which means that reentry will be smoother coming off a big sea at speed. Form stability will not be as stiff either, but the boat's displacement, which submerges the chines generously, helps redress that issue. The

keel comes to a point in cross section, which absorbs a little more horsepower than a padded (or radiused) keel—but it also slices smoothly and unequivocally when landing on a wave after going airborne. Lifting strakes run well aft, but the boat probably doesn't need them for a dry ride or for the lift—the hull form takes care of both issues. They do look nice, though, and they don't interfere with smooth waterflow to the props.

Construction

Regulator's hulls are all fiberglass, which means there's no potential for inadequately sealed wood-cored stringers, bulkheads, and transoms rotting out. The bottom is supported by a one-piece grid system that also carries the deck and liner. Regulator uses isophthalic resins throughout the laminate to provide a measure of protection against osmotic blistering, and a laminate of mat and knitted fiberglass comprises the solid bottom and sides.

The aluminum fuel tank is embedded in foam inside the grid, and Regulator ensures that there is adequate ventilation below the tank to prevent corrosion from developing. Foamed-in aluminum tanks have gotten a lot of bad press, so I'm surprised Regulator uses this method. I would go with a plastic polyethylene tank because it can't corrode and should last the life of the boat. The transom is cored with high-density foam core that resists the compression loads of the transom bracket-mounting bolts, another well-considered construction feature.

Performance Test

We had ideal conditions for our test ride: calm water inshore for the speed runs and a 3- to 4-foot chop 3 miles out. This boat is as smooth running, and perhaps the smoothest, of any monohull I've run in this size range, thanks to the well-designed hull and weight. Lighter boats are faster but not smoother running than this one. We were able to maintain 30 knots in a 2- to 3-foot chop, and I unconsciously stopped bending my knees to absorb the shock after a few minutes. In a quartering sea, I took my hand off the wheel for 3 to 4 minutes at a

Regulator 26 Center Console Performance Results

RPM	Speed, knots	Speed, mph	Fuel Use, gph	Nautical mpg	Statute mpg	Range, nm	Range, statute miles	Noise Level, dBA	Trim, degrees
1,000	5.2	6.0	4.4	1.18	1.36	251	245	69	2
1,500	6.8	7.8	6.3	1.08	1.24	229	223	73	4
2,000	8.1	9.3	9.5	0.85	0.98	181	176	77	6
2,500	13.8	15.9	12.2	1.13	1.30	240	234	81	7
3,000	23	26.5	14.2	1.62	1.86	345	335	82	6
3,500	28.8	33.1	16.8	1.71	1.97	365	355	84	5
4,000	33.3	38.3	19.7	1.69	1.94	360	350	86	4
4,500	37.3	42.9	24.1	1.55	1.78	329	320	88	3.5
5,000	41.4	47.6	34.1	1.21	1.40	258	251	92	3
5,600	44.1	50.7	40.7	1.08	1.25	230	224	93	3

time, and the boat didn't change course more than 10 degrees the entire time. The ride was superbly smooth and dry. The only time we took any spray on board, with 15 to 20 knots of wind blowing, was with the seas broad on the bow—and that was minimal.

Rolling in the trough with the engines out of gear, we took some water through the scuppers, so wear boots to keep your feet dry and catch fish at the same time. The boat lay to with the stern pointing 30 to 40 degrees into the wind, so the rolling was not as pronounced as it otherwise would have been, and the ride was better than I expected in a 24-degree transom deadrise hull like this.

Across the speed spectrum, the boat ran straight, showing no tendency to wander about its heading. I would consider adding a section of side railing adjacent to the console to bring the railing height up to a full 32 inches—as on any boat of this class. At 28 to 30 knots in the kind of slop during our test ride, it would be easy to end up overboard unless you're hanging on—imagine how easy that could happen in a boat without the Regulator's smooth, stable ride at speed.

In fact, with a flatter running angle for better visibility, a better ride, and sharper helm control, this boat does far better at 25 knots than it does at 15. Resist the instinct to run this boat too slowly when it gets rough—the hull likes to run and will

pay dividends in the process. Steering was responsive, but it took some effort; I would recommend power steering to take the work out of piloting. We used the boat's installed GPS and Yamaha fuel-monitoring system for our performance run and, because they were so easy to watch, it confirmed the ergonomic location of the electronics. The tight distance between the wheel and the port throttle was not a problem unless the engines were out of gear, at which point you're not usually trying to steer anyway.

Our speed-trial results, with 237 gallons of fuel (which included the 61-gallon auxiliary fuel tank), twin 200 hp Yamahas, and two passengers on board, are given in the accompanying table.

The Regulator is certainly a top-of-the-line outboard fishing boat, built without compromise to the high standards of the company's founders, Owen (the builder) and Joan (the president) Maxwell. I would look for a few minor changes in the helm console layout, but this boat is as close to perfection as you're likely to see. The Regulator is very well built, handles and rides superbly, and is great-looking to boot.

You can find lighter, more efficient outboard boats of the same size, but probably none that offer a smoother, drier ride, and very few that can match the quality and pizzazz of the whole package.

Expect the Regulator to be a good investment, too, to the extent that not many products depreciate as such. Like any high-quality product, it holds its value to a higher degree than many other boats.

1997 Shamrock 219 Open Center Console

SHAMROCK

Shamrock 219 Open Center Console Specifications	
LOA:	21'9"
Beam:	8'6"
Draft:	2'0"
Weight:	3,900 lb. (with standard power)
Fuel capacity:	80 gal.
Standard power:	300 hp PCM Sea Maxx 5.7-liter gas
Optional power:	Sea Maxx and Crusader 275 to 320 hp EFI and TBI (Throttle Bottle Injected); Yanmar 170 and 230 hp diesels

Since 1974, Shamrock has focused its sights on building a specialty product and attempted to carve out a niche market—in this case, small inboard fishing boats from 19 to 29 feet. Not many boatbuilders make small inboards; most buyers consider the overwhelming consumer demand for stern drive and outboard power to be irresistible.

Center Console

The two-piece center console is 49 inches high and 27 inches wide at the top, with a 12-inch-high Lexan windshield on top. The console provides adequate protection from wind and spray for one person but not for two, as we discovered on our test ride. The wheel and controls are comfortably situated for seated, leaning, or standing operation, and the instrument-control panel is well placed for easy viewing and operation. A molded footrest provides a place for your feet when you are seated.

There's sufficient clearance between the console and the gunwales—up to 26 inches—so building a wider windscreen that projects a few inches out to either side may do the trick for when the spray is flying. There's also precious little to hold onto; this console desperately needs a stainless-pipe

frame around the windshield and a couple of grab bars high up on either side. Another door in the front of the console opens for excellent access to the battery switch and the underside of the instrument panel. Inside the console, accessed through doors on either side, are the polypropylene water tank and batteries.

Cockpit

A pair of 36-by-12-by-17-inch fish boxes are built into the transom, one of which does double duty as a livewell and bait-prep center. A 32-by-9-inch hatch opens for access below the fish boxes to the rudder and the deck and fish-box drain lines leading overboard through synthetic through-hull fittings (I prefer bronze, which is stronger). The bilge is neatly fiberglassed, ground smooth, and finished in gray gelcoat.

The two 40-gallon, 5052-grade aluminum fuel tanks are bedded in foam under the cockpit. You can see them through a pair of round inspection ports. When aluminum tanks are surrounded by foam and improperly installed, the air doesn't circulate and corrosion starts from the outside if water collects anywhere against the tank. I would opt for the polypropylene plastic tanks that are available in this size range. The cockpit deck above would have to be cut out to replace the tank (or tanks); for that reason, many builders make the deck removable.

Four rod holders are built into the substantial gunwales, and mounting the stern cleats at an angle recesses them out of harm's way when fishing. The coaming bolsters add a touch of class and comfort; at 26 inches high, they offer a reasonably safe fishing environment for any landlubbers in the group. To remedy the lack of a toe kick molded into the liner, I would either tool one in or increase the thickness of the bolster by 4 or 5 inches.

Rod racks are built in under the gunwales, as are port and starboard tackle storage lockers. Lowering the recessed rod-rack liner and extending it the length of the cockpit so that its bottom is flush with the cockpit deck would provide the needed toe space along the sides, leaving only the transom liner. The nonskid is excellent—grippy without abusing the knees—and it's easily cleaned. Side gutters running the length of the cockpit lead to the recessed flush corner-mounted scuppers for easy cleanup.

A full-width swim platform is standard equipment, which means you won't be gaffing any fish over the stern, detracting from the boat's role as a pure fishing machine. On the other hand, the platform does add significant versatility for boarding when moored stern to the dock—and, of course, it's great for swimming. A folding boarding ladder is also provided and aftermarket outboard brackets that bolt directly to the platform are available for outboards up to 25 hp. For those who want it, mounting a kicker on this single-engine boat isn't a problem.

Forward of the console is a 27-by-21-by-17-inch cooler–fish box. A gutter runs all around the perimeter of the deck for easy cleanup, leading back to the flush corner-mounted scuppers and overboard. Another storage box is built in under the seat in the bow, and the anchor locker is located forward of that. Separate red and green sidelights are in the eyes of the boat (the bow); I would put them on ei-

ther side of the console (or, better yet, on the T-top if you order one) to remove them from your direct field of vision at night and to increase the range at which another vessel can see you. The hand railing forward is 32 inches high, an excellent height for safety.

Engine Compartment

The engine box is 29 inches high, but the engine only takes up two thirds of that space; the remainder is used by a storage locker and leaning post behind the helm. The aft seat cover lifts up for quick access to the fuel manifold and transmission. The engine box with its built-in seats unlatches forward and lifts easily on its hinges, assisted by gas lifts.

The engine is easily accessed and, since our engine was saltwater-cooled, there was extra space forward to get to the raw-water strainer, the seacocks for the macerator and washdown pump, and the small Rule 1,000 gph bilge pump. I would upgrade the bilge pump to at least 2,500 gph, but there are also two 1,000 gph pumps aft on either side of the prop pocket. Wiring is neatly run and protected by looming, although I would like to see a cover for the bus bar to make sure it stays dry. The engine seacock is aft of the engine, where it will get a steadier supply of uninterrupted waterflow under the boat at speed, but it's difficult to reach. A rod attached to the top of the valve handle and leading up and forward would allow easy remote seacock operation in an emergency.

Hose clamps fasten the rubber fuel lines in place, and with the TBI's supply and return lines, as well as the boat's twin tanks, a total of six fuel lines are joined at a three-way valve manifold. The inside of the engine box is acoustically insulated with contoured foam, and an automatic fire extinguisher is fastened conveniently overhead. Baffled air-intake boxes for combustion air are mounted on the engine-box sides aft. One of the brackets for the boost lift was loose; therefore, a more secure foundation or larger screws may be necessary.

The engine is mounted to boxed-in engine beds fiberglassed to the hull and stringer sides; the engine mounts are lag-bolted to the beds. The bilge-blower suction line was fastened on top of the engine bed; it should extend another 7 inches closer to the bottom of the bilge. The fuel-supply lines run through stringer cutouts; they need chafing protection where they come into contact with the rough fiberglass. Overall, though, this is a nicely engineered engine compartment detailed in quality work.

Design

Shamrock recently introduced its new PocketDrive design, which its advertising describes as maximizing performance by allowing the boat to jump on plane quicker with a flatter shaft angle. A properly designed pocket can indeed improve performance, but any pocket necessarily reduces buoyancy and hydrodynamic lift aft where you really need it.

The secret to maximizing better performance is minimizing the pocket volume, making it just large enough to incorporate the prop. This larger, slower-turning prop and, to a lesser extent, the lower shaft angle are really where the increased efficiency originates. The more slowly you can turn a prop (as long as you don't run out of pitch by increasing the diameter too much), the more efficiently a boat in this speed range will be driven.

Incorporating a pocket also allows builders to maintain the same shaft angle and move the engine aft if they so choose, but the allowance for the loss of buoyancy aft must be considered. The Shamrock's rudder is essentially transom-mounted with a transom bubble extending to the waterline some 4 inches aft. A cavitation plate is fitted to the top of the rudder—a necessity when the rudder projects as far aft of the transom as this one does. Without it, the rudder would tend to suck in air and stall in high-speed turns.

The better-designed pockets have a continuous radius or curve in cross section like the Shamrocks. This shape interferes less with steering and, for a given prop size, minimizes the loss of buoyancy. Remember that prop-tip clearance can be allowed to decrease as the hull shape above the prop starts to conform to the arc of the propeller-blade tips. Theoretically, you can drop down to 1/8-inch clearance if the pocket exactly matches the propeller-tip arc; otherwise, a 15 to 20 percent clearance is needed. The Shamrock also has recessed trim tabs to adjust for list and trim.

Older Shamrocks with a Keel Drive system have molded fiberglass skegs that support and protect the direct-drive prop. The PocketDrive, on the other hand, has no skeg, which leaves the running gear exposed to grounding damage. A pair of spray rails forward adds lift, resulting in a drier ride. Reverse chines aft also add lift at speed and stability at rest.

Construction

Shamrock uses an all-fiberglass stringer system to eliminate the possibility of rot in a wood core. According to the manufacturer, sufficient foam is blown in to provide positive flotation. Tooling is neat and well executed. With a one-piece deck and superstructure assembly stretching from bow to stern, this will prove to be a low-maintenance boat. It also results in a stronger leak- and rattle-free boat.

Performance Test

We had a great day for our boat test off Fort Lauderdale, Florida. The wind was blowing at a steady 25 knots out of the northwest, so by the time we got 4 or 5 miles offshore, we had a 2- to 4-foot chop on top of a 6- to 8-foot groundswell—a veritable boat tester's delight, to be sure. The boat only carries 80 gallons of fuel, which isn't much for a boat of this size; however, it burns less fuel than outboards, and deep-Vs need more fuel because they require more power to push.

In reality, plan on this being a 20- to 22-knot boat, both by virtue of its power plant and because of its full-bow and modest-deadrise hull design. In the low 20-knot range, we rode comfortably heading directly into the seas; cranked up to 24 knots, the ride became much harder—more than we were willing to endure. Downsea, the bow provided ample lift and buoyancy to keep us from burying our nose. In the trough at idle, the hull's form stability and low center of gravity requited themselves well; playing a fish from this boat in a 4-foot beam sea is more like angling from a dock than you would expect.

Once up on top, we were able to back off to 2,300 rpm before falling off plane. At a little more than four turns lock-to-lock, the steering was very responsive. Hard over, the boat turns on a dime—less than 30 feet at low speed. At high speed, the boat leans slightly into the turn, which is much more comfortable than a flat turn that tends to throw people around.

The trim tabs weren't needed to lift the stern for efficiency; our best speeds were achieved with no tabs. But heading into the steep chop, a bow-down attitude gave us a smoother—and wetter—ride.

I found myself looking for more grabrails to hang onto during our roller-coaster ride—I would add them to the front and sides of the console. Backing down at 1,300 rpm, a little water shipped aboard through the scuppers, but drained quickly overboard once we stopped. Laying to with the engine out of gear, the boat rolled easily and drifted slightly stern to the wind. The ride was comfortably dry with the seas on the beam; it was the wettest with the seas 20 to 30 degrees on either bow.

Back at the dock, the boat backed easily into its slip with less effect from the crosswind we encountered than most other boats of its size in production today.

According to Lauderdale Marine, many of its Shamrock customers are former sailors and trawler owners, and they are not known to make decisions quickly. Once they do buy a Shamrock, they hang onto them or trade up to a larger model. The traditional looks—with the boat's low, sleek lines and time-tested and traditional power plant—certainly appeal to old salts who value seaworthiness and dependability.

✳   ✳   ✳

If the idea of simplicity, reliability, shoal draft, a clear stern, and a less expensive propulsion system appeals to you, check out the Shamrock. This is an excellent 20-knot (in a chop) boat with a low center of gravity and excellent stability and seaworthiness. It is solidly built and pleasingly styled, and will still be looking good, aesthetically, in twenty years. You can order options such as a blue or burgundy hull, a trolling valve to slow down the shaft speed at idle, diesel power, and a T-top.

No boat is perfect, however: I would like to see increased fuel capacity to make these boats better suited to offshore use. Shamrock could combine the best of both worlds and make a skeg available on its pocket-drive boat for grounding protection.

Pro-Line's 19 CC is one of the smaller models in the builder's 17- to 30-foot center-console lineup. This is a good-running, well-equipped boat with high freeboard for added safety, a self-bailing cockpit, and—believe it or not on such a small boat—an enclosed head. A ten-year transferable warranty is evidence of the builder's confidence in its own product (the all-fiberglass stringer system is built to last); the style-conscious will like the sporty graphics.

PRO-LINE

An excellent offshore fisherman, the Contender 21 Center Console delivers a superb ride with its true deep-V bottom. It's also built light and strong for excellent performance, range, and speed with moderate power.

Boston Whaler's 17 Montauk is the original center console—or so many people say—and it's only slightly modified from the original 16-footer popular in the 1960s and 1970s. This one has a twin-sponson hull form, which means it will pound your kidneys loose in a light chop, but it's very stable and a great all-purpose, calm-water family boat. Medium-density foam injected during construction between the hull and deck liner bonds the thin fiberglass skins together. All Whalers from 13 to 28 feet are similarly built, except for the 34-foot Defiance flagship, which is also foam-filled but does not rely on foam structurally. Boston Whaler makes high-end, pricey center and dual consoles and walkarounds that tend to hold their value well.   BOSTON WHALER

This photo shows the easy access to the head compartment on the Century 2300.   CENTURY

This cutaway drawing shows how a Cobia 174 CC is built, with a fiberglass stringer system bonded to the hull and deck, foam-filled voids, and a foamed-in aluminum fuel tank on centerline.   COBIA

Besides building outboards, Yamaha builds boats (Century and Cobia) to hang them on. Like many builders, Century has switched to all-fiberglass, foam-filled stringer systems and synthetic transoms to eliminate the possibility of rot—the bane of wood-cored boats everywhere. Unlike most boats in this size range, Century models even have fiberglass ribs to stiffen the hull sides. Also in the minority is Century's ten-year hull warranty, a feature that should be standard with every boat. Century's lineup includes the 2600 CC shown here, as well as center and dual consoles, walkarounds, bay boats, and a hybrid cuddy, ranging from 19 to 32 feet.

CENTURY

Yamaha-owned Cobia produces center consoles, walkarounds, deck boats, and dual consoles from 17 to 27 feet. The modified-V hull (20 deg. transom deadrise) with its moderate 8-foot, 6-inch overall beam delivers a good ride in a light chop. Cobias have all-fiberglass hulls, synthetic rot-proof transoms, and foam-filled stringer systems. Watch out for any boat with foamed-in aluminum fuel tanks, though; they must be kept absolutely dry to prevent corrosion. A long list of features is standard and an impressive ten-year warranty is included.

COBIA

Albemarle Boats builds no-nonsense, smooth-running fishing boats from 24 to 41 feet. The 260 CC shown is available with either single gasoline or diesel jackshaft-stern-drive power, or twin outboards on brackets. That's a big difference in weight distribution—which do you suppose works better? The advantage of the jackshaft, of course, is the relatively clear transom with the engine box forward. This rig works especially well for anglers who want to trailer the boat to out-of-the-way locales and then barrel offshore in sloppy weather to catch fish. The new Albemarle 41 Open is a Blount-designed offshore powerhouse well suited for offshore tournament competition.

ALBEMARLE

Grady-White's solid reputation, built over four decades starting with wooden lapstrake models, is well deserved. Construction is conventional with plywood-cored stringers and bulkheads, and the boats are heavily laid up—a virtue many Grady owners swear by when it's time to run fast in a steep chop. The C. Raymond Hunt Associates—designed, warped-V hulls run well, with a combination of efficiency and good ride quality matched by few other builders. The 247 CC Sportfish shown is typical Grady-White with high freeboard translating into added seaworthiness and improved interior safety. These boats aren't cheap, but they tend to hold their value and are well-regarded among connoisseurs.

GRADY-WHITE

Edgewater builds rugged boats, with its Permagrid and Ramcap construction methods. The former has interlocking all-fiberglass stringers bonded directly to the hull and deck liner; the latter includes preformed foam to which the fiberglass liner is bonded. All voids are foam-filled. This is former Boston Whaler engineer Bob Dougherty's solution to avoiding or improving on the structural use of low-density foam: the fiberglass components are bonded to each other directly or the fiberglass is bonded to preformed foam. The 247 Edgewater CC shown is a good-running seaboat—not as fancy on the inside as a Whaler, but certainly built to last for generations. A full lineup of twelve models from 13 to 26 feet includes center-console, dual-console, and walkaround fishing-family boats.

EDGEWATER

A high-end builder of fast offshore sportfishermen, Intrepid has built a solid reputation for its excellent construction quality and equally good performance. Center-console, walkaround, and cuddy models from 28 to 37 feet include the Intrepid 36 CC cuddy shown here. Twin outboards, bolted to integral mounts, are shielded from the cockpit by a full-height transom. Intrepid is a believer in stepped bottoms, which can be effective at improving speed by reducing wetted surface and frictional drag at high speeds. The Intrepid's true deep-V bottom delivers a superb ride in a chop. A big-canyon runner like this boat can comfortably spend the night offshore, with all the basics in the cuddy and sufficient built-in fuel capacity.

INTREPID

Here's a boat that gives you something to talk about with the other anglers on the launching ramp. Built of polyethylene plastic in a closed mold, Triumph boats—like plastic fuel tanks—are seamless and rugged, resilient, and easily maintained. The hull color is molded in, so there's no need to worry about scratches in the finish. The Logic 210 shown is the largest in the four-boat series, which starts with an intriguing 12-foot RIB look-alike. With its close-molded construction, this boat is essentially made of one piece of cross-linked plastic, so forget about leaks and squeaks.   TRIUMPH

The Godfrey Polar Bay center-console series—saltwater boats from one of the country's biggest freshwater builders (including this 21-footer)—ranges from 19 to 23 feet. These models have more freeboard and deadrise than the builder's flats boats and somewhat less than its single 18-foot V-series offering. This boat is touted by the builder as suited for family cruising as well as fishing, with pull-out backrests for the latter and a bow sunpad for the former. An insulated fish box and lockable rod storage are available.   GODFREY

In business since 1967, Mako is one of the oldest names in center consoles, and builds eight from 17 to 31 feet, as well as walka-round, dual-console, flats, and bay boats. The 17 CC shown is an original 1960s hull with an updated interior, with extra features such as upholders and a livewell. The bottom is fairly flat, with 12 degrees of deadrise at the transom, so the hull will be stable at rest and fast for the horsepower. However, the ride will be on the bumpy side compared to a boat with a deep-V hull.   MAKO

The Sea Fox 210 is another good example of a well-built boat offered at a very fair price. Note the high (read: safe and seaworthy) freeboard and the reasonably fine entry for a good ride in a light chop. The company builds a wide range of center- and dual-console, bay, flats, cuddy, walkaround, and deck boats from 16 to 25 feet. The all-fiberglass hull-and-stringer system of each Sea Fox—foam-injected into hull voids—and a high-density foam-cored transom should last a couple of generations and then some; the warranty, at any rate, is good for a generous ten years.

SEA FOX

Walkarounds

The walkaround is an excellent layout for families that fish, ski, swim, and cruise. A cross between a cuddy cabin and a center console, the walkaround features a livable cabin suitable for a night or two onboard, and it's a safe spot for children to stay when cruising at high speed. Forward, the decks are recessed inside bulwarks for safe all-around accessibility, and a bow railing mounted on top of the bulwark offers a handhold on the way forward. The recessed side decks take away some but not much of the interior space, since the sides of the cabin are not very accessible in most small boats, anyway. You'll find little practical difference in space compared to an express cruiser of the same size. Down below, and depending on size, you'll usually find a V-berth with storage below, an enclosed head with toilet and sink, and a small galley with a refrigerator, countertop, sink, and perhaps a small microwave. The helm station is well protected behind the windshield to starboard on most walkarounds, with a companion seat and console opposite to port and a companionway door on centerline. This forward cockpit area benefits from any protection from wind and spray offered by the windshield. Most walkarounds come with or can be ordered with a bimini top; plastic filler curtains connect from the windshield to the bimini frame. Aft is an open cockpit and either outboard or stern-drive power.

1998 Grady-White 274 Sailfish

GRADY-WHITE

Grady-White 274 Diesel Sailfish Specifications	
LOA:	28'0"
Beam:	9'6"
Draft:	1'6" (hull)
Fuel capacity:	202 gal.
Displacement:	8,400 lb. (wet)

Grady-White's 27-foot Sailfish has been around since the early 1990s, having its styling tweaked for a softer look along the way, but the real news is the new diesel power plant recently introduced by Grady. Built on a C. Raymond Hunt deep-V hull, the 274 is already a classic, proven seaboat with a very family-friendly walkaround layout. What the new techy, lightweight diesel offers is economy (at least 50 percent better than outboards) and long range; excellent speed; and a very quiet, smoke- and fume-free operation. Cruising speed actually improves over a pair of 225 hp outboards.

The inboard engine and lower unit are placed lower in the hull than outboards can be, which increases stability by lowering the center of gravity. Diesel fuel is inherently safer than gasoline, and it usually costs less per gallon. You don't lose any cockpit space over the outboard version and, for all this, you pay a little more. If you already know the Sailfish, about the only difference you'll see—other than a lack of outboards—is a two-piece engine box that starts under the existing cockpit seat and continues aft, in a second section aft of the transom.

Cockpit

The 7-foot, 5-inch cockpit has ample room to land two or three fish at a time, and there's plenty of gear to help you catch them: under-gunwale rod racks, three per side; four rod holders (there's space on board to store seventeen rods); and up forward is a livewell to port and an insulated fish box to starboard. A saltwater spigot, freshwater shower, and removable storage bin aft (for access to the batteries below) complete the standard equipment list.

Attention to detail is also found in the padded coaming bolsters and recessed hull liner, which creates a safety-enhancing toe space and room for a toe board below. The nonskid is fairly smooth but it seems to grip well enough. A large section of the cockpit deck lifts out when it's time to replace the aluminum fuel tank. All of the decks and fish boxes drain overboard and, unlike new macerator pumps, gravity is free.

Foredeck

Of course, one great aspect of a walkaround is how easy and safe it is to get forward. Deep bulwarks and bow railings give you a sense of security; however, I would raise the railing at the bow to provide a 30-inch height off the pulpit and move the railings in to line up vertically with the inner bulwark for better balance. The trunk cabin offers a comfortable seat and the bolt-on anchor pulpit can be fitted with a windlass.

Engine Compartment

Grady-White was able to leave most of the tooling intact when it installed the first stern drive. Accessibility through two hatches, forward and aft of the transom, is quite good. We backed down in rough water on our sea trial, shipping a lot of water around the external engine box. However, afterward when we popped the hatch dockside, not a drop of water had made its way inside—which surprised me, considering the volume and pressure of the saltwater maelstrom back aft.

The gutterless removable storage bin is a candidate for redesign on follow-on production boats, but everything was generally accessible and neatly installed, even on this prototype. The batteries and battery switch, fuel filter, and fuel manifold are all located directly below the storage bin and reasonably accessible.

Construction

Built with basic (but not level) flotation to prevent the boat from sinking, the Grady-White's hull bottom is solid fiberglass with balsa core used in the sides for stiffness at light weight. DCPD-blend resin is used throughout the laminate with an ISO-NPG gelcoat to help prevent osmotic blistering (see chapter 6). This mix offers satisfactory but not great osmotic-blistering protection; the builder is counting on proper exotherm (resin cure) and a fully saturated skin coat (rather than a premium vinylester resin) to prevent blistering. Stringers, transoms, and bulkheads are cored with pressure-treated plywood and encapsulated in fiberglass. Limber holes are sealed with PVC tubes to keep the wood core dry, and the hull is divided into three watertight compartments, providing extra flooding protection to what is already there from the injected foam.

Helm

The helm is laid out with engine instruments and rocker switches on either side of the compass flat, immediately forward of the wheel. I would like to see the horn and wiper switches—used more often and/or more important than the others—moved closer to the seat; next to the trim-tab switches would be a better location.

The tilt wheel is mounted to the console at about 10 degrees from horizontal; putting a shim below it would allow the wheel to be tilted to a more horizontal and, in my opinion, more comfortable position. But the helm still works well as it is, with electronics in the box overhead attached to the hardtop and everything else visible and within reach when needed. The adjustable helm seat is located 29 inches off the deck for an excellent all-around view. There's storage under the helm seat and tackle drawers in the cabinet below the companion seat to port. Grady-White wraps the cushion down around the front of the seat to serve as a bolster when the operator is standing up—a nice touch.

Cabin

The Grady-White will make a reasonably comfortable weekender for a couple and, at the very least, there's ample room to get out of the weather. Everywhere is the quality and attention to detail that I've come to expect from Grady. A generous 76 inches of headroom, along with side ports and an overhead hatch in the bow, introduces a lot of light and fresh air down below. Grady now builds the 274 with a full fiberglass cabin liner, which makes for an attractive and easily maintained interior.

Up forward, a V-berth converts to a 75-inch double bed with the addition of a filler cushion; a second, 71-inch (76 in. would be more practical) berth is aft in the cabin below the helm area. To port is a small galley with a refrigerator-freezer, portable gas burner, sink, and storage bin–icebox. A microwave is optional, as is dockside power and a

water heater. Opposite to starboard is the enclosed head with a pull-out sink faucet for use as a shower spigot, and a manual toilet with a three-way valve and holding tank. The lower half of the head is tooled fiberglass; the upper is a padded vinyl neatly applied.

Performance Test

We ran our speed trials in protected waters, then headed out of the Lake Worth (Florida) inlet into some rambunctious 3- to 5-foot seas. We kept up a steady 18 knots heading right into them, the C. Raymond Hunt deep-V hull slicing through the seas solidly and comfortably. We started seeing more than a few 6-footers farther offshore, and slowed to 15 knots—still a commendable speed for any 27-footer in those conditions. We took minimal spray on board until I turned to put the seas on the beam, and then I wished for a higher windshield with taller and longer side windows, behind which the better to stay dry. Steering was silky smooth and responsive, as were the Volvo EDC electronic engine controls. With the single stern drive so deep below the hull, expect significant heel in a sharp turn, with the props' extra depth adding leverage to the lateral steering force being generated.

Drifting in this slop, the Grady proved to be stable and comfortable lying in the trough. Backing at an idle introduced a lot of water through the

Grady-White 274 Sailfish Volvo Diesel DuoProp Performance Results

RPM	Speed, knots	Speed, mph	Fuel Use, gph	Nautical mpg	Statute mpg	Range, nm	Range, statute miles	Noise Level, dBA	Trim, degrees
1,000	6.2	7.1	1.2	5.2	5.9	930	1,200	68	1
1,500	7.5	8.6	1.8	4.2	4.8	750	968	73	3
2,000	9.5	10.9	3.5	2.7	3.1	489	631	82	5
2,500	14.7	16.9	6	2.5	2.8	441	569	83	6
3,000	21.6	24.8	8.5	2.5	2.9	457	590	85	5
3,500	26.2	30.1	12	2.2	2.5	393	507	87	5
3,600	28.4	32.7	12.8	2.2	2.6	399	515	88	5
3,800	30.1	34.6	14.5	2.1	2.4	374	482	89	5

Test conditions: single 243 shp Volvo KAD44 EDC diesel DuoProp stern drive, full fuel, 20-foot-plus depth, calm seas, air temperature 72 degrees, and 100 pounds of gear. Test conducted on November 8, 1998, in Fort Worth, Florida. Range calculated using 90 percent of the boat's 202-gallon fuel capacity. Sound levels taken at the helm.

transom door; Grady-White says it will seal it with a gasket on future production hulls. The scuppers did a fine job of draining the water back overboard.

Coming back in, we ran at 26 knots in the quartering seas, with the hull strutting its stuff: tracking straight, running dry, and showing no tendency to nosedive running down the backs of those healthy seas. In fact, the boat runs, rides, and handles better at 25 knots than it does at 18. It's great to run a boat that's so well balanced with a smooth and dry ride and predictable handling up- and downsea. The table on page 301 gives the results of our performance test.

The Grady-White 274, especially when paired up with this diesel duo-prop package, is an excellent solution for the offshore angler or cruiser who wants long range; reliability; and a smooth, quiet, odorless ride. The overall design is a winner; the Grady is strongly—if conventionally—built and is an exceptional seaboat for its size. It should provide many years of good service. Grady-White is a pricey but well-regarded name with a reputation for excellent customer service. In fact, Grady-White placed first in customer satisfaction in a 2001 J. D. Power survey. The Sailfish is now called the 282; the 274 is no longer offered.

1999 Mako 293

MAKO

Mako 293 Specifications	
Length:	28'7"
LOA with pulpit:	30'10"
Beam:	9'6"
Hull draft:	19"
Transom height:	30" (C/L)
Transom deadrise:	23 deg.
Weight:	6,100 lb. (dry, no engine)
Fuel capacity:	240 gal.
Maximum power:	500 hp
Power options:	Twin Mercury/Johnson/Evinrude (up to 250 hp)

Mako has been building serious fishing boats for a long time, mostly outboards in the 19- to 30-foot range. This big walkaround fills a need in the marketplace for a high-quality family boat that also does a commendable job as a sportfisherman. I would take one of these eminently practical and versatile rigs over a center console any day of the week, but I'm decidedly in the minority on that count.

Cockpit

Measuring 7 by 7 feet and 25 inches deep, the Mako's cockpit has ample room for a couple of an-

glers to play fish simultaneously. The deck, covered with a fine but grippy, sprayed-on polyurethane nonskid, drains overboard via recessed transom scuppers, to which the in-deck fish-box gutters also feed. The single aluminum fuel tank below the cockpit is accessed for inspection by a pair of plastic hatches. The entire tank can be replaced without major deck surgery by removing a large section of the deck that is fastened in place with screws and adhesive around its perimeter. The fish boxes drain via pump and recessed sumps, so they'll usually pump dry whenever you choose. Rod racks below the gunwale and flush rod holders mounted in the gunwales are standard. Two bait wells or a bait well and a sink, if you prefer, are built into the transom aft.

Located below are the majority of the boat's mechanicals, accessed by a pair of plastic doors that folds down, out of the way. The deck scuppers feed via reinforced-rubber hoses to bronze check valves—impressive hardware for this application. The two fuel filters are mounted on the aft bulkhead, still close enough for reasonable serviceability. Some of the wiring needs a little TLC in the form of better looming (actually, there was none); less slack; and more direct routing, such as the aft starboard-deck courtesy light. The bilge is coated in white gelcoat for improved visibility, but I would like to see some more of that rough glass ground smooth to prevent splinter injuries. I also would prefer something other than gelcoat used to seal the plywood end grain, such as around the engine cableway tube cutouts. Epoxy is perfect for that application, and won't crack like the Mako's gelcoat was already doing on our test boat.

The transom door is mounted aft of the raised deck portion of the transom, making it just 18 inches high—which is too low for adequate passenger balance, especially considering the acceleration of which this boat is capable. Mounting the door would be a safer arrangement.

The integral swim platform–motor well sticks aft a good 3 feet, but the bottom of the boat does not extend aft with it; this is unfortunate because it would definitely improve the ride. Also remember that—with any boat of this design—the engines extend some 6 feet aft of the usable cockpit, so you'll have an obstruction to contend with when playing those monster fish.

Mako does a great job with its engine-control and fuel-line ducts, making them essentially watertight and mounting them well above deck level to keep everything dry below decks.

Two round inspection plates let you keep an eye on things down below in the bilge. The deck section into which they are mounted unscrews and lifts out for major maintenance or equipment replacement. This is a much better arrangement than on other boats, which have a large plastic (nonstructural) hatch that deflects underfoot and invariably leaks buckets, rusting the components below.

The Mako's motor well actually doubles as a full swim platform, too, with lots of area from which to dive or swim; just ensure that the engines are shut off. The stern cleats are recessed in the sloping transom sides, which helps to prevent both line snags and injuries to swimmers who might lose their balance. Mako also molded in a step to port to assist in climbing over the transom in the absence of a door to that side—nice attention to detail. Forward in the cockpit, a pair of insulated iceboxes doubles (make that triples) as seats and steps to the walkaround side decks.

Foredeck

One of the neatest features about a walkaround design is how easy and safe it is to get forward. The bow railing above the fiberglass bulwark is more than 30 inches high forward, which is excellent, and a variety of handrails with which to steady yourself are placed along the side decks and around the trunk cabin. An upholstered seat is molded into the front of the cabin, making this a very user-friendly and, I predict, often-visited locale while underway. The bolt-on anchor pulpit is fitted with a stainless steel insert, and the anchor stows hanging from its stocks below the opening hatch.

Helm

Mako takes an approach to its console layout different than many other builders, arraying the engine instruments along the top just below the compass, with the electronics relegated to a box below. I prefer the electronics higher up in more of a head-up display, since you'll be referring to them far more often than to the engine gauges—at least, if you pay much attention to depth, bottom contour, and position. I would also like to see the dual-reading (direct and indirect) compass 3 or 4 inches lower, which would make the direct-reading, forward portion of the compass visible when seated.

On the other hand, the wheel and throttles are well situated, although the throttles would be more ergonomic if they were inclined more horizontally than vertically. I would also like to see some type of retaining latch to hold up the folding footrest when it's not being used.

The console itself is quite high, so anyone shorter than I am might need to raise the seat a few inches for a better view over the bow, especially at 5 to 6 degrees of trim at cruising speed. The windshield is unusual in that it offers such a large area of glass relative to the supporting framework, which improves visibility ahead. The hardtop on our test boat was nicely tooled and crafted, with an additional radio box molded in above the helm.

Cabin

Despite all that walking room topsides, the Mako 293 still has a lot to offer down below. The appointments are fairly classy, with a textured-vinyl overhead liner covering the 71-inch-high cabintop. The 19-inch opening hatch lets in fresh air and daylight, and you out in an emergency. I didn't see the boat at night, but adding a few overhead lights would undoubtedly help you find your canned spaghetti after the late movie (just bring your own TV).

The forward V-berth, with its attractive print upholstery and adjustable reading lights, is definitely on the short side for adults, with 70 inches to starboard and just 53 inches to port. Unfortunately, the midcabin berth measures only 74 by 48 inches; it really should be reengineered to provide a minimal 76 inches of length.

The galley, located aft by the portside companionway entrance, boasts a long, laminated countertop, a single-burner electric stove, a small sink, and an undercounter refrigerator-freezer. There's also a trash container built into the counter aft and more storage space below. Mako's quality-control department never should have released this boat with the sloppy job of cutting out the hull liner around the refrigerator, or the even sloppier glasswork in the bilge below the cabin. This kind of poor quality

control is usually reserved for a few of the price builders, which Mako certainly is not.

The head, opposite the galley to starboard, features a toilet and lift-out sink spigot that doubles as a handheld showerhead. Unfortunately, Mako doesn't follow the industry trend by making its head of one or two seamless pieces of fiberglass. Rather, there are a couple of fiberglass components, including a floor tray that collects water around its perimeter (along the inboard bulkhead) with nowhere to drain, assorted pieces of faced plywood, and vinyl facing high up above the sink. In my opinion, this area also needs to be reengineered to provide the low maintenance and convenience that should be a given in a boat in this price range. The nicely tooled cabin liner that strengthens the hulls and reduces cleanup effort is a good start, but this all-fiberglass philosophy ought to extend to the head as well.

Performance Test

The wind was honking out of the southeast in Nantucket Sound as we headed out Bass River to run our speed trials. Unlike many outboard and sterndrive-powered boats, the Mako tracked well at high idle speeds in the channel, with little attention to the helm needed to stay on track. After working our way up to 3,000 rpm, it was apparent that we needed to find another venue for the higher speeds. The 3- to 4-foot seas took their toll, with a hard ride when the seas were anywhere near the bow—even with the trim tabs lowering the bow. With more deadrise and finer lines forward, we would have had a better time of it. I consider the low-overhead electronics box suspended from the hardtop liner a real safety hazard: both my companion (who's average height) and I had to be careful to stay well away from it in the rough seas. I would also like to see a higher windshield for greater protection from the elements and more aggressive nonskid; I slipped in my boat shoes several times in the rough seas.

On the other hand, the Mako's rather full sections bode well for efficiency and stability at trolling speeds. We took a lot of spray over the bow as well and, though you might not choose to go out in this stuff, you will likely have to beat your way home in it if you fish often enough. I did notice a tendency to chine-walk in the following seas, with the boat heeling over to starboard unless corrected for with trim tabs.

Back at the dock, the Mako showed some limitations since it was impossible to twist the boat with the twin outboards so close together. This can make docking the boat in a crosswind a challenge with a high freeboard (which provides all that nice interior volume), so make your approaches accordingly. On many such rigs, placing the rudder amidships and leaving it there lets you do just that. The proximity of the four-blade prop may also cause the high vibrations and pronounced thumping I felt from about 1,500 to 2,500 rpm. There appears to be space in the motor well to further separate the engines, which I would like to see done for both these reasons. You also could decrease draft by moving the engines outboard and up, following the hull's deadrise.

While hosing the boat off after the sea trial, I noticed a puddle accumulating at the helm station forward of the molded seat. Mako installed a drain in the bulkhead to help compensate for inadequate pitch in the deck tooling, but the drain should be recessed to do the job completely.

The Mako is a big seaworthy walkaround that will get you home safely in nasty weather, albeit at a slower speed than some of the competition. I would remove the head-banger overhead electronics box—which also interfered with my view ahead when I was standing—improve the nonskid, and further separate the motors.

The Mako has much to commend it for a family that fishes hard and also likes to do a little weekend cruising. The cockpit is well thought out; however, I prefer the higher sides and more aggressive nonskid of the new Wellcraft 290, another boat I tested recently. Access forward is great with the deep side decks; this is an ideal boat for bringing along little kids, seniors, and inveterate landlubbers who might just change their boating outlook after a few trips aboard such a people-friendly boat as this. There's a lot more usable deck area on the walkaround design, so make full use of it offshore. Mako needs to increase the quality control in a few areas, and I would want to see the changes to the helm and cabin mentioned previously—all of which would make this a fine boat that does its job well.

Mako 293 Walkabout Performance Test Results

RPM	Speed, knots	Speed, mph	Fuel Use, gph	Nautical mpg	Statute mpg	Range, nm	Range, statute miles	Noise Level, dBA	Trim, degrees
1,000	4.9	5.6	6.4	0.8	0.9	124	143	70	1
1,500	7.3	8.4	10.2	0.7	0.8	116	133	73	2
2,000	8.9	10.2	16.4	0.5	0.6	88	101	77	5
2,500	14.4	16.6	18.6	0.8	0.9	125	144	80	6
3,000	17.5	20.1	20.6	0.8	1.0	138	158	84	6
3,500	23.8	27.4	23.6	1.0	1.2	163	188	84	5
4,000	26.8	30.8	30.2	0.9	1.0	144	165	86	5
4,500	31	35.7	36.4	0.9	1.0	138	159	87	5
5,000	36.3	41.7	51	0.7	0.8	115	133	89	5
5,500	38.6	44.4	56	0.7	0.8	112	128	90	4
5,900	40.2	46.2	61.4	0.7	0.8	106	122	91	4

Test conditions: twin 250 Mercury EFI outboards, two passengers, three-quarter tank of fuel, 25-foot-plus depth, 1-foot seas, air temperature 66 degrees, and 200 pounds of gear. Test conducted October 14, 1998, in Bass River, Dennis, Massachusetts. Range calculated using 90 percent of the boat's 180-gallon fuel capacity. Sound levels taken at the helm.

1996 Pro-Line 231 Walkaround

Pro-Line 231 Walkaround Specifications	
LOA:	24'5"
Beam:	8'6"
Hull draft:	1'6"
Transom deadrise:	22 deg.
Weight:	3,700 lb. (hull only)
Fuel capacity:	140 gal.
Freshwater capacity:	15 gal.
Maximum power:	300 hp

It's not often I come across a boat that looks better the more I snoop around, but that was clearly the case with the 1996 Pro-Line 231 Walkaround. There are other walkarounds that look very similar from a few yards away, but some of them are disappointing compromises and not nearly so well thought out. It seems that Pro-Line's design team built this boat as though they intended it for their own use, and at a reasonable price.

The walkaround class has a lot to commend it, with a deep cockpit and recessed side decks leading forward—which makes it safe for the whole family, and opens up the entire LOA for topside use. A cross between a center-console and an old-style cuddy boat with a windshield forward, this layout combines some of the best of both designs. While a center console offers little protection for its occupants and most have no cabin space, the Walkaround's windshield offers ample protection from the elements for both the operator and a couple of guests—and there's more room to keep dry in the cabin. The helm is also situated far enough forward to allow a sizable cockpit aft.

Foredeck

Walking forward along the recessed side decks between the raised bulwark and the deckhouse sides, there's only one step up from the cockpit. This boat is a safe place for kids and seniors, with plenty of protection offered by its welded stainless steel bow

railing and grippy nonskid. The nonskid pattern used by Pro-Line has a fine but gritty surface, so it will keep you on your feet and still be easy to clean. The side decks are also wide and deep enough so that you can head aft for the gaff with two hands full of bent rod without hanging on, just like on a center console.

The raised trunk cabin forward, with its large opening hatch, makes the cabin roomy below, but it also serves as a nice seat for you and several of your closest friends—or it can be a great casting platform when the stripers are running in full force. Something worth mentioning about the Pro-Line is that the hardtop's forward aluminum supports mount on top of the cabin, out of the way of the side decks (a nice feature), and they also serve as a grab bar if you decide to ride up forward on the way out to the fishing (or sightseeing) grounds. The supports are positioned and sized so they don't interfere unreasonably with the operator's visibility— also a nice feature, but one that can't be taken for granted in this market.

Anchoring with this boat would be a snap with a molded-in anchor-line locker that drains overboard and an integral anchor pulpit with a stainless steel anchor-roller bracket. There's only a single 8-inch bow cleat—one too few in my opinion— and 8-inch side cleats on the raised bulwarks farther aft. The fuel fill is easy to reach just forward of the starboard side cleat.

In summary, the bow of the Pro-Line 231 is actually usable with its ample sitting and standing room and secure railing, not something you can say about many other 23-footers out there. Pro-Line's tooling, by the way, is first-rate with distortion-free surfaces everywhere in the hull and topsides.

Cockpit

This cockpit has been well thought out. Unlike other boats in this market, Pro-Line has recessed toe kicks along the sides that provide much better balance than if the liner came out flush with the coaming. There are also racks under the coaming for two rods on either side, and the flush rod holders have rubber covers attached to help keep rain and spray out of the bilge below. Cockpit coaming bolsters slide out for removal and stowage below, which means they will last much longer.

There's storage below the helm and passenger seats, and Pro-Line takes the eminently sensible but rare-in-the-industry step of recessing the drain hole so water doesn't puddle inside. Tackle drawers are located under both seats, so there's little wasted space inside. A Y-valve to port lets you fill the bait well or wash down the deck from a spigot recessed under the rail within handy reach. Access plates in the cockpit deck allow inspection of the fittings on the 138-gallon, 0.125-gauge aluminum fuel tank below. That's a lot of fuel for a boat this size; the tank stretches from the cabin's aft bulkhead to the engine.

More common sense is apparent in the layout in the stern, with a large bait well molded into the cockpit liner—there's even a perforated Plexiglas partition down the middle in case you want to segregate the bait. A sink with flip-up spigot is located next to the bait well to port back where it's needed—a very nifty design.

On the stern-drive model that we took for a spin, port and starboard lift-away seats were great places for relaxing on this dry-riding boat. They lift out for access to batteries, wiring, and bilge-blower plumbing inside. Mechanicals under the bait well area are neatly installed and should stay

dry because they are located inside a door rather than under a hatch.

Engine Compartment

A foam-lined engine box enabled good access to our test boat's 250 hp 5.7-liter LX MerCruiser Bravo II outdrive. A deck flange inside the engine-box cover keeps water out of the bilge, but I would also like to see a more effective flange where the engine box meets the aft bulkhead to keep water from dripping down on the aft end of the engine. As it is, engine corrosion could become a real issue unless this problem is fixed.

Our dealer encourages this power-plant combination because of the Bravo II lower unit's great durability, strength, acceleration, and speed. He reported that most Pro-Line 231s are sold with stern drives rather than outboards, because they are quiet, economical, long-lasting, and less expensive to buy, but he said an outboard is often cheaper to maintain.

Cabin

The Pro-Line's roomy cabin makes it an excellent family boat. It's the perfect place in which to get out of the sun or rain, and it makes the boat capable of an overnighter for a couple. There's a full-size berth, small sink, and alcohol burner; a portable toilet is tucked under the center section of the berth. The berth can also be repositioned on a stanchion for use as a dinette table. All this and a respectable 19-inch-wide companionway and 56 inches of headroom—not bad for a 23-foot boat with a trailerable 8-foot, 6-inch beam.

Construction

This boat has an all-fiberglass construction with foam-filled stringers and Divinycell-cored bulkheads and transom. The deck is fixed to the stringers with epoxy putty and the hull-to-deck joint is bonded with polyurethane adhesive for greater strength. Hull voids are foam-filled for a quieter ride and positive buoyancy.

This all adds up to a well-built boat, and it

shows in one of the best warranties in the business: a lifetime structural warranty (unfortunately, bottom blistering is not covered) that is also transferable within the first ten years. Pro-Line's tooling is first-rate with distortion-free surfaces everywhere in the hull and topsides.

Performance Test

Wherever you take the Pro-Line 231, you'll be pleased with its crisp and stable handling. Although this is not an offshore deep-V racing hull by any means, I found the ride to be very satisfactory and dry in the Sakonnet River's (Rhode Island) slight 1-foot chop. We managed 27 knots at 3,500 rpm and reached an unofficial top speed of just over 30 knots at 4,000 rpm.

The power steering was practically effortless and very responsive at 2½ turns lock-to-lock. The scuppers stayed dry when backing down—due to

floats that turn the scuppers into one-way valves— and so will your feet when closing in on a fish. The 250 hp MerCruiser accelerated strongly and put this fully fueled and outfitted 5,000-pound-plus boat up on plane easily at 2,500 rpm.

Unlike some other boats, Pro-Line's optional trim tabs have enough surface area to be immediately responsive. The helm station offers good all-around visibility through a well-designed, unobtrusive windshield. If it's maximum speed and efficiency you want, order the boat with a 5.7-liter LX MerCruiser B-3 duo-prop for about $2,000 more.

There are several other walkaround models on the market, but the Pro-Line is clearly a winner in this price range. Design details, construction materials and methods, and great handling result in a family and fishing package that's hard to beat.

1999 Wellcraft 290 Coastal

Wellcraft Marine is one of the largest U.S. boatbuilders with its line of 16- to 33-foot family fishing boats. The 290 Coastal is designed to have something for everyone: a comfortable cabin that sleeps

four, a raised bridge deck for a good view from the helm, and a large cockpit with ample room and features for the serious angler.

WELLCRAFT

1999 Wellcraft 290 Coastal Specifications	
LOA:	30'2"
Beam:	10'6"
Draft:	33" (motors down)
Displacement (dry):	9,000 lb.
Fuel capacity:	230 gal.
Water capacity:	47 gal.
Deadrise:	18 deg. (transom)

Cockpit

The boat's 9-foot-wide-by-7-foot-long cockpit is a comfortable 29 inches deep, which combines with excellent molded nonskid for a safe setting, even

with fish slime covering the deck. The recessed hull liner and the coaming bolsters create a toe kick for improved balance. Rod racks are provided under the gunwales and each side also gets a single, flush rod holder. Forward to port is a sink with storage cabinet below. Opposite is a livewell with a window and a tackle-drawer cabinet recessed behind the helm seat.

A pair of 4-foot in-deck fish boxes to either side aft drains via a nicely recessed sump. In what is probably an early-prototype problem, the starboard hatch on our boat had a too-deep flange outboard that scraped hard on the deck as it hinged open. Just aft of the bridge-deck step is a full-width storage compartment with three hatches above for excellent accessibility.

Aft to starboard is a 4-foot fold-up seat that tucks away in a molded inset along the transom. Behind the seat, which must be partially unhooked for access, is a door that opens to the motor-well interior. Inside are the battery switches, batteries, bilge pump, scupper drain lines, VRO tanks, fuel lines, and miscellaneous plumbing—all neatly installed. I would remount the battery switches (the most-often-accessed equipment inside) to port where there's a separate access door.

The fiberglass work in the bilge aft is neatly finished, with radiused inside corners where the stringers and bulkheads meet the hull. The carefully applied unidirectional fiberglass fabric is coated with a gray gelcoat for reasonably easy cleanup. I would add chafing protection where the plumbing (waterlines and wiring looms) exits the chase tube atop the hull stringer.

The 231-gallon, 0.19-inch-thick, 5052-grade aluminum fuel tank is installed on centerline below the cockpit. Wellcraft resists the temptation to foam in the tank (the easy way out), leaving ample space for air to circulate around the outside of the tank, which helps prevent corrosion and ensure long tank life. That's a good feature because otherwise the deck would have to be cut out for tank removal.

In the motor well, a plastic hatch (commonly used in the industry) opens for access to the mechanicals below. I would look for another solution, such as a gasketed and guttered fiberglass hatch, because the plastic hatch leaks—which was evidenced by the wiring loom below already showing signs of corro-

sion. Also aft are oil and gas fills, a freshwater hookup, a handheld shower, and a pair of well-recessed stern cleats to keep fishing-line snags to a minimum.

Foredeck

The Wellcraft's side decks are narrow at just 5 inches, but at least they're flat and covered with more of that great nonskid, as is the entire top of the trunk cabin. If you so choose, you can also climb up molded steps, open the center windshield, and step onto the foredeck; however, I would like to see a handrail near the windshield since the only other thing to grab onto is the light-duty anchor light atop the windshield.

The 22-inch-high bow railing, nicely crafted of flawlessly welded stainless, should be 6 to 8 inches higher at the bow, especially given the kind of casting duty this boat will see—at least in New England waters, where I tested it. I liked the simplicity and utility of the three 10-inch bow cleats, the integral pulpit with stainless anchor-roller frame, and the hawsehole leading to the anchor-rode locker below.

Bridge Deck–Helm

The single step up the bridge deck serves two purposes: increasing headroom in the midcabin berth below, and improving visibility with a greater height of eye for the skipper. The two-person, upholstered, starboard-side helm seat has the operator outboard immediately behind the wheel. Sitting down, I found legroom to be wanting, and the compass—located on top of the dashboard—was almost too high for me to see. The seat bottom flips up, creating a bolster and additional space for standing operation.

The helm console is thoughtfully laid out. The wheel and engine controls are easy to reach, whether the operator is seated or standing. Switches are above the wheel to port, followed by the engine instruments, which are arranged in pairs (my favorite layout) for easy viewing. Higher still is the electronics flat with ample space for a fancy suite of flashing digital toys for the ardent angler.

Other than the lack of legroom, my biggest complaint is that the dashboard area is all bright-white gelcoat, making sun glare a real problem—it reflects noticeably off the low aluminum-framed windshield. I would expect a serious fishing boat like this to have a higher windshield. Another potential problem is the wiring inside the console and below the wheel, which was already showing signs of corrosion and exposure to moisture, possibly a result of being located close to a plastic access door below the wheel. Opposite to port is a single companion seat, and both seats have lots of dry-storage room below.

Cabin

The companionway hatch folds neatly out of the way and the door folds open for easy access to the cabin. A full liner adds strength to the hull and makes for easy maintenance and cleanup. Carpets snap in place, which means they're also easy to remove for cleaning or eventual replacement. Generous 74-inch headroom, an off-white interior, opening ports, and a small, 15-inch overhead-opening hatch (a 20-inch would be better, providing an escape route) all help make the cabin seem bright and inviting. An inexpensive carpet-style liner covers the overhead and aft bulkhead, but it's carefully applied and gets the job done.

The galley has all the basics: a single-burner gas stove, refrigerator, space for a microwave oven above the sink in a cabinet, and plenty of storage space. Opposite to starboard is the enclosed head—manufactured in just two pieces of fiberglass for easy cleanup—with shower and vanity. Don't look for fancy joinery; drawers and doors are made of basic veneers—functional and straightforward.

Forward is a V-berth with a dinette table for two, which drops down to serve as a filler cushion to create a quasi double berth. I would extend the table insert another 4 inches to create a regulation 6-foot, 4-inch berth, but it's still not a bad arrangement for a 29-foot sportfisherman. The seatbacks also can be raised up and latched, creating a pair of single berths (74 inches to starboard and 69 inches to port,

as measured down the middle) for shorter adults or kids. This means that the boat can physically sleep six—but remember the height limitations.

Back aft under the helm, a 76-inch-by-39-inch midcabin berth makes good use of space and gets the job done for a couple or, given the modest (24 in.) headroom, two kids. Altogether, the cabin works well and offers sufficient accommodations and creature comforts for an occasional night or weekend afloat.

A small door in the forward bulkhead opens to the anchor locker, which is neatly glassed and finished, as was the rest of the hull that I was able to inspect. I would like to see some polyurethane adhesive used in the hull-to-deck joint, which would indicate a permanent, waterproof, and indestructible bond behind the self-tapping stainless screws evident every few inches. I would also prefer the use of solid backing plates rather than Wellcraft's washers to back up the bow cleats, particularly if they are used for towing.

Design and Construction

The Wellcraft has a conventional deep-V design with a pair of running strakes, the inboard pair running all the way to the transom. The bottom running surface continues unbroken aft all the way to the end of the motor well. This is a good idea because extra waterline length results in a better ride and, often, increased running efficiency (even with the extra wetted surface). The added buoyancy and hydrodynamic lift of the extended bottom results in a better trim angle as well. Reverse chines add lift and also form stability by shifting buoyancy outboard. The bottom, in station view (that is, viewing a section of the hull as though it were a slice of bread in a loaf), comes to a point at the keel; many designers round off or pad the garboard section to reduce both turning resistance and the tendency for the hull to trip in a hard turn.

Using a quality resin in a skin coat of hand-laid mat to prevent osmotic blistering, Wellcraft feels confident enough to warrant its hulls against blistering for a trendsetting five years. Foam-cored

Wellcraft 290 Coastal Performance Results

RPM	Speed, knots	Speed, mph	Fuel Use, gph	Nautical mpg	Statute mpg	Range, nm	Range, statute miles	Noise Level, dBA	Trim, degrees
1,000	4.7	5.4	4	1.2	1.4	243	438	61	1
1,500	5.7	6.6	6.4	0.9	1.0	184	332	64	1
2,000	7.6	8.7	8.4	0.9	1.0	187	337	69	2
2,500	9.4	10.8	11.3	0.8	1.0	172	310	74	5
3,000	14.8	17.0	15.6	0.9	1.1	196	353	78	6
3,500	21.5	24.7	18.4	1.2	1.3	242	435	79	5
4,000	24.9	28.6	24.2	1.0	1.2	213	383	80	5
4,500	30.2	34.7	28	1.1	1.2	223	402	84	4
5,000	34.7	39.9	35.6	1.0	1.1	202	363	85	3
5,600	38.2	43.9	50.4	0.8	0.9	157	282	88	3

Test conditions: twin Johnson 225 hp counterrotating outboards, half a tank of fuel, and two persons on board. Range calculated using 90 percent of the boat's 230-gallon fuel capacity. Sound levels taken at the helm.

stringers support the bottom of the 290's solid fiberglass hull. The transom is cored with high-density foam, practically eliminating the possibility of water absorption through bolt penetrations.

Performance Test

On our sea trial, the Wellcraft got up on plane smoothly and without fuss. Trimming the motors correctly is critical to both handling and speed. If a little too low by the bow, the boat comes out of turns unpredictably. If a little too high by the bow, seated visibility over the high dashboard area becomes an issue that I would resolve by raising the helm seat a few inches. Once properly trimmed out, the boat handled well and smoothly cut the few wakes we encountered.

The hydraulic steering was smooth but not very responsive at six turns lock-to-lock (about double the optimum, in my opinion). I found the throttle pod jockeying for position with my knee and, at 6 foot, 3 inches tall, legroom was on the short side for me. With the windshield set so far forward, I would also like to see it 8 inches higher for better protection from the elements. On the other hand, wheel and throttle positions were excellent—comfortably situated and easy to reach—and the large electronics panel allows ample space

for a fancy navigation suite. The accompanying table gives results of our performance test.

For an outboard sportfisherman, the Wellcraft 290 Coastal has much to offer. The level of fit and finish is about as good as the similarly priced competition. Deck safety, with the exception of the low bow railing, is quite good. The cockpit works well, as does the bridge deck, with the exception of the white dashboard and limited helm legroom.

The ruggedly constructed Edgewater lineup includes dual and center consoles from 13 to 26 feet, including this well-designed 22-foot walkaround.   EDGEWATER

Boston Whaler builds a full line of walkarounds, center consoles, and dual consoles from 12 to 34 feet. The unsinkable 26 Conquest walkaround shown is built using Whaler's Unibond construction, with low-density foam joining the hull and deck. This is one of the builder's newest models with an enclosed head, midcabin below the helm, and a galley; the boat will accommodate up to four people. Whalers are unbeatable for the attention to detail and, though quite expensive to buy, tend to do relatively well at resale time. As versatile a cruiser as a sportfisherman, the 26 Conquest's modified-V hull delivers a good ride in a chop, and twin Mercs up to 225 hp are available on this capable little canyon runner. BOSTON WHALER

Century is a small part of Yamaha, which can build anything from a grand piano to an outboard with equal facility. The builder produces a range of dual consoles, center consoles, bay boats, and walkarounds (like this 2300) from 19 to 32 feet. This is a good-looking, cleanly configured family cruising, fishing, or water-sports boat with the fuel capacity (130 gal.) and range to roam offshore with the big boys. The modified-V hull form delivers a good ride in a chop, and visibility from the raised helm is quite good. Well built using modern methods and materials, this model is built by a company that's steadily improving in terms of quality and performance. Up to 250 hp—Yamaha hp, of course—is available. CENTURY

Here is Century's biggest walkaround, a 3200 with a big 10-foot, 6-inch beam and a healthy 300-gallon fuel capacity to feed a pair of 250 hp Yamahas. A deep-V hull design is meant to slice through a chop with little fuss. A well-equipped boat, shore power, a full galley, and three separate handheld showerheads (for example) are included in the base price. Construction is of good quality on this offshore sportfisherman. CENTURY

Like Century, Cobia is owned by Yamaha. Cobia builds center and dual consoles, deck boats, and walkarounds like this 250. The all-fiberglass construction is engineered to last, and the boat comes well equipped for fishing and cruising. A V-berth with filler cushion, table, and optional portable toilet are located below. Single or twin Yamahas up to 300 hp are available. COBIA

Crestliner is a leading U.S. manufacturer of aluminum boats, and four walkaround models are included in the builder's extensive lineup. The 2360 SST shown here has a welded aluminum hull and outboard power up to 230 hp (stern-drive-powered walkaround models are also available from Crestliner) with a stern pocket for a kicker built in. Fuel capacity is 83 gallons, so the range won't be adequate for offshore fishing, but it's sufficient for inshore cruising and fishing. A small galley is an option, as is a portable toilet. A modified-V (17-degree transom deadrise), full-bowed hull will deliver a decent ride in a light chop if speed is moderated.

CRESTLINER

Mako has been building boats since Noah was a mess cook, and the product has been of uneven quality over the years under many changes of management, but the situation has improved recently. A wide range of walkaround, center-console, dual-console, and flats models from 15 to 31 feet are now being produced. Mako builds 23-, 25-, and 29-foot walkarounds; the smallest model, the 233, is shown here. In this type of design, with an integral motor well cum swim platform, 4 or 5 feet of the boat's length is given up to something other than the interior, which—from cockpit to pulpit—is more the size of a 19- or 20-footer with a bracket-mounted outboard. This 233 is a rugged, offshore-capable family sportfisherman-cruiser with a generous 145-gallon fuel capacity for those long runs to find the fish. A V-berth and toilet are located below.

MAKO

Here's one of Pro-Line's larger walkarounds, a 27-footer with stern-drive power and a standup head with shower. Outboard power is also available. All-fiberglass construction should result in long life and minimal maintenance.

PRO-LINE

Pro-Line builds a wide assortment of fishing boats, including four walkaround models from 20 to 30 feet. The 23 is a classic: intelligently and carefully designed, and offered for a reasonable price. Well equipped for fishing, the boat has a small galley, a two-person berth, and a sensible helm-station layout. A ten-year transferable hull warranty is included.

PRO-LINE

Pursuit, a sister company of Tiara, builds a range of intelligently designed and well-built fishing boats that double as capable cruisers. The 2870 walkaround shown here is a great fishing boat, with a deep-V bottom that delivers a good ride without requiring strenuous effort from the twin 225 hp outboards bolted on the integral motor well. Pursuit models are conventionally yet carefully built, with *practicality* and *ergonomics* the overriding watchwords. Other models in center-console, walkaround, and express layouts are available from 22 to 38 feet. The rare five-year hull warranty specifically addresses osmotic blistering, a commendable feature.

PURSUIT

Trophy, a division of Brunswick Corporation, builds center- and dual-console and walkaround fishing boats from 17 to 31 feet. The 2509 walkaround shown comes with more standard equipment than many of the other boats described in this chapter, and the hull is covered by a ten-year warranty. Fiberglass, foam-filled stringers won't rot out, and the hull design delivers a smooth, dry, and stable ride in a moderate chop. Power options include a single 225 hp and twin 150 hp Mercury outboards. The power is bracket-mounted, which means that you'll be buying a full 25 feet of usable boat with this Trophy, not a 21-footer with 4 or 5 feet of integral motor well.

TROPHY

Dual Consoles

The dual console is another excellent family day boat, with the whole boat from bow to stern available for passenger seating. There are twin consoles to port and starboard, and usually a folding windshield between the two that opens for access forward. Most boats have the helm to starboard and a passenger console to port. If the boat's big enough, say over 22 feet, the builder may even include a head compartment, usually below the port console. The dual console's open bow is one of its strong points, since passengers can be accommodated along the whole length of the boat. Most of these boats have a molded V-seat forward with storage below, as well as the centerline folding windshield we mentioned that opens for fore-and-aft access and closes to offer the cockpit some protection from the wind and sprays.

Planning ahead, on the builder's part, really helps out in terms of safety. There should be a bow railing forward to hang onto, and to prevent people from being tossed over the bow in case of a sudden stop. The helm position on a dual console is usually just forward of amidships, so the ride tends to be a bit harsher (hull designs being equal) in a chop than on a center console, the console on which is farther aft. The helm-forward design opens up the cockpit for water toys and passengers, though, so that's not a bad trade-off. Different builders divvy up the space differently, with some having a larger bow area and others a larger cockpit. Pick the one that best matches your needs. A dual console can make an excellent fishing boat, in toto, with the bimini lowered and center windshield opened up.

Edgewater 247 Dual Console Specifications

Length:	24'7"
Beam:	8'6"
Draft:	17" (hull)
Weight:	3,500 lb. (dry)
Fuel capacity:	150 gal.

Bob Dougherty, founder of Edgewater Powerboats, is something of a grand old man in certain boatbuilding circles, and not just because of the company's clever advertising campaign that capitalizes on his credentials. Dougherty built Boston Whalers for years before starting his own company in 1992, thinking—like other innovators in the industry—that he could do a better job once he was out on his own. The Edgewater 247 dual console (briefly called Marlin during the company's startup) is the result of Bob's ideas on boat design and construction; the similarities between the two lines are as striking as the differences.

To my eye, at least, there are common aesthetics between the two lines, including the convex bow sections and the windshield design. There's also their positioning in the market, with both lines priced at the high end. Boston Whalers present a higher-end appearance and are more nicely detailed inside, but the real difference is how the Edgewater is put together below the surface. Although Whaler relies on poured foam for structural integrity, as well as positive buoyancy in the event of a hull penetration, Edgewater relies on it solely for flotation—and if the fiberglass-to-foam bond still holds thirty years later, then that's great, too.

Construction

Edgewater uses what it calls a Permagrid construction process in which—once the hull is laid up and a fiberglass grid system is installed—foam is in-

jected in the grid and bilge cavities and allowed to harden; then the excess is trimmed off. The deck then goes on and it comes into contact with the top of the fiberglass grid system to which it is bonded. Fiberglass-to-fiberglass bonds, therefore, absorb the shear stresses as the boat works under load and in a seaway. Edgewater is also vocal about its use of all-fiberglass construction, eliminating the chances of wood-cored transoms, stringers, bulkheads, and decks turning into black mush due to poor quality control at the factory. There are many good ways to build boats using structural plywood, but it rots if it isn't properly built in; therefore, Edgewater is understandably and effectively trumpeting its unique woodless construction process.

Putting its money where its ad claims are, Edgewater offers what may well be the best guarantee in the business: a lifetime transferable warranty. The company also builds its boats to custom specifications, such as hull colors, seating arrangements, canvas, and railings.

Cockpit

Starting our tour aft at the integral motor well–swim platform, which takes up the aft 32 inches of the boat, a pair of plastic hatches provides access to the bilge below. Inside is the engine oil tank with a remote fill connection, gas line and filter, trim-tab actuator, bilge pump, and fish-box and bait-well drain-line plumbing. I would double-clamp the drain lines that are located below the waterline. You can clearly see how the boat is put together back there, with the foam poured in place and the deck assembly bonded to the stringer flats. I would like to see Edgewater do as good a job cleaning up inside as it does building the boat—a lot of fiberglass dust was still present after delivery to the dealer. Fuel and electrical lines lead out to the engine through a sealed flexible duct for a neat and protected installation. Grabrails are provided on either side outboard of the swim platform, where they do double duty as cleats when moored stern-to with crossed stern lines.

Built into the transom just forward of the engine well, three hatches lead to a huge 100-gallon fish box, a small bait-prep sink, and an 18-gallon livewell. Our boat also had a transom bench seat that folds out of the way, but it was mounted too low to fold down completely, which was annoying when standing far aft.

This boat has lots of deck space forward and aft, a result of the dual-console arrangement. The padded coamings aft are on the low side at 24 inches (not atypical of this class),and the 14-inch-high transom step to port definitely needs a gate of some kind, but things are functionally configured for a wide range of occupations. Side railings can be added if you're uncomfortable with the height.

The cockpit liner is recessed with inserts that create a toe kick, and three rod racks per side are built in. Two rod holders per side go with the 8-inch stern cleats, and the two pedestal chairs provided were comfortable and solid feeling. The aluminum fuel tank can be taken out through a removable hatch in the deck—an essential feature, unless perhaps the manufacturer has installed fiberglass or polypropylene tanks, which should last as long as the boat. The molded-in nonskid is excellent, just the right texture to make it grippy as well as easy to clean.

Helm

The starboard-side console is home to the helm, and it's simply yet functionally laid out. The tilt steering wheel is well positioned, so it's easy to reach whether the operator is seated or standing. The throttle is satisfactory for sitting, but a little low when the operator is standing; I would raise it a few inches, though a shorter person might find it fine as is. The compass is located atop the dashboard on a small flat, just where it should be for easy viewing. There's enough space left on the dashboard for basic electronics, although I would move the trim-tab switches to the right to make more room under the Yamaha tachometer and speedometer gauges.

The curved-glass windshield is well made, but I would like to see it about 6 inches higher to offer some protection when you're sitting down. The battery switch is below the breaker panel on the lower side of the dashboard; however, Edgewater needs to do a cleaner installation job because rough fiberglass was evident.

With the boat's two batteries under the helm console and a tackle cabinet to port, there's ample storage room under the two consoles. The radar arch will get in the way of walking fish aft from the bow, but it won't block your vision from the helm like too many other fiberglass arches can. Made of 2-inch-diameter aluminum pipe, this one will hold four rods, as well as antennas and even a radar.

Foredeck

Edgewater hasn't taken many shortcuts with this boat; however, there is a plastic deck hatch between the two consoles. The hatch gives underfoot, in contrast to the boat itself, which is sturdily built. Water also gets into the bilge compartment below. If a hatch is needed there at all, I would like to see it made of nonyielding, guttered fiberglass.

A step up from the cockpit level, the foredeck area has a pair of seats built in forward of the dual consoles, with storage space below. Another deck hatch, constructed of nicely tooled fiberglass, leads to a storage area under the raised foredeck. Three plastic access hatches in the liner lead to more storage bins and to the anchor-line locker in the bow. Two more cleats handle the bow and anchor lines, and a stiff stainless railing gives you something to hang onto forward.

Performance Test

As soon as we pulled away from the slip, I knew I liked this boat. Although many deep-Vs wander about their heading at slow trolling speeds, the Edgewater tracked like an arrow down the channel at 1,000 rpm. With a modified-V hull (20 degrees of transom deadrise), the boat was also stable when I stepped on board at the dock, and good form stability is an important ingredient in the boat designer's recipe for comfort and safety. If it's either too stiff or too tender, you automatically have an uncomfortable, tiring boat. Edgewater has also extended the hull bottom all the way to the transom, which might partially account for the great tracking and smooth ride. In fact, I have yet to see a boat lengthened on the waterline that didn't benefit from the experience in terms of range, handling, and ride.

With a 225 hp Yamaha Saltwater Series outboard, the boat was quiet and smooth-running. Our motor seemed to be adjusted a notch or two too low because it kicked up a lot of spray unless it was tilted practically out of the water—this likely made the boat slower than it otherwise would have been. Perhaps on the upside, the boat also backed very well, possibly because the prop wash was directed more completely under the boat instead of partially against the transom.

It was flat calm on our test ride out of Clinton Harbor, Connecticut, but fortunately we had a few Maine-style yachts running around. We headed for one and promptly launched off its 2- to 3-foot wake at 30 mph, landing surprisingly fuss-free. A few other boats in this size range ride every bit as smoothly—like my own 22-foot Grady-White dual console—but the Edgewater delivers a very comfortable ride indeed.

Dual-console layouts make a lot of sense because they make great fishing boats—perhaps better than center consoles with more open deck space—as well as excellent family boats for cruising and skiing.

When we went through a few ad hoc obstacle courses defined by lobster-pot buoys and channel markers, the boat consistently went exactly where I pointed it, handling very well at all speeds. Backing down at 2,000 rpm, nary a drop of water made it into the motor well, let alone the cockpit, which—like the fish boxes and storage compartments—gravity-drain overboard.

We managed 28 mph at 4,000 rpm (approximately 11 gph), 31 mph at 4,500 rpm, and 39 mph at 5,500 rpm (approximately 27 gph) with two passengers and seven eighths of a tank of fuel on board. This is certainly adequate performance for most families and hard-core anglers but, if not, the twin 150s with their added speed and fuel-burning capacity are an option. This same engine transformed the Edgewater into a credible acrobat as well, turning full circle at cruising speed in just 10 seconds at about two boat lengths. Range will be better than average for this class with a 150-gallon fuel capacity. The Yamaha was impressively quiet at just 82 dBA at 4,000 rpm, and some of that could be attributed to the wind.

The Edgewater is a boat you will want to pass down to the kids as a family heirloom. Tooling is first rate; you know this is a quality boat as soon as you step on board, and a close look generally confirms your first impression. The few exceptions included the dirty bilges, the anchor-chain pelican hook installed backward, and the windshield supports shipped with screws missing. Fixing these areas would make life easier for the dealer, who can easily remedy the problems before delivery to the customer. You might want to pay for the builder to apply an off-white gelcoat inside the boat to reduce sun glare from the bright-white interior.

The company has a lot of confidence in its product, and it shows in its lifetime hull warranty—something other builders should offer but don't, most likely because the quality just isn't there. The Edgewater is solidly built, thoughtfully designed with a smooth-riding yet stable hull form, and good-looking with classic, no-nonsense utilitarian lines.

Boston Whaler's 18 Ventura is the middle of three 16- to 21-foot dual consoles from that builder. Like all but the biggest Whalers, the 18 Ventura is built using low-density foam to support and join the hull and deck liners, which results in a very quiet and unsinkable boat. According to the builder, although the hull itself only weighs 1,350 pounds, the positive buoyancy of a swamped boat will support 4,200 pounds before submerging. Fit and finish is top-shelf and the price reflects the product's high quality, as well as the line's premium name. BOSTON WHALER

Grady-White is a well-known boatbuilder of center-console, walkaround, express, and dual-console family fishing boats from 18 to 33 feet. The firm harkens back more than four decades to its wooden boatbuilding roots in rural North Carolina. Gradys are solidly and heavily built using pressure-treated plywood structural members and thick fiberglass laminates. All Gradys have C. Raymond Hunt Associates hull designs, with warped-V bottoms that deliver a smooth ride in a chop, are stable at slow speeds, and run without trim tabs at moderate, efficiency-enhancing trim angles. The 223 dual console, one of which I have owned, is a great family fishing, cruising, and skiing boat with excellent seakeeping ability. GRADY-WHITE

Century builds walkaround, dual-console, center-console, and bay boats from 19 to 32 feet. The Century 2100 shown is the lone dual-console model, but it looks like a winner with a clean, open layout and pleasantly fresh looks. Centurys are built sans wood with all-fiberglass, foam-injected stringer systems, and the hull sides are actually supported by fiberglass ribs. The company offers an unusual ten-year hull warranty, so it must be confident in its construction quality, which has improved markedly in recent years. CENTURY

Sea Fox is a good example of a builder who is delivering better (and regularly updated) boats for a lot less money than many of the high-priced name brands. High-density, foam-cored transoms; foam-filled fiberglass stringer systems; and a ten-year warranty (including blistering) are standard. Bay, flats, walkarounds, and dual- and center-console models from 16 to 25 feet are produced, including 18- and 20-foot dual consoles. The 185 dual console shown has a modified-V bottom with a fine entry that produces a comfortable ride in an inshore chop. The boat is nicely equipped with standard features including a bait well, boarding platform, and ladder. SEA FOX

Scout offers a well-made lineup of fishing and family boats ranging from 14 to 28 feet, including three dual consoles. The 202 Dorado shown, with its distinctive broken sheerline, has an excellent fishing layout, especially with the optional bimini top lowered. The open bow makes the full length of the boat available for passengers. This is a beamy yet good-running boat with a generous fuel capacity of 70 gallons. Wood-free, rot-proof construction is used, including the one-piece hull stringer and deck system.

SCOUT

Maine-Style Bass Boats and Cruisers

Maine-style boats have been around for many years, and the class is typified by a small cabin and a large open cockpit with either a windshield and bimini top or a hardtop. These boats are often intended for overnighters and weekends afloat, so expect the cabin and amenities to be spartan. These are often very pretty boats, with their low profiles helping out in both the looks and seaworthiness departments. The Dyer 29 (in production since 1958) is an early bass boat that was as good for day cruising or picnicking as it was for fishing for stripers. This Maine-style picnic boat

has a low foredeck flush with the gunwales (and little headroom inside), an engine box amidships, and a huge open cockpit ready for a little al fresco dining in the sun. Like the Dyer 29, many of these boats have Down East roots with round bilges and full keels on their semidisplacement hulls providing a gentle, seakindly motion. Some, like the Mainship Pilot series, have hard-chine planing hulls with full keels. These traditional-looking boats relinquish interior volume for a sweet sheer line, less sail area, and a low center of gravity, improving their seaworthiness.

Dyer 29 250 HP Yanmar

Seeing change everywhere, Heracleitus tells us that you can't step into the same stream twice; the rest of us see permanence. But even the venerable ancient Greek philosopher might change his mind if he only knew about the Dyer 29. First tooled up in 1956 by Bill Dyer, the 29 was an immediate success with her sweet lines, able deep-water performance, and rugged low-maintenance—to say nothing of newfangled—fiberglass construction. This makes

the Dyer 29 the powerboat with the longest production run in the industry, and four hundred boats sold to date testify to the soundness and popularity of the design.

This is a semicustom boat, built with female fiberglass tooling and available in three basic configurations: a flush-deck bass boat and a trunk-cabin sportfisherman, both with an engine box, and a flush-deck cruiser with a windshield and either a

Dyer 29 Specifications	
LOA:	28'5"
Beam:	9'5"
Draft:	2'5"
Fuel capacity:	132 gal.
Water capacity:	28 gal.
Standard power:	Volvo TAMD 41 200 hp

bimini or hardtop with full enclosure. Cabin layouts are likewise negotiable. People who buy these boats go day or weekend cruising and appreciate a good seaboat when they see one.

The Dyer 29 is a comfortable and economical cruising or fishing boat, and it is available as a flush-deck bass boat or as an express cruiser with either a bimini or hardtop. The Dyer 29 is built by the Anchorage in Warren, Rhode Island.

Cockpit

The 7-foot cockpit sole and liner are nicely tooled of a single piece of fiberglass for no leaks and low maintenance. Epoxy-coated washboards raise the coaming height to 25 inches, which is on the low side, but a transom board and seat offer sufficient security aft for passengers in a seaway. A pair of deck hatches leads to the lazarette below, where bilges are clean and mostly dry. Hatch gutters drain via hoses to the bilge, which makes the plumbing less complicated. When we hosed down the boat after the sea trial, the deck had sufficient camber and pitch to drain quickly through the flush-corner scuppers.

Foredeck

Unlike the majority of boatbuilders, Dyer designs its forecastles to be inhabited by accident-prone humans. The stainless steel bow railings are 34 inches high at the bow, which combines with grippy molded nonskid for a very safe environment for kids and landlubbers. The bow cleats are 12 inches

long, so you won't run out of room when tying off two lines to each cleat (which happens regularly on many other boats). The teak pulpit looks classy and works well for housing the anchor, and it doesn't interfere with visibility from the helm, as on other boats with lower stations.

Engine Room

A large hatch opens to the engine room, with a second smaller hatch forward for access to the batteries against the forward bulkhead. Dyer has done a great job making the fuel filter-separator, seacock and raw-water strainer, and freshwater and oil dipsticks easily accessible.

A fiberglass drip pan helps keep the bilge clean, and dripless shaft seals keep the space relatively salt-free, boding well for low maintenance. A down-angle gear allows the engine to mount flat, reducing the necessary sole height for a lower profile. Aluminum fuel tanks are outboard and they appear to have sufficient space for airflow, which reduces the chance of external corrosion from developing. I would still like to see polyethylene tanks rather than aluminum because they last forever, essentially, and are offered in sizes large enough for this boat.

The engines are soft-mounted to the fiberglass hull stringers, which have a steel plate glassed in and tapped out to receive the engine-mounting bolts. The bilges are ground smooth and painted with gray gelcoat for a neat appearance. About the only detail I would change is to use high-pressure fuel lines rather than the soft rubber hoses and clamps for added chafing resistance and fitting security.

Bridge Deck

Flush over the whisper-quiet Yanmar, the Dyer's 7-foot-long bridge deck eliminates the need for an engine box, resulting in an uncluttered, user-friendly deck space. Our test boat had an L-shaped upholstered lounge to port. The helm is opposite to starboard on the boat's give-way side. The single pedestal helm seat leaves a lot of free deck space to starboard for congregating out of the weather, under the full soft enclosure.

Helm

It's fitting that the big Ritchie compass dominates the Dyer's helm, since there was a time when a compass and depth-sounder were all you had to navigate with—and a stopwatch. I actually prefer this kind of navigational simplicity because it makes you pay more attention to time, course, and current than you would with large-screen GPS plotters and radars telling you where you are to within the thickness of your blister-proof gelcoat.

If you want to add a GPS plotter, radar, and fancy sonar, you'll have to array them around the companionway wherever they fit best, since an electronics flat is not molded into the dashboard. This works well on the Dyer, giving owners the flexibility to mount everything where they want it, unlike on molded flats.

Our test boat had a 24-inch stainless Destroyer wheel and dual-lever engine controls comfortably situated directly at my fingertips whether I was seated or standing up. I would choose the optional bulkhead-mounted footrest; however, the seat was well positioned some 27 inches off the deck for a great all-around view through the beautifully crafted, varnished-teak windshield.

The autopilot has an electronic gyroscope motion detector mounted aft under the cockpit, which—being mounted well aft of the hull's pivot point—immediately senses yaw. It's available as an option, but there have been few takers. The secret,

according to the boat's owner, is to let the unit stabilize at the dock so it knows what zero motion is, and to mount it well aft enough to be more sensitive to the hull's lateral motion. The autopilot works off GPS for simple course corrections, which makes the boat absolutely controllable at 17 knots in a 2-to 4-foot quartering sea. That seems to solve the main bugaboo of a Down East–style, full-keel hull tracking in a following sea.

Cabin

Dyer allows the buyer to choose from many options for the cabin decor and layout. Most boats are laid out along the general lines of our test boat, which has the galley to port, with a two-burner alcohol stove, sink, refrigerator-freezer, and several drawers and cabinets. Located opposite is an enclosed head with toilet and lots of shelf space, but no shower or sink—perhaps the designer thought it redundant to have two sinks only 4 feet apart. A V-berth is forward with a filler cushion, creating a 76-inch double bed. Headroom is tight at 70 inches, but I could stand up in the galley with the companionway opening directly above. A 20-inch opening hatch above and opening side ports let in plenty of light and fresh air. Decor was distinctly nautical with navy-blue fabrics, a padded white nylon liner overhead, and teak trim and paneling. The electrical service panel is directly inside the companionway for easy access from either the helm or the cabin.

Performance Test

Bill Dyer would have been happy to see his 11-knot workhorses (originally powered with flat-6 gasoline engines or a 120 hp Perkins diesel) turn into the 20-plus-knot mini-luxury yachts they are today. Thanks to modern, lightweight, high-speed diesels (like our test boat's 250 hp Yanmar), an owner now has the option of impressive speed and range without the bulk of a cast-iron engine. Less weight under the hatch means that less fuel is needed for these speeds, so our engine-fuel consumption (in mpg) calculations happily spiral downward.

With the fuel tanks outboard of the engine, trim will change little as the liquid load changes. Placing fuel tanks under the cockpit has the opposite effect, with the boat invariably riding on its waterline only when it's full of fuel.

You have to ride on a round-bilge, semidisplacement hull like this to be reminded of how comfortable the motion is. At 17 knots—an easy cruise for a Dyer 29 with 250 hp—sound and motion levels are low, making for a pleasant cruising environment. In the 2- to 3-foot seas we encountered on Narragansett Bay, the ride in a head sea was smooth and bone dry. You'll work a little more at the helm in a quartering sea but, at a comfortable 17 knots, it's not really an issue—things get dicey only when you try to run at around 25 knots or faster downsea.

Sound levels were low—66 dBA at the helm at 1,000 rpm and 83 dBA at 3,600 rpm—which produced a continuous cruise speed of just under 20 knots with half a tank of fuel and two passengers. In fact, sitting near the helm, the exhaust noise was louder than the engine noise radiating through the well-sealed bridge deck. We managed 22 knots at full throttle. Dyer typically installs left-hand propellers (which back to starboard) in its 29s, reasoning that most people tie up starboard side-to because that's the side on which the helm is located.

For a cruising yacht that is comfortable, economical to operate, reassuringly solid in a seaway, and pretty as a picture, it's hard to beat the Dyer 29—it's a classic for all these reasons and many more. A long list of custom options is available, including a hardtop (watch the topside weight), automatic fire-extinguishing system, and teak and holly sole.

1997 Hinckley 36 Picnic Boat

The Hinckley Company is well known in yachting circles as a builder of custom and semicustom yachts—mostly sail but with more emphasis recently on power—and some people would be surprised to know that Hinckley has been building in fiberglass since 1959, when the technology was in its infancy. It seems only fitting that the company is still a leader in the use of cutting-edge boatbuilding processes. No less astute as marketers than as builders, Hinckley has hit the jackpot with a novel combination of high-tech and nostalgia in the form of its Picnic Boat.

On a side note, although *picnic boat* is a term more and more associated with Hinckley, when I was a Cape Cod Bay charter boat mate in the 1960s it was commonly used to describe any day boat with an engine box.

In production since 1994, this 36-footer's design concept isn't all that revolutionary, but the total package is. Advanced construction techniques and materials produce a very strong lightweight hull. Waterjet propulsion results in a mere 18-inch draft, low vibration and noise levels, and—with its patented control system—extraordinary maneuverability. The layout is quintessential day boat, with a large cockpit, small cabin, and just enough pilothouse to get in out of the rain. I, for one, could not remain indifferent to those sweet Down East lines complemented by exquisite joinery and a strongly built hull.

The Picnic Boat is built using a patented resin-infusion procedure called SCRIMP, which calls for stacking all the layers of fiberglass and coring materials when dry, covering them with plastic, and then applying a very high vacuum to draw the resin through the entire structure in one operation. This makes the hull a true one-piece, primary-bonded unit of tremendous integrity.

The hull's layup starts conventionally with gel-coat applied to the mold followed by a layer of resin-saturated chop to prevent print-through of the subsequent layers of fiberglass fabric. Next, the two halves of the hull mold and the transom are bolted together, and the keel area is laid up by hand. Then the high-tech part begins: successive layers of fiberglass and Kevlar are put in place dry, followed by thick (1.25 in.) balsa coring in the bottom and 1-inch Core-Cell foam coring in the sides, followed by more fiberglass and Kevlar. Finally, prefabricated foam-cored hull stringers and ribs, which come with a surrounding layer of fiberglass bonded in place, are secured to the hull.

The vacuum-assisted resin-infusion apparatus is assembled in place, with plastic tubes carefully positioned to provide a steady, even supply of resin on one side of the mold. Vacuum lines along the other side are put in place to draw the resin from the tubes and disperse it evenly through the hull laminate. The final step is placing a plastic bag over the entire works and sealing it securely; the vacuum is applied and the resin starts to flow. Hinckley has this process down to a science—it was building hull no. 82 of the Picnic Boat during my early-summer 1998 visit, but the process is no less exacting for its expertise.

Why go to all this trouble? For the workers, the air is safer to breath since the entire resin-infusion process takes place inside a plastic bag. For the owner, the 65:35 ratio of fiberglass to resin versus the hand-layup's 35:65 proportions results in an extremely efficient, rugged, and lightweight laminate. There is no need for heavy nonstructural mat between layers of fiberglass, and SCRIMP infuses the entire hull in one action so there are no secondary bonds to weaken the structure. Hinckley also uses a premium vinylester resin that is stronger and more resistant to osmotic blistering than the general-purpose polyester resins commonly used. The decks and cabin are built using the same process.

Propulsion

If construction is the first remarkable aspect of the Hinckley Picnic Boat, then the boat's propulsion system is the other. The design criteria called for shoal draft; a quiet, low-vibes environment to keep the sailors who buy these boats happy; and extraordinary maneuverability. After doing a little homework, the obvious answer for Hinckley was Hamilton waterjet propulsion.

Coupled with a quiet, lightweight, and efficient 350 hp Yanmar diesel, this is a most successful propulsion system. The waterjet on this keel-less boat keeps draft to the depth of the hull. The absence of underwater running gear practically eliminates vibration, even at speed. Once you learn to handle the boat in close quarters, you can maneuver this single-screw (or is it single-impeller?) Picnic Boat with far more finesse, control, and sheer verve than you can any twin-screw inboard. Stalling on weeds is remedied by reversing the impeller for a quick flush. There's also the simple pleasure of being able to ignore lobster-pot buoys or just run right over them.

Cabin

The Hinckley is a day boat or possibly a modest weekender for a couple. It has a small cabin with 69 inches of headroom; a V-berth forward; a hanging locker; cupboards and shelves; and a utilitarian galley with a cold-plate refrigerator, deep sink, and two-burner alcohol stove. The enclosed head opposite the galley has a sink with a pull-out faucet that doubles as a showerhead, and a manual flush head. A panel folds down for easy access to the back side of the helm station with its neat wiring and precise mechanical layout. Especially considering the price, we should see more effort spent sanding and smoothing the bilges and under-berth storage spaces, though. The accommodations are comfortable and aesthetically pleasing, and fit and finish is excellent.

Helm

If you like brightwork, you'll appreciate the boat's helm station with its wondrously wrought teak dashboard, companionway opening, and instrument panel. The helm is well designed with the wheel comfortably positioned in front of the sliding helm seat and the engine and waterjet controls at your fingertips to starboard. The compass is a little small for a 36-footer but is at the right height and directly forward of the wheel for easy reference. The electronics suite is nicely angled toward the operator, and the engine instruments are unobtrusively situated down below to port. For added comfort and flexibility, I would opt for a tilt wheel, which is affixed at a 10-degree angle from horizontal.

Opposite the helm to port is a back-to-back seat with storage space below. A pair of opening hatches overhead hinges open for ventilation, a necessity because the windshield and side windows are fixed (and, presumably, leak-proof); however, Hinckley is working on an opening-side-window design. Hinckley even acoustically insulates the hardtop undersides to diminish the drivetrain reverberation effect (engine and exhaust noise) inside the pilothouse area.

A large deck hatch, flawlessly finished on both sides, opens for access to the bilge below. A level subfloor (and deep hatch gutters) keeps everything dry inside, and there's space for a water heater and enough supplies to turn this day boat into a coastal cruiser if necessary.

Cockpit

The cockpit is really the attraction here, at least from a passenger's perspective. It comprises the majority of the boat, so there's lots of room to maneuver, even with the large engine box directly in the middle. The teak sideboards—a full 32 inches high—make this a safe and secure environment for kids, seniors, and landlubbers in general, who will be tempted to break with personal tradition and go boating with the incentive that the Hinckley offers. The cockpit is self-bailing, even with the boat's low sheerline. A very comfortable transom settee aft, which easily seats four, beckons. The nonskid on deck is excellent—it grips boat shoes tenaciously, but proves relatively easy to keep clean.

Engine Compartment

Hinckley pays attention to matters below decks as well, with more precision engineering in the engine compartment. The engine box, lined with Soundown acoustic lead and foam material (as is the bottom of the cockpit deck and the inside of the cockpit liner), protects the engine, quiets noise levels, and doubles as a staging area for a clambake. In addition to being well insulated, the engine box is gasketed where it meets the deck, eliminating rattles and further reducing noise transmission.

The 350 hp Yanmar fits neatly inside, with all service points readily accessible. Rugged, solid-fiberglass engine beds support the engine's soft mounts, an excellent vibration-attenuation combination. The seacock is difficult to reach, but a T-handle rod attached to the valve would be an easy fix. As added safety measures, I would like to see protective shields installed over the fan belts on the forward end of the engine, and a cover over the jackshaft connecting the transmission to the waterjet.

Access plates aft in the cockpit lead to the bilge, fuel filter-separator, and fuel-distribution manifold. Two transom-liner doors lift out for access to the steering gear and to the exhaust silencer, which exits through the boat's bottom—another ingredient in a very effective sound-deadening recipe.

Performance Test

First seeing the boat out of the water, I would have expected a fairly harsh ride in a chop with the low deadrise forward and relatively flat sections aft. Once on our sea trial, though, I was pleasantly surprised at how offhandedly the Hinckley tamed the 2- to 3-foot wakes we carved through at 22 knots in Southwest Harbor, Maine. Chalk it up to the boat's moderate beam-to-length ratio.

I recorded a top speed of just over 26 knots with a full tank of fuel and three passengers aboard. Figure on a comfortable 22-knot cruise at a reasonable 83 dBA helm sound level. At idle, the Yanmar's noise level was a subdued 57 dBA, making the cockpit conducive to normal conversational tones at slow speeds. Visibility from the helm was excellent, and the overhead hatches scooped up plenty of fresh air on our balmy test day.

Directional stability, or course-keeping, in a following sea was not nearly as good as most conventional inboards, which have keels and rudders to keep them pointing in the right direction; however, fins placed along the bottom at the transom helped. Maneuverability, on the other hand, was phenomenal, with the boat turning and stopping on a dime. Just drop the waterjet bucket for instant reverse, with no transmission shifting to shock and wear the engine.

Dockside, the boat is as maneuverable as a helicopter, able to move in any direction—including sideways—once you learn to back to port when the wheel is to starboard. This boat is a real pleasure to drive, and it's difficult not to show off a little. The builder has recently patented its JetStick control, which is essentially a joystick that controls both waterjet thrust and the bow thruster to simplify operation. Hinckley Yacht Holdings's Little Harbor series also uses the JetStick series in its Whisperjets.

Hinckley is at the top of its game in terms of powerboat construction and engineering quality, and the steep price reflects the brand's gravitational pull among the well heeled. It's not perfect; the print-through in the gelcoat detracts from what should be a mirror-smooth hull. On the other hand, there isn't a better-built production boat on the market. Hinckley sells direct—there is no dealer network.

The full keel on this built-down, displacement Maine-style hull offers some obvious advantages in terms of protection for the running gear. Note the faired full keel, which provides cleaner water-flow to the propeller.

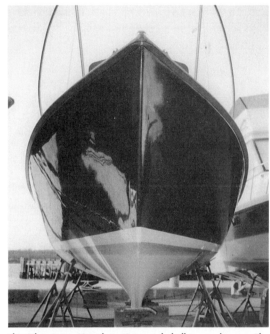

This Pilots Point 42 with its Maine-style hull is seen bow-on. The hull's clean entry and round bilges are clearly visible. This shape accounts for the hull's easy motion in a seaway and for the boat's inability to pound in a head sea, at least at semidisplacement speeds. All those curves, which blend together seamlessly in plan, section, and profile view, account for the boat's good looks and timeless appeal.

The Mainship 34 Pilot is a hard-chine version of a Maine-style cruiser, with a full keel and a hull well suited to operating at semi-displacement speeds. Mainship produces two express-style yachts, 30- and 34-footers, and 39- and 43-foot trawlers. Mainships are ruggedly built, intelligently laid out, comfortably appointed, and as reasonably priced as can be expected in today's market.

MAINSHIP

This Royal Lowell–designed, 28-foot Nauset bridge deck has much going for it. The hull form is as good as it gets in the Maine-style tradition, producing a very comfortable, economical ride, and the layout creates a large cabin with a low profile. The engine box is well aft in the saloon, and the flybridge deck is contoured to provide headroom where it's needed down below. This hull is also available with express and conventional flybridge layouts. Nauset Marine, in the boat business for more than forty years, is located in picturesque Orleans on Cape Cod.

Here's another Royal Lowell design, a Nauset 42 aft cabin. Actually, the hull is Royal Lowell's design and the aft cabin layout is Nauset Marine's. I owned one of these hulls when they were being built by Bruno & Stillman in the 1970s, and I recall the boat's superb seaworthiness as a commercial fishing and charter boat: 12 hours of charter fishing on Cape Cod consumed all of 35 gallons of fuel per day with a 265 hp GM 6:71 diesel producing a 12-knot cruise. A pair of modern 300 hp lightweight diesels—which, incidentally, together weigh about as much as the 6:71—produces a 17-knot cruise and maybe 20 knots wide open. A more comfortable off-shore-capable cruiser would be difficult to find.   NAUSET MARINE

Here's that big, beamy Carroll Lowell design, the Pilots Point 42. A great seaboat with more room (with a 15-foot beam) than the average 42-footer, it also takes more power to push one along than, say, the 13-foot, 8-inch-wide 42-footer (see left photo) designed by Carroll's brother Royal. A single 700 to 800 hp diesel with a large, slow-turning propeller is probably the optimum power for this semi-displacement hull, which operates best in the 16- to 22-knot range; its full keel and limited planing surface significantly decrease running efficiency at higher speeds. This Pilots Point 42 is beautifully finished and is a true lobster yacht.   JONATHAN KLOPMAN

Express Cruisers

Express cruisers, or open-style yachts, are a popular style for people who like the convenience of the helm station within a few steps of the lower-deck accommodations and the cockpit. About half the length of the boat is dedicated to the cabin on the lower deck; the rest is open topside space, including a bridge deck protected by a windshield and a cockpit aft. Either a canvas bimini top or hardtop provides protection from wind and rain. The express cruiser's raised bridge deck typically includes the helm station, usually to starboard, and a lounge or pilot chair opposite. The deck is raised for two reasons: to improve the skipper's visibility and to add headroom for a midcabin stateroom below.

The engine room is either below the bridge deck or below the cockpit. If the engines are below the bridge deck, then the cockpit can be low enough to easily fish from. If they are shifted aft, below the cockpit, then the accommodations can also be pushed aft, providing room for a midcabin below the raised bridge deck above. Express cruisers with aft engine rooms make excellent use of space, with either stern drives or V-drives providing propulsion power. Plus, putting the engines in the stern makes for a quieter interior. The express cruiser layout starts in the 24-foot range and now runs up to the 100-foot range. An exotic example of the Express Cruiser taken to its limit is the Sunseeker Predator 80, which has a garage in the stern to stow a tender out of sight.

The cockpit is generally down a step or two from the bridge deck, and usually features convertible lounge seating and a sunpad, an icemaker or wet bar, a transom door leading to a swim platform, a handheld shower, and a swim ladder. Without the topside weight of a big superstructure and flybridge, the express cruiser rolls and weighs less than a convertible of the same overall size. However, the express gives up the convertible's enclosed saloon and superior flybridge sightlines.

The cockpit on some express-style cruisers is rigged to fish with rod holders, bait prep stations, fish boxes and livewells, and other amenities. Sea Ray's Amberjack series and Tiara's line of cruising yachts are good examples. There's only one helm station on most of these boats; if the boat isn't properly designed, visibility ahead can be a problem if the bow rises excessively when climbing on plane (especially) and cruising.

1998 Chaparral Signature 300

CHAPARRAL

Chaparral is a leading U.S. builder of express cruisers, and our 1998 test boat was its flagship Signature 300—note that the photo is of the 2001 model. The company has a lot of experience building this type of boat, and it shows in the excellent cruising layout and arm-long list of standard features. Designed to fit as much usable interior volume as possible into a stylishly sleek profile, this class of boat—as typified by the Signature 300—

often has many features that appeal to a cruising family on a budget.

Cockpit

Let's start the tour aft. Our test boat had an extended, 2-foot-long swim platform mounted 10 inches lower than the hull's 16-inch integral platform. A cooler and fender storage brackets are built into the upper integral platform, and a carpet-lined compartment (I would change this to a fiberglass liner with a drain leading overboard) to starboard conveniently holds the battery switches and shore-power cable connector.

A plastic transom door opens to the cockpit and, at 27 inches high (6 inches higher than other boats of this class), it actually affords a reasonable measure of safety for the boat's occupants. To port, a 25-quart cooler fits neatly in a recessed bin under the coaming. Also to port is a storage bin under a double-sink unit, lined with extruded plastic—the only detail missing is a drain line. A nicely contoured U-shaped lounge seat, covered with high-quality 34-ounce upholstery, is also aft. A table with twin stanchions fits into a pair of deck sockets. Chaparral even provides cup holders and rod holders.

One feature that needs attention is the nonskid: it's too smooth to provide adequate grip, and the plastic deck hatches—which will likely be walked on routinely—are smoother still. I would either change to a more aggressive pattern in the tooling or apply an aftermarket nonskid treatment.

Engine Room

The twin 240 hp 5.0-liter EFI MerCruisers fit snugly (which means they're crowded) aft in the Chaparral's engine compartment. The aluminum fuel tank is forward of the engines, and a plywood shelf above the tank is a convenient and comfortable large flat floor from which to work. With the exhaust manifolds just 3 inches apart, changing the inboard spark plugs isn't all that easy; however, the front, top, and outboard sides of the engines are within fairly easy reach.

Three batteries are strapped down to starboard

and the 30-gallon water tank is to port. The engines are lag-bolted to fiberglass-encapsulated wooden boxes. The bilges and engine-room sides are ground smooth to remove fiberglass splinters and then coated with gray gelcoat. Chaparral even ground off the self-tapping screws fastening the hull-to-deck joint in the engine room. A few areas could use more attention to detail: I would double up the hose clamps below the waterline, such as on the air-conditioning cooling line; complete the fiberglass tabbing around the enclosed floor perimeters; and make sure the inside corners of the hull tabbing are radiused to reduce localized stresses from slamming loads in a seaway.

As for accessibility inside the engine room, the 68-by-44-inch opening is covered by four separate hatches, with gutter drain lines running directly overboard. The gutter is constructed to accommodate an aluminum insert on centerline, and water would likely leak through this cutout rather than pass to the drain lines aft. Other builders have successfully engineered single-piece hatches that open electrically, with the seats located above on articulated hinges. This makes access much simpler and faster and encourages daily maintenance checks. I would also like to see a step built in over the lightly constructed water-heater cover, which would be stepped on and damaged, given its location.

Bridge Deck

It's one step up to the bridge deck (situated over the midcabin berth below) with a two-person lounge seat to port; there is storage below, and the helm seat and console are opposite. Like the lounges aft, the helm seat is sculpted from heavy-duty vinyl. The seat slides forth and back; however, legroom and kneeroom are too tight for tall operators (the copilot's kneeroom was even tighter). The tilt wheel and single-lever Quicksilver controls are comfortably positioned at your fingertips for seated operation directly—although the throttles are likely to be a few inches too low for tall operators when standing.

The helm layout is nicely tooled and finished

with quality rocker switches and Beede gauges, but it's decidedly *not* ergonomic in layout. There's enough space for a small suite of electronics to port of the wheel. Above is a line of rocker switches ranging from bilge pump, wipers, horn, and navigation lights to the trim-tab switches immediately adjacent to the engine-room lights. The more frequently used switches, such as those for the trim tabs and wipers, should be mounted more prominently, closer to the throttles. I also would like to see the engine instruments closer together so they can be more easily taken in at a glance—rather than 18 inches apart and separated by a 60 mph speedometer—and preferably in pairs.

There are more safety problems forward. When you move forward to drop the hook, the lack of side decks makes it necessary to walk through the centerline windshield to the foredeck, where grippier nonskid and higher bow railings would be safer. The 1-inch-diameter welded stainless steel railing is certainly rugged, but at less than 20 inches high, it's too low for adequate balance. However, these are common complaints for this class of boat, regardless of manufacturer.

Cabin

For a 30-footer, the Chaparral's cabin is roomy and bright and has an open feeling. Headroom aft is 6 feet, 6 inches—and it's still 6 feet high where the trunk cabin slopes down at the forward end of the galley. Even if you don't need that much headroom, it just feels bigger and more inviting. Our test boat was finished in neutral tans, white, and beige, which should be appealing—or at least inoffensive—to most people.

The enclosed head is located to port at the base of the gently sloping companionway stairs. Inside is a manual toilet, sink with pullout shower spigot and vanity (with an off-color plastic access panel below—I recommend matching hatches), mirror, and opening port. Forward to port is the galley with its large countertop, single electric burner, sink, hideaway microwave oven and refrigerator, coffeemaker, and ample storage space for weekends afloat. The

drawers should have stops to prevent spills, though. Next in line is a small hanging locker, followed by a berth. Although the shape is difficult to accurately describe, there is well over 6 feet, 6 inches of length for at least one of the two occupants.

Aft to starboard and opposite the galley is the four-seat dinette finished in an attractive leatherette and which converts to a short, 69-by-36-inch berth (good only for kids). I would steal a few inches from the forward berth to make this dinette a regulation 6 feet, 6 inches long.

Finally, the midcabin berth is aft below the companionway stairs, and—at 6 feet, 9 inches long by 4 feet wide—it qualifies as a regular bed. The only problem is that you can't sit up as you can on many other boats of this design and size. I suggest carving out the port lounge seat above on the bridge deck, eliminating the storage space inside, and using it to create another foot of seated headroom on one side of the midcabin. A small hanging locker aft is also provided.

Construction

Chaparral starts with a premium gelcoat and a modified epoxy AME 4000 skin coat to ward off osmotic blistering. Construction is old school, with alternating layers of mat and woven roving comprising the solid fiberglass bottom; syntactic foam is added to the sides to prevent print-through and to build bulk efficiently. Plywood encapsulated in fiberglass forms the hull's stringers and bulkheads, and foam is injected in the hull voids. Balsa coring is used in the deck to build in stiffness at moderate weight.

Performance Test

Our sea trial took place on a small lake, so I can't comment on the boat's seakeeping abilities, but the hull's 20 degrees of deadrise aft should translate into a good ride in a chop. Handling was responsive and predictable, and the power steering was both easy and quick at just over two turns lock-to-lock.

Our stern-drive trim gauges were not calibrated properly; however, as expected, the boat comes out of the hole a lot faster with the drives all

Chaparral 300 Signature Performance Results

RPM	Speed, knots	Speed, mph	Fuel Use, gph	Nautical mpg	Statute mpg	Range, nm	Range, statute miles	Noise Level, dBA	Trim, degrees
600	3.9	4.5	2	2.0	2.2	269	404	66	2
1,000	6.0	6.9	3.2	1.9	2.2	258	388	70	3
1,500	7.0	8.1	6.4	1.1	1.3	151	226	74	4
2,000	9.7	11.2	9.6	1.0	1.2	139	209	78	8
2,500	17.4	20.0	12.4	1.4	1.6	193	290	78	8
3,000	22.2	25.5	16.0	1.4	1.6	191	287	80	7
3,500	29.4	33.8	19.6	1.5	1.7	207	311	82	5
4,000	34.4	39.6	26.2	1.3	1.5	181	272	83	4
4,500	40.0	46.0	37.2	1.1	1.2	148	223	89	4
4,800	42.8	49.2	41.0	1.0	1.2	144	216	91	4

Test conditions: twin 240 hp 5.0-liter EFI MerCruiser Bravo 3 stern drives, two passengers, full tank of fuel, 50-foot-plus depth, calm seas, air temperature 88 degrees, and 200 pounds of gear. Test conducted on 14 July 1998 in freshwater. Range calculated using 90 percent of the boat's 153-gallon fuel capacity. Sound levels taken at the helm.

the way down. As with many stern drives, the drill is to drop the drives, accelerate, and ease the drives back up to near level as you come up on plane. Adjust them correctly or you get a lot of porpoising if they're too high; you develop bow steer and get a wet ride if they're trimmed too low. Any boat in this class has a lot of sail area relative to the underwater hull cross section, so expect to blow around in a crosswind at low speed. But a little practice driving with the clutches and with the steering wheel left amidships allows you to put the boat almost anywhere you want. The important thing is not to try to twist with the drives anywhere but on centerline.

We were able to plane at 2,500 rpm while accelerating, and stayed on top at 2,300 rpm while slowing down, due to good weight distribution and sufficient hydrodynamic lift aft. With the tabs and drives down, I never lost sight of the horizon while coming up on plane—an important criterion. Visibility when I was standing was excellent, although the radar arches—2 feet wide at the base—take a big chunk out of the horizon (pipe arches would do the same job and let you see all around unimpaired).

The windshield, dramatically curved on either side, is remarkably distortion-free. But I would paint the dashboard flat gray or brown; the sun

glare off the bright-white surface is annoying at best and hazardous at worst (visibility is diminished when the sun is at a certain angle). The contoured seat is quite comfortable, but I would like to see the adjustable seat and molded fiberglass base moved aft 4 inches to make standing up behind the wheel more comfortable. If you like lots of electronic gizmos, space to mount them is limited, so you may have to settle for a radar or chart plotter installed to port of the companionway. The accompanying table gives performance results.

If you want to weekend aboard a quality-built midrange cruiser, check out the Chaparral. You could even take a week or two to cruise the Hudson River or explore the coast of Maine. The power in our test boat was well suited to the boat's size and displacement. As it is, the Chaparral fits comfortably into the upper third of its class, in my opinion. Attention to the constructive criticism noted would easily make this boat a standout in this market.

Our boat made good use of topside and cabin space, attention to detail was apparent in many areas, and there is significant interior volume. For safety considerations, I would add a custom non-skid finish on the topsides for a better grip on boat shoes and raise the bow railing. The 1998 base boat includes a long list of standard equipment, and options include AC, macerator, TV, cockpit cover, extended swim platform, and anchor windlass.

Dyer 40

Dyer 40 Express Cruiser Specifications	
LOA:	39'7"
Beam:	12.5"
Draft:	3'0"
Displacement:	18,000 lb.
Fuel capacity:	300 gal. (4 aluminum tanks)
Water capacity:	80 gal.

Timeless. Classic. Well proportioned. Gets better with age. The subject of this boat review is the Dyer 40, the modern rendition of a nearly forty-year-old design. One of the first production yards in the United States to build in fiberglass, Dyer has produced its 40-footer continuously since 1959—just like its bread-and-butter 29-footer. Express yachts and picnic boats are all the rage now, and Dyer has been quietly building both longer than probably anyone else.

The Dyer 40 is built on a full-keeled Down East–style hull, and its modern, lightweight, high-horsepower diesels have transformed what was originally a 12-knot cruiser into a modern express yacht capable of running fully loaded at an easily sustained 18- to 20-knot clip. As owners have become fussier about fit and finish over the years, Dyer has kept pace with plentiful use of teak and fine joinery. Although some boats are better left white because of hull-tooling flaws, the Dyer needs no such camouflage. Our two-year-old Dyer was Awlgripped a dark green to show off a practically distortion-free finish.

These semidisplacement Dyers are great seaboats. They *won't* pound and they have an easy, comfortable motion (some hard-chine boats are *too* stiff, I think). Our test ride in a 2- to 3-foot chop bore this out with a clean, flat wake. When we were back in the cockpit on the windward side, hardly a drop made its way on board due to full-length spray rails. Full-keel, semidisplacement hulls often need more attention at the helm in a quartering sea than a deep-V, but the overall ride more than compensates, especially if you run at a reasonable speed. This is also a pretty boat, with a gorgeous low sheerline, a well-proportioned trunk cabin, and a good-looking and functional teak windshield.

Cockpit

The Dyer's big 95-square-foot (9 ft., 5 in. by 10 ft., 5 in.) cockpit qualifies it as an old-fashioned picnic boat, especially with its curving, full-width upholstered transom seat. The deck is a foot off the water for lots of reserve buoyancy, and the big transom scuppers quickly drained the amply pitched, teak-soled cockpit when we hosed it down after our sea trial. With the low hull sheer and a high cockpit deck, Dyer adds fiberglass sideboards for a 24-inch height aft, to which I would add 4 to 6 inches for added safety.

A stainless steel–trimmed hatch leads to the lazarette, smoothly finished with gray gelcoat. Inside are the two rudders, supported at the upper ends by deck sockets; a teak grating to allow mooring lines to drain dry; and one of the boat's four aluminum fuel tanks. Dyer evenly spreads out the liquid load along the boat's center of buoyancy and, although you'll have to pay attention during fuel transfer, the payoff is in a remarkably level-riding hull at speed. Aluminum tanks can have a limited shelf life, so I would specify fiberglass or polypropylene to avoid major deck surgery later.

A second hatch forward provides access to the dual Racor fuel filter-separators—a pair for each engine—and dripless shaft seals. The shafts are set at a shallow and efficient 9-degree angle driven by 1.6:1 ZF gears. The cockpit and bridge deck are stick-built of wood treated with preservative, plywood subfloor, and inlaid teak planking. Hatch gutters are mitered into the framing and drain to the bilge below.

Foredeck

Wide, flat side decks lead forward to the capacious foredeck. The 1-inch welded stainless bow railings (which actually line up vertically comfortably *inboard* of the rubrail to prevent piling-induced damage) are 28 inches high at the windshield and 32 inches at the bow—specifications other safety-conscious builders would do well to emulate. The 12-inch bow cleats and three pairs of spring cleats provide all kinds of mooring options. A solid-teak bow pulpit with a Maxwell windlass and a stainless insert handles the 35-pound C.Q.R. plough anchor.

With the 17-foot-long foredeck and a comfortably high trunk cabin, you could have a party up forward on this boat. The Treadmaster tan-colored nonskid, glued to the deck in sheets, is grippy underfoot but easily hosed off at the end of the day.

Bridge Deck and Helm

The 72-square-foot (8 by 9 ft.) raised bridge deck, also finished in teak, is up a single step from the cockpit. Like any real express boat, ours had a windshield and a Sunbrella bimini top, elegantly fashioned in stainless and tan. Our test boat had a pair of forward-facing raised seats—for the captain and copilot—and another opposite to port.

Seated at the helm, the first commendable detail I noticed was the expanse of glass purpose-built to be looked through. When I was seated or standing, when the boat was at idle or running at 20 knots, the sensibly designed, beautifully wrought teak windshield is high enough so as to not obscure the view ahead. This sort of utility should be taken for granted, of course, but don't count on it on many boats on the market.

The helm station is nicely arranged with gauges farther forward and higher, and the electronics lower and nearer the operator within easy reach. I would rather arrange the gauges in pairs to make it easier to notice out-of-kilter readings. The big 6-inch Ritchie compass is perfectly positioned forward near the windshield. The vertical 26-inch stainless Destroyer wheel and single-lever Kobelt controls are comfortably positioned according to the owner's preference, although I would want a wheel closer to horizontal, akin to a busdriver's position. Our test boat had a custom swivel-mounted radar box to port of the companionway, evidence of Dyer's willingness to customize to owners' tastes.

With the seat so far off the deck (34 in.), the helm station would benefit from a recessed footrest, which Dyer would be happy to add. Color-matching the light-beige console's white-plastic access-plate inserts and instrument panel would offer a better look.

Engine Room

The 300 hp Caterpillar 3116 six-cylinder diesels fit snugly under a pair of two-piece hatches that can either hinge open for daily maintenance or lift out completely for unimpeded major-maintenance access to the engines. Centerline fluid checks make life simple, as do manual oil-changing pumps for the engines and transmissions. All-around access to the engines, even outboard where they're often inaccessible on other 40-footers, was excellent.

Structurally, making the aft engine-room bulkhead solid from sole to bilge would reduce sound levels even more, and the resulting subdivision would also add a significant measure of watertight integrity to the hull in the event of flooding. To improve weight distribution, the four batteries are forward near the engine cooling-water seacocks, which are difficult to reach forward of the engines; remote handles for the valves or relocating the seacocks is a possible solution. A second fuel tank on centerline between the engines was covered with a marine plywood box that doubles as a level floor. This is a hollow-keel hull, but most of it has been thoughtfully filled during construction with urethane foam and covered with fiberglass so the bilge water is easier to pump out.

Cabin

Sailors and nautical buffs will love this boat's elegant decor. A wide companionway and four sloping steps lead down to the Dyer 40's inviting cabin. The teak and holly sole, varnished-teak-trimmed off-white padded liners, and turquoise Corian countertops all speak of class and things nautical. Thanks to that pretty sheerline, headroom is on the low side at just over 73 inches; lowering the cabin sole would help.

The Dyer 40's salty interior is beautifully executed, with the V-berth forward, convertible dinette to port, and enclosed head and galley to starboard   BILLY BLACK/THE ANCHORAGE

The U-shaped galley is located to port with an optional Grunert top-loading holding-plate 12/110-volt reefer, alcohol stove and oven, sink, and cabinets. The drawers pull out unimpeded; I would have stops built in to prevent surprises. A U-shaped dinette is opposite the galley to starboard, and the table lowers for conversion to a comfortable 6-foot, 6-inch by 3-foot, 6-inch berth. The electrical service panel is located above the dinette on the aft bulk-

head, and the entire arrangement tilts down for convenient interior access. Another panel below folds down for access to the two battery switches.

The head is forward of the galley to port, with its electric toilet, vanity, and lift-out shower nozzle. A small overhead hatch and side port channel let in the fresh sea breeze. A small hanging locker and set of drawers are forward of the dinette. The stateroom is forward with its V-berth (convertible to a double), drawers are below, and access to the partitioned chain-and-gear storage locker is forward. A large, 23-inch Bomar hatch is overhead, letting in lots of air and light, and letting you out in an emergency via a second exit.

Construction

The Dyer's hull starts with gelcoat and is followed by a premium vinylester resin in the skin coat to prevent osmotic blistering. A solid laminate of woven and nonwoven fiberglass comprises the hull with wood-cored stringers and bulkheads. The foredeck and trunk cabin are made of composite balsa-cored fiberglass for stiffness and light weight. Decks aft are of Cuprinol-treated frames and marine plywood. Engine beds are mounted on steel plates encapsulated in the fiberglass hull stringers. The hull-to-deck joint is bonded with fiberglass, and the bulkhead and stringer limber holes are sealed with resin against moisture penetration.

Performance Test

Our sea trial aboard the Dyer was a trip down memory lane for me, conjuring pleasant recollections of many youthful days spent offshore on Down East hulls. The wake was flat and unbreaking, the rolling easy but stable. I found 18 knots and a speed–length ratio (S/L) of 2.8 to be a very comfortable cruising speed in the Dyer: slow enough so you don't have to hang on for dear life, fast enough to get you there plenty soon. It's also about as fast as you want to try to run a Down East hull, although there is the temptation to keep adding horsepower.

The Dyer proved herself nimble, taking just 22

seconds to complete a 360-degree turn at full rudder. Backing down, the cockpit stayed dry with scuppers well clear of the water. The weight distribution seemed to be excellent with the planing waterline aft a touch above the static waterline, and trim was a commendable and moderate 4 to 5 degrees. Coming up on plane, especially with 10 degrees (out of 20) down-angle on the trim tabs, the horizon stayed in view except momentarily under the pulpit. Seated or standing, I always had glass to look through rather than a too-low windshield frame. Window mullions were narrow enough that they didn't interfere noticeably with visibility ahead. We were on top with a clean wake at 1,500 rpm and 11 knots, with a companion sitting to windward on the transom seat reporting not a drop of spray.

The ride heading into Narragansett Bay's 2- to 3-foot chop was very smooth. Running in the trough offshore in a 2- to 4-foot swell and chop showed the Dyer to have good form stability and a low center of gravity (thanks to the express design). Running downsea took some attention to the helm, but not more than any other semidisplacement hull I've run. The cutaway keel offers grounding protection for the props and rudders—no small reassurance when cruising unfamiliar waters or gunkholing. I would want to check things out at night to see if the sidelights atop the pulpit railing create visibility-diminishing backscatter for the helmsman.

As for sound levels, an increasingly important issue for modern yachting families, I would want to see engine and exhaust dBA noise levels lowered significantly to the high 70s or low 80s range at cruise. This could be done with improved sound insulation and perhaps more effective silencers, requests that Dyer will cheerfully accommodate.

Dyer 40 Performance Results

RPM	Speed, knots	Noise Level, dBA	Trim, degrees
1,000	8.3	73	0
1,400	10.3	82	3
1,600	11.5	83	4
1,800	15.2	85	5
2,000	17.2	86	5
2,200	19.1	87	4
2,400	21.3	88	4
2,750	23.8	89	4

If you're in the market for a well-proportioned, solidly built, beautifully appointed, proven seaboat, take the Dyer for a test ride. Sold factory direct, the 1998 Dyer 40's standard equipment list includes teak decks, dual bridge-deck seats, and a bimini top with enclosure. Our test boat included options such as a swim platform, transom seat, teak windshield, Grunert refrigeration, and hinged Hall mast with boom. The 300 hp Caterpillars are well matched to the Dyer 40's hull design and weight. If you want to cruise at 30 knots and get tossed around a lot more, buy a hard-chine, moderate V-bottom hull; however, if a comfortable 18- to 20-knot, anywhere-anytime pace in a beautifully proportioned, true seaboat is your cup of tea, so may be the Dyer 40.

Chris Craft Constellation 26

Talk to any baby boomer who fondly remembers their grandparents' gleaming 1950s- or 1960s-vintage yacht, and likely as not they're thinking of a Chris Craft. These were the pleasure craft to have in their day—from mahogany launches to steel or fiberglass aft cabin and flush-deck motor yachts and convertibles. In fact, Chris Craft used to be the biggest builder of recreational boats in the world. They were distinctive-looking craft, too, classy-looking ladies you could recognize a mile away. Unfortunately, the company lost its way over the years, enduring changes of ownership and a loss of corporate memory. The classically styled boats of the 1960s and 1970s were forgotten, and, once you

Chris Craft Constellation 26 Specifications	
LOA:	29'6"
Length on deck:	26'6"
Beam:	8'6"
Draft:	3'7"
Fuel capacity:	97 gal.
Water capacity:	20 gal.
Displacement:	6,150 lb. (dry)
Power as tested:	320 hp Volvo 5.7 GXI DP

stripped off the decals, Chris Craft gradually became just another look-alike, ho-hum, all-white express cruiser.

All that changed a couple of years ago when the then-OMC-owned builder decided to hearken back to its roots, producing a series of three launches in the 22- to 28-foot range and a pair of express cruisers measuring 26 and 40 feet. The company did it right from the start, hiring two of the best yacht design firms in the country; Michael Peters Yacht Design drew up the three launches, and C. Raymond Hunt Associates created the two larger cruisers. We say they did it right, because more often than not builders design their own boats in-house, and judging from the product on the market today, this is an undertaking too often beyond their competence. The express boat market today consists, in the majority, of boats that are often exclusively suited for calm-water, inshore use. Too wide at the waterline, with broad, flat, shallow entries, they're seagoing bucking broncos in all but the most benign conditions. Their foredecks are more like ski slopes than forecastles, all in the interests of creating the most volume possible for the LOA. Need we say more?

OMC went bust (but not before building our test boat), and to cut through a somewhat convoluted story, Chris Craft now belongs to a consortium headed up by an enterprising Brit named Stephen Julius. Fortunately, the new owners mean to continue what OMC started. From what we've seen, the brand is on track to

being restored to its original luster.

Our test boat had a full summer's use by the time we saw it in October, which was great since we got to see how it fared over the season.

Design

This express boat has a moderately long, low foredeck with an honest-to-god trunk cabin with long, high, side windows. Those windows let in a delightful amount of light down below, just like the old Chris Craft Commanders and Constellations. Why today's express boats, with their cavelike interiors are so popular, is beyond us, but it must have something to do with 30-foot interiors in 25-foot boats. Anyway, Chris Craft was loath to give up the interior volume around the bridge deck and helm area, so the windshield and deckhouse sides are essentially full beam, with access forward through the opening centerline windshield.

The bridge deck is in the same level as the cockpit, raised more than 20 inches above the waterline. This deck height leaves plenty of headroom for the single gasoline V-8 engine aft and the small stateroom amidships under the helm. The single-level deck allows you to walk all the way from the transom door to the cabin companionway without tripping over a step. A full canvas enclosure is available, stretching from the windshield to the transom, so you can escape the rain and sun—and bugs. That the Constellation has classic origins is apparent at a glance. And it's not just the boat's looks; many practical design features also make the 26 shine ergonomically over the competition.

The Constellation 26, named after the builder's earlier Constellation line of cruising yachts, is distinctly not running with the me-too, look-alike, hard-riding crowd. It has Hunt's trademark warped-V bottom, starting with a fine, deep entry, much like that of a Blackfin 33, transitioning to 20 degrees of deadrise at the transom. The fine entry delivers one of the smoothest rides in a chop that you'll find on any boat anywhere of this size. The chine is well above the waterline forward, and the footprint of the bow at the waterline is fine compared to most of the competition.

All this deadrise gradually flattens out to a moderate 20 degrees at the transom. While a deep-V has constant 24-degree deadrise from amidships to the stern, with the chines and keel running parallel to the waterline, the warped-V bottom's chines run downhill, so to speak, all the way to the transom. Since the bottom is a little flatter at the transom, the boat develops lift more efficiently at speed, and the more deeply submerged chines create more buoyancy aft. With more dynamic lift and buoyancy in the stern, the center of gravity can be shifted aft—always a good thing for a fast planing hull. The performance benefits of this hull form are legion, including flatter running angle, or trim, when on plane—without the use of tabs to produce a smoother ride in a chop and better helm station visibility over the bow. The boat transitions up on plane smoothly, without digging a hole in the water and struggling to get on plane, as is the case with most deep-Vs. The Hunt hull planes at remarkably low speeds—around 12 to 13 knots in this case, so, as you'll read about in the Performance Test section, you can move along easily and efficiently on plane at speeds that would have deep-Vs wallowing along in a hull-high wake.

Construction

The Constellation 26 is conventionally constructed—nothing fancy in the methods or materials used to build the boat. An inexpensive anti-blister coat is made by spraying vinylester resin over the gelcoat, thereby requiring only a little of the costly and superior resin. Many builders these days apply a 3-ounce layer of mat or chop wet out in vinylester resin over the gelcoat, which produces substantially more protection since this laminate is many times thicker than a few mils of resin alone. In fact, the finest hulls get all-vinylester laminates, since vinylester is much more resistant to osmotic blistering, and it produces a far stronger laminate than general-purpose resins.

The Constellation's laminate is wet out with general-purpose orthophthalic resin, starting with 5 ounces of chop applied in two passes (which provides the bulk to prevent reinforcement print-through to the gelcoat), a layer of nonwoven roving for strength, 6 to 8 more ounces of chop which acts as a bulker and core, and another layer of fiberglass reinforcement. This produces a thick, solid-glass, low-tech laminate of consistent quality because there are no skin-to-core bond lines associated with conventional foam or balsa core materials to worry about.

The hull is supported by an interlocking stick-built network of lumber-grade plywood stringers, transverse frames, and bulkheads that's assembled on a jig and then lifted into place and tabbed to the hull. The plywood edges come into contact with the hull skin, which theoretically makes the latter susceptible to fatigue from the resulting hard spots. On the other hand, the hull skin is relatively thick and bulky, and the panel sizes are minimized on this 8-foot, 6-inch-wide hull by closely spaced framing. We'd rather see the plywood support members supported by foam cant strips strategically located on the hull's inner skin as a precaution. Foam pads are used along the hull sides to prevent the bulkhead edges from visibly distorting the topsides.

To prevent water from getting into the plywood, the wood is sprayed with resin before installation, then fully encapsulated with fiberglass after tabbing in. The limber holes are sealed with ortho resin; we'd prefer they were enclosed in fiberglass, or at least sealed with epoxy, which is not nearly as susceptible to cracking when changing moisture content causes the wood to expand and contract. The next best fix is to use pressure-treated plywood so you don't have to worry about the exterior-grade plywood rotting to start with. Better still is the use of high-density foam stringers encapsulated in fiberglass; this produces a lighter structure that allows the fiberglass (which is along for the ride anyway) to do the structural work of stiffening the bottom.

The hull-to-deck joint, with a thin backing strip of plywood, is held together with two rows of self-tapping screws and caulked with Bostic 920 sealant. Once again, many builders use a death-grip adhesive here, with the screws just serving to clamp the joint until the adhesive sets up. Relying on self-tapping screws alone in a structure that continually wracks and works in a seaway may be overly optimistic. The transom is made up of plywood encapsulated in fiberglass. The plywood end grain around the stern-drive cutout is sealed with 3M's 5200.

Decks are cored with either plywood, end-grain balsa, or high-density structural foam (in the swim platform), depending on location. Through-bolt penetrations go through the plywood core, which is best suited to resist bolt compression loads, and the holes are sealed with the Bostic 920. The cores, whatever the material, are bedded in a layer of resin-rich chop and pressed in by hand.

The cabin side windows are wide but short, and this design has lead many other builders down a slippery slope of constant cabintop flexing and leaking. But Chris Craft–Hunt made a point of specifying windows made in England that are supposed to contribute structurally to the deck, preventing the problems mentioned. Only time will tell whether they've effectively solved this problem.

Our overall impression of the Constellation's construction is that it is solid, but could stand improvement. We expected higher quality materials after seeing how well designed the boat is, and given the company's avowal to return the brand to its top-shelf roots. That's not to say that the boat won't give many years of excellent service, but when you use lumber-grade wood throughout the hull support structure in a wet bilge, seal that wood with crack-prone resin, have a plywood-cored transom, and don't bother with vinylester resin in the first 3 ounces of mat, you're asking for trouble. Chris Craft's new management has since incorporated a number of the changes recommended here.

Cockpit

You can step onto the bolt-on swim platform for access to the cockpit. A full 3 feet deep, the platform projects nearly a foot beyond the stern drive, which gives swimmers an extra measure of safety when diving aft. Once you push a button to release it, you can pull the swim ladder out of its compartment and it will drop down with three steps fully submerged. This depth is great, since you can actually climb up it without being built like Arnold Schwarzenegger. The only problem is with the ladder's width: the rungs are only 7 inches wide, which makes it as almost as difficult to climb as if it were too short. We would recommend a 12-inch-wide ladder for this reason.

The swim platform itself is one big, flat surface, so what's missing? Slots to let the water drain off. Picture this: you're backing down the ladder, or a wave breaks over the stern, and you have what is essentially an 8-by-3-foot scoop doing its best to break off the transom. If the platform were full of holes, or slots, the water would shed quickly, easing the stresses and strains caused by all that lever arm.

Though it has a toe space below, the plastic transom door is just 19 inches high—about 10 inches too low for good balance: imagine standing back there when someone unexpectedly hits the throttle. In the cockpit, the aft section of an aft, L-shaped lounge to starboard hinges up and goes along for the ride when the engine compartment hatch is raised. This makes for no-fuss access to the engine. There's storage under the seat, which accommodates up to four people. A small sink is fitted in to starboard behind the forward settee.

Molded steps also lead up to the cockpit coamings, though there aren't any side decks to walk forward on, with the windshield extending nearly to the gunwale. A table plugs in for use at the aft settee, which is a nice cruising feature, but the aluminum socket for the table stanchion on our test boat was already corroded with peeling paint.

Forward is the bridge deck area; there's a second L-shaped settee to port, with room for up to three people, and this molded seat, in fact, is what provides the seated headroom to port in the midcabin below. This seat offers a pretty good view outside the boat, and it's close by the helm seat opposite to starboard.

Access to the foredeck is through the opening windshield, as mentioned. You don't have the feeling of sliding down a ski slope when walking forward on the cabintop, either. The flat bow area distinguishes this boat, once again, from the vast majority of the competition. Once you are forward, the flat deck area is safe to walk on and seems actually to have been designed with the human anatomy in mind. The only problems, in our view, are that the molded nonskid is too slick—it barely offers any grip to deck shoes—and the shiny stainless steel bow is just 19 inches high, again about 10 inches too low to offer any real measure of protection for passengers sent forward to tend lines or drop the hook.

Engine Compartment

A 3-by-4-foot hinged hatch in the cockpit deck lifts for access to the engine compartment. Actually, it jumps up, since the two boosters put out more force than the hatch actually weighs, so when closing the hatch, you have to step on it so the latch will seat properly. But that beats having to lift a heavy hatch that can fall on your toes if you slip. Anyway, there's lots of room to move around forward of the engine, standing on top of the 97-gallon, 0.125-inch-thick aluminum fuel tank. The fuel tank, by the way, seems to be securely fastened down, but there are a couple of potential problems.

First is that the tank serves as a natural step, as mentioned. So, you're going to be walking on the exposed ground and tank level indicator wires laying on top of the tank. There should be some sort of shelf or platform over the tank to protect the wiring and to prevent the oil canning that comes with each step on the thin aluminum tank top. Second, in the interests of keeping the center of gravity as low as possible, the bottom of the tank, which is shaped to match the hull, is perilously close to the standing bilge water. As the bilge water slopped around on our test boat example, we knew the bottom of the fuel tank was getting splashed. It's no more than 1 inch from the hull on centerline, and within ¼ inch at most at its outer sections. We would redesign the tank so it's farther off the bilge; better yet, polyethylene tanks would eliminate the potential for corrosion in the first place. (Pursuit proactively recalled its boats that had fuel tanks mounted too close to standing bilge water, fixing them at the company's expense.)

Accessibility to the top and front of the engine is excellent, and the saltwater-cooled engine on the test boat eliminates one maintenance point. But why anyone would order a raw-water-cooled engine in a boat used in salt water is beyond us. Unless you have some kind of freshwater flushing system that's used every time the boat ties up, the engine will rot out well before it wears out.

The bilge is finished in gray gelcoat, applied over smoothly sanded fiberglass. Shelves built into the hull outboard serve as convenient platforms for the batteries, the water heater and water tank to port, and the holding tank to starboard. The hatch gutters lead to 1.5-inch drain lines that exit through the transom, and the gutter is flanged, so the engine and components were as dry as a bone after our rough-water test ride and thorough washdown.

Cabin

What distinguishes the Constellation's cabin from almost all the competition is the light. The long, tapering side windows flood the compartment with sunlight so that it's unusually welcoming and roomy feeling inside. Through a narrow (18 inches at the companionway's protruding sliding door) companionway down molded fiberglass stairs to the cabin, you find 6-foot, 1-inch headroom, which is not bad for a boat this size. It's not the best, but when you consider how bloated most similar boats of this size appear, this is one time we'll pardon giving up a bit of function for a reasonably proportioned exterior. Besides, this might not be that much of an issue for people who are under 6 feet tall. The cabin is conventionally laid out. Immediately below the bridge deck and helm area is a mid-cabin, which has a 7-foot-8-inch-long, 4-foot-wide berth with up to 3 feet, 3 inches sitting headroom to port. The midcabin is roomier and more accessible than that on many other boats of this size.

To port, the galley has a fiberglass countertop with a mottled pattern in the gelcoat to resemble granite or some other exotic, natural material. A single-burner stove, molded-in sink, and small refrigerator are standard equipment, and there are spaces reserved for a microwave and coffeemaker, should you wish to add them. There is plenty of room to stow enough groceries for a long weekend, and the light coming in through that long window above the galley countertop makes the galley someplace you actually look forward to being in.

The head opposite the galley to starboard is a standard all-molded-fiberglass affair with a few caulked joints that hopefully won't eventually leak. More glorious sunlight can stream in through another of those long trunk cabin windows. The VacuFlush toilet (standard equipment) is on a raised platform , and you can sit a spell without banging your knees or elbows. What a concept. The head's molded liner is shaped to direct water off the toilet platform to the deck and the deck drain, which is a novel feature, and likely a C. R. Hunt touch (the firm has designed a number of 35- to 140-foot yachts), proving that a little trickle-down is a great thing. The sink faucet pulls out to fit in a bracket high on the bulkhead forward for duty as a shower nozzle. Finally, this is a big head compartment for a 26-footer—not at all cramped feeling.

Forward is a V-berth with a V-shaped table that drops down to serve as a bed insert. Legroom varies from 6 feet, 4 inches (if you sleep pointing north and south) to 6 feet, 6 inches (if you lie along the hull side). Our 19-inch-square overhead hatch had been leaking for some time, so the dealer was in the process of replacing or rebedding it. It's just big enough to use as an escape route should you find yourself sinking by the stern in the middle of the night.

A couple of comments on decor. The overhead liner is meticulously applied; there's not a lot in this area to differentiate this boat's quality from that of a $2 million Viking convertible. The woodwork, such as the head and closet doors and the galley drawers, is simple and functional—nothing fancy or pretentious. Our only complaint is with the carpeting. Chris Craft should follow the lead of some of the other builders in this category and incorporate a molded fiberglass pan that would include the deck and V-berths, at least, topped with a snap-in carpet. The reason we suggest this is that the carpet on our test boat is stapled or glued in place—to the deck and to the vertical surfaces within a foot or two of the deck. After one season's use (which included use by three rambunctious, gum-chewing children) the carpet was dark and stained, and a little dank smelling. The snap-in carpet also unsnaps, of course, which is the point. It can be easily removed from the boat for cleaning or even replacement as needed.

Helm

The Constellation's helm station is ergonomically one of the finest we have encountered on any boat. First, the comfortable seat has an adjustable bolster that lowers to extend the seat bottom or flips up to serve as a leaning post of sorts. Legroom is generally adequate, and the seat cushion is a full 27 inches high, so visibility seated was good, even over the bow when coming up on plane. The only problem was with the top of the windshield frame, which was just about at eye level when seated; once the boat is running at 4 degrees or so of trim up on plane, the horizon bisects midwindow, so sight lines are better at speed. But the windshield frame and mullions are narrow enough that sight lines all around at all speeds are still quite acceptable, using a real-world standard.

The wheel tilts up and down through a wide arc, so almost anyone can find a comfortable position. Having the seat so high means that the wheel and engine control lever are at just the right height for either seated or stand-up operation. And the helm seat is not only high up, it's comfortable, with bolsters keeping you securely fixed even when the boat is being tossed around in a stiff chop.

What could be improved? Well, the molded fiberglass seat foundation should be 3 or 4 inches farther aft. That way, you could stand up behind the wheel without your heels jammed against the foundations and your thighs pressed against the wheel—especially when the boat is running bow-up on plane.

The instrument and electronics panels are angled so they're pretty much perpendicular to your line of sight. This is important, since too much angle makes it hard to see the gauges and displays. The dash is all gray, so neither sunlight or nighttime instrument lights will cause much windshield glare. There's also plenty of room on the upper panel for an average small day-cruiser's-worth of flush-mounted electronics. The official Chris Craft gauges looked pretty cool, but the tachometer is hard to get used to because of the stylish but impractical way the rpm indication is segmented. The multigauge (oil pressure, water temperature, volts, and fuel level) is too low on the panel, and it's partially obscured behind the steering wheel rim. Also, Chris Craft should save the speedometers for its runabouts; this one looks a little silly on a 26-foot family cruiser, and it takes up valuable (and limited) real estate on the dash.

Performance Test

We'll say up front this is certainly one of the best-running, smoothest-riding, straightest-tracking boat of this size and class that we've ever tested. Perhaps the Formula 27 and Donzi 27 are in the same

league, running at speed in a chop. In short, it's a superb little seaboat, capable of running offshore in conditions that would keep most of the competition tied to the dock. Our test boat, which had been in the salt water for six months straight, had an even growth of slime covering the bottom and a couple inches of grass growing on the outdrive. Even the propellers were covered with slime. So we'd expect a boat, with a clean, freshly painted bottom, to run at least a knot or two faster. We had three people onboard and a ¾ tank of fuel and full water, and whether the props are too big or the bottom incredibly fouled, we only managed to run up 4,100 rpm, whereas 5,000 rpm is the normal operating maximum for this small-block Volvo.

We had a 15- to 25-knot breeze blowing across Marblehead Harbor, which a few miles offshore was kicking up a 2- to 3-foot sea with an occasional 4 footer. We were able to run at 15 to 16 knots right into these waves quite comfortably. When we speeded up a few hundred rpm, or launched off one of those 4-footers, we'd land with the midbody of the hull impacting the water first. Most boats would have jarred your kidneys, but this one just sort of squished into wave on impact. It did pound when forced up over 20 knots, but what do you expect?— these waves were taller than a kitchen countertop and plenty for any 26-footer to handle.

We've mentioned that this hull slips up on plane with a lot less effort than a deep-V. In fact, we were solidly up on plane with a clean wake astern at 12 or 13 knots, so the boat's efficient operating range is exceptionally wide. With our dirty bottom, we managed to make just under 27 knots at full throttle, our 320 hp Volvo 5.7 GXI DuoProp laboring to make that 4,100 rpm. An easy cruise of 3,000 rpm produced about 16 knots at just over 11 gph. Or, if you just have to get there a little sooner, crank it up to 3,500 rpm for 21-plus knots at just under 14 gph fuel flow. Chris Craft reports the boat will hit 37 knots at WOT, 5,000 rpm, and sustain 21 knots at a 3,200 rpm cruise when the bottom and outdrive are clean. That sounds plausible.

Trim topped out at 5 degrees when coming up

on plane with the tabs and lower unit down, and the boat ran at a very modest 3 to 4 degrees without tabs at higher cruising speeds. Laying-to in the beam seas, the boat rolled comfortably, with none of the snap seen in flat-bottom, too-wide hulls and none of the excessive rolling common to many deep-Vs. Our Volvo power steering took just 2.5 turns lock-to-lock, and it was practically effortless. This resulted in superior handling at all speeds. In fact, setting the throttle at 3,000 rpm, we managed 360-degree turns to port and starboard in just 14 seconds, which is excellent. The boat heels comfortably, proportional to the turn rate, in a hard high-speed turn.

Downsea performance was just as impressive as running into them. The boat tracked very well, at both semidisplacement and planing speeds. The boat never felt as if it had a mind of its own, it was always under control, and handling was very predictable, which says a lot for a boat in a quartering sea.

Windshield wipers should be standard on this boat, as should freshwater washers. It was tough seeing where we were going in those 3- to 4-footers without them, as we had a steady deluge of salt water over the bow at 14 to 15 knots, as one would expect. We had the factory canvas on board, and it needs a redesign, too. Water made its way steadily through the gap between the canvas and the windshield frame, and the vinyl gasket, apparently added to act as a water intrusion-preventing baffle, was

cracked at every snap. There's also a gap where the opening center windshield meets the trunk cabin that allows water to blast its way through. Other than that, the windshield seems to be a good design, solid and unobtrusive with big, flat panels of glass to see through.

Our only real sea trial complaint is that this boat is loud (and it sounded louder than the dBA numbers indicate): around 90 dBA at full power, and 83 to 85 dBA at cruise. We'd much prefer the through-hub exhaust over our test boat's through-transom style. The engine exhaust just echoed and reverberated throughout the rpm spectrum annoyingly and intrusively.

We'd very much like to see this boat with a 300 hp Yanmar bolted to a duo-prop stern drive. It weighs about the same as the gasoline engine, and you could probably figure on an all-day-long cruising speed at least 50 percent faster than the gas engine could deliver while burning 40 percent less fuel.

It's too bad all the other express boat builders don't have the vision and compulsion for improvement that Chris Craft obviously has. Fortunately, Chris Craft gave the designer free reign to design a boat that does so many things well. This is an ergonomics-driven, trailerable boat that performs wonderfully in sloppy weather and looks as good as it performs. It has class, seaworthiness-inspired proportions, a top-shelf hull design, and a user-friendly layout.

The OMC-built test boat's construction, on the

Chris Craft Constellation 26 Performance Results

RPM	Speed, knots	Speed, mph	Fuel Use, gph	Nautical mpg	Statute mpg	Range, nm	Range, statute miles	Noise Level, dBA	Trim, degrees
1,000	5	5.8	1.5	3.33	3.83	290	334	70	2
1,500	7	8.1	2.6	2.69	3.10	234	269	77	3
2,000	8.3	9.5	4.5	1.84	2.12	160	185	79	4
2,500	11.8	13.6	7.7	1.53	1.76	133	153	84	5.5
3,000	15.9	18.3	11.1	1.43	1.65	125	143	83	5.5
3,500	21.4	24.6	13.6	1.57	1.81	137	157	85	5
4,000	25.6	29.4	22.2	1.15	1.33	100	115	88	5
4,100	26.4	30.4	24	1.10	1.27	96	110	89	5

Single 320 hp Volvo GXI DuoProp 5.7-liter gas. Noise levels measured at helm.

other hand, was disappointing. Our biggest complaint has to do with the boat's rot-prone lumber-grade plywood used structurally in the stringers, transom, and in the decks around bolt holes; the lack of a vinylester resin-saturated chop skin coat; the reliance on self-tapping screws to hold the hull-to-deck joint together; and the corrosion-prone aluminum fuel tank so close to the bilge. All that wood can last for decades if it stays bone dry, but therein lies the rub: boats spend most of their lives in water. Thousands of boats meet their early demise precisely because of rot.

The builder reports that it has shifted to rot-proof, pressure-treated plywood in future hulls, and that it's investigating the use of plastic tanks to replace the aluminum ones. Both these moves will produce a better, longer-lasting boat.

Michael Peters Yachts Design is now designing all Chris Craft models, and six boats ranging up to 60 feet are planned. As Chris Craft earns its way back to the top of the heap, it plans to spend what it takes to improve the construction quality to match the marvelous design work of C. Raymond

Hunt Associates. The builder indicated to us that it plans to review the overall construction materials and processes it inherited from OMC, and to upgrade them to a higher standard. We hope that will be the case. Then anyone, including our nostalgic baby boomer friends, can buy their dream boat knowing that a Chris Craft is every bit as good as she looks.

Available options include alternate hull colors, air-conditioning, windlass, camper canvas, engine room light, cockpit table, foredeck sunpad, engine compartment fire-extinguishing system, 5 kW genset, macerator with overboard discharge microwave, oil drip pan, and a remote searchlight. Chris Craft offers the new diesel Volvo KAD300 Sterndrive DP as an option, which would greatly improve cruising speed, economy, and range. The builder may also offer Yanmar diesel power if market demand dictates; that would be nice, since the Yanmar STZE B3 puts out more hp and weighs 110 pounds less than the Volvo.

1998 Formula 41 PC

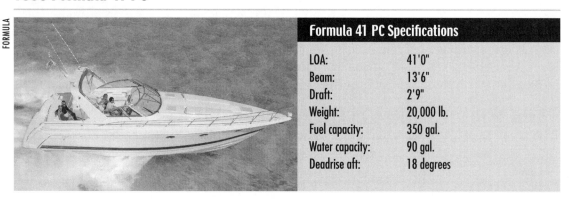

FORMULA

Formula 41 PC Specifications	
LOA:	41'0"
Beam:	13'6"
Draft:	2'9"
Weight:	20,000 lb.
Fuel capacity:	350 gal.
Water capacity:	90 gal.
Deadrise aft:	18 degrees

Cockpit

The Formula 41 PC is a good example of how well the builder understands this cruiser market. Attention to detail was evident as soon as I stepped aboard the Formula. Crossing the big, 40-inch-wide swim platform, I noticed the molded nonskid—

bold and aggressive, it's still not hard on the knees and is easy to keep clean. The swim ladder under a flush hatch lifts out on a clever articulated hinge. Three steps descend underwater, so you don't need to be a gymnast to climb it.

Conveniently, there's a 6-foot-long storage

compartment hidden behind the transom; however, the access door is just 30 inches wide, making it more difficult than it needs to be to reach all that space. To starboard is a small compartment for the two shore-power cables, the freshwater hookup, and the telephone and TV connectors. Our boat also had a dinghy davit hidden away behind a transom lid. A hot-and-cold freshwater shower is located at the two steps leading up to the 22-inch-wide, sturdy transom door.

To port as you enter the roomy cockpit is a cleverly designed rope locker with the engine-room hatch switch inside. Just forward is a molded step leading to the side deck and a large Corian-type counter area with a sink, refrigerator-freezer, and storage locker. To starboard is a U-shaped lounge; a removable seat section tucks behind the seatback to clear the way when raising the engine-room hatch. A table stanchion fits into a deck socket in the 24-by-34-inch day hatch to the engine room. The thick aft cockpit bolster turns into a seatback when you lift it up and pull out the 60-inch bench seat inside—there's room enough for seven or eight people to sit. An insert turns the lounge area into a sunpad.

Helm

Another step leads up to the bridge deck, where a three-person seat is to port and the helm is to starboard. The skipper can share his or her deeply upholstered, 4-foot-wide seat with one or two friends, with helm station all the way outboard. Sitting down dockside, I had a good all-around view through the aluminum-framed windshield. The curved glass was remarkably distortion-free, a real necessity when watching for running and navigational lights at night.

Legroom is excellent and the steering wheel is comfortably positioned, as are the rocker switches below. The Bennett trim tabs are controlled from switches up higher to starboard, and our boat had tab-position indicators, which are nice to have—and even a necessity in my opinion. I like the way the engine gauges are clustered in pairs so they're easier to take in at a glance, and the tan dashboard area minimizes windshield glare.

There is one oddity that I can't account for on the Formula: the throttles are directly at your right elbow when you're seated, but the shifts are well forward, close to the electronics panel. Using both at the same time is very awkward—and I've got long arms. To make it comfortable to use both throttles and shifts at the same time, and to do so when seated or standing, I would like to see them moved to positions on either side of the wheel—and the throttle needs to be higher. Better yet, install single-lever engine controls! I had to bend down to reach them while standing up, which is decidedly *not* ergonomic. The autopilot control, on the other hand, is conveniently located below the throttles where it's easy to reach when sitting down.

A handrail and a pair of steps lead up to the nonslip dashboard on centerline and out through the opening windshield to the foredeck. This layout is satisfactory when it's calm, but once out on the foredeck you're in a no-man's-land with nothing to hang onto. A centerline railing is definitely called for to provide safe all-weather access to the anchor. The same excellent nonskid is found forward on a 2-foot-wide strip down the center and on the narrow (6 in. wide, but at least they're flat) side decks. The stainless bow railing is sturdy and attractive, but otherwise it's almost useless at 16 inches high—it is something to trip over or from which to hang onto the boat at the dock: the bow railing should be at least 28 inches high for safety.

Cabin

Down the companionway stairs is an open, roomy interior, finished brightly with shades of tan and white for a neutral tone. Headroom is well over 6 feet, 5 inches throughout much of the cabin. An elliptical lounge or dinette is to port, with a table that lowers to create a filler to convert the lounge into a 7-foot-long-by-3-foot, 8-inch berth. The electrical service panel is located to port near the companionway, but out of the weather and up at eye level for easy use.

The galley to starboard has a large Corian countertop with cutouts for a trash bin and a large double sink. A NuTone food center is built in as well, and the sink spigot lifts for cleanup. A two-burner stove, microwave-convection oven, coffeemaker, upright refrigerator-freezer, TV-VCR, and ample storage space are included.

Just aft of the galley is the midcabin with its U-shaped lounge seat and generous seated headroom. The area is well lit and ventilated, and has lots of storage space. The 6-foot, 4-inch-by-4-foot, 8-inch island berth in the master stateroom is well cushioned and comfortable. Both ends of the berth narrow considerably forward due to the hull's flare and back aft to create more room to maneuver. A hanging locker and TV-VCR are aft to port, and side lockers provide room for small treasures. A 20-inch hatch (just big enough to get through) overhead and small opening side ports let in however much air and light you want.

The boat's single head has access through a pair of doors leading from the stateroom and the cabin. An electric toilet, circular shower (a nice design that makes excellent use of headspace), and storage above and below the vanity are all well engineered in this attractive one-piece unit. It's easy to keep clean with its joint- and mildew-free structure and smooth finish.

Engine Room

Formula has applied its engineering experience down below in the engine room. The entire cockpit deck in the form of a hatch lifts on stainless hinges at the forward end. Once it was raised its full 47 inches, I could stand up straight in fully half of the engine room. A full 28 inches between the engines permits reaching the cooling-water expansion tanks, dipsticks, and seawater strainers down between the engine stringers and engine blocks.

Although accessibility to the space itself is excellent, some of its components are tough to reach. The engines' seacocks are near the forward bulkhead inside the 16-inch-deep stringers, making them difficult to access—you have to lie down on

the batteries with their exposed terminals; I would want a battery cover. The seacocks should be relocated for better access; fitting them with a remote operating handle would solve the immediate problem, but the chance of the seacock valves being maintained properly decreases in direct proportion to their accessibility. A frozen through-hull valve is of little use when an aged hose ruptures. Only a small mechanic could get to the steering gear and water heater back aft. Access to the outboard side of the engines is also difficult, with just 6 inches between them. You may think this is your mechanic's problem, but remember that neglected equipment becomes unreliable over time.

The fuel system is worth discussing. The Racor filter-separators are located above the transmissions and are very easy to reach. Although most boats in this class use compression fuel fittings, Formula still uses a fuel hose and hose clamps. Aircraft-type hoses and compression fittings are much stronger and abrasion-resistant, so they should be included on a boat of this price and size.

Wiring is neatly loomed, fastened, and routed, as are the many drain lines aft. The 80-amp battery charger, Xchanger oil-changing system, and Halon 1301 fire extinguisher are neatly installed in the forward bulkhead. On our test boat, the port main-engine seacock's through-hull had a slow leak, with a large drop of water rolling down into the bilge every 5 to 10 seconds; it may need to be removed and rebedded. Overall, the space easily accommodates daily maintenance checks and minor work, but I recommend fixing the seacock access and fuel fittings and making the aft engine-room bulkhead watertight.

Construction

The Formula is conventionally built, with a solid fiberglass hull supported by an interlocking network of plywood-cored bulkheads, intercostal frames, and stringers. The limber holes are, in effect, double-sealed by fiberglass during installation. A vinylester-based resin in the hull's skin coat protects against osmotic blistering; Coremat is used in the sides to prevent fabric print-through; and flota-tion foam is injected, mostly for sound-deadening, although an impact and holing might not sink the boat if the foam itself is not penetrated.

The shoebox hull-to-deck joint is secured by Plexus polyurethane adhesive and stainless bolts—certainly a better arrangement than self-tapping screws. Decks are cored with ½-inch Divinycell, adding stiffness and strength at less weight than could be achieved by a single skin of fiberglass.

Performance Test

On our sea trial out of Boca Raton, Florida, on a day in mid-December, we fortunately had 30- to 40-knot winds out of the northwest, which meant we had a great lee close to the beach and 2- to 4-footers riding a 6-foot swell just a couple of miles out. The two 450 hp Diamond Series Cummins took their time getting up to 1,800 rpm from idle, but then their turbos kicked in and the Formula took off like a ski boat.

Running with the seas on our quarter, the boat tracked very well, taking little effort to keep it on course; it was the same heading directly downsea. With the 4- to 6-foot seas on the beam at 25 knots, we had an active platform under us, and we took more than a little spray over the bow. However, the boat's excellent stability at speed was appreciated, and I've seen far wetter rides than this in similar conditions.

The real test for this boat came when we started heading directly into the steep chop at 18 knots. At that speed, the ride was fairly comfort-able but with some slapping and cavitation with the

shallow, recessed propellers ventilating periodically. At 24 knots, the ride didn't seem much rougher, but above that speed it got downright uncomfortable. However, this is still a better running head-sea boat than a Sea Ray type, and it's nearly as good as a British-built Fairline or Viking Sport Cruiser.

If the helm seat were only 6 inches higher, a person of average height would have been able to see over the bow with the trim tabs up. Tabs down in a head sea smoothed the ride out noticeably—and slowed the boat a couple of knots with the extra wetted surface, making the ride wetter.

Another visibility complaint is related to the wide fiberglass radar arches that cut a decent-size chunk out of the horizon—all in the name of styling. I suggest cutting a slot up the middle like Ocean does on its flybridge hardtop supports or, better yet, making them out of stainless pipe so they don't interfere with the sight lines so much.

Surprisingly, the boat ran reasonably well with full tabs when running downsea, too; that's good because I couldn't have seen ahead otherwise. There was no tendency for the boat to bow steer. The ac-companying table gives the Formula 41 PC perfor-mance results.

The engine-control layout mentioned previ-ously was awkward enough offshore, but it was far more so when maneuvering dockside. Our boat had optional power steering, and it was money well spent—the Formula handled superbly in the steer-ing department once underway at speed.

The modestly sized 23-by-26-inch props on the business end of the Aquamet 19 shafts (set at a

Formula 41 PC Performance Results

RPM	Speed, knots	Speed, mph	Fuel Use, gph	Nautical mpg	Statute mpg	Range, nm	Range, statute miles	Noise Level, dBA	Trim, degrees
630	6.3	7.2	1.9	3.32	3.81	1,044	1,201	64	1
1,000	8.2	9.4	5.0	1.64	1.89	517	594	62	2.5
1,400	10.6	12.2	14.7	0.72	0.83	227	261	67	7
1,800	18.9	21.7	21.7	0.87	1.00	274	316	69	5
2,200	25.5	29.3	30.1	0.85	0.97	267	307	72	6
2,400	28.9	33.2	35.7	0.81	0.93	255	293	74	5
2,600	31.3	36.0	44.1	0.71	0.82	224	257	77	4.5

12 deg. angle) turned by 1.5:1 ZF gears dug in fairly well at idle speed.

The Formula 41 PC is one of this quality builder's best-sellers, it's the biggest boat in the company's 26- to 41-foot lineup, and it is a well-engineered production cruiser offering good value on today's market. Unlike many express cruisers, this one has a moderate beam-to-length ratio, which means that although it has less interior volume than a comparable-quality Sea Ray, for instance, it can deliver a superior ride in a stiff chop. The boat is well-designed for its intended purpose as a family cruiser. With the optional generator and AC, the boat has the self-contained cruising capacity to comfortably cruise the Bahamas or northern climes in the summer. With a six-person sleeping capacity, the single head may seem limiting, but such is the nature of an express cruiser. The standard-equipment list is lengthy, but you'll undoubtedly want a few extras to round off the amenity list.

1999 Hunt 33

C. Raymond Hunt Associates have been refining Ray's original deep-V hull form since that pioneer's death in 1978. Today, the company is well known for designing modern deep-V bottoms carrying traditional-looking superstructures. In my opinion, these are some of the seakindliest, best-looking boats on the seven seas.

The firm has entered the production-builder's fray with its own boat, the Hunt 33—and a prettily proportioned craft it is, with a low graceful sheer, fine sections forward and amidships that promise (and deliver) excellent seakeeping, and a comfortable cabin for occasional weekending. I expected the boat to run well, with my only real questions of how comfortable can anyone make a light boat in a stiff chop, and is the quality of construction on par with the design.

Engine Room

The beauty of a single-diesel, other than being cheaper to buy and operate, is the great accessibility afforded by the engine's location amidships. A two-piece hatch on centerline folds up and lifts out, while hinged hatches outboard lift easily on boost lifts. The holding tank is outboard to port, along with the hot-water heater, which used waste heat from the engine on our shore-powerless test boat. A pair of heavy-duty batteries is outboard to starboard, but these will likely be moved aft on follow-on hulls to help submerge the chines a little more.

The wiring is neatly installed and loomed, although Hunt plans to relocate the main wiring run along the engine room's starboard hull stringer to reduce the likelihood of it being stepped on. Bilges are ground fairly smooth and coated with gelcoat, although a little more grinding was needed to produce a true high-end finish. The soft engine-bed mounts are bolted to steel plates encapsulated in the foam-cored hull stringers, which are in turn stiffened by gussets, producing a combination of rigidity and resilience that nicely reduces vibration levels. Sound insulation is carefully applied and effective, with heavy-clad surfaces resisting tears common in these materials.

Cockpit

The 6-foot, 8-inch by 9-foot cockpit is a textbook design example. Toe kicks are formed by the wide coamings that are 25 inches high forward, which is on the low side, but are mitigated by the toe kick and excellent nonskid, and 27 inches high at the transom. The deck, which is surrounded by narrow, deep gutters to quickly drain the well-sloped deck, is also easily removed by backing off a few screws. Molded steps lead to the foot-wide side decks and forward to the bow's single 12-inch cleat and hawsehole for the anchor rode. Hunt offers owners any ground tackle setup they might want, so our boat was ready for a pulpit or anchor chocks to be installed. Sections of the prototype's decks forward and in the cockpit deflected slightly underfoot; although this is perhaps more a perception than a safety or structural issue, Hunt plans to increase the thickness of the coring at negligible cost in terms of weight.

Bridge Deck and Helm

The single-diesel allows a low, flush deck over the engine, which lowers the yacht's center of gravity, reduces sail area, and results in a more pleasing profile. The 6-foot, 9-inch-long bridge deck is a single 6-inch step up from the cockpit. Our test boat had a 5-foot, 5-inch bench seat to port with storage below, and a matching 37-inch seat aft of the pedestal helm seat opposite. The helm station is comfortably laid out, perhaps reflecting Hunt's experience in building commercial pilot boats. The tilt wheel is mounted so that it's no reach at all from the helm seat—it's like driving a car. The dual-lever mechanical engine controls are to starboard of the wheel, also within easy reach, and the engine instruments are clearly visible above the wheel. This works well with the bow-thruster control to port of the wheel.

There's space for a modest array of electronics, although on this console version, they will likely need to be mounted atop the dashboard. The compass is directly in front of the wheel, as it should be, and the DC breaker panel is a foot to the right of your right knee when you're seated in that 30-inch-high upholstered pedestal seat. I was glad to see that Hunt, unlike most builders, installed trim-tab-angle indicators so you actually know their position at a glance.

The pièce de résistance has got to be the aluminum-framed windshield. It's beautifully built with large side vent windows and narrow mullions to minimize line-of-sight interference. Powder-coated for long life and with a great-looking finish, this was a windshield that I could actually see through without stooping over. An integral handrail, installed to hang onto when walking outside, makes the stiff frame even sturdier. Another nice feature is the double-jointed table, made in Sweden by Lagun, for the port seat. It hinges in several directions and lifts off and stows in a neat integrated package when not in use.

Lazarette

The same large engine-hatch tooling is used in the cockpit, resulting in a highly accessible lazarette and fuel tank. The 103-gallon aluminum tank is well strapped in and appears to afford ample room for air to circulate and prevent corrosion. Hunt is modifying the rudderboard to support both the steering gear and the top of the rudderpost for added hull protection in the event of an underwater collision.

Cabin

The cabin is finished Herreshoff-style with varnished mahogany trim and a teak and holly sole set off by the white bulkheads, cream-colored wood slats covering the hull sides, and a padded vinyl headliner. Headroom is on the slim side at 71 inches, but follow-on hulls will add another inch or so; the advantage is the low exterior profile. The opening portholes and 20-inch overhead hatch result in a light and friendly setting.

For a weekender, there's sufficient space with the convertible dinette to port that turns into a 78-by-36-inch berth. Opposite is the enclosed head, generously proportioned and beautifully finished, with a sink spigot that lifts out to become a handheld shower. A small mirror doubles as a convenient access door to the helm-console wiring.

Just forward of the head, the galley has a sink and refrigerator storage space behind and below the countertop. With the addition of a filler cushion, the V-berth forward converts to something like a queen-size bed, and there's a good 76-plus inches of legroom along the hull. Our prototype had a few rough spots, with unsealed joints and corners in the head and an exposed bow-thruster breaker below the V-berth, but Hunt has fixed those details on newer hulls. The overall quality of the cabin is very good, and the layout is simple but practical.

Design

This hull is a prototypical C. Raymond Hunt Associates deep-V hull, improved steadily over the years since the 1960 original. The boat has very fine lines forward, with radiused keel sections and a cutaway stem to improve ride and control and to reduce bow steer (yawing) in a following sea. Chine flats are 6 inches wide at the stern, adding form stability and dynamic lift for a drier ride. Running strakes also contribute to a dry ride and add lift and dynamic stability at high speeds.

With 35 degrees of deadrise below the windshield, reentry in a head sea is surprisingly smooth, especially for a boat as light as the Hunt. Transom deadrise is 20 degrees, indicating a reasonable balance between dynamic lift and form stability.

Construction

Hunt designed the hull structure to ABS Motor Pleasure Yacht rules, starting with an ISO-NPG gelcoat, followed by an anti-osmotic blister coat of 1.5-ounce mat wetted out in vinylester resin. This is followed by general-purpose, orthophthalic resin in the laminate of bidirectional, nonwoven fabrics surrounding a ¾-inch Airex-cored bottom and Divinycell-cored hull sides and decks. Stringers and bulkheads are also cored with Divinycell for high strength at moderate weight; areas subject to compression loads around bolts get a high-density foam substitute. The all-important hull-to-deck joint, which not only keeps the water out but also absorbs significant sheer loads as the boat moves in a seaway, is bonded with 3M 5200 adhesive and fastened with stainless bolts and screws.

Performance Test

Buzzards Bay in Massachusetts is probably my favorite place for a sea trial, since you can almost always find a lee for speed runs and, due to the prevailing southwest wind, sizable waves to play around in afterward. Such was the case on our test day.

We ran the speed runs first, and a couple of things caught my attention. First is the speed capability of a boat with a single modestly sized diesel, with sustained 25- to 27-knot cruising speeds easily reached. Second is the fuel economy, with the lower drag and lighter weight of the single diesel producing 2.3 to 2.7 nmpg, a full nautical mile more per gallon than many twin-diesels I've tested in this size range. Noise levels were satisfactory, but not yet at the level a quality builder can achieve with a little experimentation and persistence (our test boat was a prototype that the builder had not yet had time to tweak). The accompanying table gives the performance results of our sea trial.

Visibility from the helm was excellent with moderate, 4-degree trim at cruise, an indication of good weight distribution relative to the hull's center of dynamic lift. Running in the 3- to 4-foot seas at 25 knots made me appreciate the 35-degree bottom deadrise below the windshield area, just where you need it most to minimize slamming loads as the hull lands after becoming partially airborne at that speed. The Hunt is light for its size, and it takes a cleaver-like hull form like this one to produce a smooth ride despite the low displacement. Tracking in a quartering sea at 22 knots was quite good, although a heavier, more deeply submerged V-bottom hull will perhaps have a slight advantage. As we drifted in the trough, the roll period and amplitude were unremarkable (no more than 12 degrees to leeward that day) and comfortable. At 4½ turns lock-to-lock, steering was reasonable, but I would opt for power steering and a quicker 3 turns befitting a boat with this speed capability.

Hunt 33 Performance Results

RPM	Speed, knots	Speed, mph	Fuel Use, gph	Nautical mpg	Statute mpg	Range, nm	Range, statute miles	Noise Level, dBA	Trim, degrees
1,000	7.2	8.3	1.23	5.9	6.7	533	1,154	74	0
1,400	9.8	11.3	3.55	2.8	3.2	251	543	79	2
1,800	15.5	17.8	6.54	2.4	2.7	216	466	83	4
2,000	19	21.9	8.01	2.4	2.7	216	466	83	4
2,200	21.8	25.1	9.42	2.3	2.7	211	455	83	4
2,400	24.8	28.5	10.97	2.3	2.6	206	445	85	4
2,600	27.4	31.5	13.63	2.0	2.3	183	395	86	4
2,800	29.2	33.6	16.81	1.7	2.0	158	342	87	3
3,000	31.3	36.0	20.49	1.5	1.8	139	300	89	3

Test conditions: single 355 hp Cummins diesel inboard, three passengers, full tank of fuel, 25-foot-plus depth, 1-foot chop, air temperature 68 degrees, and 100 pounds of gear. Test conducted on October 24, 1998, in Buzzards Bay, Massachusetts, off Padanaram, Massachusetts. Range calculated using 90 percent of the boat's 103-gallon fuel capacity. Sound levels taken at the helm.

The faster-ratio steering would also come in handy dockside. Unlike a twin-engine boat on which the rudders are left amidships while docking, the Hunt 33's rudder is constantly shifting when the boat is backing into a slip, especially in the absence of a full keel to minimize sideslip in the breeze. The bow thruster offers lots of push, so there really isn't any difficulty maneuvering once you master the thruster-wheel-throttle and clutch dance. That's another good reason for specifying single-lever engine controls, which—by removing one more moving part from the equation—will make the entire evolution less accident-prone.

Hunt has since reduced the noise levels by mechanically isolating the throttle cables (with rubber interfaces) and fussing with the hatch gaskets.

Hunt has an excellent boat that will satisfy the needs of a broad niche market well. Purveyors of day boats with engine boxes beware: the Hunt in many ways goes one better with an uncluttered, flush deck; fixed underwater gear for better tracking in a following sea; an excellent, true deep-V hull form that produces a superior ride despite the boat's modest displacement; and a surprisingly competitive price.

The Hunt 33 is very well built using conventional boatbuilding methods and materials to produce a light and strong structure. The single 355 hp Cummins is a perfect match for the boat, producing a good turn of speed with almost unheard-of economy. This single-engine configuration is an excellent choice with its economy of purchase, maintenance, and fuel consumption; excellent accessibility; inherent reliability (you may want to add a second fuel filter-separator in series to make sure); and the low deck profile resulting from being mounted in the deepest part of the hull.

Little Harbor Triple–Waterjet Whisperjet 44

Rhode Island–based Little Harbor Marine, founded by sailing legend Ted Hood, is a high-end builder of mostly waterjet-powered cruising boats. Low-slung and nicely proportioned, these yachts were originally based on Blackwatch offshore sportfisher hulls. The Whisperjet 34- to 55-foot series includes this 44-footer, a 1,260 hp beauty available with twin or triple waterjets.

Little Harbor Whisperjet 44 Specifications

LOA:	44'0"
Beam:	13'7"
Draft:	2'1"
Displacement:	28,000 lb. (approximate)
Maximum cabin headroom:	6'8"
Fuel capacity:	520 gal.
Water capacity:	164 gal.

Standard power: Twin 420 hp Yanmar 6CX (M)-ETE diesels

Test-boat power: Triple 420 hp Yanmar diesels driving Hamilton 291 waterjets through 1.25:1 reductions

Engine Room

There's not much room to spare in the 44's engine room with the third centerline propulsion iron tucked inches away from its mates. A pair of 600 hp lightweight diesels would fit better and might increase propulsion efficiency. On the other hand, it looks like the U.S. Navy specified the machinery and equipment installation, with color-coded plumbing, precisely positioned aircraft-type fuel lines, and wiring and plumbing systems neatly and unobtrusively routed. Hood is fastidious about sound levels, which explains the Soundown rubber-wrap on the stringers and aluminum fuel tanks, as well as covering the Hamilton waterjets under the cockpit.

Soft engine mounts bolted to solid engine beds are the best combination for sound and vibration attenuation, so of course it's what you'll find on a Little Harbor. The bilges aren't tooled fiberglass-smooth (and they should be for the price), but they're close enough to make for easy bilge cleanup. Ideally, there should be a solid watertight bulkhead between the engine room and the lazarette for passive flooding protection, but that would be difficult on this boat with all the intervening machinery traversing the two compartments. Hood makes it easy to get to the engine room two ways: with a day hatch opening for quick access or by pressing a button so the entire bridge deck lifts cleanly out of the way for a more panoramic presentation.

Side Decks and Foredeck

The Little Harbor's long bow and graceful sheerline will unquestionably earn many a prolonged stare. From the cockpit looking forward, the foredeck stretches on forever, and it's a beautiful sight to behold. Walking forward to enjoy that perspective, the side decks are nice and wide—over a foot for the most part. The windshield, with its clean frameless windows, slopes inboard markedly, adding elbowroom and looking great at the same time. The boat is as practical as it is attractive: the bulletproof, 2-foot, 8-inch-high stainless steel bow railing, the massive 12-inch bow cleats that look just a little thicker and shinier than anyone else's, the oversized open bow chocks, and stainless steel–framed cabin hatches that hinge from either end—your choice depending on the wind situation. When you walk on the trunk cabintop or foredeck, you will think you're walking on concrete.

Back in the cockpit, the coaming is only 2 feet high outboard, and there's no toe kick at the transom to keep you on balance blasting by at 40 mph. This makes the cockpit unsafe for standing passengers at high speed. Atypically unsailor-like, there are also no scuppers to get you out of a pooping jam offshore. The deck drains through a crack in the aft end of the deck hatch through two 1½-inch-diameter drain lines. The manufacturer says it's going to add scuppers on future hulls and back-fit this one.

Accommodations

Down in the cabin, Hood squeaks more than 6 feet, 8 inches of headroom out of a low-profile 44-footer, by both adding generous camber to the deck above and installing the sole as low in the hull as possible. Cherry joinery is balanced by mostly white headliners and cabin sides; joints are tight, but the boat looks like it went out the factory doors before the last sanding and varnishing phase was completed. Hood promises to do better on follow-on hulls. Also practical—and not seen enough on boats of this size—are the separate head (with toilet and sink) to port and shower with sink to starboard. The layout is perfect for a cruising couple with a private forward stateroom; by adding an insert and a small lounge seat, a king-size berth is created. The grandkids can be accommodated with the seat and lift-up dinette backrest that converts to 6-foot, 10-inch upper and lower berths.

Traces of Hood's sailboat heritage show up in details like lots of cedar-lined closet space; numerous storage nooks and crannies; classy, leak-proof, stainless steel–trimmed portholes; and ample freezer-refrigerator capacity.

Performance Test

Part of the beauty of waterjets is their ability to run over soft lobster-pot buoys with absolutely nothing below the waterline to snag them: just three flush-mounted, slotted, bronze grills on the hull bottom sucking up seawater and the enclosed impellers shooting it out the stern. Other pluses include a paltry 2-foot, 1-inch draft, stop-on-a-dime performance, and an ultrasmooth drivetrain with a sailboat's vibration levels (due to the location of the propeller or impeller inside a tube with its inherently uniform waterflow, which minimizes the general ruckus of a conventional propeller spinning away inches below the bottom of a boat at an angle offset from the actual waterflow). The boat's infinitely variable thrust and great maneuverability in close quarters will bring out the showoff in you.

I don't recommend it, but you *can* try running at 35-plus mph, leaving the throttles set at cruise speed, and pulling the reverse buckets slowly to the full-astern position. Those waterjets are instantly and smoothly running in the other direction, with no shock on the left-in-gear transmissions. There's nothing better for collision avoidance—unless it's paying attention to where you're going—than instantly reversible waterjets.

If you actually want to dodge those little buoys, the steering is very tight at 1.9 turns lock-to-lock, but it takes some effort; slacking the system off to 3 turns might help on both scores. In very rough water, waterjets also tend to become airborne as soon as the hull does, momentarily losing waterflow and propulsion thrust. Inboard props are much deeper in the water, making this less of a problem for them.

Little Harbor Triple–Waterjet Whisperjet 44 Performance Results

RPM	Speed, knots	Speed, mph	Fuel Use, gph	Nautical mpg	Statute mpg	Range, nm	Range, statute miles	Noise Level, dBA	Trim, degrees
1,000	5.6	6.4	3.3	1.70	1.95	794	913	67	2
1,300	6.8	7.8	5.7	1.19	1.37	558	642	71	2
1,600	8.3	9.5	10.2	0.81	0.94	381	438	73	2
1,900	9.5	10.9	15.0	0.63	0.73	296	341	75	4
2,200	13.1	15.1	23.1	0.57	0.65	265	305	79	5
2,500	19.2	22.1	30.3	0.64	0.73	299	343	82	5
2,800	26.1	30.0	42.6	0.61	0.70	287	330	83	5
3,100	33.1	38.1	56.4	0.59	0.67	275	316	85	5
3,320	39.4	45.3	75.6	0.52	0.60	244	280	89	4

Test conditions: half a tank of fuel, four persons on board, 1.23:1 gears, and Yanmar 420 hp. Noise level tested at helm.

If you need a reason *not* to buy waterjets, there is the lack of directional stability, especially at lower speeds, because nothing projects below the bottom of the boat (like rudders) to keep you going in a relatively straight line—just the small keel and the hull's deadrise. Retractable rudders might help; they would be fully lowered at low speeds or in following seas, and retracted otherwise. The manufacturer has built similar rudder systems before, so it shouldn't be a major engineering challenge.

A good waterjet hull form has less deadrise and the keel is rounded in cross section forward; otherwise, the bow turns into a rudder in following seas. This means the head-sea ride on the Little Harbor will be somewhat harder than on a boat with a finer, deeper entry. The Little Harbor heels to beat the band in turns with so little underwater lateral resistance (that is, no keel or running gear).

Learning not to oversteer takes getting used to, since I found the boat very suddenly heading 40 degrees to one side. We had flat-calm conditions on our sea trial, but this directional-stability issue is more pronounced in a following-sea scenario. Visibility from the helm was good through large expanses of windshield, although the pulpit kissed the horizon consistently from my vantage point at the helm. Depressing the trim tabs drops the bow soon enough, but handling the quirkiness quotient increases commensurately with pronounced bow steer kicking in when the tabs are lowered.

Waterjets lose efficiency at low to midrange speeds, so don't expect to be able to operate in the 12- to 18-knot range—that limitation can be a problem when the going gets rough and you can't take the pounding when running at 25 knots. Waterjets also ventilate far easier in rough water than submerged props. On the other hand, the jets are very responsive when turning at speed—it took just 20 seconds to complete a 360-degree turn at 3,000 rpm, about half the normal time for a 44-footer. However, since most of my time at sea has been spent *not* running waterjets, perhaps a conventional inboard would feel sluggish to me after a month on board this boat.

Having enough get-home reserve power on just two engines won't cramp your style much—running on two engines, we made 27 mph at 3,000 rpm and hit nearly 32 mph wide open. Running on three engines, we were on top at 2,200 rpm for 14 mph, so this is one slippery hull. It also has a nicely refined bottom, with radiused double chines decreasing wetted surface and the waterline beam for better efficiency. Radiused chines and running strakes forward run smoother and drier, and are easier for the builder to fabricate than those with hard inside corners.

Docking the boat, once you learn how, is a dream. You can twist and walk the boat with a lot more grace and finesse than any inboard could. With less underwater area, just expect to get blown around more in a crosswind. Handling quirks aside, this boat is a real performer, and does the job of transporting an affluent owner and guests from point A to point B with heart-pounding alacrity.

Now owned by Hinckley Yacht Holdings, the Little Harbor line of high-end Whisperjet waterjet-powered boats, is aiming for the stratosphere with these specialty yachts, in terms of both clientele and product. First, it takes a rare boater who can afford one of these works of art—expect less than $100,000 back from your million-dollar bill on a 1999 fully equipped triple-jet LH 44. For that, you get a bow thruster, oil-change pumps, transom shower, inverter-charger, 5 kW genset, AC, entertainment center, Grunert holding-plate refrigerator-freezer, ground tackle with remote-controlled windlass, and a Pompanette helm seat. Built in Taiwan, the latest in the Whisperjet series is being offered in both twin- and triple-jet packages, with sales so far divided evenly between the two powerplant options.

Pluses include gorgeous looks, nonexistent vibrations, great ride, sensible helm layout, exquisite cherry joinery, and shiplike machinery installation; minuses include primarily the price.

No one puts together a classier-looking, better-engineered express-style yacht than Little Harbor.

You can sail away on a well-equipped Eastbay 49 for less money; the Eastbay is a bigger boat with a better ride, similar quality, and excellent engineering.

But if you want waterjets, beautiful styling, almost-as-good-as-it-gets construction, and the Little Harbor logo, there may be a 44 in your future.

1998 Mainship 30 Pilot

There aren't enough companies like Mainship that offer great value, solid engineering and construction, and very user-friendly and practical layouts. Here's a reasonably priced boat that is great-looking and well proportioned and has a seaworthy, semi-planing hull for comfortable 13- to 15-knot cruising; a terrific layout for day trips or weekending; and an attractive bottom line made possible by efficient, no-frills production lines (and a few shortcuts) and the buying power of the Mainship-Silverton-Luhrs-Hunter conglomerate.

Cockpit

Let's start the tour back aft. The 8-foot, 4-inch-wide by 5-foot, 5-inch-long cockpit is a comfortable 27 inches deep, and the deck drains quickly through recessed scuppers and aft gutters. Mainship will also offer a transom door as an option on later models, and I consider that a good investment for easier stern-to boarding from the optional swim platform.

The lazarette bilge, like the engine room, is reasonably smooth and coated with gray gelcoat. Heavy-grade wiring is used for the green-wire bonding system—no shortcuts here, either. Main-

ship gets it right with the hatch gutters too—they're a full 1½ inches deep and lead directly overboard through the cockpit scuppers. The nonskid does the job gripping boat shoes, and it should be easy to keep clean. Unlike on some more expensive boats I've been on, the glass is even ground smooth under the cockpit washboards, very likely saving you an eventual painful splinter.

Corner-mounted flush hawseholes lead to the 10-inch stern cleats bolted to the nicely tooled interior cockpit liner. Shore-power and TV-telephone connectors are to port and the freshwater hookup is to starboard.

Comfortably wide side decks lead forward from the cockpit. The rugged 1¼-inch-diameter welded aluminum bow railing is 27 inches high at the bow, which is OK, but it drops to just 18 inches farther aft. Other than that, the bow is a great place to plug for a few stripers or to sit on the raised trunk cabin and ride along at slow speed for the fresh air and excellent view.

Bridge Deck

A single step leads from the cockpit up to the 8-foot-long and 7-foot-wide bridge deck. Molded fiberglass bench seats, which are tooled in on either side, are standard, although I'm not convinced this design makes the best use of deck space. Lift up the cushions to get to the two lift-out hatches on each side to access the storage room below. This area will get wet, since the hatches aren't flanged. A single 3-foot-wide engine-room hatch runs most of the length of the bridge deck. It's so well balanced on its boost lifts that a toddler could lift it.

Helm

A pair of 32-inch helm and companion seats raised a full 33 inches off the deck are comfortable and afford a good view through the no-nonsense aluminum-framed windshield. The helm is to starboard, a conventional and sensible approach because that's the side from which stand-on vessels come, according to the Rules of the Road. The straightforward helm layout puts the wheel at a comfortable 30-degrees-from-vertical angle.

A small flat for electronics is to starboard of the wheel, with room for more atop the dashboard ahead. The wheel and compass should be in front of the operator, so they need to be moved a few inches to the right. A nice feature is the tilt-back helm console, which allows easy access to the wiring harnesses and insides of the gauges and switches. To port is a clear chart lid to hold your chart pack in place in a stiff breeze. I like the fact that the windshield is high enough so that you're not looking at the frame at horizon level; however, at idle speed, it's low enough to just see over when you're standing.

Cabin

A sliding companionway door opens 20 inches to the three steps to the cabin, which is surprisingly big, with a full 6-feet, 5 inches of headroom and an open, inviting feeling. It's also bright and sunny with opening portholes and a single 20-inch overhead hatch. The layout, designed to sleep two on a double berth forward, is fairly conventional with a convertible V-berth and dinette forward (the table lowers to support the berth's filler cushion). Just aft is a pair of bench seats with more storage underneath. The galley is located to port by the companionway, and has a large countertop, sink, two-burner stove, refrigerator, and optional microwave oven above. The enclosed head is opposite to starboard, and it has a full 6 feet, 3 inches of headroom, a folding seat over the toilet, a nicely tooled liner, a removable shower spigot, an opening porthole, and a vanity with sink and storage space. It's roomy and well engineered.

Our boat had a teak-lined interior and a teak and holly sole. With the off-white or light cream-colored fiberglass liner, the result is quite appealing and will be easy to maintain. The seat cushions were a classy-looking plaid, and there's even a leatherette-lined padded backrest around the U-shaped dinette seat.

Engine Room

The virtues of single-engine propulsion are immediately evident upon popping the hatch to the Pilot's engine room. The engine is uncrowded and there's ample space for auxiliary equipment on all sides. Part of the credit goes to the 5 kW Seapower alternator that runs off the main engine, eliminating the need for a separate generator. Immediately, you notice the clean bilges and the rugged, no-nonsense construction.

Mainship has done a fair job of getting you to the machinery, the only exception being that the molded bridge-deck bench seats reduce the opening to 3 feet wide and restrict accessibility considerably outboard of the engine. You can get to the engine itself for fluid checks, though the fuel filter-separator—mounted 6 inches or so off the bilge and outboard of the engine—is difficult to reach. The seacock and the internal raw-water strainer are both easily accessible.

The problem with the single centerline hatch is getting to the battery charger and fire-extinguisher bottle on the forward bulkhead and to the saltwater and freshwater pumps forward to port. Continuing the hatch all the way forward to the companionway would open up this area. That said, the hatch gutters are deep and well designed, so the engine room will likely stay dry. Plastic cable chases nicely hide and protect the wiring. I would like to see Mainship upgrade to compression fittings on its fuel lines; soft hoses and hose clamps are for outboards, in my opinion. Freshwater and holding tanks are to port and starboard, respectively, outboard of the engine.

The engine installation is very clean, with the 230 bhp Yanmar sitting level and compact on its vibration-absorbing mounts through-bolted to the fiberglass-encapsulated wooden hull stringers. Bilges are neatly sanded and gelcoated gray for easy cleanup.

The 175-gallon, 0.19-inch-thick, 5052-grade aluminum fuel tank is mounted on brackets to separate the bottom of the tank from its floor, allowing air circulation, which is essential to long tank life. Many builders just drop the tank on neoprene strips and strap it down. The fuel tank projects into the engine room from under the cockpit so, unfortunately, it would be difficult to construct a watertight subdivision bulkhead—essential to staying afloat in the event of a holing—around the tank.

Design

The Mainship 30 Pilot is based on Luhrs's earlier Alura, with its semiplaning (or semidisplacement) hull form; sharp, deep entry; round bilges; and soft sections flattening out aft. Small chine flats have since been added to the round bilges and the keel has been lengthened for full grounding protection, making this a sensible hybrid. These chines add some lift at planing speeds, resulting in a slightly stiffer roll and greater form stability.

The boat has a full hollow keel that gives it an added measure of directional stability except, arguably, in a quartering sea when it could actually make this moderate-speed boat more susceptible to passing-wave energy. It's also nice to be able to run aground (at least in sand or mud) without worrying about damage to the prop or rudder.

Construction

One way that Mainship keeps costs low is by keeping construction simple with a solid fiberglass hull of woven roving and mat. Mainship uses an ISO-NPG gelcoat to help prevent osmotic blistering, with DCPD-blend resin used throughout the laminate. Fiberglass-encapsulated marine-plywood stringers and bulkheads strengthen the hull and reduce hull-skin panel sizes to manageable dimensions. The hull-to-deck joint consists of two flanges bonded together with self-tapping screws and 3M 5200 polyurethane adhesive. Limber holes are sealed against water penetration with flexible gelcoat, which is not a great way to keep the water out because the gelcoat will soon crack. Decks forward and aft are cored with balsa for stiffness and light weight, and a fiberglass internal-pan assembly is used forward to form the cabin sole and liner. Just be sure you don't drill any holes through the balsa, which is like a sponge when laid bare and exposed to water.

Performance Test

With the Yanmar purring away at idle speed, we recorded some surprisingly low sound-level readings—just 67 dBA at the helm and 71 dBA in the cockpit. In fact, the generator on our sea-trial test boat (hull #1) made a lot more noise than the propulsion diesel. At higher speeds, we started developing what sounded like propeller-induced rumbling noises that overpowered any sounds the engine was making. If Mainship works through that problem, this could be a very quiet boat indeed throughout the operating spectrum. Imagine trolling at 1,000 rpm and being able to talk from the cockpit in conversational tones with someone in the cabin.

The boat managed an honest 14-knot cruise at 3,100 rpm, and topped out at just over 17 knots at 3,500 rpm. Not bad, especially considering the miserly fuel consumption. The table next page lists the Pilot 30 performance results with seven eighths of a tank of fuel, full water, three passengers, and light gear in 18 feet of water.

This boat simply will not pound going into a head sea. The entry is just too sharp and deep—almost Destroyer-like, and this is obviously not a

Mainship 30 Pilot Performance Results

RPM	Speed, knots	Speed, mph	Fuel Use, gph	Nautical mpg	Statute mpg	Range, nm	Range, statute miles	Noise Level, dBA	Trim, degrees
1,000	5.2	6.0	0.4	13.0	15.0	2,041	2,347	62	1
1,500	7.7	8.9	1.81	4.3	4.9	668	768	69	2
2,000	8.7	10.0	3.42	2.5	2.9	399	459	71	3
2,200	9.5	10.9	4.16	2.3	2.6	359	412	73	3
2,400	11.3	13.0	4.94	2.3	2.6	359	413	74	3
2,600	13.1	15.1	5.69	2.3	2.6	361	416	81	4
2,800	14.9	17.1	6.96	2.1	2.5	336	387	82	4
3,000	16.8	19.3	7.82	2.1	2.5	337	388	83	4
3,200	18.1	20.8	9.45	1.9	2.2	301	346	83	4
3,400	19.4	22.3	10.57	1.8	2.1	288	331	84	4.5
3,500	20.5	23.6	11.58	1.8	2.0	278	320	85	4

Test conditions: single 230 hp Yanmar diesel inboard, three passengers, full tank of fuel, 60-foot-plus depth, 1-foot seas, air temperature 72 degrees, and 100 pounds of gear. Test conducted on September 21, 1998, in Narragansett Bay, Rhode Island. Range calculated using 90 percent of the boat's 175-gallon fuel capacity. Sound levels taken at the helm.

30-knot boat, either by virtue of the hull form or the propulsion plant. With the big rudder, the boat should handle well even with seas abaft the beam.

At five turns lock-to-lock, the boat turned responsively and quickly on an even keel. Four turns would be better for quicker response in close quarters. It took us only 27 seconds to turn 360 degrees at 3,000 rpm, which is remarkably fast. The big hollow keel kept us pointing in the same direction with only minor helm corrections required. The hollow keel contributes to course-keeping but not to stability, since it likely displaces more than the keel structure itself.

Sitting down at the helm, the horizon disappeared behind the pulpit at higher speeds (we measured approximately 7 degrees of trim—about 2 degrees more than ideal), which is not desirable for obvious visibility reasons. A combination of three solutions could easily fix this: add trim tabs to drop the bow down, raise the helm seat, and remove the pulpit (or replace it with a pipe-framed arrangement that would allow you to see through it). Otherwise, plan on driving standing up. Other than that, the view ahead is the most important, and visibility all around was good.

This was hull #1 and, according to the builder; the seat has since been raised 5 inches. Mainship has added a wedge to decrease running angle and the boat apparently does not need trim tabs, so you can now see the horizon.

The 1998 Mainship 30 Pilot is a real bargain with a single gasoline 4.3-liter, 205 hp engine, or with optional Yanmar diesel power. Mainship delivers a sturdy, serviceable boat that is well worth the price. The boat is solidly if simply constructed and very attractively styled; it should be a capable seaboat. It offers comfortable accommodations for weekending or even weeklong coastal cruises and gunkholing. Be aware of the inevitable shortcuts, and have a prepurchase survey done so you know what you're buying in advance.

The Pilot would also make an excellent fishing boat with a big-enough cockpit that is easy to fish from and clean up—just add rod holders and outriggers. Don't plan on adding a tower because the boat is of moderate beam, especially compared to some of the 30-foot, excessively beamy barges to which you may have grown accustomed. The Pilot, on the other hand, gets the beam-to-length ratio just about right for efficiency and a good ride offshore. This is a boat that I can recommend to any family looking for a great deal in new powerboats: classic lines, a low profile for good stability, and less susceptibility to a crosswind.

1997 Sabreline 36 Express Cruiser

Sabreline 36 Express Cruiser Specifications	
Length:	36'0"
Beam:	12'6"
Draft:	3'4"
Displacement:	18,500 lb.
Fuel capacity:	300 gal.
Water capacity:	100 gal.
Transom deadrise:	14 deg.
Standard power:	twin Caterpillar 3116 300 bhp

This Maine-based builder produces classically styled, well-built, and reasonably priced express, aft-cabin, and sedan cruising yachts from 34 to 47 feet. Sabre Corporation makes good use of the Yankee work ethic, perhaps re-creating it in a highly technological application like this modern power yacht. The 36 Express is a real classic in terms of design, layout, and sheer utility. Although its hard chines mean it's not actually a Maine-style yacht, Sabre produces a comfortable ride in the mid-20-knot range, and it reaches those speeds efficiently due to its hull form and moderate displacement. It's low to the water, without a flybridge and the sheer bulk of many modern cruisers.

Sabreline's sailboat heritage is evident in the boats' pleasingly nautical interiors.

This is one of Sabre's smallest models, designed to sleep two couples for extended weekends or occasional longer trips. As the company brochure says, the boat is for people with less time to spend on the water but who want to make the most of the time they do have. Well stated, although I could see a couple spending a few weeks on board working their way up and down the coast on a relaxing, private cruise.

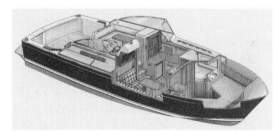

Cockpit

When I boarded through the transom door, the first thing that caught my eye was the cream-colored deck and liner. It really cuts down on the glare—a vast improvement over the bright white seen on too many boats. At 7 feet, 4 inches long, 10 feet wide, and a full 30 inches deep, the cockpit offers a hospitable spot to kick back and relax on the two-person, aft-facing lounge seat. The fact that the entire cockpit deck unbolts and lifts out will be appreciated by the owner who will eventually be confronted with replacing the fuel tanks.

Three well-guttered hatches (with clog-resistant ¾ in. drain lines) lead to the bilge below—and it's a long way down, creating lots of storage area for longer trips. The bilges and hull stringers are coated with beige gelcoat for a neat appearance, as are the underwater exhaust lines. The single aluminum fuel tank conforms to the shape of the hull to maximize capacity and available space. It's mounted on neoprene strips to provide air circulation on the tank bottom for longer life. Sabre has even created an enclosure for the steering gear, which doubles as a convenient seat.

The nonskid pattern is excellent—grippy yet cleanable. Molded-in steps lead to the 16-inch-wide side decks. In fishing terms, this means you can stroll down the side decks with a gaff full of striper in each hand without hanging on. The tooling on this boat is beautifully wrought, nowhere more evident than on the bow with its gorgeous trunk cabin.

The welded stainless double-pipe bow railing, 26 inches high forward, is secure and rigid to the grasp. Two line lockers aft of the anchor pulpit provide a place to stow the bow lines at sea; the straightforward bolt-on pulpit holds the plough anchor firmly in place.

Bridge Deck and Helm

It's up a single step to the 8-foot-long bridge deck, home to a beautifully crafted stainless steel–framed windshield, a forward-facing lounge seat to port, and raised pedestal seats forward to port and starboard. The starboard-side helm is nicely laid out with the wheel 10 degrees from vertical, and separate shifts and throttles located just forward. Assorted rocker switches are on a flat panel just ahead of the wheel, immediately followed by the engine gauges (I would relocate the tachometers so they're next to each other rather than separated 18 inches by the various gauges—the port tach is also obscured by the shifts). An electronics flat is higher up and just forward, properly positioned for easy viewing. The compass sits atop the electronics flat, ideal for easy reference when you're watching the water ahead. The entire arrangement tilts aft for gauge and electronics maintenance, a savings for the owner in reduced labor rates.

A chart table with a folding plastic cover is opposite to port, and Sabre has included thoughtful touches: well-placed grab bars, a centerline opening vent window (although I would like to see a narrower frame around this window to reduce interference with the view ahead at speed), and a companionway door that actually folds back out of the way. Like the cockpit, the bridge deck also lifts out for major engine maintenance.

Engine Room

To get down to the engines, you pop open another well-fashioned guttered-and-gasketed hatch. Oil checks and oil changes are carried out from centerline. Seacocks, raw-water internal strainers, and the fuel filter-separators are all located along the aft bulkhead (as are the batteries and battery switches) and reasonably accessible. The engine freshwater expansion tanks are actually up under the bottom of the electronics console, a more accessible location than the engine room could afford. An electrical inverter is aft and outboard of the port engine—a little difficult to reach, but manageable considering the minimal maintenance requirements.

This is one boat that actually has a watertight aft engine room bulkhead. It also appears that, by sealing a couple of hoses passing though the forward bulkhead, it too could easily be made watertight. The 2:1 ZF gears lead to 1¾-inch Aquamet 22 shafts (as good as they get) set at a fairly steep 14-degree angle through dripless shaft seals. Soft mounts support the engines, which in turn are bolted atop the hull stringers. A flat diamond-tread floor between the engines makes for a comfortable working surface. All told, this is a well-engineered and accommodating engine room—I wouldn't make any changes, which is unusual for me.

Cabin

The Sabreline 36 cabin showcases the company's experience in the cruising and sailing markets. Our test boat had what the company calls its "Herreshoff look," with a balanced blend of cherry and white that highlights both to good advantage. The effect is of understated beauty and elegance; undoubtedly, this is one area that owners will show off with pride to their cruising guests. Its sailboat origins are revealed in a positive sense, but its essence is very much that of a contemporary powerboat.

With its 6-foot, 4-inch headroom, the cabin is light and airy with small stainless-framed opening portholes and overhead hatches. Look elsewhere for exotic woods and joinery; the Sabreline's is neatly constituted and precisely executed with great care by Sabre artisans. Joints are tight and doors close firmly, and the teak and holly sole is a class act. On the foot-high trunk-cabin sides, I might opt for larger side windows for more light and a better view, but this is a matter of preference.

The U-shaped galley is located to port at the bottom of the companionway stairs. It makes excellent use of space with a built-in undercounter refrigerator-freezer, gas range with a two-burner stove, stainless sink, ample cupboards and drawers, and a functional white countertop with a fiddle-board to keep everything in place in moderate sea states. More cupboards could be added above the sink against the head bulkhead if an owner wished.

Opposite to starboard is a U-shaped dinette that easily seats four or five with a maple table and some classy-looking sea-green upholstery and storage below. It converts to a double berth of generous proportions: 6 feet, 8 inches by 4 feet. The electrical service panel is above the dinette and convenient to the companionway, but well out of the weather.

The head, just forward of the galley to port, is entered from either the main cabin or the master stateroom forward. It's a nice size, with a manual toilet, molded fiberglass sink and vanity, and storage lockers behind sliding doors. The sink's pull-out faucet doubles as a showerhead that fits the bracket provided. An attractive teak grating lifts up for access to the bilge below, which doubles as a shower sump. I would add a second clamp to the toilet flushing–water seacock. A lip on the bottom of the clean-fitting maple door would keep the shower water completely contained inside the low threshold.

The master stateroom usually comes with a queen-sized island bed, but ours had an owner-specified V-berth with a filler cushion. This really has its merits because it opens up the stateroom on centerline where it's really welcome; the result is a larger berth at night. There's lots of room below for lockers and drawers; in fact, Sabre puts the space to good use holding the AC unit conveniently up forward. Storage lockers behind sliding doors are to port and starboard under the gunwales, and there's also a three-quarter-height cedar hanging locker to starboard. A 20-inch opening hatch above lets in fresh air and daylight—and you out, in an emergency. I might opt for one of these larger hatches to replace the smaller one in the main cabin.

Even so, this cabin is brighter than most boats in this class just as it is. An older couple might want to rearrange the companionway steps to ease the rise and run by adding a third stair. At 13½ inches, the top step is a stretch for some seniors, to whom this boat will surely appeal, and Sabre would gladly accommodate such a request.

Performance Test

We had just a small chop for our sea trial, so I can't comment on the boat's rough-water capabilities. In the 1-foot chop of the Severn River near Annapolis, Maryland, the boat sliced its way onward without missing a beat. The relatively sharp entry and the moderate beam were responsible for the ride and efficiency. I measured perhaps the tightest turning circle ever: at 2,200 rpm, we came around 360 degrees in just 20 seconds. There are several similarly sized boats that easily take twice that long at the same speed. Credit goes to the amply large rudders and proper rudder angle (35 degrees) at full rudder, neither of which can be taken for granted.

This is a solid 20-knot cruiser, which should make the majority of people in this market quite happy. Not many boats are very comfortable at higher speeds anyway, even in calm water—there's just too much motion to be relaxing. This boat gets the priorities right.

Sabreline 36 Express Cruiser Performance Results

RPM	Speed, knots	Speed, mph	Fuel Use, gph	Nautical mpg	Statute mpg	Range, nm	Range, statute miles	Noise Level, dBA	Trim, degrees
800	6.1	2.49	1.8	3.39	3.90	915	69	1	69
1,000	7.3	3.39	2.3	3.17	3.65	857	73	1	73
1,400	9.2	6.52	5.9	1.56	1.79	421	78	2	78
1,600	10.6	9.33	8.3	1.28	1.47	345	79	4	79
1,800	13.4	12.29	10.5	1.28	1.47	345	81	5	81
2,000	16.3	15.05	12.2	1.34	1.54	361	82	5	82
2,200	18.8	22.67	14.6	1.29	1.48	348	83	5	83
2,400	20.6	35.67	18.6	1.11	1.27	299	85	5	85
2,600	23.7	45.98	22.5	1.05	1.21	284	87	4	87
2,800	24.6	58.66	28.8	0.85	0.98	231	87	4	87

Test conditions: three passengers, ¾ tank of fuel, full water, light gear, and 20 feet of water. The range was calculated at 90 percent of fuel capacity; sound levels were taken at the helm.

Backing at 1,000 rpm into the chop, a little water made its way through the transom door, but quickly disappeared into the gutters and out the scuppers, which allowed not a drop aboard. While sitting down, I never lost sight of the horizon when the boat was coming up on plane. Get-home capability is about 10 knots on one engine at 2,000 rpm. The single engine would max out at 2,400 rpm, so the 2,000 rpm seems reasonable and likely won't result in overheating during extended periods. Just be sure the gears will free-wheel without damage for extended periods before trying it.

The rugged windshield has narrow, unobtrusive mullions and interferes very little with the skipper's sight lines. I would recommend trimming down the 3-inch-wide horizontal vent-window frame on centerline because it bisected the horizon with the trim tabs raised and the bow up. As in any express boat with the sole helm station down below, be sure to specify freshwater window washes on all three windows to remove the glare-inducing salt smear.

The bimini top on our test boat deserves an honorable mention, mostly to alert readers to the availability of some superb craftsmanship and innovative design. Price Canvas in St. Michaels, Maryland, produced a beautiful top on our boat, and the forward 3 feet of the top rolls back and tucks inside an ingenious flap without snaps or Velcro. This is a real work of art and well worth investigating.

The Sabreline 36 handled beautifully in the chop and also at the dock, where it backed into the slip with natural ease.

The Sabreline 36 Express is a well-designed, beautifully crafted yacht that offers excellent value, particularly when compared with some of the higher-priced competition. You get 90 percent of the very best for 70 percent (or less) of the cost. Options include teak trim, a teak windshield, an inverter or a 5 or 8 kW genset, AC, full electronics, an anchor windlass, a swim platform, a trawler mast, and a bimini top.

I don't know where else you can find a similarly appointed yacht of this quality at this price. The boat is also nice to look at: it is well proportioned and has clean, crisp lines. Any problems I've noted are minor and easily rectified. This boat is also available as a hardtop sedan cruiser.

1998 Sea Ray 400 DA, Gasoline Power

The Sea Ray 400 Sundancer, or DA for short, is a cruising boat, and no one knows this market better than this megabuilder from Knoxville, Tennessee. Research, including focus groups for owners and dealers, presented evidence that owners of express cruising boats in this size range like to cruise with friends, but they need elbowroom and privacy. The solution is to provide two staterooms, each with its own head, separated by a saloon. In a pinch, two more can sleep in the cabin's dinette. On this boat, accommodations are first on the priority list.

The spacious room down below is due in part to the V-drive propulsion arrangement back aft, which allows the engines to be placed an engine length farther aft than is possible with in-line gears. Of course, the problem with allowing accommodations to drive a boat's design is that seakeeping often suffers; the laws of physics—specifically, the vertical accelerations resulting from such a design—remind us that you can't have a voluminous interior and a great seaboat.

Construction

Sea Ray backs up a skin coat of premium vinylester resin to prevent osmotic blistering with a five-year prorated blister warranty, transferable to a new owner. Alternating layers of woven roving and mat comprise the solid bottom, with overlaps at the keel and chines. Balsa coring is used in the sides and decks to reduce weight. Plywood coring is used in

the way of bolt penetrations to resist compression loads. Bulkheads and stringers are fiberglass-encapsulated plywood; Sea Ray says it keeps the water out of the wood by glassing the limber holes before the stringers are installed in the boat. Bulkheads are glassed to the hull and to the deck above for extra rigidity. Foam is injected into bilge voids for a quieter ride and to provide a little positive buoyancy in the event of hull rupture.

Helm

The helm is raised 16 inches above the cockpit so you're a little higher off the water for improved visibility; this also opens up the midcabin below. The frame on the well-crafted stainless steel windshield doesn't hinder the view. Moderate bow rise means you would always see plenty of blue water between the boat and the horizon. Sea Ray put a chartlet area between the oversize gauges forward under the compass. The electrical switches are directly in front of the wheel and easy to reach. The gauges are 4 feet or so forward of the helm, and might otherwise be difficult to see, but they're oversized and clustered in pairs by function, so they're easy to read. If I ordered one of these boats, I would specify the two-tone color option to reduce the windshield glare from the white dashboard and compass.

Engine Room

If you like to do your own engine maintenance, you'll love this boat—at least in the forward part of the engine room. In fact, I've never seen an engine room that's easier to get into—initially. All you do is push a button and wait a few moments for the 90-by-61-inch hatch to lift hydraulically and afford you walkaround, stand-up engine access. Large gutters keep the machinery dry; fuel hoses are high-pressure, premium aircraft-type with compression fittings; two Rule 2000 bilge pumps are provided with two-tiered float switches; and Racor filter-separators are easy to reach, as are the five batteries.

I have one criticism that I'm not sure why Sea

Ray has not already addressed: the hatch's single mechanical boost on centerline does an excellent job of lifting the hatch out of the way, but it also restricts access aft between the engines, making it difficult to get back to the seacocks, strainers, and steering gear. Twin boosts or outboard hatch props would easily resolve this problem.

Cockpit

Stepping across the large swim platform and through the transom door, there's a handy light switch, a shower, and a large U-shaped cushioned settee with an adjustable table. A section of the settee to starboard lifts out for access to a small storage locker, and the table stows out of the way under the engine-room hatch. Other clever features include a fold-down cockpit step, battery switches, a breaker panel, a sink, and an icemaker. The foredeck is easily reached from comfortably wide side decks; fine but aggressive nonskid and rugged 27-inch-high bow railings provide acceptable security forward.

Cabin

Entering through the wide (24 in.) companionway, the saloon's cavernous 79-inch headroom, pleasing sandstone decor, and opening side ports and overhead hatches result in an open feeling. Sea Ray knows how to put a cabin together with ample space and a pleasing upscale decor.

To port is the well-designed galley; I'm no chef, but everything seems to be arranged for optimal performance. Sea Ray's fiberglass galley countertop blends seamlessly with the Corian sink cover, the result of a flawless Sasfas Grandcoat one-step finish—a nice display of fiberglass tooling and finish know-how on Sea Ray's part. The galley features a large 6.3-cubic-foot Norcold upright refrigerator-freezer (with a TV-VCR above for easy viewing), three-burner stove, and microwave oven. A garbage receptacle, a NuTone combination blender–grinder–can opener, a hideaway coffeemaker above, and a lazy Susan and dish racks below make excellent use of space in this nicely equipped galley.

Opposite to starboard and in close reach of the galley countertop, the dinette seats six for dinner. A platform below the dinette seat slides out for conversion to a large double berth. Etched glass panels behind the dinette are an attractive detail.

The master stateroom has a queen-size berth and all the amenities, including AC and TV. Guests in the midcabin won't feel slighted, since closing the door essentially makes their domain private. This stateroom also doubles as a handy reading or eating lounge, or play area for the kids.

Sea Ray's attention to detail shows everywhere down below: stainless steel companionway threshold, stainless-ringed hatches, opening hatches with sliding screens and shades, gold-accented push-to-open latches that work effortlessly, and access panels that let you go everywhere for maintenance.

Performance Test

Accommodations may be the raison d'être of this boat, but we'll first look at how the Sea Ray 400 DA requited itself on a sea trial. We left port with a 10- to 15-knot breeze out of the southwest and headed offshore. The first noticeable thing about the drivetrain was the uninspiring, sluggish response elicited when the engines were clutched in. The Sea Ray's small, 22-by-23-inch props just don't have enough blade area to deliver adequate responsiveness at marina maneuvering speed, at least not without using a generous amount of throttle. Steering response, both dockside and cruising, was likewise lethargic, both because it took six turns lock-to-lock and the small rudders weren't capable of easily turning such a large twin-propeller tunnel boat. My impression was that I was driving a stodgy limousine, not a sports car.

That said, the MerCruiser state-of-the-art 7.4-liter MFI (multiport fuel injection) gasoline engines' performance was impressive, especially in terms of mpg on a 40-footer. In fact, these engines, with their increased efficiency and reliability and reduced maintenance, may put a new twist in the diesel-versus-gasoline debate. What any cruiser should do well, of course, is transport its occupants safely and comfortably to their destination. Exceptional ride quality and commodious accommodations are usually mutually exclusive attributes, and this Sea Ray clearly emphasizes the latter.

Swinging those four-blade propellers through 2.5:1 V-drive gears, the 400 Sundancer can keep both the long-range cruising enthusiast and the speedster satisfied. Not that this boat would be run for hours at this speed, but at 1,000 rpm, we reached 6.2 knots for a range of 869 nm. We stepped it up to 3,000 rpm to 18 knots for a range of 366 nm. A little more engine speed—3,500 rpm—gave us 24 knots for 333 nm, and top speed at 4,200 rpm zipped us along at 29 knots for 232 nm. Most people will likely cruise in the lower end of the 3,000 to 3,500 rpm range to extend the useful life of their engines, so figure on this being a 17- to 19-knot boat with a load of fuel, passengers, and gear on board with these big-block gasoline engines running easily. Throughout the speed range, the boat had an efficiently level ride and never exceeded 5 degrees of trim once on plane.

While diesels certainly get more work out of a gallon of fuel, they also weigh more than these MerCruisers (though Yanmar 300s weigh about the same and deliver a much-improved cruising speed at their continuous cruising rpm). In nmpg, the gasoline engines are actually more efficient at some speeds than the heavier 350 hp Caterpillar diesel-powered 400 Sundancer I ran in Florida. Those Cats add significant weight in the stern, which might account for some of the surprising performance results. For the average New England boater who puts in less than 150 hours each season, these gasoline engines make a good deal of sense.

On our sea trial, the ride was smooth and mostly dry while running downsea in a 1- to 2- foot chop. We reached the Race, the infamous locale where the Atlantic Ocean and Long Island Sound noisily meet—their conjoining made quite a racket in the form of a 3- to 4-foot dancing chop. Of course, this was a great place to test a hull's mettle, especially with waves nearly as close together as they were high. The Sea Ray is by no means a seakindly hull at speed in a stiff chop; it simply has too little deadrise forward and too full an entry where the hull absorbs most of the slamming loads on plane in a seaway. In a beam or following sea, you'll be a lot more comfortable.

But for a cruising yacht that stays in moderate conditions, and as long as you don't push it too hard—say, running at the gasoline-powered boat's natural comfortable cruise of around 18 knots—the ride is comfortable enough in a light chop. I found that running directly into the 2- to 3-foot seas at 22 knots with trim tabs fully depressed made for a comfortably smooth and reasonably dry ride. Running at slow speeds back in the marina, it was a pleasure to drive the boat with 360-degree visibility from a sitting position (except for the annoying and unnecessary blind zones created by the wide fiberglass radar arches).

I definitely would like to see the boat respond better to the wheel and to the clutches. Whether the props and rudders are too small, and the tunnels too deep and slab-sided—all of which I suspect—the result was sluggish handling. Backing the starboard engine, the bow actually fell off decidedly to port until I applied a good burst of power. Backing into a tight slip in a crosswind was uneventful, but single-lever controls might be more appropriate for a novice running this boat in tight quarters.

The Sea Ray 400 Sundancer has much in its favor in terms of solid construction, a very workable design, and commendable performance with gasoline power. Quantitative improvements could be made in handling, ride quality, engine-room access, and a few other areas, but this boat will please many as it is. Also, despite my usual preference for diesel engines, this boat—by virtue of its size, V-drive configuration, and intended use—makes a strong case for gasoline power, especially for the Northeast market's more limited cruising season. The Sea Ray 400 Sundancer is pricey compared to some of the competition, but its sales and service network is second to none—a big consideration.

Tiara 3800

Tiara 3800 Specifications	
LOA:	40'9"
Length on deck:	38'4"
Beam:	14'2"
Draft:	3'6"
Displacement:	22,500 lb. (dry)
Fuel capacity:	411 gal.
Water capacity:	110 gal.
Deadrise (transom):	18 deg.

Tiara has earned an enviable reputation as a builder of high-quality open express yachts. Most striking is not the materials or methods used to build a Tiara, but rather the attention to detail that goes into each model's design and construction. Tiara is just as well known for its conservative and enduring styling, which has always put form at the service of function; a ten-year-old Tiara is just as good-looking and contemporary as one freshly minted.

Nonetheless, Tiara's latest models, starting with the superb 5000 Express and continuing with the 3800 (introduced in 2002), have given a distinct nod to trendy Euro styling, with curves, radii, and reverse transoms replacing hard corners everywhere on the yachts' exteriors. They're not any better-looking, in my opinion, but they answer the call to the modern for many prospective owners. In one or two areas, the curves show the balance tilting in favor of form, as we'll see, but the soul of the 3800 remains true to its origins.

S2 Yachts is parent to Tiaras and Pursuits; the former are open cruising yachts that fish, the latter are fishing boats that also cruise. Our 3800 open devotes half of its LOA to the lower-deck accommodations: a single-stateroom and single-head arrangement with a large saloon and well-equipped galley. Amidships is a raised bridge deck with the engine room below and aft is an open cockpit, large enough to fish from but emphasizing cruising, with its lounge seats and padded coaming bolsters.

Design and Construction

The Tiara 3800, like the rest of the builder's lineup, is based on a modified-V hull with reverse chines and spray strakes forward. Tiaras are beamy boats, a trait dictated by market demand, but the builder does a commendable job with the 3800, producing decent ride quality despite the challenges imposed by so much breadth at the waterline. Deadrise at the transom is a moderate 18 degrees—probably an ideal figure for a 30-knot boat like this—combining moderate vertical accelerations in a seaway with efficient and effective dynamic lift at speed. More important in this constant-deadrise bottom, the deadrise at stations 3 to 5 (approximately 30 to 50 percent of the way aft from the bow) is generous enough to diminish slamming in a chop to very low levels. In fact, the reentry launching off 4- to 6-foot swells at 25 knots on our test ride was surprisingly cushiony.

Tiara's laminators start with a vinylester-resin skin coat over a thick gelcoat to prevent osmotic blistering. The hull is solidly if conventionally built (unlike the techy wet-preg, postcured Epoxy 5000) with a solid-glass bottom laminate of biaxial and triaxial knit fabrics. For added stiffness at moderate weight, hull sides are balsa-cored above the waterline, as are the decks and superstructure.

Stringers are made of fiberglass-encapsulated foam except in way of the engines, where plywood better attenuates engine vibrations and resists local bolt loads at the engine mounts. Engine-room and lazarette bulkheads are vacuum-bagged, balsa-core fiberglass, a process that eliminates "fat" (that is, plywood along for the ride) and reflects Tiara's increasing interest in putting the advantages of the I-beam principle to good use (sandwich-composite construction mimics the I-beam with the glass skins absorbing compression and tension loads, and the core efficiently resisting shear stresses).

Plywood and aluminum replaces the balsa in way of deck-bolt penetrations. The hull-to-deck joint is bonded with polyurethane adhesive and fastened with self-tapping screws, followed by another row of screws when the PVC rubrail is installed.

Cockpit and Deck (Topside)

This boat has a great cockpit for fishing, measuring 80 inches long by 138 inches wide and a safe 29 inches high, and with toe kicks to port and starboard created by the 10-inch-wide coaming above. A two-piece 27-inch-wide transom door opens from the optional swim platform, which has freeing ports (slots, actually) molded in to shed water quickly; some builders neglect this important detail. Decks are covered with Tiara's trademark non-skid pattern.

The boat's cruising emphasis is evident in all the cockpit seating; a 5-foot-long transom seat with room for three people pulls out from under the coaming, and forward to port and starboard are two more fixed upholstered bench seats. Be aware that the Tiara's topsides are all bright white, so expect to need dark sunglasses to ease eyestrain in the sun. As antidotes, Grady-White's and Albermarle's cream-colored fiberglass, for example, is a lot easier on the eyes, but Tiara's white is obviously meeting market demand.

An inspection hatch forward provides access to the tops of the twin 0.19-inch-thick, 5052-grade aluminum fuel tanks. Two other hatches aft lead to an insulated 6-foot fish box and an insulated livewell above the lazarette; these boxes are removed for access to the lazarette below. The gutters drain directly to the cockpit scuppers, which consist of two 2-inch drain lines in each corner; they're also recessed to eliminate standing water.

The rudderposts are stoutly supported by aluminum channels bolted to the tall hull stringers. Water collects in the bilge outboard of the prop pockets; this area should be filled in to eliminate the standing water that was present on our new test boat. For improved flooding resistance, the forward lazarette bulkhead should certainly be watertight, rather than leaving a pair of 4-by-12-inch openings above the propeller-shaft strut-pad backing plates. The genset muffler and an EMI Suppressor are also mounted in the lazarette.

Wide (10 in.) flat side decks lead forward via molded cockpit steps and a stiff, welded, stainless steel bow railing that's a comfortable 26 to 28 inches tall forward. A pair of 12-inch bow cleats and a 10-inch anchor cleat for the molded bow pulpit are forward, and two 10-inch side cleats are located below the windshield to port and starboard. One 19-inch deck hatch forward and a pair of 12-inch hatches aft lead to the cabin.

Cabin

Tiara's accommodations are always a delight, and the 3800's five-sleeper cabin was no exception. Through the 23-inch-wide companionway (and past the sliding screen and door), it's down four steps, below which is the yacht's electrical breaker panel. (The AC-DC master panel with shore-power and genset controls is mounted separately forward above the dinette.) The cabin is open and inviting, and the 6-foot, 7-inch headroom adds to the feeling of roominess.

The galley is immediately to port, and our test boat had an L-shaped Corian countertop with a two-burner stove and a deep double sink. Corian covers for the stove (a microswitch secures power when the cover goes down) and sink stow away in a purpose-built cabinet, and a lazy Susan makes good use of corner space below. Also included are three drawers with push-to-open latches, a Norcold refrigerator-freezer, a coffeemaker, and a microwave oven.

Opposite to starboard is a dinette that converts to a 6-foot, 9-inch double berth; the seatback flips up to serve as a single bunk. The TV in the forward bulkhead swivels 180 degrees so it can also be used in the stateroom forward. All these elements combine to add cruising versatility and enjoyment for the yacht's owners.

This boat has a large head (6 ft. long total) with a separate circular shower, so the saloon gives up some space to port, but there's still ample open deck space, mostly attributable to the yacht's significant 14-foot beam. The radiused bulkhead at the circular shower makes the most of the space—both inside and outside the shower compartment—and has a pleasing appearance.

The teak and holly sole looks salty, and classicists will appreciate the teak veneer on the flat and curved bulkheads. I prefer the lighter and richer-looking cherry that's available only on the Tiara 50 for now. But a great-looking honey-ash veneer is also available—its lighter color would likely make the interior seem a little larger still and more contemporary.

If you're looking for fancy joinery work, you'll find it in the double-leaf dinette table that is framed in teak and has a bird's-eye-maple veneer inset. The flat finish does little to bring attention to the fine workmanship evident when you look closely at the table, which lowers easily on its spring pedestal to support the berth's filler cushions.

The forward stateroom includes a 6-foot, 4-inch queen-size island berth with gas shocks that make light work of getting to the storage space below. The 19-inch hatch above serves as an alternate exit in case of emergency, and lets in a fresh sea breeze. To port is a cedar-lined hanging locker and, as elsewhere in the cabin, the vinyl liner overhead and along the hull sides is smoothly applied with arrow-straight seams.

The yacht's single head, entered from the saloon or directly from the stateroom forward, is quite large, so there's ample space to get around the VacuFlush toilet and Corian-topped sink vanity. A two-piece fiberglass liner presents a clean appearance and should be easy to keep clean since mildew-attracting seams are minimized.

Engine Room and Fuel Tank

The bridge deck is raised on a pair of out-of-the-way outboard electric screw-lifts. A gasket around the perimeter of the engine room helps to seal in engine noise (though on our test boat, the gasket was coming loose aft at the corner of the recessed step on centerline). When the deck is fully raised, there's 30 inches of clearance outboard and 24 inches on centerline in way of the molded step.

The 450 hp Diamond Series Cummins diesels fit nicely in the engine room; there's ample room all around these inline-6 engines for maintenance. The seawater strainers and fuel filter-separators are mounted aft on either side of the Onan 8 kW genset. The starboard sea strainer is easy enough to reach, but everything else is a stretch, especially the starboard fuel filter-separator, which is behind the strainer. Engine maintenance checks can all be done from centerline.

The fuel system features compression hoses and fittings, except for the genset, which uses rubber hoses and hose clamps. All hose ends are clearly labeled, even at the engines, and the hoses are securely clamped in place and routed away from traffic areas. An optional Glendinning Cablemaster is outboard of the starboard engine, as is the water heater, and a pair of galvanic isolators prevents stray shore-power voltage from wreaking galvanic-corrosion havoc. Strong dripless shaft seals help keep the bilge dry.

The engines are supported by soft mounts bolted to the fiberglass-encapsulated plywood stringers. Tiara traditionally uses a drift-pin arrangement, wherein a pair of 1-inch bronze drift pins inserted horizontally through the stringers is drilled through from above and tapped out; the engine mounts then are bolted through the stringer top to them.

The batteries are below the centerline deck platform, low in the bilge, where they best contribute to stability and are well out of the way. The overhead is tooled fiberglass, the space is well lit, and a channel above serves as a cableway and structural stiffener. The bilges are sanded smooth and painted with white gelcoat for easy cleanup, and the wiring is neatly routed and protected by looming.

The two 200-gallon aluminum fuel tanks under the cockpit are made of 0.19-inch-thick, 5052-grade aluminum. Except for their tops under the forward centerline cockpit hatch, the tanks were inaccessible, so I don't know how well they're mounted or how much airspace there is around them.

Bridge Deck and Helm

Up two steps from the cockpit, the 6-foot, 3-inch-long bridge deck is raised well above the waterline for an excellent all-around view. Both the four-person L-shaped lounge to port (32 in. high) and the person-and-a-half helm seat (35 in. high) offer a great view outside the boat. While the helm seat is usually raised for obvious reasons, the passengers also get consideration from the builder: even the footrest is raised 1 foot off the deck.

At the nicely sculpted starboard-side helm, which tilts aft for access to the console's wiring, the engine gauges are at just the right angle to be clearly seen when the operator is standing or seated, and there's an open area below for owner-specified electronics. A rubber detent holds the console firmly in place, dispensing with the metal latches on earlier Tiaras. The compass is located atop the console, making it a little difficult to see when you are seated.

The molded-fiberglass windshield's curved glass panels on this model are distortion-free, a definite plus in my opinion. However, the black-painted border around the window edge of the windshield frame's corner posts is an effective 8 inches wide, blocking off sight lines unnecessarily; the old angular aluminum windshields were more functional. The gray-colored dashboard under the windshield helps to minimize the glare off the windows above.

Performance Test

We had a great day for our sea trial: it was in the high 70s and a ground swell was still making its presence felt with the occasional 4- to 6-footer rolling in across the 10-fathom line. This is a big, rugged, and seaworthy boat that I would take offshore in all but the most extreme conditions. We had a full load of fuel on board, and our boat was powered by 450 hp Cummins diesels turning 24-by-28-inch four-blade cupped nibral (an alloy that's stronger than bronze) props through 1.72:1 ZF gears.

Turning 1,600 rpm for 14 knots left a clean wake astern; 1,800 rpm put us fully on plane at 18 knots. Backing down at 1,000 rpm, no water made its way on deck, and the swim platform was solid as a rock slapping those waves down. The ride quality was excellent running at 24 to 26 knots in the 4- to 6-foot swells, with minimal slamming loads and a dry, stable, and very controllable ride. The yacht's sense of ease in those sea conditions was impressive; for me, that's the bottom line.

Steering was reasonably responsive at 4½ fairly low-effort turns lock-to-lock, and better than previous Tiaras I've tested (5½ turns on the 3500, for instance). We made 360-degree turns in an average of 31 seconds (with the throttles set at 2,400 rpm and slowing to 2,150 rpm in the turn), about average for this size inboard. But I would still order the boat with power steering, an additional (well-spent) $2,000, according to Sea Star. It's hard not to feel this way after operating so many of the 30-knot European 60- and 70-foot motor yachts that would run circles around most manual-steering boats half their size.

Running along in the chop while seated at the power-adjustable helm seat (it slides forward and aft at the push of a button), I could consistently see the horizon above the bow pulpit—which is, of course, essential to safe operations, even while coming up on plane. The high helm seat and bridge deck place your line of sight well above the waterline.

Having such a high helm seat was beneficial,

since this boat runs at a bow-high 7 degrees of trim in its cruising midrange. A natural running angle of 3 to 5 degrees would be more efficient for a zero-degree buttocks hull like this one, but that's difficult to accomplish with a hull this length.

Dropping the tabs helped, of course, but trim-tab angle indicators are definitely in order, and should be standard on any boat of this size and cost; tab angle is an annoying guessing game otherwise. The aft-oriented LCG helped with directional stability with seas abaft the beam.

Noise levels were very low at trolling speed but on the high side at cruise. Tiara has done an excellent job reducing radiated noise through the engine-room overhead and bulkheads; it's the exhaust noise that predominates throughout the operating range, which is where further sound-deadening engineering efforts should be focused. Nevertheless, we were able to carry on a conversation in slightly raised tones while running at cruise rpm.

I know of several high-end custom and production builders who have shifted to linear mufflers for two reasons: they're fairly quiet and, because they're comfortably mounted outboard of the cockpit fuel tank, they free up space in the engine room.

The Tiara 3800 is a well-built family express cruiser with pleasing lines and solid offshore seakeeping manners. Where would I look for improvement? Improve the sight lines interfered with by the windshield and radar-arch designs, improve the mufflers to reduce exhaust noise levels, and move the fuel filter-separators and raw-water strainers so they're easier to access. The Tiara's mechanical systems and overall engineering are cleanly executed, space utilization is commendable, and the boat's versatility is compelling.

Standard equipment includes stainless steel bow railings, anchor pulpit, bridge-deck wet bar, saloon stereo, TV-VCR, and a fully equipped galley with Corian countertops.

Options in 2001 included the swim platform with ladder, genset, reverse-cycle AC, radar arch with side curtains, teak and holly sole, anchor windlass, and Glendinning Cablemaster shore-power handler. A hardtop (without the radar arch) and a half-tower are also available.

Tiara 5200 Express

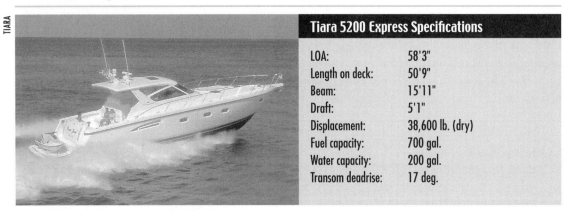

TIARA

Tiara 5200 Express Specifications	
LOA:	58'3"
Length on deck:	50'9"
Beam:	15'11"
Draft:	5'1"
Displacement:	38,600 lb. (dry)
Fuel capacity:	700 gal.
Water capacity:	200 gal.
Transom deadrise:	17 deg.

Tiara's founder, Leon Slikkers, has been building cruising yachts since the late 1950s, and he's undoubtedly got things down to a science at S2 Yachts, Tiara and Pursuit's parent company. Certainly, his art is also present in the company's new 50-foot flagship, as well as that of his son, David Slikkers, the company's president.

This new 50-footer is certainly one of the most

advanced production boats being built in the United States, with a wet-preg, vacuum-bagged, postcured epoxy hull and deck laminate. Wet-preg means that the glass-to-resin ratio is carefully controlled. Vacuum-bagging ensures sound bond lines between the fiberglass skins and the balsa core. Postcuring aids in cross-linking, making the laminate even stronger and more durable. Epoxy is the strongest resin and the best glue available, and is very resistant to osmotic blistering.

Cockpit

Starting the tour aft, the Tiara's cockpit is loaded with features, including a pair of tables recessed in the deck with a choice of three heights: dining table, cocktail table, and sunpad extension. The deck hinges up to improve both access to the lazarette below and engine-room light. Two lounges offer up to 16 feet of upholstered seating. Twin transom doors, 29 inches high like the coaming bolsters, make the cockpit a safe place to hang around, even at cruising speeds—especially with Tiara's excellent molded nonskid.

A 100-cubic-foot aft transom garage holds scuba gear, bicycles, and other assorted essentials. On the swim platform, an optional davit (with optional passarelle, or gangway, capability, which will allow you to board the stern by a davit-mounted ramp) lifts up and swings out to handle the swim platform–mounted tender. Recessed grabrails in the swim platform give you something to hold onto as you're getting in and out of the tender, but they're low enough to walk over without tripping.

Foredeck

Molded cockpit steps lead to the flat, 11-inch-wide side decks where a bow railing extends nearly to the cockpit and several deckhouse-mounted handrails lead forward to the foredeck. Located there are a large anchor-chain locker and an optional shore-power-cable locker for use when mooring bow-to—a nice feature because to use the tender, the stern has to be free of the pier. A sunpad for two is recessed into the foredeck, with a

wraparound gutter and grabrail, all 316-grade stainless like the rest of the boat's deck hardware. The sidelights are mounted on the pulpit railing; relocating them atop the hardtop would prevent backscatter from interfering with the operator's night vision and would increase the range at which they could be seen from another vessel.

Bridge Deck and Helm

Raised two steps up from the cockpit, the bridge deck is a model in ergonomics with a huge L-shaped lounge to port, raised well off the deck to afford a fine view for five or six people. To starboard is a wet bar with a refrigerator and icemaker below, hidden behind flush cabinet doors connected to the appliance doors for simplicity.

A Tiara tradition, the raised helm is a nifty feature. The unit hinges aft for easy maintenance access inside, and the entire unit, as well as the surrounding dashboard area, is finished in dark gray textured fiberglass to reduce windshield glare. Starting atop the console, lining up the compass with the wheel and moving it closer to the operator would make it easier to view, especially for a shorter person. Next, electronics are arrayed across the top half of the angled console, directly near your line of sight when piloting. Engine gauges and rocker switches are located below—easy to read and reach as needed. Throttles are to starboard and shifts are to port of the stainless Destroyer wheel. The Stidd two-person helm seat adjusts vertically and horizontally, and tilts back to suit any frame; especially when it is raised all the way, visibility is excellent and a class leader.

Engine Room

Entered directly from the cockpit or from a bridge-deck hatch, the engine room is roomy and well lit and has a comfortable 5-foot, 2-inch headroom. Maintenance checks are all conveniently conducted from centerline. The engine-cooling-water seacocks are easy to access, and feature bilge-suction capability with fail-safe valves that prevent accidental back-flooding from sea to bilge (the only acceptable kind).

Dual fuel filter-separators on the forward bulkhead allow shift-on-the-run operation; relocating them closer to centerline would make them easier to reach and to check visually. The electrical service panels are also on the forward bulkhead in the engine room—according to Tiara, to encourage frequent visits by the owner to this critical space—a well-considered strategy.

Tiara continues with its tried-and-true engine-mounting system involving mounting bolts tapped into bronze retaining pins below. A combination of soft mounts and rugged fiberglass engine beds helped produce the low vibration and sound levels we encountered on our sea trial. Tiara's excellent engineering includes loomed wiring and plumbing, neatly labeled high-pressure fuel- and oil-changing lines, and dripless shaft seals. The V-drive-engine installation makes possible the yacht's huge cabin, while keeping shaft angle to 11 degrees. Of course, the trade-off with the big cabin is a smaller engine room; a lot has to be engineered into this area, but Tiara does a fine job of working with the available space.

The tooled fiberglass liner and foil-backed insulation overhead combine to produce exceptionally low noise levels. As a result of the vacuum-bagging process, bilges are very smooth and are coated with white gelcoat for good visibility and easy cleanup. The aft bulkhead is not continuous to the deck above; I would want to ensure that it's high enough to prevent progressive flooding from the engine room aft or from the lazarette forward in the event of a hull penetration.

Cabin

As a cruising yacht, the 5200 is really in a class of its own. Tiara has escalated into a new echelon with this boat, not only in terms of construction quality, size, and utility, but also in the sheer quality of interior appointments and joinery. Cherry cabinetry and softly radiused paneling is beautifully finished, approaching levels seen in European imports and custom American yachts. The level of fit and finish is especially commendable considering that

our test boat was hull #1; expect follow-on hulls to be more impressive still.

The cabin is accessed from a wide (23 in. opening) companionway fitted with a sliding screen (another focus-group request). Headroom is an exceptional 6 feet, 10 inches, which—in combination with the chrome-plated stainless steel opening portholes and three 20-inch hatches overhead—really opens the interior up nicely. With 26 feet from the forward bulkhead to the companionway, there is an extraordinary amount of living area, as well.

At the companionway entrance, the L-shaped galley is immediately to port with a hunter-green Corian countertop, deep sink, three-burner stove with dishwasher below, coffeemaker above, and cabinet storage everywhere. Separate refrigerator and freezer units are located aft, tucked under the bridge deck and staggered in height to accommodate an ergonomic microwave oven and a pots and pans storage area. Under the companionway stairs, which lift effortlessly on boosts, is an optional single-unit washer-dryer.

Forward of the galley is a big U-shaped lounge luxuriously upholstered in Connolly leather and outfitted with a bird's-eye-maple- and cherry-trimmed table. A pair of barstools drops into deck sockets when the need arises. Forward and across the wide cherry sole to starboard is a second L-shaped lounge, an arrangement that lends itself to uncrowded, comfortable cruising for a family. In keeping with the company's intent (grounded in the real world of everyday cruising) that this be a four-sleeper, neither lounge converts to a bed.

The accommodations include two staterooms; the master is forward and has a queen-sized island berth with a real mattress and storage below, cedar closets, and a huge en suite head with separate shower. The second stateroom is opposite the galley to starboard with an ingenious arrangement that borrows from and improves on the Europeans. Twin single berths convert into a single king-sized-plus by raising one berth up and folding out another below that has a mattress attached to the bottom. There's a cedar hanging closet and private access to the yacht's second head, which is also reached directly from the saloon. Tooling in the heads, like everywhere else onboard, is beautifully and artistically done.

Construction

The way this boat is built is really the story behind the headlines. In fact, the Tiara 5200 is built like no other production boat—and like no other Tiara, for that matter. Two words make all the difference: *epoxy* and *postcure*. Quadaxial fiberglass and balsa coring is used throughout the hull, stringers are fiberglass-encapsulated foam, and the entire structure is laminated with epoxy resin. The fiberglass is preimpregnated with resin before being applied to the mold. The wet laminate is vacuum-bagged until it sets up and then is postcured at 150 degrees for 20 hours. The result is a structure 3,000 pounds lighter and 50 to 75 percent stiffer than a conventional hull, in part because the glass-to-resin ratio is an impressive 60:40 percent, precisely the opposite of conventional layups. The superior strength and moisture resistance of epoxy results in an incredibly durable and long-lasting structure.

Performance Test

For the sea trial, we had perfect weather in Narragansett Bay: clear skies, lots of wind kicking up 3- to 5-foot seas, and a lee when we wanted it for the speed runs. The boat's generous beam argues against a record-setting pace in a head sea, but the hull design incorporated enough deadrise (17 degrees at the transom) to allow us a comfortable 22-knot cruise upwind without pounding. Downsea, the Tiara tracked straight with little helm input.

A 360-degree turn at 2,000 rpm took 38 seconds, slightly better than average for this class vessel. However, it took between 5½ and 11 turns lock-to-lock on the wheel; power steering would drop that down to a more responsive and still low-effort 3 to 4 turns, more suitable to a 30-knot boat of any size. I prefer a more horizontally inclined wheel than the Tiara's vertical setup—it makes spinning the wheel more comfortable, especially when I am seated, and there's a lot to be said for single-lever controls.

With four passengers and half a tank of fuel, a leisurely 1,600 rpm produced 20.7 knots, and 2,000 rpm made for a continuous 28.3-knot cruise; range was some 300 nm at 90 percent capacity. Full throttle—2,330 rpm—yielded 32.6 knots. Sound levels were low to moderate at the helm: 79 dBA at 1,600 rpm and 82 dBA at 2,000 rpm, testimony to Tiara's unusually effective sound-deadening treatment.

Seated visibility was very good, especially with trim tabs depressed to lower the bow. The windshield glass sections were clean and undistorted, even in the 90-degree curves in the corners. The only impediment to visibility was on centerline with the 6-inch-wide windshield mullions and the vent window's horizontal support and lifting mechanism. Otherwise, I never lost sight of the horizon while coming up on plane, due in part to the moderate 5-degree trim at cruising speed, ideal for this hull form and indicative of near-perfect weight distribution.

Tiara's engineers and marketers have worked together to produce a superbly designed and built flagship. The Tiara 5200 is the hands-down winner with the best express-yacht accommodations I've yet seen in this class. Included is a classy combination of beautiful colors, innovative and complementary woodwork (cherry, teak, and maple), and a very sensible, roomy layout. Engineering is top-notch and the 5200's well-balanced hull design makes for great seaworthiness and comfort in a capacious yacht.

Options on our test boat included a cherry interior and cabin sole, davit with passarelle, full electronics, forward shore-power cable, dishwasher, washer-dryer, and hardtop.

Regal, a proponent of stepped bottoms in many of its models, builds well-appointed cuddy, bowrider, sedan, and express boats from 18 to 42 feet. The 4260 shown here is the company's flagship. Regal express cruisers deliver a better ride than many others, with deeper deadrise and a sharper entry that smooth out the chop.   REGAL

Bayliner is one of the biggest boatbuilders in the world, producing everything from a 16-foot runabout to a 57-foot pilothouse motor yacht. The builder does a good job turning out low-priced boats of fair to good quality. Vinylester-resin skin coats, standard on Bayliners, are lacking in many name brands costing half again as much. Note that the bow railing on the Ciera 2855 express cruiser shown here will actually help keep you from falling overboard, and the big cabin sleeps up to six during weekends afloat.   BAYLINER

Donzi is a well-regarded, go-fast race and fishing boat builder, but it also turns out some of the nicer express cruisers around, like this 39ZSC. Like Formula's PC line, this is a good-running boat with a deep-V bottom and moderate beam. Donzi adds a stepped bottom to the equation, which reduces frictional drag once you get above 30 knots or so. Donzi produces go-fasts, cruisers, sportfishermen, deck boats, bowriders, and runabouts from 16 to 45 feet.   DONZI

Cruisers Yachts, in business since the early 1950s, has made a name for itself producing well-built boats at a reasonable price. Express, sedan, and pilothouse motor-yacht models now range from 28 to 53 feet, including the impressive new 5370 express. The new-for-2001 3572 express shown illustrates a comfortable helm station with an adjoining companion seat. This builder has a talent for designing commodious boats that nonetheless look proportionate and even sleek, and that deliver a surprisingly smooth and dry ride in a 2- to 3-foot chop.   CRUISERS INC.

Chaparral is a large builder of quality 18- to 35-foot express, cuddy, bowrider, and deck boats, but it's probably best known for its Signature express cruiser line. The 260 shown is a trailerable (8 ft., 6 in. beam maximum without a permit) family weekender that sleeps four and can double as a skiing or fishing boat. Like most boats of the genre, the 260 could use higher bow railings and a taller windshield, but there's a lot to like about the layout.

CHAPARRAL

Part of boatbuilding conglomerate Brunswick Corporation, Maxum builds a long list of bowrider, cuddy, express, aft-cabin, and sedan cruisers from 18 to 46 feet. Maxum produces a lot of boat for the dollar, due in part to shared buying power and tooling capability with its sister companies. The 2700 SCR shown here is one of Maxum's midsize offerings with a large interior for the LOA, and with a full hull form well suited to running in a light chop.   MAXUM

Larson builds bowriders, deck boats, and express cruisers, including its flagship Cabrio 330 shown here. The stepped bottom is something of a marketing gimmick in this moderate-speed express cruiser, but the boat runs through a light chop with little fuss. The maple woodwork below gives the Larson an upscale look, the separate shower is a bonus, and there's enough room for a couple with four kids to spend a comfortable weekend on the water.   LARSON

This Italian number looks like a sedate canal cruiser when backed into a slip, but the rounded stern camouflages a deep-V bottom extension on this performance cruiser. The boat feels like it's made of steel—it's that solid—and quality is top-notch throughout. By no means meant for families clipping coupons, the Aprea Mare lineup includes this 35-footer and several other high-end models from 25 to 52 feet.   APREA MARE

The Dutch-built Linssen 45 features a convertible Variotop that folds back into the wide radar arch. The arch takes a good-sized chunk out of the operator's horizon; otherwise, this is an impressively designed, well-built, and good-looking offshore cruiser.   LINSSEN

This high-end Linssen 45 express has a comfortable two-stateroom layout with a salty, old-world decor. This new fiberglass yacht from a well-regarded steel-cruiser builder is purportedly based on a European pilot boat hull.   LINSSEN

Sea Ray builds almost fifty models from 17 to 66 feet, including this entry-level 24-foot express. This is the smallest express boat that can feasibly incorporate a habitable, even comfortable cabin with something close to standing headroom. Sea Rays are priced above much of the competition, but they're well engineered and nicely appointed. The builder also scores points for encouraging investment in service infrastructure in some locales by its dealer network, and by following up on owner satisfaction through internal customer satisfaction surveys.   SEA RAY

One of the high-end boats in our express-cruiser sampling, the 55-foot Viking Sport Cruiser is built in the United Kingdom by Princess Yachts and distributed in the United States by Viking. Three staterooms accommodate six comfortably, and the elegantly appointed saloon has all the comforts of home, but the real news is in this boat's exceptionally good performance. A moderate 14-foot, 4-inch beam and a deep-V hull form deliver one of the smoothest rides found on this class of boat. Express, flybridge, and motor yachts from 40 to 105 feet are available.   VIKING

Open/Hardtop Sportfishermen

Open sportfishing boats look a lot like express cruisers at first glance, but the emphasis here is on cockpit size and outfitting and overall fishability. Since the cockpit must be within a foot or so of the water for landing gamefish, the engine room is situated forward below the bridge deck, which reduces the amount of room available for accommodations. Although the boats have a raised bridge deck and tall windshield (taller than average for styling-driven express cruisers), most of these boats have hardtops, full plastic enclosures, and at least half-towers, so they're not so open after all. This layout has found favor with owners of large outboards moving up and with the cruising couple weary of hiring a crew for their bigger yacht. The captain is just a few steps from the cockpit, can see well enough from the elevated bridge deck to catch fish,

and there's always the tower when visibility isn't quite good enough from the main helm station. A half-tower, with its platform forming the frame for the canvas or fiberglass top, is a popular option. Older couples can easily handle the open layout, with no bridge stairs to climb.

Some open sportfishermen are based on manufacturers' existing convertible models (Viking, Ocean, and Bertram, for example), only modified with the deckhouse and flybridge removed and the bridge deck raised. Removing this topside weight, as with the express cruiser, makes the boat faster and more seaworthy with a lower center of gravity and less sail area. The bigger open sportfishermen are anything but day boats, with some of the 50-footers featuring two-stateroom, two-head cabins complete with a saloon and fully equipped galley.

Luhrs's 36- and 38-foot and Pursuit's 30- and 34-foot open sportfishermen are good examples of the production genre with their beamy hulls and solid seakeeping abilities.

Albin 28 Specifications

LOA (on deck):	28'4"
Beam:	10'0"
Draft:	38"
Deadrise (minimum):	16 deg.
Displacement (dry):	7,500 lb.
Fuel capacity:	132 gal.
Water capacity:	36 gal.
Cabin headroom (maximum):	74½ in.
Power as tested:	Peninsular 280 hp V-drive inboard diesel

Like its big brother, the low-profile 32-foot sport-fisher, the Albin 28 Tournament Express has personality. It occurred to me that this boat is reminiscent of the more recent British Coast Guard rescue boats. In fact, it just looks like the kind of boat you would want to be in when the situation starts to get nasty (if you had to be in a 28-foot civilian-type boat, of course). It comes as a practical hardtop version (like our test boat) or as a sleeker-looking open boat with just a windshield.

This boat is as gimmick-free as I've yet seen— it must be a breath of fresh air for the marketing department to have a boat like this to sell. It's evident that this boat is intended to be used—for serious fishing, cruising, sightseeing, and entertaining. The boat has a large cockpit interrupted by a low-profile engine box, a functional enclosed pilothouse, and an accommodating cabin. Everywhere you look is antiseptically clean fiberglass and everything has a function and a place. The bottom line is that you'll get your money's worth with this boat.

Design and Construction

Although the emphasis with this boat is on the cockpit, the pilothouse is designed to keep you dry and protected from wind and sun. For the size and layout of this boat, the cabin is also exceptional, with sleeping room for two couples.

Like the bigger 32 sportfisher, the Albin 28 has a fiberglass hull and deck using efficient bidirectional and unidirectional glass. A vinylester resin is used to prevent blistering in the first two laminates. The bottom and decks are cored with balsa except under the engine and on parts of the side decks. The sides and keel are solid glass. Stringers are made of fiberglass cored with four layers of plywood from the center bulkhead aft (where they support the engine). Forward of that, foam replaces the plywood to reduce weight.

Deck and Cockpit

The heart of this boat, the cockpit is accordingly large and well organized. The cockpit bolster is a nice feature, as are the flush-mounted rod holders and rods racks on either side under the rail. The cockpit has ample storage space under several deck hatches, which also improve access to the engine when needed. The transom rail has four hatches covering an aerated live-bait well to port, and a large insulated fish box and a storage box to starboard. The bait-well pump and seacock are accessible under a cockpit hatch aft, as are the steering gear and trim-tab machinery.

The swim platform (with ladder) might be convenient if you want to go swimming, but you might not want it on a fishing boat. The deck is fairly low at under 6 inches above the waterline at the transom—which means the boat doesn't have great weight-carrying ability—but it allows for a reasonably low hull sheer aft with sufficient cockpit rail height left for safety (29 in.). And the deck is still high enough to keep everything dry when you are backing down on fish or just drifting.

Molded-in steps lead to the side decks. There's a saltwater washdown spigot and an emergency hand bilge pump in case you need it when the lights go out. The fuel tank sits under the cockpit deck aft of the engine; you don't have to worry about mixing up the fuel and water fills—they're color-coded and on opposite sides and ends of the cockpit. You can even fit a paper cup under the fuel fill vent so you don't get to know your local coast guard members in a nonsocial setting. The waste connection is within easy reach near the starboard spring cleat.

There's not a lot of deck pitch and camber, but the deck drains well, mostly through deck hatch drains, as well as through the cockpit gutters and scuppers. And draining through the hatch gutters is OK since they in turn drain overboard, not into the bilge.

The side decks on the Albin 28 are wide, with an easy to reach grabrail along the top of the pilothouse, which is a good feature since the bow railings on our test boat leaned too far outboard (several inches farther than the outside of the rubrails) to do much good. I would pull them in 4 to 6 inches—which would also prevent damage to them when you pull alongside a high dock or pilings—and I would raise them a couple of inches at the pulpit (although, at 28 in., they're already better than average). I liked the well-made, understated aluminum radar arch on the aft end of the hardtop.

Large, no-nonsense sidelights were recessed in pockets several feet aft of the bow out of the operator's field of vision at night. This boat has a good ground-tackle arrangement with an anchor pulpit, bitt, and two line lockers, but the line cutout on one locker hatch on our test boat had bare balsa exposed. The balsa had been painted with gelcoat

rather than properly glassed, which I would fix ASAP. All six of the cleats on this boat are 10-inch, as they should be, with recessed spring and stern cleats. The two bow cleats are several feet (too far, I think) aft of the bitt.

Helm

In the pilothouse I noticed the headroom first—all 79 inches of it. This boat can get away with this extravagance since the deck isn't raised for a flush engine-hatch installation. Large glass windows help with visibility, but the window frames are unnecessarily large compared with most other boats, obstructing visibility somewhat. The side windows slide open and the center windshield opens for probably the best ventilation you'll find on any boat short of a Hobie Cat. I also liked the three windshield wipers.

The overhead electronics box gets in the way when you're standing at the helm if you're over 6 feet tall—I would trim its depth from 11 to 6 inches. The single-lever Morse control, steering wheel, and bow-thruster control are properly located. The instrument panel is easy to read and it's a mini-command-central, with all controls for lights, blowers, horn, trim tabs, bilge pumps, bait tank pump, and windshield wipers a short reach away. I found the molded bucket seats to be a little snug at 16 inches wide, but other seats are available if you want them. The port seat has drawers built in underneath and sits on a large box with an opening port light that houses a midcabin berth underneath. There's also storage under the helm seat.

Two plastic companionway covers stow behind the port seat when not being used, but I would prefer to see some type of sliding-hatch arrangement for greater convenience. A single-handed owner will appreciate the full-sized spring cleat within reach of the cockpit.

Engine Compartment

Access to the single V-drive 280 hp Peninsular diesel is through a boost-assist hinged engine box located in the middle of the cockpit. Maintenance points are easy to reach, but side access is cramped, which is why the side panels leading from the outboard storage bins are removable. Fuel lines and filters are easy to reach aft.

The two batteries (with a splashproof cover) and charger, along with the engine's bronze seacock and strainer, are forward of the engine within easy reach under another hatch. There's sound insulation on many surfaces under the deck and the bilges are all smoothly gelcoated. When you're finished checking the oil and water, the engine box secures snugly in place with rubber ties. Sturdy welded aluminum mounts through-bolted to the stringers support the engines. Hot freshwater taps off the engine when it's running or is heated by 110 volts when dockside.

Cabin

I like this cabin with its bright, cheery layout. Stepping over a 3-inch coaming and down two steps leads to a comfortable-looking haven. The large, inviting convertible dinette forward is a snap to convert to a 77-inch double berth with its telescoping table stand. Seatback cushions lift up and latch overhead for extra bunk legroom. There's a compact galley to port complete with refrigerator, sink, alcohol stove, and microwave oven. Headroom, at a maximum of 74½ inches, is fair for a 28-foot boat; ideally, I would prefer an inch or two more.

Aft of the galley, Albin has surpassed the generic midcabin cruiser with its 76-by-45-inch berth tucked under the passenger seat topside. Pressurized hot and cold water comes from a removable 36-gallon tank to the galley sink, as well as to the head to starboard with its sink and shower nozzles. There's ample storage space in the cabin, including a hanging locker forward of the head.

This cabin is well lit and ventilated due to a 20-inch hatch overhead and six side ports, two of which are in the head. Overhead lighting and electrical receptacles are plentiful and hardware is top-notch. A door panel can be removed for unimpeded access to the instrument-console wiring, and the battery switch is located under the companionway steps. The fiberglass cabin liner is bonded to the hull for extra strength.

Performance Test

In my opinion, this is one of the easiest steering, straightest running boats in this class in a following or quartering sea: you point it and it goes. The unique cutaway keel may be part of the explanation—I would adopt that design for the Albin 32, as well. The full, fairly shallow entry forward helps

Albin 28 Performance Results

RPM	Speed, knots	Speed, mph	Fuel Use, gph	Nautical mpg	Statute mpg	Range, nm	Range, statute miles	Noise Level, dBA	Trim, degrees
1,800	9.2	10.6	4.30	2.14	2.46	254	293	81	1
2,000	10.5	12.1	5.30	1.98	2.28	235	271	83	2
2,200	12.3	14.1	6.10	2.02	2.32	240	276	83	2
2,400	14.5	16.7	7.31	1.98	2.28	236	272	85	3
2,600	16.5	19.0	8.45	1.95	2.25	232	267	88	4
2,800	18.8	21.6	9.83	1.91	2.21	227	263	89	4
3,000	21.0	24.2	11.10	1.89	2.16	225	257	89	5
3,200	23.1	26.6	13.10	1.76	2.03	210	241	91	5
3,400	25.6	29.4	13.78	1.86	2.13	221	254	91	4
3,450	26.2	30.1	14.56	1.80	2.06	214	246	91	4

All tests: approximately half the advertised fuel capacity on board; rpm measured with a dwell meter; speed measured using differential GPS. Range was based on 90 percent of the 132-gallon total fuel capacity (119 gal. usable). Sound levels were measured at the helm station. Trim tabs adjusted for best performance. Test-boat power: single 280 hp Peninsular diesel.

with seas abaft the beam, but it also results in a bumpier ride going into a head sea than on finer-bowed boats.

Dockside, the payback for those good following-sea handling characteristics (with the shallow entry and cutaway keel) is a tendency to blow with the wind. The simple-to-use optional bow thruster makes up for most of that, though, so you just have to learn to use the thruster with the single left-hand prop, which backs to starboard. Although the boat has a very tight turning circle with its well-placed rudder and minimal lateral resistance underwater, this boat would benefit from a larger rudder to help it back down with more directional control. Minimal water came in through the scuppers when we were backing down.

The steering setup on this boat was very good—practically effortless and acceptable at 4½ turns lock-to-lock. The hull sides were dry when on plane, so a combination of light overall weight, moderate deadrise, and good chine design contribute to an efficiently driven hull form.

At a very reasonable base price, the Albin 28 is a well-built, thoughtfully designed boat able to handle a long list of duties ranging from dockside cocktail parties to tuna fishing on Stellwagen Bank. It's made to last and, with the extra fuel capacity, I wouldn't hesitate to take it offshore on an overnighter for a little extended fishing. Just remember to plan on reasonable speed limitations (around 16–20 kt.) going into moderate chop. A deep-V racer it's not, but that's obvious from the good mileage figures in the performance data.

I liked the sensible helm layout, standard windshield wipers, recessed cleats, wide side decks, comfortable cabin, no-nonsense cockpit, strong construction, and five-year structural warranty. This arrangement will work for anyone who wants a unique, low-profile hardtop or who just likes an engine box to sit on.

I would get the extra 60-gallon fuel tank—it will increase the range by almost 50 percent. But I would ask Albin to plumb this tank so the engine can take a suction directly from it rather than having to use a fuel-transfer pump; I also advise getting the bow thruster. Other options include a macerator, swim platform, and stereo. I would add windshield washers and narrower window frames for better visibility forward. I also would pay Albin to upgrade the sound insulation—perhaps with double lead-foam insulation—the noise coming through the deck from this not-especially-loud diesel was tiring after a while. Albin has added a bulkhead forward in the engine compartment to reduce the noise level.

I would straighten out the bow railing (which Albin says is a supplier's error), and I would try a larger rudder to help with better steering control when backing. You can also order a half-tower but not a flybridge—too much weight for the hardtop. If you're a serious angler, consider the half-tower for better visibility.

You can order the boat with a more water-resistant closed-cell foam core instead of balsa and with watertight bulkheads. Any way you fit it out, you'll get decent value for your dollar.

1997 Blackfin 40 Combi

There's probably not another big-beamed 40-foot express I would rather be aboard doing 30 knots in 4-foot seas than a Blackfin Combi; hardly any other boat constitutes serious competition. Stand forward of the bow when it's high and dry, and you'll see part of the reason in the narrow, deep entry with 49 degrees of deadrise. Sure, some cabin volume and running efficiency is lost with this deep-V hull, but the Blackfin is designed to take offshore abuse that many boats couldn't even begin to tolerate—while keeping you comfortable in the process.

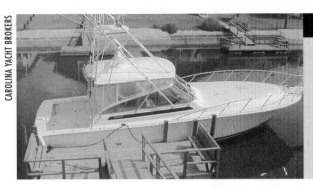

Blackfin 40 Combi Specifications	
LOA:	40'5" (without pulpit)
Beam:	14'6"
Draft:	3'7"
Displacement:	34,700 lb.
Fuel capacity:	510 gal.
Water capacity:	120 gal.
Deadrise (transom):	18 deg.

With its open layout—no deckhouse or fly-bridge to add topside weight and sail area—the Combi is low and stable. It may be the ultimate canyon sportfisherman in its class, with an unmatched ability to slug it out in sloppy weather, getting there and back without knocking fillings loose. Once comfortably 80 to 100 miles offshore, with the helm only a few steps from the cockpit, the captain can help out whenever it gets too busy for the mate to handle alone.

Cockpit

The cockpit is the ideal size for a full-fledged fighting chair or a pair of smaller deck chairs. At 8 feet long and 11 feet, 5 inches wide, it has ample room for serious fishing. Its 26-inch depth, excellent nonskid, and toe kicks all around make it safe and secure for the sport; the generous pitch, large flappered scuppers, and full 15-inch height off the water make it easy to keep hosed down and dry when backing down. An icebox (available as a freezer) and bait-prep station with sink and drawers are forward next to the engine-room door, and a huge livewell is an option to starboard. The coaming bolsters are a nice detail, and they're in tracks for easy removal and stowage out of the sun and weather. The 50-amp shore-power service and TV-telephone connections are to port; the saltwater and freshwater washdowns and a freshwater hookup are to starboard forward.

Three deck hatches lift for access to the 60-by-16-by-12-inch fish box and the 18-inch-square storage bin, which lift out for access to the steering gear and fuel tanks below. A 72-by-18-by-12-inch transom fish box is also available next to the 29-inch-wide transom door.

Two 255-gallon aluminum fuel tanks are forward of the deck hatches, and the fuel manifold to starboard allows either engine to take a suction from and return to either tank.

Foredeck

The 10-inch-wide side decks lead forward with the windshield frame providing a good handhold as you work your way to the solid-feeling, 1¼-inch aluminum railings, a full 28 inches high at the bow. The 10-inch bow cleats and two pairs of side cleats handle any mooring configuration you come across. As in the cockpit, the nonskid is excellent—grippy underfoot yet easy to keep clean, and Blackfin covers the entire foredeck, including the trunk cabintop. The Danforth anchor fits snugly in its pulpit, remotely controlled from the helm station.

Engine Room

This is one of the smallest boats around with cockpit access to the engine room, and it's reasonably well thought out, but I would add a couple of grab bars and make a few modifications for better accessibility down below. Tattletale lenses on the engine cooling-water expansion tanks let you know when to add water; however, the tanks are situated directly against the overhead so you can't pour water in the conventional way. Oil dipsticks are on centerline—easy to reach—and the fuel filter-separators and seacocks (which need valve-handle extensions for better accessibility) are above the drip-less shaft seals. They would be much easier to reach if the deck stanchions were reengineered out of the way and the companionway sides were trimmed back.

Thin, deep fiberglass-encapsulated plywood frames (1960s-era construction!) support the hull sides and surround the battery boxes outboard of the engines, which would be a tough spot to reach. Another fluorescent light on centerline would brighten the area between the engines. Wiring and plumbing are neatly routed out of the way; however, for more security, the fuel lines should have high-pressure connectors to the flare-fitting terminals rather than hose clamps.

The 1.45:1 model MG-5090-A twin disc gears on our Volvo Penta diesels angle down to the 2¼-inch shafts set at a 12-degree angle. With a boat as heavy as this one, steeper gears—say, 2:1—and larger, slower-turning props would undoubtedly increase efficiency and midrange speed and responsiveness, especially when running at full load. The down-angle gear permits a more level engine installation and a lower overhead above. The engine beds are fiberglass-encapsulated plywood, with aluminum angle stock through-bolted from the inboard side; soft engine mounts sit atop the beds. The Northern Lights generator below the ladder aft is probably in the best possible location, although you have to watch out for the fuel-filter plumbing that juts out between the steps.

In summary, it's a livable engine-room layout that could benefit from further tweaking: for example, an overhead hatch on centerline would open up the area between the engines.

Bridge Deck and Helm

Two gentle steps lead to the 7-foot-long bridge deck. A sink and countertop are to starboard with lifejacket storage below, and a huge L-shaped lounge, located up high to port for a good view, has lots of storage space below. A small recessed chart table is to port, and the helm station is forward to starboard.

The 40-inch helm seat has room for two, and it's a full 34 inches off the deck for a great view. No lover of mindless trends, Blackfin designed the 70-inch-high, powder-coated, aluminum-framed windshield so it affords protection from wind and spray; it also looks great. Large flat panels of glass and narrow mullions make it easy to see through, although the 16-inch wiper blades are far too short for the 30-inch-high glass, and freshwater washes are a necessity.

When you sit all the way to port on the helm seat (complete with an icemaker built in below), the wheel is still offset to the left a few inches. Ergonomically, the wheel, shifts to port, and throttles to starboard work fine when you're standing, but even a tall operator has to lean forward when seated, so some fine-tuning is needed. You should be able to reach all of the controls without leaning or bending down.

There's ample room for a large electronics suite on a tri-panel console, where the instruments would be mounted high for easy viewing. The compass is at a reasonable height for me, but, like the wheel, it should be directly in front of the operator position. Everything would work much better if the seat were extended 4 inches to port!

Cabin

Blackfin does as good a job with cabin layouts as it does with hull designs. Immediately down the teak companionway stairs to port is a U-shaped dinette that converts to a 78-inch double berth when the beautifully inlaid teak and holly table is lowered. The electrical service panel is against the aft bulkhead, and the large TV is forward so it's visible from anywhere in the cabin living area.

The galley is opposite to starboard with a two-burner Princess stove and a stainless sink built into the Corian countertop. A microwave oven is at eye level over the stove, and a two-thirds-size upright refrigerator-freezer is to the left (forward) of the sink. Composite doors, half-moon in cross section, give the Blackfin's well-executed joinery a distinctive flair.

I would add large opening hull portholes to let in a little more light and air. A minimum 22-inch overhead hatch rather than the 9-inch-square version provided should be specified, to double as an additional escape route.

Despite the hull's fine entry, the forward stateroom has sufficient room for a 76-by-55-inch island berth, soffit cupboards, a built-in TV, a hanging locker with tight joints in the cedar liner, and private access to the head. With the white cabin liner, 77-inch headroom, and 19-inch hatch letting in daylight and fresh air, these are comfortable environs.

The yacht's head, roughly 54 by 50 inches, is nicely finished with a sink and vanity, an electric toilet, a small hatch overhead, and an enclosed shower stall. The shower is raised 6 inches above the head's sole, so headroom is limited, but the molded seat compensates and the high threshold keeps the water contained.

This boat is well designed and expertly crafted, so you definitely don't have to rough it to take advantage of the performance it delivers.

Construction

If you're most comfortable with tried-and-true, low-tech construction—which, in this case, includes a heavy solid-glass hull layup (no coring is used in the hull bottom), wood-core stringers and frames, and plywood bulkheads—you'll like the Blackfin. (New Blackfins, after 2000, incorporate composites that cut down the weight.) The boat is ruggedly built and should provide many years of faithful service.

Remember that a deep-V like our test Blackfin, especially one that's as heavy as this boat, takes more power to push than a flatter-bottom boat. Composite construction would save a lot of weight (an especially critical factor in a deep-V), add impact resistance to the hull bottom, and result in a quieter ride. But composite hull bottoms, in production boats only, are difficult to market because doing a poor job has had dire (and highly publicized) results. Of course, the problem with a heav-

ier hull is that it requires bigger engines, which weigh more and need more fuel—a downward design spiral.

However, some boaters and boatbuilders will tell you they like weight and that a heavier boat rides better. This is true to the extent that the more mass the hull has, the less susceptible it is to acceleration by a given force—such as waves. However, weight for its own sake is an expensive and counterproductive way to make a boat ride well, especially a planing boat. I would opt for lighter, stronger, properly cored construction—add ballast tanks to a light boat if you want more weight when the going gets nasty.

Performance Test

If you clutch in both of the 610 hp TAMD 122 EDC Volvo Pentas at the same time, you better hang on—1,220 hp is major-league propulsion for a 40-footer. Heading out through Miami's Government Cut, the Blackfin rode smoothly when running into the 2- to 3-foot chop, showed excellent form stability laying to in the trough, and ran arrow-straight and bone-dry through the wake of several 60-footers that we overtook occasionally.

With the engines running, especially the Caterpillars, the Blackfin was plain *loud*; this needs to be addressed since continuous noise levels above 84 dBA necessitate hearing protection. You will lose sight of the horizon while the boat climbs up on plane: the boat aims for the sky. I would like to see the steering down around 3 turns versus the 4.3 turns lock-to-lock on our test boat. A tighter ratio results in a quicker response to the helm, appropriate in a boat as fast as this one. I would also add a rudder- and trim-tab angle indicators to eliminate some of the piloting guesswork.

Remember when comparing performance figures that our Caterpillar-powered boat had more weight and considerably more wind resistance in the form of a tuna tower and hardtop; it might easily pick up a knot or more stripped of these options. Our Volvo-powered Blackfin was clad in just a windshield.

Blackfin 40 Combi Performance Results

Windshield Only, No Tower or Riggers[1]

RPM	Speed, knots	Fuel Use, gph	Nautical mpg	Range, nm	Helm Noise Level, dBA	Saloon Noise Level, dBA	Trim, degrees
600	7.8	2.76	2.82	1,297	72	74	0
800	9.0	6.56	1.37	630	77	73	1
1,000	10.0	11.51	1.87	399	82	78	3
1,200	13.1	18.62	0.70	323	80	79	5
1,400	16.7	24.93	0.67	307	84	80	6
1,600	21.1	29.84	0.71	325	84	81	6
1,800	25.5	36.21	0.70	323	88	82	5
2,000	29.8	44.44	0.67	308	84	83	4
2,200	32.4	55.82	0.58	266	85	84	4
2,300	34.6	65.00	0.53	244	86	87	3

Hardtop, Tower, and Outriggers[2]

RPM	Speed, knots	Fuel Use, gph	Nautical mpg	Range, nm	Helm Noise Level, dBA	Saloon Noise Level, dBA	Trim, degrees
600	8.0	2.50	3.9	1,791	78	69	0
800	9.4	6.21	1.51	695	80	71	1
1,000	10.2	11.93	0.85	392	84	77	3
1,200	13.4	18.89	0.71	326	84	78	5
1,400	17.7	25.00	0.71	326	91	80	5
1,600	22.6	31.89	0.71	325	92	82	6
1,800	27.0	37.09	0.73	334	91	87	5
2,000	30.3	44.78	0.68	310	93	87	4
2,200	33.3	55.07	0.60	277	92	88	3
2,310	35.0	67.03	0.52	240	93	89	3

1. Volvo TAMD 122 EDC, 610 hp, 1.45:1 twin disc gears, 26-by-32-by-4-inch blade props, half a tank of fuel, quarter tank of water, three passengers, light gear, 70 degrees, 70 percent humidity, 35-foot depth, calm seas, and 5- to 10-knot winds.
2. Caterpillar 3196 660 hp, five eighths of a tank of fuel, quarter tank of water, three passengers, light gear, 70 degrees, 70 percent humidity, 35-foot depth, calm seas, and 5- to 10-knot winds.

The Blackfin is a good-looking, well-designed, stoutly constructed boat meant for serious fishing and cruising—you'll be able to keep on cruising when many other boats in this class have headed for the nearest lee. Noise levels are too loud, so be prepared to pay for improved noise insulation. Acoustic insulation in the engine room and under the cockpit (exhaust line cutouts in the aft engine-room bulkhead let engine noise travel aft under the cockpit deck practically unabated), exhaust noise, and noise leaks in places like the engine-room access door should all be addressed.

The Volvos were quieter and seemed to vibrate less in our tests, and they produced nearly the same cruising speeds as the bigger Caterpillars. Vibrations could have been attributable to engine design, or perhaps to shaft misalignment or unbalanced props. Efficiency was nearly identical between the two makes. Your decision about which engine to specify should also include the proximity of engine-repair facilities in your area.

In summary, the highs are great looks and layout, solid construction, and a superb ride. On the other hand, sound levels are deafening, the speed is disappointing for all that power, and the boat aims for the clouds when coming up on plane.

Henriques 38 El Bravo

Henriques 38 El Bravo Specifications

LOA:	38'0" (without pulpit)
Beam:	13'10"
Draft:	3'10"
Deadrise:	13 deg. (minimum)
Displacement:	28,000 lb. (dry)
Fuel capacity:	415 gal.
Water capacity:	60 gal.
Power as tested:	twin 500 hp Isotta Fraschini diesel inboards

Pretty boats you can find at any marina, but what about midsize canyon-running battlewagons, built to withstand daily abuse? A quick tour and ride aboard this boat will tell you where Jack Henriques's priorities lie. Few boats are more sturdily built for years of serious sportfishing or commercial abuse than the 38-foot Henriques El Bravo. This is a popular model among offshore anglers determined to get to where the fish are and back again in nasty weather. And when you're beating your way back through 8-footers, you'll likely give little thought to whether the boat can take it—the passengers will be the limiting factor in how much ground this boat can cover.

Design and Construction

Like other boats of this genre, the El Bravo favors a wide-open cockpit, a large raised flush bridge deck over a pair of diesel inboards, and a cabin that will sleep four in comfort. This model is also available from Henriques as a convertible sportfisherman with an enclosed flybridge, but the express version appeals to anglers who want to stay close to the action in the cockpit. Compared to a convertible, the express model offers a lower center of gravity with improved stability, less overall weight, and—therefore—greater speed and efficiency for the same power. You also get less interior room, of course.

The 38-foot Henriques has a hard-chine planing hull with a moderate 13 degrees of deadrise at the transom. This makes the boat easier to push than a deep-V and smoother riding than a flatter-bottom boat. A fairly sharp entry results in a smooth ride in a 2- to 4-foot chop at moderate speeds of up to 22 knots or so. At higher velocities, you're better off in a true deep-V than in a boat like this since at these speeds, so much of the hull comes out of the water so often, including the flatter aft sections. Running strakes forward and reverse chines help make for a dry ride, while contributing lift at speed. The Henriques has both a low center of gravity and hard chines for good form stability, so the ride is stable without any deep rolling associated with slack-bilge boats, even at slow speeds.

Henriques spares no effort putting together the 38. In fact, with some of the hull features (like the double chines), its rock-solid construction, and fiberglass fuel tanks, Henriques boats remind me more of a Viking than anything else.

Osmosis prevention is addressed by a Glidden isophthalic gelcoat followed by vinylester resin in the first few layers of fiberglass laminate. The bottom is a solid layup of alternating mat and stitched roving; Divinycell coring is used in the sides and decks to save weight. Overlaps of 16 inches at the keel and 24 inches at the chines enhance the hull. Henriques takes pains to keep structural wood dry: Microlam wood stringers are impregnated with epoxy and then encapsulated in fiberglass; plywood bulkheads are tabbed in and also encapsulated. Limber holes are cut through solid glass, so there's little chance of water infiltration. Bolt penetrations are bedded in polyurethane adhesive to keep the core dry.

The hull-to-deck joint is fiberglassed together, making the boat a very strong and leak-proof structural unit with a single-piece liner from bow to stern. The boat comes with a five-year structural hull warranty, but osmotic blistering is not included. Like Viking a few miles down the road, Henriques builds its own fiberglass fuel tanks. This adds some weight but eliminates corrosion problems often experienced eventually with aluminum tanks.

Engine beds are constructed of heavy ½-inch aluminum angle stock through-bolted to the stringers. The fiberglass fuel tanks, built in-house at Henriques, are held in place with a jig; then closed-cell foam is poured in, it expands and oozes out, and is trimmed off. The tank is then tabbed and fully fiberglassed in place, with the tank sides effectively becoming integral to the hull.

Deck and Cockpit

Being a true fishing boat, it's only natural that the cockpit is allocated the lion's share of the deck plan. With plenty of unobstructed deck space in the 10-foot, 3-inch-by-11-foot cockpit, there's enough room for any kind of angling imaginable; Henriques even glasses a steel plate into the deck into which a fighting chair can tap. The coaming is a generous 29 inches high for good balance when you're leaning overboard to reach a fish. A 30-inch transom door opens inboard, which is the safest way. The door makes it easier to land king-size gamefish while serving as a convenient boarding point when moored stern-to. Two insulated 53-by-22-by-23-inch fish boxes are included, so fish can be iced down for overnight trips to the canyons. Saltwater and freshwater washdowns, significant deck pitch aft, and deep gutters make for easy cleanup. Four rod holders are provided, as are under-the-rail rod racks to port and starboard. Lock-

ers forward provide ample storage space, and a livewell is available to port.

For a better footing, I would enlarge the 3½-by-7-inch cockpit steps leading forward; however, the side decks are over a foot wide, making this a well-designed and safely traversed foredeck. The bow railing is constructed of solid-feeling 1¼-inch-diameter aluminum and is a full 28 inches high for good security forward. Water and fuel fills are on separate sides, minimizing potential for mishaps at the fuel docks.

Helm

The raised bridge deck results in good visibility from the starboard-side helm and allows an extra measure of headroom in the engine room below. Molded seats on either side have ample room for locked rod storage below. A two-person helm seat, raised 39 inches off the deck, provides a commanding view through the large sections of flat glass in the sturdy windshield. When you're seated, the steering wheel is a bit of a reach, but the helm station is laid out so instruments, switches, and electronics all angle ergonomically toward the operator.

The compass is directly in front of the helm for easy viewing, even at night. A centerline vent window provides fresh air when needed; a remote actuator would come in handy since the window is fairly difficult to reach. The windshield frame is rugged but efficiently engineered and spare in dimension so it doesn't interfere with the captain's vision. There's sufficient room for chart work to port. A tower with a fiberglass hardtop 88 inches above the bridge deck is standard equipment, as is a full canvas enclosure. Above are a sunshade and full controls, an upholstered bolster, halogen cockpit lights, and a rocket launcher (tower-mounted rod holders) for those standby rods.

Engine Room

Access to the engine room is through a flush centerline deck hatch aft on the bridge deck. The engine room, with 54 inches of headroom, is painted white and well lit. A 4 kW Onan generator is aft on centerline, and there's enough space between the big Isotta Fraschini diesels for routine maintenance. Three hatches provide a level and dry working surface on centerline, lifting up for access to the bilge below. The engine-room machinery and equipment is neatly installed with aircraft-type fuel hoses and compression fittings, and easily accessible Racor fuel filter-separators on the aft bulkhead.

A freshwater hose makes engine-cooling top-off and general cleanup a cinch. There were no sea-water strainers leading to the engines; in some locales, builders think you're better off without them—at any rate, not having them certainly saves room. Both engine-room bulkheads are watertight for passive flooding protection, and there are five watertight compartments.

Cabin

The teak and white cabin interior is smaller than those found on other 38-foot express cruisers, but this is a sportfisherman—and it is still comfortable and pleasantly finished. Reverse-cycle AC is standard and two overhead hatches open for ventilation or an emergency escape. The feeling of roominess is enhanced by good lighting and a full 6 feet, 6 inches of headroom, which continues forward. The finish is applied in a quality manner; it's very well fitted out for its intended purpose and has an attractive appearance. A four-person 74-by-48-inch convertible dinette located immediately to port opposite the galley converts to a twin-size berth.

The compact but functional galley features a sink with hot and cold pressurized water, microwave oven, refrigerator-freezer, and adequate countertop and storage space. Just forward of the galley is the enclosed head with an electric toilet with macerator pump and Y-valve for dual discharge, handheld shower spigot with shower sump and pump below the cabin sole, and a vanity with sink and storage space. Forward is the stateroom with four 76-inch single V-berths (a queen size is available) and storage space below, a 19-inch cedar hanging locker, AC, and a privacy door.

Performance Test

Our sea trial took place under ideal conditions with calm protected waters off the Jersey shore for the speed runs and a 3- to 4-foot chop offshore. In this sea, the boat had a smooth, dry ride up to about 22 knots. The ride became harsh as we approached 28 knots, with the full entry forward and moderate-V sections amidships and aft showing their limitations at higher speeds. This happens especially when the waves are 30 to 40 degrees on the bow—the ride seemed smoother heading right into them. At 20 to 25 knots, the Henriques tracked very well

Henriques 38 El Bravo Performance Results

RPM	Speed, knots	Speed, mph	Fuel Use, gph	Nautical mpg	Statute mpg	Range, nm	Range, statute miles	Noise Level, dBA	Trim, degrees
800	7.1	8.2	4.3	1.65	1.90	616	708	92	1
1,000	8.3	9.5	8.7	0.95	1.10	356	409	98	2
1,200	10.2	11.7	15.9	0.64	0.74	239	275	98	3
1,400	15.0	17.3	20.3	0.74	0.85	276	317	98	4
1,600	19.7	22.7	25.3	0.78	0.90	290	334	101	6
1,800	23.5	27.0	29.8	0.79	0.91	294	338	101	6
2,000	25.8	29.7	36.1	0.71	0.82	267	307	102	6
2,200	29.3	33.7	43.6	0.67	0.77	251	288	102	5
2,350	31.2	35.9	51.8	0.60	0.69	225	258	104	5

Test conditions: test-boat power, twin 500 hp Isotta Fraschini diesels; 450 gallons of fuel, 65 gallons of water, four passengers on board, 15-foot depth, wind 5 to 10 knots, and air temperature 70 degrees. Range calculated using 90 percent of 415-gallon total fuel capacity (373 gallons usable).

downsea with little helm effort required. This hull seemed like a natural for cruising at 18 to 22 knots; smaller 380 to 400 hp diesels will push the hull comfortably at that speed.

At almost six turns lock-to-lock, the steering took little effort, but it was also slow and not as responsive as it should have been. Power steering would reduce the effort and increase responsiveness to the wheel with just three turns possible. Backing down offshore, the scuppers stayed dry, but a lot of water made its way aboard through the transom door. Dead in the water in the trough, the boat was very stable and comfortable, and showed it to be an excellent trolling platform. The windshield allowed unimpaired visibility all around and was high enough to offer ample protection, keeping clear glass—not the frame—between the horizon and my sight line.

The Isotta Fraschini diesels provided power galore, but whether it was lack of sufficient acoustic insulation, ineffective exhaust silencers (in fact, there were none on this boat), or inherently noisy engines, this was one of the loudest boats I've recorded. Something needs to be done before spending extended periods offshore on this boat; the U.S. Navy, among other authorities, considers extended periods of exposure to more than 84 dBA, as well as intermittent exposure up to 104 dBA, harmful to human hearing. Standing in the cockpit, noise levels from the engine room and from the overboard exhaust seemed to be at about the same level; therefore, it seems that both insulation and silencers are needed.

As it is, I can't recommend this power combi-nation without somehow reducing sound levels. Performance, though, was instantly responsive—maybe too responsive at low speeds, actually—even at a low idle speed, the effect of clutching in the engines is immediate. The single-lever Micro Commander controls worked superbly, with ample neutral detents and smooth throttle operation. They do take some getting used to, though, since there is so little throttle travel from idle to full power (WOT); better do your experimenting well clear of the dock the first few times.

I heartily recommend the El Bravo to anyone looking for a well-built offshore sportfisherman capable of moderate cruising speeds in rough water. If you need higher sustained speeds in rough water, find a boat with a sharper, deeper entry (Blackfin-style) and more deadrise. The El Bravo is well-constructed and solidly engineered. Before buying this model new, I would require much quieter sound levels in the mid-70s to low-80s dBA range; I'm not sure how much of the noise is due to the design of the Italian diesels and how much it could be reduced with improved sound isolation.

Several combinations of basic options are available to the builder to get the job done, including installing effective exhaust silencers. I might choose smaller engines such as Caterpillar 3126s or Yanmar 440s, since larger diesels will likely be operated throttled back much of the time offshore to save fuel. In the end, you'll have a boat built to deliver a lifetime of safe and dependable oceangoing service.

1997 Luhrs 36 Express

Luhrs has been in the business of building serious fishing boats for decades. Although the comfort level has increased lately to keep pace with customers' expectations, the emphasis is still on value and fishability. The trend continues with the new 36, but the comfort factor is rapidly gaining ground to the point that this new model offers serious com-petition for cruising yachts in its class. This is also a pretty boat with a graceful profile and seductive lines, perhaps more so than any previous Luhrs.

Design

The Luhrs has a modified-V hull with a fairly fine, deep entry twisting to a fairly flat 13 degrees of

Luhrs 36 Express Specifications

LOA:	38'11"
Length on deck:	36'2"
Beam:	13'10"
Draft:	3'5"
Fuel capacity:	400 gal.
Water capacity:	94 gal.
Height:	16'6"
Sleeping capacity:	6

transom deadrise. Double chines narrow the wetted waterline for greater planing efficiency (at higher cruising speeds), while contributing to form stability at rest with the upper, wider chine submerging at moderate angles of heel.

Construction

Luhrs uses tried-and-true construction methods to produce rugged boats of moderate weight. The Luhrs hull laminate schedule includes isotropic gelcoat 25 mils on the bottom, 20 mils on the sides, and 18 mils on the decks. General-purpose orthophthalic resin is used throughout the layup. The hull is solid fiberglass; the decks are cored with balsa. Plywood stringers are encapsulated in glass and limber holes are sealed with resin, rather than fiberglassed over for a better seal.

The hull-to-deck joint is fastened with 3M 5200 polyurethane adhesive clamped together with stainless steel screws on 8-inch centers. A nonstructural rubber toerail is added with more screws, strengthening the joint.

Cockpit

It's immediately evident that the 8-foot-long-by-10-foot, 6-inch-wide cockpit is exceptionally user-friendly for several reasons. First, the coamings are 30 inches high, so you would really have to work at falling overboard, even when playing a monster fish. Second, the nonskid is very grippy and should

be so even covered with fish slime. Third, cockpit bolsters and toe kicks will keep you on balance, even when you are leaning over those extra few inches to gaff a prize fish. With an aft gutter and a recessed 2½-inch PVC pipe scupper to starboard, and the transom door for drainage to port, the deck is easy to hose down.

Equipment includes shore power and TV-telephone hookups, saltwater and freshwater washdown spigots, stern cleats mounted below flush stainless hawseholes, a tackle drawer, rod holders, a big fish box, and storage bins under the molded side-deck steps.

Just forward of the fish box is the lazarette hatch with gutters draining overboard through the cockpit's aft gutter—you won't have to worry about leaves clogging up the drain lines. The bilges below are ground smooth and painted gray, and the steering gear is readily accessible. The wiring for the Bennett trim-tab actuator wasn't loomed, nor was the bilge-pump wiring.

The aluminum fuel tank below the cockpit appeared to be mounted in such a way as to allow sufficient air circulation, always important for minimizing the chances of exterior corrosion developing. If and when the 5052-grade aluminum fuel tank has to be replaced, the deck will have to be cut out since there's no built-in removal hatch. Overall, the cockpit does its job very well indeed for fishing or cruising.

Side Decks and Foredeck

Walking forward to drop the hook will be more of an adventure than it should be, however. The side decks slope noticeably outboard, and the bow railing is 25 inches high all the way forward—4 or 5 inches too low for really good security and balance (Luhrs will build a higher version at a customer's request). The nonskid only covers the side walkways, not the entire foredeck. You don't always stay on the walkways, so why cover only them with nonskid?

Helm

It was three steps, or 2 feet, up from the cockpit to the bridge deck, which put the starboard-side helm on our test boat high enough off the water for good all-around visibility. Although not the most rugged in the industry, the windshield will probably provide good service over the years. It's a full 30 inches high off the dashboard, and the mullions supporting each glass window are narrow but still stiff. The overall result is that the mullions don't overly interfere with your sight lines.

If you're not too broad-beamed yourself, there's room for two on the 37-inch-wide helm seat. The seat is centered on the steering wheel with the shifts to port and the throttles to starboard. With the seat pulled ahead on its track, I could reach the wheel and engine controls without leaning; with the seat pushed back, I had plenty of legroom with the recessed foot pocket.

Forward of the wheel is an electronics flat, and the entire console—wheel, controls, and electronics flat—hinges aft when five screws are removed. Forward another foot or so are the instruments, laid out asymmetrically with the fuel meter between the tachometers. Forward of the instruments and a full 4 feet forward of the operator is the compass, which I would raise; I could barely see its lubber line and I'm over 6 feet tall. I would also mount it directly over the instruments to bring it in a little closer for easier viewing. Criticisms aside, this is a helm station I could easily live with, although I would also have Luhrs paint the entire dashboard area a darker color in flat paint to reduce glare.

Across to port on the bridge deck is a 6-foot lounge that could double as a berth in a pinch. There's storage below the cushion—I would like to see the access hatch, two thirds the length of the lounge, enlarged to make it easier to get to the forward section. Aft of the helm seat is another 39-inch seat with a 30-gallon livewell just aft of it, making it easily accessible from the cockpit. The height of the livewell is especially convenient, making it easy to reach inside to grab baitfish.

Engine Room

Luhrs has refined the art of engine-room access over the years, and the 36 Express is a case study in how to do it right. With 39 inches of vertical clearance aft, there's plenty of room for a large person to access the machinery. The boost lift is offset to port as far as possible, making it easier to reach the neat array of equipment on the forward bulkhead. There's also an inspection door leading from the cabin forward. Forward and outboard of the engines are batteries and the hot-water heater, and the well-insulated water tanks are directly outboard of the main engines.

Those Caterpillar diesels were the easiest imaginable to hook up fuel meters to for the performance test—and that says something about overall machinery accessibility, as well as about how easy it is to trace the fuel lines to make sure that the supply and return lines were straightened out.

Of the two engine seacocks and fuel filter-separators, only the starboard seacock is easy to access. Both filter-separators are difficult to reach, especially to port, and it would be difficult to see water and sediment in the clear bowl provided for that purpose. Neither are they high enough off the bilge to get a bucket or even a can underneath to drain them off. The Kohler generator is under the aft removable ladder, easily accessible when the ladder is out of the way. Make sure it stays dry so it doesn't start to rust—it's located just under the bridge-deck flange and it isn't enclosed.

Cabin

I was impressed with both the size and the classy look of the 36's cabin. No glistening white fiberglass everywhere on this boat; instead, our test boat was finished in cherry, including a beautiful quarter-cut inlaid table for the dinette. The Ultraleather lounges look and feel great, and there's no bulkhead separating the forward stateroom from the rest of the cabin. Instead, a curtain from inside a locker pulls across to provide privacy, adding to the cabin's sense of spaciousness. There's even rod storage below the cabin sole—another excellent idea.

Immediately down the companionway steps is the well-laid-out galley to starboard; our test boat had a custom black Corian L-shaped countertop. Two burners are hidden below a microswitch-equipped cover—this arrangement really opens up the counter space when the lid is down. There's also a turntable microwave oven, small refrigerator-freezer, deep sink, and generous storage space.

The head is to port of the companionway, and it's done right with a separate shower with a molded seat. There's a large vanity with a large mirror above and storage room below. The smooth liner is easy to clean up, and there's also a vent hatch overhead and an exhaust fan.

To port forward of the head is a lounge that converts (by lifting and pinning the seatback in position) into an 80-by-36-inch upper berth; the lounge seat becomes an 80-by-24-inch single.

Across to starboard and forward of the galley, the lounge seat converts to a 76-by-40-inch berth.

Up forward is the master berth, which is undeniably oddly shaped, but there's well over 80 inches of length to stretch out for a good portion of it. There's also a 16-inch-wide cedar hanging locker to starboard and a TV to port—all the essentials. The cabin on the 36-footer elevates this boat to plausible competition for the likes of Sea Ray and Tiara and similar express boats, although Luhrs boats are usually thought of exclusively as fishing boats.

Performance Test

We had a bit of a chop in Boston Harbor, enough to tell me that the boat has a stable ride, if on the stiff side due to its great beam. You'll be able to cruise along comfortably at knots in the high teens or low twenties when the wind picks up, but it's unreasonable to expect that you'll keep up with a narrower, true deep-V like a Blackfin or Bertram. We were up on top at 1,400 rpm, a speed that offers excellent fuel economy if you're not in a hurry. The Luhrs had a fairly flat mileage curve, an indication of a well-chosen power drain and a well-designed efficient hull bottom.

The Teleflex engine controls were silky smooth and removed the engine-status guesswork from close-quarters maneuvering. I would definitely want a taller windshield because I found myself

Luhrs 36 Express Performance Results

RPM	Speed, knots	Fuel Use, gph	Fuel Mileage, nmpg	Range, nm	Noise Level, dBA	Trim, degrees
1,000	8.2	4.6	1.78	642	78	2
1,400	11.5	9.5	1.21	436	83	4
1,800	18.7	16.0	1.17	421	88	6
2,000	22.0	19.2	1.14	412	89	5
2,200	24.3	21.88	1.11	400	89	5
2,400	26.7	27.08	0.98	355	91	5
2,600	29.6	33.0	0.90	323	92	5
2,800	31.6	38.4	0.82	296	92	3

Test conditions: twin Caterpillar 3126 rated at 420 bhp, 2:1 twin disc gears, 24-by-32-inch four-blade props; two passengers, half a tank of fuel, full tank of water, light gear, clean bottom, calm seas, and depth over 25 feet.

staring directly at the frame while standing up with the boat up on plane. When I was seated, the visibility ahead wasn't good unless the trim tabs were lowered. It would be worse, of course, for a shorter person.

Luhrs definitely needs to resolve the noise-level problem on this boat too. At a 2,400 rpm cruise speed, 91 dBA is just too loud for comfort or to prevent hearing loss, for that matter. The U.S. Navy requires "single" hearing protection (either earplugs or muffs) if the sound levels are continuously above 84 dBA, which should put sound levels in perspective.

All told, the boat handled about average for domestic models of its class; that is, not too well when compared with many similar yachts produced overseas and some in the United States. The steering should be practically fingertip-easy and certainly not more than four turns lock-to-lock, two less than on our test boat. Our boat turned ponderously and the steering required significant effort, especially the last turn or so. Backing and twisting with the engines were another matter, with the boat spinning around quite well offshore and backing into a slip predictably and smoothly.

Handling and noise-level criticisms aside, the Luhrs shows every sign of being an excellent offshore seaboat with a well-balanced, comfortable hull form, solidly constructed and well engineered. You can take it to the canyons with confidence.

Luhrs lets you have things your way: an Open model with no windshield, an EX with a high windshield (like our test boat), or an SX with a low windshield. The colder the climate you live in, the more protection you're likely to want—remember that you can't put windshield wipers on plastic filler curtains. The SX and EX come with our test boat's starboard-side helm; the Open model has a center console situated aft on the bridge deck, close to the cockpit.

The Luhrs has much to commend it: lots of standard features and creature comforts, solid construction, and a decent ride. I would add power steering to improve steering responsiveness. I encourage you to consider it a serious contender for your attention if you are in the market for a dual-purpose 36-foot express sportfisherman/cruiser.

1997 Pursuit 3000 Offshore Express

A great open sportfisherman, the Pursuit 3000 makes good sense for anyone moving up from a center console, and also for the owner of a larger boat who's grown tired of all the maintenance and expense that goes with it. The only thing missing is a windshield.

Like a battlewagon-size sportfisherman, the Pursuit is designed to head to the canyons at 20-plus knots, catch a boatload of fish, and beat it back home just ahead of a front. The Pursuit 3000 can do it safely while providing all the basics: a place to eat, sleep, and take a shower. Of course, there's less room on the smaller boat and the ride is bumpier, and you may even have to give up the 25-inch TV—you get the picture.

On the other hand, if you own a 20-something powerboat but you want more range and seakeeping ability, the Pursuit may be just what you're looking to move up to. This is a boat originally designed for southern climes with its open helm area, but many

Pursuit 3000 Offshore Express Specifications

LOA:	31'2"
Beam:	12'0"
Draft:	3'0"
Fuel capacity:	250 gal.
Water capacity:	40 gal.
Power as tested:	twin 230 hp Volvo TAMD 42 diesel inboards
Boat weight:	11,500 lb. (dry)

Northerners are apparently taking a liking to it. There's no windshield, so any protection you need has to come from a canvas and plastic enclosure.

Construction

Pursuit uses a thick 30-mil gelcoat (22 to 24 mil is more commonly used in the industry) and a skin coat of premium vinylester resin, which is very resistant to osmosis. This treatment allows Pursuit to offer one of the best hull-blistering warranties in the industry. Quality isophthalic resin and high-strength knitted and woven fiberglass reinforcements are used in the hull and deck layup. The Pursuit's bottom is solid glass; sides and decks are cored with balsa ranging from ½ to 1 inch thick to combine light weight with strength.

Stringers are 1½ to 3 inches thick and are built up using ¾-inch Techlam unidirectional plywood coated with resin and gelcoat to help prevent water absorption in the limber holes. A better method, certainly, is glassing over the limber holes entirely before the stringers go into the boat, or using PVC tubes glassed in place; gelcoat and resin alone crack when the wood shrinks and swells with varying moisture content. The stringers are completely encapsulated in fiberglass, with the tabbing serving to increase the thickness of the hull bottom. (Incidentally, all this concern about sealing wood against moisture penetration is one reason so many builders have shifted to all glass-and-foam construction. However, many builders still use wood to excellent advantage, as long as it stays dry.)

The 1-inch-diameter horizontal brass pins 2 inches from the top of the stringers are tapped out to receive the engine-mount bolts, resulting in a very solid engine foundation. The hull-to-deck joint is bonded with adhesive and stainless screws every few inches.

Cockpit

The business end of this boat is cleanly laid out and uncluttered with all the essentials for safety, including excellent nonskid, a coaming that's a full 28 inches high aft, and a generous toe kick to keep you on balance, thanks to a separately tooled coaming that extends inboard several inches out from the cockpit liner. The deck drains aft and out through oversized, 6½-by-2½-inch scuppers, with side gutters deep enough to channel water in the right direction. It's a small point, but since a ½ inch of water will stay trapped forward of the scupper, I would like to see Pursuit bring the bottom of the scupper flush with the bottom of the recessed scupper pocket.

Don't worry about snagging a taut fishing line anywhere aft on this boat: the stern cleats are bolted in place below the flush-mounted hawsepipes, and the two hinged covers on the large transom fish box won't present any obstacles to getting your trophy safely aboard. Forward in the cockpit, the tackle and bait-prep center is both well designed and close to the action. It includes a live-bait well, a sink with washdown nozzle, and five tackle drawers.

The aft deck hatch swings up and a prop affixed to the hatch bottom swings down to hold it in place. This makes for good access to the twin rudders, which are ruggedly installed with a heavy metal channel 5 inches above the bottom of the boat. This gives the rudder assembly the strength to resist being torn out of the bottom of the boat during grounding; it's better to bend the rudderstock than open up the bottom of the boat. The bilge is ground reasonably smooth and painted white, which improves visibility below decks.

Bridge Deck

If the cockpit got first dibs at the designer's table, the bridge deck must have been next on the list. Two steps and 18 inches up from the cockpit, the flush helm area features a centerline helm station. Pedestal seats sit atop a storage box to port, and tackle drawers and a lined cooler are to starboard.

The helm seat is comfortable and you're high enough off the deck to have a good 360-degree view, but legroom is tight. My legs were cramped even with the seat all the way back—a foot pocket would have helped. The compass is directly in front of the helm and at just the ideal height. The tachometers on our test boat were next to each other, where they should be for easy simultaneous viewing. There's room below on the instrument panel for a selection of electronics, and a chart table with a Plexiglas lid is to port.

Headroom under the standard hardtop is a generous 78 inches, so the helm has a very open, airy feeling. The engine controls are close at hand, as is the steering wheel. Trim-tab switches are below the wheel—it would be nice to have trim-tab angle indicators there too. Finally, the helm console tilts back for easy access to wiring inside. This accessibility will reduce labor costs and encourage maintenance inside. With the bridge deck's aft fishing center only 18 inches high, it needs a 12-inch-high handrail on top; it wouldn't take much to get tossed over it into the cockpit during hard acceleration.

Foredeck and Tower

A large molded cockpit step leads to the side decks and foredeck where the nonskid is less aggressive but still adequate. The bow railing is 24 inches high along the sides and 26 inches high forward—I would like to see it a few inches higher for better balance. For some reason, the anchor-line-locker hatch has no gutters, just a flange, so the anchor line is apt to be damp much of the time. The foredeck, however, does provide an unbroken expanse for casting, which anglers in search of surface fish will certainly welcome.

The optional walk-in tower is strongly made and easy to climb up to—maybe a little too easy to get into, though, with a walk-in entry. I would add a gate on either side so you don't end up back in the cockpit in one step.

Engine Room

The entire bridge deck hinges up 18 inches for cockpit access to the engine room; a 26-by-17-inch deck hatch also lifts up to allow getting to the engines quickly. As expected, Pursuit has done a good job of engine-room layout and equipment installation. The engine room is quite accommodating for a 30-foot boat, even with the bridge deck down. A wide flat shelf on centerline provides a comfortable working surface between the engines, and bilge surfaces are smoothly sanded and painted white. Toggle-pin through-bolts mounting the engines, Norscot dripless shaft seals, aircraft-style compression fittings on some of the fuel lines: these all speak of quality. Not so impressive were the engine-mount shim plates sticking out at various angles rather than being straightened upon engine installation. The raw-water strainers are on the aft bulkhead above the shafts; moving them closer to centerline would make them more accessible.

Cabin

Owning a Pursuit 3000 means you'll lose all bragging rights about roughing it offshore. The cabin on this boat will keep you comfortable, indeed, with room to sleep four comfortably—and it seems roomy with 80 inches of headroom aft. I did find it a little tight getting down the 19-inch-wide companionway; many boats in this class have 2 to 3 more inches of elbowroom.

The forward V-berth sleeps two and the back of the lounge flips up to make a pair of bunk beds. In case the comfortable surroundings make you forget you're on a fishing boat, there's storage below the berths and in an upright locker next to the galley with room for ten rods. The enclosed head to port has a fold-down seat over the toilet, a shower-curtain track overhead, and a sink spigot that lifts out to do double duty as a showerhead. There's a 10-by-2½-inch opening side port above the sink that is quite narrow; I would like to see it replaced by one twice that width. In fact, I missed not having a couple of large side windows in the cabin to see what's going on outside. There are three opening hatches above the V-berth to let in daylight and fresh air.

The galley is next to the companionway; that's a good place to put it on a fishing boat—closer to the action. There's a single-burner electric stove, sink, microwave oven, refrigerator-freezer, and fairly ample storage space. There's more storage near the port seat and in a small hanging locker next to the companionway. Pursuit might match the angled floorboard grain more closely to that of the sole; the difference in color and grain was quite noticeable. All in all, it is a comfortable cabin that would be almost perfect with the addition of side ports and overhead lights forward.

Performance Test

Even with the engines just clutched in at idle speed, the boat handled very responsively. However, I would opt for more responsive steering than our test boat afforded at five turns lock-to-lock; three to four turns is more like it for a high-powered boat such as this. Rapid course changes to avoid collision take more time to execute at higher speeds, so a commensurately faster steering response is needed.

We moved into open water and increased speed to 3,000 rpm. With the 230 hp Volvo TAMD 42 diesels providing brisk acceleration, we were soon cruising at a steady 21 knots. I advanced the throttles to 3,400 rpm, a comfortable cruising speed

with these engines, while measuring 24 knots on the GPS. The full enclosure offers protection from the elements, but spray can't be cleared off with windshield wipers on plastic. You can see small objects far better through glass that's been wiped clear than even the best quality plastic that's beaded with drops of water. If you like everything else about the boat, one solution is to install a custom windshield.

When we finished our high-speed runs, I dropped down to an idle and backed into the slight chop as though backing on a fish. The boat backed well, steering readily with the rudders or the engines. Water came in through the scuppers and the transom door, but it drained quickly. In the cockpit, the 28-inch-high padded coaming bolsters were comfortable to lean against, and they were high enough for reasonable balance and security.

For owners who put more than 200 to 300 hours a year on their boat, the diesels make increasing sense. Range with the diesels improves significantly, they last longer than gasoline engines, and diesel fuel is far safer than gasoline. The only kicker really is the higher up-front cost for the diesels, but you'll recoup much of the extra investment at resale time; Pursuits tend to hold their value well.

Across the speed spectra, the Pursuit 3000 handled predictably and smoothly. Bouncing across the occasional wake, the boat seemed to be ruggedly put together with no discernable rattles or squeaks anywhere. For its length, this is a fairly wide boat, which provides a lot of room for a 30-footer. But keep in mind that narrower beam-to-length ratios generally do better in a short, steep chop. Wide open at 3,800 rpm, the Pursuit 3000 averaged 28.3 knots on two runs.

Expect a moderately smooth ride and a comfortable 15- to 18-knot cruise capability in 3- to 5-foot seas. Back in the marina, I took the time to back into a couple of slips, and there were no surprises there. The Pursuit handled well, with little tendency to wander sideways. The Volvos provided sufficient power at idle, and visibility from the helm was excellent—this is one boat you can easily drive around the marina while sitting down.

This is a fine boat, well designed and strongly built. I was surprised to see untreated, bare plywood in several of the limber holes aft in the bottom; this is not a good sign in a boat that's intended to last indefinitely. And to make the bridge-deck–lift concept work well, allowing squeeze-free engine-room accessibility, the bridge deck should lift up farther than it did on our test boat—just 18 inches. However, these are relatively minor complaints; the Pursuit 3000 is a well-proportioned, high-quality fishing machine with all the tools for serious angling.

The Pursuit will be easy to keep clean with tooled fiberglass everywhere from head to cockpit, and its rugged engineering will pay dividends, making the boat both reliable and durable for years to come. Pursuits command a good price on the used-boat market, holding their value well and increasing their appeal as an investment. I would take this boat and head for the canyons in a heartbeat.

Stamas 370 Express

Stamas 370 Express Specifications	
LOA:	38'6"
Beam:	13'2"
Draft:	2'4"
Fuel capacity:	372 gal.
Water capacity:	90 gal.
Displacement:	21,000 lb. (wet, with diesels)

Stamas has been building fishing boats that also cruise for some fifty years. With their emphasis on these fish-cruise boats, they're positioned in the same market as Pursuit and Rampage. This is the builder's largest effort to date, and I'll say up front that I see evidence of a boat that is well conceived, and clearly a success in many ways, with a unique sportfisher layout that will suit some families well. In some ways, though, it's not as well executed as I would have hoped; there's evidence of an outboard-powered boat manufacturer recently having moved up to the big leagues—with, for instance, cut-and-pasted cockpit details, more than a few bubbles and bristles in the varnish, and not-so-tight joints in some of the woodwork down below.

Design
The Stamas 370 has a unique layout. For its size, the boat has a big cockpit, and the cabin is well proportioned, as well. So what gives? Well, the bridge deck is only 4 feet, 2 inches long, which is small for a boat this size and just big enough to hold the helm and companion seat. But since the low-profile 420 hp Yanmars are under the cockpit, there's room for a midcabin under the elevated bridge deck. And it's this midcabin, and the engine location, that makes the Stamas unique in its class of express sportfishermen.

The Stamas is a good running boat, ruggedly built with a modified-V hull delivering a better-than-average ride and good performance and efficiency. The modest height and compact dimensions of the Yanmars makes this design possible. The tanks are outboard of the engines and extend aft, keeping their center of gravity nearer to the hull's center of flotation, so trim will change little as fuel is consumed. That in turn means ride quality is improved, since excessive trim, or bow-high attitude increases vertical accelerations, otherwise known as *pounding*.

The boat's hull design is by Pete Stamas; it's a modified-V with a fairly fine and deep entry. A full docking keel projects about an inch below the running gear—it's about 10 inches deep below the bottom. This is another unusual feature for a V-bottom express boat, and a welcome one if you value grounding protection (as I do) for the running gear. Of course, the extra wetted surface and weight adds drag and slows the boat, but not to a significant degree, and I think the running gear protection is well worth it. Prop pockets, which allow the propellers to tuck up into the hull, thereby reducing draft, are radiused to match the arc of the blade tips. This pocket design has been shown to be the most efficient, as buoyancy and dynamic lift are little affected, and waterflow to the props is quite smooth. There's one bottom strake per side to deflect spray and add lift forward. The hull sections have slight convexity to increase strength and help decrease slamming loads.

Construction

The Stamas 370 is conventionally built, with a few twists. The hull starts with an isophthalic gelcoat followed by blister-barrier coats of two layers of mat wet out in vinylester resin below the waterline. Vinylester resin cross-links more completely than general-purpose orthophthalic resin (which is used in the rest of the laminate) making it more resistant to water penetration at the molecular level, and it has better physical properties, meaning it can stretch as much as the fiberglass reinforcement without failing, increasing the laminate's strength and impact resistance. Ortho resin is the weak link in a fiberglass laminate, but it's used by most builders since it's cheaper to buy. Additional layers of hand-laid mat and 24-ounce woven roving and Coremat to help prevent reinforcement "print-through" complete the solid hull sides and bottom. Chines and the keel are reinforced with additional layers of reinforcement, and the docking keel is poured solid with poly-

ester putty and capped with 1.5- and 24-ounce woven roving.

The hull is supported by fir stringers encapsulated in fiberglass, tabbed to the hull while it's still in the mold to help hold its shape—this is standard procedure for most builders. Limber holes are cut through the wood-cored stringers and coated with resin and gelcoat, according to Stamas; the problem is that the gelcoat is eventually likely to crack as the wood shrinks and expands with changes in moisture content. Sealing the holes with fiberglass or epoxy would be a good idea, especially with the wood-cored, rot-prone wood stringer core. Using either pressure-treated wood or foam as the stringer core would help address this potential limber hole–related problem.

Bulkheads are fiberglass-encapsulated plywood; rather than stand the bulkhead edges away from the hull skin using jigs during tabbing-in, Stamas builds up the hull skin thickness locally with strips of reinforcement to manage the bottom-panel impact loads. I'd still rather see a slight gap between the bulkhead edge and the hull skin to help eliminate potential hard spots, though the extra hull skin reinforcement is a step in the right direction.

The hull-to-deck joint is puttied with a fibrous polyester bonding compound and mechanically fastened together with rivets, which essentially serve to clamp the parts against the putty while it is curing. The vessel's inner liners (supporting the hull sides from the transom to the cabin bulkhead) and decks are fiberglassed to the stringers, hull, and transom for additional structural integrity. A cabin liner adds structural integrity and stiffness forward.

The aluminum fuel tanks are mounted on neoprene strips (to provide an airspace around the tank bottom) resting on flat fiberglass-covered shelves and affixed with aluminum angle stock welded to along the bottom of the tanks' perimeter. When these aluminum tanks need to be replaced, the engines would have to be removed first. The seven-year hull warranty does not cover blistering, which in today's marketplace it certainly should, as an indication of the builder's confidence in the product and as a practical matter for the owner. The vinylester resin skin coat should make this a moot point, in any case.

In the cockpit and side decks, plywood is used as a core material; this makes for heavy deck sections, put they're arguably preferable to balsa from a water absorption and rot perspective. The cabin-top forward, a core of 1-inch end-grain balsa helps reduce weight while maintaining adequate strength and stiffness. Stamas also uses four layers of cloth rather than a bulkier reinforcement, believing that the glass-to-resin ratio and both strength and weight are improved as a consequence.

Cockpit

The 11-foot, 9-inch-wide by 9-foot, 6-inch cockpit is 27 inches high along the sides and 26 inches high aft along the fish box. This is a big cockpit, by any standard, for a 37-footer. Though Stamas is not generally thought of as a builder of tournament sportfishermen, the square footage back aft puts this boat in the big leagues. The cockpit deck is 17 inches above the waterline, which is high for any mate trying to gaff or leader a fish alongside, but the elevation is necessary due to the Yanmars residing below the cockpit. In fact, that you can put 880 hp below a cockpit this low to the water is remarkable. The extra height also improves the boat's seaworthiness, since the watertight volume resulting significantly increases reserve buoyancy.

We'll speak about engine room access in a moment, but suffice it to say that the cockpit deck is made up of some nine removable deck sections that screw down to the deck perimeter and cross frames. In itself, this is a good thing, since the deck looks to be watertight, and you can't have too much access belowdecks come major repair time. Our problem is with the hodgepodge way the whole thing was put together, as if existing components were taken from other models and used in this one. For instance, the cockpit drainage is through channels in gutter voids under deck section edges; if these were to plug up with debris—almost assured given their small dimensions (leaves, pine needles, and bass scales are likely offenders)—the hatches might have to be removed to clear them out.

Same goes for the drainage back aft, where small holes cut through the plastic baseboard (for lack of a better word) around the cockpit liner lead under the enclosed liner and forward to the round drain holes in the liner sides. This convoluted water drainage path is problematic at best, both because of the indirect drainage, and because of the potential for blockage. We also have a problem with the aforementioned plastic baseboard; why not just mold the liner and deck as a single unit, as almost all other builders do? It will also be hard to clean under the transom fish box and livewell, which project over the deck with a hard-to-reach opening below. George Stamas responds that their priority is to provide access to the bilge and below-deck components, hence the many removable deck sections, at their customers' request. We think that's a worthy goal but feel that the execution could be cleaner.

The hardware holding the boosts for the fish box and livewell covers was coming loose already on our test boat, which hadn't even been used to fish yet, and they are not powerful enough to keep the lids open. The hatches themselves are well made, finished on two sides in an all-molded process. These are mostly convenience issues, though plugged deck drains could quickly become a safety issue in the wrong sea conditions. Clearly a personal safety issue, though, is the transom door mounted flush with the transom and made of a single skin of fiberglass about 1 inch thick, so it's recessed 6 inches or so aft of a raised coaming at deck level. This would have the opposite effect of a toe kick, giving the angler something to trip over when working a fish over the stern. The raised coaming should be eliminated and the door built with a liner that projects inboard of it to eliminate the tripping hazard and create a toe space. The door is too low, too, to do much good, at only 22 inches high above the raised coaming, and about 25 inches above deck level. You don't want to count on it keeping you on board, especially when the throttles are shoved forward unexpectedly on this powerful boat.

The pop-up stern cleats are great for their accessibility when raised, and clean profile when recessed. We'd just like to see the next larger size used, since these 9½-inch models filled up quickly with a pair of ⅝-inch lines attached.

Also included are a sink, icemaker, and drawers below the helm seat aft, and more drawers to port under the portside seat.

Though the boat is large and fishable, its cockpit ranks as one of the more cluttered (in terms of components) we have seen on a boat this class. The one-piece cockpit liner and one-piece washboard construction used by Ocean, Cabo, Viking, and everyone else should be incorporated here to improve the ergonomic, structural, and drainage issues mentioned.

Side and Foredeck

A bolt-down step leads to the 10-inch-wide side deck, which you can actually walk along (when it's not too rough, at least) with a rod or mooring line in hand. Walking forward, a 4¼-inch-high bulwark adds some security along the side decks, and the half-tower supports give you something to hang onto. The problem is the bow railing height; at the windshield, the stainless-steel 1¼-inch-diameter rail is very low, just 18 inches, but steadily climbs until it reaches 34 inches at the pulpit; a 26- to 28-inch height aft, gradually rising to 34 inches at the bow, would add a healthy measure of safety while maintaining the required aesthetic. A pair of 10-inch bow cleats straddle the pulpit, which has a Starboard chafing plate screwed down over it, and which the anchor shank has already started wearing through it. This needs a redesign, possibly with a repositioned metal roller doing the trick.

Cabin

The big cabin in the Stamas 370 looks upscale, with a teak and holly sole, teak veneer bulkheads, molded fiberglass hull and overhead liners that look sharp and ease maintenance, and a vinyl over-

head liner (with the adhesive unfortunately coming loose in places) contrasting pleasantly. The well-equipped galley is to port, with an L-shaped Granite Coat molded countertop, three-burner electric stove, sink, undercounter refrigerator, and drawers (some of which tended to open autonomously during our sea trial). A microwave over the countertop and a small opening port are also standard.

Another neat feature is the rod storage locker below the teak and holly cabin sole. You'd have to remove 14 screws to lift the molded liner out to get to the bilge below, but at least it's accessible, unlike on many similar boats.

The head is to starboard off the companionway. The sole in the head is raised a full 5 inches above the cabin sole, which is too bad since headroom inside is down to 5 feet, 11 inches versus 6 feet, 5 inches in the saloon right outside the door. It looks like the head sole could be flush with the cabin, with just the toilet raised on a platform to make it more comfortable to sit on and to conform to the hull deadrise below. The fiberglass liner makes cleanup easy, though, and the separate shower, which in a change of pace also holds the toilet, is quite roomy. Be careful, because if the cowling around the base of the toilet comes loose, as it did on our boat, hot electrical leads are exposed. The bifold aluminum and glass shower door came open a couple of times on our bumpy sea trial—it needs a latch of some sort to hold it against the bulkhead.

The L-shaped dinette opposite the galley converts to a short (5-foot, 10-inch by 3-foot, 4-inch) berth, which will be big enough for younger children but shouldn't be counted as a berth suitable for adults. At this length, it also shouldn't even be advertised as a berth by the manufacturer, at least not without a clear caveat as to its length. Fact is, it would be a simple matter to carve another 8 inches or so out of the forward berth by cutting a slot in the bulkhead. The lounge seat should seat three people comfortably, and in useful arrangement, a pair of bar stools screw into their recessed sockets on the inboard side of the twin-leaf table, meaning that in a pinch you could probably seat five people at this table.

The forward enclosed stateroom has a double berth that parallels the hull side to starboard. It's over 6 feet, 5 inches long for most of its 4-foot, 11-inch width, so you get a big bed for a small space. The only downside here is that you have to crawl over your bedmate or dog or whoever to get in and out of bed in the middle of the night, but it beats putting in a space-robbing island berth that would carve another foot or so from the saloon. The Formula 37—about the same size as this boat—took a different approach by eliminating the stateroom bulkhead, which opens up the cabin quite a lot. Our Stamas has a teak veneer bulkhead that maybe improves the privacy, but also chops the cabin up into distinct areas. Pay your money and make your choice. This is strictly a matter of preference. Anyway, for a 37-footer, this is a big cabin, stretching over 20 feet from midcabin to forward mirrored crash bulkhead.

A pair of 19-inch-square Bomar hatches are just big enough to serve as escape routes and let in fresh air and daylight above the forward berth and the dinette table. Four opening portlights contribute to the open and airy effect. Headroom is on the low side for a 37-footer at just over 6 feet, 4 inches aft, and under 6 feet near the dinette forward. Compare this with a Formula 37 PC's headroom of up to 6 feet, 9 inches. In fact, for whatever reason, Stamas seems to have a propensity for short berths and low headroom, in our experience, especially when compared to other builders' same-size models.

Aft of the saloon is an open and accommodating midcabin, with 4-foot, 9-inch headroom, which is plenty when you're sitting down. The two seats convert to a 6-foot, 11-inch by 4-foot, 2-inch berth, which is a comfortably proportioned bed; there's also a 20-inch-wide hanging locker, and storage space below the seats. In that storage space is more wiring that's secured along the upper side, but it needs to be protected against chafing with looming or plastic wire tracks.

Engine Room

Engine room access doesn't get much better than this. A 5- by 8-foot cockpit hatch opens to nearly vertical on an electric lift, with shock stabilizers outboard to help steady it if you're rolling around offshore. Almost everything is out in the open, including the Racor fuel filter-separators mounted on the aft bulkhead, though the seacocks are very difficult to reach and close in a hurry; the starboard seacock is especially difficult to get to, and essentially physically impossible for me because of my height and heft. George Stamas reports that they are looking into relocating the seacocks for better access.

The engine room hatch opening is 2 feet short of the forward bulkhead, though, so getting to the seawater strainers near the forward bulkhead is harder, especially with the deck support stanchion on centerline; moving the stanchion against one of the engines would open things up, making it easier to get to the forward end of the engines. The ladder, also on centerline, pulls up out of the way, which helps. A wide, flat floor on centerline is comfortable to work on.

The 420 hp Yanmar (350 bhp at 3,100 rpm) 6LY2-STEs are bolted to 1.96:1 ZF gears and 1¾-inch Aquamet shafts turning 22 by 28 four-blade cupped propellers in shallow pockets. We would recommend sealing the bulkheads to make them watertight and better contain engine noise, add chafing protection for the engine exhaust hoses where they pass through the sharp-edged holes in the plywood-and-glass bulkhead, add a second hose clamp to the exhaust riser's seawater hose (there are two clamps on the other seawater hoses), replace the fuel lines and hose clamps with aircraft-type high-pressure hoses and compression fittings, relocate the seacocks to make them (more) accessible, and add looming to the wiring runs for a measure of chafing protection. The exhaust exits the hull sides aft, bypassing the optional Ecosound muffler system; this is important, since at low speeds, the backpressure-reducing venturi created by the underwater exhaust outlet shape is lacking.

The 0.19-inch-thick, 5052-grade aluminum

fuel tanks are outboard of the engines, and they extend aft into the lazarette. They're supported by and welded to aluminum angle brackets that run along their sides along the bottom. This design works well, since the brackets keep the tank bottom up off the shelf, working to prevent water from collecting and corroding the tank from the outside. The fuel tanks would be completely accessible without removing the engines, in fact, if not for the fixed hatch frame just aft of the engine room. Why Stamas didn't just make the whole thing removable I don't know, but that would have made it easier to replace the aluminum fuel tank when the time came. I always prefer fiberglass or polyethylene fuel tanks to aluminum because they make corrosion, and eventual replacement, a nonissue.

Helm

Raised 17 inches above the cockpit (reached via an 8- and a 9-inch stair), the bridge deck is 4 feet, 2 inches from the step to the forward bulkhead. This means that the 9-foot, 3-inch-wide bridge deck gets the least amount of acreage overall, with the cockpit and the cabin getting the lion's share of the LOA.

Visibility from the helm is excellent all around—about as good as it gets in this class, in fact, for a couple of good reasons. The helm is positioned well off the waterline, thanks to the raised bridge deck, so sight lines are improved and the horizon is farther away, of course, the higher you get. The windshield has narrow, but strong, aluminum mullions, which don't obscure your forward view. The high helm position also provides a great view over the bow, with the horizon always well above the pulpit, even when coming up on plane without tabs.

As with most express boats (except, for instance, the Pursuit 38 and Rampage 38), the windshield is too low to protect much from the elements; when you stand up, the top of the frame is at about chest level. And though the glass is 32 inches high, Stamas only provides 14-inch wiper blades to keep it clear, about half the length that's appropriate. The premium EZ2CY plastic curtains, ordered by the dealer, are relied on to keep you dry then, and ours were of a very high quality, made by MacDougalls Marine in Falmouth, Massachusetts. The vent windows outboard are a welcome feature, providing a steady blast of fresh air at speed.

All that bridge deck height creates the necessary headroom in the midcabin below, which makes this usually confining space seem relatively expansive and accommodating. On the downside (there always are downsides in the boat design business), it's quite a climb up from the cockpit, forward a few feet, then down five steps, and four feet, to the cabin. So you have to give up an easy trip from cockpit to cabin to gain all that midcabin headroom and the excellent helm visibility.

Headroom below the hardtop at the helm is a full 6 feet, 9 inches, and the helm station itself is comfortably set up with the wheel and engine controls well positioned for convenient seated or standup operation. The tilt wheel had a suicide knob, necessitated by the steering system's excessive 6.5 turns; the knob hits the operator's thigh, too, since the helm seat doesn't slide aft far enough so you can stand clear. Power steering, which we feel should be *de rigueur* in a boat with such a hefty price tag, would easily cut this down to a more responsive three turns. The engine gauges are spread out all over the lower panel, directly above the wheel, so you have to do a lot of looking around to keep tabs on temps and pressures. Clustering the gauges in pairs would be a better, more user-friendly arrangement. The large tachs are on centerline, though, behind the wheel rim when sitting, and in clear view when standing.

Single-lever Morse electronic controls shift comfortably with a detent mechanism that makes it clear when you're in neutral. I'm taller than average, so I'd prefer the controls to be mounted a couple of inches higher, but they're at a good angle for smooth operation. The helm seat comfortably holds two people, and an L-shaped seat opposite to port holds three.

The helm console of the Stamas tilts back, but since it doesn't open far enough for you to actually get at the wiring, the rationale for the tilt feature is obscure. When you try to close the console by tilting it forward, it's an awkward fit: it scrapes against the console edge against the fixed bulkhead, and there's no flange or gutter around the forward edge to keep water away from the wiring. It also pinches the wiring when it closes, and the wiring bundles inside are not as neat as much of the competition's.

Performance Test

We had a great day for our sea trial: a stiff southwest breeze was blowing across Nantucket Sound and Vineyard Sound as we pulled out of Falmouth, Massachusetts, en route to Martha's Vineyard. The boat climbs on plane with little fuss, transitioning over the hump with less bow rise than many of Stamas's competition. The rudders are small, but they deliver a surprisingly good bite at speed; it took us just 19 seconds to make a full turn to either port or starboard, which is remarkably fast in a boat of this size. It took a little longer than we'd like to get the rudders hard over, though, at 6.5 turns lock-to-lock. That makes collision and object avoidance more difficult than it ought to be on this 32-knot boat. Handling dockside was crisp and predictable.

Running at 25 knots in the 1- to 2-foot chop (with an occasional 3-footer), the ride was quite smooth, and the boat's natural running angle, or trim, was a moderate 3.5 to 4.5 degrees. Credit the

bang-on weight distribution and intelligently conceived hull form, and the shallow, radiused prop pockets. And even with the strong breeze broad on the bow, you could count on two hands the number of saltwater drops that hit the windshield. This is an impressively dry-running boat.

At idle, noise levels were 69 dBA at the transom and about the same at the helm. We had a good bit of smoke in and around the cockpit at low speeds, especially at startup, due to the side-dumping exhausts. Once we were moving faster, we stayed ahead of the exhaust, which in any event, at speed, is diverted to the underwater exhausts and then directly out the stern. The Ecosound EPS 1,000 muffler glassed to the bottom of the hull is used on Boston Whalers, Formulas, Pro-Lines, and other boats, the builders favoring its simplicity and efficiency of installation. Our basic problem is that sound levels at the helm were up in the 88 to 90 dBA range at high speeds, noise levels that necessitate hearing protection if exposed for longer periods of time. The boat needs to be reengineered here to get engine noise levels (which seemed significantly louder than the radiated noise through the deck) down to acceptable levels, and at least to the high 70s at cruise.

The good-looking Stamas 370 Express offers a good ride, a strong turn of speed, a unique raised-cockpit

Stamas 370 Express Performance Results

RPM	Speed, knots	Speed, mph	Fuel Use, gph	Nautical mpg	Statute mpg	Range, nm	Range, statute miles	Noise Level, dBA	Trim, degrees
800	5.1	5.9	1.5	3.40	3.91	1,224	1,408	68	2
1,000	6.1	7.0	2.8	2.18	2.51	784	902	62	3
1,500	8.6	9.9	7.2	1.19	1.37	430	495	81	4
2,000	13.1	15.1	10.7	1.22	1.41	441	507	82	5.5
2,200	15.7	18.1	13.2	1.19	1.37	428	492	84	5.5
2,500	21.7	25.0	19.6	1.11	1.27	399	458	85	5
2,700	24.9	28.6	22.8	1.09	1.26	393	452	87	4
2,900	26.5	30.5	27.5	0.96	1.11	347	399	88	4
3,100	29.3	33.7	32.4	0.90	1.04	326	374	89	4
3,300	31.8	36.6	38.7	0.82	0.94	296	340	90	4
3,450	32.4	37.3	44	0.74	0.85	265	305	91	4

layout that makes a midcabin possible, and a roomy cockpit for serious offshore fishing. It has a lot to offer, though we'd advise any buyer to specify certain changes as a condition of purchase. We'd like to see the builder retool the cockpit liner out of a single piece of fiberglass, integral to the rest of the deck superstructure, which is how almost every other builder in this range puts a boat together, for better drainage and maintainability.

Especially for the price, more attention needs to be paid to the quality of the woodwork finish in the cabin, which is below the standards set by Tiara, Pursuit, and others in this class. George Stamas says that the new supervisor in the varnish department is addressing that issue. Same goes for the fuel fittings, electrical installation, and seacock accessibility. The windshield wipers, cabin convertible dinette, bow railing, and pulpit would all benefit from redesign. I'd also insist on lower engine noise levels at cruise. The boat comes with a good, seven-year warranty that would be better still if it explicitly covered osmotic blistering.

The Stamas 370's standard equipment list includes bottom paint, a vinylester resin skin coat, built-in fire suppression system, cockpit bolsters, a teak and holly cabin sole, toilet with macerator and holding tank, dockside water connection, a fire extinguisher, battery selector switch, battery charger, shore power hookup, hot water, microwave, refrigerator, stove, CD-radio-stereo, TV-VCR, and transom shower. You can buy the boat with 8.1-liter, 370 hp MerCruiser gas inboards, but the more costly Yanmar 420 diesels are certainly the way to go with a planing boat this big.

Test boat options include a dealer-installed hardtop and marlin tower with electronic controls and canvas top, Rupp Gold outriggers, 5.5 kW diesel genset, Ecosound engine exhaust system, icemaker, navy blue hull, EZ2CY side curtain enclosure, full-color, large-screen electronics package, aft cockpit seats, anchor windlass/rope/chain/anchor, air-conditioning, dealer prep, and freight.

The Albemarle 27 is a rugged little offshore battlewagon, with a deep-V hull capable of keeping up a good pace in a chop on the way to the canyons. The jackshaft stern-drive propulsion allows the engine to be located forward under the raised flush deck, while the stern drive makes for a clear transom, at least compared with a twin outboard. ALBEMARLE

This 45 Open is the smallest model in the North Carolina–based Davis Boatworks line of semicustom open and convertible sportfishing boats to 74 feet. With their Donald Blount–designed bottoms, Davis yachts deliver a superb ride.

Albin builds affordable fishing-cruising boats from 28 to 35 feet, including this 35-foot Tournament Express. The Albin 32 + 2 is also worth a look for anyone who values a large cabin in a low-profile boat. See also the flybridge version on page 411. ALBIN

This Bruce Alderson cutaway rendering of a Rampage 36 shows some interesting engineering details. BRUCE ALDERSON

Pursuit's single or twin stern-drive-powered, well-built 2860 is a sort of seagoing SUV, with a small cabin for the occasional weekender and a large cockpit for fishing and day cruising. PURSUIT

The beamy, well-equipped Luhrs 32 Open is a pocket canyon-runner built to fish. Luhrs's lineup of sportfishing convertible and express fishing boats ranges from 29 to 50 feet. LUHRS

Pursuit's lineup of 22- to 38-foot fishing-cruising boats includes this 3400 Express. Pursuits (like sister-company Tiara) are well regarded for their quality construction, practical layouts, and ergonomic design features. PURSUIT

The Pro-Line series of fishing boats, which ranges from 17 to 34 feet, includes this twin gasoline- or diesel-powered 33 Express, a solidly built boat that offers a generous standard equipment list and good value. PRO-LINE

The Blackfin 29 Saltshaker is one of the very best rough-water rides in its class. The deep-V hull has a very fine entry and a moderate waterline beam, which delivers the great ride. The boat is also ruggedly built and good-looking—a very functional sportfisherman.

The low profile of the Blackfin 29 Saltshaker is made possible by the use of engine boxes (with integral seating) that keeps the deck low to the water. This makes getting from cockpit to helm easy and fast.   BLACKFIN

Convertibles

Convertibles have been around as long as the cuddy cabin, and with good reason: this design allows a two-deck design in a relatively small boat, providing a large interior for cruising, a flybridge for good visibility, and a big cockpit for fishing. The early convertibles had an uncovered flybridge as the secondary control station (the main station was below in the pilothouse) with steering and engine controls, compass, and depth-sounder. Now it's rare to find a convertible with a windshield and lower control station; instead, windshields are made of leak-proof fiberglass and the space below is outfitted with large TVs, full-height refrigerators, and microwave ovens.

The species has evolved to the point where the flybridge is the main operating station, with full electronics, seating for six or more, and a hardtop with full plastic enclosure. The bigger cruising convertibles are also available with a two-deck superstructure creating an enclosed, climate-controlled flybridge reached from both internal and weather deck stairs. But the pure fishing convertibles stick with the aft console arrangement on the bridge so the skipper can keep an eye on the cockpit action. An aluminum tower 30 feet or more off the water is *de rigueur* for spotting fish below or on the surface at some distance from the boat. Plus, it's just cool to run a boat from the tower. The downside is that all the air drag from a big tower can slow a

sportfisherman by 2 to 3 knots and absorb 10 percent of the propulsion power.

The business end of the convertible is the cockpit, which is outfitted by the builder with every imaginable fishing amenity, from gaff storage lockers to saltwater icemakers for chilling the catch. Although a 12-foot-long cockpit on a 60-footer only represents a fifth of the boat's LOA (a smaller percentage than on the older, smaller boats), they're still bigger than ever because of the greater beam. A transom door allows a 1,000-pound tuna or marlin to be pulled aboard, and cleats are mounted below hawseholes in the washboards to reduce snag potential when playing a fish. A coaming height of 29 to 30 inches is ideal.

A tournament-ready sportfisherman must be able to maneuver quickly on agile gamefish, and the freeboard aft and cockpit deck must be relatively low to the water to handle big fish alongside. These boats also must be fast to have any chance at winning a big-money tournament; some sportfishermen can cruise in the high 30-knot range with a full load of fuel and supplies, sea state permitting.

The same seakeeping qualities that allow a convertible to make it over a hundred miles offshore in a little more than 3 hours, fish all day in sloppy conditions, and race home for the weigh-in make them excellent offshore cruising boats as well. With many production and custom convertibles being built in the 55- to 80-foot range, these are true liveaboard cruising yachts as well as fishing boats. A 60-foot convertible has less interior volume than a 60-foot motor yacht, but it's also a better, faster seaboat.

The saloon, just forward of the cockpit, is the yacht's living room, with a lounge (convertible to a pullout berth), TV, stereo, galley, and dining area. The cabin forward on a 65- to 75-foot convertible might have three or four staterooms and as many heads, all luxuriously appointed. The engine room on a convertible is usually generously proportioned compared to strict cruising yachts, first because the engines tend to be so big, and perhaps also because the owners do some of their own maintenance and appreciate being able to maneuver around all that machinery.

1998 Ocean 40 Super Sport

OCEAN

Ocean 40 Super Sport Specifications	
LOA:	40'4"
Beam:	14'2"
Draft:	3'8"
Fuel capacity:	408 gal.
Water capacity:	90 gal.
Displacement:	27,500 lb.
Height to hardtop:	15'4"
Standard power:	twin 420 hp Caterpillar 3126 diesels
Test-boat power:	twin 410 hp Volvo 73s

As a well-known builder of fast convertible sportfishermen, Ocean knows what its customers want: speed, seaworthiness, fishability, and value are at the top of the list. Ocean delivers all this and more in its fixed-price 40-footer. The boat comes standard with everything you need to cast off and head offshore—except for your lunch, tackle, and bait.

Cockpit

The Ocean's 8-foot-long-by-10-foot-wide, 29-inch-deep cockpit is clean and simple in design. Recessed cleats lead to transom hawseholes, a tuna door opens outboard when it's time to land the big one, and side storage compartments are convenient for keeping gaffs and swabs out of sight. Forward is a nicely tooled integral assembly with a bait-prep station to port, and a freezer, engine-room access, and a cleaning-gear locker or space for a dealer-installed cockpit control station to starboard.

Two deck hatches open to the large two-part fish box forward and another—with gutter drain lines leading directly to the bilge—to the lazarette aft. This is an unfortunate arrangement since the deck has little pitch aft to it; therefore, much of the deck water ends up draining to the three hatches, where it eventually has to be pumped overboard. Glasswork in the bilge is rough in places; another hour or two of grinding before the deck goes on would make the difference. The rudderboard is rugged and securely fiberglassed in place.

A cockpit coaming bolster along the transom is a nice feature, and I would like to see the same treatment along the sides to create a toe kick for better balance when you're leaning overboard. You can also get a swim platform, which makes stern-to boarding easier—but adds an obstruction aft when playing fish in close.

Bridge

An athwartships ladder leads to the open bridge with its helm console situated slightly forward. A healthy bridge overhang nicely extends the deck area, and the view below is still quite good, especially in the aft half of the cockpit and also through the ladder opening. Getting to the outboard helm chair is a tight squeeze, but something has to give with the limited space and the console-layout requirement.

I often find legroom to be at a premium because of my height, but not so on this Ocean 40 Super Sport. The adjustable seat is well positioned and at the ideal height. The wheel and shifts to port and throttles to starboard were directly at my fingertips, especially with the seat slid forward. I would tilt up the engine instruments more to make them easier to read when the operator is seated. (Note that shorter operators would have a longer reach in all these cases.) I would also locate the switches on the console where they're more visible, rather than above the recessed footrest. The compass is conveniently located directly forward of the wheel, and an electronics flat to starboard will hold a large suite of toys to keep offshore anglers happy. If you need even more room, overhead electronics boxes are built into the optional hardtop.

Forward of the console is a lounge seat to port and an L-shaped seat to starboard with generous storage below. Tooled gutters will keep the water on the deck where it belongs and everything will stay dry inside. This is an excellent bridge layout.

Foredeck

A handrail follows the saloon side-window contour forward where you hand off to a 24-inch-high, 1¼-inch aluminum bow railing, which I would like to see 4 to 6 inches higher. Three bow cleats and a single side cleat well forward handle mooring chores, and a windlass leads to the stainless steel–lined anchor pulpit. The nonskid is very smooth but still seems fairly effective, just like in the cockpit.

Saloon

A sliding door to starboard leads to the Ocean's 14-foot-long (overall)-by-11-foot-wide saloon. Headroom is about 6 feet, 4 inches on centerline, less to either side due to the cabintop camber. Our test boat was finished mostly in off-white and tan with Ultraleather upholstery, teak paneling, and mini-blinds tucked behind carefully fitted soffits. A large window overlooks the cockpit, so you can keep tabs on what's going on there while enjoying the plush, air-conditioned interior.

The saloon has a novel layout with a half-round dinette forward on centerline raised 10 inches above deck level. This creates headroom below in the aft stateroom, and gives the settee occupants a good view out the side windows and aft. An L-shaped lounge is aft to port (a pullout sleeper bed is an option) with storage below. Opposite and immediately inside the cockpit door is a cabinet with an icemaker and electrical panel, a stuffed swivel chair, and the classy-looking Granite Coat fiberglass galley countertop with refrigerator below, large sink with instant hot water, and a convection-microwave oven above. Forward of the dinette is a TV with a built-in VCR and flanking storage lockers. Like the rest of the yacht, the saloon's layout makes excellent use of space while remaining open and airy.

Engine Room

Cockpit access leads to the Ocean's cleanly engineered, well-designed engine room; in fact, I can't think of a 40-footer with better all-around accessibility. All white and well lit overhead, there's ample room (especially for a 40-footer), including an unobstructed platform forward that hides a pair of batteries to either side forward. Easily accessible seacocks next to the shafts aft lead directly to the engine-drive cooling pumps. Oil dipsticks are inboard for quick checks, and expansion tanks on the forward bulkhead are in plain view and easy to top off. An Xchanger oil-changing system is also located forward, encouraging owners to keep clean oil in their diesels. A 12-gallon electric water heater is forward of the port engine outboard of the Halon bottle and 40 amp battery chargers, all well placed for easy access.

The 5052-grade, 0.19-inch-thick aluminum fuel tanks are outboard of the engines and near the hull's longitudinal center of buoyancy to keep trim to 6 degrees or so at cruise speed. They're also painted to retard exterior corrosion. Replacing these tanks would be an expensive proposition, necessitating the removal of the engines and saloon floor; therefore, it's important that sufficient air circulates around them so they stay dry.

The engines are well secured with engine mounts bolted to ⅝-inch-thick-by-4½-inch-wide steel plates encapsulated in fiberglass atop the hull stringers. For added convenience, a floor covered with easy-to-clean diamond-tread aluminum provides a level work surface on centerline.

Back aft under the companionway are the Crusair AC compressors and, against the aft bulkhead, the fuel filter-separators, a bit of a stretch to reach but with sediment bowls in plain view and still accessible. Aircraft-type high-pressure fuel lines and compression fittings supply the engines, and Ocean looms them where they pass to and from the tanks. The generator is aft of the port engine, shrouded in a soft enclosure (a sound shield is also available) to help attenuate sound levels dockside. Stuffing tubes are shielded to keep dripping water from spraying around the engine room.

Cabin

A companionway to port in the saloon leads past an open rod-storage bin, over an equipment space with an AC compressor and freshwater pressure tank inside, and down to the two-stateroom, one-head accommodations. Entered through an unobtrusive sliding pocket door, the cleverly designed master stateroom is under the dinette; headroom ranging from 7 feet to 6 feet, 4 inches makes it seem larger than its already generous proportions. A 6-foot, 4-inch queen-size walkaround berth fits easily inside, and there's also a large cedar-lined hanging locker, drawers and cabinets, and a TV. To port, a hanging locker under the companion-

way can accommodate an optional washer-dryer unit.

The large head with electric toilet, sink with vanity and storage above and below, and a separate molded fiberglass unit is forward, with private access from the master stateroom. Teak joinery is tight and precise, and executed with attention to detail.

Forward is the guest stateroom with a full-size, 6 foot, 8-inch-by-4-foot berth to starboard and drawers below, a small (12 by 17 in.) hatch above (I would increase it to 22 in. square so it can double as an escape route), under-gunwale lockers, and access to the chain locker forward. Both staterooms and the head have several overhead and reading lights where needed. With the portside companionway allowing such a large master stateroom, Ocean provides the accommodation of a 45-footer in a shorter boat in a commendable package.

Construction

The Ocean 40 Super Sport is built of quality materials, starting with a premium vinylester skin coat to prevent osmotic blistering. This is followed by stitched, nonwoven fiberglass in the solid bottom and cored (½ in. Divinycell) hull sides. The use of nonwoven roving allows (at least theoretically) a lower resin-to-fiberglass ratio for a more efficient laminate and improved interlaminar bond lines.

Using modern methods and engineering principles, Ocean's fiberglass stringers are foam-filled, eliminating the possibility of wood rot. Plywood bulkheads are fiberglassed to the hull and decks, and limber holes are sealed against moisture penetration by PVC inserts. The hull-to-deck joint is mechanically fastened and fiberglassed from the inside. The decks and superstructure are also constructed of nonwoven fiberglass with Divinycell coring for rigidity and light weight.

Performance Test

With a 2- to 3-foot confused chop running and the occasional ferry wake to cross in Nantucket Sound, we had a good day for a sea trial. At six turns lock-to-lock, the steering was slow to respond; otherwise, the boat handled very well at speed and dockside. Heading into the chop at 16 to 18 knots with trim tabs putting the bow down, the ride was smooth and a little wet. At 22 knots, I raised the tabs to keep from bow-steering; the ride got bumpy, but we didn't pound. We crossed a 3- to 4-foot wake at 24 knots and landed hard, reminding me of the hull's moderate deadrise forward; a rough-water-eating deep-V this is not, but neither will you be paying for a deep-V's fuel consumption.

Downsea from 16 to 24 knots, the Ocean 40 ran straight with little helm input needed to keep us on track. The running angle averaged around 6 to 7 degrees—a degree or two more than is optimum for efficiency, perhaps, but still in the moderate range, due to the midships-mounted fuel tanks.

A 15-knot breeze was blowing, and the boat twisted and backed where I wanted it to, reacting very responsively to the helm and engines. Dockside, the Ocean 40 was a breeze to maneuver, doing exactly what I expected it to and without blowing around inordinately in the stiff crosswind. Also worth noting are the Ocean's quiet sound levels in the saloon when underway: just 62 dBA at 700 rpm and 79 dBA at a 2,200 rpm cruise. The accompanying table summarizes performance results for the Ocean 40 Super Sport.

The Ocean 40 Super Sport is well built and solidly engineered with an excellent division and use of space throughout for a convertible sportfisherman. In fact, the interior design is its most impressive attribute among many that are noteworthy. The large interior dimensions and innovative layout make it a fine cruising yacht as well. This is a good seaboat in the 16- to 24-knot range, and I would not hesitate to take it offshore.

At a very reasonable price, which includes a soup-to-nuts equipment list with AC, generator, central vacuum, engine synchronizers, and an Awl-gripped engine room, this boat is also an excellent value on today's market. Options include a swim platform, anchor windlass, cockpit freezer and bait well, and Rupp outriggers. Here's a boat you can show off at a price that many can afford; just ask the sixty people who bought an Ocean 40 in its first two years of production.

Ocean 40 Super Sport Performance Results

RPM	Speed, knots	Speed, mph	Fuel Use, gph	Nautical mpg	Statute mpg	Range, nm	Range, statute miles	Noise Level, dBA	Trim, degrees
600	5.5	6.3	1.6	3.4	4.0	1,241	1,427	70	0
800	7.2	8.3	2.8	2.6	3.0	928	1,068	73	1
1,000	8.3	9.5	4.7	1.8	2.0	638	733	74	5
1,400	10.5	12.1	9.3	1.1	1.3	408	469	79	6
1,800	16.6	19.1	18	0.9	1.1	333	383	82	6
2,000	21.1	24.3	22.6	0.9	1.1	337	388	83	6
2,200	25.3	29.1	28.8	0.9	1.0	317	365	84	6
2,400	28.1	32.3	35.1	0.8	0.9	289	332	86	6
2,525	29.6	34.0	42.6	0.7	0.8	251	288	88	6

Test conditions: twin 410 hp Volvo 73 diesel inboards, three passengers, two thirds tank of fuel, 50-foot-plus depth, 1-foot seas, air temperature 85 degrees, and 200 pounds of test gear. Test conducted in Nantucket Sound on July 14, 1998. Range calculated using 90 percent of the boat's 408-gallon fuel capacity. Sound levels taken at the bridge helm.

Post 42 Convertible

Post 42 Convertible Specifications	
LOA:	42'10"
Beam:	15'9"
Draft:	4'0"
Displacement:	42,996 lb.
Fuel capacity:	520 gal.
Water capacity:	120 gal.

Post is one of the best known of the New Jersey production convertible builders, along with its neighbors Viking, Ocean, and Egg Harbor. With four models from 42 to 56 feet, the 42 is Post's smallest offering, but you wouldn't know it from the careful engineering and attention to detail that goes into the beautiful fit and finish and well-considered layout, as well as the timelessly appealing profile. The engine room is intelligently arranged for easy maintenance. The low-deadrise bottom delivers a good turn of speed for the power, but it's also a rough ride in a chop.

Cockpit

The 8-foot-long-by-11-foot, 8-inch-wide cockpit is cleanly laid out with 12-inch cleats mounted upside down under the coaming, a design that I certainly don't recommend since they're awkward to access and difficult to see. Added on forward are a bait center with sink and drawers, a storage locker, cockpit access under the saloon stairs, and a freezer to starboard; most modern convertibles make these units integral with the superstructure mold to eliminate the possibility of leaks and squeaks.

Our boat also had a nifty Glendinning Cablemaster that automatically retrieves and pays out the cable with the push of a switch. I would like to see a more aggressive nonskid pattern and higher coamings (they're just 25.5 in. high aft), especially given the boat's acceleration and speed capability.

The side decks leading forward are wide and flat, and handrails are something to hang onto all the way forward. The rugged aluminum bow railing is a full 30 inches high forward, providing excellent security on the foredeck.

The deep lazarette below the cockpit holds the single 520-gallon aluminum fuel tank, supported by angle brackets so as to provide sufficient corrosion-inhibiting air circulation outside—a nice construction detail. The tank also comes within a foot of the transom, though, so there will be a marked shift in static and dynamic trim as fuel is consumed. Ideally, to reduce reliance on drag-inducing trim tabs for proper trim, liquid loads are centered farther forward over the hull's longitudinal center of buoyancy.

Flybridge

This is definitely one of the more comfortable helm stations around, with the pedestal seat high enough for a good view and close enough so you can easily reach the nicely positioned, 20-degrees-from-horizontal steering wheel and engine controls. I would make some changes, such as adding a gate by the ladder, which would make it less likely to unexpectedly drop in on the cockpit crowd below. To make it more user-friendly, you may want to order the Post 40 with the engine instruments together in pairs rather than separated a couple of feet by the alarm panel and switches.

The electronics panel is to starboard; angling it more would let you mount everything closer for easier operation. The boxes should all be on a plane tangent to the operator's line of sight. I would also relocate the compass, which is about 9 feet forward and down too low for me to see easily when I'm seated. There's ample room forward on lounge seats, and our boat had a beautifully finished, crystal-clear soft enclosure that will extend the cruising season well into fall in colder climes. Altogether, this is a comfortable and roomy bridge that could use a little helm-station tweaking.

Saloon

One of the highlights of touring a Post boat is experiencing the interior decor, which is invariably beautifully finished and tastefully selected—in fact, the Posts always remind me of high-end Vikings inside. The saloon seems open and spacious with its generous 79-inch headroom and large side and aft windows. An L-shaped lounge with a pullout bed below is aft to port. An icemaker and electrical service panel are immediately to starboard, and an L-shaped dinette with TV above is just forward.

Two steps down and forward to port is the galley, with an upright refrigerator-freezer, a microwave-convection oven, a large Corian countertop with a cover (I would add a microswitch to shut off power to the burners) over the two-burner electric stove, and a sink. Simply lift up a hatch in the beautiful teak and holly sole to access the large dry-storage area below.

Cabin

Down two more steps from the galley, the wide companionway leads to a washer-dryer immediately to starboard. The portside guest stateroom has a pair of 75-inch bunk beds, an overhead hatch, and a cedar hanging locker. Many European boats have large side ports as well, and I would welcome them in this American boat. The Post's single head is directly opposite to starboard, and it is nicely designed and finished with an enclosed shower, electric toilet, hatch, mirrored overhead,

and dual access from the companionway and forward stateroom.

The master stateroom is comfortably situated in the bow with a 6-foot, 4-inch-by-5-foot island berth. Drawers and storage space are below; cedar lockers put nooks and crannies to good use as additional storage space. I would like a little more natural light, but both staterooms—like the saloon—are very well finished with designer fabrics, teak paneling, and carefully installed vinyl liners. For safety, I recommend replacing the Post's small 16- and 18-inch hatches with larger models (20 to 24 in.) so they could double as escape routes in an emergency.

Engine Room

Unusually comfortable cockpit access leads to the engine room, and accessibility has never been better on a boat of this class. The 73 series Volvo diesels—compact engines for their horsepower to start with—make an already large space seem positively commodious. The 1.74:1 ZF down-angle gears allow the engines to be mounted fairly level. In fact, the saloon floor above could be lowered a good 6 inches if engine clearance were the only consideration, but the 54-inch headroom will please your mechanic. The engines' soft mounts are lag-bolted into the solid mahogany encapsulated atop the fiberglass stringers.

Routine maintenance is a breeze, with bronze seacocks, dipsticks, dripless shaft seals, freshwater cooling tanks, and fuel filters all easy to access. Post's tooled-fiberglass battery boxes are a nice touch too. The genset is forward and easy to work on, and the mirror-smooth fiberglass overhead includes two removal hatches when the engines need to be replaced. The bilges are smoothly finished and painted with white gelcoat for an easily cleaned, attractive finish.

There isn't a loose wire in the place: they're all hidden inside cableways mounted out of the way in the overhead. The same attention to detail shows in the use of heavy-duty high-pressure fuel lines and fittings for added safety. In summary, the Post's engine room is among the finest of its class I've yet come across in terms of accessibility, fit and finish, and quality of components.

Construction

Post uses a solid glass hull laminate and balsa coring in the decks (except in the way of bulkheads, where plywood coring resists the added compression loads) and superstructure to reduce weight and add stiffness. The hull-to-deck joint is fastened with stainless self-tapping screws secured to a mahogany backing strip and permanently bonded with polyurethane adhesive.

Performance Test

The Post is a capable offshore cruiser with a lot of "command presence," as we used to say in the navy. Loosely translated, that means it handles competently, tracks well and predictably in a light chop, and has a very stable ride.

The Post is a wide boat for its length—though much narrower at the waterline—and deadrise forward and aft is minimal in old-style New Jersey fashion for efficiency and beam-sea comfort. In fact, the builder tells us that the 42's hull mold was taken from a plug made from the decades-old original wooden boats. That would explain the Post 42's quite flat, or low-deadrise, bottom design. Boats in those days didn't have the horsepower available to make them move out like they do with today's high-speed, lightweight diesels, so they didn't need as

much deadrise to ride easily through the waves with acceptable ride quality.

That also explains the Post's stiff ride in a chop. In the short, steep, 2- to 3-foot seas we encountered in Nantucket Sound on our test ride, I found that the Post pounded unrelentingly when running at 18 to 20 knots, making the ride very uncomfortable. Forget about trying to keep up with the rest of the fleet when the going gets rough on this boat—with their deeper deadrise forward, many (and maybe most) other boats of this size ride much more smoothly.

According to Post, the weight of the fuel tank in the stern helps provide a bow-up attitude for good following-sea control, with the generously sized trim tabs leveling things out for a smoother head-sea ride. But what happens to following-sea control when the fuel level runs low and the stern comes up a few inches? Trim tabs can't lower the stern: they can only raise it. But if the boat's numerous other strengths win you over, and you're content with modest cruising speeds when the going gets rough, then I think the otherwise well-engineered and beautifully finished Post may be worth considering.

The Post's drivetrain is superb, with some of the lowest vibration levels (subjectively speaking) that I've seen on this class of boat. It's also quiet at just 83 dBA in the saloon at a 2,200 rpm cruise. Backing down, the deck stayed reasonably dry with the scupper flaps doing their job well. I would like

Post 42 Convertible Performance Results

RPM	Speed, knots	Speed, mph	Fuel Use, gph	Nautical mpg	Statute mpg	Range, nm	Range, statute miles	Noise Level, dBA	Trim, degrees
1,000	8.5	9.8	3.3	2.6	3.0	1,205	1,386	72	2
1,400	11	12.7	12.64	0.9	1.0	407	468	74	5
1,600	13.6	15.6	16.84	0.8	0.9	378	435	75	7
1,800	17.3	19.9	21.76	0.8	0.9	372	428	78	7
2,000	21.6	24.8	26.92	0.8	0.9	376	432	79	7
2,200	24.6	28.3	32.06	0.8	0.9	359	413	80	7
2,400	27.1	31.2	38.92	0.7	0.8	326	375	83	8
2,600	29.8	34.6	48.36	0.6	0.7	291	335	83	8

Test conditions: twin Volvo TAMD-73P 430 hp diesels, one-third tank of fuel, half tank of water, and three passengers.

to see the steering's excessive and ponderous six turns lock-to-lock reduced to three or four; it takes too long to react in a collision-avoidance situation, for starters, and it makes steering more work than it needs to be when power steering is available. Once the rudder was hard over, the turning rate was very good, with the boat managing a 360-degree turn at cruise speed in a commendable average of 31 seconds. Handling dockside was predictable, which is to say, good. The accompanying table summarizes performance results of the Post 42.

Well-engineered and solidly built to last, the Post 42 makes a handsome and comfortable cruiser-sportfisherman. But if it's all-out rough-water performance and a smooth ride you want, buy the Bertram or Blackfin. The Post's wide-body design and flat bottom will run fine in a light chop or gentle swell at moderate, below-20-knot speeds. The interior is superbly finished and offers excellent volume for the boat's length, as befits a family cruiser.

Albin produces rugged cruising sportfishermen for a reasonable price, ranging from 28 to 35 feet. The 35 shown, a sedan sportfisherman, has a big saloon with lower helm station surrounded by a four-person cabin, galley up or down, and a roomy cockpit. Wide side decks, a big flybridge, high railings, and cockpit coamings speak of the Albin's overriding practicality. The 35's glitz-free sensible design extends to the boat's impressive seaworthiness, with single or twin diesels providing speeds to around 30 knots. See also the version without the flybridge, page 401. ALBIN

North Carolina builder Albemarle produces a range of open and convertible fishing boats from 24 to 41 feet. The 325 shown is about as small as a workable convertible gets, with the bulk of the LOA given over to the all-business cockpit. There's room for two couples to spend the night in the forward stateroom and on the convertible sofa in the saloon. A modified-V hull delivers a good ride in a stiff chop, making this boat well suited to the canyon fishing for which it was intended. ALBEMARLE

Bertram Yachts is gradually taking on the European styling of its Italian parent company Ferretti, which also claims to be improving the structural engineering to produce a lighter, stronger hull. The superstructure styling and the trendy new three-digit hull numbering scheme may be glitzy Italiano, but the sheerline and hull form are all Bertram. These great-running hulls have survived the Euro transformation, and the Bertram 60 shown here is the best seaboat of them all. The Bertram 60 has a three- or four-stateroom lower deck, galley up or down, and an optional enclosed bridge. BERTRAM

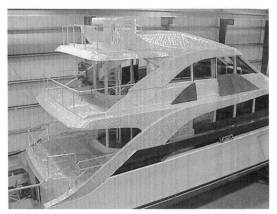

Aluminum cruising-yacht builder Broward, which specializes in 85- to 125-foot cruising yachts, has lately been building high-end, oceangoing sportfishermen like this 100-footer under construction. Four staterooms, including a full-beam master suite with his and hers heads, and two crew cabins are included. Fishing in faraway foreign waters is one advantage this large yacht has over its smaller counterparts, not to mention its significant comfort factor and seakeeping abilities.

The Hatteras 65 is one of eight convertible models from 50 to 90 feet. Based on the tried-and-true Hatteras 60, the 65 is heavily and conventionally built. Substantial displacement and a deep entry make the 65 a capable, smooth-riding seaboat, while deep reduction gears and large-diameter propellers summon impressive responsiveness to the engine controls. Three-stateroom accommodations, a large saloon, and an optional enclosed bridge provide exceptional comfort for offshore cruising. A proven sportfisherman, the Hatteras 65 has everything it takes to win on the tournament circuit.   HATTERAS

Cavileer is a new boatbuilder with some centuries-old roots, at least in name. Cavileer produces 48- and 53-foot convertibles, the latter shown here. Based on Don Blount–modified-V hulls, these yachts track exceptionally well in rough water and are very soft-running in a head sea. Premium vinylester resin is used throughout the laminate, including the solid fiberglass bottom, and balsa coring is used in the hull sides and decks. The engineering details are as impressive as the joinery; attention to detail is evident everywhere on board.   CAVILEER

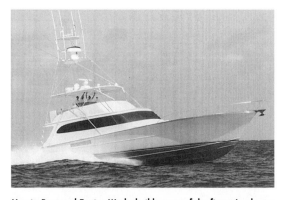

Merritt Boat and Engine Works builds some of the finest (and most expensive) custom sportfishermen in the world. The 80-footer shown, the larger of the two models currently available (the other is a 72-footer), is a marvel of engineering. It's constructed using vacuum-bagged Core-Cell coring, Kevlar, fiberglass, and epoxy resin, which produces a strong damage-resistant hull that weighs in at a moderate 130,000 pounds when fuel and water tanks are full. An excellent hull form, fabulous interior joinery (including fossilized fish on galley countertops in previous models), and sweet looks combine to make any Merritt the perfect cruising or sportfishing yacht for very wealthy outdoor enthusiasts.   MERRITT

Ocean Yachts is one of the great success stories of our recent boat-building past. Since its formation in 1977, Ocean has grown to become one of the largest builders of production convertibles in the United States. Oceans have earned a reputation for delivering a good turn of speed using modest power, with later hulls delivering a good ride, as well as plush—sometimes ingeniously arranged—accommodations. The 70 shown is Ocean's flagship, with a four-stateroom, four-head cabin (including his and hers closets and a bathtub in the master suite), an enclosed air-conditioned bridge, and well over 30-knot cruising speeds with optional power.

OCEAN

This Bruce Roberts—designed sportfisherman, shown in the later stages of construction, is a good example of an aluminum convertible built for speed and comfort. A traditional layout includes a roomy saloon with large, all-around windows and a flybridge with aluminum arch. This planing hull is capable of well over 20 knots with suitable power.

BRUCE ROBERTS

Boatbuilder Riviera is Australia's largest exporter of midsize cruising and sportfishing powerboats, including the builder's latest model: this great-looking, superbly designed 40-foot convertible. For anyone who favors a windshield in a convertible (as I do), this boat has it all: an open layout, cockpit access to the engine room, sturdy construction, and solid offshore performance with a modified-V hull. With more new models like this one, Riviera may become the Viking Yachts of down under.

RIVIERA

Saltshaker produces four Blackfin models: the 29 Combi (see Blackfin 40 Combi on pages 378–82), 29 Flybridge, 31 Combi, and the 28 Sport. These boats are a good example of what can be accomplished when the boat and its accommodations are designed around a hull form, rather than the other way around. The 29 Flybridge shown here has a surprisingly open and bright interior and a low-profile flybridge that's easily reached from the cockpit and keeps the center of gravity reasonably low. The deep-V, fine-entry hull can maintain 25 knots in a 2- to 4-foot chop. The fine, destroyer-like entry seen here shows why.

BLACKFIN

Silverton builds an extensive range of wide-beam, commodious cruising yachts that have a decided emphasis on interior volume. The builder's convertible series, though, including a 35- and a 42-footer, places as much emphasis on seakeeping and ride quality as on accommodations. The 42, shown here, is a good-looking, well-proportioned, offshore-capable cruising sportfisherman with welcome features, such as safe and accessible molded stairs leading to the flybridge and a split master head. SILVERTON

Lest there be any doubt, Viking builds some of the best high-end production convertibles in the world. A good-running hull form, a utilitarian fishing layout, benchmark engineering, great styling, and a responsive dealer-service network make for a no-brainer combination. No one can accuse the Viking 55 of being a lightweight, and most owners like their Viking that way. Most Vikings cruise at well over 30 knots with standard power. VIKING

Sedans and Hardtops

It's not too often you hear the term *sedan* on the waterfront these days, but it used to refer to what was basically a convertible with a small cockpit and big saloon. Whether this is the in-vogue label or not, it works for me. These boats usually have a flybridge, like the convertible, but the cockpit is sparsely equipped, if equipped at all, for fishing. The saloon may well have a windshield instead of a fiberglass deckhouse front, which is great for those who like to see where they're going as well as where they've been, from down below. Sedans may or may not have the seakeeping and sustained speed capability of a convertible. It all depends in their hull form, and (as on any boat) whether ride quality or acreage won out in the design phase.

Alden 60 Tournament Express—Ingrid

Great things happen when experienced owners come to Alden to have it build the semicustom yacht of their dreams. Starting with a base hull, deck, and superstructure, the sky's the limit when it comes to floor plans, woodwork, and machinery—within reason, naturally. Of course, any good

Alden 60 Specifications

LOA:	60'0"
Beam:	15'4"
Draft:	3'10"
Displacement:	40,000 lb.
Fuel capacity:	540 gal.
Water capacity:	200 gal.

builder will avoid building counterproductive features into the boat. When everything just clicks, as it did on this project, the process is a pleasure for all involved.

The owners of our test boat, Alden 60 #11, had previously owned some fifteen boats, from a 36-foot Bruno & Stillman lobster yacht to a crewed, 70 Hatteras motor yacht. When they got the urge to resume the nautical lifestyle after a brief hiatus from boatowning, this couple knew what they wanted: a comfortable yacht that could cruise at 24 knots in rough water, easily be run by the two of them, fish without looking like a sportfisherman, and had a classic New England look. We'll look at some of the owners' criteria and how Alden addressed their needs.

Cockpit and Topsides

Back aft in the 6-foot, 7-inch-by-9-foot, 1-inch cockpit, easy line handling was important. So instead of mounting the stern cleats under the coamings with the line leading through flush hawseholes, the stern cleats are flush mounted on the coamings and lead through custom, stainless chocks for ease of use.

Since this was to be an occasional sportfisherman, yet was not intended to look like a fishing boat, ingenious storage arrangements were worked out. Lockers under the 33-inch-high cockpit coamings were built in to store fishing tackle and rods.

The saloon's 72-inch portside lounge was specifically designed for rod storage below, the length determined by the owners' longest rods. Also, in keeping with this "incognito sportfisherman" approach, the cockpit's two integral lounge seats forward contain the yacht's fish box and livewell. Along with the crew-less, ease-of-yachting theme, Glendinning Cablemasters were installed to make light work of handling shore-power cables.

On any sportfishing boat, the cockpit must drain quickly and be easy to clean. So, gutters on the outboard edge of the cockpit lead to large, recessed, flush-mounted, overboard-draining scuppers. It appears that there are two cockpit courtesy lights per side, but the top lights are actually caps that conceal plugs for the downriggers; this arrangement was specified by the owners to reduce visual clutter.

Down in the lazarette are a few clues to Alden's solid engineering. Rugged rudder shelves well above the hull bottom fix the rudderstocks in place in the event of a grounding, helping to prevent hull rupture. Inside, the corners where stringers and bulkheads meet the hull skin are gently radiused to prevent hard spots, an important structural consideration. And the propeller pockets carved into the hull are gently radiused, permitting shallower draft and shaft angles without detracting noticeably from buoyancy and dynamic lift aft.

Access to the foredeck is comfortable and safe

with 18-inch-wide side decks and 31-inch-high lifelines leading forward. A stainless steel anchor pulpit holds the yacht's 66-pound plow-type anchor. Located several feet aft is a crash bulkhead that forms a large storage compartment accessed by a translucent hatch.

Bridge Deck and Helm

Since the owners spent most of their time aboard on the aft deck, they specified extending the pilothouse by 42 inches, with the aft portion of the saloon under the hardtop open to the weather, yet enclosable with plastic side curtains—which, incidentally, are secured with bungee cords for easy handling. At just over 14 feet long, the convertible aft deck is the focal point of the yacht, and it's laid out to the owners' exact specifications.

The custom helm station is to port to accommodate the southpaw owner-operator, and Alden's attention to detail shows in the large electronics panel, ergonomically angled to present a surface tangent to the operator's line of sight. The owners bought the custom stainless steel steering wheel on the Internet and had it engraved with the ship's logo before installation. Designed to be piloted from the saloon, the boat has large windows (including opening windshield-vent windows); the relatively narrow mullions provide an exceptional all-around view. In fact, the Alden 60 can comfortably be maneuvered around a marina (while sitting in the adjustable Stidd helm seat), which cannot be said about most boats. Everything is first-class: the searchlight is a Carlisle and Finch Xenon 2000, and the horn is a Kahlenberg mounted on the mast under the searchlight.

Even with the saloon's cambered interior teak and holly deck, there's still more than 80 inches of headroom on centerline, which combines with the large windows for a spacious feeling. Since the one detail lacking on many boats is a place to stretch out, the owners had Alden build the portside sofa so the cushion on the forward end hinges up to form an oversized adjustable chaise lounge, allowing one owner to read a novel while watching the other fish.

The dinette was positioned opposite to starboard, which opens up room in the master stateroom just forward on the lower deck. This also provided enough room just aft for a cabinet with a bait freezer below and a sink with storage cabinets. Also aft and overlooking the cockpit are a refrigerator with icemaker to starboard and a Splendide combination washer-dryer unit to port. Two AC units cool the saloon, even when the side curtains aft are open.

Also specified by the owners was interior access from the saloon and aft deck leading directly to the flybridge. The owners wanted more of a staircase than a ladder, making for easier and safer accessibility. Because the stairs would take up too much space in the cockpit, the owners specified custom Nautical Structure stairs that, using an electric winch, hinge up against the overhead when not at sea. Appreciating classic yacht-styling extended to specifying athwartships-oriented varnished-teak battens between the headliner panels overhead.

Engine Room

Entered through a hatch on the saloon's aft deck, the all-white, brightly lit engine room has many shiplike features. Headroom is comfortable at 62 inches, stainless railings between the engines provide something to hang onto, and the wiring and plumbing are unobtrusively routed with protective runs. Seacocks, dual fuel filter-separators, and daily maintenance checkpoints are all easy to reach, and the bilges are ground smooth and painted white for easier cleanup and better visibility. The owners, who have had a lot of experience cleaning out generator cooling-water intake filters in port, pointed out that "they even included plugs for the seacocks."

Bridge

The bridge, also enlarged by the extended pilothouse, has a centerline helm forward and a megayacht-inspired mast to support the navigation lights and electronics, with folding teak tables at the base. The owners specified that the mast be tall enough to keep the radar's RF (radio frequency) energy well away from the humans below. Wraparound railings add extra security in rough weather, and the owners chose a full seat across the aft end of the bridge to enclose the area, which adds seating for four people.

Accommodations

The owners' goals were to make the cabin visually pleasing, easy to maintain, and functional for living aboard. Ash woodwork with teak accents and a teak and holly sole were chosen for the cabin interior. The light-colored ash prevents all that wood from becoming visually overpowering, while keeping with the yacht's salty, classic ambience. Headroom is more than 6 feet, 4 inches throughout the interior, enhancing the roomy feeling in the cabin.

The owners usually cruise alone, but a guest stateroom to starboard of the companionway accommodates two people on single berths, and an en suite head is directly forward. In the galley, opposite the guest stateroom to port, the owners specified a four-burner, ceramic cooktop with flush burners and controls—a KitchenAid option. An electric convection oven is below, and a space-saving microwave oven slides out of the aft bulkhead on tracks when needed. Sub-Zero refrigerator drawers prevent anything from falling out when the doors are opened after a rough ride. A chart drawer, a large stainless sink, and a brushed-stainless Franke recessed trash receptacle were also specified.

Because they experienced a fire years ago while sleeping on board a friend's yacht, the owners had Alden install a 27-inch opening hatch forward in the yacht's cabin, ensuring a means of emergency egress. For the same reason, they installed a remote surveillance camera in the engine room.

Forward of the galley is the main saloon's seating area, in which the owners' designed a quartet of facing seats, with storage bins in the corners and a high-low table in the middle. Other clever details include a single locker that holds all the battery-charger–dependent accessories, such as cell phones. Behind one of the lower saloon seats, a door opens to reveal a TV projector that displays the picture on a pull-down screen opposite, creating a space-saving (and enhancing) entertainment center. Extra storage space and the stereo system's sub-woofer are also hidden below the seats.

The master stateroom, with its large island berth, hanging lockers, and private head with a separate shower, is located forward. Alden designed a clever, clean-looking shower floor that has gutters around the perimeter but no visible drains.

Construction

The Alden 60 is built with a vinylester barrier coat to prevent osmotic blistering, and it is backed up with an almost unheard of ten-year full warranty against blistering. General-purpose resin follows in the laminate of nonwoven fiberglass fabrics for a mostly solid bottom and balsa-cored sides. Decks are cored with Core-Cell foam; hull stringers and bulkheads are cored with Divinycell foam for a lightweight, rugged bottom grid. The hull-to-deck joint is fastened with bolts on 10-inch centers and bonded with 3M 5200, a tenacious polyurethane adhesive.

With its C. Raymond Hunt Associates–designed hull, the Alden 60 is a superb seaboat. The ride into a 4-foot chop is ultrasmooth and bone dry, and the boat tracks downsea as if on railroad tracks. The motion at rest, laying-to in the trough, is comfortably stable but not too stiff.

Performance Test

The 660 hp Caterpillar 3196 diesels deliver a cruising speed of 28 to 29 knots at 2,150 rpm, which is extraordinary for moderate-sized engines in a boat this size, and well in excess of the owners' expectations. Top speed at 2,335 rpm is 31 knots. Sound levels throughout the yacht are low, and vibrations are tamed by an effective combination of the hull's stiff, gusset-supported stringers and soft engine mounts.

The Alden 60 will hold its own among the best yachts of its size being built in the world today. The superb hull design is as good as it gets—very smooth and dry-riding and economical to propel, with naturally low trim angles for reduced vertical accelerations and improved efficiency. The Alden's fiberglass tooling, joinery work, and attention to detail are top-notch throughout. A great-looking yacht, the Alden seamlessly blends form and function, proving that a craft with timeless looks is inevitably practical as well.

The ability to extensively customize a semi-production hull to specifications has great appeal for many people. This is especially true for owners with extensive cruising or fishing experience and who have a very clear idea of what constitutes their ideal yacht. These owners noted that computer communication contributed to the success of their Alden 60, because close contact with the yard could be maintained and a paper trail of change orders was created. The result is a yacht that perfectly meets the proud owners' expectations in every possible way. "And everything works," note the pleased owners.

The owners picked the Caterpillars because of their reliability, parts and service availability throughout the East Coast, and the optional five-year extended warranty.

1997 Bayliner 3788 Command Bridge Motoryacht

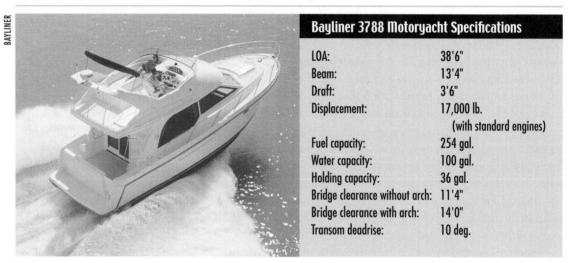

BAYLINER

Bayliner 3788 Motoryacht Specifications	
LOA:	38'6"
Beam:	13'4"
Draft:	3'6"
Displacement:	17,000 lb. (with standard engines)
Fuel capacity:	254 gal.
Water capacity:	100 gal.
Holding capacity:	36 gal.
Bridge clearance without arch:	11'4"
Bridge clearance with arch:	14'0"
Transom deadrise:	10 deg.

Bayliner has for many years addressed the need for "affordable," no-frills boats in the mass market. It is ideally poised to do so; as part of an industry giant, U.S. Marine, Bayliner has the purchasing power and high-volume manufacturing acumen to mass-produce boats for less than just about anyone else, while keeping quality to acceptable levels. Any observer in the industry would tell you that Bayliner has had its share of problems with quality, longevity, and resale values in the past, but today things seem to be changing for the better. You still can't expect to get a Rolls for the price of a Chevy, but Bayliner knows this market intimately and has responded with a variety of model lines with ramped-up quality and attention to detail.

Bayliner's Motoryacht series, which just recently added a 57-footer, includes the 3788 Command Bridge Motoryacht. This boat handily fills a niche market for what used to be called sedans—so-called because as cruising (not fishing) yachts, they had a large saloon and a small cockpit (for a little fishing on the side). This is a very practical layout for a variety of reasons.

Cockpit

As I came aboard our 3788 test boat from the solid swim platform and through a well-fitted molded two-sided transom door, it was obvious to me that Bayliner has its fiberglass-tooling procedures well in hand. The boat is built of two components: the hull, and a one-piece assembly that includes the foredeck, superstructure (minus the bridge), cockpit, and cockpit coamings. This simplifies construction since there are only two major pieces to join together. This is also an advantage for the owner since it eliminates (or should eliminate) the chance of leaks and squeaks, cuts down on weight by eliminating secondary bonding materials, and maximizes strength—all as a result of CAD-CAM design and manufacturing.

The 10-foot-long-by-5-foot-wide-by-32-inch-deep self-draining cockpit allows ample room for sunning, water sports, and even a little nontournament fishing. It's nice and deep with high coamings, making it safe for kids; if it had toe kicks all around, it would be perfect. However, this lack is a function of the deck and coaming one-piece construction; a small draft or continuous angle is necessary to remove parts from their molds, and toe kicks would interfere with this requirement. Padded side bolsters protruding 4 to 5 inches would be a good substitute for a toe kick, as would bolt-on wash rails.

The cockpit is flawlessly tooled, like the rest of the Bayliner's exterior, with a gleaming white gelcoat—be sure to wear sunglasses when the sun is shining. Storage bins are provided, but drainage is needed to keep the water from either going into the lazarette below or sloshing around inside. There's a sink for cleanup to port, and diesel fills (I suggest color-coding the caps) are on the side decks within reach of the cockpit. The shore power hooks up 3 inches forward, making it a little less convenient to hook up the cables when moored stern-to. Nonskid everywhere topside is excellent—a bold pattern that is very cleanable yet grippy when mated to boat shoes.

Lazarette

Located below the cockpit, the large lazarette is easily reached through two big 44-by-32-inch boost-lift hatches. The lazarette holds three large battery boxes, two engine silencers, generous storage space for cruising, and the steering gear. Many of the steering-post bolts protrude through the transom 1½ inches; they should be cut off to prevent injury. The limber holes through the stringers in this area appeared to be covered with only resin and gelcoat to keep the water out. Unfortunately, over time, this will not be sufficient because the resin and gelcoat will crack as the wood contracts and expands with changing moisture content. Glassed-in PVC tubes would be a big improvement. Shallow gutters should keep everything dry down below by draining the water overboard through a network of hoses.

Foredeck

Two molded cockpit steps and the excellent nonskid lead forward on 8-inch-wide side decks. A 56-inch-high grabrail is just at the ideal height for most people, but it needs to be extended another 24 inches forward for an added measure of safety. This addition, along with raising the 1-inch-diameter stainless bow railing 6 inches higher than its present 24-inch height, would make the foredeck a remarkably safe place to traverse. Bayliner provides a single 12-inch bow cleat (two are essential on any boat, especially one of this size); two pairs of 12-inch spring cleats go with the 12-inch stern cleats.

Bridge

The ladder from the cockpit to the bridge is too steep to use comfortably; it's nice to be able to climb one-handed when necessary. I would move the base out a foot or so to add a little run to the rise. The bridge itself is very roomy and nicely laid out with the helm station to starboard. To port is a big settee that should do very nicely at party time, and there's storage room below with overboard drainage and gutters aft—a nice touch. Access to the electronics requires some crawling, either through an opening under the console or through the side of the console on the port side. The console does not hinge back, which would be a more convenient arrangement but that also requires extra tooling and added expense.

Saloon

The saloon is entered from the cockpit through a 22-inch-wide sliding aluminum-framed glass door. As you might expect, the saloon is huge for a 37-footer: a cavernous 14 feet, 7 inches long by 10 feet, 10 inches wide. Forward to starboard is the lower helm station, raised 18 inches off the deck for excellent visibility through the spacious windows. Four of the eight side windows slide open for natural ventilation, as does one of the three aft windows. The only real impediments to visibility are the 9½-inch-wide sedan-top corner supports, which are especially restrictive to starboard just in front of the helm. You will have to compensate for this blind spot by moving your head around to catch objects on a steady bearing at sea.

Bayliner, as far as I know, makes no claims to fine joinery, specializing as it does in the efficiencies of low-cost mass production. However, some of the mitered joints were just as precise as some I've seen on the familiar high-priced nameplates. But there are weak areas: I would like to see some adhesive (at least) backing up the lone pair of screws that hold on the galley drawer fronts, and the marginal drawer slides will likely fare poorly in time.

Aft of the helm seat is a large U-shaped settee that should hold six linebackers; it converts into a 7-foot, 7-inch-by-4-foot berth when the 5-by-2-foot, 6-inch table is lowered. Across to port is room for a TV and entertainment center with a pair of wing cabinets. The electrical service is aft near the cockpit door, where it does the most good. Headroom in the saloon is a very generous 79 inches, adding to the roomy feeling. Lighting is excellent, with both direct overhead lights and valance lights along the perimeter. The durable-looking vinyl overhead and side liners are installed in a quality manner.

Lower Helm

Bayliner provides a 40-inch-wide, two-person soft leatherette helm seat, with the guest situated inboard. At first glance, this might seem annoying because the captain has to move every time the guest does; however, by being seated outboard, the cap-

tain can respond quickly in an emergency, which is even more important. The helm station is cleanly organized and ergonomically laid out. The compass is directly in front of the wheel—but a little distant at 56 inches away. The gauges are neatly organized, but I would prefer to see them more tightly organized in pairs, for easier comprehension at a glance.

A 31-by-11-inch chartlet area is between the wheel and the instruments. The individual throttles and shifts are close at hand to the right of the wheel, and switches under the wheel are easy to reach. The seat is comfortable and there's generous legroom, which is good since you can't drive standing up down there. The light-brown dashboard area cuts the sun glare adequately and should reduce light glare at night as well. Before you buy any boat, take a nighttime test drive just to be sure.

Galley

One of the nice features about the lower station is that you can drive the boat in the company of family and friends even in lousy weather. A few feet to port is the U-shaped galley with its optional teak and holly sole and designer countertops that add a touch of class. Also included are an upright 56-inch-tall refrigerator-freezer (just short enough so it doesn't get in the captain's line of sight), microwave oven, three-burner stove, double sinks, and a variety of drawers and cabinets. A couple of the door hinges showed signs of corrosion, as did two of the three burners.

Master Stateroom

It's three steps down to the companionway and the forward stateroom with its 77-by-60-inch island berth. Below are six drawers and lots of storage space in painted bins (which are also awkward to reach). Two opening portholes and a 19-inch-opening overhead hatch let in sea air resulting in a nice bright effect. The overhead and hull liner is of a woven fabric; the aft bulkhead is a heavily textured (and perhaps difficult to clean) wall covering. A locker with shelves is to port and a 17-inch hanging locker is to starboard.

A guest stateroom is partially tucked away under the raised helm station. There's a hanging locker, storage cabinet-dresser, opening porthole, and ample headroom forward; under the helm is a 6-foot, 3-inch-by-4-foot, 2-inch berth with 41 inches of vertical clearance—adequate for sitting up to read in bed. There's more storage in the bilge below. The bottom side of the berth was somewhat damp, so make sure you have adequate bilge ventilation, either natural or forced—especially if it's used for storage. Access panels lift out for direct access to the engine room and auxiliary-equipment room forward to port, so don't expect this to be a quiet area when the engines are running.

Head

Aft of the master stateroom to port is the head with a real surprise: a bathtub, of all things, in a 37-foot boat. Be sure you don't try to fill it when you're out cruising because you'll use up most of the water supply. The one-piece head itself is nicely tooled and easy to keep clean, but it needs a drain, as does the cabinet under the vanity. A large area for knick-knacks inboard of the opening porthole could benefit from a large fiddleboard to keep everything in one place (that's a custom feature). The large vanity above the sink holds the GFI 120-volt receptacle; it would be more conveniently located on an exposed bulkhead.

Engine Room

You access the Bayliner 3788 engine room through a pair of 52-by-32-inch hatches over each engine. The hatches, in turn, are supported by a framework of wooden two-by-fours that can be removed for major engine work. There's 42 inches of headroom in the engine room, good for this class, and the engines actually have about 6 inches more room than they need vertically. This means that Bayliner could have lowered the overall profile by 6 inches while also lowering the center of gravity; as it is, it makes for a roomier engine room. That said, I would like to see a centerline hatch added forward of the engine to make it easier to get down there in the first

place. You have to either crawl over the guest berth or contort yourself over the engine, which is impossible for a person my size.

A clearly labeled fuel-flow control panel is aft within easy reach, as are a pair of Racor fuel filter-separators. Oil- and coolant-level checks can all be made from the inboard side of the engines. Bilge plates elevate you 2 inches above bilge level, which keeps your feet and knees dry. Wiring and plumbing is neatly routed, but much of the wiring—such as the wires leading to the fuel-tank sensors and the exposed engine-wiring connector—was missing essential shrouding that helps prevent accidental cuts and abrasions. The bilges are all neatly painted white and are reasonably smooth for straightforward cleanup. Lighting needs to be enhanced; I wouldn't want to do much work down there with only the installed lights, particularly outboard.

The two 5052-grade, 0.125-inch, 127-gallon tanks outboard of the engines appeared to have adequate ventilation and room for airflow around the bottom of the tanks, which are essential to long corrosion-free tank life. Bayliner continues to use rubber hoses and hose clamps for its fuel lines; high-pressure hoses with hydraulic fittings would provide an added measure of security. Bayliner uses dripless shaft seals in this boat, a nice "yachty" feature designed to keep salt water out while minimizing corrosion problems.

The engines are bolted to vibration-dampening mounts that, in turn, are hard-bolted to heavy-angle steel, which is bolted through the 2-inch-thick, wood-cored, fiberglass-encapsulated stringers. The stringers are gusseted in place, resulting in a sufficiently rugged system. Limber holes through wood-cored stringers appeared to be adequately sealed with PVC tubes glassed in place.

The engine cooling-water seacocks and strainers are aft of the engine room in a semiseparate compartment forward of the lazarette. That location makes them only indirectly accessible; the preferred situation is to have all the machinery and related components accessible from the engine room to reach them quickly. The starboard strainer and the fourth battery box to starboard in this compartment would be difficult to reach under any conditions. The AC compressor is forward of the engine room to port and reasonably accessible. The inverter is on centerline aft of the engine room and difficult to reach.

Construction

Bayliner uses conventional tried-and-true construction methods, starting with an isophthalic resin-based gelcoat and a premium vinylester-resin-saturated skin coat of chop fiberglass to prevent blistering. (That's more than many builders do to ward off blistering, by the way.) It is followed by alternating layers of woven roving and continuous-strand mat (chop) and general-purpose orthophthalic-polyester resin. The hull bottom and sides are constructed of solid fiberglass, which is heavier and less efficient than a composite structure, but it is also cheaper to build and less susceptible to delamination and other complications than a cored composite. The stringers are fiberglass-encapsulated plywood and yellow pine; the limber holes are sealed with PVC tubes, sealant, and fiberglass. Bulkheads and stringers are marine plywood tabbed to the hull.

The hull-to-deck joint is bonded with 3M 5200 polyurethane adhesive and then screwed and bolted together. The rubrail is sealed with silicone. Chop and woven roving is used in the decks with ½- to 1¼-inch foam coring used as a stiffener, depending on the distance spanned.

Performance Test

Our test boat was provided by the Bayliner Boat Center in Madison, Connecticut, which covers Bayliner Motor Yacht sales from Maine to Connecticut. A pair of 250 hp Cummins diesels driving Hurth 1.56:1 gears and 1½-inch Aquamet stainless steel shafts (set at a moderate 11 degrees) turned 22-by-22-inch four-blade propellers on our test boat. Even with the shallow gear ratio, this drivetrain produced some impressive stop-start capability. With 6 or 7 knots headway on, I just shifted the clutches into reverse—there was no need to advance the throttle, either—and the boat stopped on a dime. When I shifted them both back into gear, the boat was moving—immediately. This translated into excellent no-throttle maneuverability dockside. The boat was moderately susceptible to the wind dockside, but no more so than other keel-less boats of this class.

Offshore on our test ride, it was flat calm, so we had to settle for crossing our 2- to 3-foot wake. This exercise told us that a 2- to 3-foot chop could be comfortably handled at maybe 16 to 18 knots; at 21 to 22 knots, we started to pound noticeably. The ride in calm water was exceptionally vibration-free, testament to a well-aligned drivetrain, effective engine vibration isolators, well-balanced props, and maybe also the properly faired and recessed prop-strut pads.

The steering is an area that needs to be addressed by Bayliner. First, it was difficult, taking a lot of effort to turn the wheel, especially past the first half turn or so. Second, response was sluggish, with a slow-as-molasses 6½ turns lock-to-lock; I was very aware of my role as a pump motor. This boat needs power steering or better-balanced rudders and a tighter-ratio steering. Rudders should be balanced so that it takes very little effort to turn them at any speed. However, the big wedge-shaped (in cross section) rudders help take up the slack there once the rudders are where you want them; with the rudders hard over, the boat turns on a dime.

On the bright side, the boat planed easily and quickly, leaving a flat clean wake at any speed above 13 knots, even with no tabs. The boat was also very quiet, even without extensive sound-dampening measures. A lot of credit goes to the Cummins's quiet design.

Performance results on our Bayliner 3788 test boat with the 250 hp Cummins are summarized in the accompanying table.

As the performance curves indicate, expect an easy 17-knot cruise with a 22- to 23-knot cruise possible—very reasonable figures indeed. The

Bayliner 3788 with 250 hp Cummins Performance Results

RPM	Speed, knots	Saloon Noise Level, dBA	Galley Noise Level, dBA	Master Stateroom Noise Level, dBA	Cockpit Noise Level, dBA
1,000	8.3				
1,500	10.6				
2,000	14.6				
2,200	17.4				
2,400	21.7	82	81	75	84
2,600	24.9				
2,780	26.8				

Cummins are helped here by the boat's moderate 9-ton (approximate) displacement. As we returned to port up the narrow winding channel, minor course changes took little effort, and the boat handled well. Also noteworthy, the wheel and throttles are positioned so you can drive comfortably when seated or standing.

For comparison, the builder's performance figures with gasoline engines and a larger diesel power plant are summarized in the accompanying table.

Although top speeds are about the same, note the *huge* difference in cruising speeds and range between the gasoline and diesel options—a great reason for opting for the diesels if you want to pay the extra cash up-front.

Bayliner locates the rudders well aft to minimize the shaft angle, necessary in this installation given the absence of V-drives, which is the other way to keep the shaft angle down. With the rudderposts actually protruding vertically through the Bayliner's transom, it's important to prevent rudder-stalling at higher speeds. This occurs when rudders are so close to the transom and an air source that they effectively draw the air in by vacuum, creating a loss of rudder-blade lift. Bayliner uses the best solution under the circumstances, with anticavitation plates fixed at the top of the rudders like mini-wings. I noticed no problems with

the steering, even at WOT at hard rudder; to the contrary—it was very responsive while producing a tight turning circle. Visibility is great, as one might expect, with the controls and gauges all conveniently situated.

Bayliner has put together a well-conceived, very affordable package in its 3788 Motoryacht. It offers a commendably comfortable layout with a bright, cheery interior and generous room topside for the whole crowd. If the use of a premium vinylester barrier coat in the hull laminate is any indication, then Bayliner is building a far superior product today than it did a few years ago.

The boat is ideally matched to the Cummins power and handles well, with the exception of the steering problems noted. The engine room has deficiencies, including component accessibility and lack of wiring shrouds, and I recommend that they be addressed. To offer this boat at a low price point, Bayliner had to cut corners—don't expect a Viking interior or engineering—so plan to spend some time working the bugs out of the systems. If you're aware of where savings have been made and become a proactive practitioner of preventative maintenance, you should enjoy years of pleasurable service from your Bayliner 3788 Motoryacht.

Bayliner 3788 Manufacturer's Performance Results: Gasoline and Diesel Engines

	Speed, knots	Total Fuel Use, gph	Range, nm
7.4-liter Merc inboard 340 hp			
WOT	27.7	58.4	106
cruise	17.1	29.0	132
Cummins 330 hp			
WOT	27.2	37.4	165
cruise	24.2	29.6	183

1997 Dettling 51

Dettling 51 Specifications

LOA:	51'4"
Beam:	14'6"
Draft:	3'6"
Headroom:	6'6"
Displacement:	30,000 lb. (half load)
Fuel capacity:	500 gal. (100% consumable)
Water capacity:	300 gal.

When you combine an offshore-capable hull, a classic-looking deckhouse, and a pragmatic interior, you could well come up with the quintessential cruising yacht. Company founder and owner Ed Dettling, a retired lawyer from Maryland who had some definite ideas about what made a good owner-operated cruiser, might actually have been the inspiration for those "relentless pursuit of perfection" ads by an upscale automaker.

Design

C. Raymond Hunt Associates, a well-regarded offshore commercial and pleasure-boat designer, was chosen to come up with an efficiently propelled yacht that can keep steaming in rough water. Dettling also wanted a classic look and self-sufficiency. The result? Forward is an aggressive-looking, fine deep-V entry with Hunt's trademark bottom strakes for a dry ride and added lift. Back aft, the bottom-V moderates to a stable and lift-generating running surface with wide-reverse chines. The chines increase the hull's form stability by providing buoyancy outboard and, along with the moderate-V aft, they add lift at planing speeds. The moderate beam-to-length ratio helps improve both ride and efficiency. The deckhouse is good-looking and practical: from the outside, you see proportion and balance; inside is just the right amount of room to get the job done.

Construction

With the design firmed up, Hinckley Yacht Company was chosen to build the hull, deck, and superstructure (although the yachts are now built in Maryland). This shell was then trucked to the Dettling Yacht Company in Easton, Maryland, where Dettling's hand-picked twelve-person crew put in the 19,000 or so hours needed to finish each boat.

Topsides

This is a no-shortcuts type of yacht. You step aboard the Dettling through any of five boarding gates in the flawlessly welded 1¼-inch-diameter stainless steel railings. Two or more handrails at each gate assist you. The teak aft deck, well protected by a roof extension, is surprisingly quiet and exhaust-free at cruising speeds, so it will serve well when outdoor entertainment is in order. Good access for major engine work is afforded by removing the entire deck in three sections. Walking forward is accommodated by the Dettling's unusually wide side decks (treated with Awlgrip nonskid), which you can actually traverse without hanging on. The nine deck hatches and opening side ports are trimmed in polished stainless steel for a pleasingly pragmatic approach to aesthetics; railings are through-bolted and blind-fastened.

The forecastle hasn't escaped Dettling's attention: a 65-pound anchor fits snuggly against its blocks, and when it's on the way up, a spotlight is positioned to let you inspect the chain at night. The chain is washed clean by a clever integral washdown system fed by a pair of seawater spigots. Two deck hatches open to reveal large storage bins above the chain locker for dock lines, swabs, and buckets. Everything drains overboard through a network of hoses to a single through-hull. Mooring versatility is addressed by three pairs of bow chocks and seven pairs of cleats.

Helm

Making this a user-friendly family cruiser meant eliminating the bridge ladder (and so the bridge); therefore, the helm is situated a few steps up from the main saloon on the same level as the flush-deck cockpit. Large opening windows and an ingenious natural-ventilation system mean there will always be a lot to see and generous amounts of fresh air. For a real sea breeze, just pop open the sliding overhead hatch and stand up on the helm sole—you've suddenly got a clever upper helm station.

Visibility from the lower primary helm station is very good, with a comfortably raised four-person seat that allows captain and guests to socialize in a quiet setting. The hinged console makes quick work of electronics installation, and the seat placement puts the large teak steering wheel with its rudder-angle indicator and the MMC electronic engine controls at your fingertips. The only downside is you can't stand at the helm because you're sitting on a raised deck above the master stateroom below.

Saloon

When you walk down the companionway steps from the bridge deck to the saloon, the transformation to a time past is complete. Rich teak joinery finished with six coats of hand-rubbed Epifanes varnish, attractive color-coordinated designer fabrics, and thick carpeting greet you. Large polished stainless steel–rimmed windows make you feel like you're still part of the great outdoors. An L-shaped lounge settee has a pedestal-mounted fold-out teak table that raises and slides into position. The settee is available as a convertible double berth to accommodate another couple in the saloon.

The saloon's teak interior is complemented by an off-white fabric overhead with teak battens in between removable sections. The step-down galley behind its teak serving counter lets the chef be involved with guests while still providing privacy. Included are two sinks—one oversize and the other fitted with a garbage disposal and a faucet fed by either salt water or freshwater. Dettling places instant-hot-water heaters by the mixing valve in the two heads and in the galley so you don't waste water. Two of the burners and the full-size electric oven below use 220-volt power; the third burner uses 100-volt power supplied by the inverter, as does the microwave oven, coffeemaker, and toaster oven.

The commercial-quality top-loading holding-plate refrigerator-freezer requires one 40-minute cycle a day from the high-capacity seawater-cooled compressor to keep the temperature down; the Dettlings had milk last for three weeks when it was kept at 30 degrees. Placing the compressor in the engine room makes it quieter in the saloon.

Accommodations

Old salts know the value of privacy, so the two staterooms are well separated, which enhances rather than strains friendships after a week or two on board together. The forward stateroom's 78-by-60-inch berth, generous storage space, 78-inch headroom, private head with Italian tile and shower, four opening side ports, and an overhead hatch will make you feel right at home. Behind the cabinet doors, you can see that all of the boat's interior bulkheads, countertops, and even shelf dividers are fiberglassed to the hull before finishing for extra integrity. Back aft, the guest stateroom offers complete privacy, another 78-inch queen-size berth, a large vanity with sink and mirror, three opening ports for lots of daylight and fresh air, and a private head with separate tiled shower and a washer-dryer built in. AC plenums are effectively but discreetly located throughout the yacht.

Engineering

Dettling put the engines in the stern, which leaves room for the fuel tanks over the center of buoyancy and effectively isolates engine noise from the people compartment. The Dettling's aft engine room contains all of the yacht's noise-generating machinery—and most of the noise: I recorded 67 dBA on the bridge and 69 dBA in the saloon, some of the lowest readings I've seen on any yacht. A 3-inch-thick sandwich of foam and two spaced layers of lead, as well as sealed cableways in the forward engine-room bulkhead, get the credit.

Trouble-free cruising demands solid engineering, and Dettling pays significant attention to the need for reliability and system redundancy. For ease of maintenance and to preserve access outboard of the engines, Dettling keeps everything either aft of the engines or inboard. The Cruisair compressors—two 16,000 Btu units and a 7,000 Btu unit—are on a shelf at the aft end of the engine room with the 8 kW Onan sound-shielded genset between them—all are easily accessible for maintenance.

Four stringers run the length of the boat—they're laid up over foam cores and then glassed in place. The engine beds are built the same way, mounted on top of the stringers and then tabbed into place. The entire assembly is a full 18 inches deep, and the design allows superb access around the engines. The engines are suspended on gusseted ½-inch angle aluminum stock through-bolted to ¼-inch aluminum backing plates. This area of the stringers is cored with wood instead of foam to resist bolt compression and to help absorb engine vibrations. A shiplike fuel manifold is fed by aircraft-type fuel hoses through two sets of Racor fuel filter-separators that permit cleaning without stopping the engines. Fuel suction is taken from the lowest point of the epoxy-reinforced fiberglass tanks, which keeps the tanks clean and lets you use every last quart of fuel.

The 2:1 ZF V-drive reduction gears allow the aft engine placement; connected to Aquamet 22 shafts at a steep 15-degree angle, they drive 26-by-30-inch five-blade props recessed in 5-inch tunnels.

The shafts are short—just 98 inches—so they're supported by just the V-drive transmissions at one end and the shaft struts and the propellers at the other end. Eliminating the need for a through-hull cutlass makes the drivetrain easier to align, more efficient, and less prone to vibration. ZF 302V-LD gears are used to take advantage of their accessibility—each reversible shaft (tapered on both ends) right through the gear to the forward end, so they're accessible for maintenance. The tapering reduces alignment problems, and the shaft can be reversed if needed.

Groco safety seacocks are used to take a suction in the engine room for emergency dewatering if needed—and the seacock has to be closed before you can open the bilge suction, which eliminates the chance of flooding the engine room, effectively resulting in a sailor-proof check valve. Aluminum ¼-inch diamond plate covers the bilge over the keel. Three Rule bilge pumps—one 360 gph and two 3,700 gph—have float switches at staggered levels. All the pump hoses feed a common manifold, discharging overboard through a bronze through-hull, and the top of the hoses are designed to prevent syphoning. The engines have pre-lube pumps that come on when the starter switches are partially turned; after 30 to 45 seconds, a warning light goes out and the engines are ready to start. The pumps are also convenient when you change the oil.

Performance Test

Our performance test took place inshore, but I've been in enough similar Hunt designs to know they do very well offshore. The boat handled well, responding snappily to the MMC engine controls and Hynautic steering. From the helm, the ride was unusually quiet, smooth, and level at all speeds. Bow rise—even during the transition to plane—was minimal, indicating good weight distribution and a balanced hull form. Visibility all around was unimpeded; you can drive this boat in a crowded marina without the urge to stand up for a better look around—which is a good thing. Performance numbers were impressive, even with a full cruising com-

Dettling 51 Performance Results

RPM	Speed, knots	Speed, mph	Fuel Use, gph	Nautical mpg	Statute mpg	Range, nm	Range, statute miles	Noise Level, dBA	Trim, degrees
1,000	7.5	8.6	2.16	3.47	3.92	1,736	1,960	65	0
1,250	8.6	9.9	5.28	1.6	1.87	814	933	62	2
1,500	9.3	10.7	8.60	1.1	1.24	540	622	63	3
1,750	15.0	17.3	11.76	1.3	1.46	637	731	64	2
2,000	19.7	22.7	17.06	1.1	1.32	559	662	65	2
2,250	22.8	26.2	25.28	0.9	1.04	451	518	68	2
2,500	25.6	29.4	33.04	0.8	0.89	387	446	70	2
2,600	27.3	31.4	42.20	0.6	0.74	323	372	71	2

Tested with twin 420 hp Cummins engines.

plement on board including spare parts, davit with dinghy and motor, spare props, a large assortment of tools, diving compressor, and food and supplies for a two-month cruise. This was especially true of fuel efficiency, with moderate beam and no-fat, vacuum-bagged, and cored construction getting much of the credit.

Twin 420 hp Cummins 6CTA8.3-M2 inboard diesels driving 2.2:1 ZF V-drives and 26-by-30-inch five-blade nibral propellers produced the performance figures for the Dettling 51 that are summarized in the accompanying table.

Of note, this builder lends new meaning to the concept of conducting sea trials: the Dettlings cruise extensively on their boats before delivery to new owners. They take good care of the boats, of course—no street shoes on board and so on—and enjoy themselves while dreaming of ways to build an even better boat. When the owners take delivery, they get a boat that has been thoroughly debugged and is as trouble-free as possible.

The Dettling 51 is as close to perfection as I've seen. Standard equipment in the 1997 base price includes an 8 kW Onan genset, 2,500-watt inverter, two sets of Racor fuel filter-separators, Mathers engine controls, Cruisair three-zone AC, three water heaters, Ultrasonic Acoustics insulation, VacuFlush toilets, and a Maxwell anchor windlass.

Options on our test boat included Seafrost holding-plate refrigeration, teak aft deck sole, full-size washer-dryer, Awlgrip hull and deck finish, air-cooled refrigeration compressor, Marquipt lo-boy davit on extended hardtop, Novurania 10-foot RIB with 15 hp Johnson, auxiliary control station, pre-lube system, spare props, Copperclad bottom applied in mold, five-blade nibral propellers, diving compressor, tool set, and complete electronics.

The Dettling 51 adds up to a high-end, no-compromises, long-range fast cruiser for yachters who have the experience to appreciate and the money to pay for the very best.

1999 Eastbay 49 Express

Grand Banks has been in the cruising-yacht business since Noah was a mess cook, or so I'm told, and has built a solid reputation for the quality and seaworthiness of its semidisplacement trawler yachts. Its Eastbay series of planing yachts—de-

signed and engineered by C. Raymond Hunt Associates and developed to capture the burgeoning planing yacht market—has caught the attention of some of the most seasoned yachters out there. The 49 is the latest and largest in the Eastbay series, and

Eastbay 49 Specifications

LOA:	49'11"
Beam:	16'0"
Draft:	4'1"
Displacement:	43,300 lb.
Fuel capacity:	775 gal.
Water capacity:	160 gal.

the combined efforts of the well-regarded Hunt design firm and Grand Banks have created what can only be described as a superb open cruising yacht with a low, graceful, classic-in-the-making profile.

Cockpit and Topsides

Starting the tour aft, you'll find the cockpit is a safe (30 in. coaming height with teak nonskid) and user-friendly place to be: molded steps leading to the wide side decks and bridge deck; molded lounge seats; large one-piece inboard-opening transom door; boost-assisted, walk-in engine-room access; and big well-guttered lazarette hatches. Four hawsepipes lead from the corner-mounted cleats set just above deck level, which works fine when moored to a floating dock. Lifting one of those beautifully tooled, seamless fiberglass and teak hatches revealed a pleasant surprise: a fiberglass fuel tank that should last as long as the boat does, unlike the aluminum tanks on some boats. I would just add a shield for the soft plastic fuel-sight gauge. The steering shelf is another indication of Eastbay's megayacht engineering—rugged and no-nonsense.

Wide teak side decks lead forward where rugged, unyielding 1¼-inch stainless steel bow railings are a full 30 inches high for excellent security. Two pairs of spring cleats with chocks let into the teak bulwark provide mooring flexibility, as does the Delta anchor's beautifully fashioned anchor-handling tray. More boatbuilding savvy (usually missing on other boats) is evident in the trunk-cabin's hatches—a 25-inch Bomar forward hatch and two 22-inchers amidships—providing not only

lots of daylight and fresh air, but also three emergency egress routes if the need arises.

Bridge Deck

For any boat with a single helm station on the main deck, visibility is essential since there's no bridge vantage point to fall back on when the going gets congested. Eastbay's designers have done a splendid job of creating a wide-open view for the captain and more than a few guests, with large sections of windshield glass interrupted only by reasonably proportioned varnished-teak mullions. The bridge deck is enclosed in glass forward with thick EZ2CY plastic curtains aft, which can be removed for an added sea breeze.

The 11-foot-long, teak-clad bridge deck is also raised well off the water—three steps up from the cockpit—creating an excellent height of eye for the mariner. To port are an L-shaped lounge with storage below and a forward-facing, two-person seat raised for a good view, with an icemaker below. The dashboard area has a covered chart table and storage lockers for bottles and sundry gear. To starboard is a storage locker, bench seat, and a raised pedestal helm chair. The helm station, dominated by large Caterpillar instrumentation and electronic displays, features user-friendly single-lever engine controls to starboard and a large vertical ship's wheel, which could be ergonomically enhanced by a smaller wheel set more bus-like at 30 degrees from horizontal. A large expanse of white dashboard—which I would like to see a darker, less glaring shade—and the overhead boxes provide ample room for a fancy electronics suite. The electrical service panel is easily accessed behind the companionway door next to the helm console.

Engine Room

Entered from the cockpit via a lift-up door and stairs or by lifting a bridge-deck hatch and climbing down a ladder, the Eastbay's engine room is one of the best I've seen in terms of machinery and equipment accessibility. Seacocks and strainers, freshwater fills, fuel filter-separators, oil dipsticks, and the oil-changing system are all located on or near centerline for quick maintenance access. The raw-water strainers and fuel filters are ergonomically mounted sufficiently high above the bilge.

Headroom is a full 62 inches, making the space seem larger than it is and more shiplike. Neatly routed and carefully bundled wiring and plumbing looms, well-designed combustion air-intake boxes, and aircraft-type high-pressure oil-change and fuel lines lend a military precision to Eastbay's engineering. The teak grating on centerline is comfortable to walk on; however, access outboard of the big Caterpillar diesels is a problem, especially getting to the water heater located to starboard. Eastbay might want to investigate switching to linear mufflers under the cockpit to free up engine-room space aft (where the vertical lift mufflers currently reside) for the auxiliary equipment.

The engines are soft-mounted to an aluminum plate that is encapsulated in the top of the large, high-hat fiberglass hull stringers and tapped out to receive the mounting bolts. The engine beds are capped with a bedded aluminum cover for an overall neat, vibration-absorbing installation. The 1.92:1 twin disc gears transition to Aquamet 22, 2½-inch stainless steel shafts, which exit the engine room at a hefty 13-degree angle through dripless shaft seals. The all-white bilges are sanded reasonably smooth for easy cleanup. The engine-room overhead and bulkheads are lined with acoustic insulation, and shielded overhead lighting is liberally provided for good nighttime visibility.

Cabin

Eastbay arranges every feature of the 49 for comfort and utility, including the 25-inch-wide companionway leading to the roomy, airy, and well-lit teak and white cabin. Our test boat was nicely outfitted with several large high-quality overhead lights, teak battens dividing the thick vinyl headliner sections, and large stainless steel opening ports with privacy curtains. There's room for two to work comfortably in the U-shaped galley to port with its Grunert undercounter refrigerator-freezer, three-burner electric range and oven, dual deep sinks, a small microwave oven overhead, an opening port, and generous storage space in cabinets and drawers. Opposite to starboard is a U-shaped dinette with storage below, a teak drop-leaf high-low table, built-in drawers, cubbyhole storage behind, and a large TV cabinet opposite.

Forward to port, an unobtrusive sliding door leads to the guest stateroom with generous 78-inch-long single berths arranged athwartships, with drawers and lockers below and reading lamps above, a hanging locker with louvered door, and two ports and an overhead hatch letting in lots of daylight and fresh air. Opposite the stateroom is the guest head with its teak grating, portlight, shower nozzle, wraparound shower curtain, and a long vanity with storage room inside.

The master stateroom is located forward, where the bright, open-feeling theme continues with the large overhead hatch, opening portlights, and generous headroom. The island berth forward raises easily on boost lifts for access to the roomy storage area below. Teak slats line the hull and match the teak built-in dressers and hanging and storage lockers. The private master head has a separate shower and a well-proportioned molded fiberglass and Corian vanity.

Design and Construction

Designed by C. Raymond Hunt Associates, the Eastbay 49's deep-V, warped-bottom hull has a fine entry with chines arching well above the waterline forward. Flat chines and a moderate 20 degrees of transom deadrise contribute to excellent form stability at rest and efficient hydrodynamic lift at speed.

The hull is ably built, starting with a skin coat of vinylester resin to protect against osmotic blistering. The bottom is solid glass except forward, where Divinycell coring is used locally to better resist slamming loads. The sides are cored with Divinycell; the decks and superstructure are cored with balsa for stiffness at light weight. Bulkheads are plywood but the bottom grid is wood-free, using instead glass-encapsulated foam hull stiffeners to reduce bottom panel sizes. The hull-to-deck joint is ruggedly fastened with a polyurethane adhesive, bolts, and screws.

Performance Test

The highlight of any boat test on a Hunt-designed hull is the sea trial, and the Eastbay 49 didn't disappoint. Although seas were too calm to assess seakeeping, this hull form is well-proven offshore and the boat was a delight to drive. It handled crisply, turning 360 degrees in 32 seconds with a full 35 degrees of rudder swing. With our twin 660 hp Caterpillar 3196s, we made 29.3 knots/64 gph fuel flow/88 dBA helm noise levels at 2,300 rpm, and just more than 27 knots/53 gph/84 dBA at a comfortable 2,100 rpm cruise—that's an excellent showing for a 1,320 hp 49-footer. The Cats also delivered strong acceleration above 1,500 rpm, although noise levels indicate a need for improved quieting to put the Eastbay in the desirable and achievable below-80 dBA range at cruise. Visibility throughout the speed spectrum was excellent with just 4 degrees of trim at cruising speed; handling dockside was likewise worth writing home about.

Eastbay has hit a home run with its beautifully styled and proportioned 49 Express. This is my personal favorite in this size range, with its world-class engineering, solid construction, and superb hull design. In fact, it's difficult to exaggerate the superiority of this boat's hull design and performance. This 49-footer will run as fast as some other express yachts with 30 percent more power.

There isn't a better-designed or (in my opinion) better-looking boat of its kind being built today. Base power is twin 435 hp Caterpillar 3208s and test power was twin 660 hp Caterpillar 3196s. Options included reverse-cycle AC, holding-plate refrigeration, an 8 kW generator, and VacuFlush heads. You get a lot of value in this boat for about the price of a Hinckley 44—this one's a keeper.

Dave Gerr is another of those talented and multifaceted naval architects who's an ardent proponent of long and narrow hulls. Here's a great example of one of his fast, efficient, and narrow cruisers with a pillow-soft ride: the Gerr-Westbourne 44. The wheelhouse, where captain and mate spend most of their time running offshore, is situated well aft, where vertical accelerations are further minimized.   DAVE GERR

Here's a baby sedan from one of the world's largest boatbuilders, the Bayliner 2858 Ciera. There's a V-berth forward, a saloon with a second berth under the dinette, helm station, enclosed head, windows all around, an easily accessed bridge, and a cockpit that is big enough from which to fish. Single gasoline or diesel MerCruiser stern-drive power is available, with an aft engine room that frees up room in the saloon and creates a reasonably low-profile design. Bayliner has something for everyone from 16 to 57 feet.   BAYLINER

Long time Maine-based boatbuilder Sabre Yachts builds both sail-boats and powerboats. The sailboat part is relevant to this book because sailors claim to know considerably more than any power-boater ever did about storage space, portholes, berth arrange-ments, and other such salty topics. And this expertise shows—I have to admit—in the Sabreline powerboat lineup of express, aft-cabin, and sedan cruisers, which ranges from 34 to 47 feet. The Sabreline 42 Sedan—which I can barely distinguish from a convertible by its cruising heritage and outfitting, and its larger saloon relative to the cockpit—is a two-stateroom, galley-down family cruiser with a pleasing well-proportioned Down East look. Molded stairs replace a more strenuously ascended ladder to the bridge.

Grand Banks saw the need for speed a while back, or at least its customers did, and the venerable trawler builder responded with its upscale line of C. Raymond Hunt–designed 30-knot (top end) ex-press and sedan cruisers. The Eastbay 43 Flybridge shown here, one of the best running boats of its kind, is in the middle of Eastbay's 38- to 49-foot lineup. Available with or without a bridge, this mod-erate displacement (33,000 lb.) yacht comes with a wide range of twin-diesel options and features a two-stateroom, galley-down cabin layout. A smooth, dry, and stable ride and excellent helm visibility are hallmarks of this exceptionally well-engineered cruiser.   NEIL RABINOWITZ

Maxum's flagship 4600 is a good-looking, roomy, and light-filled family cruiser, the largest in a lineup of boats starting at 18 feet. The large, long saloon makes for an equally big flybridge deck above, and the radar arches are blessedly far aft so they don't in-terfere too much with visibility from the helm. The two-stateroom, two-head layout is comfortably situated forward, and a lower helm station is an option. Ultraleather upholstery and VacuFlush toilets add an upscale feeling to this big family cruiser. This 35,000-pound boat is way too heavy for gasoline power; they're listed just to keep the base price down. If you can't afford the *de rigueur* twin-diesel option, you're probably better off getting a smaller boat or a used one. Osmotic blistering is covered for five years by the transferable warranty.   MAXUM

The saloon on a Sea Ray 450 Express Bridge, one of the most clev-erly laid out yachts to date from this or any other builder. The dinette is raised a foot or so, which allows a good view through the side windows but mostly creates headroom in the *two* state-rooms beneath—talk about carving space out of nowhere. A three-stateroom, two-head cabin; safe and easily navigated molded stairs to the bridge; and two intelligently laid out helm stations are included. One of the biggest and most model-prolific boatbuilders in the world, Sea Ray produces four boat lines from 18 to 68 feet, including ten 38- to 48-foot Sport Yachts, of which the 450 is one.
                                                              SEA RAY

Sabre Yachts builds this 34-foot sedan, a classic design with a modern planing hull form, which features an open and airy saloon with adjoining cockpit and a single large stateroom forward. SABRELINE

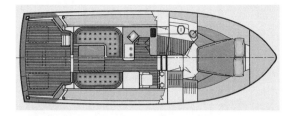

The Sabreline 34 floor plan, with perhaps more emphasis on storage than some other builders. Note the size of the saloon relative to the cockpit, which is what makes this a cruising sedan. SABRELINE

Manufactured by an express-cruiser specialist, this Regal Commodore 3780 is the builder's very first sedan—and a Euro-styled version at that. The saloon takes up the lion's share of the LOA, and the single helm station is topside on the bridge. A pair of topside sunpads, molded stairs to the bridge, full-beam saloon with lower (versus Silverton's sidewalk access) side decks, and a two-stateroom, one-head cabin are included. This Michael Peters–designed (it's great to see more production boatbuilders using real naval architects) aft engine-room hull performs quite well in a chop, but make sure to get the diesel option; this is really too much boat, at well over 20,000 pounds, for two gasoline engines to push effectively. Even with the diesels, the fast-turning 22-inch props are on the small side for delivering optimum propulsion efficiency. Bow railings are nice and high, saloon headroom is exceptional, and the cockpit overhang is a nice feature to have on hot or rainy days in port. Regal builds a wide range of quality cruisers from 18 to 41 feet. REGAL

The Silverton 410 is one of the builder's Sport Bridge series, and it's a good-looking boat considering the design's larger-than-life premise. The full-beam saloon design (which is about the size of the average 50-foot convertible) opens up extra room inside, and there are even two queen-berth staterooms that share a clever split-head arrangement, with shower to port and toilet to starboard. Silverton builds an array of space-enhancing cruisers that are well equipped, competitively priced, and built to last. These recent Silverton hull designs are better capable of offshore cruising than much of the competition—and more so than older Silvertons, for that matter—with a smoother-riding hull. This is an honest 41-footer, too—the boat is 46 feet long, 5 feet of which is taken up by an extended swim platform and a pulpit—but Silverton has the good grace not to include the two overhangs in the LOA figure.

SILVERTON

Ted Hood sold his Little Harbor marina and boat line to Hinckley Yacht Holdings in 2000, but not before establishing the line as one of the most prestigious in the industry. The Little Harbor Whisper-jet series—all waterjet-powered—includes this 44-footer, a high-end single-stateroom cruiser with a convertible dinette. The boat's sailboat heritage shows everywhere to good effect—Ted was a sailmaker and sailboat designer, among many other things—with lots of storage space, a teak and white interior (à la Herreshoff), wide side decks, and a tall, beautifully proportioned teak or stainless steel windshield. The waterjets minimize vibration and (to some extent) sound levels, minimize draft to the depth of the keel-less hull, and allow an owner to head with impunity right for those thousands of lobster-pot buoys off Newport.   LITTLE HARBOR

Pilothouse Motor Yachts

The pilothouse motor yacht is certainly one of the more popular cruising-yacht layouts. Above 50 feet or so, it makes a lot of sense. In the bow is a stateroom or two with a head, followed by the master stateroom with the pilothouse directly above. Being able to create a two-decker in this area creates a lot of interior living space. The trick is to keep the master stateroom deck as low as possible in the bilge so the pilothouse isn't too high for the boat's beam. The saloon is down a few steps and aft, and a flybridge tucks neatly above the saloon and just behind the raised pilothouse.

These yachts not only work well in terms of space; they also look like little ships. The pilothouse is the primary helm station, and it's high enough to afford a good all-around view. Aft-facing windows should be fitted so you can see what's going on behind you and to make backing into a slip less of a hair-raising experience. Doors leading out to the weather decks make it easy for a couple to handle a big pilothouse motor yacht alone.

Because the pilothouse is only a few steps from the cabin, flybridge, and saloon, it's the heart of the ship, and it makes a good family boat. Everyone is close enough, yet privacy is afforded by the multi-level layout. Seaworthiness is improved since the saloon is relatively low, directly over the engine room, which reduces topside weight and sail area. A main deck-level cockpit is usually included with a transom, and perhaps a pair of side-bulwark doors, leading to the swim platform and dock.

1998 Bayliner 5788 Motor Yacht

Bayliner, one of the largest boatbuilders in the world, produces seven motor yachts from 34 to 57 feet. As the largest U.S. boatbuilder, Bayliner has apparently been paying attention to customer expectations. Bayliners are still price-point boats, but they're surprisingly better than some of the higher-

Bayliner 5788 Motor Yacht Specifications

LOA:	59'4"
Beam:	17'2"
Draft:	4'11"
Fuel capacity:	800 gal.
Water capacity:	222 gal.
Holding capacity:	76 gal.
Bridge clearance:	19'7"
Transom deadrise:	10 deg.

priced competition, though quality limitations are still evident in some areas. This question of Bayliner quality has long been an issue with the boating press and public, but quality tends to improve as the boats get bigger. Engineering and design can be surprisingly good, while shortcuts and oversights can be aggravatingly frequent, depending on the model. It often seems with Bayliner that just a little extra effort would produce a boat that's basically above reproach, for the money.

Good value for the money is a starting point, but lately Bayliner has also been delivering more room, range, and comfort, as well as a little Euro-styling flair, in its motor yacht series. Bayliner's stylish and well-proportioned new flagship 5788 motor yacht is its largest and most complex effort to date, and it has a lot to offer for the money. The layout is open and airy, as expected by the U.S. cruising market, and performance is quite respectable with twin MAN 600s.

After my inspection, it became apparent that experienced sailors—of the powerboat variety—had significant input in the 5788's layout and design. Styling is at the service of function, deck features emphasize safety and mooring chores, helm stations stress visibility and utility, the saloon is designed to be lived in, and the staterooms and heads are large and comfortable.

Cockpit and Foredeck

Port and starboard transom doors lead from the rock-solid integrated swim platform to the cock-

pit, protected by the coach-roof overhang and with its high bulwarks adding a welcome measure of safety. Nonskid is excellent, beautifully tooled, and grippy yet easy to clean. A Glendinning Cablemaster, a high-end amenity that seems right at home on the Bayliner, feeds through a port in the transom liner to the storage drum below. Two large hatches, well guttered and with ample-sized drain lines to resist clogging, open to the lazarette, which holds the enclosed generator, battery banks, rugged steering gear, and smoothly finished white bilges.

Molded stairs lead to the side decks with high, 1¼-inch-diameter stainless bow railings transitioning to bulwarks forward. Two pairs of spring cleats and three bow cleats add mooring flexibility, as does the anchor windlass. A sunpad area is recessed into the trunk cabin, and Bayliner's excellent fiberglass tooling work is shown off to good effect on the nicely contoured cabintop.

Engine Room

I'll say up front that the Bayliner 5788's engine room is easily one of the most spacious in its class. Entered from the cockpit by folding up the bridge stairway, the aft half of the space is wide open with the DC and fuel-system accessories along the aft bulkhead. The engine gears are a full 7 feet forward, and there are 6 feet between the engines, which contributes to the boat's excellent responsiveness when maneuvering dockside.

The bilge serves as a (usually dry) walking surface, and the seacocks are close at hand and easy to operate, as are the internal raw-water strainers comfortably positioned alongside the engine beds. All this space results in a mechanic's paradise, more like working in a workshop than an engine room—headroom excepted (but which is still good for a 57-foot boat). Bayliner reduces engine-room clutter with its underwater exhaust system—which eliminates the need for silencers—and by installing the genset in the lazarette.

A few comments on structure follow. The hull stringers serving as engine beds are supported by the forward and aft bulkheads and by a low intermediate bulkhead just aft of the gears, which is notched out to make way for the shafts. If this bulkhead had shaft holes instead of notches, the intermediate bulkhead would do a better job of carrying the foot-deep stringers. The notches prevent the support from acting as a beam, which would efficiently absorb compression and tension loads. Due to the hull's deadrise, the outboard engine beds—with soft engine mounts bolted on top—are only 5 inches deep. The existing structure is adequate for the most severe conditions, but moving them outboard a few inches—making them deeper and higher—and side-mounting the engines on brackets would add strength, structural efficiency, and rigidity, as well as further attenuate engine vibration levels. I would also like to see watertight bulkheads that contribute to the boat's ability to stay afloat in the event that one compartment floods. Holes are provided in the bulkheads for water drainage in the present design, which guarantee that the boat will sink with a single major leak.

The carefully installed aluminum fuel tanks outboard are well supported with ample room for air to circulate outside, and they appear to be far enough forward and close enough to the hull's longitudinal center of flotation to minimize trim variation as the fuel load changes. For a yacht of this size, price, and quality, there is no reason that Bayliner should not be expected to use safer, more chafe-resistant, aircraft-type, high-pressure fuel hoses and fittings instead of the rubber hoses and hose clamps seen on an average 20-foot outboard.

Saloon

Entered from the cockpit through a sliding door, the saloon is welcoming with large windows; soft, neutral tan and cream colors in the Ultrasuede upholstery, headliner, and carpeting; Corian countertops and tables; and beautifully sculpted valances and liners overhead. An L-shaped lounge with table is to port, and opposite is a wet bar with icemaker and sink, and an entertainment center with stereo and large TV. Forward to starboard opposite the galley is a U-shaped dinette with a table that seats six comfortably.

Bayliner gives its customers a great deal for their money in terms of size and amenities, but don't expect seamless joinery and exotic woods. Joints and reveals between cabinet doors are nicely crafted, but fit-and-finish flaws are found here and there; this is an area that separates a large production builder like Bayliner from the high-end competition.

Galley

Forward to port in the saloon, the galley has enough room for two to work comfortably. There's a large U-shaped island counter with twin deep sinks, dishwasher, trash compactor, electric oven with a four-burner range, microwave oven, upright refrigerator, and lots of storage space. A large window provides a good view outside the boat. The galley design is thoughtful, lending a measure of privacy while keeping the chef very much a part of the saloon's activities.

Pilothouse and Bridge

Raised three steps above the saloon (which improves visibility outside and provides headroom in the master stateroom below), the pilothouse is well laid out for piloting with large expanses of glass in the windshield and side windows and a sensibly designed helm console. The electronics panel, directly in front of the wheel and engine controls, takes center stage (as it should) with room for a comprehensive suite of electronics. A row of gauges is farther forward with the compass partially obscured behind it (it needs to be raised a few inches). I prefer a more horizontally inclined wheel for better ergonomics, but the layout works well enough as it is. Visibility is excellent, with a clear view (even when the operator is seated) from ahead to a good 40 degrees abaft the beam. Weather doors lead topside, which is great for shorthanded cruising; a comfortable lounge is raised to provide five guests a good view of the passing scenery; and stairs lead directly up to the bridge tucked behind the pilothouse.

Accommodations

The companionway to the three-stateroom, two-head accommodations is entered via curved stairs from the pilothouse. The full-beam master stateroom is aft, just forward of the engine room and below the helm. At 6 feet, 3 inches, headroom is limited, but the space is roomy and pleasantly appointed with teak paneling and the light cream-colored bulkhead and ceiling motif continued from the saloon. To port is an athwartships queen-size bed with reading tables and drawers below and surrounded by a hanging locker, built-in dressers, and entertainment center. To starboard in the stateroom is a vanity with sink and more storage; the head with bathtub is adjacent. The stateroom could use more natural light, which is easily accomplished by installing larger portholes to port.

Forward is a washer-dryer off the companionway and next to a guest stateroom (also to port) with crossed single berths, a nice wide one below, and a small hanging locker with shelves. Opposite is a roomy guest head with enclosed shower. Forward and up a couple of steps (which increase the sole width in the bow) is the guest suite with a large island berth, hanging lockers, private head access, and lots of light from two overhead hatches and four side ports.

Design and Construction

The Bayliner has a modified-V hull with double chines and moderate 10-degree deadrise aft, creating a stable, easily driven vessel. The well-built hull starts with a vinylester-resin skin coat for blister protection, is laminated with unidirectional knit fiberglass and a foam core, and then is vacuum-bagged, as are the two main structural bulkheads. Stringers are marine-grade wood and foam, encapsulated in fiberglass. Decks and the superstructure are constructed of marine wood- and foam-cored fiberglass. All through-bolt points are supported to resist compression and add strength. Stringer and bulkhead limber holes are sealed PVC, laminated in place.

Performance Test

Our sea trial on the upper Chesapeake Bay was a sedentary affair with little wind and only a few wakes through which to slice. The boat did indicate good stability and a decent ride in a chop. The hull's full, broad entry would limit the boat to moderate (though still respectable) speeds in rough conditions, but also bodes well for a good following-sea ride with generous buoyancy and dynamic lift forward. Handling was good, although power steering, which Bayliner should offer as an option on a boat of this size, would help significantly to increase responsiveness from a fairly stiff 4.5 turns lock-to-lock on the bridge. Once you've run a boat with power steering, you won't want to go back. The hydraulic Hynautic engine controls worked well with minimal resistance and good sensitivity.

The 600 hp MAN diesels are an excellent choice for the Bayliner because of their compactness, excellent power-to-weight ratio, and low vibration and noise levels. The quieter an engine is to start with, the easier the builder's sound-deadening job will be, and I observed commendably low noise levels. The Bayliner gets comfortably up on plane at 1,500 rpm and 14 knots. At an easy 1,800 rpm cruise, we made 18.2 knots and measured just 70 dBA at the lower helm, 78 dBA in the saloon directly above the engines, and 73 dBA in the master stateroom. A 2,000 rpm/22-knot cruise and 2,290 rpm/24½ knots full throttle saw just a 2 to 4 dBA increase.

Dockside, the Bayliner handled well when using just the transmissions and bow thruster to back our way into a tight slip. All-around visibility from the bridge helm was good. Our test boat's owner ran a 5788 through driving rain and high seas, and reported nary a leak through all those windows, which is a comforting report indeed.

It is apparent that experienced powerboaters had some real input in the Bayliner 5788's layout and design. Styling is at the service of function, deck features emphasize safety and mooring chores, helm stations stress visibility and utility, the saloon is designed to be lived in, and the staterooms and heads are large and comfortable. If more people were aware of how much Bayliner delivers for the same investment, perhaps the premium-yacht builders would feel the heat. Compared to premium yachts, you give up the exquisite joinery, higher-quality components, aircraft-type fuel lines, and mirror-smooth bilges; however, the design has great merit, the fiberglass tooling is superb, and Bayliner's basic construction and engineering capably pass muster. The overall quality is surprisingly high, and durability is certainly built in for the long haul.

Our 1998 test boat was equipped with 600 hp MAN diesels, a bimini top, reverse-cycle AC, a hydraulic davit, a Glendinning Cablemaster, a 15 kW Westerbeke diesel, and a 4 kW inverter. I don't know of any builder that delivers as much boat for as little money—and that, of course, is Bayliner's forte.

1998 Carver 530 Voyager Pilothouse

CARVER

Carver 530 Voyager Pilothouse Specifications

LOA:	53'9"
Beam:	15'4"
Draft:	4'9"
Displacement:	42,500 lb.
Bridge clearance:	19'0"
Fuel capacity:	800 gal.
Water capacity:	200 gal.

Carver charted a new course into murky waters when it decided to design and build the new 530 Voyager Pilothouse. First, it was its biggest boat yet, and the costliest to design and tool up, with more than 40,000 hours invested in the project. Then there's the styling—distinctly Euro—and the layout: an innovative, quasi-pilothouse motor yacht. But Carver's gamble has paid rich dividends since the boat was introduced in the summer of 1997, with seventy-three of the 530s sold in the first year of production. This unexpectedly strong demand prompted Carver to expand its facilities to boost production.

Carver has long been known for building roomy powerboats, but the emphasis on European styling is taking on increasing importance. Carver is positioning the 530 to be marketed worldwide, having already built one boat with crew quarters aft, with a single berth, sink, and head. There's little doubt that the styling will hold appeal for European as well as U.S. consumers. My only questions are about hull form and why a 53-footer should have as many limitations in offshore conditions as this one does.

Carver offers significant customization for its customers, more so than many other production builders. Do you want a different galley arrangement or an office in place of the port stateroom, or perhaps a hydraulically lowered swim platform? All you have to do is ask (and be willing to pay) for it. At any rate, the basic three-stateroom, two-head layout with a two-level saloon, cockpit, engineroom access through the lazarette, and large flybridge has much to commend it.

Construction

Carver is selling the 530 as an offshore-capable boat, and it points to a ruggedly built hull as meeting the structural requirements of seagoing service. The hull starts with 20- to 22-mils of gelcoat followed by 30 mils of black vinylester gelcoat and a 2- to 3-ounce skin coat to help prevent osmotic blistering. The hull is a solid laminate of five layers of Knytex (six layers with the larger engines) and a 32-ounce fiberglass fabric stitched to a layer of mat, resulting in an average bottom thickness of 0.52 inch. The bottom is strengthened by a one-piece interlocking fiberglass gridwork of ribs and stringers that is molded separately, then held precisely in place on a jig, and tabbed in place to the hull. The hull sides above the waterline are stiffened with a core of ¾-inch balsa. Along with the plywood structural bulkheads, cabin subassemblies are also tabbed to the hull, integrating the interior with the hull.

The hull-to-deck joint is impressively engineered with its shoebox flange bonded together using polyurethane adhesive, fastened with two layers of self-tapping stainless screws, and then fiberglassed from the inside. This joint absorbs the longitudinal hull stresses in shear, so a solid bond is essential to both structural and watertight integrity.

Decks—supported in the cockpit and saloon areas by aluminum framing—and the superstructure are also cored with balsa for stiffness and reduced weight. Bolt penetrations for deck hardware are tapped into ¼-inch aluminum backing plates, which results in a clean installation and prevents water from migrating to the balsa core.

One upscale feature on the yacht is Carver's use of frameless windows prevalent on high-end production and custom boats. The glass is bonded directly to the fiberglass superstructure, eliminating the need for aluminum frames and the accompanying corrosion potential, and resulting in a cleaner exterior look. Carver also enhances the window frames with aluminum stock fiberglassed in place during construction, allowing narrower side-window mullions, while also maintaining strength and stiffness.

Hull Design

To really be counted as a true offshore vessel, any hull has to be not only built but also actually shaped to handle heavy seas. The Carver is quite limited in this area, with the comparatively flat and full sections forward limiting sustained speed, particularly in a demanding head sea. Although the boat evidently has a generous measure of reserve buoyancy and initial form stability, the 530's too-flat-bottom hull form makes the boat suitable only for occasional forays offshore in nice weather, but not for extended passagemaking in demanding conditions. Inshore cruising in commodious surroundings has long been Carver's forte, but the hull design won't satisfy the reasonable offshore cruising expectations many owners will have of a boat this big—that's a significant shortcoming.

Engine Room and Lazarette

The engine room is entered via the lazarette through a large, well-guttered, 55-by-31-inch cockpit hatch. A pair of heavy-gauge, 0.25-inch-thick, 400-gallon aluminum fuel tanks are located directly at the entrance. They are well secured to the hull stringers, with ample room all around for air circulation, which should help prevent the accumulation of standing water that causes exterior corrosion. Hose clamps hold the fuel lines in place; I would like to see Carver upgrade to high-pressure compression fittings and hoses—appropriate on a yacht of this class—for an extra measure of security. Single Racor fuel filter-separators (one per tank) are easy to access for service.

Also in the lazarette is the optional 13.5 kW Kohler genset in a sound shield, large enough (according to Carver) to run all electrical systems simultaneously. I would like to see a stronger, longer (for better leverage) valve handle on the 1-inch genset's cooling-water seacock. A Glendinning Cablemaster tub is to port aft and rudderboards made of carbon-fiber-reinforced hybrid polymer are through-bolted to the stringers. A pair of house batteries is mounted on the aft hull extension platform a full 3 feet above the bilge, which will allow a little extra transmit time for the radios in the event of flooding. Eleven batteries provide separate power sources to engine starters (which can cross-connect) and house, genset, and bow-thruster loads. Batteries are charged by engine-driven alternators and by charger-inverters fed by the genset or shore power. Space also is reserved for a 200 GPD watermaker aft of the port fuel tank.

The bilges are reasonably fair and neatly finished in gray gelcoat. There are a few spots where water can collect uphill from the stringers; more limber holes or, better yet, filling in the low spots to allow the existing limber holes to do their job would allow all the standing water to drain to the bilge pumps on centerline.

There's a full 59 inches of headroom in the engine room and about 3 feet between the engines, so it's a roomy environment in which to work. The 18-inch-high, 5-inch-wide stringers form the engine beds, which are capped with through-bolted ¼-inch angle steel to which the engine-mount supports are welded. Oil-level dipsticks and expansion tanks are accessible inboard, but the starboard engine's oil filters are outboard, making them much more difficult to reach. I would opt for the Volvo remote oil-filter option for better accessibility.

The starboard engine's cooling-water seacock hand valve was cut short to allow it to clear a nearby wiring bundle; I would relocate the seacock or the bundle. The trouble is that when the valve becomes difficult to operate over time, you might need the extra leverage of the longer handle. Both seacocks are also hard to reach and would benefit from the in-stallation of remote handles or relocation closer to centerline. The 1.75:1 ZF 7-degree down-angle gears drive 2½-inch Aquamet 17 shafts and 28-by-35-inch four-blade props set at an 11½-degree angle.

The saloon deck above the engine room is framed in aluminum and covered with plywood above and sound-deadening material below—an effective acoustic-isolation combination, judging from our sea trial results. The space's aluminum diamond-tread grating is a comfortable, easily cleaned working surface. Another smart feature is the gray-water system that collects from the sinks, showers, and air-conditioner condensate drain lines into a common sump and then is pumped overboard aft under the swim platform.

The 610 hp Volvo 122Ps (450 hp Cummins are standard) on our test boat are the largest engines available, so the space is more cramped than it would be with the standard Cummins 450s. Still, it's a generally roomy and accommodating engine room that should encourage regular maintenance.

Cockpit

Boarded from the integrated swim platform through the transom door, the 78-inch-long cockpit with its 5-foot deck overhang above offers a good spot to enjoy the fresh air out of the sun. The coamings are 28 inches high, which is perhaps adequate, but I would like to see a thicker bolster to create a toe space below for better balance in the absence of a recessed liner. Another concern is the hawsehole design above the stern cleats, formed by a single piece of stainless plate with a hole cut out above the cleat, which creates a potential for line chafing over time and especially under heavy strain. Nonskid in a neat molded pattern is effective at gripping deck shoes yet still easy to keep clean.

A single ladder leads up to the bridge; it is steep enough that you'll want to face it when climbing. For seniors and small children, the saloon's stairs are the way to go topside. Molded steps (on the narrow side at 6 in. wide aft to accommodate the wide-body saloon) lead to the side decks and on to the foredeck. The bow railing is well built of 1¼-inch rails and 1-

inch stanchions; however, it's too low at 21 inches aft and it leans well outboard, making the railing susceptible to piling damage and decreasing its effectiveness at the bow. A sunpad snaps in place on a recessed foredeck area to let you catch a few rays.

Saloon

As I entered the saloon from the cockpit through a classy, sliding stainless steel–framed door, my first impression was of light and space, and lots of both. Overhead lights are plentiful, headroom is an exceptional 7 feet, wraparound windows (with custom cherry blinds) are huge, and the combination of off-white headliners and flat-lacquered cherry cabinetry is both aesthetically pleasing and space-enhancing. Climate-controlled air (there are four different units and zones throughout the yacht) is introduced through cherry soffits overhead to eliminate cold spots and evenly diffuse airflow.

The saloon is divided into two distinct areas defined by the galley in between; aft lower (above the engine room) and forward upper (above the master stateroom). Aft, just inside the sliding door, a TV entertainment tender is immediately to port; the L-shaped lounge opposite is covered in Ultraleather like the rest of the yacht's interior seating, and has a pair of nifty recliners built in. A loveseat with a sleeper bed underneath is also available to port.

Galley

Located aft on the saloon's lower level, the L-shaped galley is well equipped with a microwave-convection oven, three-burner range with oven, side-by-side refrigerator-freezer (drawer-style pull-out units are also available), Karadon countertops, numerous drawers and cabinets, push-to-open door latches, chrome and brass faucets and fiddleboards, and an optional trash compactor. Two island-counter layouts to increase counter and storage space are available as well.

Forward Saloon

Up two steps and forward of the galley is the saloon's upper level, with the main electrical panel

immediately at the stairs for quick access. An L-shaped lounge is to port with room for five or six guests to keep the captain company. Stairs lead to the bridge above the lower saloon, and forward is the yacht's main helm.

Lower Helm Station

The futuristic-looking centerline lower helm offers good all-around visibility from the Flexsteel Ultraleather-covered electric helm seat. The windshield mullions are wide, though, noticeably reducing the captain's field of vision outside the yacht compared to other yachts in this class. However, this type of design will extend your boating season with a helm station in climate-controlled surroundings.

The seated helm position is a lot like driving a bus; that is, quite comfortable. The problem is that you can't drive or see standing up with the low-profile windows, which is why this is not a true pilot-house motor yacht—a lot of that headroom is carved out of the flybridge above. Four-function gauges indicate the essentials, and a combination engine-sync and rudder-angle indicator is on centerline. DDC-Volvo tachometers announce engine speed digitally. The windshields are large and clear, and are kept clean with large wipers, freshwater washes, and dash-mounted defrosters next to the saloon AC vents.

An electronics console is located overhead, along with a variety of rocker switches for the running lights, windshield wipers, horn, and bilge pumps—it must be like flying a plane. All these switches would be better located near the wheel. If you want to get fancy, you can order an autopilot system that's controlled from a joystick on the armrest. Unlike the aft saloon with its fabric overhead liner, the forward saloon overhead is all fiberglass. A sliding door leads directly to the starboard side deck opposite the helm station.

Flybridge

Reached from the saloon stairs or cockpit ladder, the flybridge offers something for everyone with a two-person helm seat to port, and a sink with icemaker and bottle storage area to starboard. Farther aft is a U-shaped lounge and a high-low table for conversion to a large sunpad; a second two-person seat is opposite to starboard. Aft on the cockpit overhang, an owner has the choice of a 600-pound-capacity davit with tender storage or a railing with sunpad.

Happily, the aluminum radar arch, made in-house by Carver, is far enough aft so as not to interfere too much with the captain's sight lines. Carver minds the details on the bridge, too, with electrical outlets, plastic screws holding the arch access plates in place to prevent corrosion, DC outlet adapters, and room for repeater electronics at the helm. The boat can be ordered with a bimini top but not a soft enclosure.

Accommodations

The gently curved companionway to starboard of the lower helm leads to the three-stateroom, two-head accommodations. The big master suite takes up the yacht's entire beam. It's beautifully appointed with cherry paneling all around, carefully crafted fabric headliners, and Karadon countertops. One cedar-lined closet holds the central-vacuum system, another holds separate washer and dryer units. The island bed's innerspring mattress is a full queen, and there's ample storage space in a built-in bureau, his and hers cedar lockers, and under the berth. The head is cleverly designed with separate tub-shower and toilet compartments and a sink-vanity in between, making excellent use of space. Headroom is 77 to 78 inches.

The yacht's second head is to starboard, with a separate one-piece shower with molded seat and access from both the companionway and the forward guest stateroom. The guest stateroom includes two 78-inch single berths, a locker, and an end table. Forward is the VIP guest stateroom with an island berth, hanging locker, overhead opening hatch above, and a pair of sidelights. The accommodations were impressive, and the nautical motif was carefully worked out by Carver's designers in a very tasteful setting. Four decors and four kinds of wood are available.

Performance Test

Our sea trial took place out of Staten Island Boat Sales facility on the south side of the island in 2- to 3-foot seas. I sat at the lower helm while we initially came up on plane; when we were at 1,500 rpm with the boat just barely on top, the horizon neatly bisected the windshield, offering an excellent view over the bow. The side windows are large, affording an excellent view abeam, and you also can see aft close aboard.

The sound levels in the saloon at the lower helm at 1,500 rpm with those muted Volvos were an impressively low 72 dBA (and 79 dBA at 2,200 rpm), encouraging conversation in normal tones. This was an excellent showing for Carver's sound-deadening crew and for Volvo.

There may not be a roomier 53-foot interior around, but the trade-off is that the hull's full, flat sections forward showed their limitations in the short, 1- to 2-foot chop with noticeable pounding. With trim tabs fully extended, the ride smoothed out somewhat, and handling in the small following sea seemed acceptable; I can't comment on the boat's heavy-sea handling. Laying-to in the trough, the boat showed good initial stability.

There are a few complaints to mention. On the bridge, the bright-white dashboard took its toll in the form of significant glare off the curved windshield, making it necessary to stand up and look over it. A darker color with flat gelcoat or paint would help. I would also like to see the helm seat pushed back a few more inches for more comfortable standing. The steering was quite stiff, taking significant physical effort to get the rudders to move at speed. The turning agility was unimpressive compared to similar yachts, taking a full 50 seconds and a large chunk of ocean to turn a full 360 degrees at cruise speed. On the other hand, the DDC-Volvo engine controls were a pleasure to operate, and made handling the yacht in the tight marina a breeze, even without resorting to the yacht's optional bow thruster.

✳ ✳ ✳

Carver put a lot of work into the 530 concept, and it has paid off in a very well-designed, ergonomically attuned package. The accommodations are well executed, the saloon offers a family-friendly layout for extended cruising, the galley has everything you could reasonably want for at-sea living, and the yacht is sturdily built for years of safe, low-maintenance service. The steering system needs improving, and don't expect to keep up with some of the British-built cruisers and U.S. convertibles in a 3- to 6-foot sea offshore. In fact, this hull form is the yacht's most significant drawback, limiting the yacht's usefulness, and is the only thing that prevents me from enthusiastically recommending it. However, you'll look in vain for a yacht with the interior space, smart styling, solid engineering, and comparatively low price of this recent offering from Carver.

Hatteras 6300

Hatteras 6300 Specifications

LOA:	63'0"
Beam:	18'3"
Draft:	5'6"
Displacement:	115,000 lb.
Fuel capacity:	1,290 gal.
Water capacity:	280 gal.

The name alone hints at the changes going on at Hatteras in 2001. This is the new Hatteras 6300, not the Hatteras 63, and it's a raised pilothouse motor yacht, not the flush-deck type that defined the builder's big Hargrave-designed floating palaces for so many years. In another nomenclature departure for Hatteras, this is really a 59-footer with a 63-foot running surface provided by the integral swim platform. Then there's the styling, distinctly Euro in every respect. This boat squarely meets evolving U.S. market demand. The construction, engineering, and propulsion systems are all vintage Hatteras, and the cherry interior woodworking (makore, also known as African cherry, is standard; maple is also available) shows a steady advance in the builder's fit-and-finish standards.

Hatteras may have incorporated Italian flair in the curvaceous superstructure, but not with the exaggerated, form-over-function predilection common to many Italian offerings. For instance, the side windows in the pilothouse, although shapely, are also large and offer excellent sight lines abaft the beam from the centerline lower helm station. And this yacht, designed specifically for the American upscale cruising market, has a wide-open main deck interior; the pilothouse, although raised well above main-deck level, is more a continuation of the big saloon than a separate space. This design works well on several fronts, including opening up the helmsman's visibility aft and making an already roomy interior seem larger still.

Hull Design

This hull, a departure in several ways for Hatteras, was tank-tested at Davidson Laboratory at Stevens Institute of Technology. The hull has a slightly warped bottom, which means that—relative to the waterline—the chines continue downhill as they approach the stern, with deadrise constantly decreasing aft. This feature contributes to the yacht's modest trim angle on plane, since buoyancy and dynamic lift aft are greater than on a constant-deadrise hull.

Forward, the hull has convex sections. This curvature delivers a smoother ride, with lower vertical accelerations especially noticeable in a head sea, and it makes the hull stronger—much like an eggshell is strong for its thickness. Convex curvature also makes for a wetter ride, though, since spray isn't so readily directed outward—an issue that Hatteras addresses with spray rails.

Swim Platform and Aft Deck

As with many production boats, the 6300 tipped the scales heavier than anticipated. In fact, the extra weight was evident with a glance at the submerged boarding ladder recessed under the swim platform. The yacht's heavier displacement also resulted in the swim-platform surface being just a few inches above the static waterline. If follow-on 6300 hulls are not to be made lighter, retooling to raise the platform surface and the ladder pocket would be a logical remedy. The yacht's transom incorporates the shore-power cable handlers and a large integral storage locker with a powered hatch for effortless access.

The aft deck, reached via a short flight of molded fiberglass stairs to starboard, is well protected from the elements by the extended upper deck. A seat spans the transom, molded steps lead to the side decks, and a hatch opens to the engine room and lazarette below. There are no stairs to the upper deck but they're available as an option, according to the builder. The unyielding 1¼-inch-diameter stainless steel bow railing starts at the cockpit's molded steps to the side decks, but it's quite low at just 25 inches (this is a catch-22 for many builders since market demand calls for low bow railings, but the builder's legal exposure increases as the railings get lower). To compensate, Hatteras is now adding a deckhouse-mounted handrail.

Engine Room

Down through that deck hatch, the cavernous lazarette (also available as crew quarters) features a pair of high-density composite rudderboards supporting the tops of the thick rudderposts. Located forward through an aluminum watertight door, this engine room takes its design from the builder's convertibles; that is, it's large, well lit, uncrowded, and superbly laid out for easy accessibility. There's lots of room all around those 1,400 hp Caterpillars, which actually look diminutive in the 5-foot, 7-inch headroom space. Fuel filter-separators, two per engine, are front and center for easy maintenance. Wiring is neatly routed and well protected from chafing. The Reverso oil-change system, immediately at the space entrance, is clearly labeled and ready to go. The twin Onan gensets are equally accessible, and the engine-gauge panels are angled just right for easy viewing from centerline or from the engine-room entrance.

The yacht's low vibration levels are accounted for, at least in part, by the very high, wide-based engine beds, integral to the hull's one-piece continuous stringer system. Not to belabor the point, but you don't see reduction gears this big on much else than a Hatteras or a tugboat. This would be the perfect boat with which to pull out old-growth stumps from the front yard of your waterfront home.

Saloon

When you come inside from the aft deck through the heavy stainless steel–framed sliding door, you'll see that the saloon has a U-shaped lounge to port and an icemaker and entertainment center opposite. The coolest feature here, at least for this antediluvian evaluator, is the plasma, flat-screen TV that appears out of nowhere from the starboard sideboard cabinetry. Hatteras has continued to refine its decor, and this 6300 is perhaps the builder's best effort to date with fit and finish. The overhead liner is nicely sculpted, Euro-style, with two shades of cream-colored vinyl cut in a circular dartboard pattern. Speaking of overhead, there's more than 80 inches of headroom in the saloon, which is both generous and space-enhancing. Indirect lighting is partially hidden by the cherry soffits above the side windows, which are large and extend low enough so you can see outside while seated.

Galley

Taking up 7 feet, 4 inches of the 16-foot, 10-inch-long saloon, the step-down galley forward in the saloon features a wraparound U-shaped Avonite countertop. A large sink with detachable spigot, four-burner electric stove, microwave-convection oven, dishwasher, and Sub-Zero drawer-type refrigerator-freezer were fitted on our test boat. The galley sole is finished with an Amtico faux teak and holly laminate, which Hatteras says it chose for its durability and ease of maintenance.

The galley is separated from the saloon by a low bulkhead that projects a foot or so above the countertop, and the result is a pleasant combination of privacy and social inclusion for the chef, with a clear all-around view of the proceedings from cockpit to pilothouse. There's no adjacent dinette, which is actually a bold departure from convention; instead, dinner is served at the pilothouse table just forward or back on the aft deck.

Pilothouse

Located a few steps up from the main deck level, the pilothouse is very much open to the saloon. This design makes the yacht's interior seem even more spacious than it already is, and the all-around, large windows create a pleasantly airy effect. People who love the great outdoors will love this layout. The real benefit, though, from this ship-driver's perspective, is the great visibility from the helm. You can back the boat into a slip from the lower helm, which is more than you can do with the vast majority of pilothouse motor yachts. The high-strength, green-water-resisting, tempered windshield panels are fashioned of huge sections of ⅜-inch frameless glass. In fact, all the topside windows are frameless, which means they won't ever leak because there are no frames to corrode, and the glass actually contributes to the stiffness of the deckhouse structure.

Do you ever wonder why more boats don't have helm stations laid out like a car or, better yet, like a truck, since that's the most comfortable po-sition from which to drive a boat? Well, the 6300's tilt wheel is ideally positioned right over your lap when you are seated. I'm not wild about the tachometer positioning immediately behind the wheel rim, and I prefer gauges to be lined up by pairs so you can see them more readily at a glance. But unlike more than a few other motor yachts, this one has an ergonomically angled electronics panel and a cream-colored dashboard that minimizes reflections off the big windshield above.

The throttles arguably should be mounted closer to horizontal to accommodate a more natural arm motion, but everything else about the helm station layout works well enough. I can't drive this boat without slouching when I'm standing up (the top of the windshield frames are just 5 ft., 1 in. high), but keeping the exterior profile within the stylist's bounds dictated a commensurately low window line.

The only downside to visibility, in fact, is the windshield mullions, which (unnecessarily, structurally) have boxy, visibility-hampering 6-inch-square cosmetic frames over the 2-inch-wide-by-6-inch-deep metal supports they enclose. Plus, the windshield wiper blades are long, but not quite long enough to reach the upper section of the windshield, which is precisely the part you'll be looking through if you are standing up to drive. Combined with the relatively short distance from the helm seat to the pulpit and the ample height of the seat above the waterline, the horizon is consistently visible above the anchor pulpit.

An expensive-looking aluminum door with an articulated hinge leads to the starboard weather deck, which makes getting forward from the pilothouse easy and quick. Our test boat's door didn't have a latch to hold it open, but the builder is making that standard equipment. Just behind the electrically operated helm and companion seats is an L-shaped lounge with dinette table. A seated guest's view through the windows would be improved by raising this seat, but the captain might lose some of the clear view astern.

Bridge

Up the flawlessly welded, polished stainless and teak ladder to the bridge, you open an inch-thick, smoke-colored Lexan door and walk out onto the upper deck. The bridge is tucked behind the raised pilothouse, which is what makes the pilothouse yacht such a great design: you get two levels of living space above the lower deck, but the profile is still fairly proportionate and the center of gravity manageable, at least on well-designed craft above 47 feet or so.

Hatteras has done a great job ergonomically at the upper helm station: the tilt wheel projects out from the console so it's easily and comfortably reached from the raised helm seat, and the single-lever engine controls are at just the right angle—approximately 20 degrees from horizontal—for precise throttle control. The bow-thruster control is exactly where it belongs, opposite the throttles to port of the wheel. The Caterpillar engine displays and start-stop panels are at the operator's fingertips, and the engine gauges are tangent to the operator's line of sight for clear viewing. The rudder-angle indicator is on centerline, just where you would expect it to be on any well-found vessel.

The windscreen is too low and far forward to offer any real protection from wind and spray, but its pipe frame provides a good handhold, and the low profile is a nice styling detail. There's ample room to starboard for electronics, though the panel is not angled toward the helmsman as might be expected.

The bridge deck is very roomy, with an L-shaped lounge to port and aft of the helm, and a large cabinet to starboard with a sink and two refrigerator-icemakers. A dramatic aluminum and fiberglass radar arch will support any possible combination of antennas and running lights. It also takes a significant chunk out of the captain's horizon, particularly to port, and it adds significant topside weight, so perhaps a mast would be more appropriate for this yacht. As it happens, Hatteras is investigating a lighter-arch design. The cantilevered aft deck, supported by a fiberglass-encapsulated aluminum framework, is as solid as a concrete slab, and offers a secure foundation for the yacht's tender. A cleverly concealed 1,100-pound-capacity davit appears out of nowhere to launch or recover the tender.

Cabin

Curved stairs lead down from the pilothouse and past the washer-dryer to the three-stateroom lower deck, which has an open and roomy feel to it. The full-beam master suite is amidships, and its 7 feet, 1 inch of headroom and generous dimensions combine with the double entrance doors to make it an unusually commodious suite. I don't think I've ever seen a yacht this size with so much master-stateroom headroom and such a comfortable layout.

From an engineering perspective, it's the height of the master-stateroom sole above the hull that drives the height of the pilothouse sole above, and ultimately defines the yacht's exterior profile. Hatteras has done an excellent job of blending generous headroom with a good-looking profile; to put it another way, the yacht's significant height is camouflaged by the curvaceous styling.

The master's queen-size island berth, more than 6 feet, 5 inches long, is oriented athwartships like the other berths, and is surrounded by a multitude of beautifully crafted, matched-grain cherry drawers and cabinet doors. Hatteras's joinery craftsmanship is really on display down there. The private head is also appealing, with a separate tub-shower and ample room to maneuver. Worth mentioning, too, are the 10-by-19-inch opening portholes, which are larger than usual and most welcome in dispelling the cave-like feeling aboard lesser yachts. A little larger, like on the Hatteras 75, and they could actually be used for emergency egress.

Forward to starboard is a guest or crew stateroom with bunk beds, and opposite is a second head with a separate stall shower. The guest suite with island queen and private head is forward.

Construction

The builder's smallest cruising yacht, the Hatteras 6300 is conventionally built with a 3-ounce skin coat of mat in the hull bottom and wet out in vinylester resin to prevent blistering. The heavily laid up hull is solid fiberglass below the waterline, and the hull sides, bulkheads, stringers, superstructure, and decks are cored with Divinycell structural foam for greater stiffness at a more moderate weight. The interior soles are vacuum-bagged to ensure a sound outer-skin-to-core bond line. The hull-to-deck joint is ruggedly fashioned, being screwed, bonded, and then fiberglassed from the inside. Interior cabin module subassemblies and cabinetry are solid-wood laminates.

Performance Test

Hatteras yachts, most notably the convertibles, are well regarded for their seakeeping abilities, so let's see how the 6300 fared by comarison. Massive displacement resulting from heavy construction and deep reduction gears driving large-diameter, six- or seven-bladed propellers are factors in every Hatteras yacht's performance equation. The all-new 6300 is no exception, as we found out on our calm-water sea trial. We cast off from Hatteras's New Bern, North Carolina, waterfront manufacturing facility and headed down the Neuse River with a full liquid load and six passengers and light gear on board.

I'll say up front, this is one fast pilothouse motor yacht; weighing in at an imposing 115,000 pounds, we made an honest 31.5 knots at full throttle, 2,350 rpm, with our optional twin Caterpillar 3412s cranking out 1,400 hp each. At a comfortable 2,000 rpm cruise, we averaged 25.5 knots, and made 22 knots throttled back to 1,800 rpm. The boat was comfortably on plane, with a clean wake astern and a rise in center of gravity, with 1,450 rpm producing 16 knots.

That the boat performed so well despite its considerable displacement is testimony to the propulsion efficiency inherent in large, slower-turning propellers moving a huge volume of water; to the hull's low-deadrise sections aft; and to the yacht's extended running surface provided by an integral swim platform. Another benefit of this deep-geared drivetrain, which is largely unique to Hatteras, is that (according to Hatteras) hull speed is less sensitive to weight changes and sea state; the boat just keeps bulling its way along, come hell or high water. The larger shafts and propellers add weight and cost, and require larger propeller pockets, but the improved performance—in Hatteras's view—makes it all worthwhile.

The power hydraulic steering was responsive and reasonably low effort, at 3.7 turns lock-to-lock. We averaged 48 seconds making 360-degree port and starboard turns at 2,000 rpm, which is about average for a motor yacht this size. The yacht banks away, initially, and then slightly into the turn—the latter being a welcome characteristic. In addition to the yacht's sheer speed capability, the steep 3.45:1 gears and 39-by-73½-inch seven-blade props dug in at the Caterpillars' idle speed of 700 rpm better than many convertibles do at 1,000 rpm. The result, when docking and undocking, was instantaneous clutch response and wonderfully satisfying dockside handling.

Sight lines from the flybridge are excellent, except close aboard directly aft, so backing into an unfamiliar slip would be better undertaken—believe it or not—from the pilothouse helm station. The boat seems to be well balanced longitudinally, so it comes up on plane without tabs at up to 7 degrees of trim, and then settles out to run at about 4.5 degrees at cruise speed. During the transition to plane, the bow stays well below the visible horizon from the lower helm, so sight lines ahead are unobstructed at all speeds and conditions of loading.

In addition to the vessel's appropriately located longitudinal center of gravity, the modest bow rise is due to the extended running surface, which compensates for the loss of buoyancy and dynamic lift created by the voluminous propeller pockets. Those pockets allow the propellers to be recessed farther into the hull, reducing draft and delivering more horizontal thrust with shaft angles set at an efficiency-enhancing 6 degrees. The exit region of the pockets can be shaped to focus and deflect thrust downward, lowering the bow, which is a nice ace up the builder's sleeve when it comes to influencing trim on plane.

Compared to other yachts, the 6300's internal sound levels were especially muted at low speed: in the saloon I recorded 64 dBA at 700 rpm, idle speed; 79 dBA at 2,000 rpm; and 80 dBA at 2,100 rpm, which—although fairly quiet considering there's 2,800 hp rumbling away right under your feet—is about average for high-end yachts of this class. The master suite just forward of the engine room is the real acoustic-isolation star in Hatteras's 6300 galaxy, with just 76 dBA at 2,000 rpm, significantly better than many similar yachts. Though not measured, vibration levels seemed satisfyingly low, a big point for Hatteras with its oversized gears and slow-turning, many-bladed props.

Hatteras has long been an industry legend, and the company intends to regain its leadership standing by producing all-new models that hit squarely that moving target known as market demand. The 6300, with its 40-knot hull form, is the first fruit of this effort. This new yacht has much to commend it, but there's also room for improvement. I would like to see the flawless, ripple-free tooling being produced by much of Hatteras's competition (this yacht's exterior finish was lacking in that department); higher bow railings; substantially lighter displace-

ment through the use of modern boatbuilding methods and materials; a higher swim platform; and narrower windshield mullions to improve helm station visibility.

A few years ago, Hatteras's joinery wasn't on a par with the finer European and custom U.S.-built yachts. It still isn't, but it's much closer in quality now; there are just enough barely detectable, epoxy-filled joinery gaps to drop it down a notch from the very best. All in all, however, Hatteras has produced a wonderfully ergonomic, family-friendly, and seaworthy mini-megayacht. The interior layout is intelligently executed, especially with the spacious and airy saloon-pilothouse. The AC, incidentally, could quickly turn the boat into a large refrigerator in a tropical climate.

The exceptional headroom, huge engine room, comfortable master suite, sheltered aft deck, and large bridge deck are all pluses. And the convertible-like performance is marvelous to behold. Hatteras has managed to design the boat with grace and style, without overdoing it and losing sight of what's most important in a practical seagoing vessel.

An electronics package and 800 hp Caterpillar 3406 diesels are included in the base price. If you need more speed, the 1,400 hp Cat 3412s I tested or the DDC 1,480 hp 12V 2000s are available.

1998 Krogen 49 Express

Krogen 49 Express Specifications

LOA:	49'6"
Beam:	14'9"
Draft:	4'0"
Weight:	39,000 lb.
Fuel capacity:	600 gal.
Water capacity:	300 gal.

Shown here is the Krogen 53, which is the same as the Krogen 49 except for its larger cockpit.

Kadey-Krogen has been building small ships, otherwise known as displacement trawlers, for a long time. But if you want to go faster than 10 knots or so, you need a planing hull. That led Krogen to start the Krogen Express line, much like Grand Banks started up Eastbay.

The Krogen 49 Express is a plumb-bow, hardchine cruiser that combines something of the classic (and classy) looks of a commuter yacht with the user-friendliness of the pilothouse motor yacht. This interior arrangement works well because the pilothouse is centrally located just a few steps away from both the saloon and the bridge, yet it's high enough off the water to create a more distant horizon.

Cockpit

Starting the tour back aft, the 6-foot, 6-inch-by-12-foot, 10-inch cockpit is about the safest you'll find anywhere with its 39-inch-high bulwarks that keep your feet firmly planted on the genuine teak sole. Massive stainless steel hawsepipes with integral cleats are mounted on the hull sides and transom in each aft corner, giving you a chafe-free fair lead in any direction.

Freshwater and saltwater washdowns are provided, and molded steps lead to the 20-inch-wide side decks with rock-solid 38-inch-high side rails and 31-inch bow rails, all crafted of flawlessly welded stainless. The 12-inch bow and spring cleats handle mooring duties and a beautifully executed pulpit makes quick work of anchoring; two sets of ground tackle can be accommodated in double chain lockers.

The lazarette below the cockpit has sufficient room for mooring lines and fenders. The rudderposts are affixed to massive support members; one is fitted for an emergency steering tiller.

Saloon

A pair of double swinging doors leads from the cockpit to the 13-by-11-foot, beautifully crafted saloon. With huge side windows—complete with blinds and draw curtains—and 6 feet, 11 inches of headroom, these proportions make you feel like you're in someone's home library. Our boat was heavy on nicely worked teak that contrasted attractively with a soft-white padded headliner. To port is a pair of stuffed chairs, storage bins, and built-in hutch with bookshelves.

Across to starboard are an L-shaped lounge with storage below and a drop-leaf table that lowers to support a berth insert to create a full-size bed. Forward to starboard is a bar-height countertop that separates the galley from the saloon. The height is fine for standup eating and meal preparation, and the entertainment center fits inside.

Galley

The galley is laid out to provide privacy for the chef (the high countertop) and proximity to the saloon. A full-size refrigerator is forward, as is a microwave oven. Outboard to starboard is a four-burner ceramic cooktop with pan holders and an oven below. A large sink is built into the island counter with its Corian countertop, and an icebox-freezer is built in below, making efficient use of the counter's inside corner. Wraparound cabinets are built in overhead, a trash receptacle is built in next to the oven, and more storage space and drawers are provided below the sink. This is a galley that's clearly set up for serious cruising, trawler-style.

Saloon Storage

There's a huge dry-storage space in the bilge below the saloon, accessed through a hatch that is in a machinery-removal deck section. Inside are house batteries, a Glendinning Cablemaster cable-storage bin, and two engine mufflers. A panel in the forward bulkhead comes out so that tired machinery in the abutting engine room can be removed and sent up through the big hatch in the saloon for repair.

Krogen would do well to add hatches outboard in the saloon deck so you can get to the capacious bilge areas outboard of the mufflers—and Krogen would be glad to accommodate such a request if asked. Cockpit vents admit combustion air, creating a continuous airflow through the lazarette and saloon bilge area and on the engine room, keeping everything dry and well ventilated belowdecks while cruising. The bilges are ground smooth and gelcoated white for good visibility.

Pilothouse

Three finely crafted companionway steps next to the galley lead up to the teak pilothouse, which looks in scale and purposeful layout like that of a small ship. The centerline helm is well laid out with its 24-inch stainless wheel surrounded by gauges and switches that are easy to see and operate. Our test boat had custom electronics boxes (added by the owner after delivery) in cabinetry that perfectly matched the original woodwork. Even if you lose your glasses overboard, you'll be able to stay on course with the big 6-inch Danforth compass up on the dashboard.

Visibility through the large glass windows was good, although blind zones are created by the 9-inch-wide windshield mullions—these should be narrower. A small overhead hatch opens to let in a little fresh air, and (slightly sticky) sliding side doors lead directly out to the weather decks.

Behind the helm is a very salty-looking and extremely comfortable lounge seat situated a full 40 inches off the deck for a good view. The seat bottom slides out and is supported by the telescoping table for conversion to a watch berth for the captain or first mate. As in the saloon, the teak and holly sole is beautifully crafted.

Bridge

A ladder leads to the bridge from the pilothouse. The helm is on centerline with a large stainless wheel (6½ turns lock-to-lock) and optional Mathers controls perfectly positioned to starboard. The instrument panel would benefit from being tilted up 20 degrees or so (for when the operator is standing), but the overall layout with electronics forward and aft of the gauges works well. Visibility is excellent, although you'll want to have someone relaying from the cockpit when you're backing into a slip. A large L-shaped lounge is built in and, back aft, our boat's owner had installed two center-facing lounge seats and a spot for the tender and davit.

Cabin

Another set of steps leads from the pilothouse—in this case, down to the cabin with its master stateroom forward and guest stateroom or office to starboard. The well-designed and nautically appointed master suite has up to 94 inches of headroom. The berth has generous storage room below in drawers and a storage bin. Hanging lockers are provided to port and starboard, and a dresser is built into the aft bulkhead. Access panels allow inspection of hidden wiring and plumbing running behind the finished surfaces. Four chrome-plated opening ports ring the side of the trunk cabin above, and a hatch overhead provides an escape route.

The master head to port has a vacuum toilet; Corian countertop with sink and storage cabinets; and a separate one-piece shower with teak grating, a molded seat, and an opening porthole.

The guest stateroom, located immediately at the foot of the companionway stairs, can accommodate three on an L-shaped lounge that converts to a 6-foot, 4-inch berth and the 6-foot Pullman overhead. A dresser with drawers and storage locker below is next to the lounge, and a linen locker and hanging locker are built into the aft bulkhead. Krogen now offers an alternative guest-stateroom arrangement that is worth asking about. The guest head, equipped much like the master, is across the companionway to port, and a washer-dryer unit is aft of the guest stateroom, readily accessible from the companionway.

Engine Room

The engine room is entered from the forward companionway, and its proportions and headroom (6 ft.) are enough to make any chief engineer happy. Back aft (under the galley) are the intermediate shafts connecting the engines to the thrust bearings, which are supported by massive gusseted aluminum foundations bolted to the stringers. These remote thrust bearings allow the engines to float freely on their beds for maximum vibration attenuation, while also minimizing noise-induced rumblings throughout the yacht.

Near the aft bulkhead a Westerbeke generator is mounted in its acoustic enclosure. The fuel filter-separator and seacock are outboard to port over the propeller shaft with manageable but not great accessibility. Copper fuel-return lines (I prefer aircraft-type hoses and compression fittings) run overhead back to the aluminum fuel tanks. Perforated stainless panels that cover acoustic insulation line the engine room, making the yacht's interior very quiet indeed. The main fuel manifold is to port, and it allows either engine to take suction from either tank. Our test boat also had a fuel-transfer pump and an oil-changing pump installed.

The engines are mounted on heavy aluminum channels through-bolted to the top of the hull stringers. The engines are soft-mounted on Aquadrive vibration isolators, topping off an extremely rugged engine foundation. Thoughtful features abound, like the diamond-pattern deck plates that create flat working surfaces, and the drip pans provided under the engines that make the bilges easier to keep clean. Access between the engines is excellent, so routine daily checks and maintenance will be undemanding. The engine cooling-water seacocks and strainers are forward of the engines, recessed in the bilge—which, unfortunately, would make the seacocks difficult to reach in an emergency.

Construction

The Krogen has a solid fiberglass bottom with two layers of 1.5-ounce mat in a premium vinylester resin to prevent osmotic blistering. Fiberglass high-hat stringers are laid up in a male mold, tabbed in place, and then encapsulated in fiberglass. The stringers are hollow except in way of the engine room, where they are cored with mahogany to absorb the engine-mounting-bolt compression loads and to help attenuate vibration. Stringer limber holes are lined with PVC pipe sections sealed in place with fiberglass putty.

Divinycell foam-cored bulkheads, superstructure, and decks and Airex foam-cored hull sides cut the weight down in this semiplaning vessel while increasing strength. A cored bottom would increase impact resistance and further reduce weight- and wave-induced sound levels, but it's a difficult feature to market because of a few well-publicized bad examples. The hull-to-deck joint, subjected to great stress as the hull works through a seaway, is screwed together and then fiberglassed in place from the inside for a permanent, waterproof, and high-strength bond.

Performance Test

We had a good day for a sea trial, with 20-plus-knot winds kicking up a 3- to 5-foot sea atop a 4- to 6-foot groundswell. As soon as we cleared Florida's Jupiter Inlet, we were in 6-footers breaking across the bar. The Krogen's deep, sharp forefoot paid instant dividends with a smooth, stately ride, completely unperturbed by the rollers rushing by us. At 17 knots heading right into the sea, the boat rode extremely well, more like a small ship (not to overdo the comparison) than anything else.

The boat handled reasonably nimbly, managing a 360-degree turn at 16 knots in just over 30 seconds. With moderate tabs in a head sea or with the seas broad on the bow, the ride was reasonably dry, with occasional spray hitting the windshield. Performance data for the Krogen 49 Express is listed in the accompanying table.

Sound levels were moderate in the saloon and pilothouse. The saloon started out far quieter and ended up about even with the pilothouse, probably due to the increasing exhaust noise levels. Our 350 hp Caterpillar 3116s turned 26-by-22-inch four-blade props on 2-inch Aquamet 17 (economy-grade) shafts. Steeper gears (say, 2.5:1) with larger-diameter, slower-turning props may well be better suited to this semidisplacement hull and might have improved the performance numbers—but at the cost of commensurately increased draft.

Running the boat from the pilothouse left me wanting better visibility ahead. The bow is very high for a boat this size, which makes it difficult to see over it, especially with the pulpit projecting beyond. If the pilothouse deck were 6 or 8 inches higher, it would have helped.

Krogen 49 Express Performance Results

RPM	Speed, knots	Speed, mph	Fuel Use, gph	Nautical mpg	Statute mpg	Range, nm	Range, statute miles	Salon Noise Level, dBA	Helm Noise Level, dBA	Trim, degrees
800	5.7	6.6	1.6	3.6	4.10	1,924	2,212	60	66	0
1,000	7.6	8.7	2.5	3.0	3.50	1,642	1,888	62	67	0.5
1,400	9.0	10.4	5.1	1.8	2.03	953	1,096	67	70	1
1,600	9.8	11.3	8.0	1.2	1.41	661	761	68	71	1.5
1,800	10.3	11.8	11.9	0.86	1.00	467	538	70	73	2.5
2,000	12.4	14.3	15.7	0.79	0.91	426	490	72	75	3.5
2,200	14.2	16.3	19.9	0.71	0.82	385	443	74	78	3.5
2,400	16.6	19.1	25.5	0.65	0.75	351	404	78	78	4
2,600	18.4	21.2	30.3	0.61	0.70	328	377	78	78	4
2,780	19.7	22.7	35.5	0.55	0.64	300	345	81	79	5

The Krogen 49 took the seas in stride from any direction, and had a very solid, capable, trawler-like feel to it. This boat instills confidence quickly in its seakeeping ability. With its 17-knot cruise capability, it has an excellent blend of seaworthiness and rock-solid stability with speed and good handling characteristics. Running in a following or quarter sea, the boat wandered a little around its heading, but not unreasonably so.

The steering's 6½ turns lock-to-lock should be reduced to 4 turns, and it would be great to have power steering on this boat.

All told, I was satisfied with the Krogen's handling; it is a good running boat in any direction to the sea. The bow is deep and sharp enough to slice effortlessly through some nasty chop, but not so much so that it lacks the necessary lift and buoyancy in a following sea.

For anyone in the market for a fast trawler, the Krogen is well worth considering. This 49-footer is built to a high standard, and the Krogen is by any measure a well-found, solidly constructed vessel of excellent craftsmanship. My only real complaints concern a few engine-room issues, the visibility restriction over the bow, and the 6½ turns steering. Offering a good compromise between a true displacement trawler's unparalleled range and seakeeping and an inshore boat's flat-out speed capa-

bility and shoal draft, the Krogen Express does many things very well indeed.

Dutch-Canadian yacht builder Neptunus builds high-end cruising yachts ranging from a 41-foot express to an intriguing 65-foot enclosed flybridge motor yacht. The Neptunus 60 motor yacht shown is a good-performing yacht with a luxurious interior. A midships full-beam master suite and a big, open saloon-pilothouse give the builder bragging rights to an appealing design. This is one of the relatively few North American production builders that almost matches the Europeans at their own woodworking game. The modified-V hull form delivers a smooth and dry ride offshore, and modest displacement (due to intelligent structural engineering) delivers good propulsion economy and speed.   NEPTUNUS

Carver's 570 pilothouse motor yacht is the flagship of its fifteen-model lineup, which starts at 32 feet. The 570 is a stretched version of the 530, which adds room to the saloon and master suite, and improves the boat's performance in a seaway. Carver's joinery and interior-accommodation plans have come a long way in the last decade. Its use of frameless windows, structural aluminum, and composites has produced some of the better-engineered boats in their class. Low-deadrise, hard-riding hull forms are really the only limitation, detracting from the yachts' practicality as cruisers in sloppy offshore conditions.   CARVER

Silverton, part of the Luhrs-Silverton-Mainship-Hunter boatbuilding conglomerate, is a well-regarded builder of relatively affordable family cruising yachts. Its motor-yacht series ranges from a 32-footer up to this flagship Silverton 453 aft-cabin motor yacht. Silverton's "sidewalk" design widens the deckhouse to the hull's beam, creating the large interior so much in demand in today's market. The sidewalk is used to navigate from bow to stern via the flybridge. These are some of the better-running yachts of their class, with ample deadrise to smooth out a stiff offshore chop.

SILVERTON

Hatteras Yachts is a well-known builder of high-end semicustom flush-deck and pilothouse motor yachts, as well as production sport-fishermen. The product range is from 50 to 100 feet, although the company built larger yachts for a few years; the 92 motor yacht, part of Hatteras's Elite series, is one of the largest the company builds. It has a raised-pilothouse configuration with a full-beam master stateroom on the lower deck and a saloon and "country kitchen" forward on the main deck. The 100-foot motor yacht adds an 8-foot cockpit.   HATTERAS

Here's an example of Silverton's latest handiwork, the saloon of a 453 pilothouse motor yacht. Note the starboard side helm station, positioned so the operator has a better view of the give-way side according to the Rules of the Road. Windshield mullions are narrow yet strong, causing little interference with the captain's sight lines ahead.   SILVERTON

Here's one of metal-boat designer Bruce Roberts's latest creations, the Trawler Yacht 57 pilothouse motor yacht. It's available in steel or aluminum; either way, it's a sturdy little ship ready for extended cruising. Roberts provides boat kits with precut frames, plates, and other hull and deck components ready to weld together, or CAD cutting files. STEVE DAVIS ILLUSTRATION, COURTESY BRUCE ROBERTS

Aft-Cabin Motor Yachts

For the cruising family, the aft cabin motor yacht makes a lot of sense. The master suite, including the stateroom and head, are separated from the rest of the staterooms by the saloon, offering privacy. The guest staterooms are forward and the saloon amidships, with the engine room below the saloon. This layout is ideal for two couples or for a couple with kids. What you may give up is a cockpit with all its conveniences and utility, though some manufacturers offer aft-cabin yachts with cockpits, too. More than a few builders have produced aft cabins initially and then added cockpit extensions in response to market demand. Convertibles have also been produced in aft-cabin versions, with the master suite replacing the cockpit. The most successful such designs include exterior exhaust lines with the exhaust exiting the hull at the engine room and ducted aft via fiberglass tubes incorporated in the hull side at the waterline. This frees up more space in the master suite, the sole of which is placed as low as possible in the hull to minimize the height of the cabintop.

Variations on the aft-cabin theme include the Dettling 51, which places the master suite under the pilothouse, aft of the saloon, with the engine room in the stern (see review beginning on page 424). Carver, Silverton, Mainship, Viking, and Hatteras are among the builders who have produced successful aft-cabin designs.

1997 Carver 445 Aft-Cabin Motor Yacht

If you're looking to make the most of your seagoing real estate, it's hard to beat the sheer internal volume of the aft-cabin cruiser layout. Not only do you get the cabin and saloon of a conventional sedan cruiser, but you also gain an extra stateroom and head in an area that's relatively secluded from the rest of the boat and its occupants. Carver's 445 aft-cabin motor yacht is a well-built, contemporarily styled yacht that will be as appealing ten years from now as it is today, both from a practical and an aesthetic perspective.

Aft Deck

You board the Carver from its full-beam swim platform and walk up the integral staircase. The 8-by-13-foot aft deck is a natural hub of activity,

Carver 445 Aft-Cabin Motor Yacht Specifications

LOA:	44'7"
Beam:	15'0"
Draft:	5'1"
Displacement:	32,000 lb. (full load)
Fuel capacity:	500 gal.
Water capacity:	165 gal.
Holding:	80 gal.

midway between the bridge above and the saloon below. This split-level arrangement is ideal for many cruising families, with the aft deck serving as a great place to entertain dockside or offshore. It's fully enclosed by a hardtop and side curtains with screens, so unless the snow is flying, it should be usable. A refrigerator, icemaker, and storage cabinet with sink comprise a very workable wet bar forward. The Carver's excellent tooling is nowhere more evident than on the hardtop's mirror-smooth headliner.

Bridge

There is room for five to seven guests to join you on the bridge. The helm's raised pedestal seat puts you way up there off the deck, so you can see well all around except close in aft; for backing into a slip, you'll need a spotter aft.

The separate engine controls are located on either side of the wheel: shifts to port and throttles to starboard. The instruments are easy to read, spread out to their corresponding engine's side; however, I prefer clustered instruments lined up vertically in pairs (for example, both oil-pressure gauges together) since they're easier to read at a glance. The Carver has a rudder-angle indicator—a convenient feature—and the compass is mounted directly in front of the operator, rather than higher up and closer to the skipper's sightlines. There's room for electronics to starboard on a panel that's perpendicular to the operator's line of sight.

On either side, clear Lucite doors open to the 16-inch-wide side decks, which have effective non-skid and one of the best stainless railings I've seen: it's 32 inches high forward and exceptionally stiff. The molded anchor pulpit is sturdy and well designed; two bow cleats, two pairs of spring cleats, and two stern cleats—all 12 inches—handle mooring chores with ease.

Saloon

Two outward-swinging doors (a bifold might be more convenient) open on the aft deck to access the saloon companionway's five steps. I can't think of another 44-foot boat with a larger saloon than the Carver's. At 20 feet long by 11 feet, 6 inches wide, there's room for a dinner party, dance, or perhaps a rodeo. The furnishings and decor are conservative and a lot like my living room at home. It's also bright and cheery with space-enhancing maple woodwork, large windows, and excellent headroom throughout. Divided into two open areas on different levels, the living area is aft with a single seat and entertainment center to port, and a large L-shaped settee to starboard with a pull-out berth beneath.

Down another four steps forward (these steps swing up for good engine-room access) is a U-shaped convertible dinette to port. To starboard is a user-friendly galley with a full-size refrigerator, optional dishwasher, carousel microwave-convection oven, three-burner range with oven, and a coffeemaker. A washer-dryer unit and lower helm are options.

Accommodations

Forward of the galley is the nicely detailed guest stateroom with a full 82 inches of headroom, a twin-size berth, a cedar hanging locker, and private head access. The head has a separate shower, manual-flush toilet, and large sink with storage below. Some of the yacht's more complex joinery is in this area, and all of it is impressively executed with satin-smooth finish and tight joints.

Located down four steps from the saloon, the aft master stateroom is reasonably roomy at 8 feet long and 10 feet, 6 inches wide. It's also light and pleasant with the bleached-maple interior, large opening side windows, and a full 78 inches of headroom. The 6-foot, 6-inch by 5-foot island berth has ample room to walk around, and there's lots of storage space in hanging lockers and cabinets. However, it's worth noting that there aren't so many cabinets, especially at eye level, that you start feeling closed in as you do on other yachts. A sliding mirrored door leads to the large private head with its separate shower, 6-foot countertop, vanity, and manual-flush toilet.

The lazarette and steering gear are accessed through a pair of hatches and by lifting the berth top out of the way. I was impressed by the scantlings of the rudderpost support—very heavy-duty aluminum well spaced vertically to give the rudderstock excellent support and prevent hull damage in the event of its striking an underwater object.

Engine Room

The galley steps lift up for access to the engine room. Carver makes you feel like you're the owner of a small ship with its generously proportioned engine room. With 57 inches of headroom and nearly 4 feet of space between the engines, you or your mechanic won't feel too crowded. Nevertheless, my comments on the Carver's engine room will prove my ambivalence; as on most boats, many things are done very well but there is always room for improvement. I'll start with machinery access: the space is large and roomy, but the scantlings of the huge integral molded engine beds, stringers, and cross members represent overkill. These engines are only 450 hp and a little more than 2,000 pounds, after all. Access to the engines—and forward and aft within the space—would benefit from more modestly and appropriately proportioned structural members.

The enclosed 9 kW Kohler generator (standard equipment) is immediately to port as you enter the engine room, just forward of the main engine; across to starboard is the 20-gallon Raritan water heater with holding tank immediately outboard. The main engine cooling-water seacocks are off the beaten path below the respective flywheels (and inside those big stringers). Long hoses run aft to the nearly inaccessible raw-water strainers and then to the engine pumps, a tortuous path to be sure. The bottom line is: for safety in an emergency, seacocks and strainers should be close to the engine room entrance and readily accessible. The fuel filter-separators are inboard of the engines farther aft above the stringers, and the petcock on the starboard drain bowl is directly above the stringer, which would make it difficult to drain into a bucket. A new bracket could easily fix that. Carver is looking into making the seacocks, strainers, and fuel filter-separators more accessible.

There is no fuel manifold on the Carver, which means you can't cross-connect fuel suction and return from one tank to the other. A fuel-transfer pump keeps the tanks level if the need arises. The flared aircraft-type fuel fittings should ensure many years of worry-free fuel lines.

The engine-bed stringers are really oversized, making it more difficult to maneuver around them. The engine stringers are part of an all-fiberglass unitized structural gridwork of trapezoidal members that extends from one end of the engine room to the other. The aluminum engine-mounting brackets supporting the engine-isolation mounts are gusseted for greater strength and less chance of metal fatigue over time. This is an excellent system structurally, with no chance of rot because a wood core (with all its superfluous weight) doesn't exist.

The 250-gallon, 5052-grade aluminum fuel

tanks outboard of the engines appeared to be securely installed, although there was a hard spot where the tank bottom angles up forward and meets the lip edge of its foundation. Wiring is generally neatly routed and protected by either looming or plastic cableway boxes.

Construction

The Carver is solidly built, starting with a premium gelcoat and a skin coat of hand-laid mat and vinylester resin to prevent osmotic blistering. The bottom is a solid laminate; the sides are cored in Coremat and balsa core. The hull's stringer grid system is a one-piece laminate laid up in a female mold and then inverted, tabbed, and fiberglassed to the hull bottom. This method results in a solid hull structure, the integrity of which can't easily be replicated by a stick-built structure of the same weight; it also locks the hull into shape, effectively preventing wracking and distortion.

Plywood bulkheads are set into the liner and glassed in place. The decks and superstructure are cored with balsa to save weight, which is an efficient engineering structure. Be certain you don't drill holes through any of these composite structures, though. Water penetration into the balsa, which can easily result from improperly bedded screw and bolt holes, will result in delamination and loss of physical properties of the composite sandwich. The hull-to-deck joint is bonded permanently by Sikaflex polyurethane adhesive clamped together by stainless self-tapping screws.

Performance Test

Our sea trial took place on a warm August day out of Plymouth, Massachusetts, in a 10-knot wind with a full liquid load and two passengers on board. Getting underway from the dock, the boat handled crisply with the rudders amidships, easily spinning around and predictably threading through the mooring buoys that encroached right up to the dock itself. It may be because I had just tested a couple of mid-30-foot boats, but this seemed like a very big, solid, and stable boat throughout our sea trial.

The twin Cummins 450 hp Diamond Series diesel engines were impressively quiet throughout the speed spectrum, making this boat very comfortable on the ears as well. This is no doubt due to the excellent job Carver has done with sound insulation plus the inherently quiet, well-balanced Cummins diesels. The accompanying table summarizes performance results for the Carver 445.

Carver 445 Performance Results			
RPM	Speed, knots	Saloon Noise Level, dBA	Aft Deck Noise Level, dBA
1,000	8.0	70	80
1,200	8.9	71	81
1,400	9.8	72	82
1,600	10.9	73	82
1,800	12.6	75	83
2,000	15.7	76	84
2,200	19.0	80	84
2,400	21.8	82	84

This is no speed boat—even with respectable power being developed by the two Cummins diesels—but a 16-knot cruise will prove adequate for many cruising families. The Carver has quite full and flat bottom sections forward, which was apparent when we crossed the 3- to 5-foot wakes of the Plymouth whalewatching boats at 17 to 19 knots—we pounded noticeably. From a passenger's perspective, the ride was very stable and comfortable (in calm water), with an easy motion. Dockside, it seemed less susceptible to a crosswind than other aft-cabin yachts of its size, making for less thrilling approaches to the fuel pier; the foot-deep keel helps in that respect.

For a boat with 900 hp, I was surprised at the below-22-knot speed, especially given the yacht's moderate weight, nearly flat bottom, and inherently efficient drivetrain. This boat's shafts were set at a reasonably efficient 12 degrees (8 to 12 degrees is fine for a 25-knot boat) with relatively deep 2.9:1 reduction gears and large 32-by-38-inch props; that's moving a lot of water. The Cummins diesels are rated at 2,600 rpm, so some of the lack of speed was due to either a need for engine-tuning or a too-large propeller. In any event, the engines weren't developing rated power. Carver thinks the solution lies in trimming 2 inches of pitch off the props, which it will address with its dealers. That seems like a reasonable solution for achieving rated rpm and for increasing full-power speed. The Carver factory reports achieving 24.3 knots at 2,700 rpm.

The Carver 44 is a well-finished yacht squarely at the head of the class (quality-wise) of high-volume production boats. There's nothing out there in this price range that's any better in terms of interior fit and finish with very good woodwork, tight-fitting headliners with arrow-straight seams, sumptuous leatherette settees, and good component quality.

The only limiting factor is the flat-bottom hull design that significantly limits speed in a seaway. This model has been in production since the mid-1980s, so most of the bugs should be worked out by now. If you like the idea of extended-season cruising, order the yacht with a lower station. Based on our sea trial, I would recommend the largest engines available.

1998 Maxum 4100 SCA Aft Cabin

MAXUM

Maxum 4100 SCA Specifications	
LOA:	41'6"
Beam:	13'10"
Draft:	3'2"
Displacement:	22,075 lb. (with gasoline engines)
Displacement:	31,000 lb. (full load as tested with Cummins 330 hp)
Fuel capacity:	290 gal.
Water capacity:	90 gal.
Holding capacity:	74 gal.

One of the largest U.S. pleasure-boat manufacturers, Maxum (a division of Brunswick Marine) builds boats that generally fall between Sea Ray and Bayliner in quality and price. One of Maxum's bigger models, this good-looking 41-foot aft-cabin model has a family-friendly layout. Styling is quite radical—which means its appearance may be transitory—and it's reasonable to say that interior volume is higher on the priority list than offshore seakeeping. Maxum builds runabout, express-cruiser, sedan, and aft-cabin models ranging from 18 to 46 feet.

Being built to a price point entails compromise, such as using less expensive components and even tooling from other models. But that's often fair enough with the price-conscious shopper. When this review was written, a Maxum 4100 sold for 30 to 40 percent less than a same size Euro-built sport cruiser model. But you (mostly) get what you pay for in fit and finish, seakeeping, and engineering.

Our test Maxum 4100 was a brand-new, aft-cabin, two-stateroom, two-head model, and it promises to be a great party and inshore-cruising boat.

Aft Deck

Board the Maxum 4100 from the integral swim platform with its fender and shore-power cable locker, handheld shower, waste and water connections, boarding ladder, and water fill. Then it's up five circular molded steps to the fully enclosed aft deck. From the centrally located aft deck, one short set of stairs leads up to the bridge, another to the saloon below; acrylic doors lead to the side decks. The topside decks are covered with grippy nonskid, though the 22-inch rails are too low. A washdown spigot is provided near the anchor pulpit, and a sunpad for two is atop the foredeck.

Bridge

Up just four steps from the aft deck, the flybridge is nearby and set up for entertaining. From the island console with its well-placed controls and steering wheel, I could drive sitting down, but there wasn't enough room to stand up with the fixed seat. Sight lines were still quite good, although you have to duck down to see aft. There's no place for a chart, but there's room for three guests to sit comfortably forward of the console and for three more on the helm bench.

Saloon

This boat has a terrific saloon, so I'll dispense with the couple of criticisms right away. Maxum says the hard-to-open sliding door is a temporary production problem, as is the uneven riser height of the stairs leading down to the saloon. The saloon itself is a roomy, pleasant space with shades of white and cream accented by cherry paneling (maple is available). The overhead padded liner is gold-trimmed with inset matching lights—very classy-looking. There's lots of glass to keep things bright and airy, including a full windshield. Immediately to starboard is an L-shaped settee with seating for five or six; down a step to port is a U-shaped dinette with a table for four.

Galley

Opposite and down two more steps is a full galley with a three-burner stove, double sinks, Avonite countertop, refrigerator-freezer, combination oven, coffeemaker, hardwood sole, and opening port from which to watch the passing scenery. This galley-down arrangement gives the chef a little privacy behind a lunch counter, but it's open enough to make the galley appear as to be an extension of the saloon.

Opposite the galley, the forward head is accessed from both the companionway and the forward stateroom. The complex and flawlessly executed tooling that produced this head was done well: just a couple of seams, easy to clean surfaces, and loads of open space. There's a separate shower with a circular acrylic door and a clever baffled vent, exhaust fan, raised toilet platform, and sink with large mirror.

Accommodations

The forward stateroom has a 78-by-64-inch island berth with storage below (including a drawer that wouldn't stay closed on our sea trial), two cedar-lined hanging lockers, an overhead opening hatch, and opening side ports. Reading and overhead lights were more than adequate (for our daytime test), as they were throughout the rest of the boat; a nicely hospitable stateroom.

Maxum has done a good job with the master stateroom aft, fitting in a bona fide (80 by 60 in.) queen-size bed with a real mattress and ample room to walk around. There are separate head and shower units with a cabin sink in between. Headroom everywhere is sufficient at 76-plus inches, and a large opening transom window with louvered shade—and smaller side ports—lets in lots of light and fresh air. The only real drawback in the master-stateroom layout is the minimal hanging space.

Maxum used the head and shower units from its 46 aft-cabin model to save money; the result is a significant amount of wasted space outboard of the molded-fiberglass units. There's more unused space under the molded transom stairs—another unfortunate shortcut—as well as some sloppy glasswork on our test boat, with large chunks of unsaturated roving behind the head assembly. Maxum needs to improve its engineering in these areas. Nonetheless, the overall design of the aft stateroom works well.

Engine Room

As with most sport cruisers, the Maxum engine room is tight because the emphasis is on accommodations. On this boat, Maxum fits a lot of equipment in just a few cubic feet. Access is tight and it takes three or four different entrances to reach everything; even then, it's not satisfactory. The result is that it makes maintenance difficult for your mechanic, makes it more expensive to keep the boat properly maintained, and detracts from possible damage-control efforts in an emergency.

The engine room is accessed through a 37-by-21-inch hatch in the saloon sole. In an engine room, it's important to have accessibility to the engines and other equipment. The Cummins's remote coolant reservoirs are hung from the hatch coaming, which means they're easy to top off but they restrict access to the engines. The starboard Racor fuel filter-separator is easy to reach on the forward bulkhead, but the one to port next to the fuel manifold (nicely labeled on the forward side) requires crawling way over the port battery box to reach. Getting to the port raw-water strainer and seacock necessitates lifting the aft-stateroom steps. The starboard seacock and strainer are more remote still, requiring the removal of four screws holding a pair of plywood panels in the aft-stateroom bulkhead. The engine room and its components need better accessibility.

The 145-gallon, 0.125-inch-thick, 5052-grade aluminum fuel tanks are outboard of the engines, typical of the genre. If and when they need replacing, it won't be a simple undertaking. This makes the issue of adequate ventilation that much more important since the tanks tend to corrode from the outside if moisture collects and stays there for prolonged periods. The ends of the rubber fuel lines are held in place with hose clamps; high-pressure hoses with hydraulic fittings would add durability and reliability.

The Cummins diesels drive 1.96:1 ZF in-line gears through 1¾-inch Aquamet 22 shafts (2 in. is now standard with the diesels) turning 24-by-26-inch four-blade cupped props. The 2-inch shafts are set at a moderate 11 degrees, adding to drivetrain efficiency.

A small utility room forward of the engine room to port contains the fuel-distribution manifold, the hot-water heater, and an access door leading to the forward end of the engine room. This area might hold the solution to some of the accessibility problems by relocating equipment here, especially if the dinette was raised closer to the level of the rest of the saloon, creating more room below.

The bilges are sanded smooth and gelcoated white for good visibility and easy cleanup. The engine stringers are 19 inches high, probably twice as high as they need to be, which also restricts access forward of the engines. However, they are well sealed against water intrusion by fiberglassed-in PVC limber holes at bilge level. I would like to see a deck grating in the bilge or the bilge pump mounted lower; I couldn't stand up forward of the batteries to work with 1½ inches of water left in the bilge after the pump shut off.

The unshrouded Westerbeke generator is on centerline aft of the engines. The generator mounts—attached to the engine stringers—are constructed of painted mild steel (as are the main engine's), so you can expect them to rust. Using aluminum or stainless up-front would reduce aggravation later. Wiring and cables are neatly and mostly unobtrusively routed; the battery switches and 12/120-volt distribution panels are located high up in the saloon at the master-cabin entrance for easy use. I couldn't see any evidence of engine-removal hatches built into the saloon sole, unless they're hidden under the insulation.

Construction

With an emphasis on keeping costs down, Maxum's construction is straightforward with a solid hull bottom and sides. To provide adequate stiffness, Maxum keeps panel sizes (that is, unbroken expanses of hull skin) down with a conventional grid work of longitudinals and bulkheads. A skin coat of chop saturated in vinylester resin greatly reduces the chances of blistering. Nida-Core is used as a coring material above the aft cabin to create a stiff, beamless aft deck while maximizing headroom below; vacuum-bagging helps assure a good skin-to-core bond and true surfaces.

Those obtrusive high hull stringers I mentioned are used with the efficiencies of design commonality in mind; they can be used for any of the engine options with minimal alteration. The hull-to-deck joint is bolted, bonded, and then fiberglassed from the inside for a permanent high-strength bond.

Performance Test

The boat has a lot of sail area compared to its underwater cross section, but on our calm test day, it still handled very well dockside, aided in part by the well-regulated hydraulic engine controls. The thick plastic drop curtains on the bridge were practically distortion-free (a pleasant change from the wrinkly stuff I often see), making it easy to see lobster-pot buoys and swimmers from afar. I would order the curtains with U-shaped roll-up sections, though.

We headed offshore into the light 1- to 2-foot chop. At 18 knots, we got knocked around some but didn't pound. It was quickly apparent that this is no rough-water deep-V, but it should be an acceptable inshore boat. Part of what you get with your extra money for a Fairline or Princess, for instance, is better handling and a smoother ride with a superior hull form.

With steering set at 5.2 turns lock-to-lock, the boat turned 360 degrees in 31 seconds at full throttle with a very respectable turning radius. No apologies are necessary for Maxum's steering system (rudder size, placement, design, and maximum angle), although the steering effort was moderately high; power steering would lower the effort *and* produce a snappy three turns lock-to-lock. The boat was exceptionally dry in every direction, with nary a drop hitting the side-deck weather doors.

According to Maxum's factory figures and sea trials, the 4100 delivers 18.4 knots at 2,400 rpm (with a range of only 175 nm), 21.4 knots at 2,600 rpm, and 25.5 knots at 2,900 rpm. On one engine, we got up to 2,250 rpm, and then backed off to 1,900 rpm for an estimated get-home speed of 8 to 10 knots. Sound levels throughout the yacht were reasonable, ranging from 77 to 83 dBA, including the interior and the aft deck. Drifting in the small trough, the boat rolled comfortably with a full load of fuel, full water, five passengers, and light gear. At cruising speed, tabs-up trim was within acceptable limits, even with the extra weight of the aft cabin.

The Maxum comes standard with a pair of 310 hp MerCruisers, but performance figures are not yet available. Regardless, these gasoline engines are too small for any 16-ton 41-footer; unless you don't venture past the breakwater, get the diesels. I was comfortable with the boat's handling dockside and at sea; however, remember to establish reasonable cruising expectations—this is not a rough-water boat due to its full, broad, low-deadrise entry and large sail area.

It will be hard to beat the Maxum's combination of interior layout, standard features, outstanding tooling, good handling, and dealer support. Be aware of where the money has been saved during construction and you won't be unpleasantly surprised later. Maxum has bugs to work out, such as making better use of interior voids for added storage, improving the engine-room layout, improving the component quality in a few instances, and fixing the bow railing. Refinements such as relocating fittings and using better quality components cost little in the long term but result in a longer-lasting, more reliable boat.

As mentioned, you'll pay a lot less money for a Maxum than for a European cruiser of similar size, and the Maxum offers some competition for U.S.-built, similarly priced boats. You'll appreciate the many amenities (like the burl-elm helm station) and the entertaining and cruising lifestyle that this yacht affords. Base power is 7.4-liter gas MerCruiser, while test boat options included 330 hp Cummins Diamond Series diesels, 8 kW generator, reverse-cycle AC, and a cockpit entertainment center. The Maxum 4100 is a well-equipped boat for a family that fully appreciates the yacht's distinctive capabilities and that can live with its limitations.

1998 Silverton 372 Motor Yacht

Silverton 372 Aft-Cabin Motor Yacht Specifications	
LOA:	40'6"
Beam:	14'1"
Draft:	3'3"
Displacement:	23,600 lb. (approximate dry weight)
Fuel capacity:	286 gal.
Water capacity:	100 gal.
Holding capacity:	60 gal.
Power:	320 hp Crusader 454 gasoline engines

More than a few U.S. production boatbuilders are lately showing evidence of originality; it shows up in the styling, to be sure. But there is styling for its own sake and then there's styling that's meant to serve a practical purpose. The latter is what I've found to be the case with the boldly styled Silverton 372 motor yacht. You may either love or hate the looks of this boat, but let's have a close look at it on its own terms.

Focus groups told Silverton that safety topside was a primary concern. Owners wanted to know when someone ventured topside, so the centrally located raised helm layout affords a good view all around. They wanted foredeck access to be as safe as walking down a sidewalk, which it is on this boat. And they wanted lots of room, which this boat delivers convincingly. People tend to spend more time on their boats, it seems, and they want the space to spread out in comfort.

The 372 is designed to improve traffic patterns and increase interior livable space. You can't have everything, but let's look at how Silverton managed to fit two staterooms and two heads comfortably in a 37-foot package.

Aft Deck

Boarding the Silverton is easy with a full-width swim platform and gently sloping molded-fiberglass steps (with a handheld shower on the way up) leading to the aft deck. This 6-by-12-foot area has side boarding gates as well, and there's a sink and optional icemaker built into a cabinet forward. It's a great place to sit and relax well protected from the elements (and bugs) by the hardtop and the optional full plastic and screen enclosure. The only gripes I have are the rough glasswork in parts of the aft liner, some sloppy caulking, and the recessed steps at the side entrances that could cause a sprained ankle.

Bridge

Two steps from the aft deck up to the bridge make this real split-level living for the cruising family. There's seating for six to eight around the large island helm console. The raised helm position is on centerline, affording an excellent all-around view, especially ahead and to the sides. The window in the hardtop helps to see aft at close range, but you'll still have to back slowly into a slip.

The console dominates the bridge, and it will be perfectly adequate for many cruising families without modification. It's made for seated operation, at least if you're taller than average and have to stoop to reach the engine controls like I do. The shifts to port and throttles to starboard are mounted at about 10 degrees from vertical, an uncomfortable angle to be sure and one that provides less positive control than more horizontally inclined controls. The tachometers, which you'll use the most often, are directly behind the wheel, so unless you're standing, expect to have to duck to read them clearly. There's room on either side for electronics, although because the tachometers are used more than the gauges, I think they should be more proximately displayed directly in front of the operator. For my height, I would also want more legroom, but it may be adequate for most people. The compass is well placed in a heads-up position and directly in front of the wheel.

Foredeck

Besides the sheer interior volume of this well-thought-out yacht, the pièce de résistance is definitely the foredeck access, which is down a flight of port and starboard stairs. How much easier and safer can it get? The nonskid is excellent, so you won't be slipping and sliding, and the sturdy stainless side railings atop the molded bulwarks are 30-plus-inches high, so you won't be taking an unexpected dip. The 10-inch bow cleats and integral bow-anchor pulpit are forward, and two pairs of side cleats and stern cleats address any likely mooring scenario.

Saloon

Five steps down from the aft deck take you to the Silverton's cavernous 15-plus-foot-long-by-13-foot-wide saloon—that's as big or bigger than an average mid-40-footer yacht's saloon, due to the wide-body design of the full-beam deckhouse. Immediately to port of the companionway is the electrical service panel, conveniently situated at chest height—by far, the best place for it. Next is a countertop with cabinets below for the TV and plenty of room for an entertainment center. Across to starboard is a large L-shaped settee that converts to a twin bed.

Walking forward, it's another step down to the second L-shaped lounge-dinette to port and the galley opposite to starboard. (The extra height below the aft section of the saloon is needed for the fuel tanks and engines below.) The galley has ample room for meal preparation on the 6-foot Corian countertop, and a three-burner range with oven, microwave oven, coffeemaker, and upright refrigerator-freezer are all included. A lazy Susan below the large sink makes good use of the available space, and storage room in general is excellent. You can order the boat with a lower control station, which shrinks the galley correspondingly.

Our test boat's saloon had a very neatly installed white headliner, blue leatherette soffit trim, cherry-wood-laminated interior, green carpeting, and a simulated-wood galley sole. Plenty of light is allowed in through the windshield and side windows, and installed lighting appeared quite adequate. Joinery was generally precise and attractive for this class of boat, push-to-open cabinet hardware functioned well, and the overall ambiance was pleasing. The feeling of sheer space was enhanced by the headroom—up to 88 inches of it. I would like to see strategically placed overhead grab bars added since there's little else to hold onto in the wide-open saloon.

Head

Down two more steps and to port is a good-sized head with enclosed shower, electric toilet, and sink—and a full 82 inches of headroom. A couple of comments need mentioning: the shower unit is part molded fiberglass, part paneling, and part fabric stretched under the opening porthole. Since the paneling eventually leaks, seams mildew, and fabric tears, a one-piece tooled fiberglass shower is a better solution and one that Silverton should be considering. I would like to see higher doorsills leading to the companionway and the stateroom forward to keep the inevitable head and sink overflows contained inside the nicely tooled head sole.

Accommodations

The guest stateroom is forward, where you'll find an athwartships-mounted 7-foot-by-4-foot, 6-inch berth with storage below, two cedar lockers, two opening side ports, and a 20-inch overhead hatch to let fresh air and daylight in—and you out, in an emergency.

The bright and aesthetically uplifting master stateroom is aft, as might be expected, and it won't disappoint. The 75-by-55-inch berth (complete with innerspring) runs athwartships so you can reach either side without crawling over your bedmate. Two hanging lockers are provided, as well as generous storage space, room for a TV, and a private head with separate shower. A large opaque window faces aft, letting in daylight while maintaining privacy. Access panels lead to the engine room, which will keep your mechanic happy if he has to work on the transmissions. Another access panel leads to the steering gear aft.

Engine Room

Accessing the big-block gasoline engines on our test boat was easily accomplished. If you want to do daily checks, just pop open the centerline hatch in the saloon to inspect oil and coolant levels. For major maintenance or engine change-out, large hatches directly above each engine can be removed.

Steel angle-iron mounting brackets support the engines with vibration-isolator couplings. The brackets, in turn, are solidly through-bolted to the hull stringers and engine beds (the steel was already rusting on our test boat—I recommend aluminum or stainless to prevent a perennial corrosion problem). Color-coded aircraft-type fuel lines feed the engines through a well-labeled and neatly routed fuel supply and return manifolds affixed to the forward bulkhead, although there were no external fuel filter-separators on our test boat. The battery switches are mounted horizontally on a ledge below the forward end of the hatch for easy access from the saloon; a better solution might be to locate them forward in the port storage locker using heavier cable to accommodate the extra run. This would make them even more accessible while freeing up access to the fuel manifolds below.

The engine seacocks (there are no internal strainers, which is probably fine) are outboard of the dripless stern tubes, so they're difficult to reach in a hurry. Silverton takes the unusual extra step of providing plugs for the PVC-insert limber holes so you can control liquid flow into the keel area. Cableways were neatly routed, secured, and loomed for chafing protection, except on the aft bulkhead,

where looming was missing and large cables remained unsecured outboard to starboard. The boat's wide beam helps down there as well; even with the outboard 5052-grade aluminum fuel tanks, there's ample room to change the spark plugs. As with most boats, there's room for improvement, but this is still a mechanic-friendly engine room.

Forward Auxiliary–Machinery Room

Forward of the engine room in a separate compartment (easily accessed through a hatch next to the galley), Silverton has installed the enclosed Kohler 6.5 kW generator, batteries, polypropylene water tank, hot-water heater, and battery charger. This arrangement, in fact, is what makes the engine room so hospitable—it is freed up to hold just the engines. Everything is accessible—the only change I would make is to attach the ladder with removable pins (like the engine room) rather than screw it in place, which would make accessing the water heater easier. There are even level shelves outboard for add-on equipment, tools, or spare oil.

Construction

The Silverton is conventionally constructed with a solid fiberglass bottom and Coremat in the sides (the Coremat adds bulk and stiffness without significantly increasing weight). The bottom stringer gridwork is made of fiberglass-encapsulated plywood laid up in a steel jig in one piece. The gridwork is then inverted and fiberglassed to the hull while it is still in its mold, ensuring that the entire hull structure keeps its shape.

The decks and superstructure are cored with either balsa or Divinycell foam up to 1½ inches thick in the deck spans. Plywood insert rings surround hatches and stanchions to prevent the possibility of water penetrating the balsa core. The hull-to-deck joint is made of turned-out deck and hull flanges sealed in butyl tape and fastened with self-tapping screws. The hard PVC rubrail is then screwed in from underneath. Finally, and this is what makes it an excellent joint, the entire affair is fiberglassed from the inside.

Silverton uses CAD to a large degree when bringing its new products on-line. CAM is being used increasingly, such as when making the plywood sections for the tooling used to build the molds and for making interior cabinetry components. Silverton does all its own tooling in-house, and it does it well.

Performance Test

Our sea trial out of Plymouth, Massachusetts, was conducted on a hot August day with very little wind and only an occasional whalewatching boat's wake to cross. The accompanying table summarizes the Silverton 372's performance results with twin 320 hp EFI Crusader 454-cubic-inch gasoline engines, a full liquid load, and two passengers onboard.

Silverton 372 Performance Results

RPM	Speed, knots	Aft Deck Noise Level, dBA	Saloon Noise Level, dBA	Aft Stateroom Noise Level, dBA
1,000	4.5	67	59	62
1,500	6.9			
2,000	8.2	75	66	70
2,400	9.3			
2,600	10.3 (on plane)			
2,800	11.1	80	71	79
3,000	12.5	81	72	81
3,500	17.1	83	75	83
4,000	20.7	86	83	87

Let's face it: this is really way too much boat for gasoline engines. If you want a 12-knot cruise, get the diesels! A performance yacht this is not, and a lot is asked of the big-block gasoline engines in pushing this beamy aft-cabin rig, but the base engines do go a long way toward making the purchase price affordable for more people. Figure on a realistic cruising speed of 12 to 15 knots, depending on how far forward you ordinarily push the engines and how much gear migrates aboard over time.

As with the majority of cruisers, the steering response was delayed by the six turns it took to go from hard port to hard starboard. Four turns would be more appropriate and easily achievable with a well-designed steering system and properly balanced rudders. The steering effort should be easier than it was on this boat, especially with the mechanical advantage afforded by all those turns. Once the rudders are hard over, however, the boat banks well and turns quite sharply. The boat's motion was comfortable lying-to in the passing wakes, evidence of good stability despite the large superstructure. The generous beam and reverse chines help out in this regard.

The boat was just as easy on the ears as it was on the sea legs, with quiet sound levels throughout the yacht across the speed spectrum. Expect to make 12 to 14 knots in a 2- to 4-foot head sea; higher seas will likely require slower progress with full hull sections forward. With all that sail area and without a full keel, the boat is quite sensitive to a crosswind, as you would expect (and as I discovered), so plan accordingly when making tight approaches in a crowded marina. This boat, like others in its class, could benefit by the addition of a bow thruster.

The Silverton is at once in the avant-garde of styling and at the forefront of pragmatism. It blends form and function successfully in a way that will be a pleasant surprise to many boating families that never thought the two could coexist. Be sure to buy the boat with diesels, or wait a few years and buy a used one. You'll recoup a lot of the extra up-front expense when you sell the boat.

Our test boat included at 6.5 kW generator, anchor windlass, 32,000 Btu two-zone AC, and full canvas. If you like the looks and can live without real offshore capabilities, you'll love this boat's roomy wide-body saloon and all-around topside safety and accessibility. Silverton has a winner in this cruising design and, especially by addressing the areas mentioned, could have what will be for many a nearly ideal coastal-cruising family yacht.

Carver's 396 Aft Cabin represents this builder at its best in the small aft-cabin cruiser market segment. A recent entry featuring Carver's streamlined, even futuristic styling, the two-stateroom, two-head 396's walkaround layout opens up the interior to almost full beam. Carver's aft cabin, cockpit, and sedan motor yachts range from 34 to 57 feet. Wide beam and low deadrise limit speed potential in rough water, but the builder is doing a fine job with its solid engineering, exceptional joinery, and intelligent use of innovative construction methods and materials. CARVER

The Wisconsin boatbuilder, Cruisers Inc., produces beamy family express and sedan cruisers from 28 to 53 feet, including one of my personal-favorite layouts, this 4450 Express. Cruisers does a fine job delivering the goods, with comfortable and roomy interiors, an emphasis on topside safety, and a reasonably good offshore ride, all for a competitive price. Fortunately, Cruisers hasn't gotten carried away with the Euro-styling craze, so its boats are still practical yet attractive-looking. CRUISERS INC.

The Linssen GS 430, a steel coastal cruiser built in the Netherlands, has its aesthetic charms as well as bulletproof construction and a pleasingly salty interior. If you expect to eventually run up on the rocks, be sure you do it in a steel boat. LINSSEN

Here's a rugged, good-looking steel cruiser from the Netherlands, the Linssen 41 aft cabin. Modern paint systems have made the high maintenance associated with steel hulls almost a thing of the past.

This Silverton's decent motor-yacht ride is attributable to the relatively fine and deep entry and high chines seen in this photo.

The Sabreline 47 is one of the builder's five express, sedan, and aft-cabin models ranging from 34 to 47 feet. A planing hard-chine hull form delivers a decent ride and good economy offshore in the 22- to 25-knot range. The builder's sailboat heritage is evident in the attractive interior finish and intelligent use of space. SABRELINE

Silverton's 442 aft-cabin model offers a lot of room for the LOA and, unlike a few other aft-cabin yachts in its class, the ride is as good as a typical beamy sportfisherman's with its convertible-style hull form. Silverton models come in aft-cabin, sedan, and motor-yacht layouts ranging from 32 to 45 feet, and the price is within reach of many boaters. SILVERTON

Trawlers

The redoubtable trawler conjures up images of a stout displacement hull powered by a single diesel traveling along at jogging speed for thousands of miles. These yachts usually have a forward pilothouse, accommodations forward on the lower deck, a saloon aft of the pilothouse, and a small cockpit in the stern. Some include a flybridge above the saloon, and those over 50 feet or so might have a full-beam master suite directly below the pilothouse, as in the pilothouse motor-yacht design. Other trawlers have been built with aft-cabin designs.

Although trawlers used to be based pretty much exclusively on heavy displacement hulls, a couple of trends have developed to address owners' need for speed. The displacement hulls in some cases have been lightened and lengthened, allowing them to achieve cruising speeds above a speed-to-length of 1.4. Their lighter weight decreases resistance, and their longer length increases their hull

speed. The next step is to build the trawler on a semidisplacement hull, which is able to get up on plane and achieve S/L ratios of around 2.5. Of course, the slower the hull moves through the water, the more efficiently it can be driven. But many owners want to be able to have the option of running at 18 knots occasionally to meet a cruising schedule, so a hard-chine or Maine-style semidisplacement hull works well for these applications.

When a boat has a semidisplacement hull and a conventional pilothouse or aft-cabin motor-yacht design, the builder may still call it a trawler, even though the lines are blurred at this point. Some trawler aficionados, in fact, protest that only full-displacement hulls qualify a vessel for the label, and that range must be measured in the thousands rather than hundreds of miles. If it does have a displacement hull, it will also need a means of stabilization, since this hull type's slack bilges have little form stability (though great *weight* stability). Paravanes or flopper-stoppers suspended from outriggers do the trick, as do active, gyroscope-guided fin stabilizers mounted at the turn of the bilge. Although the fishing vessels on which "true" trawlers are based have relatively low decks and small superstructures, trawler *yachts* often have large, boxy deckhouses that enhance interior space but also amplify roll, and increase the need for stabilization.

So, if you're not in a great hurry to get there, you appreciate a seaworthy vessel underfoot, and you enjoy the process of cruising as much as reaching your destination, the comfortable, economically propelled trawler may be the boat for you.

1998 Grand Banks 42 Classic

NEIL RABINOWITZ/COURTESY GRAND BANKS

Grand Banks 42 Classic Specifications

LOA:	43'3"
Beam:	14'1"
Draft:	4'2"
Displacement:	34,000 lb.
Fuel capacity:	600 gal.
Water capacity:	265 gal.

Classics of all descriptions are deemed so because they've proven themselves over time—or at least because they've convinced a lot of people that they have done so. In my opinion, our test boat, the Grand Banks 42 Classic, is aptly named because it does so many things well. What it doesn't do so well or at all—like cruising at 20 knots, delivering a dry ride, and having a shoal draft—most people don't expect of trawlers anyway.

Built originally in wood in 1965, and in fiberglass since 1973, Grand Banks has in recent years offered larger power plants, making possible 20-plus-knot (with twin diesels) top speeds versus the original single-screw's sedentary 9 knots. Even with the twins, you can throttle back to displacement speeds for decent economy and long range—although, of course, not as decent and long as the single's. The venerable name Grand Banks is, in some circles, synonymous with the term *trawler*, even though many of the builder's models are based on semidisplacement rather than full-displacement hulls. This is a semiplaning hull with hard chines

and fairly flat buttocks aft. Just don't expect a round-bilge displacement hull's efficiency or a true planing hull's performance with the Grand Banks 42.

Not that it makes any difference to any but the most myopic trawler enthusiasts, but this shows how builders have modified their products (with hard chines and twin diesels) to meet evolving consumer demand for more speed. It seems fewer buyers want displacement hulls with their 7- or 8-knot cruising speed limitations, so the builders improvise; witness Grand Banks's excellent Eastbay series of 30-knot planing yachts. Most Grand Banks models, which range from 36 to 66 feet, will cruise at 12 or more knots with twin-diesel power, putting them comfortably in the semidisplacement league. The 42 Classic has gone through modifications over the decades, and several aft-cabin configurations are available in this two-stateroom yacht.

What you get with the Grand Banks 42 is a good little seaboat, albeit somewhat tender in a following sea—as is the wont of more than a few full-keel boats. Accommodations are excellent, the ride is comfortable and reassuring, and sound levels are low enough to praise. Our test boat was hull #1399, so you would be justified in thinking that Grand Banks should have it down to a science when it comes to building its 42 Classic. My findings indicate that the Grand Banks 42 lives up to those expectations.

Topside

The Grand Banks's shiplike qualities are nowhere more evident than topside, where 18-inch-wide side decks, deep bulwarks topped with varnished-teak caprails, and 33-inch-high life rails lead to the forecastle. The oiled-teak strip planking makes for very pleasant-looking and effective (and high-maintenance) nonskid. A Lofrans chain windlass, controlled from the bridge and lower helm as well as locally, hoists the anchor; the pulpit handles two anchors, in fact. Docking bow-to is not a problem with shore-power, telephone, and TV connections forward.

Forward on the trunk cabin, a teak seat flips up for access to an integral storage bin. A 20-inch Lewmar hatch lets in plenty of fresh air and daylight in the cabin below, and is large enough to double as an emergency exit.

Also of note topside, exterior teak window frames are sealed in epoxy and coated with Awlgrip to reduce maintenance. (Frameless windows would be a sign that Grand Banks is embracing the twenty-first century.) Three 20-inch wipers work together with freshwater washes to keep the windshields clear and streak-free in the salty environs.

Back aft, the spacious theme continues with lots of line-handling and lounging room on the fantail. A large teak hatch opens to the lazarette, which provides storage for fenders, lines, and other gear. As in the engine room, bilges are ground smooth and painted white for a visibility-enhancing and agreeable appearance. The best thing about cable steering, other than its simplicity, is the fact that you can pop out a deck socket and plug in an emergency steering tiller.

Nowhere are the stainless and teak railings less than 31 inches high, which makes this yacht's topsides entirely suitable for human habitation. Atop the aft trunk cabin, a sliding hatch opens for access to the master stateroom below, and teak stairs lead from the immaculately tooled fiberglass top up to the flybridge forward. A boom and mast make easy work of handling the tender.

Back aft, the swim-platform ladder leans against the transom, making it easy for someone to deploy it from the water.

Flybridge

The bridge helm comes with a 30-inch vertical teak wheel, separate shifts and throttles (like down below), a big compass, start/stop, and full instrumentation. A companion seat is opposite to port, rear-facing seats are aft, and an L-shaped lounge with table aft is to starboard (another lounge seat would fit aft to port if you need it).

Saloon

Open, airy, and decidedly trawler-like, the 15-foot-long saloon takes up a good portion of the yacht's length. A full 77 inches of headroom, white perforated overhead liner, and lots of windows keep the parquet teak sole and teak cabinetry from overwhelming the space. It's a very pleasing effect—the teak and the white—although a cherry or maple treatment would brighten up the saloon.

The saloon has an L-shaped lounge to port opposite the helm. Our test boat had a three-burner gas stove, microwave oven, refrigerator-freezer, and Corian countertops. Aft of the helm seat, the console hides an icemaker and glassware storage.

Back aft in the saloon, the settees in the living area are to port and starboard, and they open remarkably easily for storage access. Both seats convert to 72- and 68-inch berths.

Engine Room

A 20-by-30-inch saloon-sole hatch provides entry to the yacht's large, all white, and well-lit engine room. A single engine would make this space seem even larger, but accessibility is still satisfactory with twins.

The rugged fiberglass-over-foam hull stringers and engine beds support the engines via Soundown's soft isolation mounts. There's also a rubber isolation coupling between the gear and the shaft to minimize engine-transmitted vibrations in the drivetrain.

General accessibility is quite good: seawater strainers and seacocks are on centerline forward out in the open, oil dipsticks and freshwater tanks are easy to reach, and the fuel filter-separators are a snap to check and drain on the inboard side of the black iron fuel tanks outboard and aft of the engines. Grand Banks has provided a sight glass in the form of a clear hose; I would add a shield to protect the tube from accidental damage because the tank would drain to the bilge in the event of a hose leak.

Fiberglass oil pans keep the bilges clean, dripless shaft seals control the salt water and mist, drain lines tie into common overboard discharge fittings above the waterline, and the bilges are ground smooth and coated with gelcoat for good visibility and easy cleanup. However, I would like to see mat added over the last layer of woven roving in the hull sides for a smoother, more uniform appearance and easier maintenance.

The vertical lift mufflers let you stand on the dock with the engines idling and talk in conversational tones with someone 15 feet away. The yacht's wiring is especially noteworthy, being exceptionally well routed and loomed, while remaining accessible and numbered for quick troubleshooting and maintenance. I would just add looming along the section attached to the port engine stringer for added chafe resistance. All told, this is a very well-engineered layout.

Accommodations

Located down the stairs from the saloon, the forward guest stateroom includes a V-berth, sliding side windows and opening overhead hatch, a large cedar closet to port, and an even larger head opposite with a sliding window with screen, teak grating, and a shower curtain to contain the water.

Situated aft of the saloon, the master stateroom has cedar closets and separate toilet and shower compartments. The 80-inch queen-size berth has a real mattress and generous storage space below. A dresser and dressing table are included. Sliding windows let in more daylight, and a companionway leads directly up, aft, and out. This aft retreat provides ample privacy away from the guest stateroom.

Construction

The chop-strand-mat skin coat applied over the gelcoat is saturated in isophthalic resin to ward off osmotic blistering, followed by Coremat to prevent print-through, and then finished with mat and woven roving wet out in general-purpose orthophthalic resin. Clear gelcoat is used below the waterline to make it easier to spot voids in the laminate. Hull sides and bottom are solid glass, stringers are foam-cored, and bulkheads are constructed of plywood tabbed to the hull. Decks are built of fiberglass cored with plywood. The hull-to-deck joint is joined with self-tapping screws and bonded with polyurethane adhesive.

Performance Test

We had a sloppy 2- to 4-foot sea running in Long Island Sound out of Rowayton, Connecticut—perfect conditions for our salt-bestrewn sea trial. These are the kind of seas a boat like this should be able to handle with aplomb and impunity at low (13–17 kt.) planing speeds.

I want to say a word about the principal helm station in the saloon, which featured an array of electronics, gauges, and gadgets. Surrounded by large sections of clear glass, visibility is great, even for backing into a slip. In fact, the only problem with visibility is ahead on the port bow, where the steering-cable pipe, hefty windshield mullion, and bow pulpit combine to take a significant chunk out of an important part of the horizon. Cable steering is standard, by the way—get the optional power hydraulic steering to eliminate the paunchy pipe, reduce steering effort, and increase responsiveness.

I found that with the seat back far enough for

adequate legroom, the vertical wheel is too far forward, so this is an ergonomic problem that could be resolved by installing a 20-degree-from-horizontal wheel. When I was standing up, the wheel and engine controls were both at my fingertips. Noise levels were low, in the mid- to high-70 dBA range at cruising speeds, so I could carry on a conversation with my shipmates in the aft end of the saloon while driving the boat.

When driving into those 2- to 4-foot head seas at a continuous cruise of 17 knots at 2,400 rpm, this is one wet boat; our three windshield wipers were kept busy clearing away the steady stream of salt spray—it's as if the hull is protesting being driven so unnaturally fast, which it is. But we found the ride much drier at a less strenuous cruise speed of 10 knots; not a drop of water made it inside the boat, either through the opening windshield or the starboard-side weather-deck door. Once in a while, you have to take a ride on a fast trawler like this to recall just how comfortable it is, particularly when compared to some of the ultralights being built of high-tech composites. Sheer mass in a hull does a lot to tame bodacious seas.

Incidentally, we managed a top speed of 22 knots with full fuel and three passengers on a fully outfitted boat. For those performance numbers, we had commendably deep 2.5:2 reduction gears and commensurately large props to thank. The accompanying table shows the builder's performance estimates with smaller 375 hp Caterpillars, with range calculated at a 90-gallon fuel capacity.

The tabs have a good amount of effect on trim, perhaps dropping the bow by 2 degrees at cruise speed, which improved visibility over the bow when running the boat from the lower station. But don't expect to use trim tabs in a following sea because bow steer becomes more pronounced. As with most boats, full tabs smooth out the ride in a head sea, but also invite a lot more spray on board in the process.

Up on the flybridge, the view is better still, but the steering also takes more effort, likely due to the friction of the added cable run. I'm taller than average and found the wheel to be too low for comfort. In a full-rudder turn at 17 knots, we took a mere 38 seconds to turn 360 degrees—not bad at all for a semidisplacement hull with a full keel.

Rolling in the trough was not much of an adventure with fairly good form stability keeping our leeward rolls to a confidence-inspiring 12 degrees. Backing into the same sea was not a problem either, with the waves flowing unimpeded right through the slots in the laminated-teak swim platform. Try that with a cantilevered, solid-fiberglass version and you will likely return to port with something seriously broken. To summarize, the Grand Banks 42 is a boat you can take to sea and justifiably feel secure.

Back at the dock, I backed into the narrow slip with little fuss. The highest compliment I can pay any boat is that it handles altogether predictably on all counts, just like the Grand Banks 42.

The Grand Banks 42 Classic lives up to its name with a commendable mix of speed, livability, and seakeeping. If you like the hull but want to investigate different layouts, check out the Europa (larger saloon, two forward staterooms, and no aft cabin)

Grand Banks 42 Classic Performance Results

RPM	Speed, knots	Speed, mph	Fuel Use, gph	Nautical mpg	Statute mpg	Range nm	Range, statue miles
1,800	12.3	14.1	10.6	1.2	1.3	627	721
2,000	13.3	15.3	13.8	1.0	1.1	520	599
2,200	14.5	16.7	18.6	0.8	0.9	421	484
2,400	16.2	18.6	24	0.7	0.8	365	419
2,600	18.3	21.0	30.6	0.6	0.7	323	371
2,800	21.5	24.7	42	0.5	0.6	276	318

or the motor yacht (wider aft cabin, two forward staterooms, and no fantail).

Single or twin 375 hp Caterpillar 3208s are available. We tested it with a laundry list of options, including Vacuflush heads, inverter-isolator, L-shaped galley, Grunert freezer, and reverse-cycle AC) on top of a lengthy standard equipment list. Yes, you're paying for the name, but you gain a good, seaworthy boat, resale values are typically strong, and you get to join the Grand Banks club.

Krogen 58

ROBERT HOLLAND/KROGEN

Krogen 58 Specifications

LOA:	62'11"
Length on deck:	58'0"
Waterline length:	52'3"
Beam molded (hull):	18'1"
Beam overall (over rubrails):	18'10"
Draft:	5'3" (with twin engines)
Displacement (full load):	104,000 lb.
Ballast:	7,000 lb.
Fuel capacity:	1,760 gal. (four tanks)
Water capacity:	450 gal.
Waste capacity:	100 gal.

Once in a while, a yacht comes along that makes me sit up and take notice—one that is so well thought out, carefully engineered, and meticulously crafted that it clearly stands apart. The Krogen 58, the new flagship of this line of ocean-crossing displacement trawlers, is one of those.

Why a displacement hull? The well-designed full-displacement trawler yacht has the great advantages of seaworthiness and efficiency. Speed potential is a function of waterline length (the square root of which is multiplied by 1.4 to get hull speed), since a displacement hull cannot climb up on its bow wave (that would be planing). Fuel consumption is a small fraction of a similar-size planing vessel, and the economies of buying and maintaining a 58-footer with twin 154 hp diesels rather than a 2,400 hp planing yacht of the same size are obvious. Then there's the matter of range: the Krogen 58 will cover nearly 1,300 miles at 10 knots; just throttle back to 7 knots for 3,300 nm, ocean-crossing range.

Topside Aft

Back at dockside, I started my walkthrough in the cockpit (a back porch, really), which is well protected by the boat deck overhang above. I didn't need to look far to see the high standard to which this Krogen is built: the stainless steel railing welds are ground smooth and polished, for starters. Standard equipment includes hawseholes with integral cleats, oversized scuppers for quick water shedding, teak-inlaid decks, a pair of Glendinning Cablemasters, molded seams in the internal bulwarks—the list goes on. The asymmetrical deckhouse extends flush to the port side, creating more interior room, and leaving space for a weather-deck passageway to starboard that leads to the pilothouse and foredeck.

Saloon

A Freeman watertight double door opens to the 17-by-14-foot saloon, which features 6 feet, 9 inches of headroom and some very fine cherry cabinetry. Krogen's design philosophy emphasizes lots of light and cross-ventilation inside; the large, opening side windows get the job done. The saloon's neutral colors, cherry parquet sole, and cherry and white siding coexist harmoniously. In my opinion, the cherry is pleasing and doesn't overpower the senses, as teak tends to do. The saloon, much like a comfortable sitting room or library, easily swallows a big L-shaped lounge to starboard, a large double-leaf table that will seat six or eight, and a pair of reclining armchairs opposite to port.

Galley

Situated at the forward end of the saloon, the galley is colocated yet private. The Corian-topped island counter, a full 9 feet long, includes a deep sink, Miele dishwasher, GE trash compactor, and assorted storage cabinets below and above at head level. Forward is a four-burner gas stove with range below, a GE combination microwave-convection oven, and a full-size Jenn-Air side-by-side stainless steel refrigerator-freezer. A watertight Dutch door leads to the starboard weather deck.

Cabin

Forward is the three-stateroom, two-head cabin, reached by no ordinary companionway: this one measures more than 4 feet wide in places, making it seem more like a foyer or antechamber than a passageway. The master stateroom is forward: big and airy with more than 6 feet, 10 inches of headroom, a pair of large opening hatches overhead, and four large polished-stainless opening portlights. The island berth is a full 7 feet long, and it is raised easily on gas lifts for access to the storage space beneath. His (2 ft.) and hers (5 ft.) hanging lockers and sixteen clothes drawers are also provided. The en suite head has a separate stall shower with molded seat and is very roomy, in keeping with Krogen's fewer-yet-larger-compartments theme.

The amidships starboard guest stateroom also has a queen-size berth, as well as a pair of hanging lockers and six clothes drawers. Bookshelves above

the head of the berth make this a natural navigator's quarters. There is private access to the second head, which is also entered directly from the companionway opposite the washer-dryer compartment. Just aft of the master stateroom off the companionway is an Asko washer-dryer unit stacked in a closet. The third guest stateroom to port has a desk and doubles as an office; the settee converts to a double berth.

Engine Room

Down and aft is the shiplike engine room, well lit and roomy with two John Deere diesels looking a little lost in all that space. These engines are derated to 154 hp, which means that a life expectancy of more than 20,000 hours is a distinct possibility. Watertight doors forward and aft seal the space off for an extra measure of damage control. A workbench is located immediately inside to starboard, and there's standing headroom at the entrance, 5 feet or more elsewhere. From a mechanic's perspective, this is one of the half dozen best engine rooms I've seen.

The Deeres drive powerful 32-inch props through 2.88:1 twin disc gears and 2-inch Aquamet 22 shafts with Aquadrive intermediate thrust bearings that greatly reduce vibration levels. The enclosed gensets are aft of the engines, and all maintenance points—including seawater strainers and fuel filter-separators—are in plain sight and easy to reach.

Pilothouse

Up in the pilothouse is the ship's electrical control panel, and inside, the wiring looms are a picture-perfect, precisely run, clearly numbered work of art. Anyone who doubts the ability of the top Taiwanese yards to produce world-class work need look no farther for the evidence.

What's immediately striking here is the shiplike utility evident everywhere. Visibility from the centerline helm seat is clear from dead ahead to 60 degrees abaft either beam, and a pair of small opening portholes affords a view directly aft.

Watertight gasketed dogging Dutch doors lead to the two bridge wings; the two-piece doors, in addition to giving a homey feel to the boat, allow you to catch a sea breeze while keeping passengers safe in heavy weather. An L-shaped lounge aft, which is 7 feet long and converts to a double berth, is raised a foot and a half off the deck to let the guests enjoy that spectacular view.

The centerline helm station is intelligently laid out, including a big 6-foot Danforth magnetic compass atop the electronics console. Chart tables and chart-sized drawers are to port and starboard, and the dashboard perimeter is bordered with fiddle-board handrails.

Foredeck

The foredeck, also very businesslike, has a pair of plough-type anchors, twin anchor-chain windlasses and a capstan for line handling, two pairs of 15-inch bow cleats, and four more of those closed chocks with integral cleats. If you find yourself mooring bow-to, three shore-power cable hookups are provided forward, along with a freshwater hookup and both freshwater and saltwater spigots. The 44-inch-tall bow railing creates a very safe topside environment.

Outside the port pilothouse door, a set of molded stairs leads to the upper-boat deck and then up to the flybridge. With the bimini top to protect from the elements, this is a pleasant place to spend an afternoon. The mast folds easily to avoid passing bridges, and a tender fits comfortably across the boat deck aft above the cockpit.

Construction

The bottom of the hull is solid fiberglass, including a skin coat of vinylester resin in the first two laminates to prevent osmotic blistering. Kevlar is used to add impact resistance at the stem and stern. Bulkheads and stringers are plywood-cored, and a full 7,000 pounds of lead ballast is encapsulated in the keel area to increase ultimate stability and stiffen up the roll period. Airex foam is used to core the hull sides above the waterline, and end-grain balsa and Divinycell foam are used to keep the decks and superstructure light and stiff. This use of composites topside contributes significantly to the yacht's impressive sense of initial stability.

Performance Test

The owners of our newly commissioned test boat were getting underway for their temporary home-port, so we joined them for a sea trial en route. The seas were calm, just 2 to 3 feet, but it was apparent that the beamy Krogen has a surprising degree of form stability, as well as a very comfortable motion. But like most displacement trawlers, this one has active stabilizers to steady her in a trough. Heavily built and ballasted for supreme seaworthiness offshore, Krogens are patterned after rugged commercial-fishing trawlers that persevere through the worst kind of weather. While the average planing hull will capsize if it rolls much beyond 40 degrees, the Krogen 58 will come back for more after an 85-degree roll.

The Krogen 58 is available with either single or twin engines, but I would take the twins any day. The twins draw a foot less water than the singles, they're completely protected by full skegs, and they have the added benefit of redundancy and improved maneuverability. There's so much hull under water that a fresh breeze has very little effect on the boat when docking, and the response to the rudder and engines is very predictable.

This 58's ride is authoritative and solid, with none of the extreme accelerations to which high-speed yachts continuously subject their occupants. Better still, the noise levels throughout the Krogen 58's interior were probably the lowest I've ever recorded on any yacht: just 68 dBA in the pilothouse, 73 dBA in the saloon, and 68 dBA in the aft staterooms at full power.

The big windows in the pilothouse offer excellent visibility, and the forward-sloping windshield increases room while eliminating glare. The horizon is always above the pulpit from the captain's perspective; the Portuguese bridge with its wraparound bulwark is salty and functional, especially in heavy weather; and the starboard bridge wing and docking station are nice features. Visibility from the raised flybridge above the boat deck is not impeded by radar arches and smokestacks, and you can get almost anywhere on this boat via molded stairs, not ladders.

The yacht is remarkably well outfitted from the factory, and it's all absolutely top-notch stuff. Standard equipment includes Aquadrive thrust bearings, 8 and 20 kW gensets and a 4 kW inverter, Mathers engine controls, twenty-four house and starting batteries, Freeman watertight doors, Gebo sliding windows, windlass, Glendinning Cablemasters, 1,000-pound davit, 78,000 Btu AC, fully equipped galley, VacuFlush toilets, and washer-dryer units. Price as tested with options, including the hydraulic bow thruster, twin-anchor windlass, and active stabilizers, was just under $1.7 million.

The elegantly appointed Krogen is the last word in comfort and safety for a cruising couple (and the dog and the kids): easily handled, superbly engineered, with redundant systems, and authentic open-ocean capability. Whether you want to spend a week onboard close to home or cruise the world for a year, this winner of a yacht could be your sanctuary.

Nordhavn 40

NORDHAVN

Nordhavn 40 Specifications

LOA:	39'9"
Beam:	14'6"
Draft:	4'9"
Displacement:	50,000 lb.
Fuel capacity:	920 gal.
Water capacity:	200 gal.

Although it's the smallest model in trawler-builder Nordhavn's lineup, the full-displacement 40 is designed and built to transport its passengers safely in open-ocean conditions.

Design

In overall design, the Nordhavn 40 has a raised, flush foredeck; a Portuguese bridge protecting a raised, western-style-rig pilothouse; a main-deck-level saloon aft; and a small cockpit. Geographically, the master stateroom is below the forecastle, the head and guest stateroom are below the pilothouse (which allows full headroom in these spaces), and the engine room is below the saloon.

This is a seaworthy vessel for a number of rea-sons. The Nordhavn 40 features an exceptionally high freeboard forward: 6 feet to the gunwale and 7 feet to the solid bulwark. A larger interior volume results, making the yacht more livable than might be expected of a mere 40-footer. The Nordhavn also has large forecastle bulwark scuppers designed to shed stability-impairing topside water quickly.

Equally important is the underwater hull design; the Nordhavn's deep, buoyant forefoot should minimize the amount of time the underbody spends drying out in a heavy sea and eliminate pounding for improved ride quality. The range of stability of the Nordhavn 40 is close to 180 degrees, assuming an intact superstructure.

Other seaworthiness-enhancing features include a Portuguese bridge, which consists of a bulwark forward of the bridge intended to deflect green water that makes it over the bow—or, at least, diminish the force of impact against the deckhouse and windows. Forward-facing tempered glass windows are designed to resist the pressure of seawater breaking against them at high velocity. They're a full ⅜ inch thick.

Cockpit

Let's start the tour of the Nordhavn 40 by boarding from the stern. The cockpit is entered through either transom or starboard-side doors, giving the owners some boarding flexibility when moored stern- or starboard side-to. It's shiplike in its depth, at 3 feet from deck to gunwale, and it measures 5 feet, 7 inches long by 12 feet wide.

Below the cockpit, the lazarette holds four batteries, a battery charger, and cockpit drain lines that lead overboard from the hatch gutters. The rudder installation is a textbook example of how to install steering gear: well supported and with hard stops set at 35 degrees.

Saloon

Entered from the cockpit, the saloon—nicely finished in teak veneer and joiner work—is the yacht's focal point. The saloon is fresh and airy with large opening windows around three sides and daylight streaming down from the bridge forward. An L-shaped lounge with storage below and table are to starboard. Opposite is a countertop with cabinets below.

The Nordhavn's galley is forward to port in the saloon, with a U-shaped countertop forming an island that separates the two spaces. The double sink is amply proportioned at 12 by 12 inches per section and 8 inches deep. The cabinets directly overhead on a plane with the forward edge of the sink become head-knockers when you lean forward to wash the dishes. Our test boat had a three-burner propane stove with oven, trash compactor, refrigerator, and microwave oven. Storage cabinets and drawers provide adequate space for supplies, and a Sub-Zero freezer is opposite to starboard by the stairs to the bridge.

Engine Room

When you walk down a ladder from the saloon to the lower deck companionway, just to port is a narrow, 17-inch watertight door leading to the Nordhavn 40's engine room. At 12 feet from forward to aft bulkheads, this is one big engine room—but it's narrow (about 74 in.) between the 460-gallon, fiberglass fuel tanks where the 130 hp Lugger L668D, six-cylinder, naturally aspirated diesel resides. Based on a John Deere tractor engine, an engine life of 30,000 hours is not uncommon; up to 85,000 hours has been recorded, according to Lugger.

Those twin fiberglass saddle tanks will never rust or corrode, which means they should never have to be replaced. They shouldn't cause fuel-system clogging, either—a significant improvement over black iron or aluminum tanks, both of which are susceptible to those problems.

The engine has soft mounts attached to large (14 by 5 in.) gusset-supported, wood-cored hull stringers. This combination of soft and hard is a great vibration-attenuating combination, and helps explain the boat's noticeably low vibration levels. A single seacock leads from the engine to the keel-cooler, providing a closed-loop cooling system for the main engine. Located aft is an 8 kW Northern Lights generator and a 27 hp Yanmar get-home diesel swinging a folding propeller. This engine is good for maybe 4 to 5 knots.

Water and fuel hoses are neatly run and well labeled, the space is well lit, perforated-aluminum paneling reduces noise levels outside, and the fuel-tank sight gauges are surrounded and protected by aluminum extrusions. Cooling hoses are neatly and gently radiused to prevent chafing around machinery and limber holes. Overhead panels lift out in the unlikely event that the engine needs to be replaced, eliminating the need for major surgery. Everything that needs to be is accessible, and the engineering in the engine compartment is commendable.

Accommodations

The Nordhavn 40 has a two-stateroom, one-head cabin layout forward. The master stateroom is forward and up three steps, a design that takes advantage of the yacht's 6-foot-plus freeboard at the bow. The master island berth, 6 feet, 6 inches long and 4 feet, 11 inches across at its widest point, opens easily on gas boosters for access to the bow thruster and battery, as well as to the significant storage space below. The opening hatch overhead is 20 inches across, and a ladder leads up to it so you have an exit if the boat goes down stern-first. Back in the master stateroom, his and hers hanging lockers, a built-in vanity with drawers, under-gunwale lockers, and additional counter space add the extra storage room needed for longer voyages.

Moving aft to the guest stateroom to port, there is a pair of 78-inch bunks, a built-in vanity with drawers, a small hanging locker, storage under the lower berth, access to the engine room, and a combination Splendide washer-dryer unit made in Italy. This stateroom, about as big overall as a queen-size bed, is there just to sleep or to do the laundry in, and it handles those activities well enough. The yacht's single head is functional and has a shower unit with a built-in seat.

Bridge

Our Nordhavn 40 had a small bridge that, as our test boat's owner put it, doesn't quite have room for a pilot's chair. The lack of interior room in the bridge results from leaving enough room forward and topside for the low forward bulkhead of the Portuguese bridge.

The flat finish in the helm area minimizes glare, there's ample room for electronics, and a chart table hinges up when needed to port. The mullions between the glass windows are as wide as 7 inches, though, and take a cumulative chunk out of the operator's horizon. A raised observation lounge seat is aft on the bridge, with a sea berth above and behind.

Port and starboard bridge-wing doors lead to the weather decks, where 40-inch-high bulkheads make this little boat seem more like a U.S. Coast Guard cutter. An 11-foot tender is hoisted aboard by a mast and boom and stowed atop the saloon, aft of the pilothouse. The outriggers used to suspend the paravane stabilizers are supported by the same mast.

The railings forward are solid; farther aft on the foredeck, they transition to less-secure lifelines supported by 29-inch-high stanchions. I would prefer solid 1¼-inch-diameter, 32- to 34-inch-high stainless steel railings throughout for the added security they provide.

Construction

Nordhavn builds the 40 with a solid fiberglass hull. A skin coat of chop wet out in premium vinylester resin prevents osmotic blistering and print-through of follow-on woven fiberglass. General-purpose orthophthalic resin wets out subsequent alternating layers of woven roving and mat that build the hull bottom to a nominal thickness of 1¼ inches and the hull sides to ½ inch or more at the gunwales. For greater stiffness and light weight, hull stringers are constructed of fiberglass-encapsulated Divinycell foam except near the engines, where wood is used to resist compression loads from engine-mounting bolts. The hull stringers in way of the engine, where they serve as engine beds, are cored with marine plywood and encapsulated with fiberglass; this method resists engine-mounting-bolt compression loads and helps absorb engine vibrations.

The hull-to-deck joint is as bulletproof as any I've seen; it's mechanically fastened on 4-inch centers (every other fastener is a through-bolt), bonded with a polyurethane adhesive, and then fiberglassed from the inside. The deck and superstructure are cored with Divinycell on vertical surfaces and balsa (which is more impervious to thermal heating and stiffer than PVC foam) on the decks to keep the topsides light and stiff. The hollow keel has a steel channel fiberglassed in as part of the structure to resist grounding-impact loads. A cast-bronze shoe projects past the keel, forming a skeg that supports the bottom of the rudder.

Nordhavn 40 Performance Results

RPM	Speed, knots	Speed, mph	Fuel Use, gph	Nautical mpg	Range, statute miles	Range, nm	Statute mpg	Noise Level, Helm, dBA	Trim, degrees
1,200	6	6.9	0.98	6.12	5,830	5,069	7.04	68	1.5
1,500	7	8.1	1.84	3.80	3,623	3,150	4.38	68	2
1,900	8	9.2	3.89	2.06	1,958	1,703	2.37	70	3
2,200	8.5	9.8	5.78	1.47	1,400	1,218	1.69	75	4
2,400	9	10.4	8.74	1.03	981	853	1.18	81	4.5

The Nordhavn 40 is covered by a transferable two-year comprehensive structural warranty; blistering is not covered in writing, but Jim Leishman, one of Nordhavn's owners, says the company will stand by its product in this area. OEM-installed components are covered for one year or longer.

Performance Test

As is too often the case, the day of our sea trial dawned calm and sunny, with hardly a puff of salt air, so we didn't get to experience firsthand the Nordhavn 40's vaunted seakeeping abilities. A few comments, though: our test boat required seven turns of the wheel to go from hard port to hard starboard. Certainly this is excessive, even for a boat that tops out at 9 knots. Once the rudder was against the hard stops set at a full 35-degree angle, the Nordhavn turned very sharply in just over a boat length; we managed 360-degree turns in an average of just 31 seconds. The pivot point at hard rudder is just about at the pilothouse, so the boat is easily and intuitively maneuvered around close-aboard objects, such as lobster pots.

Our torque-y Lugger diesel, driving a 28-by-24-inch, four-blade Michigan propeller, provided good responsiveness to the throttle, particularly given the vessel's modest power-to-weight ratio. I didn't try out the Naiad stabilizers, which are only effective at speed, or the paravanes, which also function at anchor. But count on either system to dramatically reduce the rolling particularly inherent in any displacement-hull design. Nearly 3 tons (5,600 lb.) of fuel in the full tanks low in the hull also helped.

As I walked around on deck underway, the predominant noise source varied from one area to another. When I leaned back over the transom and out from under the overhang above, the engine's dry exhaust—exiting through its pipe terminus some 20 feet above the waterline—was the loudest noise detected. When I moved forward a few feet, the exhaust noise diminished and the propeller discharge started to catch up and assert itself, dBA-wise—which means this is one quiet boat back aft. The other welcome benefit of the dry exhaust exiting at altitude, in addition to low machinery-noise levels at cruising speed, is the total absence of smoke in the cockpit. The accompanying table summarizes the performance results of our sea trial.

Note the futility of trying to drive a displacement vessel above its hull speed; increasing speed from 8 to 8.5 knots cuts efficiency by approximately 25 percent. Noise levels in the saloon ranged a few decibels higher than in the pilothouse; however, the yacht was commendably quiet everywhere on board and throughout the vessel's speed range.

Of the 40-foot yachts that could potentially cross an ocean safely, the Nordhavn 40 is certainly among them. Ruggedly built, well engineered, and comfortably appointed, this is a well-found seagoing vessel that many trawler types would be proud to call their own. The Nordhavn 40 meets the standards of seaworthiness implicit in the builder's claims, and provides the means for long-range cruising in comfort and style.

Here's the sturdy little American Tug 34, a good-looking, full-keel, semidisplacement cruiser with a full-beam saloon and raised pilot-house forward. A flybridge is molded to look like a tug's smoke-stack (a nice effect), and aft-facing windows in the pilothouse open up visibility astern—a point often overlooked on modern seagoing craft. A single 355 hp Cummins (a lot of power for a 34 ft. trawler) produces a 21-knot top end and a solid 18-knot cruise. It's a small boatbuilding world after all: the company is owned and operated by three former Nordic Tugs employees.

Krogen's smallest displacement trawler, the 39 is a solid little ship with 2,000 pounds of lead ballast and an 80 hp John Deere trac-tor engine for long-range dependability at a leisurely 8-knot pace. A 700-gallon fuel capacity will last a while (2,500 miles to be ex-act, according to the builder, at 7 knots) with the diesel sipping fuel at hull speed. Built for a couple to cruise comfortably aboard, the single bow stateroom is comfortable and spacious, and the for-ward part of the engine room has stand-up headroom. Other Kro-gen trawlers to 58 feet are available, as well as a pair of semidis-placement pilothouse yachts. KROGEN

The Grand Banks 52 Europa is one of the builder's latest efforts with three or four staterooms, depending on whether an aft cabin is fitted. Essentially a flush-deck motor yacht with a large, airy sa-loon continuing forward and transitioning to the pilothouse, the 52 is capable of making 18 knots with optional twin-diesel power.

NEIL RABINOWITZ/GRAND BANKS

Mainship's 390 Trawler is a semidisplacement full-keel vessel that has proven popular in the charter industry. Comfortable for a cou-ple with simple systems and a relatively low price, the 390's prac-ticality is undeniable. A lower helm station allows comfortable, cli-mate-controlled piloting in hot or cold weather, and a second stateroom allows another couple to come along for the occasional weekend afloat. Single or twin diesels providing speeds to 16 knots are available; hull speed is about 8 knots. MAINSHIP

Here's a shot of the doughty Nordhavn 40 with flopper-stoppers and paravanes deployed. See previous page for more on this sub-ject. This is as close to looking like a ship as any 40-footer ever gets. NORDHAVN

The 53-foot displacement yacht Selene is the result of a joint effort between Taiwanese builder Jet Tern Marine and Florida's David Marlow Marine Sales. The boat has a 1,000-gallon fuel capacity and carries 350 gallons of water. It has two sisters, 47 and 50 feet in length. The owner's suite on this Selene 50, which is finished in teak like the rest of the interior, can be ordered with a private entrance; a third stateroom/office is available. A Portuguese bridge, all the rage in trawler yachts for its salty effect and sometime (rough-water) practicality, is included. Also included are forward-raked windows in the pilothouse, which adds space for electronics and reduces or eliminates windshield glare. With a single 280 hp Cummins, the Selene 53 cruises at 9 knots and hits 11.5 knots wide open.   SELENE

Nordic Tugs produces solidly built semidisplacement trawlers in an ever-expanding lineup that now ranges from 32 to 52 feet. The 37 shown here is a midrange, two-stateroom, one-head, single-diesel cruiser with a salty look and pleasant sea manners. Hull length is close to 38 feet—including the extended running surface created by the integral swim platform—which improves ride quality, efficiency, and adds to hull speed. The hull is driven by 55 hp to 8 knots (at 3.5 nmpg); wringing all the power out of a Cummins 330 produces just over 17 knots (at 1.2 nmpg).

Here is a Steve Davis rendering of a Bruce Roberts–designed Voyager 55 raised-pilothouse trawler. The nearly plumb stem and raked transom make an attractive and surprisingly congruous combination. A Portuguese bridge, western-style flybridge, and forward-swept pilothouse windshield make this a businesslike long-range cruiser. This aft-master yacht is designed to be constructed of either aluminum or steel. A 200 hp diesel produces a 9-knot cruise, and fuel capacity is a generous 1,700 gallons. A planing-hull version of this yacht is also available.   STEVE DAVIS

Mainship has tapped into a strong market for budget-conscious buyers of planing and semidisplacement trawlers. The beamy 430 trawler shown here is an aft-cabin design with a two- or three-stateroom layout and galley up or down, depending on the number of staterooms. The profile is contemporary yet won't be dated in five or six years. A good-running boat, the 430 makes about 18 knots with a pair of 350 hp diesels.   MAINSHIP

Other Yachts: Marine Medleys

Many yachts and boats don't fit neatly into any of these vessel-type categories. There are combination walkaround-center consoles, pilot-house outboards, flybridge yachts, sedans sans fly-bridges, aft-superstructure expedition yachts, and so on. Variety truly is the spice of life!

1997 Fairline 65 Squadron

FAIRLINE

Fairline 65 Squadron Specifications

LOA:	65'0"
Beam:	17'4"
Draft:	4'9"
Displacement:	74,000 lb. (dry)
Fuel capacity:	1,105 gal.
Water capacity:	336 gal.

Fairline is a highly regarded British builder of high-end express, flybridge, and motor yachts from 30 to 65 feet. The 65-foot Squadron became my new benchmark of performance when I tested it in 1997 off Miami: high- and low-speed steering respon-siveness, lower helm station visibility, and downsea tracking were on par with many 30-foot outboards. This is British naval architect Bernard Olesinski's hull design, which delivers an exceptionally com-fortable ride in rough water.

Fairline's line of Squadron 43- to 65-foot cruis-ing motor yachts is designed to appeal to the U.S. market, which, in part, includes owner-operators moving up from smaller yachts. On this boat, Fair-line freed up more room by eliminating the crew quarters common to European models. Although this approach to yacht design might not be so radi-cal on this side of the pond, the Squadron 65 has a lot going for it with its good looks, family-friendly interior, and exceptional handling.

Fairline clearly sees a future for its flagship, having recently built a dedicated 30,000-square-foot facility for its production. With sights set on expanding its U.S. market, Fairline is building yachts with interiors that are plushly appointed with matched-grain, lacquered, and inlaid wood-working. Styling is fresh and contemporary, but still practical; American cherry woodwork, silk fabrics, and Connolly leather upholstery are now included as standard equipment.

Design

Fairline has added 3 feet to this model, which was originally built as a 62-footer. The extra waterline length has naturally improved ride, handling, and performance, which has resulted in more storage space for fenders and assorted water toys. It also provides more interior space, including room for a larger master-stateroom arrangement and a larger aft cabin. Fairline's largest model has a moderate beam-to-length ratio, which promises (and delivered in our sea trial) significantly improved sea-keeping ability—especially the ability to cruise at higher speeds when the going gets rough. Moderate beam also means improved efficiency over wider hulls. The Squadron 65's sharp entry and high chines forward taper to a moderate 19 degrees of deadrise aft. This combination provides a smooth ride heading into a chop, good tracking in a following sea, and an easily driven hull.

Like other builders that know how to do it right, Fairline uses propeller pockets to keep the shaft angle to 11 degrees and to reduce draft without detracting from efficiency or speed—which may even be improved. In fact, prop pockets make in-line engine placement this far aft possible.

Construction

Fairline does a good job keeping the weight down, and there's nothing like cutting fat to improve speed. The hull starts with an isophthalic-resin skin coat over the gelcoat for blistering protection. A hand-laid laminate of mat, woven, and directional roving is reinforced by hollow, interlocking stringers and intermediate bulkheads. Decks are cored with foam for further weight savings. The hull-to-deck joint gets its share of attention too, being both through-bolted and glassed together for a high-strength, leak-proof bond.

Everywhere I looked in the engine room and under hatches, I saw evidence of solid engineering and attention to detail. The large engine beds are bored out to eliminate wood and fiberglass that is just along for the ride structurally. To minimize vibration and noise transmission, the engines float on soft mounts. Shafts are connected to transmissions by soft couplings, which avoid metal-to-metal contact. Engine-room exhaust blowers, manual-

backup bilge pumps, a fixed fire-extinguishing system, and emergency steering are all included.

Saloon

Inside the saloon, the satin-lacquered American cherry sheen looks like it's ¼ inch thick, and every grain pattern in the wood is eye-catching. The sliding door and window frames aft are framed in polished stainless steel, which—along with the handsome woodwork—nicely sets off the off-white carpeting and fabric liner overhead. Plentiful fresh air is courtesy of the aft electric window and sliding side windows.

The saloon is a two-tiered arrangement, designed around headroom requirements in the engine room (aft) and the full-width master stateroom (forward) below. Headroom forward in the saloon is on the slim side for a 65-footer, but it keeps the profile and topside weight manageable in this two-deck interior. The wraparound leather lounge seats, TV, wet bar, and icemaker aft on the cockpit level will spoil those who fancy themselves mariners.

Located up three stairs (which could use a little more clearance overhead) to the forward saloon area is a huge lounge and burr-elm table for sit-down dining. Across to starboard is a fully equipped teak- and holly-soled galley tucked behind a glossy cherry partition that runs from overhead to deck. This design cuts off the chef from the saloon's festivities and it reduces visibility aft from the helm seat. On the other hand, some chefs like the added privacy this layout affords, to say nothing of the extra cabinet space.

A side-by-side refrigerator-freezer is concealed behind cabinet doors with an Avonite countertop and storage space above. A lid lifts off and stows behind the four-burner range when it's turned on; as a safety feature, I would like to see a microswitch to cut power to the stove when the lid is in place. One of the two sinks has a garbage disposal, and most anyone will feel at home with features like a trash compactor, dishwasher, multifunction oven, exhaust ventilation, and silverware storage included in the galley layout. The galley window slides open as does a decidedly shiplike weather door next to the counter, which also allows easy topside access from the lower helm.

One of the great features about cruising yachts is that families can cruise together instead of having to choose between bridge and saloon camps. This cruising plan presupposes a functional lower helm station, and what is needed for that—above all else—is good visibility outside the boat, especially at the high speeds this boat is capable of making.

Lower Helm

The Fairline's lower helm station is forward of the galley on centerline. I liked the large, high windshield with its narrow, unobtrusive mullions; you'll see everything you need to forward of this boat. On some other boats of this style (apparently designed by people who have never had to operate them), I've had to duck when seated at the helm to see straight ahead, at least when the boat is at zero trim. The same goes for the small tapered side windows on other boats (especially the Italian-made) of this genre, which happily are functionally large on the Fairline.

From the helm seat, you can easily see outside from about 210 to 120 degrees relative; the biggest obstruction is the galley partition behind the helm seat. You can see out the back of the boat without moving from the contoured helm seat, but for backing into a slip, you'll want to take up station at the cockpit controls or up on the flybridge. Being up high enough off the water to accommodate a stateroom below also enhances the scenic view.

The controls were laid out like a contemporary truck cab, directly at my fingertips, and it was good not to have to lean forward to reach them. However, the engine gauges would be easier to read if they were about 2 feet closer. The compass is situated up high, so you can keep your eyes on the road while steering the course you've laid out on the adjacent chart table. The radar and the electronic navigator are off to starboard below the chart table; in fact, they would benefit from being angled

toward the helm for easier viewing. The dashboard area is exquisitely finished in burr elm, and the small-diameter cherry steering wheel is a nice detail. There is ample room for keeping tide tables, chart packs, and other necessities in a huge storage locker next to the companionway.

Flybridge

A classy cherry staircase winds its way from the saloon up to the flybridge, or you can use the teak cockpit ladder if you've just parked the Jetski on the swim platform. There's room for two at the centerline helm seat and more room for lots of company on nearby lounges. The view from the bridge helm is excellent.

Topside

Teak steps lead from the bridge down to the teak cockpit, which is a great place for dockside cocktails and for showing off all the toys in the stern. Two doors (which could use stronger latches) open to the large teak swim platform with its own storage compartment and concealed swim ladder. The cockpit has a few secrets of its own: a hood lifts open for access to a 300 kg tender davit and cockpit shower, and a hidden gangway (or passarelle) extends and raises or lowers electrically. Fenders and mooring lines stow in cockpit lockers to port and starboard, and the Glendinning Cablemaster is to starboard aft. There's also an optional crew or kid's stateroom aft of the lazarette with its own head that has a shower and fold-down seat hiding the toilet. The head is accessed by raising one end of the aft lounge seat and climbing down a ladder. Engine-room access is from the cockpit, and there's plenty of storage room in the commodious lazarette.

Side-deck safety is excellent with wide walkways, handrails, and high stainless steel bow railings. There's more sunbathing area forward, along with more fender storage in power-ventilated storage lockers. If you've ever wished for a large forepeak storage locker for lines, fenders, and cleaning supplies, your search has ended with the Squadron 65. For mooring, sturdy stainless pipe cleats and chocks provide plenty of flexibility, and the chain locker is accessible through a large opening hatch next to the dual-purpose windlass. Contoured covers fold down to conceal the fuel fills—a nice touch.

Accommodations

The four-stateroom, three-head cabin features independent climate controls, stereos and TVs, and opening portholes. This might be a small yacht to have a full-width master stateroom, but it works well as executed by Fairline. There's a queen-size bed, sofa, walk-in closet, entertainment center, and something else you don't see enough of on many U.S.-built boats: large opening side ports. I would increase the wattage on the overhead lighting in the cabin in general, though. Another nice detail, in addition to the seemingly acres of gorgeous cherry wood, is the contoured overhead liner. The private head features a toilet and bidet, enclosed shower-tub unit, and Avonite countertops.

The starboard guest stateroom has two single berths and a private head. The port stateroom has over and under bunks, and shares a head with the forward stateroom, which has a queen-size island berth, hanging and storage lockers, and a large concealed overhead hatch. A washer-dryer unit is located off the companionway concealed behind a large cherry door. An optional layout eliminates the port stateroom in favor of a larger master stateroom and head.

Performance Test

With Fairline's John Skubal and Russ Pearson on board, we found ideal conditions for our performance test. We had the calm inshore waters of Port Everglades (Florida) for fuel consumption and speed measuring. Fairline has its hull design and weight distribution in sync; there's no more than 5 degrees of bow rise in the transition to plane, and trim stayed at acceptable levels without the need for trim tabs.

For the seakeeping part of the test, an easterly wind had been blowing at over 20 knots for the last few days on this early March day, so we didn't have to head too far past the jetties to discover that the prediction for 7- to 9-foot seas was fairly accurate. These were ideal conditions that, incidentally, match those often seen in the open English Channel waters, which helped refine and shape this hull design. At 1,000 rpm, the bow dipped about every fifth wave, but as I increased power, the boat came up on plane quickly. Surprisingly, I was able to easily maintain 19 knots heading into the seas once past the sea buoy. Half of the boat's length came out of the water on occasion, but there was no pounding; the hull landed gently and without protest. The forward sections also made for a dry ride, especially given the sea state. When I saw the boat out of the water a few days after our test ride, the reason for the exceptionally smooth ride became clear: the Fairline's bow reminded me of no boat so much as a Bertram with its high chines, bottom strakes, and deep fine entry.

Drifting in the trough, the boat proved to have generous form stability: rolls averaged just 10 to 15 degrees to leeward. The power steering allowed a very tight and responsive three turns lock-to-lock, which I think is almost perfect for any boat of this size or smaller. Heading downsea, the Fairline handled exceptionally well, needing only an occasional turn of the wheel to keep her between the buoys. The Squadron 65 handled nimbly, much more like an outboard-powered center console than a 30-ton motor yacht.

Idling up the Intracoastal Waterway and down the Dania cutoff, handling at no-wake speed was sure and predictable. So was backing into our slip, with the crisp MMC controls and a responsive bow thruster—this despite stiff winds and a megayacht bow 50 feet in front of our slip.

Visibility from the bridge was good all around, although I couldn't see the starboard quarter from the wheel. A cockpit control station solves part of that problem if what's back aft is all that counts. The upper helm is designed to be used sitting down, which means you have to stoop to use the controls when you are standing. I would like to see

Fairline 65 Squadron Performance Results

RPM	Speed, knots	Speed, mph	Fuel Use, gph	Nautical mpg	Statute mpg	Range, nm	Range, statute miles	Bridge Noise Level, dBA	Trim, degrees
1,000	10.6	12.2	12	0.88	1.02	879	1,011	60	1
1,250	12.6	14.5	21.8	0.58	0.66	575	661	62	2
1,500	16.0	18.4	33.4	0.48	0.55	477	548	67	4
1,750	20.5	23.6	51.7	0.40	0.46	395	454	68	4
2,000	25.1	28.9	69.9	0.36	0.41	357	411	70	4
2,250	28.2	32.4	106.4	0.27	0.30	264	303	72	4

a sliding helm seat because my knees pinched up against the wheel and legroom was on the tight side. The instruments are easier to read on the bridge than they are down below, and there's also room for chart work up there to starboard.

There's ample room for company on the bridge on comfortable, contoured lounge seating, and the storage space inside is the only place on the boat where I saw any slipshod glasswork. A sunpad area is aft along with a refrigerator, storage space, and small table. Sound levels in the saloon were very quiet, with readings of 70 dBA at 1,000 rpm and 75 dBA at 2,000 rpm.

You won't find a better-running, more efficiently propelled, and richly finished boat from any other builder, at least for anything like the same money. The sooner the big U.S. production boatbuilders start designing hulls like this one, the more they'll sell and the happier their customers will be.

The Renwick Group, owners of Marine Projects, which builds Princess motor yachts (sold in Americanized versions in the U.S. as Viking Sport Cruisers), now also owns Fairline. However, the two companies remain competitors under separate management. The accompanying table summarizes performance results for the Fairline 65 Squadron.

Lyman Morse 74

BILLY BLACK

Lyman Morse 74 Specifications

LOA:	74'0"
LWL:	67'4"
Beam:	18'2"
Draft:	4'10"
Displacement:	82,500 lb.
Power:	twin 1,300 hp MAN D2842LE 404 diesels

The 74-foot Lyman Morse–built, Mark Setzer–designed *Magpie*, which I first saw in an artist's rendering, was absolutely gorgeous: beautiful, well-proportioned, classical lines in a hardtop express motor yacht. But, as I found out on the sea trial, the exterior profile was matched line for line by an

interior just as impressive, with exquisitely crafted woodworking the likes of which I hadn't seen in my years of writing boat reviews. So how did this one-of-a-kind gem come into being?

Owner Nardi Suydam was looking for a unique yacht, unlike anything else he had seen. This yacht was to have a four-stateroom, three-head cabin layout to accommodate eight people, suitable for long-range cruising to Bermuda and in the Caribbean. The cabin was to reflect the luxurious sailing-yacht interiors of the 1920s and 1930s, finely crafted in mahogany and teak.

A 25-knot cruise at full load was required, and the hull was to deliver a comfortable ride in moderate offshore sea conditions at speed. The range was to be 1,000 nm while cruising at a comfortable 20 knots. "She made 34.5 knots on sea trial with a little over a half load of fuel, and that's without tweaking the propellers," commented Nardi. The boat was to be easily handled by two people, including a professional captain, and not so large that it couldn't get into smaller marinas. "We came in at a draft of 4 feet, 10 inches, which just beat my goal of 5 feet," he said. As is evident in the final product, this yacht was to be crafted without compromise to the very highest standard, using the finest materials available.

Design

When Nardi first spoke to the people at Lyman Morse about the project, it soon became clear to the builder that *Magpie* was to be its most sophisticated yacht project to date, and this from a yard well regarded for its high-end custom power and sailing yachts.

J. B. Turner, general manager and part owner of Lyman Morse, talked at length with Nardi, and recommended naval architect Ward Setzer. Nardi, who had already interviewed several design firms, was impressed, and the owner-designer-builder team was soon complete. Nardi found in Setzer Design a top-notch firm eager to give substance to his vision of the perfect yacht. Setzer, a specialist in larger yachts, was—as far as Nardi was concerned—perfect for the job because he didn't have a lot of preconceived ideas about how to design a 74-footer. He was very impressed with Setzer's first rendering and, needless to say, he was very pleased with the final results. "We added some height to the pilothouse, along with tumblehome aft and a raked

transom," noted Nardi. "Other than that, his first drawing was right on target."

Early on in the design phase, Lyman Morse built a full-scale interior mockup to fine-tune the layout, which resulted in the hull design being stretched from 65 to 74 feet. To achieve the speed and range that Nardi had specified, it was evident that *Magpie* must be built both light and strong. Building such a yacht is certainly achievable, but at a premium. So, the hull was built using the SCRIMP resin-infusion process, with premium vinylester resin used throughout the laminate. SCRIMP minimizes the resin content of the laminate to improve its strength-to-weight ratio, and produces a sound skin-to-core bond between the inner and outer fiberglass laminates and the core. Janicki Machine of Sedro-Woolley, Washington, was chosen to build the multipart molds for the hull and superstructure using its state-of-the-art, five-axis milling equipment.

The hull itself is cored with a lightweight end-grain balsa, and the bulkheads and stringers are of composite-sandwich construction to keep the weight down. Not surprisingly, the deck superstructure is also built of a lightweight composite sandwich. So far, so good; however, to meet the targeted speed and range goals, Setzer Design further specified that the interior furniture and cabinetry be built of lightweight foam- and balsa-cored construction, along with galley countertops of aluminum honeycomb-cored granite.

The result is a 74-foot yacht that weighs in at a remarkable 86,000 pounds at half load. For comparison, conventionally built yachts in this size range with hand-laid fiberglass hulls and solid joinery can easily reach a displacement of well over 100,000 pounds.

Thousands of board feet of mahogany and teak were hand-selected to produce bookend-matched cabinet and drawer fronts. Galley cabinets and end tables were sent to Heritage Company in England to be inlaid, and ebony was used by Lyman Morse as an inlay in much of the yacht's interior. The mahogany cabin-stairway baluster, itself a work of art, extends from the pilothouse down two decks to the master stateroom, and was brought on board in one piece, ready to install. Soft radiuses define the interior's wood paneling and settee foundations, creating soft lines that seamlessly blend the different areas of the saloon (inspired by Herreshoff and John Mumford), galley, and staterooms together. The varnished mahogany valance above the saloon windows is curved to three different radiuses, and it's flawlessly fashioned together. There's also a lot of impeccable hand carving, including the end-table and settee legs, and the rope and scallop detail in the master-berth headboard. "I love good woodworking, and so did my father before me," noted the owner. "That's a big part of what attracted me to Lyman Morse."

The owner specified that no screws or other fastenings were to be visible, so Lyman Morse devised a removable system of king planks held in place with gem catches. And the CNC-cut and Awlgrip-painted, removable okoume plywood overhead panels in the yacht's interior look like they're made of molded fiberglass. "Nardi came to us with three photos of other boats' interiors, and we did a lot of research into 1920s styling. That's how the classical interior styling came into being," said J.B. "With the exacting weight-control efforts and the quality of joinery in this yacht, this is our most sophisticated project to date."

Setzer Design drew the boat with an aft engine room, which has the advantage of effectively isolating machinery noises while allowing the vessel's 1,800 gallons of fuel to be centered over the hull's center of flotation. This minimizes trim change as fuel is consumed, delivering consistent ride quality offshore and unimpaired visibility over the bow, regardless of fuel load. Propeller pockets help achieve the design draft target, while still allowing the use of 32-by-44-inch propellers, well-matched to the yacht's 1,300 hp MAN diesels. At just 3,900 pounds, these engines have an unmatched power-to-weight ratio of 3:1 pounds per horsepower. The diesels are connected via jackshafts to remote-mounted 2:1 gear-ratio ZF V-drive transmissions. Remote-

mounting the gears allows the engines to be placed well aft in the hull, while permitting an efficient shaft angle of 11 degrees. And since the gears, rather than the engines, absorb the propeller thrust, the engines can be soft-mounted, helping to further diminish hull-generated vibration levels.

Other weight savings came from the selection of 16 and 30 kW Panda generators. "The electrical system is something we're very excited about," said J.B. "Every wire is labeled at both ends, and there is an entire back plane in the mechanical space under the saloon so we don't have to pull panels off for troubleshooting. There's about 5 miles of wiring in this boat, and it all runs through easily accessed wiring chases down one side of the boat." A pair of Glendinning Cablemasters below the cockpit makes light of shore power cable handling.

Two tanks hold 475 gallons of water, and a 1,500 GPD Sea Recovery watermaker keeps the tanks topped off at sea. A central climate-control system pipes chilled or heated water to quiet air handlers that are individually controlled throughout the yacht's interior.

Cockpit and Engine Room

The first clue to the yacht's joinery is when you are standing back at the stern, where the varnished-teak transom planking is let in to the hull precisely the thickness of the wood, producing a flush finish. The transom's compound curvature is beautiful to behold, especially the way it blends in seamlessly with the radiused transom corners and hull-side tumblehome. Traffic flow from the dock to the cockpit to the pilothouse is clear and straightforward, with port and starboard boarding gangways leading through wide, recessed cockpit doors. The cockpit is high-sided for safety and includes storage under the aft molded benches. In fact, topside safety was evidently a priority in the design phase: side decks are wide and flat, and railings are stout and high enough to do the job well.

Engine-room access is through a well-balanced, easily raised aluminum Freeman cockpit hatch in the cockpit's teak deck, and wing hatches provide for engine removal as needed. The engine room, with 5 feet, 7 inches of headroom, is well lit and cleanly laid out with the big MANs taking up most of the available space. Plumbing and wiring are neatly bundled and routed out of harm's way through chafe-resistant looming and grommets. Triple Racor fuel filter-separators for each engine provide shift-on-the-fly capability in case cleaning is needed offshore.

Delta T-louvered combustion air intakes in the cockpit sides provide combustion air to the engines, and a Van Cappellen engine-room air-intake system includes de-mister pads to isolate moisture and salt. Van Cappellen also did the noise-control engineering, which includes a mixture of solid (reflective) and perforated (absorbing) materials, depending on location. The forward end of the engine room, for instance, includes a solid sheet of aluminum to reflect sound away from the adjacent master stateroom. Dampening tiles were molded into the sides of the engine beds to attenuate vibrations. The engines' soft mounts and drivetrain jackshafts were provided by Aquadrive, and a Kushal damper plate on the flywheels further reduces vibrations and absorbs torsional shock when the gears are shifted. The engine beds are a composite of fiberglass-encapsulated ¾-inch plywood and high-density foam with a stainless steel cap into which the engine bolts are tapped. Solid beds and soft mounts do the best possible job of reducing vibration and sound levels.

If you want more evidence of uncompromising quality and attention to detail, Nardi specified custom-made, 316-series stainless steel screws and hardware topside to eliminate—or at least minimize—bleeding from all the metal components exposed to the elements. Screws were custom-made, and the polished stainless steel stern chocks and railings were manufactured in-house.

Pilothouse

Up a few steps from the cockpit, the teak-soled pilothouse features a pair of L-shaped settees and tables, all raised 6 inches above deck level to provide a good view through the large side windows. Raised port and starboard companion and helm seats are forward. Sliding side windows made by Freeman and overhead hatches let in plenty of fresh air, and the three frameless windshield glass panels, in addition to being leakproof, minimize the window-mullion width for uncluttered sight lines ahead. All-around visibility from the helm is excellent, and the boat could easily be backed into a slip without moving from the helm seat. The Glendinning electronic engine controls shift smoothly, with just the right amount of resistance at the forward-neutral-reverse detents, which are backed up by hardwired mechanical cables. The helm station includes a computer screen that can be used as a display for the engine-room monitor camera, as well as for the GPS plotter and radar. A second portable maneuvering-control unit, which includes steering and bow-thruster controls and a 30-foot umbilical cord, stows away in the cockpit.

Saloon

Down and forward from the pilothouse, the saloon is entered on varnished-teak stairs fitted with the mahogany baluster. The teak- and holly-soled space is full of natural light with its large side windows and many overhead opening hatches. To port, a plasma-screen TV is raised into position and lowered out of sight with its Auton lift system. In addition to DVD music videos, TV, and movies, the screen can display the radar and GPS plotter navigational pictures in the saloon.

Finished in rich leather, a settee is to port, below the TV; forward to starboard is a raised, U-shaped settee with an adjustable-height table complete with folding leaves. A stereo system above the electrical-system panels to starboard pipes music throughout the yacht. Another classy touch: the AC vents are crafted from a single piece of mahogany in a graceful wooden filigree pattern.

The portside galley is forward and down a few steps, wide open to the saloon. In fact, you can talk to the skipper at the helm station while boiling an egg on the four-burner cooktop. In addition to the composite-granite countertops, the galley features a U-shaped countertop, a large porthole at eye level over the sink, an oven, a dishwasher hidden behind a mahogany cabinet door, a trash compactor, and a Sub-Zero refrigerator-freezer. Stacked washer and dryer units are located just forward inside a cabinet.

Accommodations

In addition to providing a good seated view, the raised saloon dinette has another purpose: to create headroom for a stateroom situated directly below and just opposite the galley. This nifty European stateroom arrangement has a pair of twin beds down two steps from the lower saloon level. A head just forward is provided for use by this stateroom's occupants and as a day head.

Forward are port and starboard staterooms with stacked singles to starboard and a double berth to port. A doublewide sliding door (running forward and aft near the centerline) separates the two staterooms for privacy, and they also open wide to make one large space out of the two areas for daytime use. Forward in the bow is another head, with another separate shower. Even in the forward end, the cabin is bright and cheerful, with plenty of natural light coming in through the many opening portholes and overhead hatches.

The master stateroom is under the pilothouse and just forward of the engine room. In this location, when running in a seaway, the owner experiences minimal motion and accelerations, but also higher noise levels than forward in the yacht. The full-beam master stateroom includes a queen-size island berth with a headboard of hand-carved mahogany rope and burl cypress. A full-length countertop and desk are to port, and a deep cedar-lined closet is aft. The private owners' head is to starboard, and it has an inventive, user-friendly layout: you walk into a sink-vanity area in the middle, and separate toilet and shower areas are on either side. Finally, teak stairs lead back aft from the master suite and directly topside to the cockpit.

On our sea trial, *Magpie* delivered as promised. Handling was crisp and predictable, and the ride superbly smooth and dry in the stiff offshore chop, due to a 4.4:1 waterline-length-to-beam ratio and a fine entry. Bow rise coming up on plane was minimal, indicating well-balanced weight distribution for the hull form. The boat handled very well dockside, and sound levels throughout the interior were muted. "I wanted the performance and ride of a sportfisherman," concluded Nardi. "Speed, range, and woodworking. That's what this project was all about."

1997 Nauset 33 Bridge-Deck Cruiser

It's nice to know that Yankee ingenuity is alive and well—thriving, in fact, in the form of Nauset Marine's new 33-foot bridge-deck cruiser. Nauset Marine, a small Cape Cod, Massachusetts, boatbuilder and dealer, saw the possibilities in this former Cape Dory 33 hull, which had already been offered in flybridge and sedan configurations. But the appeal of the bridge-deck layout was irresistible for Nauset Marine owner, Phil Deschamps, and son David, the company's boat designer and builder. They had made it work in their successful 28-foot Down East lobster-style hull, so the greater interior volume of the 33 made it a viable candidate for successful

transformation when Nauset Marine bought the Cape Dory tooling several years ago.

The Nauset 33 combines the best of an express and a sedan with an aft engine room under the cockpit, a wide-open saloon-cabin below the bridge and trunk cabin, and a flybridge—just four steps up from the cockpit, with good visibility. Available with either single or twin diesels, this is an excellent 18- to 24-knot cruise hull design with a low-profile, stable layout. Nauset Marine builds custom cruising and fishing boats from 24 to 42 feet.

This bridge-deck cruiser does away with the pilothouse and expands the cabin back to the cockpit,

Nauset 33 Bridge-Deck Cruiser Specifications

LOA (on deck):	33'0"
Beam:	12'2"
Draft:	2'11"
Fuel capacity:	150 gal. single, 300 gal. twin
Water capacity:	60 gal.
Partial options list:	Onan 6 kW generator, twin 210 hp 6BT5.9-M Cummins diesels, 17,000 Btu reverse-cycle AC, bridge enclosure, Raytheon electronics suite, dual water-lock mufflers, Teleflex trim tabs

with the twin engines in our test boat protruding a foot or so into the cabin. This results in a huge single-level living area, more like a sailboat down below than anything else, only bigger. The cockpit is halfway (vertically) between the cabin and bridge, making either area easily accessible. Many people have likely shied away from the flybridge layout because of the typical seven or eight steps to the bridge. Families with small children and well-seasoned mariners will especially appreciate the chest-high bridge deck, which is on the same level as the trunk cabin, and just four steps up from the cockpit.

As I found during our performance test, the other distinct advantage of this low-profile design is excellent stability due to a low center of gravity. If you've ever thought that adding a conventional flybridge and tuna tower to a boat made little difference in its ride and stability, a sea trial onboard this rock-solid bridge-deck cruiser will make you think again.

Cockpit

The Nauset 33 can be boarded either over the side or onto the swim platform and through the transom door. The cockpit is roomy at 8 feet, 10 inches long, 9 feet, 11 inches wide, 27 inches deep, and 8 inches off the water. Three hatches lead to the lazarette over the rudders on centerline and to in-deck fish and storage boxes to port and starboard. A pair of corner-mounted 10-inch stern cleats is

reached through flush hawseholes in the teak coaming. A gutter around the cockpit perimeter forms a flange for the removable deck, a nice feature when it's time for major generator or engine work.

The sound-shielded generator was located on centerline just aft of the aft engine-room bulkhead. Nauset Marine went to great effort to keep the center of gravity far enough forward where it belongs (the lazarette is huge and, except for the generator, mostly empty), and it shows in the ease with which the boat gets on plane and runs at moderate trim with no tabs. The recessed cockpit liner makes a generous toe kick for good balance when you are leaning overboard. The 12-inch-wide side decks lead up to the foredeck, with grippy nonskid and rugged, 29-inch-high, 1¼-inch-diameter aluminum bow railings to keep you on a solid footing. Stainless or aluminum railings come in any shape and length. Any combination of side and bow cleats is available—our test boat had a single 12-inch bow cleat and a pair of 10-inch side cleats.

Flybridge

Just four steps take you to the Nauset 33's 7-foot, 8-inch-wide flybridge—a very approachable layout for the novice or landlubber. The helm is forward on centerline, well positioned for exceptionally good visibility forward when running and aft when backing into a slip—all while sitting down if you like. The helm was easy to operate when I was standing or seated, and the compass was at a good height in line with the tilt steering wheel. The instruments and various switches were conveniently situated; Nauset leaves enough room for a fancy array of electronics forward of the wheel. The entire console tilts back for easy electronics maintenance. Bench seats to port and aft accommodate several visitors; the area to starboard is left open—probably a good idea so it doesn't get too crowded topside. Our test boat's bridge was to be fully enclosed with thick, clear EZ2CY plastic side curtains, which allowed the owner to add climate control to the bridge with the 17,000 Btu AC unit installed under the bridge forward. A table drops down as a filler for the port bench, converting it into an extra berth for an overflow crowd.

This bridge arrangement provides an excellent combination of neighborly accessibility to make guests feel welcome topside and a remarkably user-friendly navigating bridge for the captain. The boat tends to be dry underway, so the natural objection to a low bridge is muted. It's also quiet, located away from the engines and the exhaust noise, and it lets the ship's company divide naturally into two or three convenient settings, if so desired.

Cabin

It was quite an experience stepping into this 20-foot, 6-inch-long cabin for the first time before it was finished. It was more like the cabin on the average 40-plus-footer. Of course, the trade-off is that the Nauset 33 gives up a pilothouse/saloon. The trunk cabin allows up to 79 inches of headroom forward and 75 inches aft, along with an 8-foot, 8-inch-wide sole, so the space seems very roomy, particularly with the six portholes, two sliding side windows, and large aft-facing windows overlooking the cockpit. The arrangement and size of the windows is a matter of choice, to a degree; for me, the more glass the better.

We took the interior photos a month or so before the boat was completed, but it had taken shape nicely, with all the details there to see. The owner had opted for V-berths forward, a galley to port, a huge enclosed head and shower to starboard, and convertible settees all the way aft to either side. The fiberglass waste and water tanks are under the forward V-berth and cabin sole, respectively, and the twin 5052-grade aluminum fuel tanks are outboard of the settees. They're well above bilge level, so they should stay dry for a long life.

This layout seems to work very well, making good use of the considerable interior space. But even that's a matter of preference, since the owner and Nauset Marine went through several plywood mockups before settling on this configuration as best suited to the owner's needs.

Engine Room

The boxes for the twin Cummins diesels protrude about 18 inches into the cabin. The tops of the boxes lift off to check the cooling-water level in the expansion tanks. For other engine checks, the cabin steps lift for access into this compact but efficiently laid out engine room. I would like to see the forward deck section hinge up—or at least a large removable hatch—to expose more of the engines for routine maintenance and to let them cool faster when you have to work on them. Oil dipsticks are inboard, as are the cooling-water seacocks and strainers. The fuel filter-separators are on the aft bulkhead, also easy to see—and clean—when needed. The engines are ruggedly mounted on ½-inch-thick aluminum plates through-bolted to the engine beds.

Construction

Like many semicustom builders, Nauset Marine has its hulls and decks fabricated by a subcontractor—in this case, Shannon Yachts of Bristol, Rhode Island. This allows Nauset to concentrate on mechanical, electrical, and joinery work. Shannon uses a polyester gelcoat followed by a general-purpose resin throughout the laminate. If I were ordering a Nauset 33 for the long term, I would specify a high-quality vinylester resin in a skin coat to guard against blistering. However, the general-purpose resin will also work well if properly applied preventing osmotic blistering from starting in any air voids.

Hand-laid mat follows, then a layer of 1808 (18 oz. roving stitched to ½ oz. mat) stitched roving, more mat, ½-inch balsa core (in the sides only—the bottom is solid glass), and two final layers of 1808. Using stitched roving saves weight by minimizing the use of unnecessary resin. Fir stringers are encapsulated in two layers of 2415 that overlap to cover the entire bottom; ¾-inch plywood bulkheads are tabbed in with three or four layers of 1808. Limber holes are coated with three coats of epoxy and gelcoated to keep the water out. The hull-to-deck joint is ruggedly fastened with bolts on 6-inch centers clamping 3M 5200 adhesive. The decks and topsides are also cored with balsa, with plywood backing plates used around bolt holes.

Some construction-related observations: I would make a couple of small changes underwater to fair things up; the keel is 5 inches wide at the top and 3 inches at the bottom, so it should be faired rather than left flat for less drag at higher speeds. Nauset Marine does this on its single-engine installations with the prop directly behind the skeg. I would also fair the flat-faced shaft-strut pads. If you opt for a dark hull color, don't expect the hull sides to be as flawless as many CAD-CAM boats coming off the production line these days; however, they're still as good as some of the big names being built exclusively in white (which better hides the ripples).

Performance Test

The Nauset's low-slung profile paid off during our mid-October performance test. Conditions were perfect as we left Meetinghouse Pond (the extreme northernmost part of Cape Cod's Pleasant Bay) with two passengers and three quarters of a tank of fuel. During the hour-long run to open water, we ran reciprocal courses for our speed run, producing 13.5 knots at 2,000 rpm, 17 knots at 2,200 rpm, 20.2 knots at a steady 2,400 rpm cruise, and 23 knots wide open at 2,600 rpm. Without using the tabs, trim ranged from 5.5 to 6.5 degrees. This test was done with an unfinished cabin, so expect slightly flatter trim and a little less speed when the extra weight is added, mostly forward.

When we arrived at Chatham Bar, Pleasant Bay's outlet to the Atlantic, the seas were running at 5 to 7 feet, just as the captain had predicted. We quickly reached the deeper water beyond the bar and kept up a steady 15 knots directly into the 4- to 6-foot seas. The Nauset didn't even begin to pound, offering a very smooth and stable ride in a head sea at those moderate speeds.

Most of my own cruising at these below-20-knot speeds has been in a Down East–style, round bilge, full-keel 42-footer, which likewise did not pound—but did it roll and throw spray! The Nauset, on the other hand, was as stable as a concrete slab and, for the most part, bone dry. The stability was extraordinary, with this low-slung cruiser just hanging there like a duck with the waves coming from any direction. Running downsea at 20 knots, the boat went where I pointed it with very little attention to the helm needed. The full keel probably helped there, as did well-placed, correctly sized rudders and a bow with moderate deadrise that generated buoyancy without digging in going downhill.

I slowed to a trolling speed of 800 rpm and steered right down the trough, but the boat only averaged 10-degree rolls to leeward, which is remarkable. Backing down in the trough, the scuppers and the cockpit deck stayed dry. Heading back over the bar with the seas on our quarter, the Nauset tracked true and without protest. Speeding up slowly, the boat came up on plane at 1,700 rpm and 11 knots.

Coming into the marina, I left the rudders amidships and maneuvered around several boats on their moorings using just the engines. Dockside, you don't have to stand to back into a slip; visibility is excellent all around. The boat had very little lateral slip due to its low sail area and full keel, so close-quarters maneuvering was predictable, even in a moderate breeze—all told, an excellent performance by the Nauset 33. Just resist the temptation to double the power and turn this into a 30-knot boat; you would have a rough, uncomfortable ride on a hull that can take you comfortably through almost anything at 20 knots.

The Nauset 33 is a remarkably simple yet innovative cruiser that is as well suited to sportfishing as it is to cruising. With only moderate power—420 hp total in our twin-engine test boat—the Nauset produced a very respectable 20-knot cruise and proved itself to be an exceptional seaboat. Easy accessibility to the bridge makes this an excellent craft for older sailors or families with children. The layout of the huge cabin is your choice, but remember to select something that you can sell someday.

Well-built, handsomely proportioned, and solidly engineered, the Nauset 33 bridge-deck cruiser can be ordered with a single gasoline engine or a variety of single or twin gasoline or diesel engines. Flybridge and express models are also available. The sky is the limit when it comes to finishing your boat—this is where you find out that the term *semicustom* applies to almost everything except the hull and deck.

Rhode Island–based Albin Marine builds 28- to 35-foot cruising boats that fish, and for a reasonable price. The 32 + 2 Command Bridge shown here has a low-profile layout, with the bridge essentially sitting on the trunk cabin and the engine room in the stern. This is a great family-cruiser design, with a spacious single-level accommodation level and a flybridge within a few steps of the cockpit. Albin's sailboat heritage is obvious in both the decor and the efficient use of interior space with plenty of storage. Side decks are wide and easy to navigate, the cockpit—although a couple of feet above water level with the engine immediately below—works fine for casual fishing. ALBIN MARINE

While this book expounds on the virtues of a long and narrow hull's superior seakeeping, ride quality, and propulsion efficiency, here's a boat that makes the point most eloquently. The Penn Edmonds–designed, Eric Goetz–built 68-by-11-foot commuter yacht *Fayerweather* has a pillow-soft ride in a 3-foot Buzzards Bay chop at 30 knots, and can make 35 knots in 4- to 5-footers without treating its passengers unkindly. Modest power—a pair of Yanmar 420 diesels driving waterjets—consistently delivers 40 knots at full load. *Fayerweather's* extreme 6:1 length-to-beam ratio can be toned down to 4:1 and still deliver the goods, though in somewhat diminished form. This boat has about the same interior volume (a good measure of a vessel's size) as an average 3:1 length-to-beam ratio 50-footer, which requires half again as much power to make the same speed in the same sea conditions. BILLY BLACK

Here's a one of a kind: an Italian-built, 36-foot Aprea Mare flush-deck cruiser called the Don Giovanni. Solidly built to high standards of fit and finish (for example, the heavy stainless steel bow railings have ground and polished welds), this yacht feels like it's made of steel topside, but the yacht's performance belies the notion that it's overbuilt. The two-berth, one-head interior is finished in cherry with teak trim, and teak decks are standard topside. Viewed from astern when docked stern-to, the boat looks like a sedate displacement trawler with its rounded transom. However, an immersed, out-of-sight extension of the hull bottom's running surface makes this a true planing hull capable of 35 knots. Aprea Mare builds boats from 25 to 40 feet. APREA MARE

Premium production builder Cobalt significantly extended its size range when it introduced the new 360. The 360 is a top-notch express cruiser with a Mediterranean-style cockpit, an angled helm station with room for a flush-mounted electronics suit, and a plush cabin that highlights the builder's newly ramped-up woodworking abilities. A moderate 10-foot, 6-inch beam and deep-V hull form deliver excellent performance in choppy sea conditions. A wide range of single and twin, diesel or gasoline stern-drive propulsion types is available. Cobalt, which is as well regarded for its after-sales support as for its boats, also produces high-quality, gorgeous-looking cuddies, bowriders, and deck boats from 19 to 29 feet. COBALT

Broward Marine is a well-established and -respected Florida-based builder of aluminum semicustom yachts ranging from about 85 to 125 feet. The yard builds to order, and also starts hulls on spec to reduce the lead time for delivery. Everything from high-end, 85-foot pilothouse motor yachts and 100-foot convertible sportfishermen to 125-foot tri-deck motor yachts are available. The beautifully styled 100-foot Broward shown here has a VIP suite forward and a three- or four-stateroom layout with additional crew quarters. A deep fine entry and hard-chine hull form deliver a comfortable and stable ride in offshore conditions; soft-mounted interior decks tame machinery vibrations; and the integral tanks add to the yacht's seaworthiness. BROWARD MARINE

Alden Yachts of Portsmouth, Rhode Island, builds high-end, semi-custom sedan, express, and aft-cabin cruising yachts from 40 to 56 feet. Resin-infused and vacuum-bagged laminates with premium epoxy and vinylester resins form the hulls designed and engineered by C. Raymond Hunt. Top-notch joinery is ample inside, and Alden goes to great effort to minimize machinery noise and vibration levels. Superb seaboats, Aldens can keep up with the best (and run ahead of the rest) convertibles in rough water. The 30-knot 56 Hardtop Express seen here has a custom interior arrangement, finished in flawless cherry cabinetry. ALDEN YACHTS

Other Yachts: Marine Medleys 493

This Lou Codega–designed, Mirage Manufacturing–built coastal cruiser takes interior volume to the max. Designed to cruise in protected inshore waters, this shoal-draft, 23-ton Great Harbor 37 come with a heavy-weather trawler's Portuguese bridge as an aesthetic feature. The 15-foot, 6-inch beam and full-beam deckhouse create a voluminous interior, with two full levels (the pilothouse is over the galley and second stateroom) and more room than many 55-footers. The pilothouse comes with a raised settee to offer your guests a good view of the shoreline passing close aboard. A two- or three-stateroom layout is available. The builder claims a range of 2,400 nm at just under 8 knots with a pair of 39 hp Yanmar diesels.

Huckins has been building boats since 1928, and the company produced many of the wooden World War II PT boats that saw service in the Pacific. Nowadays, Huckins builds classic-looking 44- and 58-foot production hulls constructed of decidedly modern Core-Cell, fiberglass, and premium vinylester resin. The Linwood 58 is the newest hull with two 44-foot models available: the Ortega 44 and the Atlantic 44, shown here. The saloon is light and airy due to big side windows, a one- or two-stateroom layout is available, and the flush-deck pilothouse offers excellent all-around visibility. Huckins's Quadraconic PT boat hull design has a full entry with low chines forward and flat sections aft; as a result, the Huckins planes easily and runs efficiently. However, vertical accelerations in a seaway at high speeds are higher than on a modern hull with a finer bow and greater deadrise for the length of the hull.   HUCKINS

The Parker 2520 is a versatile family fishing boat, with an enclosed pilothouse that extends the boat's cruising and fishing season. A pair of berths and a head forward encourage the occasional overnighter in this highly functional model, and the full transom adds seaworthiness. Well built with conventional, hand-laid laminates, this boat confirms Parker's solid reputation in its niche market.   PARKER

With a flat sheerline and classic deckhouse with trunk cabin, the John Kiley–designed Naushon 34 obviously draws its styling inspiration from the classic Huckins yachts from the 1950s and 1960s. The hull form is thoroughly modern, though, with enough deadrise continuing to the transom to improve tracking downsea, and a relatively fine entry for a smooth head-sea ride.   DANIEL FORSTER

Palmer Johnson, a Wisconsin-based builder of aluminum sail and power yachts and megayachts, earned the distinction of having built the largest aluminum yacht ever, as well as the largest yacht built in the United States in seventy years: the 195-foot *La Baronessa*. The heavily built 151-foot expedition yacht *Turmoil* shown here displaces 730,000 pounds, cruises at 14 knots with a pair of 1,400 hp Detroit diesels, and has a range of up to 10,000 miles. Built to withstand severe sea states, the hull, deck, and superstructure scantlings are very heavy, and windows, for example, are thick triple-pane glass. PALMER JOHNSON

British yachtbuilder Sunseeker just keeps building bigger and better boats. Four classes of models include more than sixteen models from 34 to 105 feet. The Manhattan 84 shown is the largest of the flybridge motor-yacht series. Two main-deck arrangements and two four-stateroom, four-head layouts plus crew quarters are available. A modified-V hull design and moderate beam-to-length ratio give this superbly finished yacht a pillow-soft ride in a rough chop. SUNSEEKER

Go-Fasts

High-performance boats, whether used for racing or recreation, are often referred to as *go-fasts*, which is apt for a boat that is meant to do just one thing—which the name suggests—well. Long and narrow, these hulls are strongly built to take wave impacts at speeds of 60 to over 100 mph. Deadrise on a go-fast monohull hovers right around 24 degrees all the way to the transom. Deep-V deadrise at the transom is an important ingredient for a very fast hull, since the boat comes clear out of the water on a regular basis, and rides on a narrow, V-shaped section of hull within a few feet of the transom.

Go-fasts are usually monohulls, but catamarans are also popular, especially at the very high end, very fast segment of the market.

No one in this go-fast world talks about knots as a unit of speed, even though these are saltwater boats, since 80 mph sounds more impressive than 69 knots.

Go-fasts have little functional purpose; most of the hull's length is given over to the engines back aft and a long, low, sloping foredeck. What's left, maybe 30 percent of the hull's length, becomes the cockpit and helm area. If there is a cabin at all, it probably has very little headroom, since the bow deck is kept low to reduce air drag, and to help with the sleek look. You don't want to be riding forward in one of these boats at high speed, anyway, since the vertical accelerations forward would be hard to tolerate.

One unfortunate consequence of the go-fast culture is noise pollution. Even though mufflers could be added, or switched on, that would drop exhaust levels on these high-horsepower (usually gas) engines considerably without sacrificing significant horsepower, many owners of these boats think it's a good thing to run around with exhausts blaring, loudly audible from literally miles away.

But if you get a kick out of pure speed, a go-fast may be just the thing for you. They're not for amateurs, by any stretch. Because their speed makes them inherently dangerous, they take a lot of skill and experience to operate safely.

The Baja 40 Outlaw, a 75-knot offshore performance boat, is one of the larger craft in the builder's lineup. The hull has an 8-foot, 6-inch beam and 24 degrees of deadrise at the transom, a standard recipe for offshore race boats. Up to triple 550 hp MerCruisers are available to take advantage of the hull's speed potential, but with no windshield to deflect the 85 or so mph wind, be sure to keep your head low.   BAJA

Formula's forte has long been offshore race boats, and the Fastech line of 27- to 41-footers is its answer to the racing crowd. The posh 382 is built for serious speed with a needlelike 8-foot, 3-inch beam, a stepped bottom, and 24 degrees of deadrise at the transom. A one-piece foam-filled fiberglass grid system supports the hull and deck liner.   FORMULA

Reggie Fountain is the one-man brand, one-man leather-loving legend who single-handedly turned the offshore racing world on its keister. Seen here is his high-performance 38 Sport Cruiser with a surprisingly roomy cabin and 61-plus-knot speed potential. The 10-foot, 6-inch beam means that this is no race boat, but its design roots are in racing. The extra 2 feet of beam creates the interior volume required in the cruising market.   FOUNTAIN

Velocity builds high-performance outboard- and stern-drive-powered boats from 20 to 41 feet. The 390 Velocity shown can reach 75 knots with optional power. According to the company Web site, Velocity's owner, Steve Stepp, thinks little of stepped bottoms on race boats, asserting that they cause instabilities resulting in spin-outs and rollovers at high speeds.   VELOCITY

Here's a real offshore race boat, the Fountain 42, capable of speeds in the 121-knot range, a speed at which most commercial aircraft can comfortably stay aloft. The impact-resistant canopy is there to reduce air drag and to provide much-needed occupant protection in the event of a rollover. Fountain's civilian lineup ranges from 25 to 65 feet, and includes fishing, cruising, and racing models.

FOUNTAIN

Donzi's 38 ZX is one of seven high-performance ZX models from 22 to 45 feet. This one can reach speeds of over 80 knots with up to 1,200 hp worth of MerCruiser stern drives. The hull has 22 degrees of transom deadrise; a 9-foot, 3-inch beam; and a stepped bottom to decrease drag and increase speed. The foredeck roof has a little more slope to it than others in this class, adding some welcome headroom in the long cabin below.

DONZI

Art Bibliography

The following bibliography is for art reproduced in this book.

Armstrong, Bob. *Getting Started in Powerboating.* 2nd ed. Camden, Maine: International Marine, 1995.

Beebe, Robert P., Captain. *Voyaging under Power.* 3rd ed. revised by James F. Leishman. Camden, Maine: International Marine, 1994.

Brewer, Ted. *Understanding Boat Design.* 4th ed. Camden, Maine: International Marine, 1994.

Gerr, Dave. *The Nature of Boats: Insights and Esoterica for the Nautically Obsessed.* Camden, Maine: International Marine, 1992, 1995.

Gerr, Dave. *Propeller Handbook: The Complete Reference for Choosing, Installing, and Understanding Boat Propellers.* Camden, Maine: International Marine, 1989, 2001.

Larsson, Lars, and Eliasson, Rolf E., *Principles of Yacht Design.* 2nd ed. Camden, Maine: International Marine, 2000.

Marchaj, Czeslaw A. *Seaworthiness: The Forgotten Factor.* Camden, Maine: International Marine, 1986.

Phillips-Birt, Douglas. *Naval Architecture of Small Craft.* New York: Philosophical Library, 1957.

Steward, Robert M. *Boatbuilding Manual.* 4th ed. Camden, Maine: International Marine, 1994.

Index

Numbers in **bold** refer to pages with illustrations

exhaust systems, 146, **172**
express cruisers, **327–74**

Fairline 65, 155, 225, **480–84**
Fayerweather, **492**
fiberglass, **80–81**; blistering,
  100–101; fatigue, 81, 82;
  glass-to-resin ratio, 86,
  103; hull construction,
  81, **84**; laminate, 86; metal
  vs. fiberglass, 123–24;
  sandwich laminate,
  90–92, 95–97; secondary
  bonding, **88**
fiberglass planking, 117–**18**
fiberglass-reinforced plastic
  (FRP), 81
fiberglass reinforcements:
  bulking materials, 84–85;
  chop and mat, 81–82;
  cloth, 84; exotic, 85–86;
  knitted, 83–84; planking,
  117–**18**; woven roving,
  82–83
fiddle rails, 219–20
fin stabilizers, 17–**18**, 20, 182
fire protection, 31–32,
  114–15, 123, 180
Fisher models: 16 Sport
  Avenger, **261**; 180 Fish,
  266; 2210, **259**
flare, 51–**52**
flat-bottom hulls, 53–**54**
flats boats, **273–75**
floodable length, 24
flood prevention, 25–27,
  180–**81**
flopper-stopper (paravanes),
  18, 19–20
flotation, 22–25, **23**, **112**–13
foam core, 93–95, **94**
foredecks, 206
forefoot, 50–**51**
form stability, 11, 13
Formula models: 41 PC,
  342–46; 260, **246**; 280 SS,
  255; Fastech 382, **496**
Fountain, Reggie, 496
Fountain models: 38 Sport
  Cruiser, **496**; 42, **497**
four-stroke outboard en-
  gines, 135–36
Four Winns, **198**
frameless windows, 117
frames, 124–**25**
freeboard, **22**, 27, 28
free communication, 28

free-surface effect, 27–28
frictional resistance, 53
frictional wake current, 17,
  35
Froude number, 44–**45**
fuel systems, **139**, **142**,
  175–**77**, 231–32
fuel tanks, 68, 113–16, 182

galley design, 218–20, **219**,
  234
galvanic corrosion, 128
gasoline inboard engines,
  138–40, **139**
gelcoat, 100–101
generators, 178–79
Genmar Holdings, 103, 223,
  243, 244
Gerr, David, 19, 430
Gerr 34, **55**
Gerr-Westbourne 44, **430**
get-home kicker, 137
girder, 125
Glacier Bay models: 260 CC,
  276; 2680, 275–79; catamaran, **77**; center console
  boat, **279**
glass-reinforced plastic
  (GRP), 81
GM: 315 hp gasoline engine,
  137; 671 two-stroke
  diesel, **144**
Godfrey models: Fundeck GS
  170, **257**; Parti Kraft
  Commander 220 SC, **266**;
  Polar Bay, **298**
Goetz, Eric, 492
go-fasts, 495–**97**
Grady-White hull, **109**
Grady-White models: 223,
  27, **318**; 247 CC Sportfish, **297**; 248 Walkaround, **224**; 274 Sailfish,
  299–302
Grand Banks models: 42
  Classic, **467**–71; 52 Europa, **478**
graphite fibers, 85
Great American Concepts, 93
Great Harbor 37, **494**
Groco through-hull fitting,
  181
gutters, **203**, **209**, **210**

habitability, 32
Halon gas fire extinguisher
  systems, 32, 180

Hamilton waterjets, **156**, **157**
hard-chine planing hulls:
  deep-V, **54–55**, **56**; flat-
  bottom, 53–**54**; modified-
  V, 55; stepped, **56**, **57**–58;
  warped-V, 55–**56**
hard chines, 13, 17, 50, **54**
hardtop express motor
  yachts, **484**–88
Harris Kayot models: 228,
  259; Flote Bote 220 Fisherman, **267**; Flote Bote
  Classic 24, **267**
hatches, 218, **220**
Hatteras models: 65, **412**;
  6300, **442**–47; Elite 92,
  452
head and shower, 214–16,
  215, 235
headroom, 218
heave (boat motion), **16**
Heckaman, Doyle, 280
helm station design, 184, **194**;
  electronics, 195; engine
  control placement,
  192–93; inspection,
  232–33, 235–37; instru-
  ment placement, 189–91,
  190, 193–95; seating,
  188–**89**; steering wheel
  placement, **191**–92;
  switch placement, **193**;
  visibility, 184–**88**
Henriques 38 El Bravo,
  383–86
Hewes models: Maverick,
  275; Pathfinder 2220V,
  274; Redfisher 18, **274**
Hinckley 36 Picnic Boat,
  322–25
honeycomb core, 95
Hood, Ted, 51, 349, 351, 352,
  433
hook, **52**–53
Huckins models: 40 Sportsman, **225**; Atlantic 44, **494**
hull loading, 70
hull shapes, about, 3–4; directional stability and,
  29–30; performance, 59;
  seakindliness and, 18–**19**;
  stability and, 11–14, 21;
  transom design, **202**–3;
  trim and, 10
hull shapes, types of: catamarans, **75**–78, 79; deck
  boats, 257; displacement,

33, **35**–38; flats boats,
  273; go-fasts, 495; hard-
  chine planing, 53–58;
  metal boats, **126**–27;
  planing, 58–59, 63–**64**;
  radius-chine, 126–27;
  round-bilge planing,
  62–**63**; ski boats, 268;
  trawlers, 466–67; waterjet-propelled, 157–58
hull-to-deck joint, 111–**12**
Hunt, Ray, 54, 56
Hunt 33, **346**–49
C. Raymond Hunt Associ-
  ates, 27, 49, 56, 224, 297,
  299, 318, 335, 346, 417,
  424, 427, 431
hybrid boats, 129
Hydra 38, **280**
hydrodynamic lift, **45**
Hy-Lite, 129

ice removal, 31
impregnators, 99
inboard engines, 138; cooling
  systems, 142, 145–46;
  diesel, **140**–44; drivetrains, 146–**49**; exhaust
  systems, 146; gasoline,
  138–40, **139**; gas vs.
  diesel, 144–45; steering,
  170–71
inertia, 16–17; free-surface
  effect, 27–28; mass, 16–
  17; and roll damping, 17;
  waterplane, 16; wave, 16
initial stability, 7, 10–14
instability. *See* dynamic instability
interlaminar bonds, 81
Intermarine, 102
International Maritime Organization (IMO), 31,
  123
Internet sites, 223, 227
Intrepid 36 CC, **297**
isophthalic polyester resin,
  87

Javelin 18 Venom, **243**
Jersey 40, **51**, 59
Jetskis, 263
Julius, Stephen, 335

Kawasaki models: 900 STX,
  264; PWC, **263**, **265**
keels, 17–18, **325**